UP AGAINST THE CORPORATE WALL

SIXTH EDITION

UP AGAINST THE CORPORATE WALL

Cases in Business and Society

S. PRAKASH SETHI

Baruch College, The City University of New York

PAUL STEIDLMEIER

Binghamton University, State University of New York

With contributions from
Thomas W. Dunfee, Karen Paul, Janet Rovenpor,
Paul Shrivastava, and Iwao Taka

PRENTICE HALL
UPPER SADDLE RIVER, NEW JERSEY 07458

Acquisitions editor: Natalie Anderson
Marketing manager: Sandra Steiner
Managing editor: Carol Burgett
Production editor: Edie Riker
Cover design: Kiwi Design
Manufacturing supervisor: Arnold Vila
Editorial assistant: Crissie Statuto

Library of Congress Cataloging-in-Publication Data
Sethi S. Prakash.
   Up against the corporate wall : cases in business and society / S.
Prakash Sethi, Paul Steidlmeier : with contributions from Thomas W.
Dunfee . . . [et al.].—6th ed.
   p. cm.
   Includes bibliographical references.
   ISBN 0-13-488371-3
   1. Industry—Social aspects—United States—Case studies.
I. Steidlmeier, Paul, [date].   II. Title.
HD60.5.U5S47 1997
658.4'08—dc20   96-895

Prentice-Hall International (UK) Limited, London
Prentice-Hall of Australia Pty. Limited, Sydney
Prentice-Hall Canada Inc., Toronto
Prentice-Hall Hispanoamericana, S.A., Mexico
Prentice-Hall of India Private Limited, New Delhi
Prentice-Hall of Japan, Inc., Tokyo
Simon & Schuster Asia Pte. Ltd., Singapore
Editora Prentice-Hall do Brasil, Ltda., Rio de Janeiro

Printed in the United States of America

10 9 8 7 6 5 4 3 2 1

CONTENTS

PREFACE

Business institutions are an integral part of the social system in a market economy. No matter how much one may try, the nature and dynamics of business institutions, and the rules of the game that govern markets, profoundly influence other societal institutions, and the growth and development of its individual members. The relationship, however, is not undirectional. No matter how much business might yearn for the unfettered marketplace, there is no businessperson or institution whose very aspirations and behavior are not governed by the internal gyroscope of society's values and cultures.

The twentieth century has been a turbulent century. Not only for its wars, but for the dizzying pace of its scientific discoveries and applications, its unprecedented generation of economic wealth, as well as it experimentation with new forms of culture. It has been a century of opulence and failed expectations. As business prospers, it would do well to recall the "complaint against the belly" that Shakespeare wrote about in *Coriolanus.* Many in today's world have cause to rebel against the belly, "that only a gulf it did remain in the midst of the body, idle and inactive still cupboarding the viand, never bearing like labor with the rest . . . ." (I, ii).

The last three decades have been especially turbulent in the evolving relationship between business—especially the large corporations—and society. In Eastern Europe and Russia, entire economic systems have fallen. New systems and institutions are only beginning to be experimented with. It would, however, be presumptuous to declare "the victory of capitalism," for capitalism itself is in the process of being refashioned. Living through these events as we are, it is too soon to add up the gains and losses from the experience. For this, we must await the mature perspective that only distance from the present can afford.

Instant history, however, has its uses. For neither now nor in the future can we ignore the recent past. It provides us with a point of departure from which we can measure progress or deflection from it. On the one hand, we are encumbered by the recent past in our perceptual biases about the behavior and motives of the people and institutions we must deal with. On the other hand, however, it provides the context in which we articulate the goals we wish to achieve and the means we would like to employ. History repeats itself precisely because we do have short memories.

We are all captives of our imaginations, which are constrained to a large extent by our living environment. Societies survive and civilizations flourish because people of wisdom can judiciously combine the lessons of the distant past with the human and material resource constraints. To build a future based solely on historical antecedents that ignore the real concerns of living persons is like casting a grand illusion. There is always a sense of motion, but no progress. To build a future as if it were an incremental step determined solely by the step just taken is ineffective. There is a continued sense of progress but, in an endless chain of actions and reactions, nothing substantive or lasting is ever accomplished.

It is instructive to examine the ways in which business and society have evolved since the 1960s. The conflicts between business firms and various elements of society during the early 1960s arose from longstanding grievances of various disenfranchised groups. They felt that their rightful share of the opportunities, aspirations, and fruits of American society were being denied by powerful vested economic interests supported and protected by a captive political system. Their rebellion was born out of the desperation of those who had nothing to lose. Issues were seen as black or white, groups as villainous or virtuous, causes as holy or satanic, and leaders as saints or charlatans.

The social and political upheavals of the 1960s forced us to face the injustices inflicted on certain social groups in our political and economic order. This was nothing new. We have experienced similar cycles throughout our history, starting with the Industrial Revolution and ending with the Great Depression. During the 1960s, the inequities in opportunity, the lack of caring, and the high proportion of society's rewards going to a few combined to make people doubt the legitimacy of the large corporations that were identified with the socioeconomic order. We saw well-being not only in terms of society's grand design but also in terms of the disenfranchised who did not seem to count at all.

The 1970s brought a partial resolution of these problems: large-scale, overt inequalities were outlawed. In an effort to prevent future inequities and provide fair compensation for past inequities, inequality of opportunity was measured, in a large number of cases, by inequality of outcome. These resolutions of past inequities have become institutionalized in a plethora of new rights and entitlements. We all claim rights to education, a decent standard of living, support for the family, privacy, a cleaner environment, old-age support, and protection from failure. When divorced from any individual obligation or reciprocity, these rights become absolutes with politically strong constituencies to protect and expand them.

An inevitable outcome of this approach surfaced in the 1980s with the emergence of single-issue causes and narrowly based political groups as a dominant feature, and not necessarily a beneficial one, of the American sociopolitical arena. Now mature and ever more sophisticated, these single-issue advocacy groups have brought about a shift in power alliances and yielded highly visible benefits to groups who were previously not so fortunate. The shift in power from producer to consumer groups, and those who proclaimed the poor and the disadvantaged as their constituency, also brought about a shift in outlook concerning the future of society. This reflected a fundamental shift from a perspective of eternal optimism and growth to a mood of pessimism and finite resources. Instead of everyone sharing a common endeavor, we viewed society as a zero-sum game where one's gains must come at someone else's costs.

The 1980s began under the banner of the "me-generation." This self-centeredness was elevated by some to the status of noble calling. We became cloistered in our self-ordained virtues. We disdained compromises because we feared that to see reason in an adversary is to sully one's own reputation.

The 1990s have been dominated by two overwhelming events that are still unfolding: the collapse of socialism in the West and a shift of the economic center toward South and East Asia. While the first suggested to the naive an irreversible victory for capitalism, the second has called into question the legitimacy of Western models of society and human values. No doubt, many are right to see the collapse of stagnant socialist regimes and the emergence of South and East Asia from mass poverty as very positive events. But the collapse of an unjust system does not make our system just and the emergence of viable non-Western systems challenges the hegemony of Western values. All of this adds up to an exciting new set of challenges. There is no social system that can remain just as it is. For business people, the challenge is to embrace fair opportunity and commitment to moral value-added in all relationships.

Business has not been immune to these changes over the past three decades. Both as a measure of self-preservation and as a consequence of a narrow perspective, business has answered its critics largely with strident intransigence and an uncompromising attitude. Instead of defining corporate interests within the larger framework of the public good, it has often resorted to defining the public interest as if it were a secondary and incidental outcome of corporate interests.

During the early 1960s, when social pressures on business had barely gathered momentum, the business response to opposition groups was generally one of lofty disdain. Business felt that paying these groups any attention would be legitimizing their social credibility. This stance reflected a simplistic approach: Pretend they are not there, and they and their complaints will go away.

In the 1970s, business displayed a more conciliatory response to societal concerns. Although corporations were aggressive in formulating the national agenda, they nevertheless attempted to narrow the gap between societal expectations and corporate performance. Substantive gains were made, some of them only after changes were institutionalized and mandated by law. During the 1980s, corporations became far more sophisticated in managing their relations to society. Confronted with well organized and articulate adversaries, corporations began to use some of the same tactics. Rhetoric was substituted for substance. Compromises and consensus were discarded in favor of holding firm. Corporations began to speak out on social issues not only by advocating specific public policies, but also by questioning their opponents' motives and even branding them misinformed and ignorant. The polarization of viewpoints had become almost complete.

The tragedy has been the failure of both the corporate community and the social activists to work as partners in finding and developing commonly acceptable solutions to societal problems. Too often, the relationship has been an adversarial one, with each side attempting to persuade the American public that the opposition is the villain. Each seems more interested in directing attention to deficiencies and labeling the opposition than in acting in the public interest.

The problems of the 1960s and 1970s concerned the correction of flagrant imbalances in the allocation of costs and the distribution of benefits among various societal groups. Business bore the major burden of enacting social changes because it was the repository of the nation's economic resources; it had the management expertise to bring about those changes; and it was most susceptible to public and political pressures for change because it comprised large, private collectives with weak external constituencies.

In the 1990s, our problems are infinitely more complex and their solutions immeasurably more difficult. We seem to have reached a watershed in terms of conflict between business and social groups. We have come to realize that big government can be just as insensitive to individual needs as big business. Although big government has solved some problems, it has created others equally ominous: social and economic inefficiencies, erosion of purchasing power through inflation, allocation of increased proportions of Gross National Product to public sector spending, and even invasion of individual privacy. There is a growing aversion toward increased reliance on the government to solve all our problems.

There is also some questioning concerning the viability of solutions offered by social activists. We no longer accept on faith every activist group that purports to speak for the public interest. It is becoming apparent that, often in their strident intransigence and uncompromising attitudes, the activists may be advancing only their own self-interests. They frequently speak for those who directly and immediately stand to gain from their positions.

The pendulum seems to be swinging against those who believed in an activist government seeking to provide a social safety net—as a matter or right or entitlement—for all of the nation's citizens in general, and its disadvantaged and disenfranchised in particular. Instead, the new conservative mood in the populace and the Republican majority in the Congress, seeks to place increased responsibility on the "individual" to be held responsible for its actions and the consequences thereof. Where government intervention does take place, it seeks to facilitate individual action rather than to ensure desirable outcome. Unfortunately, a great deal of debate on both sides seems to be mired in ideological rhetoric in which specific details, and indeed self-serving vested interests, are often presented as objective analysis and a search for rational outcomes.

The contours of the new society remain undelineated and yet it is certain that a change in direction is in the offing. Such a change, however, must take into account the ever increasing complexity of the social system, as well as the rise in technology and its attendant needs for a more highly skilled work force. The technological revolution, and, concomitantly, the information revolution, are changing the social organism, the body politic, and economic arrangements in many ways that are as yet unclear. Such changes are likely to give rise to new classes of social and economic elites. At the same time, a growing segment of society—those already on the margins, will be pushed into deep poverty from which no amount of individual initiative or hard work is likely to rescue them. The challenge for the American society, and, for that matter, the entire world, is not to create more classes of dependent people. It is essential that we create support systems to assist present and future generations in attempting to escape a life of poverty and hopelessness. Supportive social systems are essential to provide avenues of hope and means of attainment for more productive lives.

The ethical problems of the 1980s and 1990s, which stem from the conflict between business and society, do not concern obvious right and wrong or guilt and innocence. These problems pit one type of inequity over another, giving more to one group while taking from the other. The virtue of frugality squares off against the sin of accumulation; the morality of principles confronts the morality of situations. In an unjust world, the distinctions between the guilty and innocent have become ambiguous. We are faced with the realization that we live in an increasingly interdependent society where individual good is not possible outside the context of common good. It makes no sense to separate moral principles from institutional behavior, political power from economic influence, or environmental values from material rewards. To do so is to divorce the social system from its basic element: the human being.

The emerging global economic order has once again brought capitalism and its principal actor, the multinational corporation, to the apex of social institutions. Unlike the 1960s, when the multinational corporation was seen as a threat to national sovereignty and political freedom, the new world views the multinational corporation as an agent of positive change. However, underneath the thin veneer of hope and expectation lies the ever present danger of the unaccountable power of the corporate behemoth and its potential for doing harm through abuse of that power. The paradox of economic globalism has inevitably created two societies, which are quite disparate in their needs and resources, as well as their aspirations and the potential for fulfillment.

The large multinational corporation must become an active agent for social change if it is to make the world safe for democracy and, indeed, for capitalism. For the latter can survive only in an environment of unfettered individual choice voluntarily exercised in the political and economic arena. The corporation cannot confine its role to responding to societal goals advocated by other groups. As a dominant institution in society, it must assume its rightful place and contribute to the articulation of the public agenda. In today's pluralistic society, corporate participation in social policy formulation is not a luxury but a necessity; it must receive the attention of top management, as well as the corporate resources to do it right and to do it well. The cost of being wrong can be very high. Participation simply to defend the corporate position on a given social issue, to support a political candidate considered friendly to the firm, or to sell the free enterprise system is not sufficient. Effective participation demands the advancement of a coherent political process until each organization can articulate who and what they are socially and what role their products and services play culturally. This demands positive political strategies, not improvised responses to impending crises.

The sixth edition of *Up Against the Corporate Wall* presents case studies that capture the most critical issues of conflict between business and society in the 1990s. The challenge is for the business student and business executive to develop innovative and constructive approaches to resolving these issues. The cases represent, in our view, the major areas of concern that will involve the business community and larger segments of the American society in the 1990s. We would have liked to have covered a great many more issues and more cases, but this would have been impossible given the constraints of space and time. We recognize that there may be differences of opinion as to our choices of issues and cases; however, we would hope that such differences are minimal.

Public policy has come to exert an increasingly powerful influence on business strategies. While all of the cases we present reflect this dynamic, seven are particularly centered around public policy regulations and processes. The sociopolitical dimension is reflected in issues affecting personal security. The National Rifle Association and gun control case captures the conviction and emotion surrounding the desire for safety in the streets, with protagonists taking radically different approaches to law and order.

Religious institutions and various public interest groups have traditionally been viewed as the defenders of individual rights, nurturers of the poor and disadvantaged, and protectors of the environment. In the past, there has been a general tendency for the public to accept, rather uncritically, the legitimacy of their public purpose. However, human failures are not confined to the leadership of business institutions. Other social institutions may also fall prey to the temptations of power or to the pursuit of a narrow goal that might be inimical to the larger public interest. Nowhere is this dilemma more apparent than in the case of Eli Lilly and its product, Prozac, which was attacked by the Church of Scientology despite overwhelming scientific evidence as to the effectiveness of the product and the professional and ethical manner in which the product was marketed by the company. This is an apt example (if a reminder is needed), that the temptation to rush to judgment with regard to corporate behavior must be resisted. This is especially true when an issue touches scientific evidence on the one side and core beliefs on the other side. In a somewhat similar vein, the case studies of Xerox and McDonald's illustrate efforts by large corporations to go beyond what is minimally required by law; to work with environmental groups and, in general, to display enlightened corporate leadership.

Socioeconomic dimensions of corporate policy have riveted the public's attention with the drama of plant closings as corporations struggle for survival in an increasingly competitive world. The case of GM in Norwood, Ohio, focuses on this issue. At the same time, the public has been stunned with disbelief as layer after layer is peeled away from the scandal of insider trading. The saga of Dennis Levine, Ivan Boesky, and the firm of Drexel Burnham Lambert took four years to come to light, and even as this book goes to press the end is not in sight. On the other hand, the multibillion-dollar stakes of the turbulent world of corporate takeovers leave the common person to try to piece together what happened long after the action has been played out. The drama is epitomized in the struggle that took place between Goodyear and Sir James Goldsmith.

Corporations do not simply adopt a reactive approach to public policy. Increasingly, they take the offensive to assert their power, defend their turf, and justify their public policy position. One approach to accomplishing this objective has been through the use of advocacy advertising. The Chemical Manufacturers case illustrates the tactics economic agents increasingly employ to shape public opinion and their operating environments.

In the past decades, responsibility to corporate social performance has increasingly been placed on top management. Often, when a scandal is uncovered, top management does a disappearing act, leaving subordinates or the nameless system to shoulder the blame. This is examined in the General Dynamics defense-industry profiteering case, and the Bank of Boston money-laundering case.

It is not unusual for corporate wrongdoing to escape detection. In such cases, whistle-blowers play a key role. We present a study of the role of whistle-blowers with respect to environmental issues in the Alyeska Pipeline case. To provide a different perspective in managing environmental issues, we have chosen to present the example of McDonald's, a company that has attempted to "get it right," by integrating environmentalism into its core business mission.

Since the origins of capitalism, the worker has occupied a central place of concern. Our case selection reflects this longstanding orientation, as we devote four cases to workplace safety and one to employee rights. The Warner-Lambert case examines specific industrial accidents and raises the question of management responsibility. In the IBP case, the focus shifts from a specific accident to a regular pattern of accidents. This case raises classic questions of management practice in a cost-cutting industry when there is a ready supply for unskilled labor. The Film Recovery case focuses on the responsibility of top management when industrial hazards result in the death of an employee.

Our cases on employee rights concern sex discrimination (comparable worth), race discrimination (Sears, Roebuck), age discrimination (United Airlines), and alleged race and sex discrimination against American employees by two Japanese companies, C. Itoh & Co. and Sumitomo. All of these cases raise fundamental questions concerning the dignity of the individual, a concept that is at the root of democracy. Too often in this area, we focus on what companies are doing wrong. We have added a study in proactive management: how Xerox manages diversity.

Two cases focus on the rights of consumers. The case concerning GM's X-car examines the issue of auto safety. At the same time, it draws attention (along with the Sears case) to the problem of regulatory excesses and their impact on affected businesses. The case concerning the role of the tobacco industry in the United States examines consumer welfare and choice in the face of the legal production and marketing of a harmful product.

Finally, we examine the role of multinational corporations in developing societies. The business and society field today is incontestably international. In addition to C. Itoh & Co. and the Sumitomo corporation, we examine five others. The securities scandal in which Japan's House of Nomura was embroiled provides a cross-cultural perspective on fairness in financial markets. The South Africa case examines the role of American corporations in societies that explicitly avow principles of discrimination. The Bhopal case focuses on industrial accidents in settings where the likelihood of implementing safety precautions is marginal, at best. The case concerning the tobacco industry in the Third World examines what the tobacco multinationals seek to do in the Third World that they are forbidden to do at home. We also add a proactive case: the donation by Merck and Co. of a drug to cure river blindness.

We are grateful to our colleagues who generously contributed of their time and effort in preparing special case studies for this volume. Professor Janet Rovenpor of Manhattan College was responsible for preparing a penetrating case study of Alyseka Pipeline and also co-authored the Prozac case. Professor Karen Paul of Florida International University authored the case on South Africa, and Professor Paul Shrivastava of Bucknell University prepared the case on Union Carbide and the industrial plant accident in Bhopal, India. Finally, Professors Iwao Taka of Reitaku University in Japan and Thomas Dunfee of the Wharton School have contributed the case on the House of Nomura and its involvement in securities scandals in Japan.

We also wish to acknowledge the research support provided by a number of doctoral students at Baruch College, notably: Leo Giglio, Ramesh Gehani, and Linda Sama. In addition, we would like to thank the staff of the Management Department, Baruch College of the City University of New York as well as the staff at the School of Management of Binghamton University of the State University of New York for their willing and able assistance in undertaking typing and other administrative chores in putting this manuscript together.

S. PRAKASH SETHI
New York, NY

PAUL STEIDLMEIER
Binghamton, NY

UP AGAINST THE
CORPORATE WALL

GENERAL MOTORS AND
THE CITY OF NORWOOD, OHIO

Plant closings and their impact on affected communities

General Motors has "turned the corner" and is beginning to realize the expected economic results of the reorganization of its North American Automotive Operations. Its $10-billion plant construction and modernization program, and other actions are designed to create a trimmer and more competitive company.[1]

These were the opening comments of GM's chairman, Roger B. Smith, in a major press conference on November 6, 1986. This upbeat statement, however, was only the prelude to the grim news that was to follow:

A fundamental part of our "Strategy of the Eighties" plan has been to replace obsolete facilities with new or modernized plants. Just as with our reorganization moves, we recognized that for a transition period there would be an inevitable overlapping of capacity and personnel. Now we have progressed to the point where the new plants and equipment are coming on stream and the expected efficiencies can begin to pay off.[2]

GM's chairman stated that the resulting modernization reorganization would result in the closing of eleven plants that had become redundant with the construction of six new assembly plants and the total refurbishing of twelve others. GM officials also confirmed that eleven automobile assembly and metal fabrication operations would be closed

in the United States and would affect 29,000 employees.

GM estimated that cessation of these operations would result in fixed-cost reductions of $500 million annually. However, these actions would benefit all who had a stake in the continued well-being of General Motors. This statement was a follow-up to an earlier statement by GM, in which the company had indicated that it was in the process of reducing its salaried workforce by 25% by 1989 to reduce costs and increase it competitiveness.[3] Over the years, GM had been losing its market share. The statement went on outlining the details of the various plants scheduled for closing (Table 1).

To the city of Norwood, the announcement of the GM plant closing came as a thunderbolt from the sky. Its economic impact on the community was nothing short of catastrophic. At one time, the city officials even contemplated declaring bankruptcy. However, this idea was not seriously pursued.

Although the direct impact of the plant closure would be the dislocation of the plant's 4,300 workers who relied on General Motors for their livelihood, the indirect impact would be even greater. The plant closure would result in a direct loss of $2.7 million in earnings and property tax revenues to the city of Norwood. This tax loss represented approximately 25% of Norwood's annual

TABLE 1. GM Assembly and Stamping Plant Closings

Plant/Div.[a]	Location	Model	Employees	Closing Date/ Remarks
1. Assembly (BOC)	Clark Street, Detroit	Cadillac Brougham	3,500	End 1987
2. Stamping (BOC)	Conner Stamping, Detroit	Body Panels for Cadillac Brougham, Olds '88 Wagon	700	1990
3. Stamping	Fleetwood	Body Panels for Cadillac	3,000	—
4. Assembly (CPC)	Pontiac #2	Supreme, Regal, Monte Carlo	1,270	End 1987
5. Assembly (CPC)	Norwood, Ohio	Firebird, Camaro	4,000	Mid-1988
6. Stamping (CPC)	Hamilton/Fairfield, Ohio	Body Panels for Camaro, Firebird	2,500	1990
7. Stamping (Chicago, BOC)	Willow Spring, Illinois	Lux, reg. midsize car body panels	2,900	Phase out
8. Stamping (BOC)	Flint (Mich.) body assembly	G-car Bodies	3,230	End 1987
9. Assembly (T & B)	St. Louis, Missouri	Pick-up, crewcab	2,200	Mid-1987 (Move to Janesville)
10. Assembly (T & B)	Pontiac central	Heavy trucks	2,200	Aug. '88—trucks sold to Volvo Sept. '87—buses sold to Greyhound
11. Assembly (T & B)	Flint line	Pick-up	3,450	August 1987

[a]BOC = Buick-Oldsmobile-Cadillac division   CPC = Chevrolet-Pontiac-Canada division   T&B = truck and bus division
SOURCE: Statement prepared by United Auto Workers (UAW) research department (Xerox) based on publicly available information (January 24, 1987, Norwood, Ohio, p.79). Hearing of Committee on Labor and Human Resources, U.S. Senate 100th Congress, reviewing the reasons behind GM's decision to close 11 plants in four states, and to determine ways to keep these plants operating and the employees working.

operating budget. In addition, the Norwood City School System would lose $2.3 million in property tax revenues. The city was already in the throws of an economic downturn. Several other Norwood industries had recently announced layoffs and possible closure or relocation. Shortly after General Motors' announcement, the U.S. Playing Card Company announced the layoff of 105 workers, and the Siemens Corporation announced the layoff of 75 workers. These developments had followed an announcement earlier that 114 jobs were being eliminated at the Leblond Makino Company. The city had also suffered a loss of $600,000 in federal revenue sharing funds due to the elimination of the federal revenue sharing program at the end of 1986. It was estimated that the loss of income from GM jobs would remove over $100 million annually from the greater Cincinnati economy. The multiplier effect of this income loss would further impact service and supply industries throughout the region.[4] The feel-

ings of the city were best captured by a commentary on a local radio station:

Listen to the Heartbeat, Mr. Smith

You became one of the world's largest and richest corporations on the sweat and labor of the people who live in our town. And in the process, the people who made you became dependent on you. They put down their roots, took on 30-year mortgages on 50-foot lots. And whatever else they might have been, or wherever else they might have settled, they didn't because you were here. And, at least for most of them, they gave you everything they had. . . .

There are ways to keep the plants open. The state can help, and the workers are willing to make concessions. True, you might make a little less money, but you can add a human touch. You say, in your commercials, "Listen to the heartbeat . . . listen to the heartbeat of America."

To this commentary, I can only add my hope and prayer that the corporate leadership of General Motors will listen to the heartbeat. Listen to the heartbeat of those who built their company—the heartbeat of the workers, families and communities that they are now leaving behind.[5]

ISSUES FOR ANALYSIS

In a changing competitive environment, businesses must relocate plants and facilities and consolidate and expand in order to adapt to changing market conditions. No one challenges the right of business to have operational autonomies in making investment and marketing decisions. At the same time, it is also clear that any sizeable move on the part of a business entity has serious economic and sociopsychological impact on the affected workers, and also on the communities and all those who are directly and indirectly affected by the plant closing. This is particularly true in cases of small communities such as the city of Norwood, where a particular business may represent a disproportionately large proportion of its employment and tax base.

The situation is not always one-sided or dismal. Laid-off employees may find new and often more rewarding jobs, pursue new careers, or move to new areas, which prior job commitments may have prevented them from doing before. Similarly, communities may find new vigor by bringing in new, high-growth industries, a diversified economic base, and an increased sense of optimism that comes with the process of change.

The primary responsibility of a company in making investment decisions, including plant closings and relocations, is to protect the interests of the owners, i.e., the stockholders, and to ensure the survival of the organization. The next most important group is, of course, the employees. Responsible companies make all possible efforts to minimize, if not completely eliminate, the adverse impact of plant closings on their employees. Good employee relations are important to the success of a business. Furthermore, over the years, a large body of law, as well as employment contracts and union agreements, have succeeded in defining and protecting employee rights.

The situation with regard to the affected communities, however, is not entirely clear and considerable controversy exists with regard to the rights of communities and the obligation of corporations in the event of plant closures, downsizing, and consolidations.

Some of the important issues for analysis are as follows:

1. What are the legal, social, and moral obligations of a company toward the community where its plant closing will have an adverse economic impact?
2. To what extent would the responsibility of a departing corporation be affected under one or more of the following conditions?
   a. whether or not a company is profitable or is losing money;
   b. the company has been operating in the community for a long time (e.g., over 20 years), or a short time (e.g., less than 10 years);
   c. the company is among the largest, if not the largest employer in the community;
   d. the production is being moved to a poorer and cheaper labor area within the United States;
   e. the production is being moved to a Third-World country with cheap labor, or more efficient and economical operating conditions;
   f. the company has recently assumed a large amount of debt as a result of a takeover, leverage buyout, or in an attempt to thwart a hostile or potentially hostile takeover;
   g. the company's management made some poor strategic choices, or did not anticipate market changes correctly, and must now undertake radical action to rectify the situation.
3. The adequacy of a company's dealings with the community in the event of a plant closing must be analyzed both in terms of process and outcome. How might one evaluate the negotiating process used by GM in its dealings with the city of Norwood officials?
4. Similarly, how might one evaluate the negotiating stance and process used by the city offi-

cials? Could the situation, or the final outcome, have been different if either one or both of the parties had used different negotiating strategies and tactics?

5. How adequate was GM's offer of help to the city given the overall economic environment and its need to deal with a large number of similar situations?

6. How reasonable were the demands the city of Norwood made on GM?

7. What are some of the mechanisms that might prove useful in protecting the legitimate interests of the affected communities and in smoothing out the transition process in the event of plant closings that would not unnecessarily harm the process of "creative destruction" that is an indispensable part and inevitable consequence of technological change, human growth, and economic rejuvenation?

THE CITY OF NORWOOD

The city of Norwood is a small town of 2.3 square miles, with a population of approximately 25,000. It is surrounded on all sides by the city of Cincinnati. Norwood is 100 years old and is very proud of its history and traditions. Compared to Cincinnati, it provides a superior level of municipal services including an excellent public school system. The city's population is 95 percent white. It is almost completely built and no large vacant tracts of land are available for new industrial development, plant expansion, or multiple-unit, high-density housing.

Norwood is highly industrialized and has a number of plants, of which GM has been by far the biggest. Most of the workers employed in the city's plants, however, do not live there and instead commute from Cincinnati and other neighboring communities. For example, of the 4,300 GM workers employed in the plant, less than 500 lived within the Norwood city limits. Unlike most other cities in the United States, property taxes are not the primary source of revenue for Norwood. Instead, the city levies an "earnings" tax that is imposed on all wages earned within the city limits. This allows Norwood to provide an unusually high level of services to its residents without burdening them with heavier property taxes.

Even before the current economic slowdown, suggestions had been made that Norwood was too small to sustain itself as an independent town and that it should merge with its larger neighbor, Cincinnati, which after all surrounds it from all directions. However, the City officials vehemently rejected such a notion and expressed their determination and that of the citizens of Norwood to remain an independent municipal entity.

CHRONOLOGY OF EVENTS

Soon after the GM announcement, officials of the State of Ohio and the City of Norwood initiated discussions with company executives to explore the possibility of keeping the plant open. On January 15, 1987, the governor of Ohio met with GM's chairman, Roger B. Smith. This was immediately followed by a congressional hearing held by Senator Howard W. Metzenbaum (D-Ohio) on January 26, 1987, at Norwood Junior High School. The hearings included witnesses and testimony from, among others, GM representatives, city officials, UAW representatives, and some affected employees.[6]

GM's Reason for These Plant Closings

In testifying before Senator Metzenbaum's Committee, GM's president and chief operating officer, James F. McDonald, outlined his company's position for plant closings and restructuring. He argued that his company had no choice but to close obsolete plants and consolidate production in order to meet the competitive challenges faced by the U.S. auto industry in general and his company in particular.

The American automobile industry, more than any other industry, faced the heaviest burden of restructuring and downsizing as a result of changing economic conditions, manufacturing technologies, and fierce competition from Japan and other countries. GM, being the biggest of the "big three" U.S. automobile manufacturers, faced the worst situation. In less than ten years, its U.S. market share had gone down to 45 percent from over 60 percent, leaving it with a large proportion of redundant capacity, some of which was quite old and economically and technologically inefficient. To meet the new economic and competitive reality, GM launched a $10 billion-plus plant construction and modernization program, which eventually wound up being a $40 billion program, and took other actions designed to create a trimmer and more competitive company.[7]

An integral part of this strategy had been to replace obsolete facilities with new or modernized plants. The strategic plan called for the closing of eleven plants that had become redundant, with the construction of six new assembly plants and the total refurbishing of twelve others. The operations scheduled for closing would affect 29,000 employees. The assembly plant at Norwood, Ohio, was among those scheduled for closing. It would affect directly approximately 4,300 workers.

Although GM has apparently turned the corner in its drive to regain profitability and competitive health, it is by no means out of the woods. Financial analysts and industry observers insist that GM would need further trimming in order to bring its domestic manufacturing capacity in line with its sales prospects. It is estimated that GM will have to adjust downward from a current market share of 43 percent to an eventual sustainable market share of 35 percent. To achieve this, GM will probably have to close six additional plants during the next five years affecting over 100,000 workers.[8]

GM's management accepted that plant closings caused stress and disruption in the fabric of communities, but felt that unless these very painful decisions were made, the long-term health of the entire domestic manufacturing base would be at stake.

GM outlined the following reasons for its plant closings:

1. Each of the 11 plants included in the current plan had a different reason for closing. Some plants making rear-wheel-drive cars were to be displaced by more modern plants making front-wheel-drive cars. Plants in the truck and bus division were sold to Volvo and Greyhound. Some critics, on the other hand, asserted that GM was closing many plants in order to relocate substantial production capacity overseas—especially for auto parts—and that GM was sourcing more and more automobiles from Korea and Japan.

This point was, however, vigorously denied by GM's president, James F. McDonald. According to his testimony, none of the Norwood city plant's production was to be replaced by overseas production. He also stated that no other American manufacturer could match GM's "commitment to the manufacturing base of this country and to maintain American jobs." (Hearings, p. 6)

2. The Norwood plant was an old three-story plant that could not utilize the latest developments in efficient production systems. Furthermore, as the plant was landlocked, it could not be reconstructed into a modern single-story production facility. According to GM's president, James McDonald, Norwood was one of the oldest and least efficient of GM's plants. Therefore, there was no question that in the long run the Norwood plant had to be closed: "It was a matter of when." (Hearings, p. 7)

3. The Norwood plant produced midsized and sporty cars: Chevrolet Camaro and Pontiac Firebird models. These were also being simultaneously produced at GM's Van Nuys, California, assembly plant. The Van Nuys plant was built in 1947, about 25 years

after Norwood, and was updated at a cost of $22 million in 1985.

4. GM argued that it had to maintain a presence in the highly competitive California market. The company felt that by closing the Norwood plant, and moving the work to the Van Nuys plant, the latter could be consolidated and made more competitive. GM stressed that they were not sacrificing local production in favor of foreign operations. (Hearings, pp. 6–25)

United Auto Workers' (UAW) Viewpoint

Owen Bieber, president of the United Auto Workers of America, felt that GM, while addressing the erosion of its market share, "flirted with one quick fix after another." He agreed that in a dynamic economy, some plants are likely to close—but was convinced that far too many plants were closing needlessly. In his opinion, when a plant closing was justified, its cost must be shared equitably.

From the UAW's point of view, GM invested heavily for a time to gain its market-share from domestic and foreign competitors. GM pursued a risky as well as costly strategy —adding capacity at a time when Ford and Chrysler were retrenching, the industry was going through a recession, and imports were increasing. GM ran into numerous problems with the expensive technology-intensive strategy. According to the UAW chief, the idle auto capacity in 1986/87 amounted to about 2 million units. General Motors' announcement of its plant closing was likely to reduce about a million units of work capacity. With the addition of imports and transplants, the excess capacity by the end of the 1988 model year could be up to 40 million units. This was equivalent to 15 assembly plants, each corresponding to two shifts of 6,000 people per plant. Furthermore, for each job in a domestic American auto assembly plant, 11 additional supplier jobs were created (whereas the trans-

plants generated only 3 jobs). Even leaving aside the nonauto jobs, the numbers added up to between 300,000 and 400,000 auto workers' jobs.

Bieber accused GM of diversifying into unrelated industries and buying off its critics when it should be devoting these resources to gaining competitive strength in the automobile industry. In 1984, GM's Hughes Aircraft acquisition cost $5 billion and its Electronic Data Systems acquisition cost another $2 to $4 billion. In December 1986, an additional $750 million was incurred to buy out Ross Perot, EDS's owner.

The UAW chief also charged GM with exporting U.S. jobs. According to Bieber, GM was likely to service 400,000 vehicles offshore by 1988, equivalent to two plants, and produce 100,000 to 200,000 vehicles in a GM-Suzuki plant in Canada, to be shipped to the U.S. under the U.S.-Canada Auto Pact. In 1987, 1 million engines were imported, compared to only 800,000 in 1981. This was equivalent to building a whole new engine plant.

There were some rumors, although denied by everyone at GM, that GM considered the Norwood plant to be afflicted with labor troubles and, therefore, was not anxious to put more money into it. Mayor Sanker admitted that in the past the plant had had more than its share of labor problems, but that these had since been resolved and that labor relations in the plant were excellent. The union felt that workers were not getting "a chance to gain back what had been lost through foreign imports." The union was keen to cooperate with the management, as "for instance, during 1984 the Local Agreement was settled on September 10, four days sooner than the National Settlement on September 14. (Hearings, p. 102)

The local UAW challenged GM's rationale for the Norwood plant closing. Cleon Montgomery, a representative of UAW local 674, contended that "they could build the 1987 model of Camaro and Firebird for $112 million a year cheaper than their sister plant in Van Nuys, and could build the 1988 model $200 million cheaper." Thus, he could not understand General Motors' logic in moving its work to California where "only one out of five automobiles purchased is a General Motors product." He felt that without their "General Motors jobs," they would not buy "General Motors products." Quoting from an article written by the former plant manager Charlie Miller, Montgomery stressed that whereas the media was given the impression that Norwood was an old and outdated plant, it had in fact undergone extensive upgrading, with new equipment and facilities for quality control, checking, and production, and with one of the most modern paint facilities in the world. He also mentioned that since 1972, there had been very few labor disputes in Norwood. The union's goal was zero grievances. Regarding the Norwood plant being landlocked, Mr. Montgomery felt that with the help of the city of Norwood, more acreage could be acquired at very little cost to General Motors. With the close proximity of suppliers (70% within 300 miles), and the just-in-time inventory, they could expand and save GM money. With the proper layout of docks, the company could easily expand and make money and the workers were willing and determined to help GM do it.

City of Norwood's Viewpoint

The city of Norwood argued that GM had given short shrift to its efforts in seeking ways to keep the plant operating. According to Mayor Joseph Sanker:

> We have always worked to meet GM's needs, this included redirecting streets, building a new underpass, making zoning changes that GM wanted.
>
> Furthermore, in recent months, the employees of the Norwood assembly plant have proposed a number of changes intended to reduce costs and improve efficiency at the plant. The City of Norwood, State of Ohio,

local utilities and suppliers have joined in that effort.

> The attitude here used to be "what GM wants, GM gets." Not any more.[9]

Mayor Sanker also pointed out that while General Motors had decided to close the Norwood plant, several foreign manufacturers were building or planning to build auto plants along the Interstate 75 (I-75) corridor that provided access and proximity to suppliers, customers, and skilled labor. However, he still held out hope that GM could be persuaded to stay:

> In recent months, the employees of the Norwood assembly plant have proposed a number of changes intended to reduce costs and improve efficiency at the plant. The City of Norwood, State of Ohio, local utilities and suppliers have joined in that effort. It is our sincere hope that these proposals will be given full consideration by the management of General Motors. It is our further hope that these proposals combined with the Norwood plant's central location and experienced workforce will lead General Motors to the conclusion that closing the Norwood plant is not a prudent business decision. (Hearings, p. 93)

GM's Actions in the Norwood Plant Closing

On November 6, 1986, GM announced that the Norwood plant would be closed by mid-1988, giving the city almost 18 months advance notice. However, by early March GM announced the first date for its plant closing, which turned out to be August 26, 1987. As part of its closing effort, GM developed a comprehensive scheme of worker retraining, job placement, and transfer of workers to other GM locations. Moreover, under the GM-UAW contract, the company was to provide supplemental unemployment benefits, guaranteed income stream benefits, relocation allowances, and continuation of health care coverage. Depending on seniority, hourly laid-off employees with one year or more seniority could receive up to 95 percent of their take home pay for up to two years. The combined value of these benefits was estimated to be over $100 million.

At the behest of Ohio's Governor, GM agreed to hire independent economic development consultants, the Battelle Memorial Institute, to evaluate the best future use of the plant's facilities and surrounding land. GM also retained West Shell Realtors to market the Norwood property.

General Motors also refrained from seeking property tax reassessment on its plant site, thereby saving the City of Norwood about $2 million in tax revenues. GM also demonstrated its earlier commitment to being a good corporate citizen of Norwood City by indicating that its local plant and employees had contributed almost $500,000 to local charities in 1986 alone.

The Battelle Institute Report

In August 1987, Battelle Memorial Institute completed its study and submitted a final report. The Battelle study was designed to accomplish three tasks: (1) objective assessment of strengths and weaknesses associated with the Norwood area; (2) identification of suitable industries and services for GM sites; and (3) development of economic strategies to attract new companies.

The report identified Norwood's strengths in relation to factors such as multistate market access, transportation, and infrastructure (utilities, communications, health care, etc.) from excellent to good. It also recognized, however, Norwood's weaknesses in the form of a poor system of water transportation, the perception of the city as a location with high operating costs, etc. Based on its analysis of all relevant factors, the report identified over 100 industries and services that might be prospects for the plant site and made specific recommendations for its stepwise redevelopment. The Battelle

study concluded that the best use for the site could be served by attracting light manufacturing industries; business-supporting and administrative services; and wholesaling and distribution.[10]

Negotiations Between GM and the City of Norwood

Between November 1986 and March 1987, the city and state officials and UAW leaders made numerous representations to GM for keeping the plant open, but these were unsuccessful. The city immediately launched an effort to cut costs and contain the city's expenses while raising temporary revenues. According to Mayor Joseph Sanker:

> What really hurt us, I guess, is the General Motors announcement that they were going to leave in mid-1988. We took that to heart and immediately made cuts. We took some 1.5 million dollars out by payroll deductions. We laid off a total of 37 people. We privatized our waste collection, which saved several hundred dollars. We did various other things like letting people go through attrition, giving our appointed people 10% cuts in salary. We couldn't lay off our police and fire department personnel because they were under contract. We have economized while maintaining the quality of the fire and police departments. The 70-man fire department was reduced to 52, and the 56-man police department was reduced to 48. These were perhaps top heavy. They made the concessions and agreed to reduce the number of people. The city also tried to enact a 10 mill tax levy, but it was defeated by the local voters.

City officials viewed GM's claims of good corporate citizenship as mere puffery designed for public relations effect. They pointed out that the so-called $100 million GM would pay consisted of contractual payments that GM was obligated to pay and were in no way a magnanimous gesture designed to help the city.

In its dealings with GM, city officials at first attempted a conciliatory approach. They sought GM's help in tiding the city over its financial difficulties during this transition period. They felt that the "big" corporation should be willing to help the "little" town that had come to depend so much on GM. Accordingly, on April 17, 1987, city officials sent a letter to GM's chairman with a "wish-list." It asked that GM provide $2.3 million per year for four years in lieu of taxes, during which period the city would redevelop its tax base. GM was also requested immediately to "donate" to the city GM's 14-acre lot, two parking garages, and to demolish the plant and clear the plant site for redevelopment. In May and June, the city also asked GM to withhold payroll city taxes from the laid-off GM employees' supplemental pay (SUB-pay). The city tax commission also subpoenaed key GM plant officials to appear before the commission and provide information on SUB payments and withholding of taxes, which the tax commissioner estimated to be $2.8 million.

In its response, GM rejected the city's request for aid in lieu of taxes. GM feared it would be confronted with similar requests from all other locations with plant closings, which it simply would not be able to meet. Nor would GM withhold payroll taxes on SUB-pay, as its legality was in question. GM was unwilling to undertake an immediate disposition of its property pending the report from the Battelle Institute. Moreover, in keeping with its policies, GM wanted to undertake a complete environmental clean-up of the property at an approximate cost of $9 million prior to its disposition. Such an action was also necessary to protect GM from any potential liability lawsuits.

Between March and July 1987, discussions and meetings continued between GM representatives and city officials to resolve various outstanding issues arising out of the plant closing. On July 31, 1987, GM released the Battelle Institute report. City officials, however, were not satisfied with either the pace or the progress of negotiations. They had sought the help of state and national

political leaders to pressure GM. However, they were completely unsuccessful in their efforts. Mayor Sanker attributed the failure of these efforts to the politicians' unwillingness to confront GM because the company had many other plants in various congressional districts in Ohio. He further implied that Norwood was a Democratic city in a largely Republican state and, therefore, did not receive much help from Ohio's state and national political leaders.

Undeterred, the city made another strategic change in its efforts to make GM accede to its demands. While discussions with GM were continuing, on August 7, 1987, the city of Norwood filed a suit against GM for $318 million. The city charged GM with breach of contract and fiduciary duty by closing its plant.[11] The city's complaint alleged, among other things, that:

1. GM, during its 64 years of operation, had been storing, burying, or dumping ultrahazardous or toxic materials on its Norwood property, and intended to abandon these at the time of closing of its plant.
2. The city had granted GM many concessions on the express and implicit promise that it would retain active manufacturing facilities in the city of Norwood. As a result of the plant closing, the city claimed:

$56,000,000	for the use of tax revenue and commerce
$ 9,000,000	for increased cost of fire and police protection needed
$ 750,000	for construction of the Forest Avenue underpass
$ 2,500,000	for the cost of rededicating previously vacated city streets

$68,250,000

3. GM had created an equitable fiduciary relationship with the city of Norwood because of its largest relative size and longest (64 years) tenure in the city. Closing of the plant meant a breach of this equitable fiduciary relationship and caused damages to the city. The city asserted that GM had committed fraud by announcing a latter date of closure and then advancing the date.

GM then proceeded with the task of finding a suitable developer for the plant site who could come up with a proposal acceptable to the city, the state, and community leaders. At this point, there was some disagreement within the city administration as to the potential uses for this site. The proposed uses ranged from retail-wholesale distribution activities to a high-rise hotel-office complex. On December 12, 1987, GM announced the selection of the Miller-Valentine Group, a major developer of office and industrial buildings, to develop the Norwood property. The city officials were quite pleased with this selection. Miller-Valentine was given five months to come up with a development plan.

The Miller-Valentine Plan

The M-V group presented its plan in May 1988. It was developed in close cooperation with the Mayor's task force and General Motors. This project was named Highlands Point, after Norwood's title of "Gem of the Highlands," and was developed to meet the need for "revitalized, upscale economic development in a highly attractive urban setting." The plan called for a judicious redevelopment of existing properties and construction of several new structures for use by retail, sales/service, industrial purposes, and offices. It projected construction of approximately one million square feet of facilities suitable for industrial activity on the 40-acre main plant site, and 90,000 square feet of office development. A 163,000-square-foot retail development was planned for the Globe site—a 15-acre parcel adjoining site. The success of the plan was contingent on the city's cooperation in zoning and street closings, securing of Federal Urban Development grant of $6.2 million, the transfer of property and other financial considerations by GM.

GM officials, however, were becoming increasingly reluctant to continue working with the city while the lawsuit was still hanging over their heads. Thus, the company advised the city that GM would not make the additional financial commitment required by the V-M Group until the city dropped its lawsuit. In a letter to Mayor Sanker, Edmond J. Dilworth, Jr., an attorney and group director of CPC-Public Affairs, stated that while GM had refrained from making any public statements at the city's request, one city official publicly accused GM of "economic terrorism."

> This hysterical and inaccurate characterization unfortunately demonstrates the difficulties we've had in establishing a cooperative relationship with the city... We plan to pursue alternative users for the site, which may involve the sale or lease of the buildings. To do otherwise is a waste of our resources at a time when the corporation is cutting costs to improve our competitive position.

The city officials were stunned by GM's response. They had hoped that the lawsuit would bring added pressure on GM and force the company to provide greater financial support to the city. In that they were disappointed. Observed Mayor Sanker:

> We had been working very closely with Miller-Valentine. They had great plans and were a responsible development company from Dayton Ohio. The plan was almost ready to be wrapped up and we had a meeting scheduled. They were coming in to give us the final look at the plans. And we met. They showed us the plans, and then the bomb dropped! They said that GM had told them that if we didn't drop our lawsuit GM would not go along with Miller-Valentine.

The city officials refused to withdraw the suit and GM refused to move further. An impasse had been reached, causing Miller-Valentine to withdraw from the project.

The city suffered another major setback when on September 2, 1988, the Hamilton County Court, Ohio, dismissed the city's suit against GM as totally without merit or basis in fact.[12] In concluding remarks, the court stated:

Regrettably, there is no question that the City (and especially its people and the former employees of General Motors in Norwood) has and will continue to suffer from the withdrawal of the Company. A 64-year association that has generally been beneficial to both parties has drawn to a close, but in the broad sense government, all government, exists for the good of the people, not the reverse. The corporate entity of General Motors is one of those "people" for which government exists.[13]

APPENDIX

TABLE 1. Unit Sales of U.S.-Manufacturered Cars (in thousands)

Year	GM	Ford	Chrysler	American Motors	Volkswagen	American Honda	Nissan	Toyota	TOTAL
1979	4,887	1,475	909	148	167	—	—	—	8,213
1980	4,117	2,102	660	117	177	—	—	—	6,546
1981	3,797	1,381	730	94	163	—	—	—	6,163
1982	3,516	1,346	692	77	91	—	—	—	5,722
1983	4,054	1,571	842	193	85	50	—	—	6,795
1984	4,588	1,979	987	190	74	134	—	—	7,952
1985	4,608	2,070	1,140	124	78	146	40	—	8,205
1986	4,533	2,067	1,175	73	74	235	53	7	8,215
1987									
1988									

SOURCE: "Auto Sales Data," *Wall Street Journal*, Jan. 8, 1981, p. 17; Jan. 6, 1983, p. 10; Jan. 7, 1985, p. 30; Jan. 8, 1987, p. 13.

TABLE 2. U.S. Sales of Selected Foreign-Made Cars (in thousands) (1979–1986)

Year	GM	Ford	Chrysler (COLT)	Toyota	Nissan/ Datsun	Honda	Mazda	Subaru	Mitsubishi	Isuzu	Volkswagen	Volvo	Mercedes Benz	BMW	Audi	Porsche	Fiat	Renault	Jaguar	Saab	Hyundai
1979	—	—	—	508	472	353	157	128	—	—	99	57	50	38	43	—	37	19	—	—	—
1980	—	—	—	582	517	375	161	143	—	—	125	57	48	35	43	—	59	25	—	—	—
1981	—	—	111	577	465	371	166	152	—	—	82	64	58	42	—	62	32	39	5	15	—
1982	—	—	102	530	470	366	163	150	—	—	67	72	63	52	—	68	14	38	10	18	—
1983	—	—	104	556	522	351	173	157	33	—	77	88	71	57	48	—	—	33	16	26	—
1984	13	—	92	558	485	375	170	158	39	—	104	98	76	69	71	—	—	12	18	33	—
1985	85	9	105	620	535	406	211	174	50	27	141	102	85	85	74	25	—	7	21	38	—
1986	160	14	136	634	494	458	223	179	50	39	143	111	97	96	60	30	—	4	25	48	169
1987																					
1988																					

SOURCE: "Auto Sales Data," *Wall Street Journal*, Jan. 8, 1981, p. 17; Jan. 6, 1983, p. 10; Jan. 7, 1985, p. 30; Jan. 8, 1987, p. 13.

NOTES

1. General Motors Corporation, "Press Release," Detroit, Michigan, November 6, 1986, p.1.
2. *Ibid.*
3. *Ibid.*
4. Joseph E. Sanker, Mayor, City of Norwood, "Press Release," January 26, 1987.
5. *Ibid.*
6. U.S. Congress-Senate, General Motors Plant Closings, Hearings before the Subcommittee on Labor, Committee on Labor and Human Resources, One Hundredth Congress, 1st Session, January 26, 1987.
7. General Motors Corporation, press release, p. 1.
8. S. Prakash Sethi, "Norwood, Ohio, Battles GM Over Plant Closing," *Business and Society Review* (1989).
9. Interview with the author. Unless otherwise specified, all direct quotes or paraphrased statements are based on personal interviews or written communications to the author.
10. Battelle Institute, Final Report on Preparation of a Facility Reuse Assessment and Economic Adjustment Strategy for the Norwood, Ohio Area. Columbus, Ohio: Battelle Institute, August 1987.
11. *City of Norwood, Ohio* v. *General Motors Corporation*, Court of Common Pleas, Hamilton County, Ohio, *Complaint and Jury Demand*, Case No. A-8705920, dated August 7, 1987.
12. *City of Norwood, Ohio* v. *General Motors Corporation*, Court of Common Pleas, Hamilton County, Ohio, *Complaint and Jury Demand*, Case No. A-8705920, dated September 2, 1988.
13. *Ibid.*

GOODYEAR TIRE AND RUBBER COMPANY

Hostile corporate takeovers and the public interest

TAKEOVERS IN THE 1980s

The Extent of Takeovers

The United States has been in the throes of a merger wave during the last decade. The newspapers are replete with stories where billion-dollar companies change hands overnight, mostly through friendly mergers and management buyouts, but quite often through unfriendly acquisitions or hostile takeovers. For example, in 1986 the number of tender offers stood at 197, up from 97 in 1982. Their value was $65.1 billion, a 17% decrease from 1985 but well above the 1982 figure of $25.8 billion. On the whole, 76.6% of takeovers initiated were successful. The failure rate for uncontested bids averaged 2.45% from 1978 to 1986. The failure rate for contested bids, however, stood at 48.8%; from 1983 to 1985 the average failure rate for contested bids was 68.9%.[1] The number of hostile offers declined from a high of 42% in 1982 to 26% in 1986. On an average, control of the company (rather than a mere stake) was the objective in 73% of tender offers. Of the offers, 89.2% were cash. In 1987, the top 200 deals ranged from a value of $7.6 billion (Standard Oil of Ohio, acquired by British Petroleum) to $152 million. Of all deals 15% were for over $1 billion, while 35% exceeded $500 million. The median of the top 200 deals was for $365 million.[2] (See Table 1.)

Public Controversy

This is not the first merger wave, and it is certainly not likely to be the last one. One has only to go back 35 years to remember the "go-go" years of the 1960s that gave rise to the term *conglomerate*. Mergers and acquisitions are a rather constant feature of the market economy. What makes today's mergers different is that they arise out of the disparity between financial markets and real product markets. They are undertaken primarily out of financial motives, not for production and marketing.

This frenzy of takeovers has made celebrities of many raiders. The names of T. Boone Pickens, Sir James Goldsmith, Carl Icahn, and Ronald Perlman have become household words. The new breed of entrepreneurs involved in these activities have become multi-millionaires many times over. They have also created a new class of millionaires among those who provide support services for these ventures, namely, the arbitrageurs, investment bankers, lawyers, merger specialists, brokers, and others. Many fortunes have been made almost overnight—although not all of them have been entirely legal or ethical. This is not surprising. In the frenzy of highly pressured activity involving millions of dollars and stock transactions, it is understandable that some shady dealings and unsavory characters will slip through. What is surprising, however, is

14

TABLE 1.   Tender Offers: 1982–1986

	1982	1983	1984	1985	1986
Number of offers	97	74	147	142	197
Number of targets	76	60	125	116	181
Targets' $ value (billions)	25.8	17.3	58.6	78.3	65.1
% Completed offers	73	78	80	76	76
% Hostile offers	42	35	24	30	26
% of offers where control was at stake	73	70	68	72	82
Status (%)					
Completed	73	78	80	76	64
Not completed	27	22	20	24	20
Open	0	0	0	0	16
Target Response (%)					
Friendly	43	57	63	62	69
Hostile	42	35	24	30	26
Neutral	15	8	13	8	5
Form of Offer (%)					
Any-or-all	42	64	74	73	85
Partial	37	16	17	23	12
Two-tier	21	20	9	4	3
Control Sought (%)					
Stakehold	19	10	6	9	2
Control	73	70	68	72	82
Lock-up	4	8	14	13	11
Mop-up	4	12	12	6	5
Cash/Exchange (%)					
Cash	88	91	91	85	91
Exchange/mixed	12	9	9	15	9
Market					
NYSE	37	32	33	41	38
AMEX	16	8	12	8	21
OTC	43	50	49	40	33
Other	4	10	6	11	8

SOURCE: Securities and Exchange Commission, *Monthly Statistics*, vol. 64, no. 2 (1987), pp. 6–9.

the evidence that unethical and illegal practices were engaged in by some of the most venerable and blue-chip organizations in the financial community. Witness the prosecution of Ivan Boesky and others on charges of insider trading. Among the Wall Street brokerage, investment, and law firms involved are Kidder Peabody, Drexel Burnham Lambert, and numerous lesser luminaries.

The latest merger movement, however, is significant in another important perspective in that both sides, i.e., the acquirers, and the acquirees, claim to have similar objectives: to improve America's competitiveness, make companies more efficient and managers more responsive, and increase shareholder values. On the face of it, there cannot be such a thing as a hostile takeover from the viewpoint of the shareholders. The acquirer must offer a premium over the prevailing market price in order to induce the current shareholders to sell their stock. And these premiums, especially where there has been a bidding war, can be quite handsome.

The issue, therefore, is not merely that of a change in ownership from one group of individuals to another. Instead, it is intertwined with three other equally important issues. First, the role of the private corporations as the primary vehicles of economic activity in free market-oriented societies. Second, the relative role played by different groups in the survival and growth of the corporation and their rights in having a say in the running of the corporation. And, third, the changing nature of stockholders and stockholdings and how these might affect the welfare of the corporation and the interests of other stakeholders.

The increased globalization of competition, movement of capital, and almost instant transfer of ownership have created a wide gap between the legal theory of the corporation and its reality and have challenged the myth of shareholder control. In the process, a number of thorny questions have been raised pertaining to the organization of economic activity, the rights and obligations of various stakeholders, and the maintenance of a competitive economy for the benefit of society at large. Nowhere have these issues come to the fore so sharply as in the case of hostile mergers. They place in sharp relief the various perspectives articulated by highly sophisticated advocates. The debate has only begun and is likely to greatly intensify in the coming months and years until such time that a new social consensus emerges as to the manner in which large corporations should be organized, managed, and held accountable for their activities.

A BRIEF SUMMARY OF THE GOODYEAR TAKEOVER

The following case study of Goodyear Tire & Rubber company is typical of many such cases that have come to light. It also provides valuable insights into the arguments that are being made both for and against such hostile takeover attempts.

In November 1986, Sir James Goldsmith proposed to pay $49 a share for the 88.5% of Goodyear that he didn't already own. The deal came to about $4.7 billion. Sir James was the chairman of General Oriental Investments Limited—a company based in England. He is among the handful of well-known corporate raiders whose very name strikes terror in the hearts of CEOs of target companies and delights the imagination of those groupies, called arbitrageurs, who follow suit in the hope of making a killing in the stock market through short-term buying and selling in the stock of the target company.

Goodyear countered the Goldsmith threat by unveiling an ambitious restructuring plan. It included repurchasing of as many as 20 million of the company's common shares outstanding and also selling off three major units. The chairman of Goodyear, Robert Mercer, attacked Sir James as a greedy predator who was indifferent to the welfare of the company and its many stakeholders. In addition to using all the usual legal defense strategies against hostile offers, Goodyear also launched a public relations and political pressure offensive by enlisting the support of political leaders and labor unions, among others. When all the dust had settled, Goodyear was still independent. But it had to pay a very heavy price. Sir James was "persuaded" to sell his stock to Goodyear in the process and made a profit of nearly $100 million in greenmail. It is not known how much profit the Goldsmith group actually made. As mentioned earlier, their original offer was to acquire the 88.5% of the company they did not already control for $49 a share or $4.7 billion. According to Robert Mercer, they did acquire 12.5 million shares (while arbitrageurs acquired some 22 million).[3] That would amount to an actual outlay of some $613 million. For that stock plus what the group already owned, they received $100 million or around $56 a share. For every $49 share purchased they made $7, over a period of about four months.

The saga of Goodyear escaping the clutches of Sir James Goldsmith enraged many observers because of the alleged greenmail payments. This, along with certain other hostile takeovers, provided the catalyst that led to serious legislative discussion about the need for changes in federal and state laws governing stock transactions and takeover activity. However, to date, no significant legislation has been enacted at the federal level.

ISSUES FOR ANALYSIS

The Goodyear case raises a variety of issues pertaining to corporate governance, stockholder interests, management accountability, and the interests of other important stakeholders, notably the employees and the communities where these corporations are located. At the macro level, they are concerned with the long-term economic viability of these institutions because, more often than not, they take on a heavy debt burden either to fight such takeovers or to pay for them. An additional concern has to do with the impact of these mergers on the strength and competitiveness of the U.S. economy. Among some of the specific issues are:

1. What are some of the benefits and costs of maintaining an environment of relatively unrestrained merger and acquisition activity in the United States?
2. How effective are the current rules and regulations in maintaining an open environment for investments leading to mergers and acquisitions on a fair and equitable basis so as to minimize illegal activity, e.g., insider trading? If the current regulations are not effective or are insufficient, what additional regulation might be imposed?
3. Should we make a distinction between friendly and unfriendly mergers? Which groups stand to gain the most from friendly mergers, and should protecting these interests have a higher priority?
4. How do the current tax laws and accounting procedures help or hurt friendly and unfriendly mergers? What changes, if any, are needed in these laws and procedures?
5. What are the differences between the financial market value of a transaction and the real product market value, and how do they influence different types of merger activity?
6. How do various groups benefit or suffer from mergers and takeovers, e.g., stockholders, managers (upper, middle, and lower level), workers, lenders, communities where plants and corporate headquarters are located?
7. What are the rights of local communities and workers who are affected by a takeover?
8. What are the rights of shareholders of the target company? Are there significant differences between classes of shareholders? Are shareholders really dedicated to the well-being of a company? Alternately, why should shareholders be concerned with the welfare of a company when selling it would yield them better returns and thereby maximize their self-interest?
9. How should one evaluate the role of corporate raiders? What service do they provide to current stockholders, other corporate constituencies, and society at large? Are their rewards justified by their services?
10. What are some of the ethical and moral arguments that should be made both for and against friendly and unfriendly mergers?
11. What are some of the recent measures taken by various state legislatures and U.S. courts affecting mergers and takeovers? What do you feel is their impact on the economic activity and rights of various stakeholders affected by mergers and takeovers?

DETAILS OF THE GOODYEAR TAKEOVER

How Goodyear Became Vulnerable

In October 1986, after a month of speculation that it could be a takeover candidate, the Goodyear Tire and Rubber Company (the world's largest tire maker) said it was considering a restructuring.[4] The company retained the investment banking firms of Goldman Sachs & Co. and Drexel Burnham Lambert Inc. to assist it with a study aimed at developing a program for maximizing shareholder values over the near term. This would protect Goodyear's stockholders in the event that a suitor emerged. By October 27, 1986, Goodyear's stock closed at $44.125 a share, up from $32.75 a month earlier.

In the preceding years, its chairman and chief executive officer, Robert E. Mercer, and his management group had been attempting to diversify Goodyear through energy and aerospace. Tires accounted for 80% of operating profit. Analysts had speculated that if Goodyear were restructured, shareholders might receive as much as $45 to $52 a share. Goodyear's approximately 109.3 million shares outstanding had a book value of about $34 a share. Most analysts also thought that a restructuring would involve the sale of the company's oil and gas reserves. Goodyear had adopted a portfolio structure-type strategy. In examining what attracted the attack, Mr. Mercer found that the fact that the market value of the company's assets exceeded the stock price for the corporation as a whole left it very vulnerable. This was notably true of energy and aerospace holdings. Another area of vulnerability for Goodyear was its good cash flow, which could be "converted" by cutting back in areas of advertising, training, research and development.[5]

The Raid

It soon became apparent that Sir James Goldsmith, an Anglo-French financier and corporate raider, was interested in taking over Goodyear. He owned more than 15% of Goodyear's shares, a stake valued at $781 million based on a price of $47.75 a share. Sir James was understood to have amassed the necessary financial resources required to launch a bid for the company if he chose to. Merrill Lynch & Co., Sir James's financial adviser, was also rumored to become a principal in any bid for Goodyear.

Despite the fact that no tender offer had been made, Goodyear's chairman, Robert Mercer, said in a letter to employees that Goodyear was a takeover target. Mercer also told employees that Goodyear was taking every step to avoid a takeover. In a filing with the Securities and Exchange Commission (SEC), Sir James said that he would not immediately make a tender offer because the stock price was too high due to overreaction by the market. In addition, in a letter to Mr. Mercer, Sir James wrote that he was not interested in receiving any greenmail. A further twist was that Merrill Lynch could collect fees of $150 to $200 million, if Sir James succeeded in his quest for Goodyear. In return Merrill Lynch agreed to provide $1.9 billion in financing if Sir James decided to launch a tender offer for Goodyear. The potential fees and financing commitment were disclosed in SEC filings by Sir James. Finally, in November 1986, Sir James proposed to buy Goodyear for $49 a share. The fate of Goodyear thus depended on the company's ability to boost its stock price above the $49 offered by Sir James.

Goodyear's Defense

In his testimony before the Senate, Mr. Mercer insisted that "Goodyear resisted a takeover in the best interest of the Company" and its "real or long term shareholders, our employees, and plant town communities, suppliers, creditors and, of course, our customers, without whom there would be no business in which to invest."[6]

Stock Repurchase and Restructuring. To do this, Goodyear's restructuring plan called for repurchasing as much as $20 million of its shares outstanding and selling off units of the company. Sir James then said that he would not launch a hostile tender offer until the company had a chance to pursue its restructuring. If the stock price got above the offering price, then no deal would occur. Goodyear still refused to accept any offer because it felt that it could do a better job of enhancing shareholder value with its restructuring.

Rallying Shareholders. At the same time, Goodyear's management and its unionized employees tried to rally public opinion and state and federal government leaders to prevent a takeover by Sir James. Mr. Mercer advised union officials to make elected officials aware of the consequences of foreign takeovers of U.S. companies. In addition, Goodyear announced that as part of its restructuring program, it would offer early retirement to some of the 4,900 salaried employees at its headquarters. Due to the pressure from Goodyear and its employees, congressional hearings were quickly called to investigate this matter. Mr. Mercer indicated that he was pessimistic about fighting any acquisition bid by Sir James. The question then became whether Sir James would be willing to go ahead with a hostile takeover in the face of widespread opposition within Goodyear and political pressure from the communities in which Goodyear had plants.[7]

Mr. Mercer warned employees that a rigorous cost-cutting effort would result in layoffs, early retirements, and other curtailments. Goodyear announced that it would close two plants. These closings would result in terminations of about 3,200 hourly and salaried employees. In addition, capital expenditures for the continuing business of tires and related products had to be slashed by $275 million. All of these steps were necessary to provide cash for the debt service and early retirement costs incurred in the takeover battle.

In addition to commenting on the long-term health of the company, Mr. Mercer made a strong distinction between Goodyear's "true," "real," and "classic" shareholders who had an interest in the health of the company and the "elite band of raiders, speculators and financiers (who are. . .) perverting the free market system and dynamic capitalism into a quick money game with America's competitive position, economy and jobs as the chips."[8] It is not clear why Mr. Mercer would place a higher degree of trust in "true," "real," and "classic" shareholders. The so-called "elite band of raiders" were able to become shareholders precisely because the "other" loyal shareholders were willing to sell their loyalty and long-term interest in the company for immediate prof-

its, which were reflected in the higher prices for their stock offered by the raiders. Mercer considered the shareholders who sold 12.5 million shares to the takeover groups without knowing who they were or what they were up to, as well as those who sold another 22 million shares to the arbitrageurs, as duped, for they did not have the skills to read the signs and skills of an impending move on the company. It is also not clear that these sellers were indeed simpletons who were duped by the raiders. Studies show that raiders generally acquire their early positions in targeted company stock through the purchase of large blocks of stocks from institutional investors, i.e., insurance companies, pension funds, and mutual funds. These stockholders are quite sophisticated and make decisions with full knowledge and understanding of the consequences of their actions.

Mr. Mercer contended that raiders were not true investors.[9] He also saw Goodyear's other constituencies—mainly labor and local communities—as ill served by the raiders. He felt that the raiders' focus on shareholder rights failed to address the legitimate concerns of these other groups who had a definite stake in the business and whose destinies were interwoven in the corporation with those of the shareholders.

Aftermath

In the case of Sir James Goldsmith's attempted takeover of Goodyear, Goldsmith's track record at Crown Zellerbach led people to believe that restructuring would be harsh. Three issues came together: a socially responsible layoff policy, plant closing and relocation policies, and management prerogatives.

In the end, the local community/labor/management coalition prevailed, but the amount of greenmail paid was staggering and made Sir James much richer than he would have been otherwise.[10] It also considerably weakened Goodyear. Ironically, Goodyear ended up doing many of the things

Sir James had threatened to do. Management would add that the long-term productive capacity and competitive ability of the United States economy is held hostage to the "efficient financial trading principle" as opposed to efficient production. Thus, there are two sets of consequences that greenmail is allegedly adopted to avoid: (1) whatever adversity might befall the local corporation, community, and labor; and (2) a weakening of the competitive viability of the economy as a whole. For the most part, stockholders who are not included in the corporation-community-labor group resent the practice of greenmail. They contend that soaring debt, falling investment, and curtailed research do not augur well for profits.

In the case of Goodyear, debt rose from $2.6 billion to $5.3 billion. Planned investment fell from $300 million to $270 million and research from $1.6 billion to $1 billion. Over $2 billion in assets were to be sold off. Sir James Goldsmith walked away with a $93 million profit. Stockholders have a hard time seeing themselves as winners. Their only real choice is to stick with management or sell their stock. Management blames Goldsmith's greed for their plight and claims to have done the best it could for shareholders and local communities.

Many shareholders question the quality of Goodyear management in the first place. They also object that, in the event that greenmail seems necessary, they should at least have a say in such an important decision. They are demanding shareholder approval for greenmail, poison pills, and parachutes.[11] Furthermore, they object to the fact that takeover groups are offered premium prices not available to ordinary shareholders.[12] They are prevented from cashing in on the premium price takeover groups receive for their shares. They can either stick with the restructured company or sell their stock at the current market price. This apparent disparity between stockholder interests and those of management, labor, and the local community have raised a larger issue—corporate governance.

Due to all the political pressure and opposition, as well as opposition from Goodyear, Sir James was forced to stop his bid for the company. However, Goodyear had to buy out Sir James' stake for $618 million ($49.50 a share) and also make a tender offer for an additional 40 million of its shares at $50 a share, or $2 billion. The two purchases would total about 48% of the company's shares outstanding. They also planned to sell off their oil and gas units, their aerospace unit, and their wheel manufacturing unit. This plan left the company heavily burdened with debt. Sir James felt that he had no alternative but to be bought out once he decided against a hostile takeover. He did not feel that this was equivalent to receiving greenmail. Goodyear had to sell 25% of its assets to settle this. After the restructuring, Goodyear's annual sales dropped to just over $8 billion, from $9.6 billion in 1985.

The takeover attempt accelerated restructuring at Goodyear: a 12% downsizing, 4,000 layoffs, R&D and capital expenditures focused on projects with a short-term payoff, and a $4 billion debt which leveraged the company to 80% of debt to total capitalization. Mr. Mercer directly countered the argument that takeovers are good for America:

> In 1977, at a time when the tire business was at a low ebb, we invested $260 million in a new state-of-the-art radial auto tire plant in Lawton, to assure our future competitive position in world markets. With the same objective, in the 1970's and early 1980's, we modernized tire plants in Alabama and Tennessee and built up a highly competitive wire plant in North Carolina to provide top quality steel wire for use in our tire products. Then in 1983 we converted a Texas bias-tire plant to radial tires with costs that will meet Korean competition head-on when the start-up phase is completed later this month. Because of those investments, Goodyear's U.S. plants can hold their own today in global competition. In many foreign countries, for instance, it takes 25 to 50 man-minutes to manufacture 13-inch tire. Our modern U. S. plants do it in less than 10. Our advanced

equipment and technology make it possible to support higher American wages and benefits—more than $20 an hour versus as low as $1.60 in Korea. Now had we been the target of a takeover attempt in the mid 1970's, had we been force then into the short term planning... none of these investments would have been made."[13]

THE BATTLE RAGES

Why Takeovers Are Good

Takeovers are rationalized by proponents in terms of increasing economic efficiency. They focus upon management errors in strategic planning.

Financially Efficient Asset Use. The classic exponent of takeover benefits and the one to whom everyone defers has been Mr. Michael C. Jensen.[14] Mr. Jensen summarizes the scientific evidence of research as follows:

1. Takeovers of companies by outsiders do not harm shareholders of the target company; in fact, they gain substantial wealth.
2. Corporate takeovers do not waste resources; they use assets productively.
3. Takeovers do not siphon commercial credit from its uses in funding new plants and equipment.
4. Takeovers do not create gains for shareholders through creation of monopoly power.
5. Prohibition of plant closings, layoffs, and dismissals following takeovers would reduce market efficiency and lower aggregate living standards.
6. Although managers are self-interested, the environment in which they operate gives them relatively little leeway to feather their nests at shareholders' expense. Corporate control-related actions of managers do not generally harm shareholders, but actions that eliminate actual or potential takeover bids are most suspect as exceptions to this rule.
7. Golden parachutes for top-level executives are, in principle, in the interests of shareholders. Although the practice can be abused, the evidence indicates that shareholders gain when golden parachutes are

adopted. Mr. Jensen concludes that, in general, the activities of takeover specialists benefit shareholders.

To understand this rationale, it is important to review the main characteristics of corporate strategic planning in the preceding decades. The 1960s and 1970s marked a time of tremendous corporate structural change. Corporations grew through diversification and became conglomerates. In a sense, it was also a "takeover period"; but, in general, it was the large, established companies that were acquiring the smaller specialty companies. Many companies expanded into unrelated businesses. The underlying logic for such conglomerate diversification was based on a portfolio model of analysis. The corporation was interested in maintaining steady earnings. Diversification provided it with a hedge against losses when one sector or industry had a downturn. But the reverse was also true. Higher profit levels were sometimes foregone in favor of maintaining a steady and safe level of growth and income. To oversimplify, if a conglomerate had ten divisions, it was most likely at any given time that some would do well while others lagged behind or even incurred a loss. As long as a majority did well, steady profits could be assured. Some might even prove to be cash cows. Only rarely would all do well or fail at the same time. Contemporary takeover entrepreneurs focus very much on what they call management's strategic mistakes in acquiring unrelated businesses that ended up as underperforming and/or undervalued. Takeover proponents claim they can improve overall performance by getting rid of such assets and concentrating the business in a few well-chosen lines that promise high efficiency and return.

Interestingly enough, an SEC study that was published in 1988 contended that present takeovers are simply attempts to undo acquisitions that have failed. The conglomerate movement of the 1960s was essentially flawed.[15]

In appearing before Congress in 1985 (in connection with his takeover of Crown Zellerbach), Sir James Goldsmith decried both socialism and state corporatism and praised the free market.[16] Modern business, he asserted, has a pyramid structure. At the base are big business and big unions; at the peak is government. He sees those parties as both needing and taking care of each other, to the exclusion of small-and medium-sized business. He credits the latter with providing 35 million new jobs in the USA between 1965 and 1985 and praises their innovativeness and entrepreneurial spirit.

Goldsmith says the debate about takeovers is really about the "new entrepreneurial revolutions and freedoms that have engineered it."[17] Speaking of his experience with companies in France he added, "the best thing that could happen . . . would be that they should be taken over and that their constituent parts be liberated from the dead hands of established bureaucrats." Sir James adds, "Free market forces either force management to get to work or alternately allow new managers and new owners to take over. Artificial devices which inhibit such changes do no more than protect the unsatisfactory. They lead to ossification and decline."[18]

A second point that almost all takeover proponents focus upon is organizational inefficiency. They claim that corporate staffs are becoming bloated and inefficient bureaucracies. The term "corpocracy" has been coined to describe the bureaucratization of private enterprise. In their study of corpocracy, Mark Green and John Berry estimated that corporate organizational inefficiency costs $862 billion a year, six times the amount of government waste estimated by the Grace Commission.[19] However tendentious such estimates may be, the traits of corpocracy are more telling: the prevalence of insensitivity to employees, the encouragement of office politics over productivity, the fostering of secrecy over communication, the diffusion of responsibility through endless meetings, the production of paperwork paralysis, the neglect of potential markets, the encouragement of short-term thinking, the isolation of management from workers, the discouragement of innovation and the avoidance of employees who rock the boat. If any of the above is accurate, it is clear that capitalism has moved a long way from the ideals of Adam Smith. In such a situation, overhead costs soar while innovativeness and the ability to move quickly suffer. It is not surprising, then, that proponents of takeovers propose large-scale reorganization with reductions in management and staff along with the selling of unproductive assets.

A third target of criticism upon which takeover advocates focus is the large amounts of cash that are devoted to senior management compensation and perquisites. This has opened managers to the charge that they are primarily out for personal gain at the shareholders' expense. Raiders such as T. Boone Pickens and Carl Icahn have remarked many times that top management no longer thinks like shareholders.[20] (Their interests and the shareholders' interests no longer coincide.)

In his testimony before the House, Mr. Pickens expressed it this way:[21]

> The growing gap between ownership and control has distorted the traditional economic incentives that drive our free enterprise system, and many of our largest businesses have languished as a result. As our largest corporations matured, managers experienced more and more difficulty finding sound investment opportunities within their core businesses. But, rather than distributing returns to the shareholders who had put their money at risk, they frantically diversified into unfamiliar businesses. Slow growth combined with strong cash flows tempted managers to use discretionary income to buy whatever was for sale. The urge to conglomerate overwhelmed any inclination to return cash to owners because managers' careers and financial futures depended more on size than results. Mediocre results pacified shareholders, while an ever-increasing empire justified higher salaries, more perks, and bigger bonuses. Consequently, performance took a backseat to size.

Long-Term Efficiency of the U.S. Economy.
Another issue upon which takeover proponents focus is international competitive
advantage. In this area, they see American
industry heading downhill. The former
under secretary of the treasury and budget
director Richard Darman, as well as former
commerce secretary Malcolm Baldridge,
joined the criticism of much of contemporary
management for failing to apply and follow
through on technology that they invented.[22]
The nature of competitive advantage has
changed dramatically in the past years due to
deregulation of many domestic industries as
well as sharply increased foreign competition. This increased competition is due to a
number of factors: new cost-cutting technologies, lower labor costs, and intensity of sales
efforts. Foreign competitors are not free of
allegations of dumping.[23] In most industries,
however, it would be difficult to maintain
that their competitive advantage was due
solely to dumping. To restore the competitive
edge of the U.S., industry takeover proponents primarily propose restructuring of production operations. Most often this means a
leaner workforce. They drive a hard economic logic of cost controls and input/output
ratios. In addition, they call for tighter financial management and more efficacious sales
efforts.

A related reason for takeovers is to exp-
and capacity for production, distribution,
and sales. At present it is frequently cheaper
to buy than to build. This seems to be the
logic operative in Chrysler's $3.5 billion
takeover of American Motors as well as in
Emery Air Freight's bid for Purolator.[24] The
takeover in this context is based upon syner-
gies between related businesses and has
good historical prospects for success. A final
reason advanced for takeovers is that comparatively low interest rates make takeovers
as well as leveraged buyouts by management more attractive than ever. When low
interest is coupled with a set of undervalued
assets, the real costs for acquirers are greatly
diminished.

G. Chris Anderson made the case for
Drexel Burnham Lambert in Senate
Hearings:[25]

Further Legislation of Acquisition Activity Is Unwarranted

- Merger and acquisition activity results in a
  shifting of assets to more productive uses,
  more efficient forms of distribution, and technology transfers, which promote new research
  and development.
- Acquisitions expedite restructuring of unsuccessful conglomerates into more efficient and
  more highly valued entities.
- Acquisition activity serves to spur management to strengthen company performance
  and may result in the replacement of ineffective management. The chief executive officers
  of Walt Disney Productions, Martin Marietta
  Corp., and Phillips Petroleum Company have
  all declared that acquisition attempts on their
  companies have forced management to
  become more disciplined.
- Tender offers result in substantial gains to
  shareholders of target firms and benefit shareholders of bidding companies.
- Many defensive strategies available to target
  management increase shareholder wealth by
  evoking higher competing offers or deterring
  inadequate bids.
- Acquisitions result in transfers of wealth to
  shareholders who normally reinvest the proceeds in the capital markets or purchase goods
  and services, thereby in either case stimulat-
  ing economic growth and making money
  available for investment.
- Acquisition activity has not reduced corporate expenditures for long-term investment.
- Further regulation of acquisitions is unnecessary because the Williams Act strikes an equitable balance between targets and acquirers
  that allows the market to operate efficiently.
  The overall balance between acquirer and target has not been upset in recent acquisition
  activity. Isolated cases of abuse should not be
  addressed with broad legislative measures,
  but rather redressed on a case-by-case basis in
  the courts.

Mr. Anderson concluded:

In sum, Drexel Burnham believes that mergers and acquisitions are a valid business strategy which spurs economic growth and productivity. Acquisitions are motivated by legitimate business objectives such as achieving a better allocation of resources, substituting new management teams, and maximizing other business and economic opportunities. These advantages result, even if the objective of the challenge of the control is to divest part of the target's assets. These transactions almost invariably result in such assets being transferred to stronger or more aggressive managements which more efficiently and effectively deploy the divested assets.

Moral Justification: Self-Interest and the Common Good. The economic reasons for takeovers have a corollary in moral reasoning, which is rooted in free market ideology. Defenders of takeovers propose three dominant values: individual liberty, fiduciary duties to shareholders, and social utility.

Viewing takeovers as a type of action, proponents argue that they can have good consequences for society. The fundamental rationale of this argument reiterates the basic free market premise that individual liberty in economic decision making both protects the rights of the individual to seek his or her self-interest and is in the long-term interest of society. With respect to contemporary takeover activity, proponents argue that the long-term results are in the best interests of society, for the U. S. economy will be healthier. Shareholders are also said to be better served by such a free market. During a takeover, they may divest at a premium. If they hold their stocks, they will benefit in the long run by the improved economic performance of the company. Those taking over the company, it is argued, are themselves shareholders; their interests coincide with those of other shareholders. In the end it is asserted that a number of operating, financial, and tax benefits for both individuals and society may follow from a corporate takeover. Boone Pickens put it this way:[26]

In the wake of the recent insider trading scandal, the business establishment has raised a hue and cry that unsolicited corporate takeovers must be stopped. Business Roundtable has seized the opportunity to trot out its tired anti-shareholder, pro-management agenda one more time, and Congress has been inundated with pleas for reform.

When the good old boys of corporate America appear before you, look closely at where their interests lie. When they say they are long-termers, ask how much stock they own in the companies they manage. Ask them what percentage of their total personal assets that ownership represents. In other words, ask them if they have made a long-term commitment to their stockholders and employees.

Those in favor of takeovers argue a hard (and theoretical) market logic, primarily in terms of efficiency, competition, and shareholder profits. Their argument is both macro and long term. It is macro because their focus is upon the competitiveness of U.S. industry in an increasingly tough international environment. They argue that companies that are the object of takeovers are sick and mismanaged. In the long run, they are headed down the slope to extinction unless drastic measures are taken. The raiders come in, perform surgery, and help bring U.S. industry back to health. It is extremely important to note that the promise is not to bring this or that company back to health exactly as it was. There is a process of restructuring involved. New management may dismantle parts or all of a company while simultaneously building up others. Assets do not vanish, but they take different forms and are managed in new ways.

Anti-Takeover Forces

At the same time, there is no doubt that takeovers can be like corporate earthquakes that frequently leave formerly standing companies as a pile of rubble. Only very strong institutions withstand the initial tremor and subsequent readjustments.

Taking Care of Shareholders. Often, takeovers are justified as being in the shareholders' interests. Andrew Sigler, who is the head of the Business Roundtable, a business lobby, countered with this argument:[27]

> Now, I think we have to take a quick look at these shareholders we are all talking about protecting. The shareholders today are principally firms, professionally. Some two-thirds of the equity in the New York Stock Exchange is owned by these funds, and in a company like Champion, over three-quarters of our stock falls into that category.
>
> These are very sophisticated people. They value a company's stock based on its current earnings or its current prospects. They weigh that investment opportunity against their other alternatives. There are no speculative run-ups anymore. The end result of this kind of ownership has been reducing the P/E ratios of companies substantially in the last 4 or 5 years. Of course, that has been greatly pushed along by the high interest rates that we have had.
>
> I think the other part of the shareholders we have to look at is our ownership. We have an ownership today of the economic system of this country that feels that its principal responsibility is to the people whose money it manages, with very little feeling about what its real ownership is. In fact, if I heard him right, I think I heard Mr. LeBaron say that it might be something to think of in terms of selling that vote—renting, I think was the expression.
>
> The rhetoric of the raider is that he is doing everything for the shareholder. What we are really saying is we are willing to liquidate important parts of the strength of the economy to give more money to our pension funds. The real irony of that is that the assurance that an individual will indeed receive his pension is dependent upon the long-term viability of that institution that he works for. Annual up and down performance of the pension fund has very little to do with guaranteeing the success of that.

Financial and "Real" Market Disparities. Opponents of takeovers also underscore the disparity that exists between financial markets and "real product" markets. They assert that the intention of the takeover artists is to reap short-term trading gains, while committing nothing to R&D or to the long-term productive performance of a company or the economy. That is, the raiders skim off profits in the financial markets while creating no "real wealth" in the product markets. Andrew Sigler commented:[28]

> Behind the smokescreen of doing good for shareholders and punishing stupid, entrenched management, and using the magic cloak of the word "free market," a small group is systematically extracting the equity from corporations and replacing it with debt, and incidentally accumulating major wealth.
>
> Now, anyone who believes that there is no difference between debt and equity in the guts of the economic system just doesn't understand how the system really works. The basic unit we use in this system, basic business unit, is the corporation. We generally measure the strength of that corporation, its ability to perform its normal function to grow, et cetera, by the amount of this equity.
>
> Now, we think it is fiscal insanity to let the country go on with this type of phenomenon because the country loses. When the equity moves out, it does not go into equity of another company, so the economic system in effect is losing the fuel that makes it run.

Those arguing against takeovers focus on what they call the selfish intentions of takeover groups. Critics ask, do takeover critics really mean to increase the economic performance of the assets or are they opportunistically making a run at handsome greenmail payoffs? Major criticism comes when people suspect that those who take the company over do not intend to preserve and further it. Rather, they have in mind either to be paid greenmail or to strip the company of its valuable (undervalued) assets, pay off the bonds, pocket the difference, and get out. Those who believe in the likelihood of such a scenario, not surprisingly, see the takeover people as the first cousins of the robber barons. It is only natural that an antitakeover coalition has emerged. Moral objections are based both on the (harmful) consequences of takeover actions as well as on the greedy and selfish motivation of those launching a takeover attempt. Opposition is composed of management, labor, and local communities. They are the ones in line to bear the adverse consequences of restructuring.

Ends and Means

In his testimony regarding takeovers, Felix Rohatyn, a leading Wall Street figure, mentioned abuses bought about by what was happening and suggested the following:[29]

> The issues involved here are three-fold:
> a. The integrity of our securities markets;
> b. The safety of our financial institutions; c. The constructive use of capital as an engine for growth.
> These are all jeopardized by what is happening today.... At the same time, if takeover excesses are curbed, abusive defensive tactics must also be curbed. Not all takeovers are bad, not all managements are good, not all directors represent the shareholders' best interests. Takeovers do not have to be friendly; they have to be fair and soundly financed. The following should be considered:
>
> 1. Outlaw all forms of "greenmail";
> 2. Reestablish the principle of "one share—one vote";
> 3. Eliminate any form of "poison pill";
> 4. Require shareholder vote on any bona-fide offer for 100% of a company, or on major restructuring proposals;
> 5. Eliminate "crown jewel options," "shark repellents," and all other defensive stratagems designed to discourage a bona-fide bidder;
> 6. Override state takeover statutes which provide management and directors with almost unlimited license to turn away bona-fide bidders and entrench themselves.

Management has developed a number of tools to discourage takeovers. In doing so, they have spawned a new business vocabu-

lary: poison pills, greenmail, white knights, and golden as well as tin parachutes. These tools have one thing in common: to make a takeover so costly that no one would attempt it. It is important to examine what management is doing and whose interests it serves. The same moral scrutiny regarding the intentions of management, as well as the consequences of its actions, applies.

Takeover groups are criticized for junk bond financing. Junk bonds are highly risky in comparison with other bond offerings. They are not for novice investors. They remain, however, a legitimate financial tool. More important, junk bonds are not the driving force behind takeovers.[30] In 1985, junk bonds financed $6.23 billion of all mergers and acquisitions. This is less than 5% of the $140 billion that figured in all mergers and acquisitions and less than 10% of the $78 billion represented by takeover tender offers. In all, 38.2% of junk bonds in 1985 went for mergers and acquisitions. Even though this trend seems to be increasing somewhat, the mode of financing is not the key issue.

Poison pills have been increasingly used by management to fend off aggressive takeovers. The definition of a poison pill is by no means uniform. In general, it involves the issuance of a pro rata dividend to common stockholders. This dividend comprises stock or the rights to acquire stock of (1) the issuer ("flip-in" provisions) or (2) the "acquiring persons" ("flip-over" provisions) involved in a business combination with the issuer. In addition, poison pills may involve issuing stock with super voting rights ("back-end provisions"), which involve the right of shareholders to tender stock to the issuer for a specified securities package, and convertible preferred stock provisions.[31]

The most important provision is that acquiring persons may be excluded from the exercise of such rights, even though they are stockholders. Poison pill rights cannot be exercised by stockholders unless triggered by specified events such as a merger, the commencement of a tender offer, or the acquisition of a specific percentage of the issuer's stock. Unless triggered, they are redeemable by the issuer at a nominal price. The intent of such pills is clear: management hopes to set up insurmountable barriers to hostile outside bidders who would purchase a company's shares. Stockholders are usually not consulted. In imposing prohibitive costs on outside bidders, poison pills effectively give management exclusive authority to decide if an acquisition can proceed. Defenders of the pill say that it buys time. Without it, the object of a takeover has only 20 business days following the beginning of a hostile tender offer in which to respond. Management argues that the additional time to negotiate is beneficial to shareholders in the long run.

The Supreme Court of the State of Delaware upheld the legality of the pill in a 1985 decision, *Moran* vs. *Household International*.[32]

In the past few years, over 300 major American corporations have adopted the pill; not all have escaped takeover. Opponents of the pill include both corporate raiders and large institutional investors, who argue that the pill actually works against shareholders. Rarely are they allowed to purchase more shares at a discount. Furthermore, the lethal effects of the pill prevent the stock from rising as it normally would in the course of a takeover and, thus, deprive shareholders of profits they could make by playing the market.

Frequently, in defending itself from a hostile bidder, management will turn to a "white knight."[33] A white knight is a friendly investor who will put away a large block of stock (at a discount price) but who will not pose a takeover threat. In its efforts to avoid being taken over by The Limited, Carter Hawley Hale Stores Inc. turned to General Cinema, which invested $300 million in its stock in 1984. Eventually, in the face of a persistent bid by The Limited, Carter Hawley Hale had to come to an agreement with General Cinema. A white knight strategy does not necessarily save a company from restructuring, but it keeps it out of hostile hands, at least initially. (White knights do not always prove to be benevolent.)

Another device that management uses are golden parachutes (for managers) and tin parachutes (for labor).[34] A parachute affords the relevant party a hefty package of benefits in case he or she is dismissed. Both labor and management find these parachutes very attractive for they protect their own interests. Prospective raiders find them unattractive for they impose increased costs. In terms of the bottom line, it is the stockholder who pays the costs. By far the most controversial strategy employed by management is the payment of greenmail. When Walt Disney productions bought back Saul Steinberg's shares in 1984, it effectively paid him a $60 million premium not to take over the company. Similarly, Gencorp (in mid-1987) offered $130 per share for 54% of its stock against an investor group offering $100; the investor group netted nearly $100 million.[35] In a 1964 ruling, the Supreme Court of Delaware upheld the practice of buying back shares at a premium as long as the directors could show a "legitimate business reason" for doing so.[36] There is a great deal of controversy over what constitutes legitimate business reasons. Increasingly, shareholders are demanding that they get a chance to vote on the matter.

In addition to the above measures, a number of companies prefer restrictions tied to the length of time a stock is held.[37] Usually, it is a straightforward classification of types of common stock according to voting power. In a related move, some management groups are putting together their own takeovers by taking the company private in a leveraged buyout.[38] In either case, management severely restricts those to whom it is accountable.

Finally, a number of management groups are beginning to take a proactive stance to takeovers. They are scrutinizing their company profiles for items a raider would find attractive—large cash surpluses, undervalued assets to strip, overfunded pension funds, bloated staff—and taking the measures to correct them before anyone ever initiates a takeover offer.

CLAMOR FOR ACTION

Business Action

The shareholder is a property owner who does not have full control over his or her property. Often, shareholders are a fickle group. With little or no long-term loyalty to the company, they monitor their portfolio's bottom line and enter and exit accordingly. Any tie to the company is rendered even more remote by techniques of program trading and portfolio hedging. This point is important. Most observers appeal to management's duties to shareholders to secure an adequate return. The anonymous character and short-term behavior of most shareholders suggests that they may have no real commitment to the company. Such a reality calls into question the validity of the principle that "the responsibility of management is to the shareholders" and makes it imperative to recast the rights (and duties) of shareholders in the context of the rights and duties of stakeholders in a corporation.

Corporate Boards and Governance. The safeguarding of the rights and duties of all the concerned parties is a central responsibility of corporate governance. The weakest link in corporate governance today is found in the board of directors. In theory, the board of directors is charged with securing the best interests of shareholders and monitoring the performance of managers.

F.M. Scherer, who has developed data on over 6,000 mergers, summarized his conclusion this way:[39]

> You asked the question, how can we improve corporate governance? That is really where the problem lies. Let me make a simple proposal. The Congress ought to enact legislation that requires listed companies to have a certain fraction of their directors nominated directly by outside shareholders. This nomi-

nation would in fact be done largely by financial intermediaries who control for the larger corporations half of the value of shares. The financial intermediaries who now simply follow the Wall Street rule and bail out on short notice, would then have to devote attention to making sure that good outside directors are appointed, to make sure the performance of the corporation is in fact good.

Sir James Goldsmith views the relation between managers and corporate boards as incestuous: It must be remembered that almost always, directors are not chosen and elected by shareholders. Normally, shareholders are asked to vote on a list of directors proposed by management. There are no primaries and only very rarely, and at a great cost, is an alternative list of candidates proposed to shareholders and this is within the context of proxy fights. So, in effect, directors are co-opted by their future colleagues and shareholders do no more than ratify the proposals.[40] Shareholders have very little effective say. Annual meetings have not offered a fruitful venue for shareholders to communicate with each other, much less organize among themselves. Shareholders are routinely ignored when important issues such as poison pills or greenmail are decided upon.

In addition, a number of corporations are interested in issuing nonvoting classes of common stock. Such a move is objectionable for it would further insulate management from market forces of efficiency and competition. The only real power shareholders have is to sell off their shares. In recent years, their duties to stakeholders have been gradually acknowledged; this is reflected in the structure of boards and their committees.[41]

Over the years, an incestuous relation has emerged between top management and boards. In 75% of large companies, the CEO is also head of the board.[42] In most cases, top management appoints the majority of members. For the most part, boards of directors simply rubber stamp what management decides. For some years, there have been calls to make the boards more independent by placing more outsiders on them. The issue raised is the moral rectitude of management's intentions. It can no longer be assumed that management seeks the best interests of shareholders or other stakeholders. Nor can it be assumed that the board of directors protects shareholders or other stakeholders. Some argue that it is time for shareholders to gain control of the board. Other stakeholders, such as local communities, labor, suppliers, and consumers should also be represented.

Be that as it may, such a change in the board would make management's task more difficult. That is exactly what is needed. The prescription is simple: (1) restore a shareholder's perspective, and (2) take explicit account of the claims of the various stakeholders in the business enterprise.

Government Action

Many observers are looking to public policy and legislation to resolve the main issues. The U.S. Congress and a number of state legislatures have been very active in this regard.

Information/Disclosure. One issue that is especially significant is the ethics of information. On the raider side of the ledger, immediate disclosure of a raider's stock position (rather than the current 10-day lag) is called for. Disclosure is presently required at 5%. It is worth considering a lower threshold (1%, for example). More importantly all secret collusion between acquiring partners as well as the parking of shares, must be curtailed. Mandatory immediate disclosure at the 1% level would be helpful.

Margin Requirements. In addition, people are proposing changing margin requirements for trading, linking voting to a requirement that a stock be held for a minimum amount of time, altering the taxation of junk bonds, and installing debt ceilings. Such proposals are all debatable. For the market to be fair, the central issue is to change the rules regarding information.

Restrictions on "Gutting the Assets." A third issue that is proposed is to prevent those who take over a company from disposing of its assets for a certain period of time (for example, a year). This would commit those acquiring the company to managing successfully in the product or "real wealth" market. This measure would try to close the gap between financial and product markets.

Monitoring and Surveillance. The SEC is charged, among other things, with ensuring the quality of market information. To do this, it requires additional staff and increased data processing potential.[43] In particular, the SEC's "EDGAR" System (electronic data gathering, analysis, and retrieval) is essential for timely market surveillance and information. In addition, the monitoring of audit integrity as well as improved cooperative agreements with other countries are both essential measures.

Stakeholder Actions

Local Communities. Finally, the volatility of the world economy makes corporate restructuring an increasing likelihood. Labor and local communities must themselves begin to adopt proactive stances. How to do this is not clear in the economy in general, let alone in the case of takeovers. The point here is to bridge the gap between micro and macro perspectives. For their part, local communities would be healthier if they moved to diversify their economic base so as to reduce their risk in the face of market readjustments. One company towns are highly vulnerable. Part of the responsibility of local government to society is to build up a positive economic base by establishing a favorable business milieu.

Labor. Labor, too, must begin to build into its policy the likelihood of job turnover rather than persisting in the quest for life-long security. Job retraining and relocation seem to be basic features of modern business. There is considerable scope for labor to change the way it acts on the business scene in other ways also. For example, it can become a major shareholder through its pension funds. Most important, it must plan for the newly emergent international competitive milieu by explicitly gearing its policy and proposals to economic efficiency rather than redundancy.

One perspective of organized labor as to the impact of mergers on employees is provided by Thomas R. Donahue, secretary-treasurer of the AFL-CIO. In testimony before the Senate Banking, Housing, and Urban Affairs Committee, he listed three areas of injury and harm to workers and employees emanating from the current wave of takeovers.[44]

1. The takeovers and takeover attempts have led to the elimination of jobs, often those jobs held by long-service employees. Although comprehensive data on lay-offs and job eliminations are not available, it is estimated that at a minimum, roughly 80,000 members of unions that are affiliated with the AFL-CIO have been thrown out of work as a direct result of corporate restructuring. And clearly, hundreds of thousands more have been thrown out as an indirect result of those closures and reorganizations.
2. Corporate reorganizations lead to a reduction of wage and fringe benefits through raids on pension funds. In addition, workers are forced to try to lower their standard of living to get by on less while their retirement income is jeopardized, all in order to finance the employer's acquisitions or restructuring.
3. By substituting a new employer for a preexisting employer, takeovers destroy seniority and other expectations that employees build up in their jobs over a period of years. New employers are not bound to honor the expectations of those employees and those new employers all too often are ready to take advantage of their power in that regard. The morale of affected workers goes to an all-time low, while they have to listen to increasing lectures about labor-management cooperation.

Suggestions for Reform.

1. Abolish two-tiered offers, which clearly have a coercive impact and constitute the largest imperfection in the present tender offer system.
2. In case of hostile takeovers or other threats to their jobs, incumbent managers often resort to leveraged buy-outs involving collusive sales of a firm's assets at bargain basement prices. To minimize such abuses, corporate directors who receive an offer from incumbent management for a leveraged buy-out should be required to secure legal and investment advice from independent professionals, should be required to entertain competing offers from outsiders, and should select the offer that is in the best interest of the stockholders and the stakeholders in the company.
3. Raiders should also be denied the profits arising from the circumstance that their failed raid has inflated the value of the target stock. The mechanism for achieving that goal is quite simple. Section 16(b) of the Securities Act could be amended to grant targets the right to recover from a raider and those acting with a raider to recover any profit realized from the short-swing sales of stock acquired in connection with a tender offer and sold within a defined period of time after the offer expires or is withdrawn.

Protection of Communities.

1. Those mounting a takeover attempt should be required to disclose along with the offer the principal economic assumptions underlying their asset valuation and projections, the sources of and the conditions on the acquirer's financing, the business plans for the target, and any plans of the would-be acquirer with respect to the closing or the sale of any facilities of the target.
2. Fiduciaries, including most particularly institutional stockholders, called upon to decide how to respond to a takeover, should be permitted to take into account the likely community and social impact of their actions and should not feel legally constrained to maximize their short-term profits and to disregard entirely any longer range or broader interests.

Protection of Workers.

1. Contracts voluntarily entered into by a corporation should be binding on the corporate successors or the new owners for the term of those contracts.
2. Acquirers should not be permitted to fund an acquisition or to retire debts assumed in connection with the acquisition by tapping a pension fund and withdrawing the so-called surplus funding from the pension fund.
3. Top managers of an acquired company should not be permitted to escape from a reorganization on golden parachutes at the expense of rank and file workers who are left without any economic cushion whenever their employment is terminated. Just as employers are currently prohibited from discriminating in favor of high-paid employees in paying retirement benefits, so too should they be prohibited from discriminating against those high paid employees in the golden parachute arrangements.

NOTES

1. Donald V. Austin, and David W. Mandula, "Tender Offer Update: 1986," *Mergers And Acquisitions* (July/August, 1986) pp. 55–57.
2. *Business Week*, "The Top 200 Deals" (April 15, 1988), pp. 53–81. A similar report was issued for 1986 (April 17, 1987); from 1983 through 1985 a report on "The Top 300 Deals" was issued.
3. United States Senate, Committee on Banking, Housing and Urban Affairs, *Hostile Takeovers*. Washington, D.C.: U.S. Government Printing Office, 1986, p. 220. Hereafter cited as *Senate Hearings*.
United States House of Representatives, Committee on Energy and Commerce, Subcommittee on Telecommunications, Consumer Protection and Finance, *Corporate Takeovers*. Washington, D.C.: U.S. Government Printing Office, 1986, p. 3. Hereafter cited as *House Hearings*.
4. James B. Stewart and Philip Revzin, "Sir James Goldsmith, As Enigmatic As Ever, Bails Out Of Goodyear," *Wall Street Journal* (November 21, 1986), pp. 1, 15. James B. Stewart and Daniel Hertzberg, "Goodyear Said To Be Target of Goldsmith," *Wall Street Journal* (October 29, 1986), p. 3. James B. Stewart, "Merrill Lynch Could Get $200 Million In Fees on a Goldsmith Bid for Goodyear," *Wall Street Journal* (November 5, 1986), p. 4. Gregory Stricmarchuk and Ralph B. Winter, "Goodyear's Mercer Tries to Hold Off Sir James in a Contest for Company," *Wall Street Journal* (November 5, 1986), p. 28. Jonathan P. Hicks, "Goodyear's Uneasy Aftermath," *New York Times* (November 25, 1986), p. D1.
5. *Senate Hearings*, p.220.
6. *Senate Hearings*, p. 216.
7. *Ibid.*, p. 217ff.
8. *Ibid.*, pp. 219–20.
9. *Ibid.*, p. 244.
10. Jonathan P. Hicks, "Goodyear's Uneasy Aftermath," *New York Times*, (December 5, 1986), pp. D1, D2.
11. Tamar Lewin, "Business and the Law: Suits Aimed at Greenmail," *New York Times* (March 3, 1987), p. D2.
12. *Mergers and Acquisitions*, "SEC's All-Holders Rule" (November/December, 1986), p. 15.
13. *House Hearings*, p. 217.
14. Michael C. Jensen, "Takeovers: Folklore and Science," *Harvard Business Review* (November/December, 1984), pp. 109–21.
15. Kenneth Lehn and Mark L. Mitchell, "*Do Bad Bidders Become Good Targets?*" Washington, D.C.: Securities and Exchange Commission, 1988. Gregory A. Robb, "SEC Study Links Bad Acquisitions to Later Takeovers," *New York Times* (December 5, 1988), p. D2.
16. *Senate Hearings*, p. 1076ff.
17. *Ibid.*, p. 1078.
18. *Ibid.*, p. 1079.
19. Mark Green and John Berry, 1986. "Takeovers—A Symptom of Corpocracy," *New York Times* (December 3, 1986), p. A31.
20. T. Boone Pickens, Jr., *Boone*. Boston: Houghton Mifflin Company, 1987. T. Boone Pickens, Jr., "How Business Stacks the Deck," *New York Times* (March 1, 1987), p. F2. Steven Prokesch, "America's Imperial Chief Executive," *New York Times* (October 12, 1986), pp. F1, F25.
21. T. Boone Pickens, Jr., *House Hearings*, p. 47.

22. *New York Times*, "Look Who's Bashing Corpocracy" (November 24, 1986), p. 18.
23. Jerry K. Pearlman, "Save the Lectures—Give Us Some Help," *New York Times*, (December 14, 1986) p. F3.
24. Teri Agins, "John Emery Looks for a Better Package," *Wall Street Journal* (April 2, 1987) p. 34.
25. Anderson, *Senate Hearings*, pp. 137–138, 490.
26. Pickens, *House Hearings*, pp. 30–31.
27. Andrew Sigler, *Senate Hearings*, pp.196–197.
28. *Ibid.*, pp. 195–196.
29. Rohatyn, *Senate Hearings*, pp. 101, 109–110.
30. Richard Wines, "The Stock Watch System: Early Warning on Raiders," *Mergers and Acquisitions* (March/April, 1987), pp. 56–58.
31. Michael S. Helfer and William D. Brighton, "The Federal Reserve's Stand on Junk Bond Takeovers," *Mergers And Acquisitions* (July/August, 1986) pp. 48–54.
32. Suzanne S. Dawson, Robert J. Pence, and David S. Stone, "Poison Pill Defensive Measure," *The Business Lawyer*, 42 (February, 1987) pp. 423–439.
33. Isadore Barmash, "Talking Deals—Carter's Ally Calls the Tune," *New York Times* (December 11, 1986), p. D2. Robert Williams, "Taxes and Takeovers—When You Can't Resist a Bear Hug Look for a White Knight," *Journal of Accountancy*, 162 (July, 1986), pp. 86–93.
34. Alison Leigh Cowan, "New Ploy: 'Tin Parachutes,'" *New York Times* (March 19, 1987), pp. D1, D8. David F. Larcher and Richard A. Lambert, "Golden Parachutes, Executive Decision-Making and Shareholder Wealth," *Journal of Accounting and Economics*, 7, (April, 1985) pp. 179–204.
35. Robert J. Cole, "$1.6 Billion Buyback by Gencorp," *New York Times*, (April 7, 1987), pp. D1, D7.
36. Tamar Lewin, "Business and the Law: Suits Aimed at Greenmail," *New York Times* (March 3, 1987), p. D2.
37. *Mergers and Acquisitions*, "Failsafe Protection," (November/December, 1986), pp. 16–17.
38. Louis Lowenstein, "No More Cozy Management Buyouts," *Harvard Business Review*, 61 (January/February, 1986), pp. 117–127.
39. Scherer, *House Hearings*, p. 156.
40. *Senate Hearings*, p. 1082.
41. Louis Braiotta and A. A. Sommer, *The Essential Guide to Effective Corporate Board Committees.* Englewood Cliffs, N.J.: Prentice Hall, 1987.
42. Idalene F. Kesner, Bart Victor, and Bruce T. Lamont. "Board Composition and the Commission of Illegal Acts: An Investigation of *Fortune* 500 Companies," *Academy of Management Journal*, 29, no. 4,(1986), pp. 789–799. Idalene F. Kesner and Dan K. Dalton, 1986. "Boards of Directors and the Checks and (Im)balances of Corporate Governance," *Business Horizons*, 29 (October, 1986), pp. 17–23. John D. Pawling, "The Crisis of Corporate Boards—Accountability vs. Misplaced Loyalty," *Business Quarterly*, 51, (June, 1986), pp. 71–73.
43. Richard Wines, "The Stock Watch System: Early Warning on Raiders," *Mergers and Acquisitions* (March/April, 1987), pp. 56–58. Roger Oram, "SEC Projects the Case for Defense," *Financial Times* (December 10, 1986), p. 6.
44. *Senate Hearings*, p. 212ff.

INSIDER TRADING: THE LEVINE, BOESKY, AND DREXEL BURNHAM LAMBERT CAPER

*How and why do innovative entrepreneurs
become white collar criminals?*

Private property and voluntary exchange lie at the very core of market economy and capitalism itself. Thus, availability of information, and its uses and abuses, become critical to the success of the capitalistic system on the one hand and individual enterprises on the other hand. To safeguard public trust in the marketplace, public authorities in the United States and, in varying degrees, in other nations, have sought to regulate the process by which material information is disseminated in the public domain so that those who are privy to such information, because of their official position or status, would not use it for personal gain. In a similar vein, since material information is private property, those gaining unfair advantage from its use are in a sense stealing someone else's property. Hence, insider trading, i.e., entering into transactions for personal gain, based on information that they would not normally possess as members of the public, is considered illegal, unprofessional, unethical, and immoral.

Enlightened self-interest as espoused by Adam Smith, however, is not always enlightened and does not always serve public purpose. The line between untrammeled greed and enlightened self-interest is indeed very thin, and like reflections in water, is constantly blurred by those who create ripples to deflect its clarity.

The case of Ivan Boesky and his cohorts was a recent episode in one of the longest running morality plays in the annals of "Capitalism American Style." It had all the elements of high public drama, a sense of overriding community interest and public welfare. It was also very human in scale in that the personal greed and frailties of individuals were hidden behind the masks of professionalism, entrepreneurship, individual enterprise, and Horatio Alger optimism. Finally, the fall occured not because of the failure of vision or idealism gone astray, but because individual greed and instinct for survival triumphed over professional standards, individual ethics, or loyalty to one's employer, colleagues, and friends.

From 1982 to the fall of 1987, the United States economy experienced one of the most sustained periods of growth in its history. Many fortunes were made during this period, which was characterized by both steady growth and by unprecedented takeover activity. The takeover climate in the 1980s, however, was drastically different from a period of conservative growth in the 1950s to the wild availability of funds in the 1980s. An example of this occurred in the early 1980s, when oil was actually cheaper to buy on the floor of the stock exchange rather than to discover it in the oil fields. This atmosphere strongly supported the insiders' and arbitrageurs' positions. Their opportunities were further enhanced by the huge amounts of merger activity. Needless to say, access to information was a crucial ingredient to financial success and outperforming the market. Also arising from these new mergers was the increased opportunity for insiders—the lawyers, accountants, analysts, secretaries, and, of course, the bankers—all of whom had access to valuable inside information. Additional people who gained similar access to such inside information included: the investors themselves, the brokerage firms, reporters, and even printers of financial reports and legal documents, to name a few.

The fuel that was igniting all this growth was the easy availability of funds for the purpose of takeovers. Since these takeovers require huge amounts of financing, many forms of financing have arisen. The one form that has attracted the most attention is the use of junk bonds to finance acquisitions. The leading underwriter of these bonds during the 1980s was Drexel Burnham Lambert. Ivan Boesky's story presents an intriguing case study in this regard. He got caught. And he decided to put his former colleagues into play in order to get a good deal for himself. Boesky got his good deal and he delivered one of the major investment houses—Drexel Burnham Lambert—and the genius behind the 1980s junk bond market—Michael Milken—into securities fraud.

Boesky was the CEO of Ivan F. Boesky & Company, a holding company that held the controlling interests in many different financial services companies. However, the major company in the Boesky empire was his arbitrage unit. During the early 1980s, Boesky gained renown as a particularly skillful arbitrageur. Riding the crest of his success, he lectured frequently at leading business schools and nurtured a transformation of his public persona by becoming a patron of the arts, a benefactor of higher education, and a mover and shaker of society.[1]

In this effort, he succeeded admirably and he basked in his new social role. He was the toast of Wall Street, an upright citizen, a philanthropist, and the conscience of American business. Boesky's public persona is artfully portrayed in a piece that he authored for the book *Merger Mania* which was critical of many of Wall Street's financial maneuvers in this area. He wrote:

> My life has been profoundly influenced by my father's spirit and commitment to the well-being of humanity, and by his emphasis on learning as the most important means to justice, mercy and righteousness. His life remains an example of returning to the community the benefits he had received through the exercise of God-given talents.
>
> With this inspiration I write this book for all who wish to learn of my specialty, that they may be inspired to believe that confidence in one's self and determination can allow one to become whatever one may dream. May those who read my book gain some understanding of the opportunity which exists in this great land.[2]

The fall of Ivan Boesky was as steep as was his meteoric rise on Wall Street and the gain in his personal wealth and public adulation. His rise from a small-time operator to the peak of financial wealth and the terror of corporate board rooms lasted less than two years. His first use of inside information came about in February 1985, when he persuaded Dennis Levine, an investment banker and a rising star in the Wall Street firm of Drexel Burnham Lambert, to sell him confidential information concerning DBL's involvement in forthcoming tender offers, mergers, and other similar activities that had not yet become public. Levine supplied Boesky with inside information between February 1985 and February 1986, which yielded Boesky some $50 million in profits. Levine, however, was nabbed by the SEC as a result of a follow-up of an anonymous tip. Levine's cooperation with the SEC led to Boesky's downfall and implicated many others. Boesky was arrested on November 14, 1986, and charged by the Securities and Exchange Commission (SEC) with securities fraud. On April 27, 1987, Boesky formally settled with the SEC by paying a $100 million penalty. On December 18, 1987, he was sentenced to three years in prison and on March 24, 1988, he surrendered to federal authorities.[3]

As part of his sentence, Boesky had agreed to help federal investigators. He eagerly cooperated with the authorities in ensnaring other Wall Street operators, who had allegedly been profiting from inside information, in the federal prosecutors' net. This eventually resulted in a number of indictments, guilty pleas, fines, and prison sentences. The reverberations of the Boesky affair have also crossed the Atlantic and helped to apprehend other perpetrators in Europe, notably England and France.[4] In the process, the financial community experienced a loss of public trust.[5]

It took less than a year for the SEC to build its case against Boesky and another two years to bring charges against Milken and Drexel Burnham Lambert. On December 22, 1988, Drexel Burnham Lambert settled its case with federal prosecutors. Under the terms of the settlement, DBL agreed to plead guilty to six counts of criminal fraud, pay a fine of $650 million, and cooperate with the government in its ongoing investigation.[6] DBL also agreed to fire Michael R. Milken and also to deny him his 1988 bonus which was estimated at over $200 million.[7] Although, initially, Mr. Milken vociferously denied any wrongdoing, he eventually pleaded guilty to a number of charges and served a one-year prison sentence in addition to paying $600 million in fines.[*]

ISSUES FOR ANALYSIS

There are many principles that underlay the fairness of the market system. The debate over insider trading is concerned with access to information and that there must be a level playing field for everyone involved. Issues to be considered include the following:

1. How effective are the current laws and regulations in preventing abuse of insider information?
2. What is the proper role of the SEC in curbing the use of inside information for personal gain by insiders? How effective has the SEC been in achieving this goal?
3. What are the principles of materiality and disclosure? What are the grounds on which one piece of information becomes material and how should it be evaluated?
4. When is information considered to have been properly disseminated and, therefore, in the public domain? What are the implications of constructing a set of broader or narrower boundaries, in terms of time and channels of communication, for the dissemination of information?
5. Who can be defined as an insider and under what circumstances? What are the implications of a narrower or broader definition of insider for the financial markets, corporations, large and small stockholders, and the maintenance of general confidence in the fairness of trading in stocks?
6. What are the rights of the stockholders who have lost money as a result of trading by the insiders?
7. What is the employer's position when an employee is guilty of insider trading?
8. How is it possible to devise other than public regulatory measures that would curtail the misuse of inside information?
9. If stiffer legislation with respect to insider trading is passed, what will be the implications on the capital markets?
10. As opposed to what is legally wrong, what, if anything, is morally wrong with insider trading? What are the moral and ethical implications of the Boesky case and other insider trading scandals? What does it tell us, if anything, about our role models, our heroes, and our villains?
11. Is it logical for the securities industry to regulate itself? Legal scholars such as Henry Manne have argued that insider information is seldom risk-free. Therefore, we can largely

[*]Sobel, Robert, *Dangerous Dreamers, The financial innovators from Charles Merril to Michael Milken*, John Willey & Sons Inc., New York, 1993. (p. 210).

Also see: Benjamin Stain, *License to Steal: The Untold Story of Michael Milken and the Conspiracy to Bilk the Nation.* Simon & Schuster: New York, c. 1992 (pp. 188, 197).

negate its value and increase its risk tremendously by enlarging the number of those who can use it, i.e., by making it legal?

12. How did Boesky try to portray himself to the public as an upright citizen? What does it tell us about the American society and its value system? What do the Boesky case and other related scandals tell us about the American business creed?

13. Finally, how might one judge the behavior of federal prosecutors in settling the Boesky situation and other related cases, in terms of their equity, fairness, and vigorousness of law enforcement? To what extent should those who "cooperate" with the SEC be "rewarded" for blowing the whistle on others? How are the SEC's actions likely to act as measures of general deterrence for similar future crimes?

THE REGULATORY BACKGROUND

With the crash of the stock market in October 1929, the federal government realized the need for increased regulation of the financial markets. The first law enacted was the Glass-Stegall Act of 1933, which separated commercial banks from investment banks. Then, the Securities Act of 1934 created the Securities and Exchange Commission to police all financial markets. Later in 1940, the Investment Advisers Act was enacted to permit the courts to prosecute any operation that led to deceit or fraud of the consumer. In 1968, the Williams Act was enacted requiring that those accumulating a stock give notice. It also set a number of other restrictions.

The relevant section of the Securities and Exchange Commission Act of 1934 in regard to insider information is Section 10b5 [15 U.S.C. Sec. 78j(b)]. Section 10 of the Act reads, in pertinent parts, as follows:

(a) It shall be unlawful for any person, directly or indirectly, by the use of any means or instrumentality of interstate commerce or of the mails or of any facility of any national securities exchange . . .

(b) To use or employ, in connection with the purchase or sale of any security registered on a national securities exchange or any security not so registered, any manipulating or deceptive device or contrivance in contravention of such rules and regulations as the Commission may prescribe as necessary or appropriate in the public interest or for the protection of investors.

Rule 10B (17 C.F.R. 240) provides that

it shall be unlawful for any person, directly or indirectly, by use of any means or instrumentality of interstate commerce, or of the mails, or any facility of any national securities exchange,

(1) to employ any device, scheme or artifice to defraud,

(2) to make any untrue statement of a material fact or to omit to state a material fact necessary in order to make the statements made, in the light of the circumstances under which they were made, not misleading, or

(3) to engage in any act, practice, or course of business which operates or would operate as a fraud or deceit upon any person, in connection with the purchase or sale of any security.

Insider Information

The definition of insider trading is set by precedent and is determined by specific facts applicable to each case. In order to be guilty of insider trading, there has to be some kind of a breach of a duty to keep information confidential. Also, a person has to act with the intent to deceive or defraud, or with reckless disregard toward deception or fraud.

This definition is often very ambiguous when one considers concrete activities. For example, suppose that an arbitrageur (one who speculates on the possibility of a merger, by purchasing the takeover target's stock in anticipation of a price increase) calls executives of two companies that he suspects are merging. It would be illegal for either executive to disclose or confirm any information pertaining to the situation. However, if the executives' secretaries accidentally let slip the fact that their bosses had been meeting the night before, causing the arbitrageur to act, this would not constitute illegal insider trading. If the arbitrageur sends the secretary a gift in hopes of receiving information that he or she can profitably use, however, this activity is questionable. Of course, if the arbitrageur has the secretary on his or her payroll, paying the secretary a percentage of the profits, the arrangement is definitely illegal. One result of such legal ambiguity is the difficulty prosecutors face in enforcing insider trading laws, which in turn leads to an incredibly low percentage of violators getting caught.

In the last decade, an avalanche of insider cases have been brought against printers (Chiarelli and *Business Week*), reporters (Winans), brokerage house employees (Siegel, Wang), brokers (Jeffries), major executives (Thayer), lawyers, and arbitrage deal makers (Boesky). Major suspicion has centered on Wall Street stalwarts such as Drexel Burnham Lambert, Kidder Peabody, Merrill Lynch, and Goldman Sachs.[8]

Much of present activity goes back to a landmark case brought by the SEC against Texas Gulf Sulphur in 1964.[9] The SEC brought charges against 13 officers and employees of the Texas Gulf Sulphur Corporation, a publicly held corporation. The problem started in 1957 when TGS discovered what appeared to be a major lode of copper and silver. The first unofficial press release stated that the find was of major proportion; however, the officers of TGS later argued that this statement was full of rumors. The officers' denial of the first press release negated the excitement that had been generated by the report. Later on, however, TGS confirmed the rumors about the huge magnitude of the strike. Before that report was made public, 13 officers and employees purchased stock and options on TGS stock. Three days later, the report went public. The stock rose in price $7 in one day and in the course

of one week it rose to a new high of $57 from approximately $30.

Weeks before the actual announcement, rumors had been flying around Wall Street. This aroused the attention of the SEC. Both the wild rumors, and the way the officers of TGS handled the initial report, caused public criticism to rise. One month after the announcements, the purchases made by the officers were disclosed. They had grossed approximately $250,000 in the previous month from TGS stock increases. Later the SEC brought charges against these individuals; it charged them with buying shares and options, and disclosing information to other parties for their immediate profit. TGS management defended itself by claiming that they quelled the initial rumors because they were unsubstantiated. Then they claimed that options and stock they bought were purchased days before the confirmation of the strike. By this time, the extent of the officers' purchases was fully exposed to the public, which reacted with civil suits for damages running into the millions of dollars. The officers agreed to return the profits to the corporation, but the SEC refused. The SEC lost the initial court case and all charges were dismissed against the alleged defendants. Later, on appeal, a higher court reversed the lower court's decision and found eight of the defendants guilty. This was a landmark case. From it, explicit rules arose pertaining to how and when management can release to the public major corporate developments, the exercise of corporate stock options, and corporate-sponsored investment programs.

At least since the Texas Gulf Sulphur decision, the antifraud provisions of the federal securities laws have come to state, among other requirements, the "disclose-or-refrain" rule. This rule states that persons, or at least some persons, who possess material nonpublic information pertaining to the value of a corporation's securities, cannot buy or sell the securities unless they first disclose the information. That rule was first employed in the interpretation of rule 10b-5 of the Securities and Exchange Act of 1934, in the context of insiders or the corporation itself trading on inside information about corporate assets or prospects. But it has since been extended under rule 10b-5 and other antifraud provisions such as section 206 of the Investment Advisers Act and The Williams Act, to restrict the conduct of outsiders trading on information that affects securities prices though unrelated to corporate prospects—e.g., information that somebody is about the make a tender offer or publish a "sell" recommendation that is expected to have a sharp and immediate, if only short-term, impact on stock prices.

The TGS case provided precedents in four major areas of insider trading: (1) It gave a broad definition of who is an insider. (2) It defined "material information." (3) It clarified what is false and misleading information. (4) It stated how much time must elapse before information becomes public knowledge. Thus the road to more concise insider trading laws was being paved.

The first of these precedents gave the SEC wide latitude in determining the definition of an *insider* under SEC rule 10-5b. Insiders might include employees of a company as well as directors, officers, major stockholders, and "tippees" (i.e., lawyers, accountants, financial advisers, or independent contractors whose access to information about corporate affairs is only given for corporate purposes). In other words, a tippee is a person who purchases shares on the basis of advice received directly or indirectly.

The court's definition of *material information* pertained to securities and their values. It stated that material information was "any important development which might affect security values or influence investment decisions of reasonable and objective investors."

In addition, a ruling on false and misleading information was handed down. For fraud to be proven, it had to be shown that there was failure to correct a misleading impression left by statements already made or by not coming forth and explaining the current situation when there was a duty by law to clarify the situation.

Finally, of great importance to the SEC was the definition of how much time it took for some piece of information to become public knowledge. The courts held that material information becomes public information as soon as the announcement has been made public by the press. Furthermore, the appeals court ruled that to effectively make things fair, the time an insider places the order for the transaction, rather than the time of execution, is what the court rulings are based on.

In 1984, the Insider Trading Sanctions Act was enacted into law. It gave the SEC authority to seek monetary penalties and fines up to three times the defendant's illegal profits. The legal basis remains ambiguous. Everyone is clamoring for a clear definition. To this end, the SEC proposed a definition for the Insider Trading Act of 1987. The proposed definition combines elements of misappropriation theory with a portrait of the insider as an agent.[10] It states:

> It shall be unlawful for any person, directly or indirectly, to purchase, sell, or cause the purchase or sale of, any security while in possession of material nonpublic information concerning the issuer or its securities, if such person knows or recklessly disregards that such information has been obtained wrongfully or that such purchase or sale would constitute a wrongful use of such information. . . . For purposes of this section information is obtained or used wrongfully if, directly or indirectly, it has been obtained by, or is a result of, or its use would constitute theft, bribery, misrepresentation, or espionage through electronic or other means, or a breach of duty to maintain such information in confidence, or to refrain from purchasing, selling or causing the purchase or sale of, the security, which duty arises from any fiduciary, contractual, employment, personal or other relationships with:
>
> a. the issuer of the security or its security holders;
> b. any person planning or engaged in an acquisition or disposition of the issuer's securities or assets;

c. any government or a political subdivision, agency or instrument of a government;

d. any person or any self-regulatory organization registered or required to be registered with the commission;

e. any person engaged in the market for securities or the financial conditions of issuers;

f. any such person that is a member of a class that the commission designates by rule or by regulation where the commission finds that the activities of the members of such a class have a regular nexus to the operation of the nation's securities markets and that such designation is necessary or appropriate to effectuate the purposes of this section; or

g. any other person who obtains such information as a result of a direct or indirect confidential relationship with any persons or entities referred to in paragraphs a–f above.

A few months later, the SEC wrote the Senate Banking Committee's Subcommittee on Securities to more clearly include the misappropriation theory.[11] The Supreme Court Winans decision, while it did uphold misappropriation, proved inconclusive on stock fraud (with the justices split 4–4). Investment bankers complained that legal imprecision left too much discretionary power with the SEC.[12]

A CHRONOLOGICAL HISTORY OF THE LEVINE-BOESKY-DBL CASE

For all its seriousness and immensity, the unravelling of the Boesky affair had its origins in one of the more ordinary events in the annals of Wall Street. It started in May 1985, when Merrill Lynch & Company, New York, received an anonymous letter from its office in Caracas, Venezuela, stating that two brokers (Max Hofer and Carlos Zubillaga) in the firm's office were doing extremely well, almost too well, playing takeover stocks. Merrill Lynch's investigation led to a New York stockbroker. As it turned out, the broker was simply acting on orders he received from the Bahamian branch of the Switzerland-headquartered Bank Leu.

Following its regular procedures and policies, Merrill Lynch alerted the SEC's enforcement director, Gary G. Lynch, shortly thereafter. Mr. Lynch started pressuring Bank Leu and the Leu bankers began to worry. It turned out that Bank Leu's Bernhard Meier handled Levine's trades at the bank. Mr. Meier subsequently returned to Zurich where he faced no criminal or civil charges. Bank Leu had been dealing for years with Dennis Levine, a 33-year-old investment banker. Levine used various accounts to throw the SEC off his trail. Through these accounts, held in various names such as IGI (International Gold Incorporated), Mr. Diamond (Levine's mother's maiden name), Diamond Holdings, S.A., and Bernhard Meier, Levine made nearly $13 million in profits starting as early as 1980.

The Bank Leu men and Levine initially remained silent. Soon Bank Leu was talking about getting a lawyer. Levine suggested they obtain Harvey Pitt, who in 1975 had been a general counsel for the SEC at the age of thirty. What happened next was not at all what Levine had in mind when he made the suggestion. Pitt worked out a deal for Bank Leu, and the bank named Levine as the man who was doing the trading. On May 12, 1986, Levine was arrested. Within weeks, he was giving the SEC information about the men from whom he had bought tips for his stock transactions.

On May 12, 1986, the SEC filed a complaint alleging that over a five-year period, Levine, who was employed as a mergers and acquisitions specialist, secretly purchased and sold securities through a Bahamian bank account. The SEC alleged that Levine obtained approximately $12.6 million in illegal profits from his scheme of secretly trading the securities of 54 companies.

The Official SEC document charged Levine with two major offenses:[13]

1. The defendant Dennis Levine, and all other accounts directly and indirectly had engaged, and were about to engage in acts, practices and courses of business which constituted, constitute and would constitute violations of section 10(b) of the Securities and Exchange Act of 1934 ("Exchange Act") [15 U.S.C.ss 78j(b)], and rule 10b-5 [17 C.F.R. ss 240.10b-5] promulgated thereunder.

2. Mr. Levine directly and indirectly had engaged, was then engaged, and was about to engage in acts, practices and courses of business which constituted, constitute and would constitute violations of section 14(e) of the Exchange Act [15 U.S.C. ss 78n(e)] and rule 14e-3 [17 C.F.R. 240.14e-3] promulgated thereunder.

After paying $11.6 million initially to settle civil complaints, Levine still had to go to court to face the felony charges. In court, he pleaded guilty to four felony counts, each of which carried a maximum sentence of five years. He also paid an additional $362,000 in fines.[14] In the end, Levine only received two years in prison, because he gave information to the SEC leading to the greatest string of arrests Wall Street had ever seen.[15]

Those who leaked information to Levine included Ira Sokolow, an investment banker at Shearson Lehman Brothers; Ivan Reich, attorney for Wachtell, Lipton, Rosen and Katz; and Robert Wilkis, investment banker at Lazard Freres. In addition, Randall Cecola, a Lazard analyst, leaked information to Wilkis and to David Brown, an investment banker at Goldman, Sachs and Co., who leaked information to Sokolow.

Boesky met Levine for the first time in February of 1985. Because of his employment at Drexel Burnham, Levine learned of confidential information that concerned tender offers, mergers, and other business activities. In addition, Levine also gave Boesky information he had learned from other sources mentioned above in the mergers and acquisitions business. In the spring of 1985, they made an agreement that would give Levine 5 percent of the profits made by Boesky on stock transactions based on Levine's tips.

Levine would get 1 percent if the information helped Boesky decide how to play a stock that he already held. Through this agreement, Boesky managed to profit in excess of $4 million in just a few days based on Levine's information.

In the spring of 1986, the deal began to fall apart. Levine was charged with securities fraud. He was forced to pay fines and also faced the possibility of a prison sentence. In return for a lighter sentence, Levine gave out information to the SEC pertaining to his dealings with Boesky. Levine agreed to let the SEC tape private conversations he had after he was arrested.[16] One such conversation, according to Wall Street sources, was with Ivan Boesky. This in time brought the SEC down on Boesky.

The official complaint against Ivan Boesky pertained to securities fraud, and charged, among other things, that defendant Boesky, directly or indirectly, had engaged in acts, practices, and transactions which constituted violations of Sections 10(b) and 14(e) of the Securities Exchange Act of 1934 ("Exchange Act") [15 U.S.C. ss 78j(b) and 78n(e)], and rules 10b-5 and 14e-3 promulgated thereunder. In its complaint against Boesky, the Commission alleged that Boesky exercised investment control over certain entities which engaged in the purchase and sale of publicly traded securities. The Commission also alleged that Boesky obtained from Levine, an investment banker in New York City, material nonpublic information concerning tender offers, mergers, and other business activities. Also stated in the complaint was the fact that Boesky knew that the information was confidential and had been obtained through a breach of fiduciary duty on Levine's part. The complaint further stated that during the period from February 1985 through February 1986, Boesky made transactions in certain securities while in possession of this information.[17]

According to the SEC, the three largest trades Boesky made (on the basis of profits earned) were:[18]

STOCK	MERGER	PROFIT	DATE
Houston National Gas	with Internorth Inc.	$4,100,000	4/85
Nabisco Brands, Inc.	with R.J.Reynolds	$4,000,000	5/85
FMC, Inc.	restructuring of FMC	$ 975,000	3/85

Boesky had been bargaining with the SEC since July 1987. In September 1987, he reached a settlement with the SEC, which was announced on November 14, 1987. Boesky was ordered to return $50 million in illegal profits and was fined another $50 million. In addition, he was to plead guilty to a single felony conspiracy count. He was also barred from the securities industry for life. Similar to Levine, he gave information relating to other insiders on Wall Street who used their non-public, material information for personal profit. On April 23, 1987, Boesky entered his plea of guilty. On December 18, 1987, he was sentenced to three years in prison, with the possibility of parole after one year.

During Boesky's questioning, other persons were implicated. One of these was Boyd Jeffries, a broker who was chairman of Jeffries Group Inc. Another was Martin Siegel, who was one of the top investment bankers in the industry. Siegel, of Kidder, Peabody, was accused of passing information pertaining to mergers which he was working on at the time to Boesky in exchange for $700,000. Further, major suspicion was cast on leading figures at Drexel Burnham Lambert, notably Michael Milken, head of its junk bond department.

Great controversy ensued following Boesky's settlement. *The Economist* magazine wrote:[19] "The Wall Street crook, Ivan Boesky, pulled off his most audacious insider deal after he was nabbed by the Securities and Exchange Commission . . . . Through a series of maneuvers, his family has salted away at least $160 million." Most people in the field viewed his sentence as being very light, because after his apprehension he was allowed to liquidate a $400 million dollar portfolio and his other holdings over a period of time, without other investors being any the wiser. This was believed to have come about because of the fact that he hired as general counsel Mr. Harvey Pitt, partner for Fried, Frank, Harris, Shriver and Jacobson and former general counsel of the SEC. It was the same Mr. Pitt who got Bank Leu off the hook. Mr. Boesky also retained another former SEC official, Theodore Levine of the Washington firm, Wilmer, Cutler and Pickering. They were both well connected with the SEC and critics decried another "insider" deal.[20] Table 1 shows Boesky's sentence in comparison with some other equally renowned cases of insider trading convictions.

Suspicions were rife for some time that Boesky had traded some big fish for the relatively soft terms of his treatment. When the SEC made known its charges against Michael Milken and his associates as well as against the firm Drexel Burnham Lambert, the financial community was aghast.[21] The charges were detailed in a document nearly 200 pages long; they are summarized in Table 2. Boesky figured in all but four of the deals. Many observers questioned whether a case built on Boesky would hold up. At the same time others wondered whether he was just a front all along. Not only did the accused face SEC charges; they were also liable to civil suits brought by clients and interested parties. Furthermore, if convicted under RICO premises, they faced treble damages. Initially, DBL vehemently maintained its innocence and mounted a vigorous public relations campaign and legal effort to defend itself. According to some estimates, it spent more than $140 million in legal, public relations, and advertising campaigns—with $46 million paid by Arthur Andersen & Company to copy and collate the 1.5 million pages of documents requested by the government.[22] On December 22, 1988, however, Drexel agreed to plead guilty to six counts of criminal charges and to pay a fine of $650 million. The charges pertained to criminal activities including: insider trading, stock manipulation, "parking" of securities to conceal their true ownership, and false disclosure and bookkeeping. Drexel also agreed to have a

government-approved accountant pore over any trading records and documents requested by the government. The government agreed not to prosecute Drexel for any other past crimes. However, no Drexel employees were granted personal immunity. Mr. Milken was not a party to this settlement and denounced it claiming that some of its provisions violated his rights.[23]

TABLE 1. Comparison of Boesky's Sentence with Other Insider Trading Convictions

Insider Trader	Prison Term	Remarks
Paul Thayer	4 years	Former deputy defense secretary; LTV chairman convicted after trial; obstructed justice.
Dennis B. Levine	2 years	Former investment banker at Drexel; implicated Mr. Boesky; cooperated after arrest; illegal gain: $12 million.
Israel Grossman	2 years	Former lawyer; leaked information to family members who made $1.5 million; convicted after trial; no cooperation.
R. Foster Winans	18 months	Former *Wall Street Journal* reporter; paid about $30,000 by Peter Brant, a stockbroker who pleaded guilty but hasn't been sentenced; cooperated but didn't plead guilty; convicted after trial.
James Newman	1 year, 1 day	Former stockbroker; received tips tips from investment banker Adrian Antoniu; convicted after trial; no cooperation.
Ira Sokolow	1 year, 1 day	Former investment banker, member of Levine group; paid $120,000 for information by Levine; pleaded guilty and cooperated.
Ilan Reich	1 year, 1 day	Former takeover lawyer, member of Levine group; took no money; pleaded guilty and cooperated, implicated Randall Cecola.
Robert Wilkis	1 year, 1 day	Former investment banker, member of Levine group; made $3 million; pleaded guilty and cooperated.
David Brown	30 days	Former investment banker, member of Levine group; paid $30,000 by Sokolow; pleaded guilty and cooperated.
Adrian Antoniu	None	Former investment banker; tipped stockbroker James Newman; cooperated, pleaded guilty, implicated others.

SOURCE: "Boesky's Sentence Ends Chapter in Scandal," *Wall Street Journal* (December 21, 1987), p.2.

TABLE 2. An Outline of the SEC Charges Filed against Drexel, Milken, and Others

Transaction	Drexel Role	Boesky Role	Remarks
Insider Trading			
Diamond Shamrock/Occidental Petroleum	An Occidental's investment banker, knew that the company was proposing to merge with Diamond Shamrock.	Under instructions from Michael Milken of Drexel, purchased Diamond Shamrock shares and sold Occidental shares short.	Drexel and Boesky agreed to split the profits from the illegal trading. Diamond Shamrock's board voted not to approve the merger.
Storer Communications/Kohlberg Kravis Roberts	As KKR's investment banker, Drexel knew of a contemplated increase in a buy-out offer for Storer.	Under Drexel's instructions, purchased Storer stock before the increased offer was made public.	Drexel's profits from the insider trading exceeded $1 million.
Lorimar/Telepictures	Milken, as adviser to both companies, was informed that a merger between the two was likely. Acting before that information was public, Drexel bought Lorimar stock for its own account.	None	The purchases eliminated a short position, enabling Drexel to avoid a loss of approximately $568,000 and obtain a profit of about $1.23 million.
Viacom	Milken was asked to help finance a management buy-out. Before the buy-out was made public, Drexel bought Viacom stock and convertible subordinated debentures for its own account.	None	The purchase eliminated a short position, enabling Drexel to avoid a loss of about $1.78 million.
Fraud against Drexel Clients			
Maxxam Group/Pacific Lumber	Acted as investment banker for Maxxam. On the day Maxxam publicly announced a tender offer for Pacific Lumber, a dispute developed between Maxxam and Drexel over Drexel's compensation.	Under instructions from Drexel and Milken, purchased Pacific Lumber stock, sometimes at prices that exceeded Maxxam's tender offer price.	Drexel failed to disclose the secret purchases, and received $22 million in fees from Maxxam, reflecting, in part, the increased cost of the tender offer.
Wickes/National Gypsum	Consulted by Wickes on the possible acquisition of National Gypsum.	Under instructions from Drexel, purchased National Gypsum stock before Wickes' offer was made public.	Drexel failed to disclose to Wickes the purchases. Boesky's purchases resulted in profits for Drexel of about 6.7 million. In addition, Drexel was paid about $1 million in connection with the attempted acquisitions.

Continued

TABLE 2. *Continued*

Transaction	Drexel Role	Boesky Role	Remarks
Stock Manipulation			
Stone Container	Underwriter and manager of an offering of Stone securities that were to be convertible into common stock at a fixed premium over the closing price of Stone common stock on the day of the offering. (Stone told Drexel that it did not want to proceed with the offering until Stone shares reached $46-48.)	At the instructions of a Milken aide, purchased Stone Container stock. On the day before the securities were eventually offered, Boesky's purchases accounted for over 37% of the volume in Stone shares.	The transactions in Stone common stock were done to create apparent active trading in, raise the price of, and induce the purchase of Stone stock and convertible securities.
Wickes Cos.	Underwrote an offering of Wickes preferred stock that could be converted into common stock if Wickes common shares closed above a set price for at least 20 of any 30 consecutive trading days. (Wickes management wanted to call the preferred for conversion as soon as possible.)	Acting under the instructions of a Milken aide, purchased Wickes common stock after it had closed above the threshold on 19 of the previous 27 trading days.	The purchase allowed Wickes stock to close above the threshold price for conversion, and Wickes management was able to redeem the preferred stock. Drexel earned a fee of $2.3 million for agreeing to be standby underwriter for the redemption.
Failure to Disclose Beneficial Ownership			
Fischbach	Arranged through Milken for Boesky to purchase 10% of Fischbach shares.	Purchased the shares and filed a schedule 13-D reporting that his organization was the beneficial owner of the shares.	The purchases were part of a scheme that would allow Pennsylvania Engineering Corp., controlled by Victor Posner, to get around an agreement that limited its ownership of Fischbach to 24.9% unless a third party acquired 10% of the company. Pennsylvania Engineering eventually acquired 51% of Fischbach's voting stock and Victor Posner was named the company's chairman.
Harris Graphics	Drexel, Milken and various affiliated companies held substantial positions in Harris, much of which was acquired at $1 a share.	Under instructions from Milken, who guaranteed the Boesky organization against any loss, purchased 5% of Harris stock. Then, also at Milken's request, approached Harris management and offered to acquire the company.	Boesky should have stated in his 13-D filing that Drexel was the beneficial owner of the shares. In addition, Milken reportedly did not care whether the Boesky offer was accepted; he was encouraging other Drexel clients to attempt to acquire the company. Eventually, AM International, a Drexel client, acquired Harris for $22 a share.
MGM/UA	Represented both MGM/UA and Turner Broadcasting in a deal for Turner to acquire MGM/UA for $29 a share and then sell UA.	Under instructions from Milken, purchased MGM/UA securities when the deal was announced and again when the deal had to be restructured. The profits or losses on the purchases were to be shared equally by Drexel and Boesky.	Boesky's filings failed to properly disclose the Drexel and Milken were the beneficial owners of the MGM/UA shares. Drexel received about $66 million in fees in connection with the TBS-MGM/UA transactions.

TABLE 2. *Continued*

Transaction	Drexel Role	Boesky Role	Remarks
	False and Misleading Books and Records		
MCA/Golden Nugget	In 1984, Drexel purchased Golden Nugget's stake in MCA after Golden Nugget, following Milken's advice, dropped a planned takeover bid for MCA.	At Milken's request, Boesky's broker-dealer Seemala Corp. agreed to purchase the MCA shares from Drexel. Drexel agreed to compensate Seemala for any losses in open market sales of the stock.	Drexel and Semala's books didn't reflect Drexel and Milken's beneficial ownership of the securities.
Wickes Short Sales	At the direction of Milken and for the benefit of Drexel, Boesky's organization sold Wickes common stock short and engaged in covering transactions. Milken guaranteed Boesky's group against any losses.	Through Drexel, Boesky made a short sale of 5 million when-issued shares of Wickes common stock to Reliance Insurance.	Books kept by Drexel and Boesky's Semala Corp. failed to reflect Drexel and Milken's beneficial ownership of the Wickes shares.
Tax-Loss Trades	In a series of rigged and pre-arranged March 1985 transactions, Drexel, Milken, and Boesky sought to create fictitious tax losses for Boesky's Seemala Corp.	Drexel made purported sales of certain securities to the Boesky organization before the dividend record date, and immediately thereafter bought back the securities.	Drexel bore all market risk on the securities but neither it nor Semala's records reflected Drexel's beneficial ownership.
Lorimar Short Sales	In 1986, while Lormar was on its restricted list, Milken instructed Boesky to sell Lorimar common short for Drexel's benefit.	After the Lorimar-Telepictures merger, and its removal from Drexel's restricted list, Drexel sold short shares of the merged company to Boesky to cover Boesky's short position.	Drexel failed accurately to reflect on its books and records its beneficial ownership of Boesky's short position.
	Aiding and Abetting Net Capital Violations		
Phillips Petroleum	Bought Phillips stock in non-bona fide transactions from Seemala Corp. Boesky's company. Drexel held the stock in its own account or in customer accounts. Milken and Boesky agreed that Drexel would be guaranteed against any loss and that any profits would be divided evenly between them.	Semala had sustained substantial losses in connection with some of its transactions undertaken for Drexel and in its own trading of Phillips common stock. The losses created a net capital deficiency of more than $50 million.	The Phillips transactions enabled Seemala to show a smaller capital deficiency, and Seemala was compensated for profits made on the Phillips transactions.
	Fraud in Offering Materials		
Hudson Funding Corp.	Drexel was placement agent and Milken was responsible for reorganization and debt offering in connection with the reorganization of Boesky's arbitrage operations.	Sold certain assets to Drexel at below market prices and arranged to pay Drexel a $5.30 million fee for consulting services.	The below-market sales and the consulting payment were actually a way for the Boesky organization to pay Drexel its share of trading profits from transactions undertaken by Boesky at Drexel's request. The offering materials falsely described the $5.3 million payment.

Continued

TABLE 2. *Continued*

Transaction	Drexel Role	Boesky Role	Remarks

Additional Charges against Victor and Steven Posner

In addition to the Posner's violations involving Fischbach, Steven Posner contacted the Boesky organization and asked it to buy and hold shares in Burnup & Sims as a favor to Victor Posner in return for a 20% return on the investment. At the time, Victor Posner and companies he controlled held over 5% of Burnup & Sims common stock.		Later, a Posner representative told an official of Burnup & Sims that Burnup would have to buy shares owned by persons other than the Posner group as a part of any settlement. The schedule 13-D filed by the Posner group failed to disclose his ownership of Burnup shares held by the Boesky organization.	

SOURCE: James B. Stewart and Daniel Herberg, "Letters are Sent to Milken, Four Others in Drexel Case Indicating Criminal Charges Will Be Sought Soon." *Wall Street Journal* (September 9, 1988), pp. 3, 8, 9.

BOESKY FALLOUT: WALL STREET AS THE EVIL EMPIRE

The aftershocks of the Levine/Boesky/Milken-DBL affair are still reverberating throughout the capitalist world. Never in recent years had the fault line running between Wall Street and Main Street appeared so ominous. The giddy takeover period of the 1980s provided Wall Street movers and shakers with unprecedented opportunity. There were 1,889 companies acquired in 1980 at a total cost of $44.3 billion; in 1986 there were 3,356 mergers with a value of $176.6 billion. The head of one of Wall Street's largest investment banks put it this way:[24] "It was like free sex. You definitely saw the abuses growing but you also saw the absence of people getting caught, so the atmosphere grew relaxed. There really was a deterioration in people's caution, and there were so many deals being done that people must have felt there was plenty of cover for what they were doing."

The fallout has taken many forms. We discuss two: the moral-psychological aspect and the legitimacy of the rules of the game.

What Makes Boesky Run— Profile of an Insider Trader

The moral-psychological debate, insofar as it emanates from business and government circles, generally assumes that the financial system and existing legislation are adequate. The problem is with "bad apples." Why, for instance, would Martin Siegel, who earned in excess of $2 million a year, risk his career and reputation for $700,000? Why did Ivan Boesky need $50 million in illegal profits when he had (presumably) legitimately amassed over three times that amount? Theories range from the driving compulsion of raw greed to personal insecurity in feeling one has not really "arrived" in a grand enough way. Surely, no outsider can judge; most likely even those involved would find their actions inexplicable.

Two ingredients make for a criminal—an opportunity and the willingness to exploit it. In that sense, the only difference between the entrepreneur and the criminal is the legality of the opportunity and the means to exploit it. Clearly, given similar opportunities or temptations, only a few seem to exploit them in an illegal or criminal manner. It is easy to understand a person's willingness to resort to criminal means when he/she is driven by extremes of physical deprivation. However, it is more complex to explain in cases where apparently affluent people are driven to seek financial gain when they could do without it and not suffer any appreciable loss of physical comfort and financial well-being. The following excerpts from an article in the *Wall Street Journal*[25] are revealing:

No one on Wall Street ever flew as high or crashed as hard as Ivan F. Boesky.

Ivan Boesky and the risk arbitrage movement he dominated transformed the takeovers game. And more than any other person, Mr. Boesky and what he came to represent moved Wall Street's securities firms to stress their trading operations over brokerage, and to seek global trading. Ivan Boesky's spectacular success also helped turn Wall Street's investment bankers into aggressive deal makers rather than consultants.

Ivan Boesky's story—his rise from modest roots as the son of a Russian immigrant delicatessen owner in Detroit to wealth on Wall Street beyond ordinary measure, and his scandalous collapse—will surely become one of American business history's epical dramas.

He is a latter-day Great Gatsby—the self-made Midwesterner struggling to fit in with the East Coast financial establishment—whose compulsion to accumulate a prodigious fortune brings him down catastrophically.

Mr. Boesky came East in 1966, a 28-year old lawyer who had been turned down for jobs with several of Detroit's top firms. As he built his fortune, he studiously affected the trappings of Wall Street prestige. He habituated New York's Harvard Club, his large donations to Harvard having entitled him to club membership. He published a technical, ponderous volume on the art of arbitrage. He adorned his resume with business school lecturing posts, which he seems to have embroidered considerably.

"It's a Sickness I Have"

And he continued to make tens of millions of dollars at an obsessive pace, long after he had become one of America's richest men. "It's a sickness I have in the face of which I am helpless," he once told an interviewer. At the crest of his career, this "sickness" apparently drove him to seek still more profits with Dennis Levine through the baldly illegal insider-trading scheme to which he pleaded guilty . . .

I don't know what his devils were," said one arbitrageur who knows Mr. Boesky well. "Maybe he's greedy beyond the wildest imaginings of mere mortals like you and me,"

he said. "And maybe part of what drives the guy is an inherent insecurity that was operative here even after he had arrived. Maybe he never arrived."

He was driven by work, overzealous, and subject to severe mood swings. Intimates of Mr. Boesky say he vacillated between "being loud, and harsh and aggressive to mellifluously soft-spoken, charming and courtly, and that changes could come abruptly." He was also fiendish about his pursuit of information. "When somebody got an edge on something, he would go bananas."[26] The consistency of his trading successes was so overwhelming that he developed a large following among traders and brokers who would closely watch for clues about his trades and then imitate them. The snowball effect of these trades would create a marked frenzy, which would become a self-fulfilling prophesy. They would also serve to draw often unwelcome attention to Mr. Boesky.

When it came to money and business dealings, he was quite ruthless and pursued his goal with a single-minded purpose and extracted a high price, almost confiscatory, for his business acumen from his partners. For example, in a 1985 SEC filing, Boesky disclosed that his investors in the original partnership, which was dissolved in 1980, were assigned 45% of the profits, but 95% of any losses, leaving Mr. Boesky with 44% of the profits for a mere 5% of the risk.[27]

Although his first love was money, he hankered for genteel respectability and status that are generally denied the nouveau riche. And yet, he went about achieving it in the flashiest ways which only the new money would aspire to and the old money would despise. In his efforts to adorn himself as the business statesman, he wrote a book (with the help of a professional writer), *The Merger Mania* [28] and set about promoting it with garnishments about his professional credits. The book jacket and the promotional material describe him as serving as adjunct professor both at the Columbia and New York

University's graduate school of business. In fact, he never taught at Columbia and hadn't done so at NYU since 1984.

He also gave away millions to charities and political activities in his drive toward social acceptance. He became a trustee of New York University, the Jewish Theological Seminary, Brandeis University, and the American Ballet Theater, to name a few. He also thrust himself into Jewish causes and Jewish philanthropies. For example, in 1986, a few months before he was indicted, he became Special Advisor for Jewish Affairs to the Republic National Committee's chairman, and finance director of a Republican Jewish lobbying group. The same year he was also one of a group of Jewish leaders invited to the White House to discuss the proposed sale of American missiles to Saudi Arabia. It is inconceivable that Mr. Boesky did not know about his potential troubles with the SEC and that he was very likely to be indicted. And yet, he was not deterred by the prospect of embarrassing his supporters or the charities and causes that he was espousing to help.

Morality, however, cannot be legislated. The motivational set of the insider players raises ethical issues precisely because such activity raises the question posed by Socrates: is this any way to be good at being human? Is such a life of always wanting more and more a life of virtue? One result of the shock effect was a clamor for ethics training in business schools. To this end the former head of the SEC, John Shad, gave $30 million to the Harvard Business School. Somehow, it is hoped that people might realize the human carnage created by untrammeled greed and relentless clawing to get to the top. At the heart of the Shad approach is (1) the belief in the goodness of present institutions and (2) a realization that ethical character must be inculcated. It remains debatable whether educational institutions—and elitist ones at that—are the proper agents for such a task or even up to it.

While one aspect of the moral-psychological debate focuses on motivation and

intention, the other focuses upon consequences. One reason inside traders actually commit crimes is that they cannot see any victims because the effects of their crimes are so widely spread out.[29] They say to themselves that it is legal in Switzerland so it's not really bad. This gives them the impression that everyone is doing it.

In fact, insider trading is viewed differently across international borders. The European Community, West Germany, Italy, Switzerland, and Hong Kong have no insider trading laws. Being an insider is something like a job prerequisite! France has an $800,000 fine and a two-year maximum jail sentence; Britain unlimited fines and two years maximum jail time; the Netherlands a $50,000 fine and two years maximum; Japan and Canada are more indeterminate.[30]

The victimless crime argument has been hotly disputed by investors who have been caught holding the bag while Boesky, Milken, and Drexel Burnham Lambert got off with what to them was a mere slap on the wrist. To support the view that the consequences of insider trading are immoral and unfair, both the SEC and the legal system have left the door open to civil suits for damages.[31] A third point of moral-psychological reflection is that insiders feel they can get away with it. This is reinforced by historical evidence because white-collar criminals have been dealt with very leniently. This perception does not appear to have essentially changed despite the recent spate of criminal convictions and sentences. Gary Lynch, the SEC enforcement director and one of the architects behind an aggressive campaign against Wall Street corruption, was quoted as saying that severe insider-trading penalties were damaging new cases by discouraging potential defendants from cooperating. He suggested that the prospect of imprisonment, civil fines, and financial ruin was convincing some people that "it's better to hunker down than cooperate."[32] It is not clear whether Mr. Lynch was arguing for milder sentences or that the government could not make these cases effectively without the cooperation of the defendants. If the former is the case, then Mr. Lynch was ignoring the deterrent effect of current stiffer sentences on future would-be violators. If the latter is the case, then Mr. Lynch is either arguing for stiffer laws or better enforcement procedures and greater allocation of resources to securities laws enforcement.

The Rules of the Game

The heart of the debate over the rules of the game governing financial markets is whether new legislation is needed or whether, on the other hand, better enforcement of present rules is called for. Those arguing for new legislation focus upon rules for disclosure and greater clarity in defining the nature of fraud in this area. The federal securities laws impose a system of disclosure that is, in part, mandated and derived from the antifraud provisions of those laws. The mandated disclosure provisions (the registration and reporting requirements of the Securities Acts of 1933 and 1934) require information to be filed with the Commission or an Exchange, and, in that way, to be made available, or in other ways be directly disseminated, to stockholders. These reports come in many forms with different levels of specificity, such as the 10-K, 14-E, 13-D, and the standard report sent to stockholders. Some of the mandated information is to be furnished in connection with particular transactions or solicitations; other information is required to be furnished periodically, apart from solicitations or from particular transactions. Many observers wish to tighten disclosure requirements.

The antifraud provisions, in contrast to the mandating provisions, do not call for the filing or reporting of specified items of information. Rather they require disclosure only when the failure to disclose in particular circumstances leaves a false impression for persons who buy or sell the affected securities or receive services from an investment adviser.

There is nothing that states that the antifraud provisions expressly require disclosure when no relevant communication is made as part of a transaction or advisory service. Nevertheless, it is clear from the case law that the antifraud provisions do not merely enforce the mandated system of disclosure. "Rather they command disclosure of their own force, and without regard to whether their application is sought in support of mandated disclosure requirements."[33] This means that they function independently—in part to fill in voids left by the system of mandated disclosure, and in part to deter or prevent certain transactions in which one party has an informational advantage over the other.

At the heart of the antifraud measures is a stringent limitation of communication between investment bankers and risk arbitrageurs. This has been compared to The Great Wall of China.[34] "The potential for abuse is astronomical," says Paul A. Fisher, an attorney in Washington, D.C., with Stoppleman, Rosen and DeMartino and a former official of the S.E.C., "and the recent allegations make you think they're more common than we had thought." "Chinese Walls didn't keep the Mongols out of China," says House of Commerce Committee chairman John D. Dingell, "and they haven't kept the miscreant on Wall Street out of the honey pot either." Dingell added that he was looking at possible remedies, which he declined to specify. The most radical step would be enactment of a law similar to the Glass-Stegall Act, which divorced investment from commercial banking. In this case, investment banks would be barred from arbitrage activities.

The second aspect of the rules-of-the-game debate is how to better enforce existing regulations. This involves surveillance, subpoenaed information, and punishment. Improving surveillance relies on computer systems that efficiently and speedily police the market. The system works based on detecting patterns of trading by charting price increases or decreases. If price jumps

occur that are not easily explained and contain suspicious patterns of stock dealings,
there is a data base that tracks these trades. In
this way, the suspicious trades can be traced
back to the broker. Computer surveillance
can show when, at what price, and for whom
the trade was executed. Before the advent of
this technology, it took six weeks to detect
who had bought the stock. It can now be
done in less than two hours.

The NYSE's Automatic Search and
Match System (ASAM) was set up in 1985. It
stores information on 500,000 American executives. Unbelievably, it stores information
pertaining to the clubs they belong to, where
they live, and where they used to work.[35]
ASAM is used to point out links between
names of traders and their backgrounds. The
question of whether or not ASAM is an invasion of privacy will probably have to be settled in the courts. Through these modern surveillance techniques, the NYSE and its
modern equipment have detected many suspicious trades, which the SEC uses as the
base of their investigations. Once suspicious
patterns are discovered, the SEC has power
to subpoena witnesses for information and
may also investigate whom it wishes whenever it wishes.

Despite all this modern equipment, it
did not lead to arrests in the Levine/
Boesky/Milken-DBL scandal. It took an
anonymous postcard from Venezuela to
bring these giants down. The SEC has the
largest problems dealing with suspects who
deal under different names and accounts.
Foreign accounts pose another set of problems. To end this, the SEC, Britain, and
Switzerland have mutually agreed to divulge
the names behind secret accounts if the evidence is sufficiently strong. But the problem
remains formidable.

Many think that stiffer penalties are
called for. Currently, the maximum sentence
for a defendant is five years; perhaps ten
years would be more of a deterrent. In addition, they must enforce these penalties and
cut down on plea bargaining.

As international trading of equities
expands into the future, cooperation between
regulators of all countries will have to greatly improve. They could make these illegal
dealings more difficult by unifying takeover
rules, and by requiring prompt disclosure of
large shareholdings. Until insider trading has
a uniform definition across all borders, it will
not be eliminated. With the addition of modern surveillance equipment, the balance of
risk and reward has been pushed to new levels. These new regulations will not affect the
corporation but merely its financial advisers.
However, these regulations will affect the
speed and sheer numbers that characterized
the rash of mergers and takeovers in the
1980s.[36]

EPILOGUE

The rise of merger and acquisition activity
during the market's current growth phase
has brought to light a new wave of insider
trading violations. It would seem that the
memory of massive SEC actions and high-
profile indictments of the go-go years of the
1980s has proven to be selective and short.
Following an initial slowdown in merger and
takeover activity and the quieting of the junk
bond trade, the 1990s have already witnessed
a surge of big mergers and hostile takeovers,
with an accompanying rash of insider trading cases. One wonders what, if any, general
deterrent effect was created by the legal
actions taken against the offenders of insider
trading laws during the 1980s. Or is it possible that the opportunities for making enormous gains are so overwhelmingly tempting
that current levels of punishment do not
seem to deter individual offenders?
Alternately, is it possible that the general climate of business, and the society's tolerance
for illegal behavior, are so pervasive that people are unwilling to recognize the costs that
these actions impose on their victims and
society-at-large?

Consider, for example, the saga of Boesky's life after he completed his prison term. From all accounts, he does not seem to have suffered too badly from his crimes or the subsequent punishment. The investors defrauded by Mr. Boesky were awarded compensation from him to the tune of $31 million—a small portion of the money that they lost or the financial gains made by Mr. Boesky from his illegitimate activities. The courts further called on Boesky to testify in the government's case against Michael Milken, Drexel Burnham and the Posners.[37]

On April 4, 1990, Boesky was released from a halfway house in Brooklyn, ending a three-year prison term that he began in 1988. He was paroled for good behavior. Mr. Boesky, then 53 years old, had been transferred to Brooklyn in December 1989, from a minimum-security prison in Lompoc, California, where he was serving his sentence for one count of securities fraud. But since February 5, he had been required only to telephone the halfway house every day and to report in person twice a week. While at the halfway house in Brooklyn, Mr. Boesky worked as a consultant, earning about $200 a week. Upon his release, he moved to his 75-acre estate in Westchester County, New York, near the residences of several other Wall Street financiers and takeover artists who had once been the staple of his business.[38] Three years later, in 1993, Boesky reached a divorce settlement with his former wife, Seema, under which he received $20 million, a house valued at $2.5 million, and more than $2 million a year for life.[39] The story with regard to other famous cases of the 1980s, e.g., Michael Milken, is not too dissimilar.

Despite heavy fines and personal and financial losses, the insider trading phenomenon is far from dead. Securities regulators say they are opening investigations into insider trading at a rate not seen since the mid 1980s, the era in which the names Boesky and Milken became household names.[40] This is occurring in the midst of an outburst of merger and takeover battles, and has

involved lawyers, investment bankers, and their family members. Notorious among these are IBM's recent bid for Lotus, which invited the SEC's scrutiny of suspicious trading; Lockheed's 1994 merger with Martin Marietta, another military contractor; and AT&T's acquisition of the NCR Corporation. The first half of 1995 witnessed some 50 cases referrred to the SEC by the National Association of Securities Dealers for investigation into possible insider trading, which, by extrapolation, may mean a number of cases in 1995 exceeding the record 110 insider trading referrals made to the S.E.C. in 1987.

Why do the crimes persist even after former perpetrators have been caught and held accountable? According to some regulators and prosecutors, the lessons learned on Wall Street have not permeated the larger American conscience. The latest wave of insider trading cases are increasingly coming—not from the Wall Street financial and brokerage concerns—but from corporate officers, directors, and their families, friends, and lovers who take advantage of privileged information. Perhaps most indicative of this trend is the case of Frederick A. Moran, a money manager in Greenwich, Connecticut, who was the focus of an S.E.C. investigation that contends Mr. Moran bought shares of Tele-Communications Inc., a large cable operator, in advance of the announcement that it planned to merge with Bell Atlantic. Mr. Moran's son is a securities analyst with Salomon Brothers who was privy to information about the pending deal.[41]

Another interesting insider trading case occurred early in 1995. In this case, which is one of the largest on record, the government charged 17 people with using confidential information about AT&T's plans to acquire four companies between 1988 and 1993. This information allowed the insiders to realize $2.6 million in illegal profits.[42] The two primary players in the scheme were long-time AT&T employees, each with over 30 years of tenure, and positioned at relatively low levels in the company. In an ironic twist on AT&T's

slogan, "reach out and touch someone," their role was to provide tips to friends and relatives in exchange for kickbacks from profits realized by the actual traders.

Even the firms with immaculate reputations have been stung by the profit-seeking forays of ambitious young professionals. The blue-chip Wall Street law firm, Cravath,

Swaine and Moore, provides the most recent example. A senior associate at the firm, Richard W. Woodward, and his brother, pleaded guilty on June 28, 1995, to insider trading charges for profit scheming that went on undetected for years within the walls of this highly respected New York law firms.[43]

NOTES

1. Tim Metz and Michael W. Miller, "Boesky's Rise and Fall Illustrate a Compulsion to Profit by Getting Inside Track on Market." *Wall Street Journal* (November 17, 1986), p. 28.
2. Ivan F. Boesky, (Jeffrey Madrick, ed.), *Merger Mania*. New York: Holt, Rinehart and Winston, 1985, p. v.
3. Chris Welles and Gary Weiss, "The Man Who Made a Career of Tempting Fate." *Business Week* (December 1, 1986), pp. 34–35; James B. Stewart and Daniel Hertzberg, "Boesky Sentence Ends Chapter in Scandal." *Wall Street Journal* (December 21, 1987), p. 2; and Robert J. Cole, "Guilty Plea Entered By Boesky," *New York Times* (April 24, 1987), pp. D1,D2.
4. *U.K. News*, "Hearing Reveals More of Guinness Jigsaw" (January 28, 1988), p. 11; *Business Week*, "I Say, Old Boy, Did You Hear..." (December 5, 1988), p. 49; Blanca Riener, "Insider Trading Shock Rocks the Elysee." *Business Week* (January 23, 1989), p. 54; Steven Greenhouse, "French Report Finds Inside Trading." *New York Times* (February 1, 1989), p. D6; Steven Greenhouse, "Modest Insider Trading Stir Is a Huge Scandal in France." *New York Times* (January 30, 1989), pp. 1, D9; John Rossant and Frank J. Comes, "The Paris Bourse Calls in the Gendarmes." *Business Week* (March 28, 1988), p. 41.
5. *Business Week*, "Just How Corrupt Is Wall Street" (January 9, 1989), pp. 34–36.
6. *Ibid.*; See also, "And the Next Test Will Be Giuliani vs. Milken." *Business Week* (January 9, 1989), p. 37.
7. Ann Hagedorn and Stephen J. Ader, "Milken Challenge to Parts on Drexel Pact with U.S.— Unlikely to Prevent Settlement." *Wall Street Journal* (February 13, 1989).
8. V. Brudney, "Insiders, Outsiders and Information." *Harvard Law Review*, 93, (1980),

pp.322–26; J. Templeman, "The Insider-Trading Dragnet Is Stretching Across the Globe." *Business Week* (March 23, 1987), pp. 50–51; Gary Weiss and A. Bianco, "Suddenly the Fish Get Bigger." *Business Week* (March 2, 1987), pp.28–32; and *Wall Street Journal*, "What Happened to 50 People Involved in Insider Trading Cases." (November 18, 1987), p. 22; Chiarella v. United States, U.S., 63 L. Ed. 2d 348, 100 Stamford, CT. (1980); "Rule 1065: Birth of the Concept of Market Insider and Its Application in a Criminal Case—United States v. Chiarella." *Fordham Urban Law Journal*, 8,2 (1979–80), p. 457. Bill Sing, "Drexel Takes a Beating But 'Junk Bond' Field Appears Alive and Well." *Los Angeles Times* (December 22, 1988), Par. 1, p.1.; Stephen Labaton, "Jefferies Says He Destroyed Notes on Trades." *New York Times* (January 6, 1989), p. D4; James B. Stewart and Matthew Winkler, "Merrill Lynch Aide, Israeli Face Trading Charges." *Wall Street Journal*, March 12, 1987, p. 3; James B. Stewart and Daniel Hertzberg, "SEC Charges Insider Trading in Morgan Deals." *Wall Street Journal* (June 28, 1988), p. 3; Karen Blumenthal, "Maxus Sues Kidder, Siegel, Boesky for Damages in Alleged Insider Trades." *Wall Street Journal* (November 24, 1987), p. 2; Andy Pasztor, "Thayer Enters Plea of Guilty in Trading Case." *Wall Street Journal* (March 5, 1985), p. 4; James B. Stewart and Daniel Hertzberg, "Inside Trading Scandal Implicates High Aides at Goldman, Kidder." *Wall Street Journal* (February 13, 1987), p. 1.
9. United States Court of Appeals, Second Circuit, "Securities and Exchange Commission, Plaintiff-Appellant, v. Texas Gulf Sulphur Co., a Texas Corporation, et. al., Defendants-Appellants, 401 F.2d 833 (August 13, 1968), 446 F.2d 1301 (June 10,

1971); S. Prakash Sethi, "Securities and Exchange Commission vs. Texas Gulf Sulphur Company," *Up Against the Corporate Wall*, 4th ed. (Englewood Cliffs, N.J.: Prentice Hall, 1982), pp. 288–316.

10. Gregory A. Robb, "S.E.C. Offers Legal Definition of Insider Trading in Stocks." *New York Times* (August 8, 1987), pp. 1,34.

11. Thomas E. Ricks, "SEC Proposes Insider-Trading Measure That Includes Misappropriation Theory." *Wall Street Journal* (November 20, 1987), p. 4; Nathaniel C. Nash, "S.E.C. Submits Plan on Insider Trading." *New York Times* (November 20, 1987), pp. D1, D6.

12. Nathaniel Nash, "Stiffer Penalties on Insider Trades and Rewards for Informers Voted." *New York Times* (November 20, 1987), pp. D1, D6.

13. Securities and Exchange Commission, Litigation Release No. 11905, May 12, 1986.

14. Thomas J. Lueck, "Levine Gets 2-Year Jail Term." *New York Times.* (February 21, 1987), pp. 33, 36.

15. Diane Francis, *Maclean's*, "Business as Usual in the Greed Game," (Nov. 7, 1988), p. 11.

16. James Sterngold, "Taping by Levine Called Part of U.S. Insider Investigation." *New York Times* (November 24, 1986). pp. D1, D6.

17. Securities and Exchange Commission, Litigation Release No. 11288, November 14, 1986.

18. *New York Times*, "How 3 Insider Deals Worked, as Detailed by U.S." (November 16, 1986), p. 34.

19. *The Economist*, "Ivan Boesky—Who Says Crime Doesn't Pay?" (July 11, 1987), pp. 79–80.

20. Robert J. Cole, "Wall Street's Defensive Line." *New York Times* (March 30, 1987), pp. D1, D6.

21. Stephen J. Adler and Laurie P. Cohen, "Drexel Faces a Stockholder Suit Claiming Injury from Wrongdoing Alleged by SEC." *Wall Street Journal* (September 9, 1988), p. 8.

22. Kurt Eichenwald, "Drexel Burnham Fights Back." *New York Times* (September 11, 1988), pp. F1, F8

23. *New York Times*, "As Key Executives Face Charges, It Appears Wall Street Itself Is on Trial." (February 15, 1987), p. 38.

24. Tim Metz and Michael W. Miller, "Boesky's Rise and Fall Illustrate a Compulsion to Profit by Getting Inside Track on Market." *The Wall Street Journal* (November 17, 1986), p.28.

25. Metz and Miller, *op. cit.* November 17, 1986.

26. *Ibid.*

27. *Ibid.*

28. Ivan F. Boesky, (Jeffrey Madrick, ed.), *Merger Mania—Arbitrage: Wall Street's Best Kept Secret.* New York: Holt, Rinehart and Winston, 1985 p. 30. William Criddle, "They Can't See There's a Victor." *New York Times* (February 22, 1987), p. D1.

29. *Business Week*, "Across the Globe." (March 23, 1987), pp. 50–51.

30. Templeman, "Insider-Trading Dragnet," pp. 50–51.

31. Fred A. Bleaksdley, "Losses by 'Arabs' Put Near $2 Billion." *New York Times* (November 15, 1986), pp. D1, D9; Stephen Labaton, "Business and the Law: A Green Light in Boesky Suit." *New York Times* (November 23, 1987), p. D2; and Clive Wolman, "Boesky Partners Assets May Lead to Legal Claims." *Financial Times* (May 7, 1987), p. 7.

32. "Insider Cases and Penalties," *New York Times* (February 19, 1988), p. D3.

33. Stephen Labaton, "Drexel Concedes Guilt on Trading." *New York Times* (December 23, 1988), p. 1.

34. Chris Welles, "A Big Crack in the 'Chinese Wall'." *Business Week* (March 2, 1987), p. 33.

35. *The Economist*, "Rules for the City." (February 7, 1987), pp. 17–18, 75–76.

36. *The Economist*, "The Chairman Says." (February 21, 1987), p. 11.

37. Victor Posner and his son Steven were accused by the SEC, in 1988, of joining Milken and Boesky in an effort to improperly take control of the Fischbach Corporation, a New York electrical and mechanical contractor. Federal District Judge Milton Pollack ruled in 1993 that the Posners had violated Federal securities law by failing to disclose the plan. The Posners were ordered to repay about $4 million they had received from Fischbach. There was also a ruling barring them for serving as officers or directors of any publicly held company. In January of 1995, Victor Posner lost a Supreme Court appeal of the ruling.

38. Kurt Eichenwald, "Boesky Released on Parole, Ending 3-Year Prison Term." *New York Times* (April 5, 1990), p. D1.

39. "$20 Million Deal for Boesky." *New York Times* (June 10, 1993), p. A1.
40. Susan Antilla, "Market Place: Regulatory Alarms Ring on Wall Street." *New York Times* (June 9, 1995), p. D1.
41. *Ibid.*; Stephanie Strom, "S.E.C. Accuses an Analyst and His Father of Insider Trading on Merger Plan." *New York Times* (June 16, 1995), p. D8.
42. Kenneth N. Gilpin, "17 Cited in Insider Trading." *New York Times* (February 10, 1995), p. D1.
43. Peter Truell, "Cravath Lawyer and Brother Are Guilty of Insider Trading." *New York Times* (June 29, 1995), pp. D1, D20.

THE ALYESKA PIPELINE SERVICE COMPANY

*The role of whistle-blowers in detecting and correcting
legal and regulatory violations of environmental
protection and operational safety procedures*

RECENT TRENDS
IN WHISTLE-BLOWING

Whistle-blowing, an act that occurs when an employee discloses information about a company's wrongdoing to the public or to the authorities who have the power to initiate corrective action, is a growing organizational phenomenon and the subject of considerable public policy debate.[1]

In the business world, whistle-blowing, hitherto, has been viewed with a large measure of disapproval because it exposes the corporation to potential damage to its name and reputation, destroys group harmony and teamwork, distracts employees from pursuit of the overall corporate mission, and results in financial costs associated with litigation and restitution. Whistle-blowing has also been viewed as a potential tool for undue employee pressure and even blackmail from disgruntled employees seeking revenge under the guise of "doing the right thing." Whistle-blowers are seen as "informers" with

incorrect or incomplete information who should raise their concerns inside the corporation before going public.[2]

Public perception of the role of whistle-blowers has been gradually changing. In part, this is due to increased organizational and technological complexity, which give rise to the potential for causing tremendous harm to society through business negligence or deliberate disregard for human and environmental safety, for the economic and legal rights of others, and for the moral obligation binding on individuals to expose wrongdoings without fear of retaliation. The heightened concern for potential for serious social harm has manifested itself in new federal and state laws that shield individuals from corporate reprisals against whistle-blowing and offer government-granted rewards and inducements to blow the whistle when these allegedly illegal acts are committed against the state or in violation of specific laws.[3] (See Exhibit 1.)

One of the more controversial new laws dealing with this issue is the False Claims Act, revised in 1986. It allows employees who blow the whistle on government contractor fraud to receive between 15-30% of the amount of money recovered by the government (the actual percentage depends on whether or not the Justice Department joined the whistle-blower in the lawsuit against the contractor). In the eight years since the False

This case was prepared by Dr. Janet Rovenpor, Assistant Professor of Management, Manhattan College, Riverdale, New York, 10471 under the guidance and counsel of Professor S. Prakash Sethi, which she gratefully acknowledges. Financial support was provided by the Louis F. Capalbo Endowment Fund, School of Business, Manhattan College. Special thanks are due to librarians Thomas O'Connor and Stacy Pober.

Claims Act was revised, whistle-blowers have filed 700 lawsuits, the Justice Department has intervened in 100 cases, and the government has collected approximately $750 million.[4] The twin convergence of forces in terms of changing public opinion and rising legal protection has opened the gates to whistle-blowing involving a broad spectrum of companies and industries. During the last ten years, a number of highly publicized cases of unethical and illegal behavior have been brought to light by whistle-blowers.[5]

THE ALYESKA PIPELINE SERVICE COMPANY

Nowhere are the problems and challenges associated with whistle-blowing and its consequences more apparent for their complexity as in the case of the Alyeska Pipeline Service Company. Here was a company operating in a highly environmentally sensitive and ecologically fragile area where any wrong step would cause irreparable damage. When the issue of whether or not the pipeline should be built was being debated, the company made promises to maintain the highest standards of environmental safety. However, the company was found to have consistently violated not only federal and state safety laws but also its own internal standards. Here was a company that denied any wrongdoing despite ample disclosures by whistle-blowers and instead sought to intimidate whistle-blowers through private investigations, lawsuits and other measures using the raw exercise of corporate power.

ISSUES FOR ANALYSIS

The Alyeska Pipeline Service Company case offers a rich tapestry with which to analyze the complexity of issues pertaining to the whistle-blowing phenomenon and how it might affect business-society relations on the one hand, and business-organization-individual employee relations on the other hand. In terms of the individuals and organizations involved, whistle-blowing raises highly charged emotional issues of employee loyalty, societal obligations, institutional morale, and group relations. It also raises issues of employee rights of due process, the corporation's right to protect its property and trade secrets, and society's right to protect itself from illegal and unethical corporate behavior that may result in serious health, safety, and environmental harm that can be difficult to correct if found after the fact. As you read this case, consider the following issues:

1. What are the sociopolitical and environmental conditions (e.g., laws, public opinion, and industry characteristics) that make whistle-blowing a necessary phenomenon or at least one possible approach to deterring companies from engaging in illegal/unethical behavior? To what extent were these conditions present in the Alyeska Pipeline case?
2. What are the elements of corporate behavior and corporate culture, including institutional mechanisms, that encourage/discourage the disclosure of wrongful activities within the company? These would also include the leadership style of top management, governance arrangements, organizational structure, decision-making processes, information flows, and compensation systems. How were these conditions pertinent to the Alyeska case?
3. What are some of the potential effects, both positive and negative, of federal and state laws that encourage/protect would-be whistle-blowers? What are some of the other protections offered to whistle-blowers in the absence of specific laws? How well do you think these laws protected the whistle-blowers in the Alyeska case?
4. What motivates whistle-blowers? Are there any personality traits that separate them from others? Or, is there a convergence of events and individual employee situations that forces whistle-blowers to be different from otherwise ordinary employees? How would you evaluate the motives of the individuals who blew the whistle on the Alyeska Pipeline Service Company?
5. What are some of the strategies and tactics that corporations use: (i) to create an internal

environment that facilitates open communications, effective handling of dissent, and the establishment of corrective and proactive responses, thereby making external intervention unnecessary; and, (ii) to dissuade and discourage would-be whistle-blowers or to create countermeasures that might be developed to protect individuals from such reprisals? In the case of Alyeska, what were the company's major strategic thrust and operational mode in dealing with the whistle-blowers? How effective and desirable were these strategies and tactics from the company's viewpoint and from society's perspective?

6. How effective are the current legal procedures and types of punishments available to penalize companies for wrongdoing and to deter such behavior in the future? What role should government, the media, parent companies, and consumer watch-dog groups play in making sure that companies like Alyeska act in the public interest?

THE FOUNDING OF THE ALYESKA PIPELINE SERVICE COMPANY[6]

On November 16, 1973, U.S. President Richard M. Nixon signed a bill that authorized the construction of the Trans-Alaska Pipeline. It was to be an 800-mile pipeline that would connect the large oil reserves found in Prudhoe Bay on the Northern Slope of Alaska with the Port of Valdez which is located in the southern part of Alaska. Passage of the bill was much debated by Congress and the rest of the nation. There was concern that the project might cause irreparable damage to the natural habitat of Alaska, which sustains a large variety of flora and fauna, including such endangered species as the bald eagle. On the other side of the debate were those with ambitious plans for reducing the dependency of the United States on foreign oil. This was a goal of major importance given the then recent oil embargo imposed by the Organization of Petroleum Exporting Countries (OPEC) on the Western

countries. The approval of the pipeline came almost nine years after oil was discovered at Prudhoe Bay.

Eight of the largest oil companies in the world, including British Petroleum, Exxon, and Mobil, created a consortium named the Alyeska Pipeline Service Company (APSC). The goal of this consortium was to construct and operate the pipeline (See Exhibit 2.) A committee, consisting of members from the companies that own APSC, acted as a board of directors to oversee Alyeska's operations.

To overcome environmental concerns during the congressional debate, APSC vowed to adhere to the strictest safety and maintenance standards. The company promised to: provide high-technology pollution control systems; maintain emergency oil-spill response teams, burn off sludge and toxic vapors with incinerators; monitor the quality of ballast water spilled into the Valdez Harbor; and operate double-hulled tankers that were resistant to puncture. These types of safety measures were deemed especially important by environmentalists because of Alaska's harsh but fragile environment. The area is prone to earthquakes, which meant that, in places where the pipeline was built above ground, it had to be placed in a supportive saddle; the tundra consists of permanently frozen ground that could easily be melted by the 100-104 degree heat emanating from the oil in the pipeline.

Today, the Trans-Alaska Pipeline delivers 1.5-2. million barrels of oil per day, supplying the nation with 1/4th of its domestically produced crude oil. In 1989, it was estimated that the pipeline's owners had earned $45 billion in profits during the previous 19-year period. The oil industry in Alaska provides 10,500 people with jobs in a state where there are only 220,000 jobs and makes it possible for all 550,000 Alaskans to receive a yearly "dividend" check of between $331 and $1,000.[7] The State of Alaska also earns approximately $2 billion a year, or 85% of its revenues, from oil. The local government collects taxes based on a "wellhead" figure that represents the prices paid by refineries for the crude oil minus the costs incurred for transporting the oil. When Alyeska's operating costs rise, the tariff the pipeline operator charges for transportation increases. Thus, the spread upon which the government can collect taxes is lower. The state has estimated that every $1 increase in tariffs reduces its tax revenues by $0.25. If Alyeska spends $1 billion to repair its pipeline, the state will lose $250 million in taxes.[8]

ALYESKA'S HISTORY: A LITANY OF ENVIRONMENTAL, HEALTH, AND SAFETY VIOLATIONS

Completion of the Trans-Alaska Pipeline. There have been persistent concerns and complaints about Alyeska's failure to establish an effective quality control system. Even before June 20, 1977, the first day that oil began to flow through the pipeline, problems were noted in the way that Alyeska constructed and planned to operate the pipeline. As two federal-state inspectors stated, one month before the pipeline opened, "There is no environmental quality-control in the area whatsoever. In our opinions, it is beyond belief that the quality-control program is so lax at this late stage of construction." Another state pipeline coordinator said that, "We should have shut the whole thing down until they provided an adequate quality-control program. They never did the job they should have, and it . . . caused some inexcusable environmental damage."[9] The company was criticized for not elevating the pipeline by at least 10 feet in all 550 predesignated locations to allow for bear and caribou to pass underneath; failing to install proper culverts to prevent massive erosion of the tundra; using inappropriate equipment; and neglecting to obtain required permits. During Alyeska's early years, there were 4,000 separate incidents in which over 300,000 gallons of oil spilled. The company paid $100,000 in fines to the state for various violations.[10]

Alyeska acknowledged that it violated some of the most stringent regulations and that it had faced oil spillage and sewage treatment problems. Alyeska's manager of environmental protection, however, defended his company, stating that " . . . overall, I think we've done as good a job of protecting the environment as we could."[11] However, according to Alyeska's own internal memo dated July 24, 1975, and obtained by the *Wall Street Journal*, "Alyeska section construction management and the [contractors] have placed stipulations and requirements for the environment secondary to those for pipeline construction. Greater emphasis must be placed on the environment work to bring it into conformance with the stipulations."[12]

Water Pollution at Alyeska's Valdez Terminal 1977–1986. In 1986, Alyeska's sprawling complex of 18 storage tanks and its large southern terminal at Valdez came under scrutiny for lax procedures. Water pollution problems seem to have plagued the harbor since 1977. Oil tankers arriving at the Valdez terminal carry with them oily ballast water needed to maintain tanker stability during the voyage to Alaska. This water is pumped out of the tankers at Valdez so that they can take on the crude oil. Approximately 13 million gallons of ballast water is discharged by the tankers every day. The Valdez facility was supposed to clean the oily ballast water by using heaters to separate the oil from the water. Waste material, or "sludge," was to be burnt in a large incinerator (which Alyeska never constructed); some of the more oily substances could then be channelled into outgoing crude oil; the clean water would be discharged into the harbor. The company was also supposed to install a continuous monitoring system to test both the quality of the water being discharged into the harbor and the quality of the oil extracted from the ballast water before it was placed into the terminal's storage tanks.

It now appears that Alyeska was not following many of these procedures. The company claimed that it could not find a reliable continuous monitoring system and that the heaters were dismantled because they were difficult to maintain. Alyeska dealt with these problems by recycling sludge directly back into the ballast-water treatment tanks instead of incinerating it. The water, with amounts of toxic hydrocarbons that were much higher than allowed by federal law, was dumped into the Valdez waters. One piece of evidence indicating that at least one of the pipeline's owners knew about the sludge problem was a letter, written by a Valdez terminal superintendent to an Exxon engineer.[13] In it, the superintendent complained that the treatment plant was not removing solids properly and asked for assistance from Exxon. Although Exxon officials claimed they did not know how their company responded, Alyeska documents revealed that an Exxon official who studied the plant recommended that since sludge disposal would cost at least $1.5 million a year, more oily waste should be diverted into crude oil destined for outgoing tankers. Another internal memo from plant operators revealed that solid wastes were accumulating at a rate of 1-2 tons per day, far more than reported by Alyeska.[14] Ihor Lysyj, an EPA consultant and an expert on ballast-water treatment, estimated that the plant was spewing out 1,600 pounds of toxic and hazardous substances every day, or enough sludge to completely cover four football fields three feet deep during its eight years of operations. It's like "vacuuming your house, dumping all the collected dust back on the carpet and then starting the whole process over again."[15] Alyeska was charged with routinely falsifying documents and failing to install and, in fact, disconnecting—pollution control systems without notifying the EPA. All along, Alyeska maintained that it did, in fact, comply with all antipollution laws and that allegations of record tampering and sludge dumping were false. It claimed that its ballast water treatment facility was "probably the best and the most modern" plant of its kind in the industry.[16]

Air Pollution at Alyeska's Valdez Terminal 1978-1993. Air pollution problems have plagued Alyeska over the years. Between 1980 and 1985, internal Alyeska records showed that the company's vapor disposal system was shut down on an average of one day in five.[17] To save money, the company built only three of the four incinerators required by the U.S. Congress. Alyeska also operated the incinerators at lower temperatures than originally specified, and used carbon steel instead of stainless steel to construct the incinerators, thereby causing more rapid decay.

In 1993, EPA regulators claimed that "venting" problems had existed since 1978. Benzene, toluene, and other pollutants were escaping directly into the atmosphere through vents at three remote standby tanks adjacent to three pumping stations. These were supposed to be used only during an emergency. Unlike the standard tanks, the standby tanks are not linked to incinerators. Bill MacClarence, an air quality coordinator for the Alaska Department of Environmental Conservation estimated that faulty equipment was allowing 10,000 tons of benzene and other hazardous gases to escape into the air every year.[18] In 1990, Alyeska was obliged to spend between $15-20 million to undertake the necessary repairs.

Alyeska's Response to the 1989 **Exxon Valdez** *Oil Spill.* Alyeska's lack of sufficient concern for the environment and its poor record of contingency planning in dealing with a major disaster became all too apparent during the sequence of events that began on March 24, 1989 when the oil tanker *Exxon Valdez* ran aground in Prince William Sound. Charles O'Donnell, Alyeska's top executive at Valdez, was awakened at about 12:30a.m. by a phone call from the terminal informing him that a supertanker was possibly aground on Bligh Reef. After reflecting on the situation for a moment, O'Donnell ordered a subordinate to head for the terminal. He then rolled over and went back to sleep. (See

Exhibit 3 for a listing of major players involved.)

This was typical of Alyeska's slow and inadequate response to the catastrophe which resulted in an oil spill of 11 million gallons of oil. Crucial equipment, such as fenders—which were needed so that a second tanker could come alongside the *Exxon Valdez* and siphon off its remaining oil—could not be located for hours because they were buried under 14 feet of snow. An audit revealed that Alyeska was missing, or had out of commission, one out of three required tugboats, five out of thirteen oil skimmers, and that if possessed only 14,000 feet of containment boom instead of 21,000 feet. It took 14 hours, nearly triple the time Alyeska had estimated for responding to a spill, to repair, load, and send out a barge equipped with cleanup equipment to the site of the accident.[19]

Alyeska had originally promised a 20-person, 24-hour emergency oil-spill team. However, the team had been dismissed in 1981 and its responsibilities had been passed on to workers with other duties. Alyeska managers contended that this was a "superior arrangement" since there were now 120 employees trained to handle oil spills. Yet, at least one of these 120 individuals admitted that he had "zero oil spill training, none."[20] A former oil spill coordinator, whose last job at Alyeska was in 1983, called fire and oil spill drills a "farce, comic opera."[21] At one fire drill, for example, a fire engine arrived with a driver but no crew; in another, a fire engine's hose malfunctioned, a fire hydrant failed because the pump was not turned on, and dummies placed at the center of the fire could not be saved. Oil-spill drills did not fare any better. In one case, a containment boom sank and, in another, a boat carrying a high ranking executive ran aground.

Alyeska has consistently asserted that it had an excellent environmental record—safely directing more than 8,000 tankers in and out of the harbor—before the *Exxon Valdez* disaster. The State of Alaska, however, had another opinion. Dennis Kelso, head of Alaska's Department of Environmental Conservation, summed up the outrage felt by many when he said, "Alyeska stands as a monument to a powerful and rich industry's fundamental failure to keep its commitments. They have operated as if they were a sovereign state, with terrible consequences. As a nation, we have to ask ourselves: 'Can we trust them anymore?'"[22]

Nevertheless, the owners of Alyeska were granted immunity from prosecution in a criminal case that criticized the company for its failure to respond quickly to the *Valdez* oil spill. Attorney General Richard Thornburgh played a key role in negotiating the settlement with the Exxon Corporation. Thornburgh himself was criticized because of his $32,296 investment in two of the pipeline's owners. He received a waiver of conflict of interest rules from President Bush just a few days before signing the settlement. More recently, Alyeska paid $32 million to Alaska and the federal government to settle lawsuits. Part of the money will go towards building docks and warehouses to store emergency oil spill equipment, reimbursing the U. S. Coast Guard for its expenses, and reimbursing Alaskan towns for lost fish-tax payments. It is expected that an additional $98 million will be paid as a result of another settlement finalized in July 1993.

Pipeline Corrosion Problems Detected in 1989. The Trans-Alaska Pipeline is a 48-inch-wide tube of half-inch thick steel. It was supposed to be rust free for its first 30-40 years, the length of time it would take to retrieve all of the oil from Prudhoe Bay. And yet, only 13 years after the pipeline was constructed, serious corrosion problems were detected. Federal investigators attributed the corrosion to Alyeska's haste in applying a protective epoxy coating to the pipeline. Alyeska officials noted that the most extensive corrosion appeared in a nine mile stretch of pipe 160 miles south of Prudhoe Bay. Repair costs were estimated between $600 million to $1.5 billion. Alyeska, however, refused to assume responsibility, contending that corrosion was inevitable as the pipeline was aging. However, rust could not be detected until after a sophisticated technology, called a "pig" device, was invented.

ENTER THE WHISTLE-BLOWERS

Most of the information implicating Alyeska for violating environmental and safety regulations, and not keeping to its commitment to operate a safe pipeline, came from numerous whistle-blowers from both inside and outside the corporation.[23] (See Exhibit 3 for the cast of characters.) Many Alyeska employees chose to provide evidence of company wrongdoing to a former independent oil tanker broker, Charles Hamel of Alexandria, Virginia, instead of directly contacting state and federal regulatory agencies. Despite various state and federal laws that protect the rights of employees who come forward, Alyeska employees were afraid that they would lose their jobs. Hamel, a longtime critic of oil companies, therefore, served as a conduit between the whistle-blowers and various government agencies, congressional committees, and other organizations, including the news media.

Charles Hamel was not a professional environmentalist or even an activist. In fact, during the early 1970s, Hamel, in his role as a staff assistant for Alaska's democratic senator, Michael Gravel, was instrumental in convincing environmental groups, commercial fishers, and Native Americans that the Trans-Alaska Pipeline would be good for Alaska. He later became an oil tanker broker, selling and transporting North Slope crude oil. He claimed that his business collapsed in the early 1980s when he found that his oil contained a high percentage of water. He later sued Alyeska and its owners for $12 million but failed to collect any money.

During this period, Hamel became aware of the existence of serious gaps in Alyeska's operating procedures with regards to worker safety and environmental protection. He would later tell a congressional oversight hearing, "We were living in a conspiracy of silence waiting for an environmental disaster to occur and, as you know, it did. I decided I had to do something to prove to the public that the oil industry had violated their legal and moral obligations to Alaska."[24] Obsessed and driven, for the next ten years, Hamel would cultivate a network of contacts amongst Alyeska's employees who would provide him with written documents and letters attesting to Alyeska's wrongdoings. He also maintained an 800 telephone number for tipsters.

Hamel was one of the first individuals to warn of corrosion in the pipeline, years before Alyeska acknowledged the problem. He offered evidence of water pollution at a Fairbanks refinery and provided some of the key internal documents to Alaska's attorney general and the EPA when the ballast-water treatment plant at the Valdez terminal came under investigation. In testimony before the Senate Energy and Natural Resources Committee, he accused Alyeska of deliberately allowing its vapor recovery system to deteriorate. Information provided by Hamel resulted in: (a) a $20,000 fine imposed by the EPA on Alyeska for illegal waste water dumping; (b) a $15-20 million repair on Alyeska's vapor recovery system (completed in the summer of 1990); and (c) a $600 million to $1.5 billion program launched by Alyeska in 1989 to refurbish the corroding pipeline.

In 1987, Charles Hamel filed an administrative complaint with the Alaska Public Utilities Commission claiming that Alyeska and Exxon had sold him watered-down crude oil. Among those testifying at the hearing were: Erlene Blake, a plant laboratory technician at Alyeska from 1977 to 1983; James Woodle, a marine superintendent at the Valdez terminal from 1982 to1984; Steven Eward, an Alyeska technician from 1977 to 1980; and Philip Nicpon, former chief chemist at the North Pole Refinery in Alaska.

Blake testified that she had been instructed by her supervisor to falsify reports to the EPA whenever the volume of treated water flowing into the bay exceeded maximum federal limits and that it was "standard operating procedure" to "alter" such records. She also stated that when repeated tests of oil samples showed that it contained too much water, a supervisor would draw a sample from a "miracle barrel" whose contents always passed the tests. She apparently kept her own logs in which she recorded the correct test results. Unfortunately, she was not able to produce the logs as evidence because they were allegedly stolen from her personal locker by a supervisor.[25]

James Woodle testified that plant operators were instructed to ignore safety procedures, if necessary, in order to handle large quantities of incoming ballast water. "Just empty the tanks and make room," were the instructions.[26] Woodle further charged that Alyeska encouraged the practice of sending samples of treated ballast water to Seattle Washington, for testing. By the time the samples traveled the 1,200-mile distance, the pollutants had decayed and the water tested within limits. Not that it mattered much anyway because the water was dumped into the harbor before the test results would come back from Seattle. Woodle was fired by Alyeska.

Eward testified that he was frequently ordered to disconnect the meter that measured how much treated water was being dumped into the Valdez Harbor. Federal law sets limits on the amount and rate at which water can be discharged. Thus, "there was no other way for regulators to check it."[27] Nicpon reported that the level of water in the North Slope crude oil regularly purchased by his refinery was "significantly higher" than the official test result showed.[28] Despite the testimony of these individuals, the Commission ruled that Alyeska hadn't knowingly fabricated test results.

In 1989, Alyeska hired Thorpe Technical Services, Inc., to test the pipeline for corrosion. Thorpe's investigation spotted 622 anomalies using the "pig" device. However, a year later, Edward Thompson, a 26-year-old former employee of Thorpe, wrote to federal and state agencies that oversaw the pipeline. In his letter, he claimed that he and his coworkers were inadequately trained and improperly supervised by Thorpe and Alyeska when performing magnetic tests to spot pipeline cracks. He also claimed that workers often drank beer and used drugs at work and that supervisors deliberately ignored test results showing that parts of the pipeline were dangerously rusted. Dale Thorpe, president of Thorpe, denied the charges and suggested that Thompson was seeking revenge after being fired for misuse of a company vehicle. Robert Mengelkamp, a 19-year-old Fairbanks resident, reported that he, too, was inadequately trained and supervised. Mengelkamp said that he and other coworkers were shown an antiquated filmstrip, which kept on breaking, on how to use the equipment. This occurred only after they had already started inspecting the pipeline.

As a result of Thompson's and Mengelkamp's allegations, state and federal officials ordered Alyeska to conduct a new $500,000 retesting program in which nineteen sections along the pipeline worked on by Thorpe were unearthed and examined. No new pipeline corrosion problems surfaced and Thorpe appeared to be vindicated. The Federal State Pipeline Monitoring office, however, found that the contractor used inexperienced and poorly trained workers, and that Alyeska did not implement appropriate quality assurance and quality control procedures. Alyeska accused Thorpe of billing irregularities and refused to pay for two months of work already completed by the contractor. Thorpe sued and was later awarded $900,000 by a state superior court jury. Alyeska, in turn, was awarded $150,000 because some of the allegations regarding billing irregularities proved to be true.

ALYESKA'S ACTIONS AGAINST THE WHISTLE-BLOWERS

The negative publicity about Alyeska's operations and the resultant pressure were beginning to build up. The company was becoming concerned about its potential impact on public opinion.[29] The situation was not helped when Alyeska's executives viewed a videotape of a January 20, 1990 film called "Slick Operators." In the film, broadcast by British television, British Petroleum, Alyeska's principal owner, was chastised for not knowing that the Valdez terminal was a disaster waiting to happen, given the high standards it applies to the operation of its large Shetland Islands terminal. An internal memo was also read in which a company lawyer compared Alyeska's oil spill response to earlier Alyeska promises that its pipeline would be the safest in the world. Alyeska executives were upset that a confidential attorney work-product document had been disclosed. They felt that it was their duty to stop the flow of stolen documents and proprietary information from their company.

Alyeska's manager of corporate security, J. Patrick Wellington, contacted the Wackenhut Corporation in Coral Gables, Florida, to discuss the possibility of an investigation. He reported his conversation to James Hermiller, Alyeska's president, who authorized an investigation. Founded in 1954 by former FBI agents, Wackenhut is the third largest security firm in the United States. The firm trains all officers and managers employed by the Department of Energy (DOE), guards the DOE's nuclear facilities, handles security arrangements at 15 U.S. embassies throughout the world, and runs detention centers for the Immigration and Nationalization Service. One of its subsidiaries—American Guard and Alert (AG&A)—had a contract with Alyeska dating back to 1977. This contract charged AG&A with the responsibility for protecting the pipeline from acts of sabotage.

In 1989, the Wackenhut Corporation set up a new, 18-person special investigations division (SID) headed by Wayne Black. Black had been a criminal investigator for the Dade County prosecutor but had been suspended in 1981 for conducting illegal wiretaps and pressuring witnesses in a police brutality case. Black was given the Alyeska assignment, code named Case # 427. Throughout the investigation, Wellington spoke to Black at least twice a week to discuss progress. Wellington was also responsible for setting up a covert billing system in which Wackenhut was to bill AG&A for its investigation of Hamel; AG&A would then include those charges in the TAPS/3105 monthly billing to Alyeska.

Surveillance and Investigation of Charles Hamel. Wackenhut set up an elaborate sting operation to ensnare Hamel. Their goal was to trick Hamel into revealing his information sources, thereby undermining his credibility and effectiveness. In March 1990, Hamel attended a meeting of environmentalists held in Anchorage, Alaska, called the Frontier Thinking Conference. One evening, when he was having drinks with a friend, he noticed a beautiful woman at Fletcher's Bar, located in the hotel that was the site of the conference. A few days later, the same woman was seated near him on the first part of his airline flight back to Virginia. The woman introduced herself as Ricki Edelson, a researcher for an environmental litigation support group, Ecolit ("eco" from the word "ecology" and "lit" from the word "litigation"). She indicated that she was gathering information that could be used in lawsuits against the oil companies in Alaska. To further garner Hamel's sympathy and support, she fabricated a story saying that she was a single mother whose ex-husband was delinquent on child support payments. She expressed a fear of losing her new job if she failed to make worthwhile contacts at the meeting. Hamel was only too willing to help.

It must have been a combination of Hamel's naiveté and male ego that he was so careless about sharing sensitive information with a total, albeit beautiful, stranger. Nor did his antenna pick up any danger signals when, a few weeks later, he received a letter from Dr. Wayne Jenkins, staff researcher for Ecolit, thanking him for his assistance. One wonders if he would have been so forthcoming about sharing this information had he been contacted "cold" by the so-called Dr. Jenkins. Jenkins and Hamel set up a meeting and agreed to work together to pursue litigation of the oil industry. During their meetings, the gullible Mr. Hamel provided Jenkins with sensitive internal documents on Alyeska's air pollution problems; lack of preparedness to respond to a major oil spill; and, Exxon's illegal dumping of hazardous materials off the coasts of California and Florida. On August 19, 1990, alone, Hamel supplied Jenkins with over 500 legal documents. Hamel boasted to Jenkins about his connections with Congressman George Miller who had stayed in his house during government hearings on the *Exxon Valdez* oil spill.

Ecolit, as it turned out, was a fictitious company. Ricki Jacobson (nee Edelson) was an undercover agent working for Wackenhut. Dr. Jenkins was none other than Wayne Black himself. While Ricki Jacobson was in Alaska establishing her connection with Hamel, Black and his associate, Richard Lund, placed an advertisement in the *Valdez Vanguard* announcing Ecolit's interest in conducting confidential interviews with local residents to discuss the *Exxon Valdez* oil spill. They placed flyers on local bulletin boards and on cars parked near Alyeska offices. In fact, in one of the first conversations held between Black and Hamel, Hamel expressed surprise at Ecolit's ability to bypass Alyeska security guards in order to place flyers on the automobiles of its employees. However, this failed to arouse any suspicions in Hamel's mind as to Ecolit's veracity. This is surprising given the fact that he had personal knowledge of the high-pressure tactics that Alyeska

used to suppress dissent among the company's employees. On two occasions, Lund visited the Trustees for Alaska, a nonprofit environmental law firm, where he took photographs of the building and stole trash from several offices. When Lund witnessed a lawful demonstration at Alyeska's Anchorage headquarters, he identified the organizers, noted their license plate numbers, and took photographs.

To make the trap even tighter, a Wackenhut investigator, Sheree Rich, opened two Ecolit offices, one in Florida and one near Hamel's home in Virginia. These offices were appropriately furnished and decorated with "Save the Whales" posters and other paraphernalia of an environmental activist organization. During his visits to Hamel's home, Black allegedly removed documents from Hamel's desk and sifted through his mail. Black also installed surveillance cameras in the Ecolit office where he met with Hamel. And, in the best "spook" tradition, he used a motorized van with electronic eavesdropping equipment to tape Hamel's conversations at home. Apparently, money was no object when it came to neutralizing Hamel's effectiveness in exposing Alyeska. For at least twelve consecutive weeks, Hamel's trash was stolen from outside his home. At one point, Hamel actually videotaped masked men stealing his trash. However, he never suspected Black or Ecolit as the probable instigators. Wackenhut agents obtained Hamel's credit-card records, copies of his banking transactions, and lists of his long-distance telephone calls. They uncovered information about Hamel's divorce, his wife's medications, his ownership of property, and his business disputes with Exxon. Hamel was even offered two checks for $2,000 each from Ecolit to cover his expenses. One of the checks was personally delivered to Hamel's home by Sheree Rich, who was wearing a concealed eavesdropping device at the time her delivery was made. Hamel picked up the second check at one of the Ecolit offices. Rich reasoned that Hamel may have accepted the money because he was facing financial difficulties. She told the *Anchorage Daily News* that Black knew of Hamel's poor financial situation and may have offered to pay Hamel for the documents he had in his possession.

The Wackenhut investigation revealed the name of one apparent whistle-blower, Robert Scott, an operator at Alyeska's vapor-recovery system. Scott's number appeared 15-20 times in Hamel's telephone records. On October 24, 1990, Scott was fired after 14 years of service to Alyeska for allegedly poor performance. He was 64 years old. Alyeska also accused him of making racists remarks, and starting an argument in the company parking lot.

Other apparent targets of the Wackenhut investigation were: Dan Lawn, an officer with the Alaska Department of Environmental Conservation; Robert Swift, a Valdez bartender who befriended Wayne and Lund; and Ricki Ott, a scientist specializing in marine pollution. Wackenhut agents felt that they might be able to have both Hamel and Congressman Miller indicted for receiving stolen documents. In a memo written by Jonathan Goodman, an attorney hired by Wackenhut during the covert operation, the "best goal" for the operation would be to get "Miller and Hamel indicted for encouraging theft of property."[30]

It would appear that representatives of the companies that owned APSC were shown, for the first time, the output of Wackenhut's operations on September 25, 1990. William C. Rusnack (vice-president of Atlantic Richfield Company and president of Arco Transportation Company); Fred Garibaldi (president of British Petroleum of America and chairman of the TAPS Owners Committee); and Darrell G. Warner (president of Exxon Pipeline Company) attended a TAPS Owners Committee meeting held in Denver at the request of James Hermiller. They were told of the reasons for the Wackenhut investigation and were shown excerpts of videotapes in which Hamel described his allegations of pipeline corrosion and of toxic materials being dumped into the Valdez harbor. Hermiller indicated his desire to pursue a civil lawsuit against Hamel to get the Alyeska documents back. However, this was not agreeable to the owners. Instead, the owners ordered that the operation be shut down immediately. They felt that although the investigation had been conducted in an apparently legal manner, it was not consistent with their business standards. At the same meeting, the owners instructed Alyeska to assemble all investigative materials so that they would not be destroyed or used for any purpose and arranged to bring the matter to the attention of Alyeska's other owners at a regularly scheduled full-owners committee meeting to be held on October 3 in La Costa, California.

Instructions to shut down the operation were reiterated at the second full owners' committee meeting. The owners decided to hire an independent law firm to review the Wackenhut investigation and to safeguard the documents. Many of the owners expressed their concern at not being informed of the Wackenhut investigation at the outset. Others seemed to have felt under some obligation to report Hamel's allegations of wrongdoing to the proper authorities. Legal advice was sought on this issue as well.

Black immediately shut down the Ecolit operation, telling Hamel that Ecolit was forced to close due to a lack of funding and that Black must look for a new job. Sheree Rich was instructed to close down the Ecolit office in Miami. In a memo from Black she was told, "Effective December 31, 1990, Ecolit will cease to exist and must fade away with no trace to you or this company. Errors and mistakes with regard to forwarding addresses and slip-ups are not possible or acceptable. For this reason, please be extra careful to think ten steps ahead."[31] Hamel wanted to continue the relationship and even offered to search for alternative sources of funding.

Internal Turmoil at Wackenhut: Repercussions from the Hamel Investigation. In May 1991, Raphael Castillo, an investigator at Wackenhut, made a formal complaint to the director of personnel about Wayne Black's investigative practices. He subsequently met with Allen Bernstein, the vice-president of domestic operations and Tim Howard, an in-house counsel. Bernstein asked Castillo to conduct an independent investigation into sexual harassment charges made against Black by several female employees at Wackenhut. During his investigation, Castillo learned of the concerns held by a number of Wackenhut agents regarding the legality of the surveillance techniques used against Hamel. He played a tape of these conversations to Bernstein and Howard. When they did not seem to care, he resigned.

Castillo sought legal advice and decided to inform Hamel of the covert investigation. He also offered his assistance to Hamel if he [Hamel] were to bring matters to the attention of federal and state authorities. Castillo recalls his first telephone conversation with Hamel: "Chuck was flabbergasted. He didn't know what to say. He starts screaming on the phone... about to have a nervous breakdown. I think he had to double his ration of tranquilizers."[32] Hamel informed Congressman Miller's committee about the Wackenhut operation in July 1991. On August 7, the committee filed a written request for documents from Alyeska on the Hamel investigation. After repeated written requests and subpoenas, the committee acquired a wealth of material including letters, legal briefings, bills, telephone record logs, diagrams, an espionage manual, audiotapes, videotapes, and other information from Alyeska and Wackenhut documenting the handling of the Hamel investigation, as well as the extent of involvement of the various parties. Three-day hearings on the covert surveillance operation authorized by Alyeska and conducted by Wackenhut were held on November 4, 5, and 6, 1991.

Alyeska's Grudging Admission of Guilt. On September 21, 1991, Alyeska took out full-page advertisements in newspapers throughout Alaska, wherein Alyeska's president, James Hermiller, apologized to the people of Alaska for his authorization of the covert investigation. Hermiller admitted that "the investigation, taken as a whole does not meet the standards Alyeska strives for and Alaskans expect. Alyeska values its good relationship with Alaskans and I am sorry if I have put that relationship in jeopardy." (See Exhibit 4.)[33] The apology, however, did not seem to have gone beyond a superficial attempt at "damage control." There did not seem to be an internal investigation. No one was fired or even censured. And, despite all their expressions of concern, Alyeska's owners, the major oil companies, did not take any action to rein in the renegade management of Alyeska. It is no wonder that the Trustees for Alaska rejected the apology, as did Hamel. "There has been no apology to the targets of the investigation, no remedial action to remove the chilling effect the investigation has had on Alyeska employees who fear exercising their legal rights to contact EPA, the Alaska DEC, Congress or even me," said Hamel.[34]

The Covert Investigation of Hamel Receives Media Attention. On November 3, 1991, CBS published details of Alyeska and Wackenhut's covert surveillance operation in its "60 Minutes" television news program. Among those who appeared on the show were: Charles Hamel, George Miller, and Wayne Black. (See Exhibit 4 for transcript excerpts.)

OVERSIGHT HEARINGS OF THE COMMITTEE OF INTERIOR AND INSULAR AFFAIRS

The House of Representatives' Interior and Insular Affairs Committee, headed by George Miller (D) of California, held hearings on November 4-6, 1991, to investigate whether or not Wackenhut used illegal surveillance methods in its covert operation of Hamel and other suspected whistle-blowers. The committee also believed that the operation was intended to impede the committee's receipt of information on Alyeska's alleged environmental violations.

Officials testifying on behalf of Alyeska included Hermiller, the company president; Wellington, its security chief; and Alyeska's attorneys. The thrust of their testimony was that Wackenhut was hired to find out how, and by whom, confidential, privileged, and proprietary company documents were being stolen. The company considered these documents to be corporate "assets," which contained "secrets" regarding its operations and legal affairs. The company feared that the documents might get into the hands of competitors, terrorists, and saboteurs. Alyeska called Hamel a criminal who had stolen company documents and tried to use them to extort money from Alyeska and Exxon.

Wellington defended the covert operation as a legitimate means of trying to stop documents from being leaked from the company. He justified the creation of the Ecolit offices and the placement of flyers on the Alyeska employees' automobiles as "investigative" and not "deceptive" tools. When asked whether there were any established procedures in Alyeska's security department with regard to conducting internal investigations, he conceded that there were none. Hermiller also stated that he believed all investigative techniques used by Wackenhut were "lawful" and "proper." He believed Wackenhut to be one of the world's most prominent and reputable investigative firms. He also had obtained the advice of several attorneys regarding the legality of the investigation. Nonetheless, he complied immediately with the owners' request to stop the investigation.

A more aggressive and spirited defense of Wackenhut's operations was presented by William Richey, a Miami attorney and personal friend of Black. He stated, "The whistle-blower laws and statutes have not abolished the Ten Commandments in this country. It is absolutely improper for people to be stealing records of this type."[35] Richey apparently felt that members of the committee were closeminded. He commented that the Hearings were a little bit like "Alice in Wonderland" with "a verdict being made before the trial began."[36]

Black and Lund did not testify at the hearings, claiming the Fifth Amendment against self-incrimination. However, in a report for Alyeska conducted by the law firm of Paul, Hastings, Janofsky & Walker, Lund defended his actions with regards to Hamel by saying that he took Hamel's trash from the curbside and did not trespass onto Hamel's property. He claimed that he had acquired Hamel's telephone records from Ron Eriksen, who had advertised in a private investigator newsletter that he could provide legally obtained telephone records.

Black indicated in an interview with Steven Kroft for the CBS program "60 Minutes" that he was proud of the investigation and would do it again if he had the opportunity. He defended and justified his "investigative" techniques, which included stealing trash, obtaining telephone numbers, creating fictitious companies, and surreptitiously recording conversations saying, "People don't bring stolen documents to us if we tell them we're investigators. So it's—it's not like you can come right out and tell somebody who it is, and say, 'Please, please bring me the evidence that—you committed a crime'"[37] (see Exhibit 5).

The Committee heard the testimony of a number of Wackenhut employees, including Sheree Rich, Ricki Jacobson, Ana Contreras, Adriana Caputi, and, David Ramirez. They provided details of Wackenhut's operations and the extensive scope of surveillance activities that the company carried out against Hamel. Ricki Jacobson testified that she was asked to travel to Alaska to attend a conference on environmentalism in March 1990.

Her only assignment was to attend the meetings, find out if Hamel had registered for the conference, and observe him in the hotel bar. She was surprised that Hamel was on the same flight leaving Alaska and that he was so talkative to a stranger. The testimony showed that during a two-month period, Wackenhut's bills to Alyeska exceeded $200,000. It was shown that Lund alone was responsible for altering the company's computer program and data bases. This testimony led to the committee's suspicion that many documents, especially Wackenhut's bills for services provided to Alyeska, were destroyed.

Charles Hamel appeared at the hearings and provided testimony in the form a prepared statement. Hamel confirmed that he did indeed serve as a conduit between Alyeska whistle-blowers and the various regulatory agencies overseeing pipeline operations. He also mentioned several business disputes he had with Exxon, including the claim that he was sold watered-down crude oil. He stated that he had been approached in 1985 by the oil industry and asked what would it take to get him to "go away." In addition to seeking $12 million in compensation for the loss of his business, Hamel wanted the oil companies to clean up the environment by conducting an audit of the Valdez terminal, installing a pollution monitoring program funded by Alyeska but run by an independent group, and creating a medical monitoring fund for Alyeska technicians who had been exposed to toxic vapors. He felt that Alyeska's claim that he had stolen confidential company documents was a case of psychological projection. He did not, after all, take Alyeska's trash, tape company telephone calls, break into Alyeska offices, or pose as one of its own employees. The committee members chose not to question him because the committee's main objective was to investigate the legality of the techniques used by Wackenhut. After the hearings ended, Miller said, "Mr. Hamel had no control or operational say-so in the surveil-lance—and the focus of this hearing had to be on those individuals that were making decisions about whether or not to go forward with the surveillance."[38]

Testimony of Alyeska's Owners. Testimony was heard from the representatives from three companies that controlled a majority of equity interest in Alyeska. Darrell Warner, Fred Garibaldi, and William Rusnack all stated that they learned about the covert Wackenhut operation on September 25, 1990, and ordered it halted that day. Rusnack made the following comment about the investigation, "It scared the hell out of me . . . I didn't know what we had. I don't particularly like video tapes. I don't like going through people's garbage. I felt extremely uncomfortable."[39]

A number of inconsistencies that were uncovered during the hearings, however, indicate that at least two out of the three senior executives from Alyeska's owner companies may actually have known about the Wackenhut investigation before September 25, 1990. Steven Dietrich, an Exxon attorney, apparently stated behind closed doors that he had briefed Warner about the operation in mid-August; Garibaldi admitted that he had been advised twice by Hermiller about the investigation but had never followed up on Hermiller's invitation to view videotapes of Hamel.[40] Even if one accepts the testimony of Warner, Garibaldi, and Rusnack as being accurate—that the executives learned about the investigation seven months after it began—was it their responsibility to supervise Alyeska more closely? Committee member Harry Johnston of Florida blamed the owners for not knowing what Alyeska was doing. He said, "It seems to me that everyone is building a firewall for responsibility, knowledge, and insulating themselves from everyone else."[41]

During panel discussions at the hearings, Alyeska's owners were asked a number of questions about Alyeska's policies for handling whistle-blower complaints and about its organizational culture. Miller asked Rusnack what he did to assure employees that they could discuss their concerns with Alyeska's managers. Rusnack replied that the first step was to run the organization appropriately and to obey vigilantly all environmental laws and regulations. The second step was to create an environment so that employees would know they should take action if they were to detect wrongdoing by informing the owners or the proper authorities.[42] Miller asked Garibaldi if the leaking of confidential documents from a company was (a) a unique American problem, (b) a culture problem, and, (c) a problem for British Petroleum in its overseas operations. Garibaldi said, " I cannot make a comparison. I do not know. In my own personal experience this has been—I have never seen an organization come under as much pressure from the outside as occurred to Alyeska following the events of the *Exxon Valdez* spill."[43]

Committee Findings and Recommendations. The committee issued a 2,000-page report of its findings in July 1992. It concluded that the "Wackenhut agents engaged in a pattern of deceitful, grossly offensive and potentially, if not blatantly, illegal conduct to accomplish their objectives."[44]

In the majority report released by Chairman Miller, the committee made a number of recommendations.

1. The Justice Department should consider criminal and civil prosecution of Alyeska and Wackenhut for potentially violating federal laws that prohibit the obstruction of justice, surreptitious recording, possession of surreptitious recording devices, mail and wire fraud and access to credit, financial and other private information.
2. Authorities in Washington, D. C. and the states of Alaska, Florida, and Virginia, should consider criminal and/or civil action against Alyeska and Wackenhut under state laws.
3. Alyeska and Wackenhut should consider changes to their management and operations.

4. Alyeska's owners should increase their control over and responsibility for Alyeska's management.
5. The State of Alaska, the EPA, the Department of Transportation, and the Department of Interior should substantially increase resources devoted to regulating Alyeska and the Trans-Alaska Pipeline.
6. The Presidential Task Force should increase government oversight over Alyeska and conduct an independent audit of the pipeline.[45]

The vote by members of the committee to approve these recommendations was unanimous. Nevertheless, minority members of the committee, led by Don Young (R), the only committee member from Alaska, insisted on attaching their own 186-page response to the report to be sent to the Justice Department. Their goal was to review the evidence on the Wackenhut investigation in an "objective and dispassionate manner" and to determine whether or not the committee's inquiry was conducted in accordance with the rules of the committee and the U.S. House of Representatives. Miller was criticized for appearing on the "60 Minutes" program which had aired the night before the hearings began. During the program, he called Hermiller and other individuals involved in the Wackenhut investigation "criminals." Thus, minority members felt that Miller had already made up his mind that the individuals were guilty, before their testimony was heard. Miller's prejudices and anger at the possibility that he, too, had been a target of the Wackenhut investigation might have tainted the selection and subsequent interpretation of the evidence.

The minority report further claimed that:

1. Alyeska's concern over leaked documents was legitimate. The fact that engineering diagrams and technical data had been stolen could threaten the security of the pipeline and result in a loss of a major source of U. S. crude oil.
2. The taking of trash is an investigative technique used by law enforcement agencies. Although it is an activity that offends people,

the U. S. Supreme Court ruled that discarded trash is abandoned property in which former owners have no reasonable expectation of privacy.

3. There is a difference between attempting to identify those people within Alyeska who were contacting Hamel and those people Hamel was calling outside of Alyeska. Since the Wackenhut investigation focused on the former, the investigators were, as they said, trying to identify the source of stolen documents. The latter approach would be an invasion of privacy and an attempt to obtain information that would discredit Hamel.

4. Miller was at fault for personally deciding to conduct the investigation without obtaining the support of the entire committee as dictated by committee and House rules. He should not have released a draft report to the media in July 1992 without first giving it to committee members for corrections, modifications and/or appendages.

5. Congressional committees are not empowered to conduct criminal trials intended to punish offenders. The evidence should have been forwarded to the proper authorities without evaluation.

At the same time, it was rumored that Alyeska attorneys helped the minority committee write the part of the report pertaining to Alyeska's and Wackenhut's role in the covert operation. These charges were denied by David Dye, the Interior and Insular Affairs Committee's minority counsel and by other minority members. Young was nevertheless criticized for supporting Alyeska, leaking tapes to the media in an attempt to destroy Hamel's reputation, and badgering witnesses behind closed doors (it was noted that he receives 20% of his campaign funds for reelection from the oil industry).[46]

Wackenhut in the Aftermath of the Congressional Hearings. There are some signs suggesting that Wackenhut embarked on a campaign to harass its own employees who testified at the congressional hearings. Castillo was forced into hiding. Caputi charged Wackenhut with sending imposters who posed as *Miami Herald* reporters to her mother's home in an attempt to discover her whereabouts. This happened two days after she left for the hearings inWashington. On the advice of her attorney, Caputi did not immediately return to Florida. She was quoted as saying, "I'm nervous, because everybody is out to save their own neck, and there are some powerful people involved."[47]

David Ramirez said that his work was criticized and he was getting mysterious telephone calls. He accused Black of trying to destroy his personal reputation and interfering in his personal life.[48] Along with Jeff Freburg, another former employee, he wrote a letter to Chesterfield Smith, a Wackenhut board member, accusing Black of scattering false documents about the Hamel case in the office in order to entrap "traitors," and questioning employees on a daily basis about the actions of those who were involved in the congressional probe. "It got to the point where I didn't know what I could say to whom. I didn't even know what cases were real and what cases weren't real, what faxes were real and what faxes weren't real. There was just a general atmosphere of paranoia, and it got worse after the hearings," said Freburg.[49]

Shortly after the hearings, George Wackenhut, CEO, called a meeting at headquarters in an attempt to boost employee morale. He appeared with his entire face plastered with band-aids, his arm in a sling, and a limp. "Look what they did to me in Washington," he joked.[50] Black was forced to resign from Wackenhut in December 1991. He now operates his own detective agency. In April 1992, Wackenhut agreed to pay a $10,000 fine to the state of Virginia for using unlicensed private detectives.

Additional Whistle-Blowers Come Forward

The covert investigation launched against Hamel did not deter other whistle-blowers from reporting additional violations of worker safety and environmental laws committed by Alyeska throughout the early 1990s.

Glen Plumblee was a quality control inspector at Alyeska with 18 years of experience. He was hired in 1990 as part of a new "get-tough attitude" towards quality control after the *Exxon Valdez* oil spill. Over a three-to-four month period, he wrote 200 so-called "discrepancy reports" indicating quality control problems in his area. These compared with only 3 or 4 discrepancy reports that were written over the entire prior 13-year period. Notwithstanding, during his time with the company, Alyeska reduced the number of inspectors from 8 to 4 and demoted Plumblee from the position of senior quality control inspector to quality control coordinator. He also reported that he was forced by his superiors to visit a mental health clinic to determine why he complained so much. Plumblee was fired by Alyeska in November 1991 because he refused to accept the pay cut and demotion. Soon thereafter, he contacted the media and Hamel, passing on his allegations along with a notebook that he had kept, which documented Alyeska's refusal to address his concerns.

In a complaint filed with the Department of Labor and in an affidavit to members of the U. S. Congress, Plumblee reported that: (1) welding done during initial construction of the pipeline was never appropriately evaluated and some test results were faked; (2) only 67 out of 230 pressure vessels holding liquid or gas were ever inspected; (3) leak and vapor losses were allowed to occur often with little concern for worker health and the environment; (4) inspectors were intimidated and harassed while trying to perform their duties; (5) only 8 out of 36 bulk storage tanks had been internally inspected; (6) there was no evidence to show that any of the tanks had a cathodic monitoring system to measure corrosion as required by federal regulations; and (7) the recent replacement of segments of corroded pipeline was not performed in compliance with written specifications. "Never in my career have I experienced such misrepresentation and disregard for quality assurance/quality control as at Alyeska," claimed Plumblee.[51]

In responding to Plumblee's allegations, William Howitt, Alyeska's vice-president of engineering stated that: quality-control jobs were restructured to allow inspectors to monitor work in real time so that immediate corrections could be made; the inspectors were making less money because they no longer worked overtime although their hourly pay had been increased; cathodic monitors were used once a year; a program was in place to inspect internally all tanks by 1995; and, that neither state nor federal law dictated as to how often vessels must be inspected.[52]

James Schooley charged Alyeska with ignoring his warning that an improperly constructed fire-control system might fail during an emergency. He stated that crucial pipes had not been strongly welded together and that the foam they carried might not reach a fire ignited in the crude oil holding tanks. Schooley was accused by his supervisors of not being a team player when he refused to sign off on discrepancy reports that he had written. He filed a complaint with the Labor Department charging that Alyeska was trying to remove all company inspectors from the field and replace them with temporary contract inspectors who could be removed without cause. Schooley was fired in November 1992.

Kenneth Hayson was a former Alyeska electrical inspector. He claimed that Alyeska workers had been violating national electrical codes by incorrectly sealing equipment on a tanker-loading berth. There was the danger of an explosion taking place should vapors from the dock seep into the equipment. He resigned because he felt that Alyeska's supervisors were abusive; they prevented him from doing a good job and made his working conditions intolerable.

Richard Green had 30 years of experience as a quality control manager at nuclear plants and big construction companies. He was hired by Alyeska in April 1991 and worked there for 20 months before being fired. During his time at Alyeska, he was ordered to falsify an employee performance evaluation so that the company could justify firing an inspector, James Schooley, who had raised the issue of potential safety problems. He himself found hundreds of violations of government-mandated safety codes but was criticized when he tried to report or correct them. Inspectors were also instructed to downgrade violations instead of registering them in discrepancy reports that required prompt and sometimes costly repairs.

GOVERNMENT ACTIONS OR LACK OF ACTIONS

A review of the materials in the events surrounding this case strongly suggests that government agencies, at both the state and federal levels, may have failed in their oversight duties of the pipeline's operations, especially in its early years. Alaska's assistant state attorney general stated in 1977 that "throughout the entire [pipeline construction] project, no one has come down hard on Alyeska. State and government authorities have gone along with Alyeska when they shouldn't have."[53] Local fishermen and environmental groups were also quick to blame governmental officials with the EPA and the state. One spokesperson for a local fishing group charged that, "The regulators did a very poor job over the years by failing to devote the necessary attention and expertise to supervise plant operations."[54] Some state and federal officials admitted that budget cuts, a shortage of manpower, and pressures from other environmental work diverted their attention from Alyeska.

Furthermore, a report issued by the U. S. General Accounting Office in August 1991 concluded that the federal and state agencies responsible for overseeing pipeline operations allowed Alyeska to be self-policing. These agencies were: the Department of the Interior, the EPA, the Department of Transportation, Alaska's Department of Environmental Protection, and Alaska's Department of Natural Resources. Officials accepted Alyeska data and reports indicating that the company was meeting safety requirements without conducting their own independent analysis or testing. The report found that there was: (1) an inadequate review of Alyeska's oil-spill response plan; (2) a leak-detection system that failed to spot the pipeline's 14 known oil spills; (3) undetected corrosion of pipeline and storage tanks; and (3) inefficient coolant devices attached to portions of the pipeline.[55]

A more recent report, the 1993 Safety Audit for the U. S. Bureau of Land Management, indicates that the government may at last be attempting to take corrective action. James Baca, the director of the U. S. Bureau of Land Management, hired an engineering team to conduct a 60-day review of Alyeska's operations. The team's job was to investigate alleged safety and environmental problems that had surfaced from complaints made by whistle-blowers. The audit was presented to a House of Representatives Energy and Commerce Subcommittee on November 10, 1993. The engineers found "a lack of properly maintained and calibrated equipment, lack of professional standards and criteria for inspection, lack of inspection record keeping and documentation, inadequate inspector certification training, an inadequate inspection regime, and inadequate inspection of pipe girth welds."[56] Among the vast array of technical, managerial, and organizational deficiencies, the report found: (1) poor quality control and quality assurance procedures; (2) 20,000 electrical code violations; (3) inadequate control in the event of a major earthquake (in hundreds of places the pipeline rests directly on its vertical supports instead of on a supporting saddle); (4) a repressive atmosphere in which inspectors were punished and intimidated. At the hearing, Baca blamed Alyeska for its "adversarial attitude," which bred contempt for the concerns of the public interest. He also felt that Alyeska management was hindered by a "destructive dis-unity among the owner companies in their approach toward running Alyeska."[57] The bureau installed a confidential hotline for Alyeska employees who wished to report problems.

THE WHISTLE-BLOWER SETTLEMENTS

In May 1993 the U. S. Department of Labor ruled that Alyeska had illegally fired Green for blowing the whistle on alleged safety and environmental violations. It ordered Alyeska either to reinstate Green with back pay or to pay him his salary, including back pay, through the end of the year. Green was satis-fied with the outcome and would return to Alyeska, saying, "There's a few bad apples there, but I believe in finishing what I start. I am hopeful this ruling will be a message that things have to change at Alyeska."[58] In June 1993, Alyeska reached a settlement with five other whistle-blowers, including Plumblee, Schooley, and Hayson. Alyeska agreed to rehire the former inspectors and pay them an undisclosed sum of money. Plumblee now works as an inspector for Arctic Slope Inspector Services, an Alyeska contractor. He credits Alyeska's new president, Pritchard, with helping him get the job by writing let-ters to various contractors stating that he and the others were "eligible" for work.

In December 1993, Hamel had his day in court. Almost penniless, he spent $70,000 on an invasion-of-privacy suit against Alyeska. Before the settlement, friends were paying the mortgage on his home in Virginia. Unofficial sources reported that he received $5 million from Alyeska. Wackenhut is responsible for funding part of the settle-ment. Judge Sporkin stated that, "No one should be subjected to the kind of treatment the Hamels were." Alyeska's spy operation was "horrendous," and "reminiscent of Nazi Germany."[59] Hamel was not compelled to reveal his sources of information or desist in his whistle-blowing activities. Nevertheless,

in a prepared statement, Hamel said that he would voluntarily relinquish his self-assumed position as leading voice for Alyeska whistle-blowers. Alyeska, Exxon, British Petroleum, and Atlantic Richfield spent more that $10 million in legal fees.

LOOKING INTO THE FUTURE: THE NEW ALYESKA?

In February 1993, James Hermiller an-nounced his early retirement from Alyeska without elaborating upon the reasons for his departure. A week later, Wellington announced that he too would be stepping down. At a hearing before the House Subcommittee on Oversight and Inves-tigation held in July 1993, David Pritchard, the new president and CEO, admitted that several potential safety and environmental problems cited by the whistle-blowers, but initially denied by top management, existed. In October 1993, Alyeska hired two consult-ing groups: Booz, Allen and Hamilton to work with managers on needed improve-ments and Arthur D. Little to conduct a $6 million review of operations and manage-ment practices. In December 1993, Pritchard announced that he was creating the position of business practices officer with the respon-sibility of reviewing employee concerns and ensuring compliance with rules and regula-tions. It will be "the logical point of contact for anyone who wishes to voice concerns about any aspect of Alyeska's operations."[60]

Nonetheless, during the writing of this case, additional pipeline-related problems were reported. In May 1994, an article in the *Wall Street Journal* noted that Alyeska's elec-trical systems violations were much more extensive and serious than previously sus-pected. Several electricians received electrical shocks of 130 volts while doing repair work; others requested that they be assigned to a different project because they were not satis-fied with the way the repairs were being made. During the same month, 8,400 gallons of oil spilled at Valdez during the loading of a British Petroleum tanker, making it the third largest spill in the terminal's history. In August 1994, two additional whistle-blowers, Laura Ashby and Paul Lott, filed complaints against Alyeska with the Labor Department. In December 1994, the confidential audit conducted by Arthur D. Little criticized Alyeska's ability to respond to fires and other emergencies and found the pipeline vulnerable to earthquakes. Alyeska estimated that it will need to spend $250 million over the next few years to remedy problems found in all current audits.

EXHIBIT 1. Overview of Selected Federal Whistle-Blower Protection Statutes

1. THE CIVIL SERVICE REFORM ACT AS AMENDED BY THE WHISTLE-BLOWER PROTECTION ACT OF 1989.

Essential Features. Federal civil servants are able to file whistle-blowing claims with the Office of Special Counsel (OSC). The OSC is an independent entity, headed by an attorney, charged specifically with protecting whistle-blowers. It refers cases to the Merit Systems Protection board. The Act makes it easier for whistle-blowers to prove they were harassed by their employers and prevents the OSC from discussing employees who have sought its help with prospective employers. The Act covers such violations as race, religious, and sex discrimination; nepotism; mismanagement; gross waste of funds; abuse of authority; danger to public health or safety.

2. THE NATIONAL LABOR RELATIONS ACT OF 1935.

Essential Features. Gives employees the right to organize and bargain collectively. Protects unionized employees who testify or file charges concerning illegal or unfair labor practices. Allows unionized employees to negotiate for "just cause" firing provisions in their labor contracts so that employers cannot retaliate against whistle-blowers.

3. THE FALSE CLAIMS ACT AS REVISED IN 1986.

Essential Features. Creates strong incentives for employees to come forward with information on government contractor fraud. Uses a bounty system whereby the employee gains between 15-30 % of the money recovered by the government (the percentage is less if the Justice Department decides to join the employee in the lawsuit against the employer).

4. PROVISIONS IN THE CLEAN AIR ACT, THE ENERGY REORGANIZATION ACT, THE OCCUPATIONAL SAFETY AND HEALTH ACT, THE SAFE DRINKING ACT, THE WATER POLLUTION CONTROL ACT, AND THE OTHER SPECIFIC ACTS.

Essential Features. Covers violations of purposes of specific Act. Encourages whistle-blowers who have suffered retaliation to file a complaint with the Secretary of Labor who investigates the charges and orders corrective measures if violations are found. Among some of the remedies provided to the whistle-blowers are: a reinstatement of lost wages and benefits; recovery of litigation costs, including attorney's fees.

5 .THE CIVIL RIGHTS ACT OF 1964.

Essential Features. Discrimination in the work place on the basis of race, color, sex, or national origin is unlawful. Under Title VII, an employer cannot retaliate against an employee who files a complaint or who testifies, assists, or participates in an investigation regarding discrimination.

6. THE AGE DISCRIMINATION IN EMPLOYMENT ACT.

Essential Features. Protects employees who file charges, testify, assist, or participate in an age discrimination investigation.

SOURCES: Marcia P. Miceli and Janet P. Near, *Blowing the Whistle: The Organizational and Legal Implications for Companies and Employees.* NY: Lexington Books, 1992; Martin W. Aron, "Whistle-blowers, Insubordination, and Employee Rights of Free Speech," *Labor Law Journal* (April 1992), pp. 211-220.

EXHIBIT 2. Alyeska's Principal Owners

Name of Company	Percent of Ownership
British Petroleum	50.0%*
Arco	21.3
Exxon	20.3
Mobil	4.1
Amerada Hess	1.5
Unocal	1.4
Philips	1.4

*Standard Oil of Ohio was one of Alyeska's original owners but was subsequently acquired by British Petroleum.

SOURCE: David Bowermaster, "A Long Blotted Record," *U.S. News & World Report* (October 25, 1993), pp. 39-40.

EXHIBIT 3. Cast of Main Characters

ALYESKA EXECUTIVES

James Hermiller: 57 years old. Became Alyeska's president two months after the *Exxon Valdez* oil spill in 1989. Recruited from British Petroleum where he had been a refining and marketing executive. Many Alaskans believed he would make Alyeska more accountable for its actions. He visited environmentalists, invited fishermen to his offices, supported the creation of a citizen's watchdog group to monitor Alyeska's operations. Took early retirement on April 15, 1993.

David Pritchard: 45 years old. Became Alyeska's current president when Hermiller retired in April 1993. Previously he had been responsible for operating the Prudhoe Bay oil field owned by British Petroleum (Alaska) Inc.

Patrick Wellington: 59 years old. Former Juneau Police Chief, Commissioner of Public Safety, and Director of Alaska State Troopers. Was Alyeska's Manager of Corporate Security and Aviation from May 1978 (when the pipeline opened) until the summer of 1993 (when he retired).

WACKENHUT EXECUTIVES

Wayne Black: 43 years old. Was a criminal investigator for Dade County prosecutor's office in Miami until he was suspended in 1981 for allegedly pressuring witnesses, conducting illegal wiretaps, and illegally acting as a lawyer. He resigned and went into private practice until joining the Wackenhut Corporation in 1989 as head of its new 18-member special investigations division (SID).

Rick Lund: Wackenhut investigator; held title of "Technical Supervisor." Known for his skills in handling electronic, computer and surveillance technologies.

George Wackenhut: 72 years old. Founded the Wackenhut Corporation in 1954. Helped it become the third largest security company in the United States with sales of $521 million in 1990. Between 1951–1954, worked as a special agent for the FBI in Atlanta and Indianapolis.

THE WHISTLE-BLOWERS

Erlene Blake: Plant Laboratory Technician at Alyeska from 1977–1983.

Adriana Caputi: Joined the Wackenhut Corporation in October 1989 to continue working for Wayne Black as an investigator in the newly formed SID. In April 1991, she was given an eight-hour suspension by Black after false allegations about her character and job performance were made. She subsequently resigned.

Raphael Castillo: Trained as a military policeman by the U. S. Air Force. Worked as a police officer for police departments in Florida and Nevada. Did undercover work for the Bureau of Narcotics and Dangerous Drugs. Joined the Wackenhut Corporation in January 1991 as Area Supervisor. Was transferred to SID in March 1991. Resigned May 28, 1991.

Ana Contreras: 29 years old. College graduate with a degree in Criminal Justice. Worked for five years as a criminal investigator for the U. S. Customs Service in Florida and Texas. Began employment in Wackenhut's SID

	in May 1990 at the rate of $14 per hour. Since resigning from Wackenhut, has worked for a private medical malpractice claims investigator.
Mercedes Cruz:	Part-time employee at Wackenhut. Hired July 1990. Analyzed telephone call records. Was fired April 1991.
Steven Eward:	Alyeska technician from 1977–1980.
Richard Green:	Worked for 30 years as a quality control manager for nuclear plants and construction companies. Was hired by Alyeska in April 1991. He was fired 20 months later.
Charles Hamel:	61 years old. Former oil broker from Alexandria, Virginia. Over a period of ten years, served as a key intermediary between whistle-blowing Alyeska employees and between the public, the media, and Congress.
Kenneth Hayson:	Alyeska electrical inspector. Pointed out national electrical code violations. Resigned after being harassed on the job.
Ricki Jacobson:	Hired by Wackenhut to work as an entry-level trainee under Wayne Black in November 1989. As a former real estate agent, she came to Wackenhut with no previous investigative experience. She had been referred to Black by a personal friend.
Philip Nicpon:	Former chief chemist at the North Pole Refinery in Alaska. His company was a buyer of North Slope crude oil.
Glen Plumblee:	Hired by Alyeska in 1990 as a quality control inspector. He had 18 years prior experience as an inspector for companies in the nuclear and oil industries. He was fired in November 1991 after refusing to accept a pay cut and demotion.
David Ramirez:	Former marine intelligence officer and executive protection officer for DWG Corporation in Miami. Hired by Wackenhut in November 1990 where he worked in SID with Wayne Black in the capacity of supervisor.
Sheree Rich:	30 years old. Former Tallahassee police officer with undercover experience. Hired by Black in August 1990. Black promised that he would train her as an investigator. She worked for Wackenhut for 6 months. She was fired in January 1991 after refusing a request to steal trash in another investigation. She now investigates child sex abuse cases.
Robert Scott:	64 years old. Scott, an operator at Alyeska's vapor recovery system, was fired on October 24, 1990 after 14 years of service to the company. In September 1991, he filed a wrongful discharge case claiming that Alyeska retaliated against him for providing information about air and water pollution at the Valdez terminal to Charles Hamel. He lost his case, and the appeal of his case, in 1993.
James Schooley:	An Alyeska inspector who was fired in November 1992 after voicing concerns about worker health and safety problems.
Edward Thompson:	26 years old. Worked for one year in 1989 for Thorpe Technical Services, Inc., a subcontractor hired by Alyeska. Has a criminal record with felony convictions for robbery and larceny. Had his driver's license revoked four times and suspended two times for driving while intoxicated.
James Woodle:	Retired Coast Guard commander. Port captain of Alyeska's marine terminal at Valdez from 1982–1984.

ALYESKA PIPELINE
Service Company

James D. Hermiller
President

September 21, 1991

A MESSAGE TO ALASKANS FROM
ALYESKA PIPELINE SERVICE COMPANY

Dear Alaskans:

A great deal has appeared in the Media recently regarding a security investigation I authorized last year into the theft of documents from Alyeska. Alyeska has limited its public comment on the investigation largely out of respect to a request from a U.S. House Committee for information on how and why the investigation was conducted.

Now that Alyeska has responded to the House request, I believe it is time to let Alaskans know where we stand and how we view our actions.

First, I would like to make it clear that my instructions regarding the management of this investigation were explicit from the start. The investigation was to trace the source of the thefts using legal methods and standard investigative practices. It was not my intent to interfere with anyone's communications with Congress or to investigate any member of Congress. I believe that a full review of the record will attest that the investigation did neither.

Having said this, however, it is clear that being legally correct is not enough. The investigation, taken as a whole, does not meet the standards Alyeska strives for and Alaskans expect. Alyeska values its good relationship with Alaskans and I am sorry if I have put that relationship in jeopardy.

When the Alyeska Owners Committee was first notified of the investigation last fall, several months after it began, an open and candid discussion followed. The Owners clearly were concerned about the conduct of the investigation. The Owners and I concluded unanimously that the investigation was wrong and should be terminated. It was also agreed that all documents related to the investigation should be collected, secured by a third party and never used.

Many Alaskans have asked whether Alyeska would respond in the same fashion if faced with a similar situation in the future. The answer is no. Some action would be required, of course, because the theft of documents cannot be condoned or rewarded through inaction. But closer consultation between Alyeska management and the Owners would guide any future response.

As President of Alyeska over the last two years, I have worked hard to be responsive to Alaska's concerns and expectations. You have the right to expect the highest standards of conduct from Alyeska. Over the years Alyeska has worked hard to be a responsible corporate citizen. We hope we have not let you down and we seek your continued support and trust.

Sincerely,

ALYESKA PIPELINE SERVICE COMPANY

EXHIBIT 5. Transcript Excerpts from CBS's "60 Minutes"—November 3, 1991

Steve Kroft, Co-host: When the seven major oil companies built the trans-Alaska pipeline 14 years ago and began pumping oil from the North Slope to a tanker terminal in Valdez, they pledged to respect the environment and the safety of their workers. So when the evidence began reaching Congress and the federal regulatory agencies that those promises weren't being kept, the oil companies decided to put an end to the problem of plugging the leaks—not the leaks in the pipeline, the leaks of damaging information reaching Washington.

The Alyeska Company, the consortium of oil companies that owns and operates the pipeline, went out and hired one of the nation's largest private-eye firms to conduct an elaborate, expensive and secret undercover investigation of one man, a former oil broker by the name of Chuck Hamel. Why would the oil companies that own the Alaska pipeline go to so much trouble to silence Chuck Hamel? Well, if you visit the upstairs office of Hamel's Virginia home, you begin to get some idea. For the past decade this has been the command center for his one-man war against Alyeska. What are all these documents?

Chuck Hamel: Well, this is—is Exxon Shipping documents from some of their ships that polluted along the way, other oil companies who were doing some wrongdoings in Alaska.

Kroft: . . . Where did this stuff come from?

Hamel: Well, it comes in the mail, a great deal, and in the fax machine. I get faxes. I don't know who's sending to me.

Kroft: These documents and the information in them have cost Alyeska dearly. In 1987, it was Hamel who told the EPA about the release of cancer-causing compounds into the air at this terminal in Valdez. It cost Alyeska $30 million to correct the problem. And it was Hamel who told Congress that the pipeline was corroding. Last year, Alyeska agreed to fix it at a cost of up to $900 million.

Hamel: They're making a billion dollars a year on the Alyeska pipeline, profits, these companies. . . greed has gotten to them where that's not enough. They want a billion plus, cheat a little on the environment and make an extra nickel.

Kroft: When Chuck Hamel took on Alyeska and the oil companies a dozen years ago, he had the strongest of motivations: revenge. Hamel claimed they cheated him out of millions of dollars in an oil deal and then drove him out of the tanker business. When he began to fight back in court and in the press, Alyeska employees began slipping him information about safety and environmental violations . . . Hamel not only protected their confidentiality, he got results. And over time, he attracted a legion of Alyeska whistle-blowers.

Hamel: . . . and they'd say, 'Here's the problem, I have to do these things that are wrong, and my fellow employees and we have no choice.' 'We'd lose our jobs.' 'We have families.' 'We have children, like everybody else.'

Kroft: Tell me about the first encounter with the Wackenhut undercover team.

Hamel: That would have been in Anchorage, at the—Fletcher's Bar. It was late in the evening, and this lovely young lady somehow was getting our attention.

Kroft: How was she getting your attention?

Hamel: Well, pretty blonde, tanned, and her clothing, if I recall—I think that her blouse was rather transparent. It just didn't fit the scene in—in—Anchorage in March, 11:00 at night.

Continued

Kroft: A few days later, the same woman just happened to be leaving Anchorage on Hamel's flight.

Hamel: We sat down next to each other, and she told me she worked for an environmental group called Ecolit, Ecological Litigation.

Kroft: The woman told Hamel that Ecolit was anxious to help him by bringing lawsuits against Alyeska and the oil companies. In reality, the woman was a Wackenhut investigator, and Ecolit a Wackenhut invention set up for one purpose, to lure Chuck Hamel into revealing his sources. Former Wackenhut investigator Sherry Rich helped set up the phony environmental group. It offered Hamel office space, computer services, even cash.

Sherry Rich: He was having financial problems, and that's why they were such a good bait for him. Because they were his company that was on the same side as he was, with all this, you know, unlimited funds that could help him out. . . .

Kroft: But Wackenhut and Alyeska didn't stop there. They even stole his garbage and found out things like when his mortgage was due, that his wife was on medication, even details of his private correspondence. . . .What they did find in his garbage was an envelope from this man, Robert Scott, whose name also appeared on Hamel's long-distance telephone records. Robert Scott was an Alyeska technician stationed at the Valdez tanker terminal. He now admits that he leaked confidential Alyeska documents to Hamel. Alyeska says you stole these documents.

Ralph Scott: I'm not a thief.

Kroft: It's Alyeska property. That you stole them and sent them to Chuck Hamel.

Scott: I am not a thief. If Alyeska wants to call it stealing, that's fine. But I called it doing my civic responsibility.

Kroft: What kind of problems with Alyeska did you come across?

Scott: Air pollution, water pollution—I could sit here and tell you for an hour. I could go nonstop for an hour.

Kroft: Did you ever raise these questions with Alyeska?

Scott: For a period of about eight or nine years, yes.

Kroft: What happened?

Scott: Nothing, absolutely nothing. I might as well be talking to—to the wall . . . .

Kroft: But Robert Scott and Chuck Hamel were apparently not the only targets of the Wackenhut investigation. Ana Contreras, the former Wackenhut investigator, recalls a conversation she had with Wayne Black.

Ana Contreras: He came to my desk one day and said, 'Ana, this investigation is getting big. This investigation is so big it involves congressmen.' Hamel was making contact with congressmen about the documents he was getting, and the congressmen were using the documents at the hearings. And those hearings were hurting Alyeska and Exxon. And he said, 'We're going to get them. We're going to really get them.'

Kroft: The congressmen.

Contreras: Yes.

Kroft: Did he mention any congressmen in particular?

Contreras: He mentioned Congressman Miller.

Kroft: That's Congressman George Miller of California, chairman of the House committee that oversees operation of the Alaska pipeline system and a recipient of much of Hamel's information. Congressman Miller believes that Wackenhut was trying to compromise either him or his committee's investigations of Alyeska.

George Miller: They just decided that they were a little police department unto themselves, Wackenhut, Alyeska. They said, 'We're like the government.' 'We're worth billions.' 'Look who we represent.' 'Hey, it's just Chuck Hamel.' 'It's just one guy.' 'It's just one member of Congress.' 'It's just one environmental movement.' Come on.

Kroft: Congressman Miller says the pipeline company was out to silence its own employees, who are protected by federal whistle-blowers laws, and not, as Alyeska claims, to retrieve stolen documents.

Miller: That's not what they were after. They were about stopping the investigations of my committee, and Chuck Hamel, who make a whole series of assertions to me, to the Senate committee, to the EPA, to other people, all of which turned out to be true. All of which would be very, very bad for Alyeska.

Kroft: After Congressman Miller announced that he would hold hearings into the Wackenhut investigation of Chuck Hamel, the president of Alyeska took out a newspaper ad apologizing for having ordered the investigation.

Miller: It's what criminals usually do—do, is they apologize. They apologized after they were caught.

Kroft: You're calling them criminals.

Miller: I'm calling them criminals.

Kroft: Alyeska turned down our request for an interview, so did Wackenhut. But we did manage to catch up with Wackenhut's director of special investigations, Wayne Black...Just want to ask you a couple of questions about the Alyeska investigation of Chuck Hamel. You proud of the investigation?

Black: I'm real happy with it. I think we did a—did a good job, Our people did a good job. We'd do it again if we—if we had the opportunity.

Kroft: You're proud of going through somebody's garbage? You're proud of surreptitiously recording conversations? You're proud of setting up phony companies and giving people a lot of bogus information?

Black: People don't bring stolen documents to us if we tell them we're investigators. So it's—it's not like you can come right out and tell somebody who it is, and say, 'Please, please bring me the evidence, that—you committed a crime.'

Kroft: Your client, Alyeska, knew what was going on.

Black: Yes.

Kroft: At every step of the way.

Black: That's correct.

Kroft: . . . As for Robert Scott, Alyeska fired him for what it said was unrelated worker misconduct. Why do you think Alyeska fired you?

Scott: For blowing the whistle, if you will.

Kroft: You're sure of that?

Continued

EXHIBIT 5, *Continued*

Scott: I am positive, just as sure as the Lord makes little red apples.

Kroft: Are you sorry you did this?

Scott: Absolutely not. I would not change one thing, except that knowing what I do now, I might tell Chuck Hamel we better use some pay telephones and a different phone every time. And I won't put—I won't use—I won't put my return address on the letters, and don't you put your garbage out. That would be the only change I'd make. . .

Kroft: Starting tomorrow, Chuck Hamel, ex-Wackenhut investigator Sherry Rich, and her former boss, Wayne Black, will all appear at a congressional hearing to testify about everything they told us.

NOTES

1. For a comprehensive discussion of the definition of the term, "whistle-blower," see Marcia P. Miceli and Janet P. Near, *Blowing the Whistle: The Organizational and Legal Implications for Companies and Employees* (1992) NY: Lexington Books, pp. 13–39.

2. For a lively debate among scholars and practicing managers surrounding the issue of whether or not whistle-blowers are informers, see "Is Whistle-Blowing the Same as Informing?" The article originally appeared as an editorial survey in *Business and Society Review* (Fall 1981), pp. 4–17. It was reprinted in A. Pablo Iannone (Ed.), *Contemporary Moral Controversies in Business* (1989), NY: Oxford University Press, pp. 207–20.

3. A recent study indicates that a total of 33 states have enacted some type of general whistle-blower statues, including 15 states that extend such protection to workers in the private sector and another 9 that require prior notification of employers before a worker discloses such information to individuals outside the organization. See, Tim Barnett, "Overview of State Whistleblower Protection Statutes." *Labor Law Journal* (July, 1992), p. 448.

4. Calvin Sims, "Trying to Mute the Whistle-Blowers." *New York Times* (April 11, 1994), pp. D1 and D8.

5. Some of the more publicized recent cases of whistle-blowing involved companies such as: (a) General Electric Company (1984–88); (b) Prudential Insurance Company of America (1992); (c) Teledyne Corporation (1993); (d) United Technologies Corporation (1994); and, (d) National Health Laboratories, MetWest, and MetPath (1992).

6. The following chronology of events was pieced together from secondary sources. Especially helpful were the following articles: Richard D. James, "Price of Progress? Alaska Pipeline Opens on Time, but Shortcuts Scar the Environment." *Wall Street Journal* (June 20, 1977), pp. 1, 16; Charles McCoy, "Broken Promises: Alyeska Record Shows How Big Oil Neglected Alaskan Environment," *Wall Street Journal* (July 6, 1989), pp. A1, A4; Andy Pasztor and Robert E. Taylor, "Unsafe Harbor: Alaska Pipeline Firm Is Accused of Polluting Sea Water Since 1977," *Wall Street Journal* (February 20, 1986), pp. 1, 17; Timothy Egan, "Alaska Pipeline Faces Costly Work to Stop Rust," *Wall Street Journal* (March 11, 1990), p. 20.

7. "Alaska's Oil Pipeline: Chaos Theory," *The Economist* (December 4, 1993), p. 32; Dennis O. Olson and J. Patrick O'Brien, "The Great Alaskan Money Give Away Program." *Economic Inquiry* (July 1990), pp. 604–15.

8. Maria Shao, "Caught in the Wake of the *Exxon Valdez*." *Business Week* (August 6, 1990), pp. 74–76.

9. James, "Price of Progress," p. 1.

10. McCoy, "Broken Promises," p. A4.
11. *Ibid.*
12. *Ibid.*
13. Pasztor and Taylor, "Unsafe Harbor," p. 17.
14. *Ibid.*
15. *Ibid.*, p. 1.
16. *Ibid.*
17. McCoy, "Broken Promises," p. A4.
18. Richard Mauer, "Pipeline Company, Stung by Critic, Goes after Whistle-Blowers." *New York Times* (September 23, 1991), p. A14.
19. McCoy, "Broken Promises"; and, "Exxon Says Fast Containment of Oil Spill in Alaska Could Have Caused Explosion," *Wall Street Journal* (April 5, 1989), p. A3.
20. McCoy, "Broken Promises, p. A4.
21. *Ibid.*
22. *Ibid.*
23. Sources used for this section and the following sections include: "Alyeska Pipeline Service Company Covert Operation." *Report and Oversight Hearings of the Committee on Interior and Insular Affairs of the U.S. House of Representatives, 102 Congress, second session, parts 1 and 2* (1992), Bethesda, Maryland, Congressional Information Service (microfiche numbers 92-H441-34, 92-H442-9 and 92-H442-6); Richard Mauer, "He Spied on Spies, Blew Whistle: Man Who Bared Alyeska Campaign against Hamel Is Now in Hiding." *Anchorage Daily News* (November 3, 1991), p. A1; Richard Mauer, "The Details of Deception: Dirty Tricks Used against Alyeska Critic Hamel Leave Him Bruised." *Anchorage Daily News* (September 1, 1991), p. A1; Robert Hennelly, "Big Oil Runs a Sting." *Village Voice* (November 5, 1991), pp. 39–41; Allanna Sullivan, "Slippery Slope Alaska Pipeline Gets 'Sham' Safety Checks, Former Workers Say." *Wall Street Journal* (August 4, 1992), p. A1, A5; Charles McCoy, "Another Former Alyeska Inspector Says Oil Pipeline Ignores Potential Problems." *Wall Street Journal* (February 22, 1993), p. A5.
24. "Hamel's Statement," Oversight Hearings of the Committee on Interior and Insular Affairs, p. 260.
25. Pasztor and Taylor, "Unsafe Harbor," p. 17; "Hamel's Statement," Oversight Hearings of the Committee on Interior and Insular Affairs, p. 261.
26. Pasztor and Taylor, "Unsafe Harbor," p. 17.
27. McCoy, "Broken Promises," p. A4.
28. Andy Pasztor, "U. S. Probes Charges of Improper Billing of Buyers of Alaska Pipeline Crude Oil." *Wall Street Journal* (March 6, 1985), p. 10.
29. The description of events discussion in this section was structured primarily from the following sources: "Alyeska Pipeline Service Company Covert Operation." *Report and Oversight Hearings of the Committee on Interior and Insular Affairs of the U.S. House of Representatives, 102 Congress, second session, parts 1 and 2* (1992), Bethesda, Maryland, Congressional Information Service (microfiche numbers 92-H441-34, 92-H442-9 and 92-H442-6); Richard Mauer, "He Spied on Spies, Blew Whistle: Man Who Bared Alyeska Campaign against Hamel Is Now in Hiding." *Anchorage Daily News* (November 3, 1991), p. A1; Richard Mauer, "The Details of Deception: Dirty Tricks Used against Alyeska Critic Hamel Leave Him Bruised." *Anchorage Daily News* (September 1, 1991), p. A1; Robert Hennelly, "Big Oil Runs a Sting." *Village Voice* (November 5, 1991), pp. 39–41; Allanna Sullivan, "Slippery Slope Alaska Pipeline Gets 'Sham' Safety Checks, Former Workers Say." *Wall Street Journal* (August 4, 1992), p. A1, A5; Charles McCoy, "Another Former Alyeska Inspector Says Oil Pipeline Ignores Potential Problems." *Wall Street Journal* (February 22, 1993), p. A5.
30. Sullivan, "Slippery Slope," pp. A1–A5.
31. Mauser, "He Spied," p. A1.
32. *Ibid.*
33. Allyson Pyette and Kim Fararo, "Alyeska Makes Public Apology, Company's Statewide Ads Admit It Was Wrong to Spy." *Anchorage Daily News* (September 21, 1991), p. A1.
34. *Ibid.*
35. "Panel Discussion," Oversight Hearings of the Committee on Interior and Insular Affairs, p. 178.
36. *Ibid.*
37. CBS "60 Minutes," November 31, 1991, Program Number 2407, Burrell's Transcripts, p. 10.
38. Patrick Lee, "Alyeska Spyjinks Probe Has Surprise End." *Los Angeles Times* (September 13, 1993), p. D2.
39. Keith Schneider, "A Case of Heavy-Footed Gumshoes." *New York Times* (November 10, 1991), Section 4, p. 3.

40. William P. Coughlin, "Did Oil Executives Know of Spying Operation?" *Boston Globe* (December 3, 1991), p. 10.

41. "Panel Discussion," Oversight Hearings of the Committee on Interior and Insular Affairs, p. 245.

42. "Panel Discussion," Oversight Hearings of the Committee on Interior and Insular Affairs, p. 256.

43. "Panel Discussion," Oversight Hearings of the Committee on Interior and Insular Affairs, p. 257.

44. Minority Report of the Committee on Interior and Insular Affairs, Part I (Final), p. 4

45. "Recommendations," Report of the Committee on Interior and Insular Affairs, Part I (Final), pp. 89–90.

46. *Ibid.*

47. Heather Dewar, "Pair Posed as Reporters to Find Witness, Mother Says." *Miami Herald* (September 7, 1991), p. 3B.

48. "Chief Alyeska Pipeline Investigator Quits." Los Angeles Times (November 16, 1991), p. D2.

49. Heather Dewar, "Embattled Wackenhut Sleuth Quits," *Miami Herald* (November 16, 1991), p. 1B.

50. Lore Croghan, "Wackenhut Corporation Looking Forward to Storm's Passing." *Miami Herald* (November 23, 1991), p. 1C.

51. Sullivan, "Slippery Slope," pp. A1–A5.

52. *Ibid.*

53. James, "Price of Progress," p. 16.

54. Pasztor and Taylor, "Unsafe Harbor," p. 17.

55. Timothy Egan, "U. S. Finds Lax Regulation of Alaska Oil Pipeline." *New York Times* (August 5, 1991), p. A8; Allanna Sullivan, "GAO Criticizes Government's Role in Alaska Pipeline." *Wall Street Journal* (August 5, 1991), p. C13.

56. "Alyeska Vows to Correct Pipeline's Problems," *Oil and Gas Journal* (November 22, 1993), p. 32.

57. *Ibid.*

58. Charles McCoy, "Alyeska Suffers Blow As Ruling Backs Complaint by Fired Safety Inspector." *Wall Street Journal* (May 25, 1993), p. A5.

59. Charles McCoy and Richard B. Schmitt, "Alyeska Settles Suit by a Whistle-Blower." *Wall Street Journal* (December 21, 1993), p. B8.

60. David Whitney, "Hamel, Alyeska Sign Settlement Agreement. Terms Kept Secret How Much Money Pipeline Company Critic Will Be Paid." *Anchorage Daily News* (December 21, 1993), p. A1.

ELI LILLY AND COMPANY
vs.
THE CHURCH OF SCIENTOLOGY

The Prozac controversy

On September 14, 1989, Joseph Wesbecker entered his former place of employment, the Standard Gravure Printing Plant in Louisville, Kentucky, carrying an AK–47 assault rifle in one hand and a duffel bag filled with handguns and ammunition in the other. He walked towards the elevator that would take him to the company's executive offices on the third floor. He exited the elevator, firing his weapon. Within 20 minutes, Wesbecker shot 8 employees to death, wounded 12 others and ended up committing suicide by shooting himself. A subsequent coroner's report revealed that Wesbecker had therapeutic amounts of the antidepressant drug, Prozac, in his bloodstream. Eighteen of Wesbecker's victims and their families began a lawsuit against Eli Lilly and Company, the firm that manufactures Prozac, claiming that the drug was responsible for Wesbecker's acts of violence. Although he had a prior history of mental illness, the victims believed that Prozac pushed Wesbecker "over the edge." The lawsuit was eventually dismissed, following a lengthy trial, as were all other lawsuits filed against the company that have been litigated to date. Lilly currently faces over 160 lawsuits while

This case was jointly prepared by S. Prakash Sethi and Janet Rovenpor, Assistant Professor of Management, Manhattan College, Riverdale, New York, 10471. Financial support was provided by the Louis F. Capalbo Endowment Fund, School of Business, Manhattan College. Special thanks are due to librarians Thomas O'Connor and Stacy Pober.

78 others have been dismissed. Lilly has adopted a "no-settle" position in all pending product liability lawsuits, has offered to indemnify doctors being sued for prescribing Prozac to patients by paying for their legal defense and judgment, and has continued to defend for the safety of Prozac on radio talk shows, television programs, and in letters sent to physicians and pharmacists.

One of the most important players in the Prozac controversy, and in many ways perhaps the instigator of the controversy, has been the Church of Scientology (COS), a religious organization founded by the late L. Ron Hubbard. The organization has been a longtime foe of psychiatry and pharmaceutical companies. As part of its campaign against Prozac, one of the COS's affiliated organizations, the Citizen's Commission on Human Rights (CCHR), submitted a petition to the U.S. Food and Drug Administration (USFDA) in an effort to get Prozac banned. The group also gave its support, in the form of court testimony and literature, to defendants in criminal cases. The COS's campaign against Lilly met with some initial success. A year after the Wesbecker incident, Prozac's share of the antidepressant market dropped 4%. Many patients stopped using Prozac. Other former users jumped on the litigation bandwagon and launched their own lawsuits against Lilly, invoking what was to become known as the "Prozac Defense." The term was used to refer to claims made by (or on behalf of) former Prozac patients that "Prozac Made Me Do It." In criminal cases, this meant that defendants could argue that while they may have been depressed all their lives, they never physically harmed, abused or murdered others until being prescribed Prozac. Therefore, they should not be held legally responsible for their actions. In product liability and malpractice lawsuits, it was argued that Prozac, instead of easing a patient's depression, made it much worse until the patient eventually attempted suicide or inflicted harm on others.

Prosecutors, on the other hand, reminded the courts that the USFDA and published clinical studies had never found any cause-and-effect relationship between Prozac and suicidal or homicidal behavior. Many defendants were using other prescription drugs in addition to Prozac at the time they were involved in committing crimes. Therefore, it was argued, the "Prozac Defense" should not be allowed. Furthermore, since depression and suicide often go hand in hand, it would be impossible to determine whether Prozac, or the defendant's underlying mental state, was at fault. Prozac may simply not have worked for that particular patient; he or she may have commited suicide without any external provocation.

ISSUES FOR ANALYSIS

The controversy surrounding Eli Lilly and its drug, Prozac, raises a number of troubling questions about a system that creates massive social conflicts between corporations and other segments of society and exposes a company to very expensive and time-consuming lawsuits despite the fact that the company has met all regulatory and scientific standards in the manufacture and marketing of a useful pharmaceutical drug. At the corporate level, the case illustrates how a company deals with one of the most critical issues facing a business organization. To wit, how it should handle and respond to threats launched against a highly profitable product. It also leads to an in-depth understanding of the nature and extent of the risks and liabilities a corporation must assume as a conse-

quence of the use of its products and services in the marketplace. In particular:

1. To what extent should a corporation be held responsible for the real or alleged adverse effects emanating from the use of a particular product when the product has met all possible regulatory mandated standards of safety? What obligations do pharmaceutical companies have in placing adequate warnings on product labels? How far must a company go in protecting its products from unauthorized and unwarranted usage?

2. What is the appropriate role for activist groups, and especially religious organizations, in creating public debate and controversy on the drawbacks associated with the use of a product? On the one hand, these groups may be: (a) forcing companies to defend their products through extensive testing and thereby enhancing the overall quality and safety of these products even beyond the rigorous standards imposed by the USFDA; and, (b) making the public more aware of the potential adverse consequences of these products when people may have been all too willing to heed the advice of "authority" figures and use a product without analyzing it potential risks. On the other hand, by imposing unwarranted requirements, these groups may be making the products too expensive, thereby making some people afraid of to use them when they could benefit from their usage; and, also discouraging companies from developing new drugs with important potential benefits for members of society (e.g., finding a cure for AIDS). Negative advertising campaigns distract the attention of a company's employees, waste precious time, and divert resources that could, otherwise, be used for additional research and product development.

3. What are the social and moral obligations of activist and religious groups when their accusations appear to be unsubstantiated and may even be tainted with a measure of self-interest? In the case of Prozac, the COS was the pivotal group in generating and building momentum against Prozac. To the extent that the COS's accusations are found to be baseless, what role should other religious institutions play in support of organizations that are victims of such attacks?

4. In an atmosphere of heightened and often substantiated publicity about an essential drug like Prozac, who protects the interests of the current and future patients who may be deterred from using the drug for fear of its adverse side-effects and thereby be deprived of the medicine's benefits to their health and well-being?

5. The success of activist groups in creating public controversy about a corporation's activities depends, to a large extent, on their adroit use of news media and especially the broadcast media. What are the standards, if any, by which various segments of the mass media, and especially television, regulate themselves to ensure fairness and accuracy in their coverage of a particular event? How effective are these measures when viewed from the perspective of the Prozac controversy?

6. How well prepared was Eli Lilly in anticipating the attack by the COS? How well did the firm handle issues raised by the news media, law courts, regulatory bodies, and users of the product (i.e., health care providers and patients)? What were the major elements of the strategy Lilly used to cope with the controversy? How satisfactory were the company's responses during various stages of the controversy?

7. How should a corporation prepare itself to anticipate controversies and to deal effectively with them? What are some of the major elements of an effective response strategy in terms of early forecasting, crisis management, corporate culture, the role of top management, and the management of external communications and constituency relations?

8. And finally, at the societal level, fundamental, and even more troubling questions remain to be answered in the moral and ethical domain as a result of recent medical advances in psycho-pharmacology. For example, should high-school students be encouraged to take Ritalin before an SAT exam to help them concentrate and score higher? Should musicians take beta blockers to control stage fright before a concert? In their studies of the human brain, scientists have begun to identify chemicals that cause anxiety, impulsiveness, and poor concentration. Do the drugs developed to act on these chemicals merely enhance, or, do they fundamentally alter an individual's personality? How should these issues be framed, discussed, and decided at the societal level taking into consideration individual rights and social well-being?

ANATOMY OF THE PROZAC CONTROVERSY: CHRONOLOGY OF EVENTS

As "miracle drugs" go, Eli Lilly's antidepressant drug has had plenty of highs and lows—being at the same time characterized as a lifesaver and a killer drug. In a short period of ten years, it has entered the lexicon of American language and even pop culture where "living with Prozac," to the consternation of the company, has often become the "in" thing. According to a recent article in the *Wall Street Journal* entitled "More Are Listening to Prozac to Keep Their Business Edge,"[1]

It is often said that drugs are mirrors of a culture, its pressures and longings.

So what does it say about America today that Prozac—the household name of antidepressants—was the top-selling drug among health maintenance organizations in 1994? Overall sales of Prozac, which hit the market in 1988, now rank second to the ulcer drug Zantac, according to market researcher IMS America.

Part of the reason Prozac is so popular among HMOs is because it marries economy and convenience. Most psychiatrists find Prozac is safer and easier to give than older antidepressants, which carry overdosing and cardiac risks. Low-cost primary-care doctors can give it as well as psychiatrists—sidestepping a costly referral.

"HMOs are keeping costs down," says Tampa psychiatrist Michael Sheehan. Hospitalization is costliest, followed by psychotherapy. And though psychiatrists urge medication coupled with counseling, a year of Prozac costs only about $500.

. . . . But [Prozac like] drugs appeal to the spirit of an age as well. In the 1950s, Valium served as "mother's little helper." In the 1980s, cocaine fired the manic "Me Decade." Today, there are hints that some seek Prozac to pump up their professional personae. In the contracting economy of the 1990s, professionals feel they must keep or sharpen their edge—or die.

. . . In his book, "Listening to Prozac," psychiatrist Peter Kramer describes Prozac as "steroids for the business Olympics"—a warning label with a seductive subtext. . . . Dr. Kramer says he hasn't seen people taking Prozac "for trivial reasons." But he adds, "Clearly, it's a matter of perspective." When Valium was abused, he recalls "Everyone agrees it happened, but was difficult to document."

The paradox at the heart of Prozac is this: Experts say it still isn't reaching those who need it most. Only a quarter of depressed people ever receive treatment of any kind.

In the section that follows, we provide a brief chronology of events that depicts the public aspects of the controversy involving Prozac. This chronology shows how the controversy came about, how it was fostered, and the impact various developments had on opposing groups, on their public posture, modus operandi, and tactical and strategic goals.

Massacre at the Standard Gravure Printing Plant

The first prominent legal proceeding in which the COS, through its CCHR affiliate, played an important role was that involving the case of Joseph Wesbecker. When the coroner's report found Prozac in Wesbecker's bloodstream, the commission contacted the families of the victims and persuaded ten of them to sign a letter urging that a congressional investigation of Prozac be held. During his congressional testimony, Dennis Clarke, president of CCHR, asserted that Prozac caused Wesbecker's violent behavior. Clarke also appeared on the Phil Donahue syndicated talk show in February 1991 stating that Wesbecker had no prior history of violence and had not been involved in a job-related argument for 32 years.

It was later revealed by the *Wall Street Journal* and other sources that Wesbecker had previously tried at least twelve times to commit suicide. When not taking Prozac, he spoke about killing his bosses, bought the guns he later used, and went to a gun range to practice. Blood samples taken after Wesbecker's suicide revealed that his blood contained seven drugs, five of which were antidepressants, including Prozac.[2] At the trial, it was shown that Wesbecker had carefully laid plans for the attack several months before he had started taking Prozac, including the purchase of $3,500 worth of weapons and ammunition. Wesbecker also made sure that his financial affairs were in order, going so far as to arrange for the disposal of his remains.[3] Nonetheless, lawyers representing the widows of Wesbecker's victims alleged that Eli Lilly knew or should have known that Prozac: (a) was unsafe for use by the general public for treatment of depression; (b) could cause users to experience intense agitation and preoccupation with suicide; and (c) could lead users to harm themselves or others.[4] In December 1994, the jury in Louisville, Kentucky, found that Eli Lilly was not at fault and that Prozac did not lead to Wesbecker's violent rampage.

Martin Teicher's Study in the *American Journal of Psychiatry*

In February 1990, an article addressing some possible violent emotional side-effects of Prozac appeared in the *American Journal of Psychiatry*. The lead author, Martin Teicher, a Harvard Medical School Professor of Psychiatry, reported that 6 out of 172 of his depressed patients (or 3.5%) developed intense suicidal thoughts after taking Prozac for an average of 26 days. This state was more intense, obsessive, and violent than anything the patients had previously experienced. Five of the six patients had suffered from prior suicidal tendencies. Their suicidal thoughts did not fully disappear until an average of 87 days after the cessation of treatment.

As a result of the six clinical case studies, Teicher and his colleagues concluded: "At the present time we can only state that persistent, obsessive, and violent suicidal thoughts emerged in a small minority of patients treated with fluoxetine. Fluoxetine was the sole pharmacologic agent in only two cases; the other patients were taking a variety of other medications, which may have also contributed to this reaction and thereby complicate interpretation. The purpose of this report is to suggest the surprising possibility that fluoxetine may induce suicidal ideation in some patients. Only additional surveillance will enable us to learn whether this is a widespread or valid concern."[5]

Despite the tentative nature and limited scope of Teicher's report, Scientologists used it as the basis for their widespread claim that "up to 140,000 people in the United States have become violent and suicidal by Prozac" and "can explode any moment without provocation."[6] Teicher subsequently stated that such use of his paper was "absolutely irresponsible."[7] His patients were not representative of the average patient who uses Prozac. He himself considered Prozac safe and helpful when used properly and believed that the COS and CCHR "have their own ax to grind, and they are using my paper in a somewhat distorted way to serve their own purposes."[8]

Teicher's study was, however, anecdotal. There were other studies by medical researchers using more rigorous research design to evaluate the efficiency of Prozac. A one-year study at Rush-Presbyterian St. Luke's Medical Center in Chicago, for example, monitored 100 Prozac users and found no increase in the risk of suicide or violence among the patients. A survey intended to measure suicidal thinking among 1,017 patients treated with various antidepressants during 1989 was administered by two psychiatrists affiliated with the Harvard Medical School and Mass General Hospital. No drug was singled out as being more related to suicidal thinking than any other. These and other similar studies suggest that different people respond in different ways to drugs and that Prozac, while helping many clinically depressed patients, is not a panacea and patients need to be carefully monitored.[9]

Several Criminal Cases and Lawsuits Using the "Prozac Defense"

One of the most active attorneys in the anti-Prozac litigation has been Leonard Finz, a former New York State Supreme Court judge, and his associate, Jerrold Parker. Their firm, specializing in medical malpractice and product liability, has handled scores of Prozac cases. Peter Dock, the legislative affairs director of CCHR, told a *Washington Post* reporter that CCHR refers prospective clients, who call its hotline, to Finz and other lawyers. Finz vehemently denies any connection to COS and claims that he was unaware that some of his clients might have come through such a channel.

The following are two examples that are illustrative of cases using the "Prozac Defense." In March 1991, Kevin Callahan of St. Petersburg, Florida, came home from the race tracks one evening. He grabbed a kitchen knife and proceeded to stab his wife in the throat and back. His wife survived the attack but Callahan was charged with attempted murder. In court, he claimed that he could not remember the events that took place that night because he was using Prozac. His wife testified in a deposition that Callahan had assaulted her before ever using Prozac. Callahan, moreover, had a previous criminal record of grand theft, arson, and defrauding an insurance company. In January of 1992, he was convicted of attempted murder.

In 1990, Rebecca McStoots was convicted in Kentucky of first-degree assault after shooting her physician in the neck. She is currently serving a 10-year prison sentence. At the trial, in which Prozac was once again targeted, medical records showed that McStoots had a history of violence prior to taking the drug. These records were made public after McStoots' lawyer had asked the judge to dismiss the case because his client did not wish to endure further public scrutiny.

Some of Prozac's alleged victims were much more famous than either Callahan or McStoots. CCHR tried, but failed, to reopen the investigation into the 1989 suicide of activist Abbie Hoffman. The group claimed that Hoffman had been using Prozac, although the coroner reported that he had found no trace of the drug in Hoffman's body during the autopsy.

Formation of the Prozac Survivors Support Group (PSSG)

In April 1990, COS arranged to have Janet Sims of Franklin, Tennessee, appear on the television talk show, "Geraldo." She claimed that she had become suicidal and violent, swallowing pills in an attempt to end her life, while taking Prozac in 1988. CCHR's toll-free telephone number appeared at the end of the show for other Prozac sufferers to use. Sims went on to form PSSG with the help of CCHR. CCHR advised her on how to start the group and attract news coverage. It paid for PSSG's mailings, recruited members, and announced the formation of new chapters in news releases.

Petitions Submitted to the U. S. Food and Drug Administration

In October 1990, CCHR filed a petition with the USFDA to ban Prozac from the market claiming that Prozac was addictive and caused suicidal and violent behavior. In August 1991, a Ralph Nader consumer watchdog organization, Public Citizen Health Research Group, petitioned the USFDA to put a warning label on Prozac alerting patients that it may cause suicidal thoughts and impulses. On September 20, 1991, the USFDA convened its psycho- pharmacological drugs advisory committee. It heard the stories of numerous witnesses

claiming that their outbursts of violence against themselves and others were attributable to Prozac and not to their underlying depressive illness. The committee, which consisted of nine outside members, aided by six consultants including Dr. Teicher, unanimously decided that Prozac and other antidepressants did not cause the emergence or intensification of suicidality or other violent behaviors. The committee also decided in a six-to-three vote that no labeling changes should be made for Prozac. The USFDA's actions were supported by such major national health organizations as the National Alliance for the Mentally Ill, and the National Depressive and Manic Depressive Association. The USFDA rejected CCHR's petition to ban Prozac, concluding that "the data and information available at this time do not indicate that Prozac causes suicidality or violent behavior. There is no evidence that Prozac is associated with tardive dystonia or tardive dyskinesia (movement disorders), nor is there evidence that Prozac is addictive."[10]

CCHR's Activities Overseas

During 1990–1991, CCHR embarked on a worldwide effort to discredit Prozac in foreign countries where Prozac was being marketed. In its anti-Prozac campaign, CCHR publicized its claims of Prozac's negative side-effects and targeted the news media, regulatory authorities, physicians, and even Prozac patients. For example, in an article appearing in the Finnish media and entitled "Killer Drug Also Available in Finland," CCHR demanded the withdrawal of Fontex (the local brand name for Prozac). In the Netherlands, CCHR wrote letters to the Ministry of Health and the country's political parties calling for a ban on Prozac. The group also cautioned the queen to avoid current or future treatment of her husband (who was known to be suffering from depression) with Prozac. CCHR also circulated articles and other materials critical of Prozac to various groups and general news media in many other countries, e.g., France, Sweden, Denmark, Belgium, Germany, Italy, the United Kingdom, Spain, Canada, Australia, and New Zealand.

Scientology Battles the News Media

In May 1991, a special report on the COS appeared in a *Time* magazine article written by Richard Behar. In the article, entitled, "Scientology: The Thriving Cult of Greed and Power," Behar attacked the COS for not being a religion. He viewed the COS as "a hugely profitable global racket that survives by intimidating members and critics in a Mafia-like manner."[11] Behar claims to have obtained the information for his report from 150 interviews, and hundreds of court records and internal Scientology documents. COS members refused to be interviewed for the article.

COS retaliated against *Time* and Eli Lilly by taking out full-page advertisements for 12 weeks in *USA Today*.[12] The advertisements, costing approximately $3 million, accused Lilly and *Time* of a conspiracy to run a story full of lies and mistakes. The advertisements also suggested that *Time* supported the views of Hitler in World War II and that Lilly introduced the illicit use of heroin, methadone, and LSD into American culture. Still other advertisements promoted Scientology and praised its founder. At the bottom of many of the ads, readers were told to look for a special advertising supplement on *Time* that would appear in *USA Today* on June 14, 1994. The 80-page supplement contained detailed accounts of the same themes that had figured prominently in earlier advertisements.

The Scientology advertisements did not sit well with some *USA Today* clients, staff, and other newspaper editors. Rance Crain, editor-in-chief of *Advertising Age*, for example, complained that, "Advertising is being used in ways it was never intended and to be used. There is a real danger here that it is going to weaken the efficacy and believabili-

ty of all advertising. It concerns a lot of people."[13] Some editors and reporters at *USA Today* felt that the content of the advertisements was "low class" and that their usage to further a vendetta was inappropriate. Quite a few customers complained and some threatened to pull their own ads from the newspaper. Nevertheless, Steve Anderson, media relations manager for *USA Today*, stated that management's position was to protect the First Amendment and that this meant safeguarding the right of individuals to purchase advertising space to express their viewpoints.

COS Initiates Legal Action against Hill & Knowlton and Eli Lilly

In May 1991, COS filed a lawsuit against Eli Lilly and its public relations agency, Hill & Knowlton. Scientologists claimed that Lilly had pressured Hill & Knowlton, as well as a Chicago law firm, Baker & McKenzie, to drop COS as a client. In the Baker & McKenzie case, two former partners who had handled intellectual property matters for the COS claimed that Lilly, a long-time client, threatened to end their business relationship unless the law firm stopped representing the church. The two partners resigned after the announcement that Baker & McKenzie would no longer work with COS. Robert Cox, chairman of Baker & McKenzie, denied the allegations, claiming that he "never heard one word from Lilly; not one phone call; not one letter."[14] He said he no longer wanted his firm to represent COS because of its alleged shady activities around the world. Jury selection in the case was scheduled to begin June 13, 1994. One month later, the $40 million lawsuit was settled out of court.

Lilly Fights Back

In January 1991, Eli Lilly ran a training program for 1,700 of its U.S. sales people aimed at increasing their skills when discussing

Prozac clinical trial data and Scientology with concerned doctors. In March 1991, Eli Lilly indicated its readiness to assist prosecutors in criminal cases and also offered to pay the fees of expert witnesses, which could range from $150 to $500 an hour. Leonard Finz, one of the key litigators in Prozac lawsuits, objected to Lilly's offer of assistance to prosecutors claiming that it constituted "intrusion by a high-powered multi-billion dollar enterprise, creeping into the criminal justice system in a very insidious way."[15] Edward West, a Lilly spokesperson, countered by saying that " . . . no jury should be deprived of the appropriate medical information that is available on [Prozac] simply because a prosecutor's office may lack funds."[16] Lilly also announced that it would defend, indemnify, and hold physicians harmless against claims, liabilities, and expenses arising from personal injury alleged to have been caused by Prozac as long as the drug had been properly prescribed. The company felt that physicians should not have to defend themselves alone against a powerful organization like COS. "This is a public relations controversy, not a medical controversy. Doctors need to understand that we stand squarely behind the drug and their use of it," stated Edward West, a Lilly spokesperson.[17] Others, however, criticized Lilly's indemnification plan as being a "slick marketing ploy" aimed at counteracting declining Prozac sales.[18]

Lilly's efforts to defend itself against the COS's attack intensified in June 1991. The company's representatives began to appear on radio/television talk shows. Through a special edition of its internal employee newsletter, "Dateline," Lilly's chairman discussed the Prozac controversy, COS ads, and facts about Prozac. Lilly also sent several hundred "Dear Doctor" and "Dear Pharmacist" letters to individuals throughout the country mentioning the COS's attack on Eli Lilly and its products. The letters were accompanied by an attractive booklet intended to assist health care providers in counseling their patients about depression and Prozac. Lilly also ordered 250,000 special reprints of the *Time* magazine cover story, "Scientology: The Cult of Greed" to distribute to physicians.

The Debate Over Prozac Continues

Two recent books highlight the ongoing debate over Prozac as a drug. Peter Kramer received his M. D. from Harvard, has a private practice in Providence, R.I., and writes a monthly column for *Psychiatric Times*. In his best-selling book, *Listening to Prozac*, Kramer describes the cases of a number of previously depressed patients who suddenly became calm, confident, and cheerful after taking Prozac. Peter Breggin received his psychiatric training at Harvard and the Upstate Medical Center of the State University of New York. He has a private practice in Bethesda, Maryland and is the founder and director of the Center for the Study of Psychiatry. In his book, *Talking Back to Prozac*, Breggin argues that if Prozac can transform personality for the better, it can also transform it for the worse. He criticized the USFDA approval process for new drugs, saying that it relied too heavily on studies supervised and paid for by the drug companies. Breggin was an expert witness for the plaintiffs in the Wesbecker trial. He is a longtime critic of lobotomies, electroshock therapy, and psychiatric drug treatment. He also implied that the close ties between Eli Lilly and George Bush/Dan Quayle during their administration, put pressure on the USFDA to speed up the approval of Prozac despite Lilly's inadequate testing.

Critics of Breggin believe his arguments are dangerous. "His [Breggin's] views stop people from getting treatment. They could cost a life," says Susan Dime-Meenan, president of the National Depressive and Manic-Depressive Association.[19] During the early stages of his career, Breggin had ties to Scientology. He had also written an article in which he spoke approvingly of sexual relations among children. Although Breggin admits that he once was an ally of the COS and that his wife had been a member, he claims they both renounced the group twenty years ago. Regarding favorable attitudes towards sexual relations among children, Breggin stated, "I don't agree with that anymore. That's from a period in the '60s, and I've certainly left that far behind."[20]

INSTITUTIONS AND ACTORS INVOLVED IN THE PROZAC CONTROVERSY

The Prozac controversy is not simply a debate on the efficacy of a drug or the scientific merits of the drug testing and approval process. While this aspect of the debate is critically important from the perspective of patients and physicians, the tenor of the debate is also influenced, to an equally great extent, by the institutions and actors involved; their value set and economic and financial constraints; the role these institutions perceive for themselves in the broader sociopolitical context; and the types of strategies and tactics that they bring to the competitive arena to win in the marketplace of ideas and values. This section briefly discusses the environmental framework and institutional character of Eli Lilly and the Church of Scientology and describes their strategies and tactics within the context of their particular institutional values and norms.

Profile of the Pharmaceutical Industry

The pharmaceutical industry, with 1994 worldwide sales estimated at approximately $188 billion, has been one of the most profitable and fastest growing industries in the world. It is composed of two segments: ethical drugs (prescription drugs that are not advertised to the public and are available only from medical practitioners) and nonprescription drugs (or over-the-counter medica-

tions). In recent years, the ethical drug segment has accounted for 70–80% of the total pharmaceutical market while the non-prescription drugs segment has accounted for 20–30% of the total pharmaceutical market. The U.S. represents approximately 27% of the international pharmaceutical market. Other key markets include: Japan with 19%, Germany with 7%, France with 6%, and the United Kingdom with 3%. Exhibit 1 (p. 105) provides information on the world's major pharmaceutical companies.

The pharmaceutical industry is currently facing fundamental changes all over the world that would have a profound effect not only on the shape of the industry, but also on how health care is provided and paid for, and the extent of choice people will have in seeking health-care services. These changes have been propelled by: (a) prospects of government-mandated health-care reform with an increasing focus on cost-containment policies; (b) the growth of managed care systems that have shifted the bargaining power from health-care providers (e.g., physicians and hospitals) to health-care payers (e.g., insurance companies and employers); (c) the costs, risks, and amount of time required to introduce new drugs into the marketplace through aggressive R & D; (d) demographic trends projecting the aging of the population; and, (e) further globalization of all segments of the health-care industry.

The constant and incessant drive to discover and develop new products has made research and development expenditures critical to the success of pharmaceutical companies. In the U.S., the industry has the highest ratio of research expenditures to sales of all major domestic industrial groups. In 1993, this ratio reached 16.7%. The process of developing, testing, and getting a new drug approved by the USFDA is formidable. A recent Tufts University study indicated that it takes an investment of approximately $231 million and about 12 years to produce a successful new drug (this includes 3.5 years of laboratory and animal studies; 6 years of human clinical trials, and 2.5 years of government regulatory review).[21]

The high costs and the length of time required to move a new drug from the laboratory to the marketplace have forced pharmaceutical companies to rely ever more heavily on the profitability of "breakthrough drugs." Since these breakthrough drugs are significantly different from the drugs currently on the market, they allow pharmaceutical companies to sell them at higher margins, thereby permitting a single drug to carry the burden for heavy, and high-risk, research and development efforts of other drugs. "Me-too drugs," on the other hand, are drugs that are similar to products already on the market. Pharmaceutical companies have been criticized for investing large amounts of R&D funds in these drugs, which, although highly profitable, do not necessarily provide significant therapeutical advantages over their counterparts. Product-line extensions are also crucial for pharmaceutical companies in generating further revenues and extending the life of a product by determining its efficacy for ailments other than that for which the product was originally approved by the USFDA. Another consequence of cost pressures, and the changing dynamics of the health-care industry, have led to a worldwide trend toward consolidation in the industry. (See Exhibit 2, p. 106.) According to the Pharmaceutical Manufacturers Association, drug companies eliminated over 30,000 jobs during 1992–93. Pharmaceutical companies are forming strategic partnerships with other firms in the health-care industry.[22]

Eli Lilly: The Company

Eli Lilly and Company describes itself as "a global research-based corporation that develops, manufactures, and markets pharmaceuticals, medical instruments and diagnostic products, and animal health products."[23] It is ranked 108 in *Business Week*'s "Global 1,000" in terms of market value and 85 in *Fortune* magazine's "Fortune 500" in terms of sales.

In 1993, sales reached $6.4 billion (a 5% increase from 1992) while net income was $480.2 million (a 32% decrease from 1992 due to restructuring charges). Among some of its well-known products besides Prozac are: Ceclor, an oral antibiotic; Darvon, a painkiller; and Humulin, human insulin of recombinant DNA. Exhibits 3 and 4 (pp. 106–107) provide some information on Lilly's financial and other measures of performance.

History. The company was founded in 1876 by Colonel Eli Lilly, a 38-year-old Civil War veteran and pharmaceutical chemist, in Indianapolis, Indiana.[24] With capital of $1,400 ($1,000 in negotiable notes and $400 in merchandise), and two employees other than himself, Eli Lilly opened a small establishment to produce and dispense medications. He vowed that his company would manufacture pharmaceutical products of the highest possible quality, develop only those medicines that would be dispensed by physicians, and base all of its products on the best scientific information available.[25] Sales increased significantly after Lilly purchased the patents in 1909 to a new kind of capsule making machine. By 1920, production reached 3 million capsules a day.

In the latter years of his life, Eli Lilly spent most of his time performing civic duties to improve the quality of life in Indianapolis. Eli Lilly died in 1889 and his son, Josiah Kirby Lilly, who had started working at the company at the age of 14, took over the family business. Josiah inherited his father's sense of social responsibility. During the Depression, he maintained a no-layoff policy, creating work for people to do while keeping them gainfully employed. He also made sure his company developed a policy of promptly responding to natural disasters and the needs of affected communities. In 1932, Josiah Lilly stepped down and his two sons, Eli and Josiah, Jr., became the company's new managers. Sales rose from $13 million in 1932 to $117 million in 1948. Successful company products were: insulin developed from a hormone extracted from the pancreas of pigs; a liver extract for treatment of pernicious anemia; synthesized barbituric acids for drugs used in surgery and obstetrics; and penicillin and other antibiotics. Eli was responsible for updating the company's antiquated production systems. Josiah improved the company's sales and distribution methods, putting tremendous emphasis on the training of its salespeople. To this day, one of the distinctive features at Lilly is its well-trained and professional sales staff.

In 1953, Eugene Beesley became the first president of Eli Lilly who was not a family member. Beesley was responsible for Lilly's expansion overseas and for the development of public relations and government lobbying strategies. Because so much public attention was focused on the pharmaceutical industry's tremendous efforts to perfect the Salk polio vaccine, Lilly realized it had to make itself better known to the nonprofessional community. During the mid-1960s, Lilly established a legislative liaison office in Washington, D. C. This followed the passage by the U.S. Congress of the Drug Amendments of 1962, which expanded the USFDA's regulatory control over the industry.

Lilly doubled in size during the 1970s. When competition from generic drug manufacturers intensified, Lilly diversified, entering into agricultural chemicals, animal health products, medical instruments, and beauty care products. During the 1980s, Lilly encountered a number of controversies regarding the safety of some of its products. Darvon was attacked for its addictive qualities. The U.S. Justice Department filed criminal charges against Lilly and a former vice-president for failing to inform the government about four deaths and six illnesses related to its drug, Oraflex. Lilly was also named in a number of lawsuits filed against manufacturers of diethylstilbestrol (DES), a drug that caused cancer and other problems in the children of mothers who had taken it in the 1940s and 1950s to prevent miscarriages.

Top Management. There have been a number of significant top management changes at Eli Lilly in recent years. In November 1991, Vaughn Bryson became Lilly's new CEO, replacing Richard Wood who retained the chairman of the board position. Bryson held on to his new job for only 20 months. Although he was very popular with Lilly employees, the board, at the urging of his one-time supporter, Wood, forced him to resign. Under Bryson's leadership, Lilly recorded its first-ever loss in the third quarter of 1992, the stock price slid from the high 80s in early 1992 to the high 40s in 1993, and the product development pipeline was criticized for being weak.

Randall Tobias, a Lilly board member and a vice-chairman of AT&T, was named the new CEO. Industry analysts were initially skeptical of Tobias because he had no prior pharmaceutical experience. Tobias, however, moved swiftly to position Lilly to compete better in the new environment of the health-care industry. Believing that "there are no sacred cows at Lilly except the dividend,"[26] he announced an early retirement program aimed at reducing the work force by 4,000 employees over the next few years. To help Lilly concentrate on its core prescription pharmaceutical business, Tobias has put its Medical Devices and Diagnostics division up for sale and he also seems interested in selling Lilly's 40% interest in Dow-Elanco, a pesticide company.

In line with the industry trend toward consolidation and vertical integration, the company recently agreed to purchase the McKesson Corporation's PCS Health Systems Inc., the nation's largest manager of drug benefits programs, for $4 billion in cash. The acquisition of PCS Health Systems is expected to make it easier for Lilly to develop effective disease management programs intended to assist health maintenance organizations in the provision of less costly and better quality health-care services to subscribers. Disease management programs aim to provide "total" health-care services by alerting physicians about patients at risk for a certain disease and determining which therapies would most likely work best at each stage of a disease. The goal is to provide early interventions, before a patient's illness progresses to an advanced stage requiring more costly and rigorous treatments (e.g., surgery, repeated physician visits, prolonged hospital stays). In the case of diabetes, for example, Lilly would use PCS's customer data bases to identify, early on, patients who may require daily insulin injections to forestall the onset of more serious complications (and more invasive treatments) of the disease such as blindness, kidney problems, and the possibility of amputations.

The Globalization of Eli Lilly. Lilly has begun a systematic and sustained effort to expand its international presence and has targeted a number of newly emerging markets, e.g., China and India, for special attention. Eli Lilly's transformation into a multinational corporation evolved gradually as the firm responded to various competitive pressures in its environment.[27] In the 1980s, Lilly resembled a traditional ethnocentric company that sold its domestically manufactured products outside the U.S. market through foreign affiliates. Overseas operations were limited to providing local sales support. By the early 1990s, however, Lilly had become a single, integrated, global firm that kept decisions regarding worldwide product development, strategic planning, and product quality standards centralized at headquarters while allowing its affiliates to manage day-to-day operations and other decentralized activities (e.g., final manufacturing and marketing, and in some cases, research and development activities).

Prozac: The Wonder Drug

Treatment for depression changed dramatically in 1988 when Eli Lilly introduced Prozac. It was the first drug in a new generation of antidepressants known as selective serotonin reuptake inhibitors (SSRIs). Prozac's mode of operation is different from traditional antidepressants. It operates only on the neurotransmitter, serotonin, by blocking a nerve cell pump that removes serotonin from its site of action in the brain. Current estimates suggest that 15 million Americans suffer from serious clinical depression. Costs, in terms of lost productivity and treatment expenses, to the U. S. economy may be as high as $27 billion a year.[28] Traditional drugs prescribed by psychiatrists, from two main groups called tricyclics or monoamine-oxidase inhibitors, have undesirable side-effects. They can be addictive when used improperly, and are also toxic when taken in large amounts.

Discovery and Testing. Prozac, known by its chemical name fluoxetine hydrochloride, was discovered in 1972 by three Lilly scientists: Ray Fuller, David Wong and Bryan Molloy.[29] Molloy was an organic chemist who had developed a number of cardiac drugs for Lilly. Fuller was interested in brain chemistry research. Wong had successfully developed antibiotics for agricultural uses but now wanted to develop drugs for humans. Fuller persuaded Molloy to leave his heart research and to join him in his search for new antidepressant drugs. Molloy decided to study compounds whose chemical structures were similar to those of antihistamines (historically, research on antihistamines led to the discovery of the first major antidepressants). Molloy and Wong met at a lecture given by Solomon Snyder from Johns Hopkins University. Snyder described a new way to test the effects of various drugs on neurotransmitters using the ground-up brains of rats. Back at Lilly's laboratories, Wong applied this technique to conduct tests of Molloy's new chemical compounds. The researchers discovered that one compound, labeled 82816, selectively prevented the absorption of serotonin by transmitting cells. It turned out to be an earlier version of Prozac. Clinical trials with fluoxetine began in 1976. Lilly submitted a New Drug Application for fluoxetine in 1983 to the USFDA. Prozac was approved for marketing in the U.S. in December 1987. Lilly's subsidiary, Dista, began distribution of the drug in January 1988. In all, more than 35,000 patients have participated in fluoxetine clinical trials and more than 3,000 scientific papers have been published addressing the medication's safety and usefulness.

Prozac's Market Success. Shortly after Lilly introduced Prozac into the marketplace, it was hailed alternatively by journalists as a "wonder" drug (*New York* Magazine), as a "breakthrough" drug (*Newsweek*), and as the "personality pill" (*Time*).[30] The drug was so well received by patients and psychiatrists that one columnist joked that Prozac should be placed into the nation's drinking water.[31] Prozac was an immediate financial success for Eli Lilly and Company with sales of $125 million in its first year (1988) and $350 million in its second year (1989).[32]

Today, Prozac is used by 16 million people around the world and has been approved in over 75 countries as a safe and effective treatment for depression. Lilly sales for Prozac reached a record of $1.3 billion worldwide in 1993, an increase of 30% over 1992. It has been estimated that sales could reach as high as $1.68 billion in 1997.[33] Such potential could easily be realized since Prozac has recently been approved by the USFDA for treatment of obsessive-compulsive disorders affecting approximately 5 million Americans. A USFDA advisory committee has also voted unanimously to recommend approval of Prozac for treatment of an eating disorder, known as bulimia, which affects between 1 and 3 million Americans.[34]

Current Challenges. The maintenance of Prozac as a safe and effective treatment for depression and other disorders, so important to Lilly's future success, is by no means guaranteed. Industry statistics rank Prozac as the number two best-selling drug in the world, behind Glaxo Holdings PLC's ulcer-healing drug, Zantac. Lilly must compete with new copy-cat drugs such as Paxil offered by SmithKline Beecham and Zoloft offered by Pfizer. Sales of Paxil and Zoloft reached $225 million and $464 million, respectively in 1993.[35]

The major societal challenge for Eli Lilly lies in the drug's phenomenal popularity, which is both a blessing and a curse. There are concerns, for example, that Prozac is being overprescribed by some doctors and that it is being improperly used to treat everything from back pain and premenstrual syndrome (PMS) to obesity, gambling, and fear of public speaking.[36] Lilly has expressed concern that Prozac may become the center of a new "drug" culture.[37] In March 1994, Lilly took out full-page advertisements in medical journals and trade publications claiming that recent media attention has "trivialized the very serious nature of the disease Prozac was specifically developed to treat—clinical depression."[38]

The Church of Scientology (COS)

COS is based in Hollywood, California. It has a large branch in Clearwater, Florida, other smaller branches throughout the world, and claims to have 8 million followers. Former Scientologists report a much lower figure, however, saying there are no more than 700,000 members and perhaps as few as 50,000 members. COS has 14,000 staff members and 1,300 churches, missions, and organizations in 78 countries.[39] Among COS's many celebrity members are: Tom Cruise, John Travolta, Kirstie Alley, and Mimi Rogers.

Early Beginnings of COS. The Church of Scientology was founded by a former science-fiction writer, L. Ron Hubbard, in the early 1950s. He headed the organization until his death at the age of 74 in January 1986. A biographical sketch of Hubbard appeared in a June 1990 article written as part of a series on Scientology for the *Los Angeles Times*. The article mentioned, among other things, that Hubbard had an early fascination with hypnotism and black magic; that he suffered from some early emotional problems that prompted him to ask the Veteran's Administration for psychiatric treatment; that he was involved in a nasty divorce and custody battle with one of his wives, who accused him of subjecting her to "scientific torture experiments."[40] Hubbard had not been seen publicly for the six years preceding his death. David Miscavige assumed command of the COS after a power struggle with two COS lieutenants who had been in hiding with Hubbard.

The preachings of the COS are rooted in a new "mental science" that Hubbard invented in the 1950s. His early ideas, appearing in a book entitled, *Dianetics: The Modern Science of Mental Health*, discussed his discovery of an unconscious "reactive mind," in which all of a person's emotionally or physically painful experiences were recorded. Traumatic events, called "engrams," caused psychosomatic illnesses such as ulcers, migraines, colds, and allergies. Through the use of a technique called "auditing," a person could get rid of these engrams. "Auditing" is conducted with a device called an "E-meter," which is similar to a lie detector. It is designed to measure electric changes in the skin. Hubbard also believed in the existence of an immortal soul or "thetan" that passes from one body to another through reincarnations.

COS as a Religious Organization. COS proclaims Scientology to be an "applied religious philosophy" offering techniques to help people improve their health, intelligence, ability, behavior, skill, and appearance. One of its main tenets is a belief that man is basically good and has such inalienable rights as the right to defend himself, to speak freely, and to choose his own church. Man is forbidden, however, by God's laws, to destroy his own kind, to destroy the sanity of

another, or to enslave another person's soul.[41] French law professor, Jacques Robert, believed that Scientology could be a bona fide religion because it has a credo; stresses a belief in the Supreme Being, soul, immortality, and reincarnation; has a hierarchy, and is disciplined.[42]

In early October 1993, COS was notified by the IRS that 30 of its organizations would be recognized as tax-exempt organizations whose donation income would not be subject to federal income tax. This concluded one of the longest-running tax disputes in the history of the IRS. Documents filed with the IRS revealed that COS had assets of $400 million. Miscavige and his wife were paid $62,683 and $31,359, respectively, in salaries and did not receive a percentage of funds as commissions for fundraising. There was little evidence of private enrichment that would be barred by the tax law for religious and charitable organizations.[43] COS officials were pleased with the IRS decision and developed an expansion program. A new, 590-page book, *What is Scientology?*, was published by Bridge Publications. The book promised to give the real story behind the headlines. In advertisements, COS announced that it would welcome new members from all mainstream faiths. It also promised to help members realize their full spiritual potential by helping them understand how the mind works.[44]

COS as a Business Organization. In a special report that appeared in a 1991 *Time* magazine article, Richard Behar described COS as a highly profitable, Mafia-like organization with worldwide operations, which uses tactics of intimidation to control its members and attack its critics. Behar cited as evidence the trauma endured by several members, such as Noah Lottick, a 24-year-old from Kingston, Pennsylvania, and Harriet Baker, a 73-year-old widower from Los Angeles. Lottick spent $5,000 on auditing and then committed suicide a few months after having joined the Church. Lottick's father, a physician who had investigated the Church, said, "We thought Scientology was something like Dale Carnegie. I now believe it's a school for psychopaths. Their so-called therapies are manipulations. They take the best and the brightest people and destroy them."[45] After Harriet Baker's husband died of cancer, Scientologists offered to cure her grief with a $1,300 auditing program. She was later persuaded to take out a $45,000 mortgage on her house that would then be spent on auditing. Her children stepped in to prevent her further involvement with the Church.

Behar describes how COS keeps adding new counseling and therapy steps, each more costly than the one before, as members search for higher levels of salvation. New recruits, for example, (1) take a free personality test in which they learn of their weaknesses; (2) take a $250 communications course that involves sitting on a chair without moving and speaking to others without expressing feelings; (3) engage in auditing sessions costing $500-$1,000 an hour; (4) spend $2,800 on a course in which they become reacquainted with the world. To help pay for these services, members can earn commissions by recruiting new members, becoming auditors themselves, or by signing an employment contract to work in return for services. In one of his bulletins to church officials, Hubbard reportedly wrote, "Make money. Make more money. Make others produce so as to make money. . . . However you get them in or why, just do it."[46]

COS has brought a $416 million lawsuit against *Time* magazine and Behar charging them with "falsely labeling a judicially recognized religion as 'bogus' and 'Mafia-like'."[47] Also in dispute is Behar's claim that the COS had $503 million in income in 1987. The Church has said that this figure was falsely inflated by nearly $500 million. Scientologists believe the motive for trying to ruin COS's reputation was financial; a deal had been negotiated in which Lilly promised to order reprints of the article, adding $1 million to *Time's* profits.

COS As a Controversial Organization. There have been over 35 lawsuits brought against COS by former members charging it with negligence, unlawful imprisonment, intentional infliction of emotional stress, and harassment. Hubbard's own estranged son has called Scientology "a power-and-money-and-intelligence-gathering game. Scientology and all the other cults are one-dimensional, and we live in a three-dimensional world. Cults are as dangerous as drugs. They commit the highest crime: the rape of the soul."[48] Vicki Aznaran, one of the leaders of the COS until 1987, said of the Church, "This is a criminal organization, day in and day out. It makes Jim and Tammy [Bakker] look like kindergarten."[49] During the 1970s, eleven of the Church's officials, including one of Hubbard's wives, were jailed for burglarizing several government agencies, including the U.S. Justice Department and the IRS. The Scientologists were interested in purging government files of what they considered false information that was being circulated worldwide to discredit the church and Hubbard. At the time, federal prosecutors wrote, "The crime committed by these defendants is of a breadth and scope previously unheard of. No building, office, desk or file was safe from their snooping and prying. No individual or organization."[50]

Other accusations against the Church have included: allegations that the Church harassed reporters who wrote negative stories about Scientology; that it used brainwashing techniques to control the minds of its members; and, that it paid low wages to members who catered to the personal needs of its leaders. Robert Welkos, co-author of the *Los Angeles Times* articles, for example, claimed that he was investigated by private detectives hired by Scientology attorneys; threatened with lawsuits; sent brochures about funeral arrangements; and had his name appear in advertisements placed on billboards that gave the impression that he was endorsing Scientology. Behar has countersued the church for harassment and for illegally gaining access to his personal credit records.

Scientologists around the world have been charged with various offenses. In Spain, for example, 11 members of the COS, including Heber Jentzsch, president of Church of Scientology International, were investigated in 1988 for illegal association, tax evasion, and fraud. The judge compared the Church to a pyramid scheme that requires members to pay increasing sums of money. Its drug rehabilitation center, Narconon, cheated patients and lured them into Scientology.[51] In Italy, 6 scientologists were convicted in 1991 of deceiving confused individuals; 67 others were acquitted of charges ranging from criminal association to tax evasion.[52] In France, 4 Scientologists were charged in 1990 with fraud, illegal practice of medicine, and premeditated violence. The national president, Daniele Gounard, was accused of being responsible for the suicide of one of the Church's new members.[53]

Scientologists support Hubbard and defend his character. "Any controversy about him is like a speck of dust on his shoes compared to the millions of people who loved and respected him."[54] Scientologists admit that a small group of members engaged in illegal activities during the 1970s. However, they also contend that they were justified in burglarizing government offices because government agents had unfairly harassed and persecuted them. COS insists that it has since developed mechanisms to prevent such occurrences from happening again.

The Role of the Mass Media in the Prozac Controversy

The Prozac controversy supplied excellent material for television talk shows. They have become tabloids of the air by creating—

through a process of sensationalization—both contrived events and instant celebrities. Prozac offered an irresistible opportunity for them to "cash in." The two key protagonists were a large, respectable pharmaceutical company that had supposedly turned evil; and a religious organization founded by a science fiction writer that has sometimes been labelled a cult.

We smiled when Tom Sanders (played by Michael Douglas), the main character in the movie, "Disclosure," was asked by a coworker if he wanted a Prozac to ease his fear of losing his job. We felt sad when we read in the local newspaper that Mark Woodley actually did lose his job as Santa Claus at Macy's department store because he had AIDS and was taking Prozac. We thought it was cute when we learned that the polar bear at the local zoo was given Prozac to even out his mood swings. Nonetheless, some of these references may do more harm than good. They seem to indicate that Prozac is a "cure-all" and should be used by people to deal with life's everyday difficulties.

The February 1991 Phil Donahue show entitled, "Prozac—Medication that Makes You Kill," provides perhaps the best example of one-sided reporting and disregard for the facts. Excerpts from the show's transcripts appear in Exhibit 5 (p. 108). The list of guests included Dennis Clarke from CCHR; Leonard Finz, the key lawyer in Prozac lawsuits brought against Lilly; Bonnie Leitsch, the national director of PSSG; Prozac patients with negative experiences, and victims of Prozac users. Significantly absent from the show were Lilly spokespersons, USFDA representatives, physicians, and Prozac patients with positive experience. Although Lilly representatives were apparently invited to come to the show, the company declined and sent a prepared statement that Donahue read during the program.

Some of the more glaring omissions and distortions made by guests on the Donahue show are described below. The only possible conclusion that one might draw from such inaccuracies and distortion of facts is that the show's producers did not view it as a news event and of wide public import where a drive towards accuracy would serve an important public purpose. Instead, it was viewed as an entertainment show where facts were easily forgotten, or even fictionalized, to enhance their entertainment value.

1. The claim made by Mrs. Miller, a woman who was shot by Joseph Wesbecker in 1989, that Wesbecker was "an average nice Joe," had never hurt anyone else, and tried to commit suicide only once, is far from the truth. Also, the statement by Clarke that Wesbecker "had no history of violence and never had an argument on the job in 32 years" ignores evidence to the contrary. As a matter of fact, Wesbecker tried to kill himself 12–15 times and had been hospitalized three times for mental illness. He had repeatedly threatened people around him including his wife, children, bosses, and coworkers. These and many other facts about Wesbecker were easily available and could have been verified had someone bothered to do so.

2. Bonnie Leitsch, the national director of PSSG, blamed her 1989 suicide attempt on Prozac. She did not, however, give out any details of her earlier suicide attempts and was not questioned by Donahue as to why she had taken Prozac and whether or not she had a prior history of mental illness. Medical records, available from other sources, revealed that Leitsch had suffered from depression since 1976, had overdosed on sleeping pills in 1960, and had become depressed by the 1988 suicide of her daughter. A Kentucky judge dismissed her $150 million lawsuit against Lilly stating that her lawyers did not produce any evidence supporting their charges.

3. The statistic offered by Dennis Clarke, that as much as 7% of Prozac patients develop obsessive, violent, suicidal preoccupation, was apparently based on the article written by Martin Teicher. The statistic, however, was taken out of context and extrapolations were incorrectly made for the entire U.S. population. Thus conclusions were drawn—based on faulty sample and research design—that were totally unwarranted and indefensible.

4. Clarke contended that Prozac had horrendous side-effects, including bronchitis, lung infection, and pneumonia. Clarke was not a physician. Nor did he supply any scientific evidence or cite a single medical report that linked Prozac to these diseases. And yet, he was allowed to make these faulty statements unchallenged, which made them appear to be objective facts.

5. Only at the very end of the program did Donahue briefly mention that Clarke was a member of the Church of Scientology and that much of the criticism directed towards Prozac originated with COS. Donahue also described COS as a legal organization that endorsed mainstream medical treatments, such as surgery and blood transfusions. The program made no reference to COS's longstanding opposition to psychiatry.

With the help of COS, other alleged victims of Prozac, also managed to appear on other talk shows, for example, "Geraldo" where truth and accuracy were sacrificed with equal disdain. The Church, however, did not fare so well on two other nationally televised news programs, namely, CBS's "60 Minutes" which aired on October 27, 1991, and ABC's "Nightline" anchored by Ted Koppel, which aired on February 14, 1992. (Exhibits 6 and 7, pp. 111-117, contain excerpts from these programs.)

The Church of Scientology's Assault against Lilly: Strategies and Tactics

The Church of Scientology mounted a three-pronged attack in its fight against Lilly. It included: (a) a legal-judicial strategy, (b) a campaign in the mass media, and (c) a confrontation in the regulatory arena.

Legal-Judicial Strategies. COS has a well-honed strategy of using the legal-judicial system in the United States. The Church has filed numerous defamation-of-character lawsuits against its critics. It has also appealed judgments made in favor of ex-Scientologists, such as Larry Wollersheim, who had sued the Church for the intentional infliction of emotional stress and unlawful imprisonment. It has also filed more than 100 lawsuits against the IRS to obtain documents available under the Freedom of Information Act, in an attempt to prove that the Church was improperly targeted for audits and special investigations in the 1970s. In addition, COS has filed religious discrimination suits against the Cult Awareness Network (CAN) for not allowing Scientologists to join the group as members. CAN is an organization that was founded in 1978 by Patricia Ryan, whose father Leo Ryan was killed at Jonestown, Guyana. Its primary purpose is to educate the public on mind control by cults. CAN's organizers claim that if Scientologists were admitted as members and allowed to answer the telephones and attend conventions, no one would call or donate money to CAN.

COS pays over $4 million a year in legal fees to a hand-picked group of lawyers for litigation, contract negotiations, and trademark and other legal work. Almost 80% of the work is done by the Los Angeles law firm of Bowles & Moxon. (Four of the law firm's partners are Scientologists.) It has been alleged by detectives who worked on Church assignments and received paychecks from Bowles & Moxon that they were sometimes asked to conduct thorough investigations of people in order to find embarrassing or incriminating information about them. In pursuing its critics, COS seems to follow a "fair-game" doctrine. Established during the 1960s, this doctrine states that anyone who impedes the COS and its operations could "be deprived of property or injured by any means by any Scientologist without any discipline of the Scientologist. May be tricked, sued or lied to or destroyed."[55] Scientologists claim, however, that the doctrine was rescinded a long time ago because people had twisted its meaning.

Mass Media and Public Opinion Strategies. The most elaborate account of the mass media and public opinion strategies used by COS comes from an individual who should know—Robert Vaughn Young, an ex-

Scientologist who handled public relations and media for L. Ron Hubbard and other church leaders for 20 years. He was responsible for handling reporters, dealing with police and government agencies, creating "front" organizations, and discrediting critics. He claims that he taught other public relations representatives working for the Church the following tactics: how to respond to a question without answering; how to divert the issue; how to tell "an acceptable truth"; how to stall for time, how to "attack the attacker"; how to take control of a conversation; and how to appear to be a religion.[56]

In the "Manual of Justice," Hubbard also told Scientologists how to deal with negative coverage from a magazine article: (1) write a letter to the magazine demanding that the editors retract the story in the next issue; (2) hire a private detective to investigate the writer (not the magazine) to find out if she/he has a criminal or communist background; (3) instruct a lawyer to threaten the magazine with a lawsuit; and (4) intimidate the writer with personal information uncovered in the investigation.[57]

Regulatory Strategies. CCHR argued that more than 16,500 "adverse reaction reports" were made to the USFDA after Prozac was introduced in the marketplace. This provided sufficient justification for the USFDA to take action and ban Prozac. Further, the USFDA advisory committee that reviewed the petition failed to issue such a recommendation. Dr. Daniel Casey, committee chair, summarized the committee's view when he stated, "There was no evidence showing an increase of suicidality with any of the drugs in depressive or non-depressive patients. And regarding Prozac, we probably have looked more closely and analytically at those data than on any other antidepressant drug."[58] Other mental health professionals spoke out against changing Prozac's labeling without sufficient scientific data. John A. Smith from the National Mental Health Association declared that such a label change would "stigmatize an entire class of medications."[59] and would make it more difficult for patients to overcome their fear of the illness and seek treatment.

HOW LILLY DEFENDED ITSELF: STRATEGIES AND TACTICS

Lilly was unprepared to deal with the escalating controversy surrounding Prozac, although it should not have come as a surprise to the company given COS's history of fighting all drugs that could be used to treat depression and other psychological disorders. COS, for example, had previously been behind suits filed against the manufacturers of Ritalin (used to treat attention deficit disorder in children). Other drugs that have been attacked, not necessarily by COS, are Valium, (a tranquilizer) and Halcion (a sleeping pill). An analysis of Lilly's corporate culture and crisis management procedures might provide insight into why 21 months elapsed after the Wesbecker incident before the company made its first defensive move; why it did not immediately respond to Martin Teicher's study about possible suicidal ideation occurring in some of his Prozac patients; and why it did not send a public relations representative to the Donahue show to provide the company's side of the story.

Lilly has always been a rather conservative company, taking a reactive stance to threatening events in the past. It engaged in public relations and government lobbying activities only when it was forced to do so by external events. The company did not see itself as a consumer products company that must relate to the general public; it never marketed "over-the-counter" drugs, which would foster closer interaction with ultimate consumers; and it was located in a supportive Midwestern city protected to some extent from media scrutiny. Instead, Lilly relied on the training it gave its sale staff and on its frequent communications with health-care professionals.

When patients called Lilly for information on a product, company representatives would advise them to contact their physicians. The company was also unprepared to deal with the "popularity" of Prozac and its entry into the general psyche of the nation. This was the company's first foray into the antidepressant market and it was now required to deal not only with physical ailments affecting patients but also with the intense emotions characteristic of patients who are clinically depressed. Nor was Lilly prepared to deal with the new reality of the health-care debate which made the activities of pharmaceutical companies a matter of intense public scrutiny. The fact that, in COS, it had an adversary who was quite versed in the handling of the media, only made matters worse.

Despite Lilly's late start, two strategies emerged over time that proved to be effective in handling the Prozac crisis. They consisted of: (a) building stakeholder support; and (b) preparing for media issues.

Building Stakeholder Support. Externally, the company began its own massive campaign to inform physicians, pharmacists, patients, and media representatives about the motives of the Church of Scientology and the CCHR and about the serious nature of depression and the benefits attributable to the drug Prozac. Lilly offered assistance to physicians in the event of their being sued for prescribing Prozac and to prosecutors trying to make a case against Prozac patients charged with wrongdoing. In an effort to reach the more general public, Lilly sent Mitchell Daniels, its then vice-president for public affairs, to talk on the Bob Grant show and to meet with *USA Today*'s editorial board. In excerpts published by *USA Today* on June 11, 1991, Daniels called the COS "a commercial enterprise." He was later sued by the COS for $20 million for his remarks (the case was dismissed).

Internally, Lilly compiled a thorough report on COS and its activities around the world. Company newsletters included information about COS and about Prozac's ability successfully to treat depression. These articles were aimed at Lilly employees who may have become demoralized after reading the Scientology advertisements. The company also briefed salespeople and managers throughout the world on how to address various concerns about Prozac that might be raised by customers and the media.

Preparing for Media Issues. In June 1994, Lilly developed a checklist to help employees prepare for media inquiries on issues before they arose. The checklist included, among others: anticipating the type of media issues that are most likely to occur in a particular area (e.g., cosmetic pharmacology, Prozac, and suicide); developing fact sheets or press materials that are tailored to media's use; building contacts with key media reporters, editors, producers, etc.; providing general information about clinical depression or other illnesses; and, sending letters to appropriate associations expressing mutual concerns about media that trivializes or misrepresents depression and its treatment. Additionally, the company developed a communications training program to help its managers in dealing with reporters and journalists.

Organizational Changes— Preparing for the Future

The Prozac controversy taught Eli Lilly an important lesson: that it is not enough to have a product that is approved by all appropriate regulatory authorities and to be able to market it for patient use under the supervision of qualified physicians. Instead, the company must reach out to all types of stakeholders, and to the public-at-large, to ensure that the company's message is reaching all those people who could be helped by the product and to ensure that the product is being used properly and under the supervision of qualified physicians. Lilly also made a commitment to provide Prozac to any patient who needed it but was unable to pay for it.

Outreach Effort. Lilly has been making a major effort toward engendering greater public awareness and understanding of clinical depression. As part of this effort, the company cooperated with the National Mental Health Association (NMHA) in a nine-month campaign. The campaign, initiated in 1993, was aimed at public education about the fact that clinical depression was a treatable medical illness. NMHA's campaign had the financial support of 10 major sponsors (including Lilly) and more than 80 supporting organizations, with Lilly contributing approximately $500,000 to the effort. The mass media campaign was designed to reach the broadest possible spectrum of public. It included: national network television, radio, and print media. In addition, community education programs were organized all over the country by more than 400 National Mental Health Association affiliates. Among the activities undertaken by NMHA was a National Depression Screening Day, which was organized in a large number of cities at multiple locations.

Recognizing the need for a mechanism to handle patients calling the company directly for information on a drug, Lilly set up a customer-service unit staffed by professionals— nurses, physicians, and others who had pharmaceutical backgrounds. In a statement, Lilly's new CEO enunciated the company's need for focussing on the ultimate customer, calling it a mandate if the company is "to succeed in the new global health care marketplace. (See Exhibit 8, p. 118.) As part of its "Indigent Care" program, the company has established the mechanism whereby any physician can request Prozac for a patient who needs the drug but is too poor to pay for it. Under this program, physicians may initiate the necessary contact with the company and may request medicines for their patients. The company will continue to supply Prozac during the entire duration of the treatment, upon certification by the physician as to the patient's need for the drug and his or her eligibility to receive such medication free of charge.

Recognizing the need to protect its products from outside attacks, Lilly revamped its corporate communications and public affairs function. At the height of the Prozac controversy, Lilly had one director and four associates working on media-related issues. Today, the company has one overseeing director, two new directors with extensive public relations experience, and eight associates with backgrounds in television and journalism, most of whom were recruited from outside the company. Needless to say, the function's budget has doubled over the past four years.

Of even greater importance, Lilly has begun to anticipate possible challenges to new products early on, long before they are introduced into the marketplace. Lilly, for example, has already established relationships with various advocacy support groups representing patients with Alzheimer's disease in anticipation of its drug to treat the disease, which is still in the R & D pipeline. The purpose is not to begin to market Lilly's drug but to cooperate with these groups to help learn more about the nature of the disease and the needs and concerns of sufferers from the disease.

EXHIBIT 1.

Company Name	1993 Sales ($ billions)
A. Top 10 Pharmaceutical Company Rankings by Worldwide Sales	
Merck	6.3
Glaxo Wellcome (proposed merger)	5.8
Bristol-Myers-Squibb	5.0
SmithKline Beecham	4.0
Pfizer	3.9
Ciba-Geigy	3.8
Lilly	3.7
Johnson & Johnson	3.7
Hoecht	3.6
American Home Products/Robbins	3.2
B. Top 10 Ethical Pharmaceutical Company Rankings by U.S. Sales	
Merck	3.7
Glaxo Wellcome (proposed merger)	2.9
Bristol-Myers-Squibb	2.8
Lilly	2.5
American Home Products	2.3
Pfizer	2.3
Smithkline Beecham	2.1
Johnson & Johnson	2.1
Marion Merrell Dow	1.8
Upjohn	1.7

EXHIBIT 2. Recent Mergers and Acquisitions in the Pharmaceutical Industry

Date	Acquiring Company	Target Company	Price ($ billions)	Benefits for Acquiring Company
November 1993	Merck & Co.	Medco Containment Services	6.6	Distribution channel providing influence over prescriptions for 41.5 million patients
May 1994	SmithKline Beecham	Diversified Pharmaceutical Services	2.3	Influence over prescriptions for 14 million patients
August 1994	Sandoz	Gerber Products	3.7	Consumer infant products
October 1994	Roche Holding	Syntex	5.3	Painkillers, anti-inflammatory drugs, research pipeline
November 1994	SmithKline and Bayer	Sterling Winthrop	2.9	OTC products including Bayer aspirin in the U. S.
November 1994	American Home Products	American Cyanamid	9.7	Vaccines, antibiotics, generic drugs, Centrum vitamins, agricultural chemicals
November 1994	Eli Lilly	PCS Health	4.0	Influence over prescriptions for 55 million patients
January 1995	Ciba-Geigy	Chiron	2.1	49.9% stake. Biotech products, research pipeline
Proposed	Glaxo	Wellcome	14.9	Antiviral drug Zovirax, AIDS drug AZT
In Negotiations	Hoechst	Marion Merrell	—	Cardizem heart drug, Seldane allergy drug, generic drugs

SOURCE: ElyseTanouye and George Anders. "Drug industry takeovers mean more cost-cutting, less research spending." *Wall Street Journal*, Feb. 1, 1995, p. B1.

EXHIBIT 3. Eli Lilly and Company: Financial Performance

	1990	1991	1992	1993	1994
Return on Sales (%)	24.5	25.7	17.0 *	8.9 *	20.7
Return on Equity (%)	31.2	31.2	14.4 *	10.2 *	25.9
Return on Assets (%)	17.5	17.2	8.3 *	5.2 *	11.8
Number of Employees	23,200	23,600	24,500	24,900	24,900
Net Sales/Employee (000)	180.1	192.1	202.6	208.8	229.4
Net Income/Employee (000)	48.6	55.7	28.9	19.3	51.7
Earnings per Share	3.54	3.99	2.86 *	1.58 *	4.10

	1990	1991	1992	1993	1994
Income beforeTaxes					
(worldwide in millions)	1418.1	1626.3	1193.5 *	662.8 *	1698.6
(in U.S. as a % of worldwide figures)	70.8	69.1	64.4	67.0	62.8
(in Japan, Europe, and Middle East as a % of worldwide figures)	23.8	25.5	28.2	23.8	32.6
(in other areas as a % of worldwide figures)	5.4	5.4	7.6	11.2	6.1

* Reflects impact of restructuring, special charges, and accounting changes.

SOURCE: Eli Lilly and Company 1994 Annual Report to Shareholders.

EXHIBIT 4. Eli Lilly and Company: Net Sales and Revenue Growth; R&D Expenditures

	1990	1991	1992	1993	1994
Worldwide Net Sales (net of transfer sales)	4179.0	4533.4	4963.1	5198.5	5711.6
U. S. (%)	63.9 *	63.3 *	59.8	59.7	57.5
Overseas (%)	36.1 *	36.7 *	40.2	40.3	42.5
	——	——	——	——	——
	100	100	100	100	100
(As a percentage of overseas sales)					
Japan, Europe, and Middle East	76.8*	76.5*	74.8	72.8	72.6
Others	23.2*	23.5*	25.2	27.2	27.4
Product/Category Sales (%)					
Anti-Infectives	30.9*	30.1*	35.0	33.3	28.6
Gastrointestinal	na	na	6.2	7.6	8.5
Central Nervous System	19.4*	19.4*	26.0	26.8	32.2
Diabetic Care	10.68*	10.2*	12.9	13.2	13.6
Animal Health	6.8*	6.8*	8.6	8.5	8.1
All other	12.8*	12.7*	11.3	10.6	9.0
R&D Expenses (in millions)	549.4	590.5	731.0	755.0	838.7
R&D Expenses (as a percentage of sales)	13.2	13.0	14.7	14.5	14.7

*Estimated percentages based on selected data from previous annual reports. The 1994 annual report does not include breakdowns for years prior to 1992.

SOURCE: Eli Lilly and Company 1994 Annual Report to Shareholders.

GUESTS:

Leanne Westover, Husband Committed Suicide while Taking the Drug Prozac

Hon. Leonard Finz, Former New York State Supreme Court Judge

Jacquie Miller, Shot Four Times by a Worker Who Was Taking Prozac

Bonnie Leitsch, Attempted Suicide while on Prozac

Brenda Hargis, Had Suicidal and Homicidal Thoughts while Taking Prozac

Dennis H. Clarke, Citizens' Commission on Human Rights

PHIL DONAHUE: You've heard about the wonder drug Prozac? It was on the cover of *Newsweek* magazine. I want you to meet the people who had their lives changed or who lost loved ones because they took Prozac. They're blaming Prozac for the tragedies in their own lives.

Leanne Westover is the widow of Del Shannon, the rock star. Here is a young man who hit it big and then was coming back with a fabulous new chapter of his career when he killed himself. He did so while taking Prozac for depression.

Jacquie Miller is one of the victims of Joseph Wesbecker. He's the mass murder who went on a rampage in Louisville, Kentucky, in late 1989 . . . He shot 20 people, killing 8. He shot Jacquie Miller four times and she survived.

Bonnie Leitsch joins us. She attempted suicide while taking Prozac and was revived in the hospital emergency room.

Also with us is Brenda Hargis, who was taking Prozac to help her lose weight when she began fantasizing and actually planning the murder of her husband and children as well as her own suicide.

Eli Lilly, the giant pharmaceutical company, makes Prozac and they are not at all thrilled with this program. You should also know that Prozac is approved for prescription use in the United States and is a gigantic hit. Millions of people who are depressed are taking Prozac and it helps. Steps forward these people to say if you or someone you love is taking Prozac, you'd better keep an eye on them . . .

Ms. MILLER: (describing how she was shot four times by Joseph Webecker at Standard Gravure): What had happened was, when I went out into the hall to see what the commotion was, I had to turn, and when I turned I was eye-level with a rifle. And I just stopped and I looked up into the face of who was holding the rifle. I didn't know who he was. And as soon as I looked into his face, my first instinct was "Oh, my God, I'm going to die," because this man was totally devoid of any—any human element, any human soul . . . . He was just gone. There wasn't anything there and I knew he wanted me dead. I knew this. So I ran to go back into my office to get my gun that I had on me that day to try to stop him . . . . I stopped to help someone who had already been shot. I wanted to make sure she got back into her office because I knew if he got to her first before I could get to my gun, he'd kill her, because he had already shot her before. So it took time away from me getting to my gun, so he just basically got to me before I could get to him.

DONAHUE: You had a bullet pass through your entire body.

Ms. MILLER: Yeah. Yeah. Well, two, technically. The first one went through my chest, totally through my chest . . . .

DONAHUE: And tell me what you think you know about Mr. Wesbecker and Prozac.

Ms. MILLER: Well, I know that except for a span 10 years ago, where he had once before tried to commit suicide, he had never had any violent tendencies except for that one spell. He had never tried to hurt anyone else. Everyone who knew him, knew him to just be your average nice Joe.

DONAHUE: He was under psychiatric care at the time of the incident, isn't that so?

Ms. MILLER: Yes . . . .

Ms. LEITSCH (describing her role as national director of the Prozac Survivor Support Group and her personal experience with Prozac): As the national director of the Prozac Survivor Support Group, in little old Louisville, Kentucky, I have received over 300 phone calls with adverse side effects. And we're not talking about skin rashes, as Lilly would have you to believe. We are talking about mothers who think about killing their children. We're talking 13-year-old children throwing themselves through plate glass windows. We are talking 16-year-old girls trying to commit suicide, nice little ladies working in churches who take money from the funds to pay for their Prozac . . . .

DONAHUE: Yeah. Tell me about your—tell me—do you remember what you felt in your head.

Ms. LEITSCH: Well, Prozac is so overwhelming, you would not believe it. Your mind runs like a freight train. It constantly goes. There is—the first six weeks I was on this drug, everything goes through your mind. Like if you walk through a door, you don't just walk through a door. Everything is animated. You see every thought, every move of the door frame. Constantly, there's thoughts in your mind . . . You cannot sleep. You cannot rest. You cannot sit down. I had akathisia with Prozac . That's pacing back and forth, not being able to sit down, not being able to sleep . . .

DONAHUE: Well, let me just get this in . . . Fluoxetine is the pharmaceutical name for Prozac. More that three million people have taken it. *The Wall Street Journal* tells us that Prozac made about $700 million last year and for Eli Lilly, the gross numbers will probably be $1 billion this year. This is big business. I say again, to the protest of some of our guests, that millions and millions of people are taking Prozac without side effect and without the ensuing hallucinatory, self-destructive, overwhelming energies reported by our guests today . . .

DENNIS H. CLARKE: There's some very important points here that shouldn't be gone by. . . . There is a tremendous problem with this drug . . . in that people are killing themselves and making it appear to be accidents. They're running head-on into other individuals with their cars. They're running into bridge abutments and so on. And it appears to be accidents because the drug is producing in these people an obsessive violent need to kill and to be killed.

DONAHUE: Yes, in some—it is reported in the medical literature and the evidence has been presented to the *New England Journal of Medicine* in a letter to the journal from physicians—Mr. Clarke: And in an article.

DONAHUE:—who are following this.

Mr. CLARKE: As much as 7 percent of the people developing obsessive, violent, suicidal preoccupation.

DONAHUE: Right. Now, in the absence of Eli Lilly, who declined the invitation to be on our program, they have the good fortune of having me as their defender. Well, it's their fault. They didn't show. One more time—millions of people are taking this drug around the world.

Mr. CLARKE: Or have taken it.

DONAHUE: Violent tendencies and self-destructive imaginings have been reported in a certain small percentage of patients. These folks want you to know that the number isn't so small. Lilly says it is. And at the very least, the public health group, the Ralph Nader-founded organization in Washington, has already released its own report on this saying that at the least, the warnings on the package should now be bolder and more specific. It should be noted that this—the Public Health Research Group did not call for its removal. One of the good things about Prozac apparently is that it has a good side effect profile, which is a fancy way of saying it has very few side effects.

Mr. CLARKE: But that's absolutely not true, though . . . the side effects profile for Prozac, by the way, is horrendous. This is a drug which frequently causes bronchitis in individuals, lung infection, infrequently but not rarely causes a type of pneumonia which can be fatal, It causes high blood pressure, low blood pressure. It causes impotence and a whole catalogue of very serious problems. . . .

DONAHUE: . . . Here's what Lilly—here's the statement Lilly put together for us. Now—hey, trying to be fair here. "Many patients feel that Prozac is a wonderful, life-saving medicine and its use has improved the quality of their lives. Prozac is widely accepted by regulatory agencies and physicians in more that 45 countries as a safe and effective treatment for depression. Depression is a terrible disease that carries a high risk of suicide. Medical science has yet to discover a way to completely prevent the fact that one in six patients will commit suicide. Twenty-five thousand patients participated in Prozac clinical trials and it has been used by more than three million people world-wide. In an evaluation of more that 3,000 clinical trial patients with depression, serious suicidal thoughts occurred less often in people receiving Prozac than in people using other treatments. Clearly the weight of medical opinion throughout the world supports the conclusion that Prozac does not cause suicide.". . .

Mr. FINZ: Phil, I'd like to swing to the Wesbecker case for the moment. Joseph Wesbecker—incidentally, we represent the estate. We also represent 10 of the victims, several of whom were killed, others of whom were maimed, similar to Jacquie Miller over here . . . . The brief point is that he was on Prozac for one month. During this one-month period of time, there was a different person who emerged. Here was a person who became an overnight killer. He would stare at things with whites in his eyes. In fact, his own psychiatrist just two and a half days before the killing, said, "I'm going to take you off Prozac. You have deteriorated before my eyes.

DONAHUE: You have his notes, don't you?

Mr. FINZ: Absolutely.

DONAHUE: Here's what the notes say, notes made by Joseph Wesbecker's doctor two days before the murder rampage in Louisville . . . "Patient sees to have deteriorated. Tangential thought. Weeping in session. Increased level of agitation and anger. Question—from Prozac? Because of deterioration," the psychiatrist wrote, "I encouraged patient to go into the hospital for stabilization, but he refused. Plan: discontinue Prozac, which may be the cause. Return to clinic in two weeks."

Mr. CLARKE: And he let him walk out and three days later, he walked into history as one of the most offensive mass murderers of this century. And this is a man who in his entire life had never struck his children, never struck his wife, had no history of violence and never had an argument on the job in 32 years." . . .

DONAHUE: I should remind this audience that Eli Lilly, the one taking the heat because they are the prescribed—they have the patent on Prozac, alleges, perhaps not frontally but out loud, that much of the criticism coming against Prozac is originated by the Church of Scientology. We should say that Mr. Clarke, I believe you are a member of the Church of Scientology.

Mr. CLARKE: That's correct.

DONAHUE: And when last I looked, that was legal to be a member of the Church of Scientology.

Mr. CLARKE: That's correct. Phil, I thank God every day that there's an organization big enough and strong enough to take on Eli Lilly.

DONAHUE: All right. I just want to get it all in here. Does the Church of Scientology—it's not— does it permit surgery, blood transfusions and other mainstream medical treatment?

Mr. CLARKE: Absolutely. Normal—just—

DONAHUE: Yeah.

Mr. CLARKE: The point here is that Eli Lilly is not here because Eli Lilly knows that anything they say can and will be used against them in the court of law because they've got another killer drug on the market.

EXHIBIT 6. Transcript Excerpts from CBS's "60 Minutes"—October 27, 1991

PEOPLE INTERVIEWED:

Maria Romero, Suffered from depression for 10 years until helped by Prozac

Bonnie Leitsch, Attempted suicide while on Prozac

Dennis H. Clarke, Citizens Commission on Human Rights

Dr. Paul Riley, Medical Director at the Saint Vincent stress center in Indianapolis

Dr. Richard Greathouse, the coroner who investigated Wesbecker's death

Rhonda Hala, claims she became violent towards her doctor and herself after taking Prozac

Donna Alcorn, claims she became homicidal and suicidal after taking Prozac

Hana Whitfield, ex-Scientologist who used to be L. Ron Hubbard's assistant

Martin Teicher, Harvard University Psychiatrist

Lesley Stahl, co-host: If you suffer from depression, chances are someone has recommended that you take Prozac, an antidepressant that the medical establishment says is safe and effective. But the Church of Scientology says it isn't. Prozac, they say, causes a violent need to kill and be killed, and Scientologists are on a crusade to have it banned. . . . For the past year, former Prozac users have been going on the talk-show circuit to warn people that Prozac is a killer drug.

Ms. HALA: I went from somebody who was never depressed to a person who became violent toward my doctor, attacked him three times physically, attempted suicide six times and slashed my body over 150 times.

STAHL: These stories scare Prozac users; they infuriate psychiatrists.

Dr. RILEY: If I were depressed, it would be the first drug that I would go to . . . without any fear . . . .

STAHL: We talked to a lot of psychiatrists, and every one of them said that Prozac, when carefully monitored by a physician, is a safe drug. They all complain that a smear campaign against Prozac is being orchestrated by a religious cult and that some of their patients are afraid to take the drug and others already on Prozac are taking themselves off.

Dr. RILEY: I cannot use this medication when I should be using this medication because a group of eccentric people say it's bad and because they can influence all of television.

STAHL: The driving force behind the negative publicity, the Church of Scientology, which has been "waging war"—those are its own words—against psychiatry and psychiatric drugs for more than 20 years. The Scientologists are fighting Prozac through a group they set up, the Citizens Commission on Human Rights.

Mr. CLARKE: The drug is producing in these people an obsessive, violent need to kill and be killed. . . . Our small organization has now documented over 130 violent deaths associated with the use of Prozac.

STAHL: Dennis Clarke is neither a scientist nor a doctor. He calls himself an investigative reporter. No psychiatrist, no medical organization that we know of has agreed with him and other Scientologists about Prozac. And when Clarke's group filed a petition with the Food and Drug Administration to have Prozac banned, the FDA said, 'There is no solid evidence that the drug causes violent behavior.' Clarke's response? He attacked the FDA at a news conference . . . . To try to prove that Prozac is a killer drug, the Scientologists almost always point to the massacre that took place at the Standard Gravure Printing plant . . . The Scientologists claim that Wesbecker was a non-violent man that Prozac turned psychotic. But Dr., Richard Greathouse, the coroner who investigated Wesbecker's death, says he was mentally ill years before he ever took Prozac.

Dr. GREATHOUSE: He had violent thoughts towards the Standard Gravure Company for—and blamed them for many of his problems . . .

STAHL: Before Prozac?

Dr. GREATHOUSE: Yes.

STAHL: Before he went on Prozac?

Dr. GREATHOUSE: Long before he went on Prozac he wanted to destroy the place.

STAHL: In 1984, five years before he took Prozac, Wesbecker's medical records show that he had this conversation with a doctor. "Have you ever felt like harming someone else?" "Yes,"Wesbecker said. "Who?" "My foreman." "When?" "At work." The same medical records show Wesbecker had already attempted suicide 12 to 15 times. The Scientologists dismiss his history of mental illness. They just keep insisting it was Prozac that made him pull the trigger. But what about the other 100 plus people they claim Prozac made suicidal? We decided to look into same of those cases and what we found were people who, like Wesbecker, had already shown signs of mental instability or suicidal behavior well before they ever went on Prozac. . . . Bonnie Leitsch appears regularly with the Scientologists to denounce Prozac. She claims she had absolutely no history of mental illness until her doctor put her on Prozac as a pick-me-upper. A drug, she says, drove her to attempt suicide.

Ms. LEITSCH: . . . in an instant, I thought, 'Hey, I know a good idea, I'll just kill myself' . . . So I—I thought, 'Well, what am I going to use?' So I found my mother's arthritis medicine and I took a whole handful and—and took her medicine. And I went into the sitting room to sit down to wait to die.

STAHL: Had you ever been depressed?

Ms. LEITSCH: No, I have never—I'm not a depressed person.

STAHL: But this medical report from the hospital where she was admitted after her suicide attempt says, 'Apparently this lady has been seriously depressed for some time.' Had you ever tried to commit suicide before?

Ms. LEITSCH: No, I have not. I have not . . . .

STAHL: . . . . in this medical report from the hospital . . . it says . . . 'She has a history of suicide attempt, approximately 20 years ago, where she took an attempted overdose of over-the-counter medications.'

Ms. LEITSCH: That was not a suicide attempt. I was a 19-year old girl trying to save her marriage and it certainly wasn't a suicide attempt . . . a 19-year old trying to scare the tar out of her husband and that was it . . . .

STAHL: . . . Hana Whitfield, who was a Scientologist for 16 years, says the Citizens Commission is creating . . . smoke as part of its long-standing war against psychiatry and psychiatric drugs. Whitfield, who now takes Prozac, used to be an assistant to L. Ron Hubbard, Scientology's founder. What do the Scientologists believe about psychiatry?

Ms. WHITFIELD: That it is the foremost ill of this world, that it is the foremost group that is bringing about the—the famine, the economic disasters, the political disasters in this world . . .

STAHL: Instead of going to psychiatrists, Scientologists get counseling sessions with a device called an E-Meter, which is supposed to monitor negative thoughts. The money Scientology gets from E-meter sales—the devices cost thousands of dollars—and from the counseling sessions is a major source of income for the church. But psychiatrists call the E-Meter quackery, and that helps make psychiatry Public Enemy No. 1 for the Citizens Commission. Well, what is the Citizens Commission on Human Rights' main mission?

Ms. WHITFIELD: It is to remove psychiatry completely from the world and to put Scientology in its place as the foremost mental health therapy.

STAHL: Clarke blames psychiatrists and the companies that make psychiatric drugs for turning the country into a nation of drug addicts.

Mr. CLARKE: The medical psychiatric pharmaceutical industry has built into this country a hard core of drug addicts like we have never seen in history with all the new drugs. This is drug-induced terrorism built into our country by the medical psychiatric pharmaceutical industry.

STAHL: As part of their case against Prozac, Scientologists cite a report by Harvard psychiatrist Martin Teicher. He claims that six of his patients on Prozac became obsessed with thoughts of suicide, but none of them committed suicide. And in fact, Teicher says he is pro-Prozac and that Scientologists are distorting his report.

Dr. TEICHER: So when they talk about Prozac, they don't tell you that, with careful monitoring, you can use the drug safely and effectively.

STAHL: Do you still prescribe Prozac?

Dr. TEICHER: Yes, I do.

STAHL: Careful monitoring seems to be the key to safe use of Prozac, because let's face it, it is a powerful drug that can produce side effects such as nervousness or insomnia. But we found no scientific evidence that Prozac makes people violent ... The president of the Church of Scientology, Reverend Heber Jetzsch, called us before our story ran to complain that Hana Whitfield, the former Scientologist, was a kidnapper. She denies it. He repeated the charge about the FDA claiming that half the members of the FDA advisory board had a financial interest in the companies that manufacture drugs they're supposed to be investigating.

Ted Koppel: Some of you may recall that last May *Time* magazine did a cover story on the Church of Scientology. To say that the leaders of that church did not like the story would be a case of wretched understatement . . . .

. . . It was during that general period and in that context that we got in touch with the man who now runs the church, David Miscavige, to discuss his appearance on Nightline. The process has taken nine months. Mr. Miscavige tells us that he has never done an interview before. And I think it's also fair to say that he and the men and women who run the Scientology organization are somewhat leery of the media.

The Church of Scientology, for reasons that we will also be presenting, does not generally get a very favorable press. David Miscavige is described in one article as ". . . ruthless, with a volatile temper," in another as being " . . . so paranoid that he keeps plastic wrap over his glass of water." I was pleasantly surprised, then, when Mr. Miscavige first came to my office a few months back. He came alone, without any staff, and we had an amiable, if intense, conversation. I believe he even accepted a cup of coffee without plastic wrap. . . .

KOPPEL: I'd like to begin, Mr. Miscavige, with, I guess, the kind of broad question that perhaps folks at home may be asking themselves right now, but let me be the guinea pig for a moment. See if you can explain to me why I would want to be a Scientologist.

Mr. MISCAVIGE: Because you care about yourself and life itself. Scientology, the word means study of life, study of knowledge, and that's where it is, it takes up all areas of life itself, things that are integral and maxims that are related to life and very existence. Let me give you an example . . . the subject of communication. This is something that major breakthroughs exist in Scientology, being able to communicate in the world around you. And I think everybody would agree that this is an important subject. Well, there's an actual formula for communication which can be understood. You can drill on this formula of communication, and learn to drill, but moreover, take the person who has trouble communicating, has—well, for some reason he can't, anxiety, whatever.

KOPPEL: I'll tell you what. Let's stick with me, okay? So far in life I haven't had a whole lot of trouble communicating. Now see if you can communicate to me what it is that you're going to be able to do for me that makes me a better communicator.

Mr. MISCAVIGE: Well, I don't—in Scientology you don't do anything for somebody else. Scientology is something that requires somebody's active participation . . . .

KOPPEL: I want to participate, I want to be active completely . . . .

Mr. MISCAVIGE: What in your life, Ted—what in your life do you not feel is right, that you would like help?

KOPPEL: I feel perfectly comfortable with my life. I like my job, I'm happy with my family . . . I'm perfectly content, that's why I'm asking you what it is you can do for me?

Mr. MISCAVIGE: Well—well, number one, I would never try to talk you into that Scientology's for you. You see, that's the funny thing about this, as if I'm now going to give a sales pitch to you on Scientology. Believe me, Scientology's valuable enough that it doesn't require any sales pitch . . . . Scientology is there to help the able become more able. The guy who's going around, he's working, he's trying to make it, these people generally have something in their life that they would like to improve and, in any event, if you can increase that person's ability, the one who's chipping in, the one who's able, and bring him up higher, this sphere of influence that he affects in the world around him can be much greater and he can get on and do better.

KOPPEL: Now, Mr. Miscavige, when you and I talked the first time, a few months ago, I said to you I was going to come after you on some of these issues. I am a cynic, by nature . . . . What you have described to me there fits perfectly with the image that I have of Scientology, namely you're interested in folks who are producing. Another way of saying that is you're interested in folks who've got money and who can pay to work their way up the Scientology ladder?

Mr. MISCAVIGE: Well you see, that's where you miss the point, because in fact, you know, this subject of money comes up, but you've got the wrong issue there. The subject of money is, where's it going . . . . the money in Scientology isn't going to me, it's not going to my colleagues. That's a fact. That's a fact. You can call up the IRS and find that fact out. They've audited our records and seen all of that. . . . Our money goes to social causes that we accept . . . . we are the largest social reform group in the world, do far more than any other church. For the last two years we have been voted the community outreach group of the year in Los Angeles . . . . The Senate of California passed a resolution that's for our work with underprivileged children in California. We work on getting drug addicts off drugs. We support Narconon, which is a drug rehabilitation center using the drug rehabilitation technology of L. Ron Hubbard. . . .

KOPPEL: During one of Forrest Sawyer's[1] pieces a moment ago, we heard one of your colleagues talking about psychiatry, right?

Mr. MISCAVIGE: Right.

KOPPEL: You guys are deaf on psychiatry. The criticism that was made was that this is foreign to the United States. He referred to its origin in Nazism and Communism . . . .

Mr. MISCAVIGE: . . . .he point there is this, that those people, the Fascists, the Communists, have used psychiatry to further their ends. That's just a fact. I mean, you want to look at the studies that brought about the Holocaust of the Jews, that the Nazis justified killing the Jews, they were done at the Max Planck Institute of Psychiatry in Leipzig, Germany, and that justified the killing of six million people. If you look at the report even Forrest Sawyer did on mental institutions in Russia, several months ago he did this, you saw that that was a tool of the state . . . . 22 days after *Dianetics: The Modern Science of Mental Health* came out, the attacks from the American Psychiatric Association started. . . . These people absolutely felt that we were cutting across their vested interests, and the lengths with which they have gone to destroy Scientology and Dianetics and L. Ron Hubbard is absolutely mind-boggling. They attempted to do so through the 1950s. First they tried to attack L. Ron Hubbard's credibility, then they recruited the American Medical Association and the Food and Drug Administration, and they then proceeded to infiltrate our organization . . . .

KOPPEL: —may I stop you just for a moment, because you know, when you talk about undermining L. Ron Hubbard's credibility, and again, I have no idea whether that video and the tape that we[2]. . . .when I hear about a man talking about having been taken out to the Van Allen space radiation belt of space ships that were essentially the same thing as the DC-8, I've got to tell you, I mean, if we're talking about this man's credibility, that certainly raises some questions in my mind about his credibility.

Mr. MISCAVIGE: Okay. Well, let me ask you, have you read any books on Dianetics or Scientology?

KOPPEL: I've been reading little else over the last two days. . . .

Mr. MISCAVIGE: . . . That bit that Forrest did there pulled out of context items . . . .

KOPPEL: . . . I'm sure that there are a lot of Scientologists, and I don't want to offend anyone who truly believes this, but there are a lot of people out there who will look at that, you say it was taken out of context. Take a minute, if you would, and see if you can put it into context for us so that it does not sound ridiculous. . . .

Mr. MISCAVIGE: Okay. . . . I want you to take the Catholic Church and take right now and explain to me, to make sense that the Virgin Mary was a virgin, scientifically impossible, unless we're talking about something—Okay . . . if we're talking about artificial insemination, how could that be, if you're talking about going out to heaven . . . .

KOPPEL: . . . you were a Catholic as a child, right?

Mr. MISCAVIGE: Yeah.

KOPPEL: So you know full well that those issues are questions of faith. Are you telling me that what we have heard L. Ron Hubbard say on this broadcast this evening, that they, to Scientologists, are issues of faith?

Mr. MISCAVIGE: No, no. As a matter of fact . . . talk about the Van Allen Belt or whatever is that that forms no part of current Scientology, none whatsoever.

KOPPEL: But what did he mean when he was talking about it?

Mr. MISCAVIGE: Well, you know, quite frankly, this tape here, he's talking about the origins of the universe, and I think you're going to find that in any, any, any religion, and I think you can make the same mockery of it, I think it's offensive that you're doing it here, because I don't think you'd do it somewhere else.

KOPPEL: I'm not mocking it. I'm asking you a question, and you know, you turn around and ask me about Catholicism, I say we're talking about areas of faith.

Mr. MISCAVIGE: Well, it's not even a matter of faith, because Scientology is about you, yourself and what you do. You're bringing up something that isn't part of current Scientology, that isn't something Scientologists study, that is part of some tape taken from, I have no idea, and asking me about it, and asking me to put it in context. That I can't do . . .

Mr. MISCAVIGE: . . . I don't know if you're aware that there was a plan in 1955 in this country, Ted, to repeat what was done in Russia. There was going to be a Siberia, U.S.A. set up on a million acres in Alaska to send mental patients. They were going to lessen the commitment laws, you could basically get into an argument with somebody and be sent up there. This sounds very odd. Nobody's ever heard of it. That's in no small part thanks to the Church of Scientology. I must say, though, that when that bill was killed in Congress, the war was on with psychiatry where they declared war on us. . . .

KOPPEL: Let me just ask you to be specific on that. You are talking about a bill having been brought into Congress for setting aside of a million acres in Alaska—

MR. MISCAVIGE: You got it.

KOPPEL:—for people— . . . to send mental health patients. What was—who was the sponsor of that bill? What was the bill number? . . . .

Mr. MISCAVIGE: Well, I have a copy of it and if you want it I can give it to you.

KOPPEL: . . . what was it about the *Time* magazine story that so upset you?

Mr. MISCAVIGE: Because it wasn't reporting on anything, it was an attempt to cause something. Richard Behar is a hater . . . . That man represents himself as an objective reporter. Here he is on record a full three years before he wrote this article, stating that he felt Scientologists should be kidnapped to change their religion . . . . let's look at this article and let's not fool ourselves. It wasn't an objective piece, it was done at the behest of Eli Lilly. They were upset because of the damage we had caused to their killer drug Prozac. They set up that article, they used their advertising dollar to force it to run . . . . I then later found out— that Eli Lilly ordered a reprint of 750,000 copies of *Time* magazine before it came out, reported in the *Washington Post.* But most importantly, here's what I do have. I put in a call to the people, the advertising firm, who set this up. I called up JWT, J. Walter Thompson, in New York. I spoke to the CEO. He said he would look into it and get back to me. He never did. I called up a man over in England who owns all these advertising and PR conglomerates for Eli Lilly, a man named Martin Sorrell. Ted, I asked him 10 times on the phone to deny that he had set this up on their behalf. He wouldn't do it. . . . We put in a call to Eli Lilly. Their response was, "We can neither confirm nor deny." . . . .

KOPPEL: Why is it necessary, in order to progress [in Scientology], I mean, some of the sums that are charged, and I literally don't have them—it's not something I've tucked away in my memory, but we're talking about, in some instances, to move from one level to the next level, $7,000, $10,000, $15,000, huge sums. Why?

Mr. MISCAVIGE: Yeah, well, okay, number one, we certainly do have a different donation system than other churches, although not all other churches.

KOPPEL: Donation?

Mr. MISCAVIGE: Yeah, absolutely.

KOPPEL: You call it a donation.

Mr. MISCAVIGE: Oh, absolutely, because there's people there who are donating to the church, period.

KOPPEL: I understand, but are there people there who are making progress—I mean, what, again, to get back to the person who doesn't have any money, what does he or she do?

Mr. MISCAVIGE: He trains in the subject of Scientology, and then audits somebody else, and he can be audited by that person, and that's free. Your see, people like to pull out the sexy part, I'd like to point out, Ted. The people that are complaining about it in your introduction, the one girl there that was complaining about it, a girl named Vicki Aznaran, which, by the way, this is a girl who was kicked out for trying to bring criminal charges into the church, something she didn't mention. . . .

KOPPEL: Okay, In the few seconds that we've got left—we've got about 45 seconds left—we've heard a lot from you and I understand there's a lot more to be said, but why is all of this a religion?

Mr. MISCAVIGE: . . . . Why Scientology is a religion? Religion is about the spirit, and Scientology deals with the spirit. We are in the tradition of the much older religions, Buddhism, Hinduism, helping the person as a spiritual being improve himself. That is what religion is about. . . .

KOPPEL: And on that note, David Miscavige, let me thank you. I appreciate very much your joining us.

Mr. MISCAVIGE: Okay. Thank you.

---

[1] Sawyer is a Nightline correspondent whose report on Scientology preceded the Miscavige interview.

[2] Koppel is commenting on a video shown at the beginning of the show in which Hubbard claims to have traveled to Venus, Mars, and a distant radiation belt.

EXHIBIT 8. Serving Our Customers

As we push forward on our strategic journey, we must deepen our collective understanding of certain concepts that are crucial to leadership in a fast changing global marketplace. An important example involves the word "customer," as it pertains to both internal and external relationships.

My dictionary defines customer as "one who purchases goods from another." The customer alone makes her or his buying decision. Moreover, the dictionary illustrates the proper usage of customer with a sentence referring to a "tough customer." This suggests that customers' buying decisions are driven by their priorities—the priorities we naturally consider as customers in our dealings with our plumber, grocer, or auto mechanic.

TRULY CUSTOMER DRIVEN

I believe that we will only succeed in our new global market place if we recognize that the customer is the boss—the party who purchases goods from us. We must satisfy our customers according to their standards—not ours. If we either can't or won't deliver what our customers demand, they'll find someone else who will.

This perspective may seem like common sense. Yet, I believe it represents a major change for the pharmaceutical industry. For decades, drug companies have invested enormous resources in telling their customers *what* they should want—and *why* they should want it. Companies have stressed subjective aspects of customer relationships, like loyalty, rather than objective factors, such as performance measurements.

We must take a 180-degree turn. We must learn to understand what our customers require to meet their goals—and anticipate how we can best use our critical capabilities to supply what our customers need. We must become suppliers of choice whose grasp of our customers' needs through the world is so visionary, so comprehensive that we consistently exceed their expectations for clinically and economically optimized outcomes.

NEW MANDATE

Our ability to succeed in the new global health care marketplace will depend in large measure on how well we understand our relationships with our customers. And this understanding begins with these realities:

We are *not* our customers' equals. We are *not* simply working side by side with our customers in pursuit of common goals that comfortable address both their needs and ours.

We *are* our customers' suppliers. We *serve* our customers. We—and we alone—*are* accountable for anticipating and delivering more health care value to our customers than they expect. We must learn how to address our customers' unmet needs and, while doing so, meet our goals.

Let me hasten to add that this perspective is just as relevant to our internal customers as it is our external customers. We must serve each other with the same standards. As we begin to view ourself as world-class suppliers accountable to our internal customers, we'll develop the kind of preeminent organizational effectiveness that enables us to lead the reinvention of the pharmaceutical industry. We'll be on our way to global outcomes leadership.

Randall L. Tobias
Chairman of the Board and CEO

NOTES

1. Marilyn Chase, "More Are Listening to Prozac to Keep Their Business Edge." *Wall Street Journal* (March 27, 1995), p. B-1.
2. Richard Karel, "Members React to Campaign Discrediting Prozac." *Psychiatric News* (June 7, 1991), p. 1.
3. Nancy Blogett, "Eli Lilly Drug Targeted." *ABA Journal* (November, 1990), pp. 24, 29; Leslie Scanlon, "Reports Show Wesbecker's Mental Slide." *Courier-Journal* (September 25, 1994), pp. 1, 22. The *Courier-Journal* and *Indianapolis Star* also revealed additional information about Wesbecker's mental instability before the shootings. Wesbecker, for example, carried guns to work and threatened to kill his supervisors if he were forced to work on a piece of equipment that he found stressful and mentioned a plan to attach a bomb to a solvent-recovery system on the roof of the printing plant so as to blow up the building.
4. David J. Shaffer, "Eli Lilly Ready to Defend Prozac in Trial." *Indianapolis Star* (September 25, 1994), Section E, p. 1.
5. M. H. Teicher, C. Gold, and J. O. Cole, "Emergence of Intense Suicidal Preoccupation during Fluoxetine Treatment." *American Journal of Psychiatry* (1990), p. 210.
6. Thomas Burton, "Medical Flap: Anti-Depression Drug of Eli Lilly Loses Sales after Attack by Sect." *Wall Street Journal* (April 9, 1991), p. 1.
7. *Ibid.*
8. Gideon Gil, "Campaign to Ban Drug Is Distorting Information." *Courier-Journal* (August 25, 1991), p. 1.
9. Daniel Goleman, "New View of Prozac: It's Good but It's Not a Wonder Drug." *New York Times* (October 19, 1994), p. C11.
10. "FDA Denies Scientology Petition Against Prozac." Talk paper prepared by the press office of the U.S. Food and Drug Administration (August 1, 1991) , p. 1; and, Thomas M. Burton, "Scientologists Fail to Persuade FDA on Prozac." *Wall Street Journal* (August 2, 1991).
11. Richard Behar, "The Thriving Cult of Greed and Power." *Time* (May 6, 1991), p. 32.
12. A compilation of the ads circulated in *USA Today*, together with their captions, dates of appearance, and page numbers follows: June 7, 1991: "What U.S. Drug Company Produced a Drug Named After Adolf Hitler?", p. 11–A; June 10, 1991: "What Magazine Gets It Wrong in 1991?", p. 4A; June 11, 1991: "What U. S. Drug Company Pleaded Guilty to Ten Charges of Concealing Evidence from The FDA?", p. 7A; June 12, 1991: "History of Human Misery," p. 5A; June 13, 1991: Who Controls What Foods and Drugs the Public May Consume?" p. xxx; June 14, 1991: "Who Controls What Gets Printed in *Time* magazine?", p. 7A.; June 17, 1991: "The True Story of Scientology," p. 5A; June 18, 1991 - "The Vital Statistics of Scientology," p. 10A; June 19, 1991: "The Creed of the Church of Scientology," p. 5A.
13. Michael Tackett, "Scientologist Campaign Shakes Drug Firm, Advertising Industry." *Chicago Tribune* (June 30, 1991), p. 20.
14. "Legal Beat: Baker & McKenzie." *Wall Street Journal* (December 19, 1991), p. B4.
15. Paula Span, "The Man Behind the Bitter Pill Debate." *Washington Post* (August 14, 1991), p.C1.
16. Amy Dockser Marcus, "Prozac Firm Fights Drug's Use as Defense." *Wall Street Journal* (April 9, 1991), p. B8.
17. Jan Gehorsam, "Prozac Maker Offers to Pay Legal Costs for Doctors Sued." *Atlantic Constitution* (June 6, 1991), p. C1.
18. LeRoy Hersh, "Prozac: Jumping on the Lilly Pad." *Legal Times* (September 2, 1991), p. 25.
19. Christine Gorman, "Prozac's Worst Enemy." *Time* (October 10, 1994), p. 65.
20. *Ibid.*
21. "Rx Needed for Ailing Pharmaceutical Industry." Standard and Poor's Industry Surveys: Health Care Products and Services (September 9, 1993), vol. 161, no. 36, p. H18.
22. Stephen Moore & Elyse Tanouye, "As Drug Makers Consolidate, Will Glaxo Go Shopping?" *Wall Street Journal* (August 16, 1994), p. B4; and, Susan Pulliam and Elysse Tanouye, "Drug Industry Consolidation May Not Be Over." *Wall Street Journal* (May 4, 1994), p. C1.
23. Eli Lilly and Company, Annual Reports, 1991, 1992.

24. The description of the early history of Eli Lilly is based primarily on E.J. Kahn, Jr., *All in a Century: The First 100 Years of Eli Lilly & Company* (June 1989); and, "Eli Lilly & Company." *The International Directory of Company Histories 1988–1994*, vol. 1, pp. 645–647. Chicago: St. James Press.

25. Information, Eli Lilly and Company, May 1992.

26. Alan M. Sebulsky, "Eli Lilly (LLY): Managing the Transition: Upgrading to Buy." Morgan Stanley (October 21, 1993), p. 2.

27. T. W. Malnight, "Globalization of an Ethnocentric Firm: An Evolutionary Perspective." *Strategic Management Journal* (February 1995), vol. 16, no. 2, pp. 119–141.

28. Eli Lilly, Annual Report.

29. Peter D. Kramer, *Listening to Prozac* (New York: Penguin Books, 1993), pp. 60–64; and, Tracy Thompson," The Wizard of Prozac: Who Is This Man Who Made Me Sane?" *Washington Post* (November 21, 1993), pp. F1, F5.

30. Fran Schumer, "Bye-Bye, Blues." *New York Magazine* (December 18, 1989) pp. 46–53; "The Promise of Prozac." *Newsweek* (March 26, 1990), pp. 38–42; Anastasia Toufexis, "The Personality Pill." *Time* (October 11, 1993), pp. 61–62.

31. Andrew Tobias, "Give Greed Another Chance." *Time* (November 26, 1990), p. 74.

32. Thomas Burton, "The Promise of Prozac." *op. cit.*, p. 1.

33. Robert C. Hodgson, Stephen M. Scala, and Ian C. Sanderson, "Eli Lilly & Co." Boston: Cowen & Co. Newsletter *Perspective* (March 7, 1994), p. 11.

34. "Lilly's Prozac Approved by FDA to Treat OCD." *Wall Street Journal* (March 2, 1994), p. B10; and, Lora McGinley, "Lilly's Prozac is Cleared by FDA to Treat Bulimia." *Wall Street Journal* (April 27, 1994), p. B6.

35. Hodgson, Scala, and Sanderson, *op. cit.*, p. 12.

36. Timothy Egan, "A Washington Town Full of Prozac." *New York Times* (January 30, 1994), p. B6; Geoffrey Cowley, "The Culture of Prozac." *Newsweek* (February 7, 1994), p. 41; Milt Freudenheim, "The Drug Makers Are Listening to Prozac." *New York Times* (Jan. 9, 1994).

37. Mitchell W. Miller, "Listening to Eli Lilly: Prozac Hysteria Has Gone Too Far." *Wall Street Journal* (March 31, 1994), p. B1.

38. *Ibid.*

39. Andrew Blum, "The Meaning of Scientology, According to Church Gospel." *National Law Journal* (June 14, 1993), p. 37.

40. J. Sappell and Robert W. Welkos, "The Scientology Story: The Making of L. Ron Hubbard." *Los Angeles Times* (June 24, 1990), p. 38.

41. "The Creed of the Church of Scientology." *USA Today* (June 19, 1991), p. 5A.

42. *Le Nouvel Observateur* (July 25–August 1, 1990).

43. Robert B. Hershey, Jr., "Scientology Reports Assets of $400 million." *New York Times* (October 22, 1993), p.A12.

44. Laura Bird, "Advertising: Church of Scientology to Launch Campaign to Improve Image." *Wall Street Journal* (October 20, 1993), p. B5.

45. R. Behar, *op. cit.*, p. 32.

46. R. Behar, *op. cit.*, p. 34.

47. Andrew Blum, "Church's Litany of Lawsuits." *National Law Journal* (June 14, 1993), p. 38.

48. Penthouse, 1983.

49. R. Behar, *op. cit.*, p. 35.

50. R. W. Welkos and J. Sappell, "Burglaries and Lies Paved on Path to Prison." *Los Angeles Times* (June 24, 1990), p. 15.

51. *St. Petersburg Times* (Dec. 10, 1988).

52. *Indianapolis Star* (July 5, 1991), "67 Acquitted, 6 Guilty in Scientologist Trial."

53. *Le Nouvel Observateur* (July 25–August 1, 1990).

54. "Hubbard's Image Was Created of Truth, Distorted by Myth." *Los Angeles Times*, p. 13.

55. A. Blum, "Church's Litany of Lawsuit," *op. cit.*, p. 36.

56. Robert Vaughn Young, "Scientology from Inside Out." *The Quill* (November/December, 1993), p. 39.

57. Robert W. Welkos, "Shudder into Silence." *The Quill* (November/December, 1991), p. 38.

58. "Anti-depressants Update." Talk paper prepared by the press office of the U.S. Food and Drug Administration (October 18, 1991), p. 3.

59. John A. Smith, Remarks before the Psycho-pharmacological Drug Advisory Committee, Food and Drug Administration (September, 20, 1991), p. 4.

MANAGING CULTURAL DIVERSITY
AT XEROX

*Going beyond affirmative action
and minimal equal opportunity*

America has often been called a melting pot, a phrase celebrating its immigrant history and reflecting the diverse social origins and identities of its inhabitants. Curiously enough, diversity is a relatively new term as applied to the management of American business enterprises. Rivers of ink have been split analyzing America's social history and the dominance of white anglo-saxon protestant male culture, especially in political and business circles. Following the social activism of the sixties, however, minority and/or nonmainstream subcultures in American society have asserted themselves with new vigor. This change has been complemented on the global scale with the emergence of many newly independent states following World War II. For want of a better name these states came to be called the "Third World" [as well as "the South"] and have assumed growing importance ever since the Bandung Conference of 1956, in which for the first time they began to become organized as a significant world political force. As a result of these changes, a new global business operating environment has been forged from both domestic and global forces.

In the 1990s, mainstream American business leaders have come to recognize that "all those people who are not like us" are not only a permanent force but a growing one. Domestically, the profiles of both the labor force as well as of customers and other stakeholders reflect cultural diversity. Furthermore, as normal day-to-day business dealings become increasingly globalized, business leaders realize that their important foreign constituencies are likewise diverse. Business leaders have come to realize that it is imperative to become "culturally competent."

For all that, business circles are not all that clear whether sociocultural diversity is something to be *valued* or simply a formidable factor to be *managed* (Geber, 1990). The difference is critical. If sociocultural diversity is simply to be managed, business enterprises will simply aim to *accommodate* such forces as they come to have a direct impact upon their business or exercise significant social voice. If such diversity is valued, on the other hand, then management will seek to integrate it into strategic planning and turn it into a source of competitive advantage and a critical success factor.

The Xerox Corporation has become known for taking the latter approach. It is not alone. Significant innovations in this area have been pioneered by companies such as Corning and NYNEX, to name a few (Winterle, 1992).

In what follows we first clarify some of the various meanings attached to the term "diversity" and then present the leading issues for analysis. This is followed by an outline of some of the fundamental demographic trends that describe the sociological phenomenon of diversity and a discussion of some of the management models that have evolved to respond to this new social situation. This background sets the stage for an in-depth analysis of how Xerox corporation approaches the diversity issue.

THE MEANING OF THE TERM "DIVERSITY"

For all its common usage there is no common definition unequivocal agreement regarding what the term diversity really means. In its most general sense diversity refers to those elements in society that are not part of the sociological mainstream. It turns out, however, that "mainstream" is as difficult to pinpoint as "diversity."

Most discussions take social power, privilege, and prestige as the point of departure in differentiating "the mainstream" from "the diverse." Such an approach emphasizes questions such as who holds political office, controls the centers of business power, and is listed in the social register. Historically, the group that held the most power in American society was the male [now villainized] WASP: those of white, anglo-saxon, protestant origin. To oversimplify down the line, the social power, privilege and prestige of whites [of European origin] dominated all other races, Christians [especially protestants] assumed preeminence over all other religious groups, males over females, traditional nuclear family over other forms of family and/or sexual preference. Identification of the "diverse" became focused upon those who (1) were not at the center of institutional power and who were somewhat marginalized, and (2) represented subcultures, such as racial minorities or women.

In a strange twist, diversity also became associated with perceptions of social disability. Not without reason—the "diverse," who were defined as such in terms of gender, race, culture, age, disability, or lifestyle patterns,

were often the targets (or victims) of both individual and social bias. Their career paths were strewn with obstacles to be overcome. Their "diversity" effectively *disabled* their pursuit of happiness and success.

To better appreciate the social obstacles posed by diversity, it is instructive to view the issue of diversity through the prism of social justice. Justice is a complex ethical concept. Two components stand out: (1) rendering to each person what is due him or her, and (2) ensuring the fairness of institutions. Figuring out the normative content of the words "due" and "fairness" is notoriously difficult. No matter how one comes out on the issue, however, two basic dynamics are emphasized (Steidlmeier, 1992, ch. 3). First, **procedural justice**, which raises questions of liberty and self-determination, fair opportunity and access, and due process in conflict resolution. Secondly, **distributive justice** which deals with the fairness of outcomes; i.e., where people end up in society and what they have in the end.

In the diversity debate, both of these elements come into play. It was the historical denial of basic human rights of liberty and social opportunity to certain segments of society that strongly linked the diversity debate to human and civil rights. The diverse have generally been worse off in terms of their command of wealth, social power, and prestige. The reason they were worse off is that they were discriminated against. This perception of unfairness eventually linked the diversity issue to affirmative action and equal employment opportunity.

As a general term, equal employment opportunity [EEO] refers to federal, state, and local laws that prohibit discrimination in any aspect of employment. Federal law is principally based upon Title VII of the Civil Rights Acts of 1964, the Age Discrimination in Employment Act of 1967 and the Americans with Disabilities Act of 1991. The basic principles of EEO are: (1) nondiscriminatory access to jobs, and (2) equal treatment with respect to conditions of employment.

By way of contrast, affirmative action is a contractual obligation imposed upon those companies that do business with the government. It was formally expressed in Executive Order 11246, which was issued by President Lyndon Johnson on September 24, 1965. To gain a contract, companies had to: (1) analyze the composition of their work force and the effect of their human resource policies on minorities, women, and (qualified) disabled individuals; and (2) undertake proactive measures to remedy the "under-representation" of those target groups (where normal representation is defined by the demographic patterns of society at large). The plight of the diverse "minorities" is portrayed as similar to that of players in a poker game who lose against a stacked deck. Those advocating affirmative action state that it is now time to set things right. Opponents cry foul and claim it is like allowing the socially disadvantaged to draw cards, while mainstream players may not.

There is no doubt that discussion of equal opportunity, affirmative action, and diversity have been historically intertwined. It could be a serious mistake, however, to strictly identify the diversity debate with either affirmative action or equal employment opportunity. Approaching diversity as either one emphasized remedial solutions to sociohistorical unfairness and emphasizes *social management* of diversity through public policy choices. That may well be going off in the wrong direction because, in so doing, the insight that diversity is to be *strategically valued* is relegated to the background, if not lost sight of altogether.

ISSUES FOR ANALYSIS

1. What is new about diversity at this juncture of American history, as distinct from the traditional view of America as a melting pot?
2. To what extent is diversity something to be valued rather than something to be managed?
3. In what ways is diversity related to affirmative action programs? Does it make sense to forge such a relationship?

4. In what ways might diversity serve as a basis for a company's competitive advantage? Is it essentially an opportunity or a threat?
5. Is it likely that "market forces" will tend to make diversity a source of competitive advantage?
6. What are the management alternatives to either valuing diversity and/or managing diversity?
7. To what extent is diversity a business issue, rather than a widespread social, educational, or political issue? For example, how diverse are various churches? What is the situation with regard to university administrations and faculties? Is it really the responsibility of business to deal with this social issue?

DEMOGRAPHIC TRENDS UNDERSCORING DIVERSITY

No matter what anyone might think about diversity, it is undeniable that demographic trends are fundamentally altering the sociocultural and political landscape and related opportunities and challenges that define the business operating environment. It is not only the work force that is changing, however. The customer—the strategic focus of total quality, process reengineering, and other management innovations of recent years—is also changing. It is this second point that makes both valuing and managing diversity as a positive asset a fundamental characteristic of competitive advantage.

POPULATION AND LABOR FORCE PROJECTIONS

Due to a combination of natural growth rates and immigration, the adult population (16 and over) of the United States is projected to grow by some 21.6 million people from 1995 to 2005, almost evenly split between men and women. About 39.3% of this increase will be non-Hispanic white (male and female). The 4.6 million non-Hispanic white males will account for 21.4% of the total population increase. (Hispanics in the census are not counted as a race and, alternatively, may also be counted as either white, black or Asian/other.)

Major attention was drawn to the future composition of the work force by the Hudson Institute's report, *Workforce 2000: Work and Workers for the 21st Century* (1987), which estimated that over the 1985-2000 period, only 15% of *net new workers* (new workers added minus those who leave the work force) would be nonimmigrant and non-Hispanic white women. Furthermore, 42% would be nonimmigrant and non-Hispanic white women. Immigrants were projected to swell the labor force by 23% and nonimmigrant nonwhites by 20%. Relying, as they do, on multiple assumptions with respect to new entrants and leavers of the labor force, these projected net changes in labor force composition have been disputed (Fullerton, 1993). Yet no one seems to dispute the general outlines of the trend.

According to the U. S. Department of Labor (1994A, 1994B) the increase in the work force (calculated as those entering minus those leaving) is estimated at 18.1 million over the 1995-2005 period (Table 1). Of these, 2.7 million (or about 14.9%) will be non-Hispanic white males. 33.4% of the new work force in 2005 will be made up of non-Hispanic white women. Overall, non-Hispanic whites will constitute 47.7% of the new 2005 labor force, Blacks, 15.2%, Hispanics, 24.8%, and Asian/other 14.3%. (The figures reflect some double counting between Hispanics and nonwhites).

In the total work force, the share of non-Hispanic white men will decline from 41.2% in 1995 to 38.0% in 2005, down from approximately 47% in 1985. The share of women rises from 45.9% in 1995 to 47.7% in 2005, with non-Hispanic white women at 35.1% and 34.9% respectively. The share of blacks rises slightly from 11.1% to 11.6%, while Hispanics rise from 9.1% to 11.0%, and Asians and other minorities from 4.2% to 5.4%.

In the consumer population, non-Hispanic whites decline from 75.7% to 72.2%, while blacks rise slightly from 11.% to 12.0%, and Hispanics from 9.1% to 11.0%, and Asians and other minorities rise from 4.3% to 5.6%.

Even though a number of companies are making changes, many of occupations in the overall economy are still associated with gender and race, most notably managerial and professional specialties. (See Table 2.)

TABLE 1. Population and Labor Force Projections for Ages 16 and Over, 1995, 2005 (thousands)

Population Group	1995 Population	2005 Population	1995 Labor Force	2005 Labor Force	% Active 95/05
TOTAL	197,256	218,861	132,447	150,516	61.1/68.8
MEN	94,490	105,340	71,591	78,718	75.8/74.7
White	165,988	180,153	61,378	67,645	76.5/77.2
Black	22,695	26,228	7,241	8,355	64.5/66.2
Hispanic	17,955	24,240	7,297	9,628	80.8/79.5
Asian/Other	8,573	12,420	3,072	4,355	66.2/66.6
WOMEN	102,766	113,521	60,856	71,798	59.2/63.2
White	85,807	92,539	50,854	58,840	59.3/63.6
Black	12,471	14,441	7,396	9,040	59.3/62.6
Hispanic	8,919	12,130	4,797	6,953	53.8/57.3
Asian/Other	4,488	6,541	2,605	3,918	58.0/59.9

SOURCE: U. S. Department of Labor, Bureau of Labor Statistics, *The American Work Force–2005,*, Washington, D.C., U. S. Government Printing Office, 1994, Table A1, pp. 122–24; NOTE: Hispanic origin does not denote race.

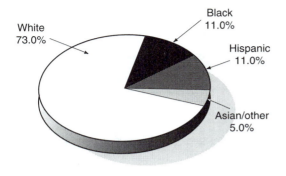

CHART 1. Composition of Labor Force, 2005

DEALING WITH DIVERSITY: LEADING MANAGEMENT MODELS

Business people who value diversity emphasize its contribution to: (1) the company's knowledge base and (2) its vision of its strategic mission, as related to the overall business environment (Herriot and Pemberton, 1995, pp. 1–7). It is argued that a company needs more than "know-how" or the capacity to solve problems in light of past experience. It needs to probe innovatively the validity of its fundamental framework of understanding. The capacity for innovation, it is argued, is to be found in the very diversity of frameworks that workers, customers, and other stakeholders bring to the analysis of the business environment. In management terms, implementation of a diversity program is: (1) a process of organizational learning that evokes a new vision of the operating environment and its opportunities, as well as: (2) flexible frameworks of action. Without an accompanying proactive transformation of management practices, diversity would simply resemble a quota system (Thomas, 1990).

The participation of women in the work force increased from 44.7% in 1973 to 57.9% in 1993. And, whereas women accounted for only about 33% of the managers in 1972/73, by 1993 they were about 50% (U. S. Department of Labor, Bureau of Labor Statistics Report, 1994, pp. 8, 23). At the same time, top management jobs still are very hard for women to break into. Table 3 lists the top fifty companies in terms of appointing women managers.

While women are making some progress in managerial ranks, very few women are to

TABLE 2. Occupational Employment for Selected Demographic Groups, 1983, 1993 (percent)

Occupation	Men		Women		Blacks		Hispanics	
	1983	1993	1983	1993	1983	1993	1983	1993
Executive, administration, managerial	12.8	13.8	7.9	11.8	5.4	7.9	5.7	7.5
Professional specialty	11.7	12.2	14.0	16.5	8.7	9.7	6.0	6.6
Technicians and related support	2.8	3.1	3.3	3.7	2.7	3.2	1.8	2.2
Sales occupations	10.9	11.4	12.8	12.6	6.0	7.8	8.2	9.0
Administrative support, including clerical	5.8	6.1	29.7	26.8	16.8	17.1	15.4	13.7
Service occupations	9.7	10.3	18.9	18.0	24.5	23.5	17.7	9.9
Precision production, craft and repair	19.9	18.8	2.3	2.1	9.0	8.1	14.4	13.2
Operators, fabricators, and laborers	20.8	19.9	9.7	7.6	24.1	20.9	25.0	22.2
Farming, fishing and forestry	5.5	4.3	1.3	0.9	3.0	1.7	5.7	5.8

SOURCE: United States Department of Labor, Bureau of Labor Statistics, 1994. *Report on the American Workforce*, Washington, D.C., U.S. Government Printing Office, p. 24.

TABLE 3. The 50 Leading Large Companies in Percentage of Women Managers

	1992 Total Women Managers	Women As % of All Managers 1992	1982	1992 Rank		1992 Total Women Managers	Women As % of All Managers 1992	1982	1992 Rank
Aetna Life & Casualty	3,484	21.9%	11.4%	16	May Dept. Stores	9,630	59.9%	56.6%	3
Ameritech	1,454	42.3	N.A.	28	McGaw Cellular	460	38.2	N.A.	34
Amer. Int'l Group	954	35.5	23.8	44	McDonald's	3,665	46.0	47.4	19
Amgen	135	33.8	N.A.	50	Microsoft	459	33.9	N.A.	49
AT&T	16,958	45.2	34.2	20	National City Corp.	1,685	51.1	35.6	10
Automatic Data Proc.	932	34.4	29.5	47	NBD Bancorp	1,667	49.8	43.3	13
Banc One	3,078	48.5	45.7	17	Nike	364	37.0	29.3	41
Bank of New York	1,424	38.1	34.0	35	Norwest	1,974	41.7	N.A.	29
BankAmerica	7,455	61.2	55.9	2	Nynex	1,831	40.0	40.0	32
Bankers Trust Co.	1,577	35.4	28.8	45	Paramount	999	43.2	18.5	25
Barnett Banks	154	38.8	N.A.	33	PNC Financial	2,060	44.5	N.A.	22
Bell Atlantic	1,124	50.2	N.A.	21	Reader's Digest Assn.	281	43.0	28.3	26
Bell South	1,189	45.1	N.A.	21	Sara Lee	2,239	36.2	26.8	42
Block (H & R)	512	50.1	68.6	12	Sears Roebuck	14,405	37.4	38.2	38
Capital Cities/ABC	1,259	37.3	21.8	40	Southwestern Bell	4,620	40.9	43.9	31
Chase Manhattan	3,450	42.5	26.2	27	Student Loan Mktg Assn.	401	55.9	23.8	7
Chemical Banking	5,732	44.4	32.9	23	SunTrust Banks	2,722	56.2	N.A.	6
Cigna	3,770	49.6	N.A.	14	Times Mirror	1,288	35.0	N.A.	46
Citicorp	3,256	41.5	35.6	30	Toys R Us	1,888	43.7	33.0	24
Comerica	897	49.0	40.1	15	Transamerica	999	37.3	N.A.	39
Dun & Bradstreet	1,734	37.7	24.9	37	U.S. West	1,416	51.7	N.A.	9
Federal Nat'l Mortgage	205	35.9	25.4	43	U.S. Healthcare	303	56.7	N.A.	4
First Interstate Bankcorp	3,222	56.7	49.8	5	Wachovia	1,503	48.0	31.5	75
First Union	2,329	53.2	28.8	8	Walt Disney	2,168	38.0	22.3	36
Gannett	1,999	34.2	22.6	48	Wells Fargo	2,907	66.1	51.9	1

SOURCE: Sharpe, Rochelle, 1994, "Women Make Strides, but Men Stay Firmly in Top Company Jobs," *Wall Street Journal*, March 29, pp. A1, A10

126

TABLE 4. Women on Corporate Boards of Directors, Top 500 Companies

Women held a total of only 26 board of directors' seats among the top Fortune Industrial 500 and
Service 500 companies last year, according to Catalyst, a New York-based group that studies women's business issues.

Industrial Companies	Number of Female Directors	Service Companies	Number of Female Directors
Chevron Corp.	1	American Telephone & Telegraph	1
E.I. du Pont de Nemours & Co.	2	Cargill Inc.	0
Exxon Corp.	1	Enron Corp.	1
Ford Motor Corp.	1	Fleming Cos. Corp.	0
General Electric Corp.	2	Marriott Corp.	2
General Motors Corp.	2	MCI Communications Corp.	1
International Business Machines	2	McKesson Corp.	1
Mobile Corp.	1	Spring Corp.	1
Philip Morris Cos. Inc.	2	Super Valu Stores Inc.	2
Texaco Inc.	1	Time Warner Inc.	2
Totals	**15**		**11**

Note: The census was for the year ending March 31, 1992. According to Catalyst, there are "no significant changes" in this year's (1992) survey, which is scheduled to be released in November. Source: Catalyst, "1992 Census of Women Directors."

SOURCE: CQ Researcher, "The Glass Ceiling," October 29, 1993, p. 940.

be found in the boardrooms of America's top 500 companies. (See Table 4.)

In the survey cited, only 16% of 200 chief executives thought it either somewhat likely (14%) or very likely (2%) that a women would succeed them in the next decade, although, when asked to project twenty years ahead, the response changed to 63% and 18%, respectively. The major reasons cited for a women CEO not coming along sooner were: (1) women lacked experience (64%); (2) women are in career paths to do not lead the CEO post (50%); (3) women lack broad experience (45%), and (4) they have not built up networks of solid connections and support (31%).

Overall, in the early to mid-1990s, 44% of U. S. corporations surveyed had diversity programs in place and 39% were planning them. At least 36% had diversity training for managers. At the same time, 17% were cutting existing programs, for budget reasons among others, and 26% were planning to do so (Eisman, 1993; citing Hudson Institute/ Towers Perrin as of October 1991). The major challenges to managing diversity are summarized in Table 5. Attitudes and accepted social and corporate cultural values pose the primary problem, leading to an emphasis

TABLE 5. Challenges to Managing Diversity

	1992	1993	1994
Overcoming deep-rooted attitudes/corporate culture	62%	56%	56%
Increased education and training needs	51%	50%	48%
Providing growth opportunities for diverse work force	48%	43%	43%
Communications barriers	50%	38%	37%
Identifying and developing role models/mentors	*	25%	29%
Language barriers	21%	15%	14%
Other	3%	2%	3%

* denotes category not covered in this survey

SOURCE: Olsten, 1994.

upon education and communication as solutions. Diversity is clearly an educational and learning process.

The general actions that management tends to take are summarized in Table 6. Of the various measures tried, training is assuming more importance as the one item that is most effective.

Overall, diversity programs do make a difference. Those companies with explicit programs report a 33% increase in minority managers and a 46% increase in women managers as opposed to 17% and 30%, respectively, of all companies surveyed. Nearly 48% of executives surveyed reported an increasing need for training and education to manage diversity. Of these, 56% explicitly targeted overall attitudes towards diversity as concrete measures to provide career opportunities as areas of major focus.

Women as managers often do better in certain industries (Sharpe, 1994, p. A10; see also Bass and Avolio, 1994). In finance, insurance, and real estate, women account for 41.4% of managers; in services, 38.9% and in retail trade, 38.5. But they clearly lag in wholesale trade (20.9%), manufacturing (15.9%), agriculture (14.5%), construction (10.4%), and mining (9.8%).

THE EXPERIENCE AT XEROX

As of 1992, 26.7% of Xerox corporation managers were women (Sharpe, 1994, p. A10), a rank of 74th among 200 large companies. By 1995, this increased to 32.3%. [See Table 7.] Xerox's diversity program has received a lot of attention because of its underlying philosophy, as expressed in the company's diversity statement:

> At Xerox, we view diversity as something more than a moral imperative—we see it as a business opportunity. For us, diversity goes beyond numbers and targets; it is the acceptance and celebration of people of all ages with globally diverse backgrounds who bring fresh ideas, opinions, perspectives, and borderless creativity that enrich the lives of others. Diversity is a global mosaic, a tapestry filled with exciting colors, shapes, designs and accents.

HISTORICAL BACKGROUND

Xerox (1994; subsequent page numbers refer to this document) sees its commitment to diversity against the backdrop of its corporate culture, as shaped by its founder Joseph C. Wilson. From the beginning "valuing and respecting our people" was one of the company's core values.

Xerox was in line with civil rights legislation of the 1960s. In 1968, then president C. Peter McColough directed managers to "heavily intensify our recruiting of negroes." He added that Xerox would "not add to the misery of the present condition of most negroes. It would not condone the waste of a great natural resource" (p. 1).

TABLE 6. Actions for Managing Diversity (percent of all companies surveyed)

	1992	1993	1994
Corporate communications	55%	41%	43%
Diversity training for managers	24	27	31
Company wide seminars	39	27	28
Translation of materials into English	20	12	16
Courses in English as a Second Language	11	10	14
Career/outreach programs	13	9	10
Restructured benefits for diversity	19	9	10

SOURCE: Olsten, 1994.

Overall, Xerox claims that "it has a long history dating back to the 1960s of aggressively recruiting women and minority candidates to fill positions at all levels of the organization (p. 5). According to the company, "During the 1970s Affirmative Action became the major focus of all staffing strategies and activities (p. 27)." This policy was implemented through education and training of managers to manage a diverse work force. In the 1980s. Xerox created a Corporate Affirmative Action Office and in 1986 it implemented its balanced work force strategy. This strategy aimed to achieve "equitable representation of all employee groups—majority males/females and minority males/females—at all levels, in all functions, in all disciplines, in all divisions." (p. 27).

In 1991, then President Paul Allaire devoted his letter to shareholders to the issue of "embracing diversity" and explained how diversity is an important factor in building a comparative advantage. He spoke of a corporate culture that "celebrates diversity" and argued that corporate culture "must be continually reshaped so that Xerox and Xerox employees alike obtain the full benefits of a workplace in which diversity is cultivated, nurtured and rewarded" (p. 2).

Historically, a number of factors figure in to the development of Xerox's diversity policy. Most important are:

1. the core values imparted by the company's founder
2. civil rights equal opportunity legislation as well as government affirmative action mandates
3. the eventual perception of the strategic and competitive advantages of diversity and a balanced work force

In the end, Xerox's efforts have been lauded by minority magazines such as *Black Enterprise, Hispanic Business, Hispanic,* and *Working Mother.* Furthermore, in a 1993 book, *The 100 Best Companies to Work For in America,* Xerox was named among the top ten companies for women and minorities.

Xerox has gained attention not only for its strategic vision and orientation, but also for the practical management measures it has adopted to make the program a reality. In what follows, we review its management resource planning process and related balanced work force strategy. This is followed by discussion of recruitment, retention, and selection policies, the use of caucus groups, and a variety of personnel measures to ensure both satisfaction and equity in the workplace.

MANAGEMENT RESOURCE PLANNING

Management resources planning (MRP) at Xerox aims to identify suitable management candidates and to lay plans for management succession. The advancement of women and minorities is an integral part of the MRP process (p. 12). Some 25 internal organizations take part in MRP reviews and a member of the corporate office participates in each organization's review. With respect to women and minorities, the review includes a listing of all such personnel at middle management levels and above, with recommendations for their next potential moves. In addition, an overview of female and minority representation for each high-potential category is prepared.

This first step is followed by a joint review conducted by the presidents of the major organizations. At this stage, the scope is broadened to include a review of the corporations' common talent resources and future, cross-organizational moves. To ensure general management talent, the presidents agree on key rotational moves for high-potential candidates in order to ensure that they gain the required cross-functional and cross-organizational experience. In this process, the upward mobility of minority and women candidates is emphasized.

The process is then moved to the corporate level. At this level, the company's "bench strength" for key executive positions is assessed, recommended candidates are reviewed, and plans are set forth to develop future executives some ten years into the future.

Xerox identifies its management candidate pool and also adopts measures to ensure their growth and development. All employees, including managers, are expected to prepare and complete a developmental action plan, which is to be focused on 23 leadership attributes. The leadership attributes emphasize various aspects of strategic leadership, organizational leadership, managing self and others, and one's knowledge base. Formal training is provided through the Xerox Management Institute, which was established in 1991.

THE BALANCED WORK FORCE STRATEGY

Xerox sees its balanced work force strategy, BWF, as a process of **inclusion** which focuses upon all employees and ensures that equitable representation is attained for all employee groups [p. 27ff]. BWF is implemented in three steps (p. 28).

First, there is a goal- and target- setting process. It requires each organization's work force, at all levels and grades, to determine the appropriate level of representation of women and minorities. The second step involves establishing clear diversity goals. Internal data are combined with external employment data. Third, once the goals are set, specific annual "opportunity targets" are established as a path to implementation.

To monitor implementation, quarterly and annual reports are demanded. In addition, some bonuses are affected by the degree to which BWF is implemented. In this process, Xerox recognizes that, while BWF is "a very viable business effort," it must "go beyond gender and race to create the kind of environment where diversity is valued and embraced."

The details of the program are very concrete. An internal memo from Paul Allaire, dated January 6, 1994, spells out how there has been, in fact, a performance gap in BWF strategy implementation. He urges managers to make better use of opportunities (hires, promotions and transfers-in), as well as the management of termination rates, in order to achieve BWF goals (pp. 29–30). Tables 7, 8, and 9 present the overall employee and management profiles for the company as of early 1995.

TABLE 7a. Xerox Personnel Data, 1995. Includes Full-time, Part-time, and Interns

Job Description	Total	No. Black Fem	% Black Fem	No. Asian Fem	% Asian Fem	No. Hisp. Fem	% Hisp. Fem	No. White Fem	% White Fem
Officials and Managers	6055	271	4.5	55	0.9	85	1.4	1162	19.2
Professionals	9035	325	3.6	237	2.6	125	1.4	2053	22.7
Sales	3787	199	5.3	37	1	88	2.3	1172	30.9
Technicians	13002	119	0.9	38	0.3	73	0.6	833	6.4
Office & Clerical	9699	1324	13.7	207	2.1	464	4.8	4428	45.7
Crafts	1040	33	3.2	3	0.3	3	0.3	85	8.2
Plant Operators	3213	305	9.5	91	2.8	165	5.1	484	15.1
Service	105	13	12.4	1	1	3	2.9	28	26.7
Laborers	606	61	10.1	2	0.3	10	1.7	214	35.3
	46542	2650	5.7	671	1.4	1016	2.2	10459	22.5

TABLE 7b. Xerox Personnel Data, 1995. Includes Full-time, Part-time, and Interns

Job Description	Total	No. Black Male	% Black Male	No. Asian Male	% Asian Male	No. Hisp. Male	% Hisp. Male	No. White Male	% White Male
Officials and Managers	6055	469	7.7	192	3.2	185	3.1	3602	60
Professionals	9035	431	4.8	521	5.8	285	3.2	5012	56
Sales	3787	293	7.7	25	0.7	108	2.9	1842	49
Technicians	13002	1275	9.8	532	4.1	1018	7.8	9009	69
Office & Clerical	9699	795	8.2	162	1.7	440	4.5	1824	19
Crafts	1040	54	5.2	12	1.2	19	1.8	821	79
Plant Operators	3213	308	9.6	88	2.7	140	4.4	1593	50
Service	105	13	12	2	1.9	3	2.9	41	39
Laborers	606	48	7.9	4	0.7	13	2.1	249	41
	46542	3686	7.9	1538	3.3	2211	4.8	23993	52

TABLE 8. Xerox Personnel Data, 1995

Xerox Corporation As of 03/13/95
Professional and Management Level Employees—Breakdown by EEO Classification

Professional or Management Level	Total	No. Women	% Women	No. Min.[A]	% Min.	No. Black	% Black	No. Asian	% Asian	No. Hisp.[B]	% Hisp.
Senior Executives	37	4	10.81	5	13.51	3	8.11	1	2.7	1	2.7
Executive Level	222	43	19.37	41	18.47	28	12.61	6	2.7	6	2.7
Middle Management	3865	858	22.2	742	19.2	372	9.62	198	5.12	149	3.86
Line Manager & Professional	5145	1207	23.46	1039	20.1	431	8.38	395	7.68	188	3.65
Professional	5800	2212	38.14	1430	24.66	662	11.41	403	6.95	335	5.78
Technicians	1615	223	14.81	316	19.57	122	7.55	89	5.51	87	5.39
Craft	1040	126	12.12	134	12.88	87	8.37	15	1.44	22	2.12
Customer Service	11328	830	7.33	2824	24.93	1267	11.18	469	4.14	1001	8.84
Auxiliary Sales Representatives	239	140	58.58	78	32.64	45	18.83	11	4.6	21	8.79
Labor Service	711	336	47.26	179	25.18	135	18.99	9	1.27	29	4.08
Office & Clerical	6299	5025	79.77	1908	30.29	1205	19.13	201	3.19	460	7.3
Plant Operators	3213	1061	33.02	1136	35.36	613	19.08	179	5.57	305	9.49
Outside Customer Clerical Service	3086	1251	40.54	1429	46.31	852	27.61	150	4.86	415	13.45
Sales	3787	1509	39.85	773	20.41	492	12.99	62	1.64	196	5.18
Other	18	5	27.78	3	16.67	0	0	2	11.11	0	0
	46405	14830	31.96	12037	25.94	6314	13.61	2190	4.72	3215	6.93

[A] Minority   [B] Hispanic

TABLE 9. Xerox U.S. Representation Data, 1995. Full-Time, Part-Time, and Intern Employees

Job Description	Total	No. Women	% Women	No. Min.[A]	% Min.	No. Black	% Black	No. Asian	% Asian	No. Hisp[b]	% Hisp.
Officials and Managers	6055	1580	26	1291	21	740	12	247	4	270	4
Professionals	9035	2751	30	1970	22	756	8	758	8	410	5
Sales	3787	1509	40	773	20	492	13	62	2	196	5
All Other	27665	9057	33	8056	29	3448	16	1142	4	2351	9
	46542	14897	32	12090	26	6336	14	2209	5	3227	7

[A] Minority   [B] Hispanic

RECRUITMENT, SELECTION, AND RETENTION

The recruitment, retention, and selection process is at the core of Xerox making progress in its BWF strategy. As mentioned, the company sees the issue in strategic terms and also as clearly going beyond the legal mandates of equal employment opportunity as related to civil rights law or affirmative action as related to government regulations.

The process of filling positions varies by operating unit. Once there is a vacancy, however, a unit must secure a "Request for Personnel" form, which functions both as the approval document as well as the specification of the job requirements. The request for personnel is then posted on the Online Job Posting System for the organization. If that does not elicit viable candidates, the search is broadened to other Xerox units, outside advertising, and other forms of internal and external search. External searches make use of the Black Liaison Managers, Hispanic Liaison Managers and Senior Management Women's networks. Xerox has also established a College Experiential Learning Program (XCEL) that brings in students on various work/study and internship assignments. These and other measures, such as networking through minority chapters of professional organizations, are adopted to ensure an inclusive breadth for the search. This recruitment process then feeds into the BWF policy implementation, which governs not only recruitment but also selection and retention of women and minority candidates.

CAUCUSES

The general literature on diversity emphasizes the importance of a mentoring process to nurture the talent and career prospects of women and minorities. Xerox corporate headquarters are located in Rochester, NY. Senior managers were galvanized into action in the aftermath of the violent race riots that tore the city apart in 1963. It was in the late 1960s that the company began to hire the first sizable group of black sales representatives [p. 18], primarily in the San Francisco/Oakland Bay Area. Once hired, these employees encountered many difficulties once they were inside the company. In 1969 they began to meet informally in one another's homes. They called their informal support group BABE, for Bay Area Black Employees. Their focus was to increase the number of Blacks hired by Xerox and also to ensure that they were of top quality.

By 1974, there were some six different Black Caucus groups. The company recognized their role and they continued to expand. By the 1980s, caucus groups emerged for Hispanics, Asians, and women, to be followed by other support groups based upon disability, sexual orientation, and functional expertise. The Xerox experience has spread to other companies.

At present the caucus groups are well organized and both employee-funded and employee-controlled, although they use Xerox facilities in nonworking hours and make use of internal electronic mail. Caucus groups have significant interaction with management at all levels. They sponsor many activities, including workshops, conferences, and mentoring. Xerox's success with caucus groups has been written up as a case by Harvard Business School (Friedman, 1991).

OTHER PERSONNEL PRACTICES

Aggressively affirming diversity represents a strategic choice Xerox has made (p. 1). It is, however, part of a larger set of personnel policies that recognize all of the company's people as a source of competitive advantage. The equation is simple: "To achieve and maintain customer satisfaction and business goals, Xerox must have a highly motivated and satisfied work force" (p. 36). As a result, specific diversity initiatives fold into a broader based set of personnel policies. A wide variety of issues are involved. Most important are the following:

1. implementation of an employee satisfaction measurement system, which surveys ten key factors;
2. antiharassment training and prevention
3. pay equity evaluations
4. work/family benefits, which include life cycle assistance, child care subsidies, child care resource and referral services, elder care, adoption assistance plans, dependent care development fund and salary redirection programs, and employee assistance programs
5. educational assistance
6. flexible benefits plan (called "A Matter of Choice") which customize benefits to individual preferences
7. compliance with government laws and regulations

CONCLUSION

Xerox has set for itself an ambitious set of goals. It recognizes that it has some clear performance gaps (pp. 29–31). Yet the company provides a positive and proactive example of dealing affirmatively with social change in a manner suited to its strategic mission. The company recognizes the close connection between ethical values of fairness and justice and the legitimate social aspirations of various diverse peoples that constitute its own ranks, but also the ranks of its customers worldwide as well as other stakeholders. Perhaps more directly than many other companies, Xerox has forged a linkage between these factors and the fundamental strategies that guide its core businesses.

REFERENCES

Adams, Bob, 1993. "Glass Ceiling." *CO Researcher*, 3, 40 (October 29, 1993), pp. 937–59.

Alster, Judith, Theresa Brothers, and Holly Gallo, eds., *In Diversity Is Strength: Capitalizing on The New Work Force*. New York: The Conference Board, Report No. 994, 1992.

American Management Association, *Survey on Managing Cultural Diversity*, 1993.

Bass, Bernard M., and Bruce J. Avolio. "Shatter the Glass Ceiling: Women Make Better Managers." *Human Resource Management*, 33, 4, (1994) pp. 549–60.

Coates, Joseph F., Jennifer Jarratt, and John B. Mahaffie. *Future Work: Seven Critical Forces Reshaping Work and the Work Force in North America*. San Francisco: Jossey-Bass Publishers, 1990.

Conference Board, The, *Availability of a Quality Work Force*, New York, Report No. 1010.

Conference Board, The, *In Diversity Is Strength: Capitalizing on the New Work Force*. New York, Report No. 994, 1992.

Conference Board, The, *Work Force Diversity: Corporate Challenges, Corporate Responses*. New York, Report No. 1013, 1993.

Conference Board, The, "Diverse Families," *Work-Family Roundtable*. New York, 3, 1, Spring, 1993.

Dobrzynski, Judith H., "Some Action, Little Talk: Companies Embrace Diversity but Are Reluctant to Discuss It." *New York Times* (April 20, 1995), pp. D1, D4.

Eisman, Regina, "True Colors." *Incentive* (August, 1993), pp. 24–28.

Fernandez, John P., *Managing a Diverse Workforce: Regaining the Competitive Advantage*. Lexington, MA: D. C. Heath and Co., Lexington Books, 1991.

Friedman, Raymond A., "The Black Caucus," Harvard Business School cases, 1991.

Fullerton, Howard N., Jr., "Labor Force Changes Exaggerated." *Population Today* (May, 1993), pp. 6–7, 9.

Geber, Beverly, "I Give Up: Is It Valuing Diversity or Managing Diversity?" *Training*, 27, July, 1990.

Henderson, George, *Cultural Diversity in the Workplace: Issues and Strategies*, Westport, CT: Quorum Books, 1994.

Herriot, Peter, and Carole Pemberton, *Competitive Advantage through Diversity: Organizational Learning from Difference*. Thousand Oaks, CA: Sage Publications, 1995.

Holmes, Steven A., "Programs Based on Sex and Race Are under Attack," *New York Times* (March 16, 1995), pp. A1, A22.

Hudson Institute Inc., *Workforce 2000: Work and Workers for the 21st Century, Executive Summary*. Washington, DC: U. S. Government Printing Office, 1987.

Jackson, Susan E., and Eden B. Alvarez, "Working through Diversity As a Strategic Imperative," in *Diversity in the Workplace*. NY: The Guilford Press, pp. 13–29, 1992.

Jamieson, David, and Julie O'Mara, *Managing Workforce 2000: Gaining the Diversity Advantage*. San Francisco: Jossey-Bass Publishers, 1991.

Johnson, Sharon, "The Diversity Challenge," Special Advertising Supplement to the *New York Times*, (May 7, 1995) 16 pp.

Johnson, Arlene A., and Fabian Linden, *Availability of a Quality Work Force*. NY: The Conference Board, Report No. 1010, 1992.

Kilborn, Peter T., "Women and Minorities Still Face 'Glass Ceiling'," *New York Times* (March 16, 1995), p. A22.

Loden, Marilyn, and Judy B. Rosener, *Workforce America! Managing Employee Diversity As a Vital Resource*. NY: Irwin Publishing Co. 1991.

Morrison, Ann B., *The New Leaders: Guidelines on Leadership Diversity in America*. San Francisco: Jossey-Bass Publishers, 1992.

Olsten Corporation, *Workplace Social Issues of the 1990s*. Olsten Forum on Human Resource Issues and Trends, Westbury, NY, 1992.

Olsten Corporation, *Workplace Social Issues*. Olsten Forum on Human Resource Issues and Trends, Westbury, NY, 1994.

Reitman, Valerie, et al. "Women in Business: A Global Report Card," *Wall Street Journal*, (July 26, 1995), pp. B1, B6.

Roosevelt, Thomas R., Jr., "From Affirmative Action to Affirming Diversity," *Harvard Business Review, 90, 2,* (March-April, 1990).

Rosenor, J.B., and M. Loden, *Workforce America: Managing Employee Diversity As a Vital Resource*. Homewood, IL: Business One Irwin, 1991.

Schwartz, Felice N., "Women As a Business Imperative." *Harvard Business Review* (March-April, 1992) pp. 105–13.

Steidlmeier, Paul, *People and Profits: The Ethics of Capitalism*. Englewood Cliffs, NJ: Prentice Hall, 1992.

Thomas R. R., "From Affirmative Action to Affirming Diversity." *Harvard Business Review* (March-April, 1990), pp. 107–17.

Sharpe, Rochelle, "Being Family Friendly Doesn't Mean Promoting Women." *Wall Street Journal*, (February 29, 1994), pp. B1, B5.

Sharpe, Rochelle, "Women Make Strides, but Men Stay Firmly in Top Company Jobs." *Wall Street Journal* (March 29, 1994), pp. A1, A10.

Sharpe, Rochelle, "In Latest Recession Only Blacks Suffered Net Employment Loss," *Wall Street Journal* (September 14, 1993), pp. A1, A12–13.

Shellenberger, Sue, "Felice Schwartz: From the Mommy Track to the Zigzag Track." *Wall Street Journal* (May 3, 1995), p. B1.

United States Department of Labor, Bureau of Labor Statistics, *Working Women: A Chartbook*. Washington, DC: U. S. Government Printing Office, 1991.

United States Department of Labor, Women's Bureau, *Working Women Count! A Report to the Nation*. Washington, DC: U. S. Government Printing Office, 1994.

United States Department of Labor, *Report on the American Workforce*. Washington, DC: U. S. Government Printing Office, 1994.

United States Department of Labor, Bureau of Labor Statistics, *The American Work Force: 1992–2005*. Washington, DC: U.S. Government Printing Office, 1994.

Warner, Fara, "Imperfect Picture: Advertisers Have Long Struggled to Adjust to Women's Changing Roles at Work and Home." *Wall Street Journal* (April 24, 1995), p. R7.

Wiersema, M.F., and K.A. Bautel, "Top Management Team Demography and Corporate Strategic Change." *Academy of Management Journal*, 35, 1 (1992) pp. 91–121.

Winterle, Mary J., *Workforce Diversity: Corporate Challenges, Corporate Responses*, New York: The Conference Board, Report No. 1013, 1992.

Xerox Corporation, *Diversity at Xerox*, (1994).

Xerox Corporation, *Agenda 88, A Journal for Xerox Managers*. (1988)

ENVIRONMENTAL POLICIES AT McDONALD'S

Proactive management yields cost savings, freedom from regulatory burdens, and customer loyalty

In 1994, McDonald's sold nearly $8 billion worth of food and beverages and made a net profit of nearly $1.1 billion. Everything it sold came wrapped in a package or held in a container together with disposable eating utensils, condiment packets, and napkins. Consumers threw much of the packaging away. Critics of the American food system contend that excessive packaging leaves a mountain of garbage for communities to dispose of and leading to an ever greater exploitation of the natural resource environment. Some of the packaging is recyclable at home via curbside programs.

On average, a McDonald's restaurant serves about 2,000 customers a day and generates 238 pounds of waste a day or 0.169 lbs/customer (McDonald's Corporation, 1994b). Interestingly enough, only about 21% of waste is "over the counter" to customers, while 79% of the waste is behind the counter, with about one-third of that being corrugated boxes.

Overall, $1 out of every $12 spent in the food industry in the United States is spent on packaging and the vast majority of that packaging is disposable (USDA, 1991). As shown in Table 1, packaging is a multi-billion dollar business. Coca-Cola leads the list of top spenders on packaging, with over $856 million in 1993. The list is clearly dominated by food and beverage companies. Environmental critics suggest that the social costs of such business practices are both onerous and excessive. They argue for alternative forms of packaging that would both better conserve natural resources and be recyclable, and, if packaging were disposed of, would truly be degradable in terms of enhancing ecological integrity.

ISSUES FOR ANALYSIS

1. What is the responsibility of a business to provide for sound ecological management of its packaging?
2. What is to be said for business "green laws," as enacted in Germany, that hold the producer responsible for the environmental effects of a product during its life cycle?
3. What are the environmental responsibilities of consumers of fast-food products? To what extent should environmental concerns guide their nutritional choices and management of time (convenience)?
4. How are the economic benefits of the fast-food industry to be weighed against environmental costs?
5. What are the boundaries of environmental analysis? Should they be the "packaging life cycle" or the "hamburger life cycle?" For example, if one includes the hamburger as well as its packaging, it would be necessary to calculate the benefits and costs of the conversion of forests to grazing lands, of animal wastes upon water sources as well as the effects upon the ozone layer from gas passed by cattle [Economist, 1993].

TABLE 1. America's Largest Packaged-Goods Vendors by Materials and Containers Expenditures

The top 50 spenders on product packaging

1993 Rank	Company	Packaging Expenditures ($ millions)	1993 Rank	Company	Packaging Expenditures ($ millions)
1	Coca-Cola Co.	856.25	26	Oscar Mayer	114.60
2	PepsiCo Inc.	754.25	27	Pillsbury Co.	112.99
3	Proctor & Gamble Co.	682.72	28	Best Food Inc.	112.40
4	Anheuser-Busch Inc.	484.25	29	Del Monte Foods	109.59
5	Kraft USA	412.50	30	Nestle USA	96.15
6	Campbell Soup Co.	400.31	31	Star-Kist Seafood Co.	90.36
7	Coca-Cola Foods Div.	358.00	32	Phillip Morris Co. Inc.	89.73
8	Kraft General Foods	331.50	33	Thomas J. Lipton Inc.	87.30
9	General Mills	312.26	34	Pet Inc.	86.93
10	Miller Brewing Co.	282.50	35	Continental Baking Co.	86.25
11	Tropicana Products Inc.	269.50	36	Keebler Co.	85.80
12	Kellogg Co.	266.70	37	Ross Laboratories	85.17
13	Nabisco Foods Group	265.73	38	Armour Food Co.	84.20
14	P&G Beverage Div.	261.00	39	Borden Inc.	82.80
15	Dr. Pepper/Seven-Up	236.15	40	Cadbury Beverage Inc.	82.72
16	Quaker Oats Co.	206.93	41	S.C. Johnson & Son Inc.	81.56
17	Ocean Spray Cranberries	195.37	42	Stouffer Foods Corp.	81.53
18	Carnation Groc. Prods.	180.32	43	Hershey Chocolate USA	81.23
19	Frito-Lay Inc.	179.40	44	Colgate-Palmolive	78.16
20	Nestle Beverage Corp.	157.08	45	Green Giant	76.96
21	Adolph Coors Co.	147.15	46	American Home Foods	70.65
22	Ralston Purina Co.	134.48	47	Kal Kan Foods Inc.	69.90
23	Lever Brothers	128.35	48	Stroh Brewery Co.	66.86
24	Hunt-Wesson	119.55	49	R.J. Reynolds Tobacco	65.61
25	Clorox Co.	115.52	50	Royal Crown Co. Inc.	63.98

SOURCE: *Packaging*, January 1994. Packaging estimates are based on Information Resources Inc. dollar sales for the total U.S. market in food outlets. Expenditure is total amount spent on packaging materials and containers, including the value of any self-manufactured containers.

6. To what extent can market forces provide acceptable solutions to environmental problems?

7. How viable are industry/environmental interest group alliances, such as McDonald's and the Environmental Defense Fund, for solving other environmental problems that we face?

8. Many of the environmental measures McDonald's has adopted have proven to be cost effective and profitable. How are environmental issues to be handled when such cost-effective measures are not apparent?

PROFILE OF THE FAST-FOOD INDUSTRY

There are over 160,000 fast-food restaurants in the United States today and over 46 million Americans patronize them every day (*CQ Researcher*, 1991, p. 827). There is nothing new about fast food. In most developing countries, for example, small shops and stalls serving anything from noodles to meat and sweet snacks are commonplace. What is unique about the fast-food phenomenon in the world today is that it is becoming an **industry** and is increasingly dominated by large corporations and franchising agreements. This transformation is driven by many factors, including changes in the workplace, family structures, and choices people make about how to manage their time, as well as economies of scale and massive advertising to grab market share.

As the largest of the fast food giants McDonald's is often the focus of any criticism and policy discussions surrounding the industry. (See Table 2.) The most important

TABLE 2. A Profile of the Leading Fast-Food Giants

Company	Major Product	1993 Sales ($ billion)*	Number of Outlets	Ownership
McDonald's	hamburgers	$7.4	11,803	public
Burger King	hamburgers	$5.3	6,200	Grand Metropolitan
KFC	chicken	$4.0	8,187	Pepsico
Pizza Hut	pizza	$4.3	8,040	Pepsico
Hardee's	hamburgers	$4.0	3,622	Imasco Ltd.
Wendy's	hamburgers	$3.3	3,727	public
Domino's Pizza	pizza	$2.3	5,376	privately held
Taco Bell	Mexican food	$3.2	3,273	Pepsico
Dairy Queen	sweets	$2.2	5,207	Public
Arby's	sandwiches	$1.4 (est.)	2,420	DWG Enterprises
Little Caesar's	pizza	$2.0	3,173	privately held
Subway	sandwiches	$1.1 (est.)	5,380	Doctors Associates Inc.

SOURCE: *CQ Researcher*, 1991, p. 829; *Business Rankings Annual*, 1995, pp. 280–81.

issues it faces are: (1) nutrition and health claims, (2) personnel policies and workplace conditions, (3) discrimination in franchising, and (4) environmental policies.

The competitive dynamics of the fast-food industry are volatile and innovative. The factors that, taken together, add up to success are in a constant state of flux. In a survey conducted by the National Restaurant Association (1993), a number of variables surfaced as principal consumer concerns. The most frequently cited were location, variety, quality, pricing, and cleanliness. At the same time, studies of packaging show that, although consumers do not rank the environmental impact of packaging as the main factor in their purchasing decisions, they do have significant environmental concerns (Baum, 1994). The strategic message is that environmental strategies will evoke a positive consumer response as long as the consumer's principal concerns are not sacrificed.

PROFILE OF MCDONALD'S

As a company, McDonald's has had a long record of success. From 1989 to 1993 it averaged 10.6% growth in net income with a 5.1% increase in sales. (See Table 3.)

In the annual report to shareholders, the chairman and CEO of McDonald's, Michael R. Quinlan, analyzed McDonald's success in the following terms:

> Getting value for your money. Value. It is what's shaping buying behavior—whether you live in London, England; London, Ontario; or New London, Connecticut.
>
> Define it as "what you get for what you pay," and value defines why consumers choose McDonald's for a meal again and again. Wherever you live in the world, getting value for your money is important.
>
> But just as the importance of value has expanded to include more countries, more languages, more cultures and more currencies, so too, has the *definition* of value expanded to include more components.
>
> It used to be that value meant just low prices. Having enough money to pay the bills at the end of the month meant you were value conscious every day throughout the month. Today, low prices are a part of value, but are no longer the entire part. Accordingly, the lau-

TABLE 3. Profile of McDonald's: Five-Year Summary

Year	Sales (000$)	Net Income	EPS
1993	7,408,000	1,083,000	2.91
1992	7,133,000	959,000	2.60
1991	6,695,000	860,000	2.35
1990	6,640,000	802,000	2.20
1989	6,066,000	727,000	1.95
Growth Rate %	5.1	10.4	10.50

rels of victory in the global marketplace are earned by those products and brands that are *adding* value to the buying experience. That is, adding more to the "what you get" side of the equation, while holding the line on "what you pay."

McDonalds' environmental policies must be understood as part of its overall value-added strategy. The management at McDonald's came to recognize that environmental integrity was a significant component of the total value package that the consumer was seeking. They also realized that packaging and waste disposal represented significant cost factors that it would be strategically important to control in terms of delivering a competitively priced quality product to the consumer. In 1993, food and packaging represented costs of $1.7 billion, or roughly 42% of the total costs of company-operated restaurants. (See Table 4.) McDonalds' challenge was to deliver more value to the customer, while not raising prices. The only alternative was to cut costs. Management began to think about what few American corporations ever consider: environmentally sound packing practices could be a money maker. They could cut packaging costs while appealing to customers' environmental values. Enter the Environmental Defense Fund.

THE ENVIRONMENTAL DEFENSE FUND

Since Rachel Carson's publication of *The Silent Spring* in the 1960s, environmental concerns have mushroomed, leading to epoch making legislation to preserve the environmental quality of water, land, and air. Much of the public policy effort has been spearheaded by not-for-profit public interest groups. In the case of McDonald's, the action of the Environmental Defense Fund assumed center stage.

The EDF was founded in 1967 and is a nationally recognized advocacy group. It is known for technical analysis of environmental impacts of policy alternatives.

In 1989 Fred Krupp, EDF's Executive Director wrote Michael Quinlan, McDonald's CEO, and suggested a meeting. McDonald's accepted and a year of discussions followed. On August 1, 1990, EDF and the McDonald's Corporation signed a written accord to work together to develop an environmentally sound policy for McDonald's. (That accord is found in Appendix 1, p. 144.) The accord preserved the independence of each participant, while providing for concrete measures to work upon substantive issues. Administratively, the most important development was the formation of the EDF-McDonald's Solid Waste Task Force. From that point on, things moved quickly. In November 1990, McDonald's decided to abandon its well-known clamshell polystyrene packing and replace it with a paper-based wrap. By April 1991 the Task Force released a report outlining some 42 different initiatives ranging from source reduction and reuse to recycling and composting (*Economist*, 1992). In 1990, McDonald's spent an estimated $53 million on waste hauling and disposal and projected a possible 20% increase for 1991. Reducing the volume of garbage was an economic as well as environmental priority. By April 1993, the Task Force reported that over half of the original initiatives had been completed and another 13 set in motion. By the following year, the original set of projects more than doubled to number 95, of which 55 had been completed (Hemphill, 1994). Both the scope and pace of change has astonished many observers, some of whom still prefer to characterize McDonald's as "McGreed" (*Economist*, 1995). Indeed, in the United Kingdom, McDonald's has been involved in a lawsuit by two environmentalists accusing the company of destroying rainforests as well as causing health problems and abusing workers (Pope, 1995). The pair began their attack some five years ago and McDonald's sued them for libel. Surprisingly, the activists have fought back very convincingly, with the actual trial entering its second year as this is written.

TABLE 4. Annual Income (000$)

Fiscal Year Ending	12/31/93	12/31/92	12/31/91	12/31/90
Net Sales	7,408,100	7,133,300	6,695,000	6,639,600
Cost of Goods	2,115,500	2,037,400	1,934,000	2,974,400
Gross Profit	5,292,600	5,095,900	4,761,000	3,665,200
Sell Gen & Admin Exp	3,370,600	3,298,300	3,196,300	2,164,600
Income Before Tax	1,675,700	1,448,100	1,299,400	1,246,300
Net Income	1,082,500	958,600	859,600	802,300
Outstanding Shares	353,700	363,600	358,700	369,100

	1993	1992	1991
Revenues			
Sales by Company-operated restaurants	5,157.2	5,102.5	4,908.5
Revenues from franchised restaurants	2,250.9	2,030.8	1,786.5
TOTAL REVENUES	7,408.1	7,133.3	6,695.0
Operating Costs and Expenses			
Company-operated restaurants			
Food and packaging	1,735.1	1,688.8	1,627.5
Payroll and other employee benefits	1,291.2	1,281.45	1,259.2
Occupancy and other operating expenses	1,138.3	1,156.3	1,142.4
TOTAL FOR COMPANY RESTAURANTS	4,164.6	4,126.5	4,029.1
Franchised restaurants—occupancy expenses	380.4	348.6	306.5
General, administrative and selling expenses	941.1	860.6	794.7
Other operating (income) expense—net	-62.0	-64.0	-113.8
TOTAL OPERATING COSTS AND EXPENSES	5,424.1	5,271.1	5,016.5
Operating Income	1,984.0	1,861.6	1,678.5
Interest expense—net of capitalized interest			
of $20.0, $19.5 and $26.2	316.1	373.6	391.4
Nonoperating income (expense)—net	7.8	-39.9	12.3
Income Before Provision for Income Taxes	1,675.7	1,448.1	1,299.4
Provision for income taxes	593.2	489.5	439.8
Net Income	1,082.5	958.6	859.6
Net Income per Common Share	2.91	2.60	2.35
Dividends per Common Share	.42	.39	.36

THE ROLE OF PACKAGING FOR MCDONALD'S

McDonald's cannot function without packaging. It is a critical input that is vital to its delivery of services to the customer. McDonald's itself has provided an outline of the strategic elements that enter into its packaging strategies (See Table 5.)

McDonald's packaging policy had to meet simultaneously the three criteria of availability, functionality, and waste reduction. In changing from the polystyrene clamshell to the paper wrapping with a thin polyethylene tissue layer for heat insulation, it was able effectively to meet all three conditions.

TABLE 5. Principal Packaging Considerations in McDonald's Business

Availability

Functionality
  Insulation
  Breathability
  Handling ability
  Appearance

Waste Reduction
  Reduction in materials use
  Reduction in production impacts
  Use of reusable materials
  Use of recyclable materials
  Use of recycled content
  Use of compostable materials

More important in the task of overall waste reduction was to come to a clearer idea of what were the various sources of waste and what was the relative importance of each source. Table 6 presents a summary of McDonalds' findings. On-premises waste averages 138 pounds per restaurant each day. This works out to 0.12 lbs per each customer served. Corrugated boxes are clearly the leader among packing materials, accounting for 34 percent. As will be shown later on, McDonalds' redesigned Big Mac containers

and carry-out bags are made from corrugated boxes. Such policies address the 11 percent waste factor deriving from coated and uncoated papers as well as the 4 percent waste from polystyrene.

McDONALD'S ENVIRONMENTAL POLICIES

Given its criteria for packaging as well as its assessment of the overall factors that generated waste, McDonald's then formulated a more comprehensive environmental policy, which would embrace every aspect of its business. The outlines of this policy are presented in Table 7.

The policy is built upon two cornerstones: natural resource protection and waste management. Implementation of these policies is to be ensured by motivating people in terms of environmental values and practices, on the one hand, and setting procedures of accountability into place, on the other.

The details of each of the four policy sets have been worked out in considerable detail. Table 8 (McDonald's, 1994a, 1994b) provides an overview of the key waste reduction policies. One priority is simply to reduce the

TABLE 6. Summary of McDonald;s On-Premise Waste Characterization Study[1]

% of Grand Total		% of Grand Total	
Uncoated Paper	4%	Corrugated	34%
Coated Paper	7	Putrescibles[2]	34
Polystyrene	4	LDPE	2
Non-McDonald's		HDPE	1
Waste	4	Liquid	2
Miscellaneous	2	Miscellaneous	6
Totals	21		79

GRAND TOTAL:
138 lbs. /per day/per restaurant
0.12 lbs per customer served

Definitions and Examples (examples are not an all-inclusive list):

Over-the-Counter:	Waste in the customer sit-down area and from outside waste receptacles.
Behind-the-Counter:	Waste behind the register counter, including kitchen and storage rooms.
Polystyrene:	Hot cups and lids, cutlery, salad containers.
Miscellaneous OTC:	Condiment packaging.
Corrugated:	Shipping boxes.
Putrescibles:	Food waste from customers, egg shells, coffee grounds, other food scraps.
LDPE:	Low-density polyethylene film wraps and plastic sleeves used as inner packaging in shipping containers.
HDPE:	High-density, polyethylene plastic used mostly for jugs, e.g. syrup jugs.
Liquids:	Excess, nonabsorbed liquids measured during the waste audit.
Misc. BTC:	Durables, equipment, office paper, secondary packaging other than corrugated boxes.

[1] Based on a two-restaurant, one-week-long waste audit performed 11/12–11/18/90 in Denver, CO and Sycamore, IL. Figures have been adjusted to reflect the conversion from sandwich foam to paper wraps.

[2] Most putrescibles and liquids are from behind the counter; the waste characterization study was not able to separately quantify customer organic waste, so all such waste is listed in the behind-the-counter category.

TABLE 7. McDonald's Corporate Environmental Policy

Effectively managing solid waste
> Reduce
> Reuse
> Recycle

Conserving and protecting natural resources
> minimize energy and other resource consumption
> not permit the destruction of rainforests for our beef
>   supply

Encouraging environmental values and practices
> relationship with local communities
> providing educational materials
> partnership with our suppliers

Ensuring accountability procedures
> environmental affairs officer
> seek the counsel of experts
> timely, honest, and forthright communications

TABLE 8. Key Waste Reduction Policies

Reusable Materials

For each packaging item, including shipping packaging, consider the option of substituting a reusable container for a disposable one.
Substitute bulk packaging for single-portion packaging wherever possible.

Recyclable Materials

For all existent materials and all new materials being introduced, seek to consolidate the range of materials used in order to maximize opportunities for recycling.
Seek to design all disposables using materials which can be recycled into high-grade products.
Minimize the use of links, pigments and other additives.
For disposable used for take-out/drive-thru packaging, increase use of materials that are included in municipal collection programs (e.g., curbside collection programs).

Recycled Content

Seek to increase recycled content in all primary and secondary packaging and food service items.
Seek to increase the use of post-consumer materials as part of the recycled content in all primary and secondary packaging and food service items.

Reduction in Materials Use

Strive to eliminate all unnecessary secondary packaging.
Minimize use of materials in all packages and food service items.

Reduction in Production Impacts

Substitute unbleached or non-chlorine bleached paper for bleached paper wherever feasible.
Select plastic resins made from relatively safer chemical feedstocks.
Use materials that are produced utilizing processes that minimize energy use and water consumption.
Ensure that all inks and pigments are of as low environmental concern as possible, and minimize use of such additives.

Compostable Materials

Where viable recycling options do not exist, design paper packaging to be compatible with organic waste composting.
Use only truly compostable materials that decompose completely and safely.

SOURCE: McDonald's 1994, 1994b.

amount of materials used, by eliminating all secondary packaging, for example.

Furthermore, of the material that is used, priority should be given to those materials that are either reusable, recyclable, or compostable. Furthermore, in the production of packaging materials themselves, priority is to be given to: (a) using recycled content in the

production of new materials, as well as to (b) emphasizing production processes that are themselves environmentally friendly.

Not surprisingly, the plastics industry has raised counterarguments stating that foam cups do less damage to the environment than paper cups (Naj, 1991) and that a polystyrene hamburger clamshell uses 30% less energy than paperboard in manufacturing processes that add up to 46% less air pollution and 42% less water pollution (Scarlett, 1991).

RESULTS OF McDONALD'S POLICIES

McDonald's policies cover just about every aspect of its business. To get an idea of the results of its policies we examine the company's efforts in the area of recycling. The breadth of the "McRecycle" Program is outlined in Table 8 with some of the major results detailed in Tables 9 and 10.

Table 9 lists the uses to which McDonald's waste materials that are collected for recycling are put. The company details over 22 applications in the field of construction and remodeling. There are also some 7 applications in the paper products area, as well as over a dozen in the supplies and equipment field.

Table 10 outlines the recycled content now used in McDonalds' own packing. It has increased from 17% in 1990 to over 45% in 1994. Almost all paper that McDonald's uses is in some measure made of recycled materials.

McDONALD'S ENVIRONMENTAL PARTNERSHIPS

In accomplishing all of this, McDonald's has moved far beyond its initial cooperation with the EDF. It has made it a policy to expand its environmental partnerships. (See Table 11).

Overall, McDonald's has been quite successful in achieving both of its goals—to significantly reduce the costs of its packaging, while positioning itself as committed to the

TABLE 9. McRecycle USA

Construction and Remodeling	Supplies and Equipment	Paper Products
Carpeting	Booster seats	Carry-out bags
Ceiling and floor tile	Cloth towels	Carry-out-drink carriers
Concrete curbing	Doors and panels for grills, fryers, etc.	Corrugated boxes
Conference room chairs	Drive-thru audio system	Happy Meal cartons
Construction lumber	(head set, battery pack, battery case)	
	Highchairs	Napkins
Decorative siding	In-store trays	Toilet tissues
Fencing and decking	Interior/exterior signage	Tray liners
Interior table tops	Mop buckets	
Insulation	Mop hands	
Landscape edging	Pallets	
Landscape timbers	Trash can liners	
Menu board frame	Trash recipients	
Office chairs and tables	Utility carts	
Patio blocks		
Patio tables and chairs		
Playland equipment and components		
Playland surfaces		
Restaurant seats		
Roofing materials		
Stepping stones		
Tire stops		
Wallboard		

SOURCE: McDonald's 1994a, 1994b.

Table 10. McDonald's Recycled Packaging 1994

Each McDonald's makes a significant contribution in recycling by using recycled material in packaging.
Each McDonald's averages spending $20,000 per year in recycled packaging.

Item	Total Recycled % Content	Post-Consumer Material %/ Post-Industrial Material %	Primary Source of Raw Material
Big Mac Container	40	15/25	Old Corrugated Boxes
Carry Out Bags	100	50/50	Old Corrugated Boxes
Napkins	100	30/70	Office Paper
4-Hole Drink Trays	100	92/8	Newspapers
Happy Meal Bags	100	65/35	Newspapers
Trayliners	100	10/90	Magazines
Sandwich Wraps	20	0/20	Industrial Scrap
Jumbo Roll Tissue	100	40/60	Office Paper
Toilet Roll Tissue	100	20/80	Office Paper
Roll Towels	100	20/80	Office Paper
Corrugated Boxes	40	20/20	Old Corrugated Boxes

McDonald's has increased recycled content in packaging to an average of 45% (compared to 17% in 1990).
McDonald's U.S. restaurants currently utilize 133,000 tons of recycled packaging per year.

SOURCE: McDonald's 1994a, 1994b

TABLE 11. McDonald's Environmental Partnerships

Smithsonian Institute (1989)
Rain Forest Trayliners
World Wildlife Fund (1989)
Five million ECOLOGY magazines for youth
Keep America Beautiful (1990–91)
Waste Reduction Action Plan: 42 Initiatives to reduce, reuse, recycle/compost McDonald's waste
Global ReLeaf (1991)
Over 9 million trees given to customers
Conservation International (1991)
"Discover the Rainforest" Happy Meal booklets
Buy Recycled Business Alliance (1992–today)
Founding member of this National Recycling Coalition group dedicated to increasing the purchase of recycled products
Student Conservation Assn. (1993–today)
Created McDonald's All Star Green Teens: high school student environmental recognition and educational program
U.S. Environmental Protection Agency's Green Lights Partner (1993–today)
Lighting energy conservation program
Environmental Defense Fund (1993–today)
Part of the Paper Task Force, with Time, Prudential, NationsBank, Duke University and Johnson & Johnson, working together to buy more environmentally preferable paper products
Conservation International/Clemson University (1993–today)
Restoring land in Central America's La Amistad Biosphere Reserve
US EPA'S WasteWi$e (1994–today)
Participating in voluntary waste reduction program
National Audubon Society (1994)
April 1994 "Earth Days" Happy Meal
National Audubon Society/The Composting Council (1994)
Participating in "Food for the Earth," a composting initiative of the food service industry

SOURCE: McDonald's 1994a, 1994b

integrity of the environment. The company was a leader in what has come to be the new environmental wisdom of enlightened corporations: "being green is good business" (Biddle, 1993; Clark, 1991; Denison et al, 1990; Kirkpatrick, 1990; Lee, 1987; Stuller, 1990).

For all that, when one looks across industries, it is not all that easy being green (Walley and Whitehead, 1994). Historically, in the United States business has always tended to chafe at environmental legislation, preferring market solutions. At the same time, many environmentalists assert that regulation will serve as a stimulus to innovate in the marketplace. Perhaps no set of environmental laws has received more attention in recent times than the stringent laws put forth by the Federal Republic of Germany.

AN ALTERNATIVE APPROACH: GERMANY'S LAWS HOLDING THE PRODUCER RESPONSIBLE

One of the most difficult issues to resolve in the environmental policy debate is determining who is to be held responsible for maintaining environmental integrity. In the case of fast food, many players are involved—the producers of packaging materials, the food outlets, and the consumers. In the early 1990s, Germany took a surprising approach in holding the producer of the product responsible. This policy has received intense scrutiny from business and political circles (Boerner and Chilton, 1993; Burt, 1993; Cairncross, 1992; *Der Spiegel*, 1993; Lewis, 1992; Ludwig and Jones, 1992; Shea 1992, Stern, 1993; Weiner and Tostman, 1991).

The discussion is complex. Obviously, in industries where companies can fairly easily pass on costs to consumers, a company will not experience competitive difficulties in complying with such regulations. When that is not the case, or when industry practices are segmented, then a company may find itself to be at a competitive disadvantage to comply. It is too soon to assess the competitive effects of the green laws upon German industry and employment. Short term, they could be quite serious. Longer term, one might expect technological and market innovations to adjust to legislation. Key factors, therefore, are both the timing and conditions that form part of the legislation. Environmentally innovative firms can well prosper. Laggards will be at a competitive disadvantage and may be forced to relocate.

To solve such a problem as it affects clean air, the United States adopted the policy of "pollution permits" (Hahn and Hester,

1989). These grant companies tradable allowances with respect to pollution. More advanced companies can sell their excess allowances to companies that lag behind. While there is a cost involved for the latter, it is more manageable in the competitive terms.

The McDonald's example provides an interesting view into how a company has creatively managed environmental concerns in light of its fundamental strategic mission. It remains to be seen whether this is a model that other companies and other industries will follow.

Appendix 1.

AGREEMENT ON A JOINT MCDONALD'S/ENVIRONMENTAL DEFENSE FUND TASK FORCE TO ADDRESS MCDONALD'S SOLID WASTE ISSUES

1. The Environmental Defense Fund (EDF) and McDonald's Corporation agree to establish a joint task force to investigate and prepare a report on options for reducing, reusing, recycling, and composting the wastes generated through McDonald's operations
2. The options report will serve as one element in a full assessment by McDonald's of the environmental impacts of its operations
    a. The report will characterize the wastes produced by McDonald's stores and operations, and explain recycling and waste reduction actions already taken or planned by McDonald's
    b. The core of the report will outline a broad range of additional operations for changes in operations and materials use that could reduce the environmental impacts of wastes generated by the company, its franchises and its associated operations (See the following Annex #1 for a list of potential options).
    c. These options will be evaluated using criteria to be developed at the outset by the task force.
    d. Where strictly proprietary business statistics, information or processes are involved, McDonald's and EDF will reach prior agreement on access to, protection of and any future disclosure restrictions pertaining to such information.
3. The task force will be composed of four EDF staff and four McDonald's staff.
4. The task force will require priority efforts and time commitments by both parties and will try to complete the options report within approximately six months.
5. Where possible, information needs of the task force will be met using expertise within or accessible to EDF and McDonald's
    a. Where outside expertise is needed, the task force will jointly agree upon and direct the work of expert consultants.
    b. The costs of hiring outside experts or other substantial information-gathering activities as jointly agreed upon will be borne by McDonald's.
6. McDonald's and the Environmental Defense Fund will independently pay for expenses incurred by their participation in the task force. Meeting locations will be chosen to result in roughly equal travel expenses among the two parties.
7. If McDonald's and EDT significantly disagree on data interpretation or particular conclusions drawn in the options report, the report may contain separate statements written by each party.

8. In the event that little or no agreement can be reached on the contents of the report or the direction of the task force's research, either party will have the right to terminate the project midstream.
9. As the work of the task force proceeds, both parties will pursue their business and advocacy activities on environmental issues as they see fit.
10. Once reviewed and agreed upon, the options paper will be jointly released by McDonald's and EDF. Following publication of the report, McDonald's and EDF will be free to state and pursue their own views and perspectives with respect to the report and task force. EDF and McDonald's will name their official public and task force spokespersons on all matters covered by this agreement.
11. McDonald's shall not refer to EDF's work with McDonald's in this joint task force, other than through the simple dissemination of the final report, in any marketing, advertising, or point of sale material without the written approval of EDF.
12. Following either the conclusion or termination of the task force both parties will be free to use the report and other information gathered during the effort in their own subsequent work, with each party maintaining exclusive control over such work, unless restrictions are mutually agreed upon prior to such time; except that the final report shall not be disseminated by either party other than in its full form without the agreement of both parties.

_____

For Environmental Defense Fund
Date: _____, 1990

_____

For McDonald's
Date: _____, 1990

SOLID WASTE REDUCTION AND MANAGEMENT OPTIONS FOR CONSIDERATION BY MCDONALD'S/EDF TASK FORCE

1. Redesign of packaging and shipping materials to use less material and use materials that are more recyclable or compostable.
2. Use of materials that generate fewer environmental impacts in their production and disposal (e.g., unbleached paper).
3. Greater recycling and composting of the total solid waste output from stores, including, for example, in-vessel composting of food wastes and food-contaminated paper.
4. Evaluation of potential for use of reusable items in stores, like cups and utensils.
5. Greater use of packaging and shipping materials (e.g., molded pulp products) that contain recycled content.
6. Steps to reduce litter problems associated with McDonald's packaging.
7. Customer and community educational efforts to promote recycling at McDonald's at home, and at work, tapping McDonald's large daily contact with individuals and its tremendous popular appeal, especially among children and young people.
8. Given the large quantities of materials that McDonald's uses, the potential for the company to use its purchasing power to help develop markets for recycled materials. As well as purchasing recycled materials, McDonald's might assist in promoting an industrial infrastructure (e.g., paper recycling mills) to supply the company and its affiliates that could utilize recyclable materials produced at McDonald's stores.

REFERENCES

Baum, Chris "10th Annual Packaging Consumer Survey 1994." *Packaging* (August, 1994), pp. 40–43.

Biddle, David. "Recycling for Profit: The New Green Business Frontier." *Harvard Business Review* (November-December, 1993) pp. 145–56.

Boerner, Christopher, and Kenneth Chilton. "Recycling's Demand Side: Lessons from Germany's "Green Dot." Center for the Study of American Business, Washington University, St. Louis, MO, 1993.

Burt, Justine, and Patricia Dillon. "What the U.S. Can Learn from Germany's Packaging Take-back System." *Resource Recycling*, 13 (September, 1994), pp. 87–89.

Cairncross, Frances. "How Europe's Companies Reposition to Recycle." *Harvard Business Review*, 70 (March-April, 1992) pp. 34–36.

Clark, Charles S. "Fast-food Shake-up: Beleaguered Chains Improve Nutrition, Environmental Impact and Job Quality." *CO Researcher*, Washington, DC, 1991.

Denison, Richard A., Jackie Prince, and John Ruston. "Good Things Come in *Smaller* Packages." Environmental Defense Fund, Working Paper (December 6, 1990) photocopy, courtesy of EDT.

Der Spiegel, "OEko-Schwindel: der Unfug mit dem gruenen Punkt." (June 21, 1993), pp. 34–37.

Economist. "Food for Thought." August 29, 1992 pp. 64–66.

Economist. "Life Ever After." October 9, 1993 p. 77.

Economist. "Burger Follies." February 25, 1995 pp. 58–59.

Environmental Defense Fund. "Adjustment of Franklin Study Figures on Paperboard to Account for the Reduced Weight of McDonald's new Wraps and Comparison of Energy Requirements and Environmental Releases for Polystyrene Foam and McDonald's New Wraps," (December 6, 1990), press release, courtesy of EDF, 7 pp.

Environmental Defense Fund. "Franklin Associates Study Actually Shows McDonald's New Packaging Requires Less Energy, Releases Fewer Pollutants, and Produces Less Waste Than Polystyrene Foam," (December 6, 1990), press release, courtesy of EDF, 3 pp.

Environmental Defense Fund. "McDonald's Says No to Foam: Why and How the Environment Benefits," (December, 1990), photocopy, courtesy of EDF, 18 pp.

Environmental Defense Fund. "Environmental Defense Fund and McDonald's Corporation Waste Reduction Task Force Workplan," (September, 1990), press release, courtesy of EDF, 15 pp.

Environmental Protection Agency. *Assessing the Environmental Consumer Market*. Office of Policy, Planning, and Evaluation, 1991.

Food Engineering. "Packaging Strategies '94 Conference Focuses on Packaging's Identity in the '90s." (June, 1994), pp. 73–76.

Hahn, Robert W., and Gordon L. Hester. "Marketable Permits: Lessons for Theory and Practice." *Ecology Law Quarterly*, 16 (1989), pp. 358–69.

Hemphill, Thomas A. "Strange Bedfellows Cozy Up for a Clean Environment." *Business and Society Review* (August, 1994), pp. 38–44.

Hinnells, Mark, and Stephen Potter. "What Next for Consumer-level Environmental Policy?" *Policy Studies*, 15 (Spring, 1994), pp. 4–15.

Kirkpatrick, David. "Environmentalism: the New Crusade, It May Be the Biggest Business Issue of the 1990s; Here's How Some Smart Companies Are Tackling It." *Fortune* (February 12, 1990), pp. 44–48.

Lee, Elliott D. "Opposition to Plastic Packaging Is Intensifying as the Nation's Solid-waste Problem Grows Acute." *Wall Street Journal* (November 25, 1987), p. 40.

Lewis, Claire Simone, "Packaging, the Internal Market and the Environment." *European Trends*, 4 (1992), pp. 68–72.

Ludwig, Kathy, and Tom Jones. "The Advance Disposal Fee: Has Its Time Come?" *Resource Recycling* (September, 1992), pp. 94–95.

McDonald's Corporation. "Earth Effort: McDonald's Commitment to the Environment, Our Resource Conservation and Energy Policy." (1994a) brochure, courtesy of McDonald's Corporation, 2 pp.

McDonald's Corporation. "Earth Effort: Facts and Resources." (1994b) brochure, courtesy of McDonald's Corporation, 2 pp.

McDonald's Corporation. "Letter to the Environmental Community." (1994c) photocopy, courtesy of McDonald's Corporation, 10 pp.

McDonald's Corporation and the Environmental Defense Fund. *Waste Reduction Task Force Final Report,* (April, 1991) photocopy, courtesy of McDonald's Corporation, 138 pp.

Naj, Amal Kumar. "Foam Cups Damage Environment Less than Paper Cups, Study Says," *Wall Street Journal* (February 1, 1991), p. B8.

National Restaurant Association. *Nutrition and Restaurants: A Consumer Perspective.* Washington, DC, 1993.

Pope, Kyle. "Charged with Libel, Pair of Activists Puts McDonald's on the Grill." *Wall Street Journal,* (July 18, 1995), pp. A1, A5.

Rathe, Todd A. "The Gray Area of the Green Market: Is It Really Environmentally Friendly? Solutions to Confusion Caused by Environmental Advertising." *Journal of Corporate Law,* 17 (Winter, 1992), pp. 419–58.

Rolfes, Rebecca. "How Green Is Your Market Basket?" *Across the Board* (January-February, 1990), pp. 49–51.

Ryan, Megan. "Packaging a Revolution." *World Watch,* 6 (September-October, 1993), pp. 28–34.

Scarlett, Lynn. "Make Your Environment Dirtier— Recycle." *Wall Street Journal* (January 14, 1991), p. A12.

Shea, Cynthia Pollock. "Getting Serious in Germany: Germans Are Reducing Their Output of Household Waste." *Environmental Protection Agency,* 18 (July-August, 1992), pp. 50–52.

Spaulding, Mark. "What Consumers Said 10 Surveys Ago." *Packaging* (August, 1994), pp. 44–45.

Stern, Marilyn. "Is This the Ultimate in Recycling? New Legislation in Germany Holds Companies Responsible for the Environmental Impact of a Product Throughout Its 'Entire' Life. *Across the Board,* 30 (May, 1993), pp. 28–31.

Stilwell, E. Joseph. *Packaging for the Environment: A Partnership for Progress.* American Management Association, Washington, DC, monograph, 1991.

Stuller, Jay. "The Politics of Packaging: What's the Best Way to Reduce the Glut of Plastic in the Environment? Not Even Environmentalists Agree on the Answer; But the States Are Pressing Ahead with Legislation," *Across the Board,* 27 (January–February, 1990) pp. 40–43.

United States Congress, House Committee on Energy and Commerce, Subcommittee on Transportation and Hazardous Materials. "Contribution of Packaging to Solid Waste Crisis," Hearing, May 16, 1991.

United States Department of Agriculture, Economic Research Service. *Food Cost Review, 1990* (July, 1991) AER-651.

Walley, Noah, and Bradley Whitehead. "It's Not Easy Being Green." *Harvard Business Review,* (May-June, 1994), pp. 46–52.

Weiner, Richard L. A. and Stefan Tostmann, 1991. "What Can the EC Learn from Germany's Bold Legislation on Packaging Waste?" *International Environmental Affairs,* 3 (Fall, 1991) pp. 282–291.

THE FIRST NATIONAL BANK OF BOSTON

*Money laundering and other activities
by banks and other financial institutions*

On February 7, 1985, the First National Bank of Boston pleaded guilty to having violated provisions regarding cash transactions of the Bank Secrecy Act of 1970[1] "knowingly and willfully" failing to report to the Internal Revenue Service cash transactions with foreign banks that totaled $1.22 million over a four-year period. The transactions involved nine foreign banks and 1,163 deposits between July 1980 and September 1984. The Bank of Boston was fined $500,000. The violations were uncovered in the process of a money laundering probe, "Operation Greenback," a Treasury Department initiative begun in 1980. It was directed at organized crime and designed to ensure compliance with the Bank Secrecy Act of 1970.[2]

In addition to its international misdealing, the Bank of Boston was also accused of domestic currency violations. Banks are generally required to report cash transactions of $10,000 or more. In this case, the Bank of Boston had placed two real estate firms, Huntington Realty Co., and Federal Investments, Inc., on the list of those exempt from such reporting. These firms were controlled by the Angiulo family, which was reputedly linked to organized crime. The Bank of Boston was not only guilty of illegal currency transactions, it was implicated in money laundering.[3]

Following its guilty plea, the First National Bank of Boston was called before congressional hearings on April 3–4, 1985. Upon opening the hearings, Subcommittee Chairman Fernand J. St Germain described the situations as follows:

> No one has come forward with evidence that the top officials of the Bank of Boston were in conspiracy with organized crime figures, and we are not suggesting that here today. However, bank officials need not be corrupt or into conspiracies for organized crime; it is enough that bank officials, such as those at the Bank of Boston, be sloppy, and that they operate without controls and without really caring.
>
> Organized crime can make use of any institution that fits that profile, even the purportedly exalted Bank of Boston, and organized crime, drug traffickers, tax evaders are delighted with a regulatory system that hears no evil, sees no evil, speaks no evil, regulators such as we will find at the OCC during this period of time. That is, the Office of the Comptroller of the Currency.[4]

The Bank of Boston case provides a unique exposé of the magnitude and complexity of illegal currency transactions. It reveals an astounding gap between legislative intent and administrative practices in both private banks and public agencies and, in so doing, raises the question as to who is really responsible and how they are to be held accountable. Further, it calls into question whether the government has any real chance of eliminating money laundering.

ISSUES FOR ANALYSIS

1. To what extent were the mistakes made by the Bank of Boston bureaucratic and administrative errors, rather than a result of benign neglect or a deliberate decision to look the other way?
2. How easy is it for those in the "underground economy" to take advantage of paperwork foul-ups and communication failures in the banking system and what can be done about it?
3. To what extent is the management of the Bank of Boston responsible for both the violations of norms for cash transactions and for money laundering? Is it true, as the chairman of the Subcommittee charged, that the Bank of Boston had made non-compliance with the Bank Secrecy Act an art form?
4. What corporate-level and business-level policies are called for in order to minimize such occurrences in the future?
5. What was the proper role of various government agencies involved and how well did they execute their responsibilities? Would you agree with the Subcommittee chairman's view that the office of the comptroller of the currency appeared to rise to a high level of efficiency only when it was protecting its own turf?
6. What measures should be undertaken that would ensure better interagency cooperation and would also improve the efficiency of the regulatory process and make it more effective?
7. What, if anything, is morally wrong with violating the administrative norms for cash transactions? Are the norms realistic in today's trillion-dollar economy?
8. What rights do individuals have to privacy regarding their financial situation? Under what conditions is it right for government to invade that privacy?

THE LEGAL AND ECONOMIC CONDITIONS SURROUNDING MONEY LAUNDERING IN THE UNITEDSTATES

Money laundering is big business. Because it is shrouded in secrecy, precise estimates are hard to come by. In his 1994 testimony before Congress, the Treasury Department's under secretary for enforcement, Mr. Ronald K. Noble, estimated that some $300 billion in U.S. dollars is laundered every year, with roughly a third of that being tied to the drugs and narcotics trade.[5] As soft as such estimates may be, they do not begin to factor in Asia and Europe. The countries most worried, of course, are those with hard currencies. The Group of Seven industrial countries and the European community set up a Financial Action Task Force in 1989 to study the problem and come up with recommendations.[6] Their forty-some recommendations now form the basis for antilaundering laws in most OECD countries. Implementation of such measures is slow. Furthermore, it is often being outpaced by modern banking technologies and means of money transfers.

The U. S. Congress has attempted to strengthen its own enforcement with the Money Laundering Suppression Act of 1994.[7] In many ways, new ingenious money laundering schemes outpace the legislation. Furthermore, key agencies are not adequately staffed with skilled personnel. The U. S. Department of State's Bureau of International Narcotics Matters issued a detailed strategy report in April of 1994, the *International Narcotics Control Strategy Report*.[8] It provides a detailed list of all the financial crimes linked to money laundering (pp. 465–538) and reviews the situation in all of the major countries involved. One interesting section (pp. 477–78) outlines the "money launderer's shopping list,"—a detailed description of the sort of operating environments in which money laundering flourishes. These include places where money laundering is not a criminal offense, where bank secrecy is strict, where financial regulations are lax, where nonfinancial institutions are prominent conduits of cash and so forth. In the Bank of Boston case, the conduit was a well-respected financial banking institution. In the ten years that have intervened since this case, electronic transfers and the uses of falsified import and export invoices have come to figure as far more popular means to get the job done.

The criminal activities of the Bank of Boston can best be understood within the legal context of the regulatory reporting requirements and their intent in terms of public policy. An added element has to be the extent to which regulatory processes are enforced and complied with. A second consideration deals with the nature of the underground economy in the United States and the vast sums it produces that must be laundered so that they can be used in legal activities by their illegal owners. And finally, the laundering activities of the Bank of Boston should also be viewed in terms of how widespread such activities are in the banking industry. In fact, the Bank of Boston is not an exception but merely a worst example. It suggests that current regulatory processes are grossly inadequate. Profits to be made from money laundering are so enormous that they tempt even the bluest of blue chip banking organizations and financial institutions; and, in the final analysis, the leaders of these organizations are not only guilty of legal crimes but also of moral and social crimes, in that they participate in the furtherance of organized crime activities in the United States that undermine the social and moral fabric of society.

REGULATORY ENVIRONMENT—
THE BANK SECRECY ACT OF 1970

The Bank Secrecy Act of 1970 was designed to assist the government in its pursuit of the underground economy, especially organized crime and the money that is used in order to attain their goals.[9] This legislation was based on the concept that if a paper trail is established around all large cash transactions, it will deter the flow of illegal funds into the normal banking channels, thereby making their legitimization more difficult. Congress felt that a strong record-keeping system would assist in criminal, tax, and regulatory investigations by tracking sources and uses of cash throughout the banking industry. All insured banks of the United States are required to abide by the rules of this Act. Banks are responsible for keeping proper records. Financial institutions are required to file a CRT (currency transaction report) for amounts in excess of $10,000 with the Internal Revenue Service (IRS) within 15 days of each occurrence. A bank also must identify and record information on the customer who conducts the transaction. The bank must also file a CMIR (Currency of Monetary Instrument Report) with the Commissioner of Customs for any transportation of currency into or out of the United States in amounts of $10,000 or more. Penalties under this Act are quite severe and can amount to $10,000 in civil penalties per violation and criminal fines of up to $250,000. These penalties can be imposed either on a bank or on an individual, even if the government is unable to bring criminal charges regarding how the money itself was accumulated. In other words, a person or a bank can be in trouble for not reporting even if the money not reported was not involved in a criminal activity.

In the area of domestic transactions, financial institutions must file a currency transaction report (CTR) with the Internal Revenue Service on each individual deposit, withdrawal, payment, transfer, or exchange of currency by, through, or to a financial institution that involves currency in the amount of $10,000 or more.[10] This report is to be made on Form 4789 within 15 days to the IRS.

The sheer size and number of transactions taking place every day in the vast banking system makes it absolutely necessary to create some exemptions in order to reduce the incredible level of paperwork that would otherwise be produced. These exemptions have been provided in those areas that are least likely to be connected with any criminal activity. Such exemptions include transactions with the Federal Reserve, Federal Home Loan Banks, transactions between domestic banks, and those between nonbank financial institutions and commercial banks. Additionally, a bank can place certain established depositors on the exempt list if they are U.S. residents and operate a retail business in the United States that generally deals in a large number of cash transactions. The generally accepted exempted businesses are those that operate a sports arena, racetrack, amusement park, bar, restaurant, hotel, licensed check-cashing services, vending machine companies, or theatres. However, these exemptions do not imply that the depositor will never have to file a CTR again; rather, a ceiling higher than that of this Act is installed (based on the average amount of cash transactions for that particular business). When this ceiling is exceeded, a CTR must be filed. Operations that are excluded from this exempt list include automobile, boat, and airplane dealerships. Such exclusions exist purely because those businesses provide an easy and effective way to enter illegal funds into the banking industry. They also supply equipment for the transportation of illegal goods. Finally, transactions by all levels of government may be exempted.

With regard to foreign transactions, the regulation breaks into two components. One, any transaction between a domestic concern and a foreign concern that involves the physical shipment of more than $10,000 of nontraceable funds, must be reported to Customs through Form 4790 (CMIR) and to the Currency Commissioner through Form 4789 (CTR). Two, any standard physical currency transaction from a domestic bank to a foreign bank that consists of at least $10,000 must be filed with the U.S. Customs officials through the use of Form 4790.

The laudable goal of winning the battle against organized crime has, nonetheless, raised questions about the means employed to do so. Specifically, what are the rights of the individuals to privacy with regard to the necessary information that must be supplied? This point raises the question of what methods may be used by the government to attain this information for use in legal proceedings. The Right to Financial Privacy Act of 1978 restricts the disclosure of information from a customer's records unless he or she has been served with legal papers. Furthermore, the

institution must wait 10–14 days before furnishing this information to proper authorities. In addition, the government must deliver a statement of compliance with the Privacy Act prior to receiving the requested information. However, this law does not restrict an institution from notifying the government of information that may be related to criminal activity.

THE UNDERGROUND ECONOMY

The real shock in the Bank of Boston case was the realization of how easily the underground economy could use legitimate banking enterprises to achieve its goals. The underground economy deals with tax evasion as well as the rewards of organized crime and other illegal activities.[11] It is estimated to be a $500-billion-a-year industry. It is also growing at an explosive rate. This economy is based on the false reporting of taxes, nonmarket activities (unreported income from home), and illegal activities (drug, prostitution, and racketeering).

False reporting of taxes can be accomplished through the nondisclosure of income as well as falsification of records. A prime example of this can be seen on the streets of New York City. It is estimated that there are some 5,000 street vendors who do not disclose any earnings from the sales of their products.

Nonmarket activities include the selling of services through unofficial routes (such as in-home service and repair work) when income so earned is not reported for tax purposes. These two types of activities are functionally legal, but the nondisclosure of income generated therefrom is illegal. The larger the amount of undeclared income, the greater is the burden of taxation placed on the declared income, assuming the need for tax revenue to remain constant. The third component of the underground economy is comprised of activities that are illegal per se, for example, selling illicit drugs and narcotics, stealing property, operating prostitution rings, loan sharking, and racketeering, to name a few. Operated by organized crime syndicates or groups, both the activities and the income earned therefrom are concealed from the tax authorities. The magnitude of these activities and their revenues are indeed staggering.

It is estimated that the total revenues of organized crime organizations in the United States are greater than the combined revenues of the iron, steel, copper, and aluminum manufacturing industries and approximate about 1.1% of the GNP. While it is obvious that this group can operate effectively underground, it also has a problem. To wit, these activities generate enormous cash flows that far exceed the needs of the illicit enterprises. As a result, some means must be found to channel these funds into legitimate enterprises where they can be invested profitably. Hence, the need for laundering this money and gaining access to the legal banking system. In order to gain entrance to this system, organized crime operates various legal enterprises such as construction, entertainment, trucking, and food and liquor wholesaling. Through these companies, the "mob" can bring the illegally generated funds into the banking system by making it seem that the cash flows are from these businesses and not from other sources. Once this money is in the banking system, it can be put to use by the mob. It enables organized crime to expand and pursue various illegal goals. The objective of the government, through regulation of banking system and reporting procedures, is to make such access difficult, if not impossible, and to reduce the flow of illegal funds into the normal banking channels.

Another problem caused by the underground economy is the skewing effects it has on the various economic indicators such as the Consumer price index (CPI), unemployment rate, and Producer Price index (PPI). This induces error in government's assessment of the economy and causes a misdirection of government programs in order to address what is thought to be a problem.

Because of these activities, the government has initiated a number of programs to reduce the impact and scope of underground economy with particular emphasis on the activities related to organized crime. These include the Organized Crime Control Act of 1987, The Racketeer Influenced and Corrupt Organizations Act of 1970 (RICO), and the Bank Secrecy Act of 1970. The First National Bank of Boston was charged under the latter.

MONEY LAUNDERING

Money laundering plays a pivotal role in organized crime activity. According to James D. Harmon, executive director of the President's Commission on Organized Crime, cash is "the life support system without which organized crime could not exist".[12] The objective of the U.S. government is to reduce the funds that would be allowed into the system itself. The main laundering objectives include the improved portability (exchanging $20s for $100s) and nontraceability of funds. This is accomplished by sending funds into little known banks offshore after converting these funds into a more shippable size. Once they are in another country, the funds are exchanged for that or another country's currency. This generally takes place in countries with strong bank secrecy laws, thereby preventing anyone from looking into the source or ownership of these funds.

The use of shell corporations that exist purely to supply a place through which to run money is another common method of arriving at the same result. There are numerous other examples of different methods that are used but a very common one is the use of "smurfs." These people simply go to various banks and branches and make deposits in amounts that are just below the flagging amount of money ($10,000 per deposit). Smurfs can be very effective in the distribution of funds (30–40 transactions a day with a value of $5,000–7,000 per deposit). Another method is the purchasing of nondirected money orders for large amounts and then depositing them into other bank accounts, thereby effectively eliminating the paper trail because these money orders were purchased with cash and then deposited into accounts as money orders.

The ultimate in money laundering occurs when a depositor can attain exempt status from the CTR lists at a bank. This is a very sought after privilege since no transactions will be reported to the authorities. All business then falls within the realm of legal transactions for the company in question. As mentioned earlier, only certain types of businesses are allowed to be on this list and those that fulfill the requirements must provide proof of the source of their cash flows. Placement on the exempt list with a fairly high ceiling is the best of schemes because the transaction costs are much lower (less transactions) and the funds can be processed without concern of federal involvement.

All this being said, money launderers are both opportunisitic and creative. They probe those areas in the environment that may be the weakest at any particular moment. For example, they will falsify trade invoices until Customs catches on. Then they shift to the next item on their shopping list, whether electronic bank transfers or personal courier, and try that out.[13]

THE CASE AGAINST THE BANK OF BOSTON

This is not the first time that the Bank of Boston has flirted with organized crime. In 1978, a loan officer of the bank arranged to finance the acquisition of World Jai Alai in Florida for Roger Wheeler, former chairman of Telex Corporation and John Callahan, former World Jai Alai president and a suspected mobster. If the deal was successful, Mr. Callahan was to have been reinstated as president of World Jai Alai. Two years later, Mr. Wheeler was murdered. Mr. Callahan became the next victim a year later. The two murder cases remain unsolved.

In the current case, the Bank of Boston was charged with two distinct sets of violations: (1) failure to correctly report international currency transactions, and (2) failure to report domestic cash transactions. The latter gained particular notoriety because it involved the Angiulo family of Boston, purported to be the most powerful Mafia family in Massachusetts, which was suspected of money laundering.

International Transactions

The first problem deals with overseas transactions with large banks. Commercial banks have long been in the business of receiving shipments from foreign banks for deposit in their own accounts. Most of the action was handled by New York banks. However, growing logistical problems at Kennedy Airport caused foreign banks to seek alternatives. The Bank of Boston sought this business, and as the letters from the FED prove, the bank had a large amount of money flowing through its doors soon thereafter. Two separate, unrelated shipments would occur. First, small-denomination bills would be received from the foreign banks for credit in their accounts. Then, a request would be sent to Bank of Boston that currency in large-denomination bills be shipped back to the requesting bank. Profits were gained by taking a small percentage of the total amount shipped.

Neither of these transactions was made or received at the explicit request of the Bank of Boston. There were no deposits made to individual or company accounts. It was all inner-bank transactions. There was the possibility that some of the money being received could have originated from illegal activity, but that was not thought to be the responsibility of the Bank of Boston because it could not be expected to find out the origins of the money. This was because the country of origin (for the most part, Switzerland) maintained its own secrecy laws.

The Bank of Boston came under the suspicion of the Federal Reserve as early as 1977 for its unusually large amount of such transactions.[14] The "Information" brief filed by then U.S. Attorney William F. Weld and the Chief Attorney of the New England Organized Crime Strike Force stated:[15]

That the defendant Bank of Boston was required to file a Currency Transaction Report for each of the currency transactions set forth in Appendix A below; and wilfully failed to file said Reports, in violation of Title 31, U.S.C. 1081 on transactions occurring before September 14, 1982, and in violation of Title 31, U.S.C. 5313 for transactions on or after September 14, 1982, and in violation of 31 Code of Federal Regulations, Sections 103.22(a) (1980) and 103.25 (1980), which offenses were committed as a part of a pattern of activity involving currency transactions exceeding $100,000.00 within a twelve-month period, to wit:

1980	—	$ 194,410,422.00
1981	—	$ 544,722,484.00
1982	—	$ 269,307,393.00
1983	—	$ 161,378,672.00
1984	—	$ 48,864,310.00
TOTAL:		$1,212,682,310.00

All in violation of Title 31, U.S.C. Sections 1081 and 1059, and Title 31 U.S.C. Sections 5313 and 5322(b).

The Angiulo Connection

The Angiulo family owned two real estate concerns: Huntington Realty Co. and Federal Investments, Inc. Both firms have been the bank's customers since 1964 at its North End branch. On various occasions, cash deposits large enough to appear suspicious were made by the two firms. Nevertheless, in 1976, Huntington Realty was placed on the exempt list and in 1979 Federal Investment Inc. was added to the list.[16] In 1980, new and stricter regulations were announced for the Bank Secrecy Act. The biggest change occurred with the type of companies that would be allowed to stay on the exempt list. In 1980, the Bank of Boston was asked why Huntington Realty and Federal Investments were still on the exempt list given the new changes that were then in effect. The Treasury Department requested a copy of the exempt list for examination in April 1982.[17] The Bank of Boston sent the full list. The Treasury Department sent back the list with annotations next to the customers' names about whom it desired more information to estab-

lish their eligibility. Huntington and Federal were among those questioned.

Mr. Hubert Cox, an officer in Banking Offices Administration, Bank of Boston, called the manager of the North End branch to ask for information about these two accounts.[18] She asked that these companies be allowed to stay on the list since they collected rent and other payments which were mostly in cash. Mr. Cox questioned if they should be on the list because he did not know if they were to be considered a retail operation. The manager reported that the accounts of Huntington Realty, and Federal Investments should be allowed to stay on the list because of the type of business that they were in, as well as because they were long-time customers. It was her opinion, from experience, that the North End residents tended to pay for their rental payments through the use of cash, which would explain the very high level of cash brought in by these two companies. She also stated that the Angiulos were the primary owners. Mr. Cox was uncomfortable with the situation and asked one of his assistants to follow up on it. This assistant did not do any followup. Mr. Cox, for his part, never asked his assistant about the outcome. The companies stayed on the list. It was asserted that this was an error of laziness and not one of illegal intent for personal gain either for the bank or any of its employees.

In May 1983, the federal government, in the course of its investigation of the Angiulo family in Boston for racketeering, loan sharking, and murder, subpoenaed the Bank of Boston to provide information regarding its domestic cash transactions. It was determined that during 1982, the Angiulos were allowed to purchase $1.765 million worth of cashier's checks, of which more than $250,000 were purchased in cash. Over $270,000 in cashier's checks were made payable to Cowen & Co. where the family maintained 37 brokerage accounts. In all, during the years 1979–1983, Huntington and Federal purchased 452 cashier's checks totalling $7,372,343.20. Of these, 163 cashier's checks totalling $2,163,457.50 were for cash and would have been reportable were those firms not on the exempt list. Huntington also engaged in large cash disbursements of the savings account balance at year end.[19]

On October 10, 1981, the Office of the Controller of Currency (OCC) requested specialized examinations of the Bank of Boston. However, because the examiners were not properly trained in the new regulations and because the new order for specialized examining did not reach the examiners, no violations were found.

In April 1982, Treasury Deputy Robert E. Powis requested that all Massachusetts banks forward their complete exempt lists to his office for examination. By June 3, Mr. Cox forwarded the list to Mr. Powis as requested. On June 8, Mr. Stankey of the Office of Enforcement of the Department of the Treasury returned the list to Mr. Cox with several questions regarding individual customers on this list. Both Huntington Realty and Federal Investments were among those questioned.

By summer 1982, OCC was informed by the Treasury Department that it was targeting nine banks in the State of Massachusetts regarding compliance in the matter of 31 CTRs (completion of Form 4789). The Treasury Department also requested the assistance of OCC in order to tabulate the currency receipts of the Federal Reserve Bank at Boston relating to the flow of currency. This task was assigned to two assistant national bank examiners.

In September 1982, a regularly scheduled examination of the Bank of Boston took place. On September 21, Deputy Powis sent a letter to the OCC chief national bank examiner with the following information:[20]

> [C]ompliance with the reporting requirements of the Bank Secrecy Act by banks in Massachusetts [was] very low. [N]otable lack of understanding of the exemption provisions in the [Bank Secrecy Act] regulation.
>
> [T]he number of and dollar amount of CTR reports filed by banks in Massachusetts were not consistent with the large volume of currency activity between the Federal Reserve Bank and its members.

> Our review indicates that the First National Bank of Boston, which appears to purchase the largest amounts of currency from the Federal Reserve Bank of Boston . . . has a very low level of compliance with the Bank Secrecy Act.
>
> The officer in charge of currency operations at the bank, in contacts with my office regarding exempt lists, has informed us that he is not completely familiar with the provisions of the Bank Secrecy Act regulations.

A task force was set up in order to assure that the problem recognized by Powis would be effectively reduced and controlled. In April 1983, a national bank examiner in the OCC examination division discussed the matter with the officials of the Bank of Boston. On April 27, the Treasury Department authorized the IRS to undertake an investigation of possible criminal violations of 31 CFR Part 103 at the Bank of Boston.

On February 7, 1985, the Justice Department filed criminal felony charges against the First National Bank of Boston alleging that the bank knowingly and willfully failed to report to the federal government the movement of $1.2 billion between the Banks and several Swiss banks. The Bank waived indictment and pleaded guilty to the felony charge. The fine imposed was that of $500,000.

Bank of Boston's Response

Notwithstanding the guilty plea, Mr. William L. Brown, chairman and chief executive officer, Bank of Boston, was emphatic that the Bank's international transactions were "perfectly legal". The Bank of Boston began aggressively to pursue this business with foreign banks in the mid-1970s when logistical difficulties at Kennedy Airport led big foreign banks to look outside New York City banking circles.[21] The Bank of Boston dealt principally with Swiss Banks. According to Mr. Brown:

> The international shipments consist of two separate but unrelated elements: first, shipments to Boston consisting mainly of small-

denomination bills; and second, shipments to foreign banks consisting largely of new $100 bills. These shipments were always made or received at the explicit request of the foreign bank, not at the instigation of the Bank of Boston. They traveled in a closed, bank-to-bank loop, and no individual depositor had access to them.

It is of course possible that some part of the cash that was deposited into the vaults of the Swiss banks originated from illegal activity … I can only say it was our understanding that Swiss banks served as clearinghouses for other European banks, and Bank of Boston provided a service . . . which we . . . believe was a legitimate one.[22]

Mr. Brown conceded that the only mistakes made by the bank were in failing to file the necessary reports. He asserted that this failure was primarily due to "defects in our management systems."[23]

Mr. Daniel Dorner, vice-president for deposit operations, gave his account of management confusion over reporting. According to Mr. Dorner, the Bank of Boston did, in fact, file Report 4790, which the Customs required; it failed, however, to file Form 4789 which the IRS required. Mr. Dorner and Mr. Brown provided lengthy accounts of how such a mistake was made. The Subcommittee found them barely credible.

In defending Bank of Boston's domestic transactions, Mr. Brown was equally cavalier: the regulations regarding legitimate exemptions from reporting were unclear.[24] In fact, he maintained that the pre-1980 regulations were sufficiently broad that the Angiulo enterprises could be properly exempted because the companies regularly dealt in large sums of cash. He concluded: "Without question, that decision represented an exercise of bad judgment; under no interpretation of the 1980 regulations should the two companies have been kept on the exempt list. Nonetheless, our inquiry has revealed absolutely no basis for believing that either the initial placement of the companies on the list or their retention in 1980 and again in 1982 was motivated by any desire for personal gain or other improper purpose."[25]

The response of the subcommittee chairman, Congressman St. Germain was one of incredulity. He queried Mr. Brown and Mr. Stoddard Colbert, first vice-president in charge of the Metropolitan Boston Branch system if they ever read the local papers' articles on the Angiulos:[26]

Mr. Brown: Does it (the article) mention the companies?

Chairman St. Germain: Yes, the companies are mentioned, but the fact of the matter is— didn't you, Mr. Colbert and Mr. Brown, know who the controlling parties were in these firms?

Mr. Brown: No.

Chairman St. Germain: You don't bother to look? You just take a corporate name at face value and say "Gee, that's a nice name?"

Mr. Brown: Mr. Chairman, it's impossible for me to look at all of our customers. We have hundreds of thousands.

Mr. Brown concluded his testimony by asserting that Bank of Boston admitted its errors and was mending its ways. As proof he pointed out that there had been a complete audit of all the transactions of the last four years.[27] This audit revealed several missing transactions and the following supplemental filings were made: (1) a filing on March 7, 1985, involving some 400 transactions that totaled $93,000,000, and (2) a filing on March 27, 1985, involving another 1,200 transactions with a total value of $110,000,000. With these reports, it was felt and attested by the examiners that the Bank of Boston was now under full compliance. To ensure that such things would not happen in the future, Mr. Brown went on to list some of the changes that would be implemented throughout Bank of Boston's management.[28] Among these were the following:

1. Final authority for those on the exempt list would be channeled through the upper levels of the law department. To get to this high point, a branch manager first had to do a background check on the customer in question. If the customer passed this test, then the request for exemption would be sent with the

branch manager's recommendation to the senior branch administration officer. Final clearance had to be given by the law office.

2. A special task force was constructed in October 1984 to develop a comprehensive compliance program that would follow the letter and spirit of all currency reporting. Currency transactions for both domestic and foreign transactions would be signed by the manager of the branch or office it originated from, as well as being signed by a central office that would control all transaction-form logging.

3. Training was made more thorough at every level of the company; this would be ongoing to ensure that training would be up-to-date with all regulations of the Federal government.

4. Manual logs were designed that all tellers were required to fill out if there were any large cash transactions. This log was then looked over by management at the end of each day every night in search of transactions that would require a CTR to be filed. This log was soon to be computerized and when this occurred it would be possible to total up all deposits for one account throughout the system for that day (thus eliminating the usefulness of the "smurfs").

5. Compliance officers had been given increased authority over the groups they managed in order to control them effectively. They had also been given the power to take compliance problems directly to top management.

These changes, as well as those recommended by the President's Commission on Organized Crime, were designed to effectively ensure that the Bank of Boston would be in full compliance with the Bank Secrecy Act.

SYSTEMS FAILURE: BUNGLING AND REGULATORY MISMANAGEMENT IN THE OFFICE OF THE COMPTROLLER OF THE CURRENCY

There is little doubt that the Bank of Boston was guilty of showing little or no concern for the various rules of compliance that were necessary for the successful implementation of the regulations of the Bank Secrecy Act. At the same time, it is also clear that the government agencies charged with implementation of the Act were falling down on the job. The Hearings showed that, while these government organizations had a common goal, there was a lack of coordination in their actions. In the absence of such cooperation, duplication of work and jurisdictional conflicts were commonplace.[29] In order to alleviate this problem, a document was drawn up between the Department of Justice, the Federal Bureau of Investigation, and the four federal banking regulatory agencies, which was designed to improve detection, investigation, and prosecution of bank fraud.[30]

This document outlined the various responsibilities of each agency, as well as restrictions on sharing information between these agencies in order to protect the account holder from invasion of privacy.[31] When and if implemented, this document would most likely aid the effectiveness of each agency. It would bring about reduced duplication of work and enhanced agency communication that would alert the appropriate agency of possible problems before they were allowed to reach crisis proportions.

NOTES

1. Subcommittee on Financial Institutions Supervision, Regulations and Insurance of the Committee on Banking, Finance and Urban Affairs, House of Representatives, *The First National Bank of Boston Hearings*, April 3 and 4, 1985; pp. 1, 139–142, 142 ff. [Hereafter cited as *Hearings* followed by appropriate page numbers]; U.S. Department of Justice, Organized Crime and racketeering Section, Boston Strike Force, "News Release" (February 7, 1985); in *Hearings* pp. 139–41, and United States District Court, District of Massachusetts, *United States of America* v. *The First National Bank of Boston*, "Plea Agreement" in *Hearings*, pp. 142–45.

2. "Appendix to the Statement of C. T. Conover, Comptroller of the Currency" in *Hearings*, pp. 386–87.

3. Permanent Subcommittee on Investigations, Committee of Governmental Affairs, U.S.

Senate, *Domestic Money Laundering: Bank Secrecy Act Compliance and Enforcement Report*, (December 1986) pp. 10ff. Hereafter cited as *Report*.

4. Ferdnand J. St. Germain, *Hearings*, p. 3.
5. U.S. Congress, House of Representatives, Committee on Ways and Means, Subcommittee on Oversight, 1994, *Hearing on the Department of Treasury's Efforts to Address Money Laundering*, Statement of Hon. Ronald K. Noble, Under–Secretary for Enforcement, U. S. Department of Treasury, p. 37.
6. *The Economist*, "Money Launderers on the Line," June 25, 1984, pp. 81–82.
7. U.S. Congress, House of Representatives, *Money Laundering Suppression Act of 1994*, 103rd Congress, 2nd Session, Report 103–438, 1994.
8. U.S. Department of State, Bureau of International Narcotics Matters, *International Narcotics Control Strategy Report*, Washington DC, U.S. Government Printing Office, 1994.
9. *Report*, pp. 1ff.; Public Law 91–508, Title 27.
10. *Report*, pp. 1–3.
11. *Business Week*, "Money Laundering," (March 16, 1985), pp.74–80.
12. *Business Week, op. cit*, pp. 78–79.
13. U.S. Department of State, Bureau of International Narcotics Matters, *International Narcotics Control Strategy Report*, Washington DC, U.S. Government Printing Office, 1994 pp. 477ff; and U.S. Congress, House of Representatives, Committee on Ways and Means, Subcommittee on Oversight, *Hearing on the Department of Treasury's Efforts to Address Money.Laundering*, 1994 pp. 101–11.
14. Federal Reserve Bank of Boston, "Memorandum" (March 30, 1977) in *Hearings*, p. 13.
15. United States District Court, District of Massachusetts, *op. cit.*, "Information" in *Hearings*, pp. 146–48.
   Bob Davis, "Bank of Boston Unit Currency Transfer Found in Probe of Alleged Crime Family." *Wall Street Journal* (February 11, 1985), p. 11.
16. "Memorandum Concerning Angiulo Transactions at the Bank of Boston." In *Hearings*, pp. 165–175.

17. Conover, *op. cit.*, pp. 386–87; Monica Langley, "Comptroller Concedes Failure to Detect Bank of Boston Currency-Law Violations." *Wall Street Journal*, (March 4, 1985), p. 1
18. William L. Brown, "Statement," *Hearings*, p. 263; Bob Davis, "U.S. Says Bank of Boston Unit Was Told It Broke Law 2 Years before Compliance." *Wall Street Journal*, (February 28, 1985), p. 11
19. "Memorandum Concerning Angiulo," *op. cit.*, pp. 170–71.
20. Cited by Conover, *op. cit.* in *Hearings*, p. 389; for full text see Robert E. Powis, "Memorandum," (September 21, 1982) in *Hearings*, pp. 77–78.
21. Brown, *op. cit.* in *Hearings*, pp. 258–71; also William L. Brown, "Report to the Annual Meeting," (March 28, 1985) in *Hearings*, pp. 177–81.
22. Brown, "Statement" in *Hearings*, p. 259.
23. *Ibid.*, p. 260; *Hearings*, p. 272; *Report*, pp. 4–6; *American Banker*, "Treasury Tightens Rules on Reporting Large Transactions." (June 15, 1980), p. 1.
24. Brown, "Annual Meeting," *op. cit.*, pp. 181ff; "Statement," *op. cit.*, p. 263.
   Bob Davis, "Bank of Boston Faces Image Problem Likely to Linger for Years." *Wall Street Journal* (March 7, 1985), p. 1; *American Banker*, "Boston Bank Chief Defends Actions in Cash Transfers" (February 12, 1985), p. 1.
25. Brown, "Statement," *op. cit.*, pp. 264ff.
26. *Hearings*, p. 252.
27. Brown, "Statement," *op. cit.*, pp. 265ff.
28. *Ibid.* p. 266.
29. *Hearings*, pp. 398–438; Bob Davis, "Bank of Boston Unit's Fine Criticized as Inadequate by House Banking Panel." *Wall Street Journal*, (April 4, 1985), p. 8.
30. *Report*, pp. 23–31; Bob Davis, and Monica Langley, "Senators Seen Backing Tougher Rules on Bank Cash–Transaction Disclosures." *Wall Street Journal* (March 13, 1985), p. 12; Lois Therrien, "An All–out Attack on Banks that Launder Money." *Business Week*, p. 30.
31. C. T. Conover, "Statement" in *Hearings*, pp. 370–381.

GENERAL DYNAMICS CORPORATION

*Defrauding the U.S. government—
overcharging on defense contracts*

General Dynamics, the second largest U.S. defense contractor, with 1987 awards of $7 billion, has been the subject of various government inquiries for almost twenty years. The current charges of fraud and mismanagement were brought out in the process of congressional hearings, Pentagon reviews, and Justice Department proceedings.[1]

The principal charges and accusations included:

1. Inadequate financial disclosures to the SEC and the shareholders, particularly with respect to the SSN 688 submarine construction contracts.
2. Stock manipulation through the cover-up of potential losses, in particular with reference to the Trident program.
3. Providing illegal gratuities to military officers (i.e., Hyman Rickover and others), and falsification of records to conceal these illegal gratuities.
4. Incorrect procedures involving millions of dollars of "undocumented" expense vouchers and related requests for the government to reimburse the company for its costs.
5. Misuse of corporate aircraft and abuse of executive perquisites.

PREVALENCE OF FRAUD AND MISMANAGEMENT AMONG DEFENSE CONTRACTORS

This was not the first time that charges had been levied against General Dynamics. The company had been beleaguered with similar charges in the past.[2] Moreover, the problem is not confined to General Dynamics in a manner that could be attributed to its organizational structure, decision-making procedures, or the caliber and character of its top management. In fact, problems of inefficient management, sloppy record keeping, and financial mismanagement including fraud, are endemic to large segments of the defense industry.[3]

Examples of such activity include the notorious $600 toilet seat, the $300 coffee pot, and the $9,000 wrench. The issue has been building for a long time. These activities and similar ones came to a boiling point in 1985. In that year, the Department of Defense (DOD) temporarily or permanently barred over 650 military contractors from doing business with the Pentagon. This was up from only 57 in 1975 and 78 in 1980.[4] The Department of Defense reports that cases under investigation have averaged over 1,000 per year during the past five years. The FBI has said that 680 cases of fraud were referred to the Bureau from October 1983 through May 1987. Of these, 286 are still pending.[5]

The post-Vietnam War years saw the emergence of more scandalous stories that coincided with the military build-up. When President Reagan came to office in 1981 and vowed a dramatic increase in defense spending, the stories of fraud and mismanagement served as cannon fodder to rouse public opinion against increased spending. Addressing the defense industry's Best Practices Forum Defense, Secretary Caspar W. Weinberger acknowledged the problem: "We all know waste, poor management, and actual criminality are present in many companies." The seriousness of the problem was underscored when he went on to add: "That unless there is [defense] acquisition reform, the defense program is imperiled".[6]

ISSUES FOR ANALYSIS

The issues raised by the General Dynamics case go beyond the narrow confines of the particulars relating to the company. They encompass a whole array of macro and micro concerns that raise questions of managing relations between business and government on the one hand, and the determination of national priorities on the other hand.

1. Defense procurement, by its very nature, often involves dealing with single-source suppliers. Competition among different suppliers is either nonexistent or nonfeasible. It should be noted here that the United States Department of Defense (DOD) annually purchases almost $170 billion in goods and services. It accounts for about 25% of the federal budget and approximately 6% of the GNP. Defense acquisition is the largest business enterprise in the world. Weapons procurement accounts for approximately 28% of the Pentagon's own budget. The Department of Defense also spends huge amounts of money on research and development (R&D).[7] Moreover, procurement often involves both development and production with uncertain technologies, unforeseen development and manufacturing problems, constant design and specifications changes, and unanticipated cost overruns. Thus, the more complex the project, the greater is the difficulty in the monitoring function under these circumstances:
   a. How can defense industry standards be effectively monitored and controlled? Will

the codes of ethics mandated by the Defense Department be adequate? Or, will they be no more than window dressing?
   b. How should the procurement process itself be structured? What changes are needed at the Department of Defense, in the Congress, in the management policy of corporations, in the Executive Branch, and in their interaction with each other?

2. A related issue has to do with the need for maintaining close DOD-contractor relations for smooth functioning of the procurement, function, and yet, at the same time, maintaining arm's-length transactions between DOD employees and defense contractors to ensure honesty and integrity in the oversight function. Under these circumstances:
   a. How does the present system of contacts, including limitations between the two groups, influence these relationships? Relevant points include lobbying by the contractors, employment of former defense personnel by the defense industry and enforcement procedures by the DOD to root out corruption, bribery and other abuses among its own employees.
   b. How should disputes in overhead, pricing discrepancies, and progress payments be resolved, and who should resolve them?
   c. To what extent does DOD encourage reporting of illegal activities among its employees and those of the contractors? How does DOD protect whistle-blowers? What additional measures are needed in this area?
   d. What measures, if any, are needed to minimize undue influence on the part of the nation's defense contractors? Does the "revolving door" policy create a conflict of interest when key decision makers at the Pentagon leave their posts to take jobs in defense industries? Do they use their position at the Pentagon to grant special treatment in order to gain future employment?
   e. How effective are the DOD procedures in detecting fraud and how energetic is DOD in enforcing these regulations, prosecuting wrongdoers, and seeking restitution? What additional measures, if any, might be needed?

4. In regard to defense contractors, what are the problems related to the situation where these companies undertake both private and gov-

ernment work? To what extent do these problems contribute toward a tendency for false claims or overbilling to the DOD by defense contractors? How might these problems be resolved or minimized?

5. In regard to General Dynamics, what are the characteristics of the company, its corporate culture, organizational structure, product mix, or the quality of its top management that might have contributed to its problems? Should felons such as Lester Crown, who was an unindicted coconspirator in bribery charges, be allowed to sit on the boards of strategically sensitive companies such as General Dynamics?

6. Apart from the legal and regulatory measures, what else can the American society do to inculcate higher standards of ethical and professional behavior in corporate executives in producing goods that are vital to the nation's defense and security?

GENERAL DYNAMICS CORPORATION

General Dynamics is one of the largest U.S. defense contractors. In 1987 its sales totaled $9.3 billion with a net income of $437 million. From 1983 to 1987 average sales grew at a rate of 9.4% while net income grew at the rate of 13.9%. Earnings per share in 1987 stood at $10.26, reflecting a 24.3% grow rate over the five-year period.[8]

The corporation is organized into several divisions. The principal ones are: (1) the Electric Boat Division, which produces the SSN 688 and Trident Submarines; (2) the Convair, Pomona, and Valley Systems Divisions, which produce missiles and gun systems, including the Tomahawk and Stinger Missiles; (3) the Fort Worth Division, which produces the F-16 as well as military electronics; (4) the Electronics Division, which produces military electronics; (5) the Space Systems Division, which contracts primarily with NASA and the Air Force for such things as the Centaur Rocket Upper Stages; and, (6) the Land Systems Division, producer of the M-1. In addition, there are other divisions that produce civilian planes, building products, and information system.[9]

CHRONOLOGY OF EVENTS

1950 to 1974

In 1959 General Dynamics acquired the Crown family's Material Services Corporation and paid Henry Crown with $2.1 million in GD preferred stock. During the early sixties, General Dynamics went through a period of financial instability. Henry Crown clashed with Roger Lewis, the General Dynamics chairman and CEO over policy. In 1965 the management of General Dynamics attacked Crown and voted to recall the family's convertible preferred shares for $105 million in an effort to remove him from the board. Crown took his money, resigned from the board, and then began to systematically acquire all the General Dynamics shares that he could.

By 1970 the Crown family had accumulated 10.5% of General Dynamic's stock and gained 6 out of 14 seats on GD's board. Crown was in control again and was determined to keep it that way. This was to have serious repercussions for the company during the 1985 congressional hearings. Crown's son, Lester, was named as an unindicted coconspirator in 1974 for bribery involving the Material Services Division and Chicago officials. The issue was settled but there was no doubt of Crown's culpability. He could not, nonetheless, be removed from the board.[10]

In 1970, GD brought in David Lewis from MacDonnell-Douglas as CEO to combat a worsening financial position. The company was facing financially difficult times and omitted its quarterly dividend. GD was indicted by a grand jury in 1971 for contract irregularities and had a badly tarnished image. As it turned out, Lewis was highly successful in turning the company around. From a $7 million loss in 1970, sales rose to almost $8.1 billion in 1985 and net income rose to $383 million.[11]

An important element of this success was the pursuit of government contracts by

General Dynamics. In 1971, GD received 7 out of 12 contracts for the SSN668 (Los Angeles class) submarine, with the other 5 going to Newport News, a Tenneco company, which also received the design award. In 1973 Electric Boat gained another 11 contracts. To gain this business GD agreed to a "fixed price" contract. It was speculated that Lewis intentionally underbid to "buy in" hoping to recover his costs and make profit through increase in DOD's purchase price resulting from "specification changes." His own corporate people thought he yielded too much power to Admiral Rickover in order to curry favor.

When it came to producing the submarine and delivering on the contracts, GD was not doing so well, however. Production at Electric Boat was chaotic. In November 1974, Arthur Barton, the comptroller at Electric Boat, predicted an $800 million overrun on the $1.2 billion bid for the 18 submarines. A bearer of bad news, he became anathema to all company officials. By December 1974, the Navy was aware of production problems and had heard of overrun possibilities. It did not want this in the press so it offered $100 million to GD. By that time Electric Boat's own internal estimate was revised downward to $500 million. During all this time, Lewis kept the extent of the overrun secret from everyone: the SEC, the Navy, the board, shareholders, and Arthur Andersen, its independent outside accountants. In January 1975, the Electric Boat Claims Team estimated a $300 to $350 million loss on the first contract alone (7 submarines).[12]

1975 to 1978

In June 1975, Lewis finally told the board there could be a $100 million loss. Gordon MacDonald was put in charge of operations at Electric Boat.[13] In April 1976, the Navy came through with $97 million. By December 1976, General Dynamics formally filed a $544 million claim with the Navy, which shocked everyone. There was a showdown with Rickover.

In October 1977, Takis Veliotis took over at Electric Boat. Veliotis, a highly energetic and exuberant Greek American, had a checkered past. He came to General Dynamics in 1973 as General Manager of the Quincy Yard, where he was very successful during his four-year tenure in turning the division around. Veliotis had hopes of eventually succeeding Lewis. Once at Electric Boat, he discovered the Lewis cover-up but decided he had to play along. The cover-up was cemented in place by the career aspirations of both men. Unknown to anyone, however, during Veliotis' tenure at Quincy, he took over $1 million in kickbacks from Frigitemp, a subcontractor. In the end, this was to prove everyone's undoing. Frigitemp went bankrupt in the early 1980s and the chain of investigations led to Veliotis' indictment in September 1983. He would flee to Greece to avoid being subpoenaed by federal prosecutors.[14] But for this investigation, the whole General Dynamics scam might well have succeeded.

By 1977, General Dynamics was losing $15 million a month. Yet it showed no losses on its books from 1975 to 1977. Its stock price hit a high of $65 in 1976. By October 1977, it was still trading around $50. The Navy auditors found that the General Dynamics claim of $544 million had only $13 million merit. Rickover was furious over the fraud and he incited his friendly contacts in the U.S. Congress, leading Senator Proxmire to hold hearings. To add to the company's troubles, in November 1979, the Navy said that the Trident program was in trouble. It was $400 million over the $1.19 billion budget. Furthermore, the delivery date was set for April 1980, rather than General Dynamics' October 1979 date (which itself was six months after the contract delivery date). General Dynamics was accused of trying to manipulate its stock price by failing to disclose the truth.[15]

After threatening to discontinue production of the SSN668, General Dynamics decided to settle the SSN688 overrun disputes in June 1978. There was pressure to do so both from the Navy and from local congressmen. The total amounted to $843 million. The company was paid $125 million for some of its claims that the Navy did not dispute. The (disputed) remainder of $718 million was to be split evenly between the Navy and General Dynamics. Future overruns of up to $100 million were also to be split evenly. But amounts in excess of $100 million were to be borne by the company.[16] In the end, the Navy paid the equivalent of nearly $639 million. After tax deductions, General Dynamics charged off $180 million against earnings. It also received $300 million in advance from the government, which afforded the company extra earning capacity. Edward Hidalgo negotiated the settlement for the Navy and later went on to work for General Dynamics.

1979 to 1985

With overrun disputes finally settled, and General Dynamics on a financial upswing, a new problem was on the horizon. The U.S.S. Bremerton, already one year late to delivery, was found to have been built with poor quality steel and poor welds as well. The problem affected a number of ships. General Dynamics was faced with massive overhaul costs. Mr. James Ashton, assistant manager at Electric Boat, estimated cost overruns of from $170 to $200 million. Both Lewis and Veliotis moved to squelch him.[17]

No submarines were produced in 1980 at Electric Boat. To pay for its overruns, General Dynamics named the Navy as the insurer in a suit to get the U.S. government to pay. The ploy was unprecedented. Rickover was furious once again and more investigations ensued. But in October 1981 there was a settlement, which was generous to General Dynamics. George Sawyer, who negotiated the settlement for the Navy, later went on to become an executive vice-president and a member of the board of General Dynamics.

During 1981, things were beginning to look up. Electric Boat turned out six SSN668 submarines and the first Trident Submarine. In addition, F-16 aircraft production was ris-

ing, thereby giving General Dynamics' profits a much needed shot in the arm. Lewis had appointed Mr. Oliver Boileau as the new president of the company. Veliotis felt that his career was being undermined by some of the moves made by Lewis and Boileau. Veliotis was in the thick of the latest overrun controversy. He threatened to resign from Electric Boat. Lewis still needed Veliotis at this point. To mollify him, he made him an executive vice-president and a member of the board in May 1980. In the end, however, the settlement with the Navy called for Veliotis' removal from Electric Boat, as well as the exclusion of Rickover from Navy contracting. The second major overrun controversy seemed to be settled by 1982 and General Dynamics was prospering.

In the meantime, the Frigitemp investigations heated up. Veliotis was indicted in September 1983 and fled the country. In cooperating with the Justice Department's investigations, General Dynamics froze Veliotis' assets. Veliotis, in turn, decided to bury the company while getting the best deal possible for himself. He had copies of key records as well as tape recordings of key conversations, more than enough to prove that General Dynamics' top management was guilty of fraud. In May 1984, Veliotis was interviewed in Greece by the U. S. Justice Department. By October, he had turned over the bulk of his evidence.[18]

In May, the Navy suspended General Dynamics and set strict conditions for future contracts, including formally instituting a code of ethics as well as new accounting and management practices. In addition, certain fines were to be paid. The company was reinstated on August 13, 1985, but was suspended again from December 3, 1985 until February 7, 1986. Lewis resigned as CEO in December and was succeeded by Stanley Pace.[19]

General Dynamics' Position

General Dynamics' position with respect to the aforementioned charges was set forth by Chairman David S. Lewis in testimony before the Subcommittee on Oversight and Investigations of the House Committee on Energy and Commerce on February 28, 1985.[20]

Lewis and MacDonald appeared together and denied most of the serious charges against General Dynamics. These included: the Lester Crown affair, the Trident controversy, and improper billing of expenses to the government. Lewis stated that "the activities of the company are guided by policies set forth in written directives that conform completely with U.S. Government laws and regulations." He went on to say that most of the allegations "have emanated from malicious and untrue allegations made by a former employee, Mr. P. Takis Veliotis, who is now a fugitive from justice in Greece."[21] In his testimony, Lewis offered the following explanations in General Dynamics' defense to various allegations:

1. *Inadequate Financial Disclosures Concerned the SSN688 Submarine contracts.* These contracts caused serious difficulties for General Dynamics. The point of contention was whether the status of incurred costs, predicted overruns, claims submittals, and settlements on the SSN688 program were disclosed in a timely fashion. In Lewis' recounting of events, he focused upon the second overrun, which followed upon the USS Bremerton problems.

It was this particular overrun, together with the Trident issue, that investigators felt provided the major basis for an indictment. Lewis stated that the accusations of overruns apparently stemmed from a telephone conversation, taped by Veliotis, between himself; Lewis; Gordon E. MacDonald, executive vice-president of finance; and Warren G. Sullivan, vice-president of industrial relations. The purpose of the telephone conversation was to dissuade Veliotis from immediately discharging James E. Ashton, who was serving as Electric Boat assistant general manager of engineering. Ashton took that position in 1980, when Veliotis told Lewis that he wanted to leave the general manag-

er's position at Electric Boat and move to a higher level job. Ashton was then brought in as assistant general manager with the goal of growing into the general manager's job. However, almost immediately after his arrival, Ashton had considerable difficulty getting along with Veliotis and others at Electric Boat.

Ashton's testimony followed the joint appearance by MacDonald and Lewis. His testimony indicated a considerable discrepancy between GD's public announcements and his own projection, which would later turn out to be far more accurate. Ashton had called Navy officials and corporate officers to tell them that he thought the management's estimates of company losses were far too optimistic. GD maintained that Ashton was not qualified to make such estimates. Furthermore, GD's outside accounting firm, Arthur Andersen and Co., was informed of all the facts and saw nothing out of line with SEC reporting requirements. In fact, Arthur Andersen gave an independent confirmation of the claims.[22] Hence, according to David Lewis' testimony, financial information was, in fact, adequately disclosed to the proper parties in a timely fashion. Lewis' case was based on what he would call best knowledge available at the time. Lewis also contended that Ashton was not doing his assigned duties. Management wanted to fire him, but was reluctant to do so because the company was involved in critical negotiations with the Navy. Thus, Ashton's dismissal, according to Lewis, might be construed as if he was being fired for being a troublemaker. It was at this point that the telephone call concerning Ashton took place.

It should be pointed out here that cost overruns are very difficult to analyze before they happen. They are based on a series of untested probabilities. One estimate of General Dynamics' first set of overruns attributed 35% to inflation, 18.5% to problems with government furnished equipment not made by General Dynamics, 20% to changes in contract design, and 26.5% to production costs.[23] Design revisions proved to be a major bone of contention. In a taped conversation with MacDonald, Veliotis mentioned 7,000 to 8,000 revisions but asserted that the added costs were negligible. In another conversation with Rickover, he spoke of 32,000 revisions and implied that the costs were very great indeed.[24] In congressional testimony, the Navy acknowledged some revisions but pointed out that, nonetheless, Newport News produced the same submarine for $50 million less. What all of this shows is that the overrun problem is a hostage to poor accounting and auditing methods. In fact, the industry culture was set in a pattern of bidding low to gain a contract and then proceeding to lock it in so that DOD would come to the rescue of the company.

2. *The stock manipulation charge was related to the delivery date of the first Trident Submarine.* The Congressional hearing opened with a Veliotis tape of a conversation with MacDonald on November 29, 1977.[25] On the same day, the Navy held a press conference which indicated that a massive cost overrun of $400 million on the Trident program was primarily the fault of Electric Boat and left a clear impression that the Trident program would be unprofitable. The Navy also indicated that its estimate of the delivery date of the first Trident was six months later than the company's estimate.[26] The issue of whether the Trident program would be profitable or would incur a loss was vital with respect to its impact on the price of General Dynamics' stock.

On the next day, Veliotis again taped a telephone conversation with MacDonald. Veliotis alleged that two statements on that tape proved that General Dynamics knowingly quoted an overly-optimistic forecast delivery date for the first Trident in order to keep the stock price from sliding. General Dynamics agreed that the stock price was sliding, but attributed it largely to confused and misleading statements made by the Navy in the press conference. General

Dynamics protested to the Navy that the press conference inaccurately assigned the whole $400 million overrun to inefficiencies at Electric Boat. In response, the Navy released a memorandum attributing only $114 million to the company. It further stated that the contract ceiling price had not been reached and that General Dynamics would earn a profit on this project.

Veliotis agreed with the company's press conference statement, except he thought the delivery date was too optimistic. He conducted his own study in November 1977, just after he took over at Electric Boat. It was not completed until February 1978, however, and he then forecast the delivery date as November 1980 or early 1981. Lewis and MacDonald were aware that Veliotis believed that the October 1979 date was too optimistic. However, they said that since others were more familiar with the status of the program, they were more confident that the company's quoted date was viable.[27] The company argued that it was the uncertainty of profits, and not the estimates of delivery dates, that were important to the price of General Dynamics' stock. The stock was trading around $41.5 by March 15, 1978, from its high of $50 in November 1977. Therefore, getting the correct information in regard to profits to the stock market was very important. Since General Dynamics' stock had declined by almost 25%, it was obvious that General Dynamics did not manipulate its stock price through a more optimistic announcement of delivery dates.

3. *General Dynamics also denied the charges of illegal gratuities in violation of the submarine contracts.* This included gifts to Admiral Hyman Rickover and other military officers.[28] The company admitted that two gifts of jewelry costing $1,125 were given to Admiral Rickover for his wife in 1977. Lewis went on to say, "It is unfortunate that the Admiral asked for things and that it is unfortunate that the company gave (gifts) to him, but there was nothing corrupt in any of it." In addition, two other categories of gifts were given. The first consisted of a large number of minor items that were provided to the Navy for Admiral Rickover's use during sea trials of submarines constructed at Electric Boat. The second consisted of gifts made at ceremonial functions at Electric Boat, principally the keel layings and launchings of submarines.

General Dynamics claimed that it understood the breach of the gratuities clause in their contract to mean "the offer of a gratuity to an officer or an employee of the U.S. Government to obtain a contract or to secure favorable treatment in the awarding, amending, or making determinations concerning the performance of a contract."[29] However, since no gift or any other thing of value was ever given to Admiral Rickover by General Dynamics with the intention of corrupting him, no breach could have taken place. With respect to the giving of gifts at launchings, General Dynamics claimed that it was a centuries old tradition, and that under Navy regulations relative to the receipt of gratuities by Navy personnel, such gifts were specifically recognized as permissible. With regard to the sea trial gratuities, the company maintained that the provisions were requested by the Navy and that they were, in effect, "contract extras" designed for comfort, convenience, and entertainment. In May 1985, the Navy instructed General Dynamics to pay a fine of $676,283.30 (ten times the amount of the gratuities) and Admiral Rickover himself was censured.[30]

4. *Allegations that General Dynamics submitted millions of dollars in "undocumented" expense vouchers to the government.* Lewis maintained that the vouchers were documented to the extent required by the government acquisition regulations. The testimony details a number of expenses.[31] Some, such as MacDonald's boarding of his dog Fursten at Silver Maple Farms for $87.25 are egregiously out of line.[32] Most of the testimony, however, was a sparring contest over

the definition of allowable costs. While admitting to some mistakes, Lewis, for the most part, maintained that the government had been asked to reimburse the cost of only those expenses that were properly allocatable to the government's business.

General Dynamics maintained that all defense contracts provide for negotiation of overhead costs when disagreements between the government and the contractor arise. The Defense Contract Audit Agency (DCAA) has access to the contractor's records and, after studying them, issues audit reports which become "advisory documents" for use by government negotiators in establishing the government's negotiating position. According to GD, in large and complex contracts, it was not unusual to find many items that would be questioned by DCAA and ultimately disallowed by ACO. However, according to Lewis, it was never the company's intention to consciously misrepresent any request for reimbursement of costs incurred.[33] The company agreed that the questions raised by the DCAA should not be considered to be the final word since the role of the DCAA was only advisory. The Administrative Contracting Office (ACO) had the ultimate responsibility for reviewing, negotiating, and settling with a contractor on the contents of the allowable overhead costs. An exhaustive review of "97 million" overhead vouchers (primarily at Electric Boat and Pomona Divisions) led to a settlement of $57.3 million in the Navy's favor.[34]

5. *Use of corporate aircraft for non-business purposes and submitting the costs to the government for reimbursement.* The company asserted that its use of corporate aircraft represented an efficient and effective use of an important productivity and security tool. Corporate personnel were required to visit divisional operations in many places in the U.S. In addition, many visits had to be made to other locations where the company had significant business to be carried out with government officials, contractors, and sub-contractors concerned with General Dynamics. The disputed cost items centered around business purposes of a more general and indirect nature, e.g., to provide travel to important business meetings and conferences and to meetings of other companies' boards of directors. According to General Dynamics, the amount of these activities had been greatly exaggerated, and, furthermore, the validity of the items was not in question, just their cost application.[35]

The Government's Position

There was not one "government position" but two, advanced by two different agencies whose objectives, strategies, and tactics were not necessarily similar. In fact, in some instances, they were diametrically opposed. The two bodies of the government in question are the Department of Defense (DOD) and Congress.

The DOD's overriding concern is stability, continuity, and predictability in procurement. This is the means of carrying out its goal of maintaining national security.[36] DOD wants stability and a reasonable division of labor in the budgeting process. As the system currently works, each year the president prepares a budget for congressional approval. Therefore, each year the amount that the Pentagon receives changes. The weapons development and production system, on the other hand, has long lead times and depends on funding commitments that are not easily changed without serious impact to costs and also facility utilization and planning by defense contractors. DOD, therefore, is hard pressed to keep systems functioning. The contractors know of this instability in government funding and thus are discouraged from making the long term investment necessary to improve productivity and lower costs. DOD tries to combat its inability to promise a long-term commitment with other inducements. It uses special concessions such as highly profitable "sole source contracts,"—thus eliminating the risk of losing a contract

to another contractor.[37] It also employs "unpriced contracts," thereby guaranteeing the contractor the reimbursement of virtually *all* the costs and removing any risk of cost over-run. DOD allows for sloppy auditing procedures that ratify unanticipated and questionable expenses "after the fact," e.g., accepting a 50-50 split (which will be further enumerated in the congressional viewpoint); of overhead charges, and progress payments—interim monthly payments that reimburse the contractor for up to 95% of his costs *before* the performance of the contract is completed.[38]

The DOD contends that these practices are necessary in order to attract high-quality contractors to take on a project, and to keep them interested once production has begun. Such means are deemed necessary because Congress cannot promise contractors any amount beyond the current fiscal year. The DOD also argues that Congress plays too large a role in the weapons development, production, and procurement process.[39] Too often, Congress's interest in a particular weapons system is correlated with the political careers of its members. It is clear that the settlement of both of General Dynamics' cost overruns had the active support of congressional representatives from the affected districts. The settlement of such disputes, as well as the landing of a contract in the first place, mean jobs and votes. The success or failure of a program not only has to do with defense but with corporate, political, and military careers. Too often, the latter forces dominate.

Congress, in return, points the finger right back to the DOD. The first claim, and perhaps the most important one that Congress makes, has to do with the need for centralization of procurement. There is no central, senior official in the DOD to handle procurement and associated activities.[40] Keeping in mind that there are four branches of the military (technically, the Marines are part of the Navy) it is not hard to fathom the consequences of having no centralized means of equipment acquisition.

Congress also accuses the DOD of "gold-plating" the weapons systems, thereby contributing to excessive cost and time overruns. Goldplating means that the specifications for any system or good are so detailed and customized, that *if* a contractor can manufacture it at all, it is usually a most inefficient process. For example, the Packard Commission reported that specifications on certain requested computer chips were so custom tailored, that they ended up costing thousands of dollars more than, and having *fewer* capabilities than, a standard state-of-the-art chip, which could have done the job to begin with.[41]

Congress also accuses the DOD of rushing weapons systems into production without sufficient development and testing of a prototype model to iron out all possible bugs and potential malfunctions.[42] This was the case with the SSN668 submarine. Before it was rigorously tested as a prototype, it was in production as a class of submarines. The SSN668 was in fact an inferior product. It passed the tests of speed and stealth but performed poorly on the depth it could reach.[43]

Another reason for cost overruns, according to congressional sources, was fraud by defense contractors and lenient treatment thereof by DOD. The $9,000 wrench provides a symbolic example.[44] The DOD's accounting procedures are considered so flawed and lax that, in some cases, R&D and engineering bills were submitted for tools that were produced and paid for under *previously satisfied* contracts.

The easy, informal alliance between the Department of Defense and the industry is further borne out in the rollover of personnel from one to the other. The House hearing devoted considerable time to the case of George Sawyer.[45] He had negotiated the second set of overruns on behalf of the Navy but very favorably for General Dynamics in 1981. By 1983 he was not only a vice-president at GD; he was a member of the board! Company testimony includes documents from Navy officials affirming the lack of a conflict of interest when General Dynamics

was in the process of considering Sawyer for employment.

MOVING TOWARD CHANGE

By 1985, it was clear to everyone that defense contracting was in a crisis. Realizing the threat to his administration's defense policy, President Reagan created a 17-member committee to evaluate the situation, and to make necessary recommendations. This committee, the President's Blue Ribbon Commission on Defense Management, was set up in July 1985 under the chairmanship of former defense secretary David Packard (This group will hereinafter be referred to as the Packard Commission.) The Packard Commission report, entitled "A Quest For Excellence," was released in June 1986 and has since become a major document for the development of future policy.[46]

The Commission focused its attention on four topics, i.e., National Security Planning and Budgeting; Military Organization and Command; Acquisition Organization and Procedures; and, Government-Industry Accountability.

1. *National security planning and budgeting.* The President and his National Security Council would set forth national security objectives and priorities and the DOD would draw up military programs accordingly. This "conforming" would consist of developing a 5-year-plan of action and a 2-year budget, both of which would fit the option the President has chosen. Congress would be asked to approve the 2-year budget, and if so, would authorize and appropriate the funds for major weapons systems only at two key milestones of: (1) full-scale R&D (including a prototype) and, (2) high-rate production (as a weapons class). The DOD would *not* be required to present its budget on a line-item by line-item basis.

2. *Military organization and command.* Several operational changes were suggested in the organization of military command to better facilitate action, and to remove some of the bureaucratic levels of command (manage-

ment) that existed. Recommended changes allow for better communication between branches, shorter chains of command for quicker action, and, in general, a better organized system.

3. *Acquisition organization and procedures.* First and foremost, in the office of the secretary of defense, it was recommended that a statute be passed to create the position of undersecretary of defense-acquisition. This person would have a solid industrial background, and would serve as a full-time defense acquisition executive. He or she would set policy for procurement and R&D, and would supervise the overall acquisition system. Further, this position would have administrative oversight for auditing defense contractors. It was further recommended that each branch of the military should create a comparable acquisition position whose job description would mirror that of the undersecretary.

In addition, the DOD would upgrade the individual acquisition position(s) so as to enable it to attract and hold on to quality acquisition personnel.

The report recommended other changes, including greater use of "off-the-shelf" items and the increased use of operational testing and prototypes. It also strongly argued for more competition in the acquisition process. Competition does not so much refer to the design of a military system as to its production. The costs of the former may too often be prohibitive. Such a policy would restrict the number of sole-source contracts.

4. *Government-industry accountability.* The Packard Commission recommended that the federal criminal and civil laws pertaining to defense acquisition must be aggressively enforced on any and all violators. Further, more effective laws should be passed to prevent fraudulent and/or unethical actions. In addition, ethical guidelines must be drawn up and implemented. In response to the recommendations set forth by the Packard Commission, many defense companies have begun initiatives on business ethics and conduct. Many companies have signed a document called the Defense Industry Initiatives on Business Ethics and Conduct. The principles in this document are: (1) a written code of business ethics and conduct; (2) the employee's ethical responsibilities; (3) corporate responsibility to employees; (4) corporate

responsibility to the Government; 5) Corporate responsibility to the defense Industry; and (6) Public accountability. It calls for the contractors to adopt and implement a set of principles of business ethics and conduct that acknowledge and address their corporate responsibilities under federal procurement laws. Furthermore, free, open, and timely reporting of violations become the felt responsibility of every employee in the defense industry.[47]

In connection with this, General Dynamics has specifically initiated an updated, strengthened ethics program to ensure that all employees practice and understand the vital importance of the highest possible standards of business ethics and conduct. Beginning in August 1985, the company's newspaper, *General Dynamics World*, has featured regular articles on its new ethics program at all levels throughout the company.[48]

In this program, and as part of a formalized education and training plan, a new booklet entitled "General Dynamics Standards of Business Ethics and Conduct" was distributed to each salaried employee. The booklet defines and discusses explicit standards of employee conduct on a number of specific subjects, including: conflicts of interest, pricing, billing, and quality/testing. A comprehensive program to communicate and implement these defined standards was introduced at all divisions.

Finally, the DOD has also begun to implement some changes. As noted earlier, suspensions or debarments of defense contractors are up dramatically. Settlement agreements now outline very specific actions to be taken by contractors to implement comprehensive corporate ethics programs and internal audit and management controls, and to enforce them.[49]

Much Ado About Nothing

How did it all end? When it was all said and done, it turned out that it was almost all said and very little, if anything, done. General Dynamics had its wrists slapped. Although investigations continued for the next two years, little happened. Finally, on Friday, June 19, 1987, the Justice Department dropped all criminal charges against General Dynamics in an investigation of its Pomona division. A civil suit against the company on similar fraud charges was also subsequently dropped. In its announcement, the Justice Department said that a review of documents, found after the original indictment was handed in, showed that General Dynamics was correct in its interpretation of contract provisions pertaining to cost overruns.[50]

If one looks at the nature and scope of penalties, three patterns emerge:

1. DOD is extremely dependent on a handful of large contractors for its purchases. The size and complexities of the purchases is such that often it is difficult to draw the line between design changes, unforeseen circumstances, cost overruns due to inefficiencies, and outright contract fraud. Moreover, DOD cannot afford to weaken the contractors, through penalties, so as to reduce their financial and operational strength thereby jeopardizing national security.

2. The long-term nature of supplying complex systems, and even simple purchases, builds a sense of comradery and cooperation between vendors and DOD personnel. While such cooperation is necessary for the smooth operation of the procurement effort, it also creates opportunities for collusion and illicit favors. The situation becomes even more complex because of the "revolving door" nature of future employment of DOD personnel with the contractors, and the no-competition or single-source nature of many procurement contracts.

3. The long and sustained relationships between DOD and vendor personnel also makes it difficult for the former to impose harsh penalties where evidence of clear-cut irregularities exist and where harsher penalties would act as general deterrence without, at the same time, seriously impacting the vendor's viability. Thus, there is a constant attempt on both sides to settle things amicably, and to "keep disagreements within the family," with the results that most penalties

do not amount to more than a slap on the wrist and have an equally negligible impact on vendor behavior.

Thus, after a few skirmishes and public squabbles, business goes on as usual and the country and society become the ultimate losers. This is amply borne out in the manner in which the charges against General Dynamics were disposed of by DOD. Moreover, as can be seen by the recent evidence in other cases, General Dynamics was not alone in getting off easily but instead followed a pattern that was only too predictable from similar events in the past and is quite likely to repeat itself in the future.[51]

On June 14, 1988, the Justice Department announced the largest white-collar crime investigation ever in the United States. It involved a number of the largest defense contractors, defense department officials, consultants, and even members of Congress. The alleged activities included bribes, payoffs, bid-rigging, and the selling of confidential information to gain competitive advantages in defense contract bidding.[52]

The drama has continued unabated into the nineties.[53] From 1988 through 1994, many major companies have been found guilty. In 1994 the government collected more than a billion dollars from such companies. There is little sign, however, that procurement practices have fundamentally changed. One of the government's most potent weapons has been the revised whistleblower law passed in 1986, that grants whistleblowers awards of a minimum of 15 percent of the amounts the government recovers. This has provided a very strong incentive for those in the know to step forward. To be sure, there is mounting controversy over the role of whistleblowers and contractors continue to lobby extensively to change the whistleblower laws. They do not hesitate to engage former Pentagon and other government officials to press their case. The "revolving door," where former government officials head off to lucrative industry positions, has not been slowed down. In the end, the whole issue of defense industry corruption is complicated by much larger issues such as downsizing and restructuring in the industry, a shrinking defense budget, and the intense battle between Congressional districts and local areas to maintain their share of the shrinking defense pie. Fundamental change will take decades.

NOTES

1. United States Congress, House of Representatives, Subcommittee on Oversight and Investigations, Committee on Energy and Commerce, *Oversight of the Federal Securities Laws and Disclosures Thereunder By the General Dynamics Corporation*, February 28, March 25, April 23, April 24, 1985. Hereafter cited as *Hearings*. *Washington Post*, March 1, 1985, "General Dynamics' Officials Grilled," pp. A1, 8.
2. *Business Week*, "General Dynamics under Fire," (March 25, 1985), pp. 70–76.
3. *Newsweek*, "How to Reform the Pentagon's Wasteful Ways," (May 27, 1985), pp. 144–49.
4. Packard Commission Report, June 1986, *A Quest for Excellence*, p. 103. (Hereafter cited as The Packard Commission.)
5. Philip Shenon, "Dept. of Justice Faulted on Drive to Combat Crime," *New York Times*, (July 3, 1988), pp. 1, 11. *Newsweek*, "Payoffs At the Pentagon," (June 27, 1988), pp.20–22.
6. Caspar W. Weinberger, "Remarks to the First Annual Best Practices Forum Conference," October 30, 1986.
7. Ruth L. Sivard, 1985, *World Military and Social Expenditures*, The Packard Commission, pp. 48, 73.
8. General Dynamics Corporation, *10-K Report*, 1988.
9. General Dynamics Corporation, *Annual Report*, 1987.
10. *Hearings*, pp. 8–14.
11. General Dynamics Corporation, *Annual Report*, 1986.
12. Patrick Tyler, *Running Critical: The Silent War, Rickover and General Dynamics*. HarperCollins 1986, pp. 135–146.
13. *Ibid.*, pp. 146–148; 159–163; *Hearings*, pp. 8–14.
14. Tyler, *Running Critical*, pp. 168ff.
15. *Ibid.*, pp. 187–192, 209–14, 220, 231. *Hearings*, pp. 15–49.
16. Tyler, *Running Critical*, pp. 139–46, 176–78, 293–294; *Hearings*, pp. 470–73.
17. *Ibid.*, pp. 258–60, 287; *Hearings*, pp. 76–97; 426ff.
18. *Hearings*, pp. 93ff; Tyler, *Running Critical*, pp. 329–41.
19. Joan Nelson–Horschler, "Stan Pace to the Rescue: Creating a New Image at a Scandal Ridden Firm." *Industry Week* (March 31, 1986), p. 81.
20. *Hearings*, pp. 8–14.
21. *Hearings*, pp. 15–49.
22. *Hearings*, pp. 470ff.
23. *Wall Street Journal*, "Cost Overruns in the Defense Industry" (December 1, 1977). p. 35.
24. Tyler, *Running Critical*, pp. 152, 239–40.
25. *Ibid.*, pp. 209–212; *Hearings*, pp. 76–89.
26. Tyler, *Running Critical*, pp. 209–14.
27. *Hearings*, pp. 92–97; 171ff.
28. Tyler, *Running Critical*, pp. 162–163, 223–224, 272–273.
29. *Hearings*, pp. 258ff.
30. Office of The Assistant Secretary of Defense, Public Affairs, News Release, (May 21, 1985).
31. *Hearings*, pp. 180–419.
32. *Hearings*, pp. 197, 205.
33. *Hearings*, pp. 13–14.
34. Office of the Assistant Secretary of Defense, Public Affairs, News Release, (August 13, 1985).
35. *Hearings*, pp. 12–14.
36. *The Packard Commission*, pp.xvii–xx. Caspar W. Weinberger, "Remarks to the First Annual Best Practices Forum Conference." U.S. Department of Defense, Press Release (October 30, 1986), pp. 3-5.
37. *Business Week*, "Caspar Weinberger Flies into Heavier Flak" (April 15, 1985), pp. 132–33.
38. Tim Carrington, "Watered–Down Military procurement reforms Will Ensure 'Business As Usual,' Critics Charge." *Wall Street Journal*, (August 13, 1985), p. 54.
39. *The Packard Commission*, pp. xx–xxi.
40. *Ibid.*, p. xxv
41. *Ibid.*, pp. 60–61.
42. *Ibid.*, pp. xxv–xxvi
43. Tyler, *Running Critical.*, pp. 52–72.

44. *New York Times*, "Another Failure to Fix the Pentagon." (November 21, 1987), p. A18.

45. *Hearings*, pp. 428–527.

46. *The Packard Commission*, pp. xvii–xxx.

47. Best Practices Forum, 1986. *Defense Industry Initiatives on Business Ethics And Conduct.* (Reprinted in the *Packard Commission Report*, 1986a, pp.41–45.)

48. General Dynamics Corporation, *General Dynamics World*, January, 1986, p.2. General Dynamics Corporation, *General Dynamics World*, August, 1985, pp.1–2.

49. Department of Defense, Office of the Inspector General, Integrity Alerts, (March 1986).

50. *The Packard Commission*, p. xiii.

51. "U.S. Abandons Fraud Case against General Dynamics." *New York Times* (June 19, 1987), p. 18. "U.S. Calls Halt to Investigation of a Contractor." *New York Times* (May 20, 1987), pp. 1, D2.

52. "The Defense Scandal: The Fallout May Devastate Arms Merchants." *Business Week*, (July 4, 1988), p. 28.

53. Jeff Cole, "Battle Over Grumman Escalates the Dogfight in Defense Industry, *Wall Street Journal* (March 14,1994), pp. A1, A6; Calvin Sims, "Trying to Mute the Whistleblowers," *New York Times* (April 11, 1994) pp. D1, D8.

THE HOUSE OF NOMURA AND THE JAPANESE SECURITIES SCANDALS*

The integrity of markets in a cross-cultural perspective

I sincerely apologize to the public and the nation's investors for the trouble caused . . . I am responsible for the firm's actions. [Employees in the future will] strictly abide by ethical rules."

Setsuya Tabuchi
The Chairman of Nomura Securities
(June 20, 1991)

These shocking statements of contrition and admission were in response to the revelation that one of the world's most powerful securities houses had been "caught red handed, offering illicit compensation to institutional clients, laundering money for yakuza (the Japanese mafia)[1] and encouraging (stock speculation)."[2] Nomura Securities, and the three other members of the "Big Four" securities firms in Japan (Daiwa, Nikko, Yamaichi), were ultimately accused of a plethora of improper activities, which also included tax evasion, ignoring the Ministry of Finance (hereafter referred to as "MOF") directives, succumbing to extortionists, and misusing confidential information.

On October 8, 1991, the MOF announced penalties against the Big Four. Nomura was banned from brokering equities in 86 offices and branches for one month, starting October 15, 1991. Nomura was further prohibited from brokering for six weeks at its head office and seven other large branches; ordered to

This case was prepared by: Iwao Taka, The International School of Economics and Business Administration at Reitaku University; and Thomas W. Dunfee, The Wharton School at The University of Pennsylvania. It is based upon public documents and media reports. Wanda Foglia, Stefan Whitwell, and Martin Rawle also provided input into the drafting of the case.

suspend activities in its research division for one month; and forbidden from bidding in government-bond auctions until the end of November 1991.[3] A month later, the Japanese Fair Trade Commission (JFTC) publicized the results of its investigation of the scandals and issued decrees against the Big Four, ordering them to promise never again to compensate clients for losses. The JFTC also clearly stated its position that similar offenses in the future would lead to criminal sanctions, regardless of motive. The Big Four signed consent decrees with the JFTC in December 1991.[4]

Nomura also made significant efforts of its own to acknowledge and atone for its role in the compensation of favored clients. Yoshihisa Tabuchi resigned as president in late June 1991, almost immediately after the scandal broke, and Setsuya Tabuchi resigned as both chairman of Nomura and vice chairman of Keidanren (The Japanese Federation of Economic Organizations). The latter also relinquished the opportunity to become the head of the Securities Dealers Association of Japan. Thirty-two senior Nomura officers were fired, and several others demoted, while the pay of those executives who remained was slashed by as much as 30%.

FORESHADOWING A CRISIS: THE GROWTH OF CORPORATE DISCRETIONARY ACCOUNTS

The core illicit activity comprising the so-called Japanese Securities Scandals was compensating favored clients for investment

TABLE 1. Trade Surplus and Foreign Assets of Japan

Fiscal Year	Trade Surplus	Japanese Yen vs. Dollar	A Reserve in Foreign Currency	(Million Dollar) Foreign Assets
1980	6,766	217.40	27,020	11,534
1981	20,358	227.38	27,231	10,918
1982	20,141	249.66	24,015	24,682
1983	34,546	236.39	25,109	37,259
1984	45,601	244.19	26,538	74,346
1985	64,601	221.09	27,917	129,821
1986	101,648	159.83	58,389	180,351
1987	94,034	138.33	84,857	240,744
1988	95,302	128.27	99,353	291,746
1989	69,999	142.82	73,496	293,215
1990	69,864	141.30	69,894	328,059
1991	113,683	133.18	68,230	383,072

* Fiscal year starts in April and ends the following March.

SOURCE: The Japanese Economic Planing Agency, *Keizai Hakusho (Economic White Paper: 1992)*, Tokyo: the Ministry of Finance, 1992, reference, pp. 68–69.

TABLE 2. Changes of the Japanese Official Discount Rate

Year	Month/Day	After Revised Rate (%)	Revised (%)
1980	2/19	7.25	+1.00
	3/19	9.00	+1.75
	8/20	8.25	-0.75
	11/ 6	7.25	-1.00
1981	3/18	6.25	-1.00
	12/11	5.50	-0.75
1983	10/22	5.00	-0.50
1986	1/30	4.50	-0.50
	3/10	4.00	-0.50
	4/21	3.50	-0.50
	11/ 1	3.00	-0.50
1987	2/23	2.50	-0.50
1989	5/31	3.25	+0.75
	10/11	3.75	+0.50
	12/25	4.25	+0.50
1990	3/20	5.25	+1.00
	8/30	6.00	+0.75
1991	7/ 1	5.50	-0.50
	11/14	5.00	-0.50
	12/30	4.50	-0.50
1992	4/1	3.75	-0.75

SOURCE: The Ministry of Finance, *Kinyu/Shoken/Kawase Key Word (Key Words of Finance, Securities, and Exchange)*, Tokyo: Keizai Chosakai, 1992, p. 47.

losses. During the 1980s, Japanese firms were collecting huge amounts of cash and were witnessing an increasingly large trade surplus. (See Table 1.) With interest rates particularly low, firms were searching for investments to soak up their excess cash. (See Tables 2 and 3.)

Changes in the Japanese tax laws in 1980 made investments in trust accounts for institutions and corporate investors particularly attractive.[5] Two types of accounts became especially popular: *tokkin* and *kingai*. Tokkin accounts enabled a corporation or pension fund to deposit a reserve with a trust bank under an agreement that specifies the length of the contract and how the portfolio is to be managed. In most cases, the investor selected an investment advisory company to provide the investment "advice." Kingai were similar accounts offered to institutional investors, but they differed in that the investors did not specify how the funds were to be invested. (See Table 4.) They let the trust bank invest on a discretionary basis.[6]

Although securities firms were not officially authorized to offer tokkin accounts, many began to proffer special *eigyo tokkin* accounts to favored corporate and institutional investors to compete with the trust banks' tokkin and kingai accounts. These accounts were similar to kingai accounts in the sense that the firms' brokers directly managed eigyo tokkin accounts and used their own discretion in deciding how to

TABLE 3. Money Supply and Price Index of Japanese Real Estate

Year	Money Supply (Tri. Yen)	Average Real Estate	Commercial Area	Residential Area
1984	277.6	67.4	60.7	71.8
1985	301.6	69.2	62.7	73.4
1986	327.6	71.6	66.2	75.3
1987	364.3	79.2	75.2	82.4
1988	403.4	84.1	81.8	85.8
1989	444.9	92.3	91.6	92.8
1990	490.1	107.3	108.1	107.0
1991	502.8	110.5	111.7	109.4

* The price index of real estate (1990.3 = 100) is that of each September. The money supply is an annual average (fiscal year average) of M2 (Cash + Deposit on Demand + Time Deposit) and Certificates of Deposit.

SOURCE: Toyo Keizai Shinposha, *Toyo Keizai Tokei Geppo (Toyo Keizai Statistics Monthly)*, Vol. 52, No. 10, Oct. 1992. The Japanese Economic Planing Agency, *Keizai Hakusho (Economic White Paper: 1992)*, Tokyo: the Ministry of Finance, 1992, reference, p. 70.

TABLE 4. Securities Investment by the Japanese Corporations (Billion Yen)

Fiscal Year	Increased Amount of Money/Deposit	Raised Capital from the Market	Balance of Tokkin/Kingai
1983	2,480	2,814	1,430
1984	1,890	3,996	2,190
1985	1,161	4,517	8,810
1986	5,299	5,781	20,430
1987	7,532	16,812	29,980
1988	9,323	17,557	35,210
1989	11,104	24,816	42,660
1990	—	10,496	36,730

* Fiscal year starts in April and ends in the following March. Money/Deposit includes short-term securities. The numbers of Money/Deposit are those of whole Japanese industries except for financial and insurance industries. The rest of the numbers are those of whole industries.

SOURCE: Uchida, S., "*Bubble Keizai de Yuganda Shoken Shijo* (The Securities Market Distorted by a Bubble Economy)," *Nihon Keizai Shinbun*, July 5, 1991.

invest the funds. The autonomy they enjoyed when buying and selling securities allowed the brokers to respond quickly to changes in the securities market.

As Japanese brokers' commissions were fixed and relatively high, these accounts made them billions of yen in commissions. (See Table 5.) In exchange, the securities firms implicitly agreed to guarantee the return on the accounts. In the mid-1980s, eigyo tokkin became very popular among brokers and

their corporate clients because of their superior return over the available domestic fixed income securities. It was estimated that the amount invested in eigyo tokkin reached over ¥5 trillion in September 1989.[7]

As long as the average price of the shares continued rising, this financial arrangement was mutually enriching. (See Tables 6, 7 and 8.) Although, as noted above, tokkin was supposed to be handled by trust banks with the help of financial advisers, by the mid-1980s, eigyo tokkin, business had become popular in the securities industry. Primarily concerned about the unorthodox form of eigyo tokkin, which could result in brokers compensating clients for market losses, the MOF asked 22 large Japanese brokers to report the balance of eigyo tokkin in October of 1986, and verbally ordered them to refrain from using eigyo tokkin.[8]

The brokers continued to use eigyo tokkin accounts despite this verbal order, and when the New York Stock Exchange suddenly plunged a year later on "Black Monday" (October 19, 1987), securities prices fell around the globe and Japanese firms were forced to compensate clients for considerable losses. However, as will be discussed more fully below, it was not until December 26, 1989, that the MOF finally issued a written directive prohibiting brokers from compen-

TABLE 5. Change of the Fixed Brokerage Commission

The Amount of Transaction (Million Yen)	1990.6 (%)	1987.10 (%)	1986.11 (%)	1985.4 (%)	1977.4 (%)
less than 1	1.150	1.200	1.250	1.250	1.250
1 to 3	0.900	1.000	1.050	1.050	1.050
3 to 5	0.900	0.900	0.950	0.950	0.950
5 to 10	0.700	0.750	0.850	0.850	0.850
10 to 30	0.575	0.600	0.700	0.750	0.750
30 to 50	0.375	0.400	0.500	0.650	0.650
50 to 100	0.225	0.250	0.300	0.550	0.600
100 to 300	0.200	0.200	0.250	0.450	0.550
300 to 500	0.125	0.200	0.250	0.350	0.550
500 to 1000	0.100	0.200	0.200	0.300	0.550
more than 1000	0.075	0.150	0.150	0.250	0.550

SOURCE: Oomura, K. and Kawakita, E., *Nihon no Kabushiki Shijo* (*The Japanese Stock Market*), Tokyo: Toyo Keizai Shinposha, 1992, p. 47.

TABLE 6. The Stock Index of the Japanese, U. S., and British Markets (1984=100)

Year	Japan	United States	Britain
1984	100.00	100.00	100.00
1985	122.35	116.87	122.29
1986	162.39	147.11	152.09
1987	240.76	174.95	198.78
1988	261.72	162.17	180.57
1989	315.07	194.81	215.08
1990	267.08	198.42	211.65
1991	226.03	223.14	230.06

* Japanese Index is based on average TOPIX of the first section of Tokyo Stock Exchange. American Index is based on NYSE Common Stock Index (all stocks), and British one is based on E. T. Actuaries' stock index (all stocks).

SOURCE: *Annual Securities Statistics (1991)*, Ed. by S. Kimbara, Tokyo: Research Department of Tokyo Stock Exchange, 1992, p. 36 and p. 358.

sating clients,[9] and it would be several more years before significant changes in investment practices occurred.

ISSUES FOR ANALYSIS

The Nomura securities scandal incident specifically invokes questions concerning what is ethical for a Japanese firm doing business within Japan. Nomura thus contrasts with cases whose focus is on how a U.S.-based global firm should act in a foreign country, or which look directly at global business practices. Japanese ethics derive from the social and religious history of Japan. A full understanding of the context of Nomura's decisions requires familiarity with the system of government regulation indigenous to Japan, captured here in the phenomenon called administrative guidance.

1. As a result of the influence of Confucianism, Japanese business ethics varies in significant ways from business ethics in the United States and Europe. In Japan, the context of the decision, and particularly the identity of the person with whom you are dealing is important. The case describes this phenomenon in terms of concentric circles—the innermost being that of the family and then moving outward through the Fellows circle and the Japan circle ultimately to the world circle. This leads to a central question in the case. Does what is ethical in Japan vary according to the circle in which the decision is made? If so, could that mean that the practice of promised compensation by brokers might be ethical in the Fellows circle but not in the Japan circle? If this is true, then to what extent is this a highly relativistic ethic? A related question involves whether it is appropriate to extrapolate from an individualistic ethic to the corporate environment. Does it make sense to think about a corporation as having a Family circle and a Fellows circle?

2. It is common for outsiders to believe that other cultures have a relatively homogenous

TABLE 7. The Aggregate Market Value and PER (Price Earning Ratio) of the Tokyo Stock Exchange

Year/Mo.	Total Value of the Japanese Markets (Tri. Yen)*	PER (1) Japan	PER (2) US High	PER (3) US Low
1985.12	196.2 (190.1)	32.44	15.4	11.9
1986.12	293.0 (285.5)	42.36	19.5	15.5
1987.12	345.6 (336.7)	69.17	19.4	12.6
1988.12	488.1 (476.9)	70.23	12.3	10.5
1989.12	630.1 (611.2)	68.42	15.3	11.9
1990.12	393.6 (379.2)	46.39	17.8	14.1
1991.12	392.0 (377.9)	41.28	29.2	21.7

* The Japanese markets consist of 8 markets: Tokyo, Osaka, Nagoya, Kyoto, Hiroshima, Fukuoka, Niigata, and Sapporo. The numbers in parenthesis are total value of the first and second sections of the Tokyo Stock Exchange. PER = (Total market capitalization)/(Total after tax profits). PER (1) is the average PER of 225 Issues for the first section of Tokyo Stock Exchange. PER (2) is the High PER of S&P Industrial Index. PER (3) is the Low PER of S&P industrial Index.

SOURCE: *Annual Securities Statistics* (1991), Ed. by S. Kimbara, Tokyo: Research Department of Tokyo Stock Exchange, 1992, pp. 66–67. Nomura Research Institute, Ltd. (ed.) *Annual of Securities Statistics*, Tokyo: the Nomura Securities Co., Ltd., 1992, p. 89 and p. 301.

TABLE 8. Equity Finance of the Japanese Corporations (Billion Yen)

Fiscal Year	Domestic Markets		Foreign Markets		TOTAL	
	Stock	CB/WB	Stock	CB/WB	Stock	CB/WB
1985	651.3	1,656.5	10.7	1,814.2	662.0	3,470.7
1986	631.5	3,572.0	0.6	2,478.4	632.1	6,050.4
1987	2,083.9	5,055.0	39.0	4,515.7	2,122.9	9,570.7
1988	4,563.8	6,994.5	16.5	6,048.6	4,580.3	13,043.1
1989	7,560.0	8,554.5	336.4	10,008.7	7,896.4	18,563.2
1990	664.3	1,306.0	-	3,138.3	664.3	4,444.3
1991	342.7	1,660.5	-	4,315.8	342.7	5,976.3

* Fiscal year starts in April and ends in the following March.

SOURCE: The Ministry of Finance, *Kinyu/Shoken/Kawase Key Word (Key Words of Finance, Securities, and Exchange),* Tokyo: Keizai Chosakai, 1992, p. 155.

ethical environment, in contrast to what they probably perceive as a very complex ethical framework in their own culture. But in this case, is it clear to a lower-level manager at Nomura as to whether it is proper to promise compensation and open an eigyo tokkin account? Which should be considered the dominant signal among the divergent signals being given about the propriety of the practice of compensation used with eigyo tokkin accounts? A related questions pertains to the surreptitious manner in which the promises are made. Why is it that a Japanese manager would signal the promise through a pat on the cheek rather than by simply stating the promise outright?

3. The issue of promise-keeping arises in all cultures, particularly in the context of economic activities. Consider the situation in which a brokerage firm such as Nomura promised compensation, the client subsequently realized losses, and the firm is now under seeming pressure from the Japanese Ministry of Finance to not follow through and provide the full promised compensation. Honoring promises, a fundamental ethical obligation, is now at odds with the long-standing cooperative relationship with the Ministry of Finance. Which of these should take precedence?

4. U.S. firms doing business in Japan of necessity encounter the practice of compensation. They may be in the role of clients seeking compensation (and at a competitive disadvantage if they aren't able to secure promises of compensation), or they may be financial

services firms directly competing with Japanese brokerage firms that are offering compensation. Several important ethical issues arise. If U.S. firms are consistently unable to secure promises of compensation (perhaps because they are not considered to be in the Fellows circle) is such a practice unethical? Would the practice of promising compensation be considered ethical in the United States? If not, then, even so, would it be permissible for a U.S. firm to follow the practice in Japan.

5. A final theme, implicit in the Nomura example, is the relationship between ethics in the United States and Japan. It is a useful exercise to try to develop a matrix which allocates practices on the following basis: ethical in both cultures, ethical in neither culture, ethical in Japan and unethical in the U.S. and ethical in the U.S. and unethical in Japan.

THE HOUSE OF NOMURA AND THE JAPANESE SECURITIES INDUSTRY

In 1872, Tokushichi Nomura started a currency exchange business under the name Nomura in Osaka, Japan. When money changing subsided due to Japanese monetary reform, Nomura began stock dealing. His son, Tokushichi II, took over the thriving business and in 1910, Tokushichi II formed his first syndicate, underwriting a portion of a government bond issue. In 1918, Nomura eventually became Nomura Bank, and in 1925, the bond department split off and was named Nomura Securities. By 1927 they opened a New York office, and continued to grow through investment trusts, retail operations, stock market investments, savings promotion plans, overseas investment capital, capital underwriting activities, floating samurai bonds, and securing international strongholds. By 1987 Nomura, became the world leader in the Eurobond market and once surpassed Toyota Motor Company to become the world's most profitable firm. Nomura had over 5 million customers, 96% of whom were individuals. Nomura had more assets than Dai Ichi Kangyo Bank, the world's largest bank, and made more money than any financial firm in the world. Furthermore, it had applied its skills and energy to other fields and subsequently became Japan's fifth largest real-estate firm and its second largest software firm.[10]

Japanese securities firms can be classified into three tiers. The first is comprised of the "Big Four," which rank among the top six in the world; they are Nomura, Daiwa, Nikko, and Yamaichi. Nomura has traditionally led the Four and is known to prefer thinking of the group as "one and three." The second tier consists of ten securities firms, all much smaller than the Big Four. There are 96 firms in the third tier: all the remaining securities firms and any foreign firms (of which there were six as of 1985). Many of the second-and third-tier firms are closely affiliated with the Big Four; 30 are affiliated with Nomura, and 19 with Yamaichi. The Big Four control 80% of all domestic underwriting, nearly half of all domestic equity and bond trading and, prior to 1986, handled nearly all the transactions involving foreign shares on the Tokyo Stock Exchange (TSE).[11] While the concentration of the industry made the actions of Nomura the most significant, it should be understood that the eigyo tokkin accounts were used by firms in all three tiers.

THE JAPANESE REGULATORY ENVIRONMENT

Most of the regulatory power in the financial sector lies in the hands of the MOF, arguably the most powerful ministry in the Japanese government. The distinction between a civil servant and a politician is important in this context. While a politician's tenure is quite short, civil bureaucrats like those in the MOF generally hold stable, continuous, life-long power, and thus exert the major influence on day-to-day regulation of the industry. The MOF is said to be the cream of the crop among civil bureaucracies, and it recruits primarily from the most eminent university in Japan: the University of Tokyo.

The MOF has several regulatory mechanisms. First, the MOF has direct regulatory power through licensing. In order to enter a certain market segment, such as domestic bond trading or underwriting, one must first obtain a permit from the MOF. The MOF determines which companies will receive licensing and thus controls entry. Firms wanting to receive a license will be cooperative with the MOF's directives, even if it means losses in the short run.[12]

Secondly, industry and government work together to a greater extent than found in the United States, reflecting differences between the cultures of the two countries. Rather than coexisting uneasily in an adversarial framework as in the United States, industry and government work with each other based upon a successful history of teamwork. In the Japanese culture, trust and cooperation are seen as paramount values, which must be upheld for the benefit of the group above the individual. This system of priorities promotes a collaborative spirit.

In addition, there is *amakudari*, which literally translates to "descent from heaven." This is a long standing tradition whereby financial services firms hire the top retiring officers of the MOF, providing them with high salaries and social status.[13] Firms thus build a strong relationship with the government through employing former bureaucrats who know how the system works and, more importantly, have pull with their friends still working for the MOF. At the same time, the MOF benefits by having people in business who understand their perspective, and with whom they can regularly communicate.

The last, and perhaps most significant means of regulation is through what is known as "administrative guidance." The opportunity for bilateral communication is provided by regular meetings between the MOF and business people from many sectors of the economy. Through these continuous discussions, the Ministry learns about the firms' needs, and informally communicates its policies. With the concentration of the securities market in the Big Four, the MOF could literally control the entire market with only four phone calls. The MOF was actually having periodic meetings with the Big Four during the 1980s to discuss mutual concerns and exercise administrative guidance.[14] The MOF's sympathetic concern for business interests has certainly been one reason for the success of administrative guidance.

Though administrative guidance rarely carries clear-cut legal punishment, it is binding, and remains compelling. Companies that have attempted to disobey the MOF have suffered serious repercussions. Aside from the MOF, no other authority was capable of exerting significant pressure on the securities industry. For example, the Securities Dealers' Association, a voluntary self-regulatory agency, could not condemn the practice of compensation since it was composed of the brokerage houses that engaged in the practice. Japanese industrial federations, such as Keidanren, could not effectively discourage the brokers from compensating, mainly because most corporate members of those federations had not become aware of unethical aspects of compensation, just as Gaishi Hiraiwa, chairman of Keidanren, mentioned after the scandal was made public.

But what we have to question now are business ethical issues in the broad sense. That is to say, there are some traditional practices which are not clearly prohibited by the laws: We cannot tell with certainty whether or not they are against business ethical standards. So at issue now are those practices . . . Business practices which traditionally have been tacitly permitted are not allowed anymore because of changes of the times. The problem we have is that some corporations have not kept up with such changes. [15]

THE ETHICAL ENVIRONMENT OF THE JAPANESE BUSINESS COMMUNITY

The Framework of Concentric Circles

Because of its cultural heritage, the Japanese people tend to conceptualize their social environment in a centrifugal order like water rings: family, fellow, entire Japan, and the world.[16] This cognitive pattern may be described as a "framework of concentric circles." Consider, for example, the place of the individual. First an individual core agent is encircled by the nuclear family. This circle is surrounded by the fellow circle, which includes friends, colleagues, distant relatives, etc. Here, material and spiritual credits and obligations are balanced over a prolonged period of time. Credits with others are regarded as implicit rights of the core agent to receive something of benefit from them. Obligations are regarded as implicit debts assumed by the core agent to return something of distinct benefit. This bilateral give-and-take relationship is viewed as "long-term reciprocity," or "long-term reciprocal ethics."[17]

In the Japan circle, people are not generally acquainted with the core agent, and "the law of the jungle" becomes dominant. In spite of that, a common cultural background binds a core agent with others, ensuring long-term reciprocity. This common cultural background makes the Japan circle quite different from the world circle. For a majority of

Japanese, the world circle is thought of as a chaotic sphere: when its chaos is conceived as something risky, the core agent tends to shield the inner circles against the world; when the chaos is viewed as a source of admiration, the door to the world is opened.

This conception is not unique to the individual level. Organizations have almost the same tendency. For example, a corporation (core agent) has a quasi-family circle that typically consists of parent or affiliated companies. In the fellow circle, the core corporation recognizes its main bank, fellow traders, distant affiliates, and long-term customers. Most of the relations among *keiretsu* corporations fall within this circle.[18] The important principle in the fellow circle is also long-term reciprocity.

Although business practices such as semiannual gifts, entertainment, transfers of staff or directors among corporations, and cross-shareholding contribute to maintenance of the long-term relationship between a core corporation and its fellows, this relationship is constructed and maintained mainly through a series of business transactions. Key to the formation and maintenance of a reciprocal coalition is how fellows respond to the core corporation's requests concerning quality, cost, the date of delivery, financial conditions, etc.; or how a core corporation meets its fellows' expectations regarding products, service, finance, etc. The Japan circle is dominated by the "principle of free competition," but the agents always remain cognizant of the importance of long-term reciprocity. In this respect, the third circle differs from the world circle.

The world circle is a space where relations among corporations become increasingly alienated and corporations are less concerned about their traditional reputations. As with individuals, the world circle is considered chaotic, so that corporate attitudes toward the world tend to become contradictory. On the one hand, a core corporation tends to exclude foreign business corporations that neither understand nor practice the long-term reciprocal ethics. On the other hand, notwithstanding these exclusionary

attitudes, there is a strong desire for excellent foreign technologies, products, and services that appear to help the core corporation become successful and competitive in the Japanese and world markets.

The Dynamics of Concentric Circles

This framework of concentric circles exerts two kinds of social influences over Japanese agents: encouraging them to do what is considered positive, and discouraging them from doing anything negative. These social influences are explained in terms of the dynamic relations of "operation base" and "battlefield." Stated otherwise, a core agent is likely to regard its outer circle as a battlefield and its inner circle as an operation base.[19] For example, when the Japan circle is viewed as a battlefield, the family and fellow circles turn into multilayered operation bases.

"Operation base" means a place where the members relax, make action programs to be applied to the turbulent environment, and receive praise. In contrast, the "battlefield," is a strenuous sphere where "the law of the jungle" is dominant. Because of these dynamic relations, individuals or organizations make efforts to acquire better results in the battlefields, hoping to be "respectable" and "acceptable" members of their inner circles.[20] To be respectable, they strive to do things considered positive; and to be acceptable, they avoid doing anything negative.

This latter, discouraging function is illustrated by what happens to individuals accused in the outer circles of wrongdoing. Both their own reputations and the names of the groups to which they belong might be damaged. If this damage is severe, it might cause individuals to lose their own operation bases. Because of this, the individuals try to avoid bringing negative impacts on themselves and their group. This discouragement function is so influential in Japanese society that the rate of crime has remained extremely low. Just as an individual loathes to commit wrongdoing, corporations are also reluctant to commit unethical conduct. To put it differently, a corporation fears that someone might recognize its wrongdoing and blow the whistle in public. Once the fact of the wrongdoing comes to light, the corporation (in practical terms: the chairman, president, vice-presidents, other executives, board of directors, middle managers, and common employees) feels strongly ashamed, being accused of dishonoring the corporate name, industrial group such as keiretsu, the image of the industry, and perhaps Japan itself. In this respect, the framework of concentric circles has often discouraged corporations from engaging in unethical conduct.[21]

On the other hand, this framework can also be used to justify corporate wrongdoing, when wrongdoing is regarded as tolerable and beneficial by other fellow corporations. Even if some fellows consider the wrongdoing intolerable and unfair, it is likely to take a long time to rectify such unethical practices. Because these fellows have been benefiting from the corporation, they can hardly force the corporation to change the practices quickly. Enforcing radical measures against the corporation might hurt a delicate balance of give-and-take, so they prefer a harmonious resolution acceptable for almost every party concerned to a confrontational approach, which might hurt interests of specific parties in the fellow circle. But once corporate wrongdoing is made public, without delay, the corporation apologizes for its mistake to the public and the corporate executives take responsibility for its involvement, because, even in the battlefields, it is very important for corporate survival to maintain the public's trust.

THE DAM BREAKS: THE JAPANESE SECURITIES SCANDAL

The Fixed Commission System and Compensation

Under the fixed commission system of the Japanese market, a securities firm could augment its earnings simply by increasing the number of transactions it concluded (Table 5). One of the most effective ways to do this was to act both as a client's main broker and as its managing underwriter.[22] Because major

corporate clients were well aware that securities firms were earning substantial profits from this fixed commission system of brokerage and underwriting businesses, these clients expected special favors from the securities firms. Each securities house understood that if it did not offer to compensate clients for investment losses, those clients would do business with other brokers who were willing to promise reimbursement.

Also, during the mid-1980s, the Japanese stock market had been steadily rising, and there seemed little danger of significant losses being incurred. (See Tables 6 and 7.) As the likelihood that extensive reimbursement would be necessary seemed slim (and in response to the expectations of the clients), Nomura and many other securities houses began to promise reimbursement whenever favored clients incurred losses. However, after "Black Monday," the brokers became obligated to compensate corporate clients on a scale never anticipated.

Although the securities firms were legally prohibited from assuring clients ex ante that they would cover losses, the Securities and Exchange Law of Japan did not prevent them from compensating trading losses ex post based on their own free will. Nomura and other brokers did, in fact, illegally guarantee their clients' investments, but in a manner in which no tangible evidence of a violation of the law existed. Patting one's cheeks became a well known method by which brokers' salespeople were able to convey the message to clients that whenever losses would occur, the brokers would compensate them for the losses.

Even though contrary to the spirit of Japan's securities laws, it was possible for Nomura and its clients to view the compensation as acceptable because of the Japanese perspective on business ethics. Nomura compensated its clients in order to justify their trust, which is considered extremely important in the Japanese business community. In addition, because of long-term reciprocal relationships, brokers were expected to assist clients of long standing that were experiencing financial difficulties. Another justification for the payment of compensation was the perception that failure to compensate institutional clients might result in serious financial damage, which could ultimately cause a recession in Japan.

The Relationship Between the MOF and the Securities Industry

The MOF has been severely criticized for its failure to prevent the payment of compensation to favored clients by the securities houses. The MOF's attempts to persuade the securities houses to repudiate their eigyo tokkin accounts were weak because of its desire to avoid confrontation with the securities industry.[23] As described above, the relationship between the MOF and the "Big Four" has historically been marked by a high degree of cooperation, both at the business[24] and personal levels.[25] It has even been suggested that the MOF's Securities Bureau often relied on Nomura to assist in the formulation of policies to enhance the development of Japan's securities markets.[26]

As noted before, in October 1986, the MOF verbally ordered the brokers to terminate their eigyo tokkin business. This verbal order did not have the binding power of law and, although the reimbursement of losses continued, the MOF did not take any significant action until December 1989. The failure of the MOF to take decisive action implied that the compensation of large institutional clients remained tolerable.

After "Black Monday"

The day after the October 19, 1987, crash on Wall Street ("Black Monday"), stock prices on the TSE began to tumble. It is reported that at one of its weekly Tuesday lunch meetings with members of the securities industry shortly after the crash, MOF officials indicated that revitalization of the Japanese stock market was a key priority, and they implicitly encouraged the Big Four to intervene and buy shares to buoy up the market. Thus, Nomura and other securities houses began buying shares to prevent the

TSE from slipping further. Such intervention did enable the Japanese stock market to recover more smoothly than other international markets, but large institutional investors still incurred heavy losses, and the securities houses felt obligated to reimburse them. (See Table 6.)[27]

Despite the existence of the verbal order barring compensation, the brokerage houses assumed that in the wake of Black Monday, the MOF's attitude had softened. There was ample evidence to support this presumption. The MOF's message at the Tuesday lunch meeting suggested that it was aware of, and sympathetic to, the situation facing large investors who had suffered great losses. This, in turn, implied Ministry acknowledgment of the fact that forcing brokers to wind up their eigyo tokkin accounts so soon after the crash would have caused the TSE to plunge even further, with the potential for a negative impact on the Japanese economy in general. (See Table 9.)[28]

This assessment of the MOF's position was also supported by another of its efforts to stimulate the TSE, in which it issued a circular notice, on January 4, 1988, permitting insurance companies to expand the percentage of total assets invested in tokkin/kingai accounts. The brokers interpreted this as implicit permission to maintain their eigyo tokkin accounts for the time being,[29] and as further evidence of the Ministry's recognition that the ideal environment in which it could mandate that the securities houses close their eigyo tokkin accounts would be when the Nikkei average was steadily rising (as at this time, clients would be less concerned about the potential for losses, and would thus not insist on being guaranteed loss compensation).

The December 1989 Directive

No further action was taken by the MOF until December, 1989, when it issued a directive prohibiting brokers from compensating clients for losses and ordering them to wind up all eigyo tokkin accounts as soon as possible. Like the earlier verbal order, however,

TABLE 9. Japanese GNP and the Balance of Governmental Bonds *(Trillion Yen)*

Fiscal Year*	Nominal GNP (A)	Amount of Issued Bonds	Balance of Accumulated Bonds (B)	(B)/(A) %
1980	245.4	14.2	70.5	28.7
1981	260.3	12.9	82.3	31.6
1982	273.5	14.0	96.5	35.2
1983	286.0	13.5	109.7	38.4
1984	305.7	12.8	121.7	39.8
1985	325.4	12.3	134.4	41.3
1986	339.7	11.3	145.1	42.7
1987	356.3	9.4	151.8	42.6
1988	379.2	7.2	156.8	41.3
1989	406.0	6.6	160.9	39.6
1990	436.9	7.3	166.3	38.1

* Fiscal year starts in April and ends in the following March.

SOURCE: The Japanese Economic Planing Agency, *Keizai Hakusho* (*Economic White Paper: 1992*), Tokyo: the Ministry of Finance, 1992, reference, p. 72.

the MOF's directive was not clearly binding, and the likelihood of being severely penalized for any violation was perceived as minimal by the securities houses.

Moreover, the directive contained an inherent contradiction: in reconciling their eigyo tokkin accounts, brokers would be forced to compensate their clients. When directed by the MOF to cease compensating clients, therefore, the securities houses began to pay clients "cancellation fees" on their eigyo tokkin accounts. This was, in effect, compensation under a different name. Although the MOF did not formally admit that it had known that such cancellation fees were being paid on eigyo tokkin, it allegedly acceded to such practices. The Ministry apparently wanted to bring an end to eigyo

tokkin in a harmonious way that was neither too harmful to institutional investors, nor too damaging to the relationships between investors and their brokers. The securities firms assumed that cancellation fees could be viewed as a short term evil that was necessary to the realization of the MOF's ultimate goal—the elimination of eigyo tokkin.[30] Since at least the securities industry interpreted it this way, even after December 1989, the industry continued to compensate its major clients for the purpose of closing extant eigyo tokkin.[31]

The Scandals Come to Light

In the rush to close eigyo tokkin accounts and pay out cancellation fees, Nomura and the other securities houses incurred abnormally high costs. Such large amounts were easily detected by the tax authorities. (See Table 10.)[32] *Yomiuri Shinbun*, one of Japan's leading newspapers, first publicized Nomura's compensation practices on June 20, 1991. At Nomura's general shareholders' meeting on June 27, president Yoshihisa Tabuchi stated that he did not think the firm had compensated clients' losses. He also, perhaps inadvertently, remarked that Nomura had already shown everything to the MOF and received its approval. Finance Minister Ryutaro Hashimoto swiftly and strongly rejected this claim, but despite Tabuchi's subsequent retraction of his statement, suspicion remained that the MOF was, at all times, aware of the continued payment of compensation.[33]

While 21 securities firms had admitted to paying more than $1.5 billion in compensation

TABLE 10. Big Four's Compensation and Additional Tax: 87.10–90.3

Name of Brokers	Undeclared of Taxable Expenses	Imposition of Additional Tax	Unexplained Expenses	(Million Yen) Amount of Compensation
Nomura	8,990	4,050	16,500	25,490
Daiwa	1,460	660	12,600	14,060
Nikko	4,700	2,120	19,000	23,700
Yamaichi	4,846	2,190	750	5,596
TOTAL	19,996	9,020	48,850	68,846

SOURCE: *Sangyo Keizai Shinbun*, July 6, 1991

by October 1991,[34] the overall total of improper payments will probably never be known. The MOF detected at least 59 cases in which clients were compensated even though they had suffered no losses, clearly suggesting that certain rates of return were guaranteed ex ante.[35] From October 1987 to March 1990, the compensation paid by Nomura amounted to ¥25.5 billion (the equivalent of approximately $186 million).[36] The biggest recipient of compensation was the Pension Welfare Service Public Corp., affiliated with the Japanese Health and Welfare Ministry, which received ¥4.9 billion (approximately $35 million) from Nomura. Showa Shell Sekiyu KK, a local affiliate of Shell Oil, received approximately ¥4.4 billion and, in the year ended March 31, 1991, alone, Nomura paid ¥3 billion each to Hitachi Ltd. and Tokyu Corp., in defiance of the December 1989 directive, to cover losses suffered in early 1990 from the slumping TSE.[37] As a result, several large American institutions considered suing the Big Four, and the United States Securities and Exchange Commission investigated whether the scandals in Japan had any U. S. implications.

THE RESPONSE TO THE SCANDALS

As a result of the penalties imposed by the MOF and the JFTC, the way in which Nomura conducts its business has been revised. This includes the erection of a "Chinese Wall" between brokerage and underwriting activities by separating the lines of command, and the abolition of rotating personnel between the two divisions. Perhaps the most significant change in Nomura policy is the decision to grant autonomy to branches, which no longer receive daily instructions from the broker's headquarters on what shares to sell. In 1991, for the first time in Nomura's history, branch performance was evaluated not on the amount of commission that they generated, but on whether they earned enough revenue to cover their overheads.[38]

The securities industry itself has also been reformed. The Interim Administrative Reform Deliberative Council submitted a report concerning the "Basic Correction of Unfair Financial and Securities Transaction" to the Japanese government in September, 1991. As a result, the government revised the Securities and Exchange Law to outlaw engaging in eigyo tokkin business and compensating clients for trading losses, irrespective of brokers' motives. The Deliberative Council did not, however, support the idea of a completely independent Securities and Exchange Commission. Instead, it proposed the establishment of a new branch of the MOF, which would be independent of the administrative division of the ministry. The council also recommended that the Securities Dealers Association play a more active role in the surveillance and regulation of the securities industry.[39]

Based upon the report of the Council, on July 20, 1992, the Japanese government established the "Securities and Exchange Surveillance Commission" (SESC). This body was empowered to inspect brokerages, and to investigate suspected violations of fair trading rules, such as insider trading, compensation, and other infractions. Critics still fear, however, that, operating with a staff of only 200 and under the umbrella of the MOF, the SESC might be a something of a toothless watchdog.[40]

NOTES

1. Although this case concentrates on the compensation of favored clients, it should be noted that the damage to Nomura's reputation was exacerbated by the revelation of its involvement in a share-manipulation scheme with one of Japan's most notorious underworld figures, the recently deceased Susumu Ishii. In 1989, a Nomura subsidiary provided more than $100 million in financing to Ishii, the former head of the yakuza, who amassed 24–27 million shares of Tokyu Corp., a railroad, retail, and real estate company. In the fall of that year, Nomura's research division issued a strong buy recommendation in

Tokyu stock, setting off a mass of aggresive buying that sent the stock soaring. Fumiko Fujisaki, "Nomura, Nikko Presidents Resign over Share Loss Compensation," *Reuters,* June 24, 1991, p. 15. "Nomura, Nikko Continuing Contact with Ishii." Source: *Mainichi Daily,* July 6, 1991, p. 14. Kei Mizusawa and Manabu Tateyama, *Nomura Shoken Scandal no Kensho (Analysis of the Nomura Securities Scandals.)* Tokyo: Kenyukan, 1991, pp. 131–42.

2. Joanna Pitman, "Nomura Struggles to Rise Again from the Ashes of Humiliation." *Times of London,* (October 16, 1992), p. 25.
3. "Unmasking Honorable IBJ," *The Economist* (Oct. 12–18, 1991), pp. 79–80, at p. 79.
4. "A Ministry Diminished," *The Economist* (Feb. 1–7), p. 86 and p. 91, at p. 86.
5. Kinyu/Shoken Kenkyukai, *Kaisei Shoken Torihiki Ho (The Revised Securities and Exchange Laws),* Tokyo: Shin Nihon Hoki Shuppan, 1991, p. 212.
6. Aron Viner, *Inside Japanese Financial Markets,* Homewood, Illinois: Dow Jones-Irwin, 1988, p. 279.
7. Shoken Chosa Group, *Shoken Fushoji Jiken (The Securities Scandals),* Tokyo: Daiichi Kikaku Shuppan, 1991, pp. 14–17.
8. Shoken Chosa Group, *Ibid.,* pp. 18–21. Nihon Keizai Shinbunsha, *Utage no Akuma: Shoken Scandal no Shinso (Dark Side of the Economic Boom: Substratum of the Securities Scandals).* Tokyo: Nihon Keizai Shinbunsha, 1991, pp. 204–06. For example, if institutional clients opened eigyo tokkin accounts, the brokers could easily transfer profits (or losses) between themselves and the investors by substituting the clients name for their own (or vice-versa) as the buyer or seller.
9. Kinyu/Shoken Kenkyukai, *The Revised Securities Law,* pp. 142–47.
10. Albert J. Alletzhauser, *The House of Nomura: The Inside Story of the Legendary Japanese Financial Dynasty,* New York: Arcade Publishing, 1990, Preface, pp. ix–xiii.
11. Aron Viner, *Inside Japanese Markets,* pp. 15–19.
12. Takahiro Miyao, "*Shoken Shijo no Kanshi Kikan ha Do Arubekika*" (How Should a Watchdog of the Japanese Securities Industry Behave?), *Keizai Seminar,* Tokyo: No. 443, December 1991, p. 12.
13. In 1990, for example, 64 of the MOF's high-ranking officials took jobs in Japanese private companies regulated by the MOF. *1992 Gendai Yogo no Kiso Chishiki (Basic Information about New Terms in 1992),* Tokyo: Jiyu Kokuminsha, 1992, p. 310.
14. In the August 21st, 1991, Hearing of the Budget Committee of the House of Representatives in Japan, Mr. Shizuo Wada asked questions about periodic meetings between the MOF and the securities houses. Kei Mizusawa and Manabu Tateyama, *Analysis of Nomura,* Appendix 5, at p. 337.
15. Gaishi Hiraiwa, "*Atarashi Kigyo Rinri wo Mote* (New Business Ethics Should Be Fair and Clear)." *The Weekly Tokyo Keizai,* Aug. 3, 1991, p. 70.
16. Junichi Kyogoku, *Nihon no Seiji Politics of Japan),* Tokyo: Tokyo University Press, 1983, pp. 191–94. Takeo Doi, *Amae no Kozo (Structure of Amae),* Tokyo: Kobundo, 1971, pp. 33–37. Iwao Taka, "Business Ethics: A Japanese View." *Business Ethics Quarterly,* January 1994.
17. *Ibid.*
18. *Keiretsu* are industrial groups or related firms that work cooperatively toward common goals or interests.
19. Junichi Kyogoku, *Politics of Japan,* pp. 195–98.
20. Iwao Taka and William S. Laufer, "Japan and Social Control: New Perspectives on Trade with a Mediator-Centered Society," *International Association for Business and Society: 1993 Proceedings,* edited by Jean Pasquero and Denis Collins, San Diego, California: Fourth Annual Conference, 1993, pp. 145–51.
21. William S. Laufer and Alison J. Cohen, "Corporate Crime and Corporate Sanctions in Japan." *Business and the Contemporary World,* vol. 4, no. 3, (Summer 1992), pp. 106–25.
22. Hiroshi Okumura, "*Shoken Scandal de Towareteirumono* "(What Are Problems in the Securities Scandals), *Keizai Seminar,* Tokyo: No. 443, Dec. 1991, p. 26. pp. 20-21.
23. This aversion to confrontation with the securities industry also helps explain why, for many decades, "the Finance Ministry tolerated stock manipulation, greenmail, covert reimbursement of trading losses, and other shady deals." Ted Holden, Karen Lowry Miller, Robert Neff and William Glasgall, "Japan Cleans House—Again." *Business Week,* July 8, 1991, p. 26.

24. For example, the brokers allegedly assisted in the marketing of government-owned shares and bonds at relatively high prices. Takahiro Miyao, *Keizai Seminar*, pp. 12–13. Kei Mizusawa and Manabu Tateyama, op. cit., pp. 189–203.
25. The "descent from heaven" phenomenon is one of the examples.
26. "[W]hen the Ministry needed a consensus from the securities industry to implement some measure or other, all it had to do was talk to Nomura. 'Nomura was powerful enough to forge the consensus,' explains one MOF official." Henry Sender, "When Nomura Was Invincible," *Institutional Investor*, July, 1992, p. 227.
27. Albert J. Alletzhauser, *The House of Nomura*, pp. 16–17.
28. It has been asserted that "Nomura probably thought its action justified because it was supporting the market. As indeed it was: but for this, the investors would have been that much more likely to liquidate their eigyo tokkin accounts, causing still more selling pressure. That may also be why the finance ministry chose to keep quiet." "Trapped in the Rubble," *The Economist*, June 29, 1991, pp. 65–66, at p. 66.
29. Nihon Keizai Shinbunsha, *Dark Side of the Economic Boom: Substratum of the Securities Scandals*, pp. 178–79.
30. Regarding this point, T. Miyao explains, "According to the MOF's guidance, compensation for the purpose of closing eigyo tokkin was implicitly allowed until December 1990." Takahiro Miyao, *Keizai Seminar*, p. 11.
31. In the August 29th, 1991 Hearing of the Special Finance Committee of the House of Councilors in Japan, Mr. Setsuya Tabuchi testified "After the December 1989 directive, I strongly felt that what I had to do was to close eigyo tokkin as quickly as possible. Because our priority was termination of eigyo tokkin, we could not consider seriously whether compensation was acceptable or not." Kei Mizusawa and Manabu Tateyama, *Analysis of Nomura*, Appendix 4, at p. 316.
32. The Tokyo Regional Taxation Bureau determined that the Big Four failed to report a total of about ¥20 billion reflecting compensation paid to favored clients from October, 1987 to March, 1990. Nomura was ordered to pay an additional ¥4,050 million for the income it failed to declare. *"Yondai Shoken ni 90 Okuyen Tsuicho Kazei"* ("Big Four Ordered to Pay Additional Tax of ¥9 billion"), *Sangyo Keizai Shinbun*, July 6, 1991, p. 1.
33. See, e.g., James Sterngold, "Japanese Trading Charges on Stock Market Scandal." *New York Times*, (June 29, 1991), Sec. 1, p. 35, col. 1: "Finance Ministry officials have confirmed that they knew Nomura and the other members of the Big Four brokerage houses were making the payments and thus discriminating against the majority of their clients." Another commentator is a little more guarded, noting, "[t]he fact that a government pension fund and a long list of blue-chip companies now admit receiving paybacks suggests, at the very least, that this was standard practice if not officially sanctioned." Garth Alexander, "Japan's Widening Financial Scandal." *Sunday Times*, (July 14, 1991), p. B1.
34. Sterngold, James, "Nomura Gets Big Penalties." *New York Times*, (October 9, 1991), Late Edition, p. D1.
35. "Under the Volcano." *The Economist*, (Sept. 7–13, 1991), pp. 75–76. *Sangyo Keizai Shinbun*, (July 6, 1991), p. 1. "Brokers Hit with ¥9 Billion Tax Bill." *The Japan Times* (July 7, 1991.)
36. Neil A. Martin, "Tremors Along the Fault Line." *Barron's* (July 1, 1991), p. 12.
37. There were also a number of "unconfirmed reports that politicians were among favored clients" who received compensation for stock market losses. Robert Whymant, "Tokyo Rocked by New Broker Disclosures," *Daily Telegraph* (July 4, 1991), p. 27.
38. "How to Grow Strong on Humble Pie. *The Economist* (Nov. 23–29, 1991), pp. 93–94.
39. *"Shoken/Kinyu Fukosei Torihiki no Zeseisaku* (Basic Correction of Unfair Financial and Securities Transaction)." *Asahi Shinbun* (September 14, 1991), p. 5.
40. *Chicago Tribune* (July 21, 1992.) The British Broadcasting Corporation, Summary of World Broadcast (July 29, 1992.)

CHEMICAL MANUFACTURERS ASSOCIATION, WASHINGTON, DC

Educational advertising campaign to change public perception and awareness of the chemical industry's activities and contributions to American society

It does not come as a surprise to any informed reader that the chemical industry has had a poor public image and has suffered a lack of public credibility about its commitment to environmental safety. The past decade has witnessed a successive increase in new laws and regulations subjecting the chemical industry to greater restrictions in product development, manufacturing, sales, and waste disposal.*

In 1979, the Chemical Manufacturers Association (CMA) convened a special Communications Task Group made up of selected industry communication managers whose objective it was to consider, develop, and revise the CMA communications program to address the industry's credibility problems. This committee decided to institute a public education/communication campaign to change public opinion about some of the negative aspects of environmental and health hazards commonly associated with the chemical industry. The campaign lasted between 1980–83 and cost almost $8 million in direct costs. This campaign, and the issue it raises for the chemical industry in particular and business community in general, are the subject of this case study.

*Adapted from S. Prakash Sethi, *Handbook of Advocacy Advertising: Concepts, Strategies, and Applications* (Cambridge, Mass.: Ballinger Publishing Company, 1987), pp. 317–336.

This was not an extraordinary action. As a matter of fact, an increasing number of corporations, industry and trade groups, religious organizations, public interest groups and community organizations, foreign governments, and even individuals have resorted to advocacy advertising and public communication campaigns to influence public opinion and government policy-makers in directions the sponsors of these campaigns consider more desirable.

WHAT IS ADVOCACY ADVERTISING?

Advocacy advertising, including idea-issue advertising, is part of that genre of advertising known as corporate image or institutional advertising. It is concerned with the propagation of ideas and the elucidation of controversial social issues deemed important by its sponsor in terms of public policy. The managerial context of advocacy advertising is that of defending or promoting the sponsor's activities, modus operandi, and position on controversial issues of public policy. The behavioral and social context of advocacy advertising is that of changing public perception of the sponsor's actions and performance from skepticism and hostility to trust and acceptance—and/or to a more neutral position. The political context of advocacy advertising is that of the constitutional safeguards for freedom of speech; a sponsor is asserting its right to speak out on issues of public importance without any regulation or censorship on the part of other private groups or government agencies. The political context of advocacy advertising would thus encompass even otherwise allegedly purely educational messages where the issues raised involve important matters of public policy, may be of a controversial nature, and the sponsor's objective is to heighten public awareness of those issues or some preferred options for their resolution.

Although advocacy advertising has been practiced for a long time in the United States, the latest and perhaps most intensive spurt came beginning with the Arab oil boycott in the early 1970s. No doubt, it was spurred in large measure by a spate of advocacy campaigns launched by oil companies, notably Mobil Oil Corporation. The late 1960s and early 1970s also constituted the period when corporations were faced with broad public attacks and more intensive government regulation because of increased national concern for a cleaner environment, health and safety, and a better quality of life. Other early entrants into the fracas, in addition to oil, were companies from such industries as chemicals, minerals, heavy (smoke-stack) industries, and forestry products.

During the mid-1970s, "big business" was also held in low esteem by the public, which gave it poor marks for credibility and responsibility. In this same period, there was a national trend toward corporations speaking out in print advertising on issues they felt to be important to the public and to themselves. It is in this environment that the chemical industry initiated its idea-advocacy campaign.

ISSUES FOR ANALYSIS

The CMA campaign raises a number of issues that deserve serious consideration:

1. To what extent can such advertising contribute to a greater public understanding of the problems confronted by American busi-ness in general and the chemical industry in particular?
2. What is the public perception of such advertising in terms of its accuracy and objectivity? Should such advertising present only the sponsor's vewpoint, or should it present other significant perspectives?
3. How important, from the public vewpoint, are the various issues selected for such campaigns? What should be the process of identifying salient issues?
4. Should trade associations, such as CMA, involve themselves in such campaigns or should it be the domain of individual companies?
5. What objectives is CMA pursuing through this campaign? To what extent are they in the public interest in addition to serving the interests of the industry?
6. What are the options available to the public to hear counter viewpoints when advocacy advertising by large corporations and industry groups overwhelms and distorts the flow of information available to the public. Is this a real concern given the large multiplicity of news media and information channels available to public? If so, what alternative mechanisms need to be considered?
7. How effective is the CMA campaign (in terms of its long-term effect) in changing public opinion?
8. How might one evaluate the effectiveness of copy and media strategies, and advertising budgets, given CMA's goals and objectives?

CMA—ORGANIZATION, STRUCTURE, MEMBERSHIP

The CMA represents the chemical industry in America. Founded in 1872, the CMA is the oldest chemical trade organization in the Western hemisphere. The association includes about 200 member companies. Most are in the United States; some are in Canada. The size of CMA's member companies and the products they make are as varied as chemistry itself. Together, they represent a major portion of the productive capacity of the industry.

The association, with headquarters in Washington, DC, has a permanent staff of approximately 165 and is headed by a full-time president. Its board of directors is composed of major executives of its member companies.

In recent years, CMA's role as the chemical industry's advocate has accelerated, becoming the focal point of many of the association's activities. CMA advocates industry positions in Congress, in the regulatory agencies, and in the executive and judicial branches. Equally important, CMA communicates information to the media across the nation.

According to a CMA brochure, the association has been in the forefront in transportation safety, occupational safety, and health and environmental protection. Recently, it has led the way in energy conservation and in solving waste disposal problems.[1] The CMA brochure describes the benefits of the association to its members in the following terms:

> Measured monetarily, CMA activities are estimated to be worth billions of dollars each year. More than $1 billion are saved annually by reducing future increases in freight charges; more than $100 million are saved each year through the development of proper engineering standards. In a recent year CMA saved several billion dollars by deflecting inappropriate environmental and workplace laws, rules and excessive taxes without endangering public health or employee safety.[2]

CMA's board and executive committees establish policy and define program areas. Responsibility for issue monitoring and development in those areas is assigned to an authorized standing committee. Each committee is usually composed of 15 industry representatives. Under the direction of the association president, the staff is responsible for implementing and communicating policy and helping the committees with their work.

The staff is organized into five function departments: (1) government relations, (2) technical, (3) communication, (4) administration, and (5) office of general counsel.

The communications department, which is responsible for public communication, is divided into the communications committee and the communications policy review special committee (now defunct). The communications committee has a major influence on the CMA communications program and comprehensive public relations activities. These programs communicate the industry's renewed commitment to doing a responsible job of protecting the public and its employees from the health and safety risks of chemicals. The communications policy review special committee was a board of directors committee that reviewed the overall direction, design, and operations of CMA's communication program. This has become the responsibility of the communications committee.

Decision-Making Process and Program Approval

The first step in developing a communications strategy to decide on the size and shape of the problem, and to come up with a tailor-made plan for remedial action. A special task force of twelve industry communication experts spent several months developing such a plan. Although CMA's vice president for public relations participated in all discussions, the plan was developed by the industry. The next step was to persuade other members to accept this proposal.

In May 1979, the thirteen-member executive committee of CMA's forty-five member board of directors approved the draft plan and appropriated funds for further development. Most important, a copy of the draft plan and a request for comments was sent to executives in member companies who act as contacts with CMA. After receiving member comments, the task force revised the plan and again sent it to all members. At this time too, a public relations consulting agency, a public opinion research firm, and an advertising agency were retained for basic polling, programming, and advertisement development.

Two months later, four regional conferences were conducted across the country to explain the program to industry personnel and to encourage involvement. Different presentations were given to lay out the basics of the plan and explain the importance of member company participation. Target audiences and major markets were pinpointed, and each communication medium was described, along with its role in the overall campaign.

ANTECEDENTS TO THE CAMPAIGN

Research data on public concerns over chemicals and the chemical industry were provided by various companies. Monsanto contributed its proprietary research in its "Chemical Facts of Life" campaign, and Shell put in data from its 1978 cancer study. Other bits and pieces were also contributed. The subcommittee reviewed the data and came to these conclusions:

1. The American public was already convinced that chemicals contributed to the high American living standard. Thus, the subcommittee felt there was no need to embark on a campaign to urge that position.
2. The American public was nevertheless apprehensive about hazards to their well-being posed by chemicals in the environment. The subcommittee, accordingly, felt this was the subject area a CMA communications campaign might address.

The task force received these conclusions and ultimately accepted them. Accordingly, the theme chosen for the CMA communications program was to increase public recognition that the chemical industry is committed to doing a responsible job to protect the public from the health and safety risks of chemicals.

LINKAGE BETWEEN CMA'S EFFORTS AND THAT OF MEMBER COMPANIES

No communication program, no matter how good, will achieve its goals if industry performance is not there to begin with. CMA argued that the industry is already paying heavily because of its poor image. For example, the chemical industry was spending more money than any other industry in cleaning up pollution, and had spent $15.3 billion (most current figure available) to date on pollution control. However, because of its communication gap, no one knew about it. Why not, instead, put some of this money into a program to achieve positive results?

CMA emphasized to its members that the association's communication effort was intimately related to the total industry communication effort, including product advertising by individual firms. The CMA communications program would emphasize issues, and more important, would undertake the otherwise difficult but necessary job of dealing with risks. On their part, individual chemical companies would continue to emphasize products and the benefits of chemicals.

This division of effort was based on the fact that associations, rather than companies, can best discuss industry wide issues, particularly major public issues. Also, an association can act as a lightning rod on controversial issues, taking some of the heat off members.

CMA emphasized to members repeatedly that advertising, while representing the bulk of the program's cost, was one part of a multifaceted program. The other parts of ChemCAP were equally important, and all were constructed to work together to achieve an impact and to meet the program's objective.[3] The association's early efforts to explain the importance of the program to members paid off. In November 1979, the CMA executive committee and the board of directors approved the communications program in principle, but it decided that one more across-the-board effort should be made to fully inform the industry on the plan's objectives, scope, and content. Finally, in January 1980, a full year after planning had begun, the board gave approval to the initial $6.1 million, two-year package.

The objective of the program was specifically spelled out to members: to broaden public recognition of the chemical industry's commitment to protecting the public from the health and safety risks associated with its products and services. Five areas were identified as topics to be discussed in the program: transportation safety, environmental protection, product safety, worker safety, and hazardous waste disposal. CMA repeatedly emphasized that the members were themselves primarily responsible for the program's success or failure because, notwithstanding the effectiveness of the communications program, it was industry performance that would lend real credibility to the program's message.

PROGRAM IMPLEMENTATION

Board approval was followed by a conference in Washington, DC, where people throughout the industry were able to discuss different ways of implementing the CMA program. The conference underscored several themes: the need for support from chief executive officers, the importance of delegating one person to be in charge of program implementation within a company, a recognition that work on this program would help an employee in his or her career, and the importance of personalizing messages in speeches and letters signed by the chief executive officer.

The CMA board next established a permanent, fifteen-member communications committee. James Sites, vice-president for communications, served as the committee's staff executive. Working with the CMA staff, the committee guides program development and implementation. A policy review group, made up of five members of the board (now defunct) was also established.[4] Once the program was developed, its implementation was monitored on a continuing basis, obviating the need for this special committee.

Once the theme was selected (see the earlier section on Antecedents to the Campaign), the task force looked at what syndicated data were telling them. The 1979 Yankelovich Corporate Priorities data, the latest data available at the time, showed that the chemical industry was seen by the following proportions of Americans as doing a poor job in complying with laws and guidelines in the following areas:

- Waste disposal   61%
- Air pollution   56%
- Water pollution   51%
- Worker safety   36%
- Transportation safety Data not available
- Product safety   32%

These topics therefore were selected as themes for the first year's campaign. A point extensively discussed by the task group was the unique position of CMA in addressing these themes. The task group agreed that acknowledging the potential of environmental pollution by the chemical industry was not something any one company would wish to do. After all these decisions had been made, the 1980 benchmark survey by Cambridge Reports was designed and carried out. The purpose of the benchmark was to establish precampaign data on the target audiences against which campaign effectiveness could be measured. It examined attitudes toward the chemical industry compared to other business sectors. Among the major findings: The public is well aware of, and appreciates, the benefits of chemicals. Most people like what the chemical industry makes but they are afraid that the chemical industry may poison them through sloppy and irresponsible operating practices. The public sees chemicals as the greatest threat to the environment and a significant cause of cancer. Fifty percent believe the chemical industry does a poor job of controlling water pollution; 44 percent believe the industry does a poor job of controlling air pollution; and 38 percent think the industry does a poor job of observing worker safety rules. More than 50 percent believe there is now more cancer than ten years ago; 47 percent see chemical food additives as a cause of cancer; 44 percent see chemical plant air pollution as a cause of cancer; 42 percent see pesticides as cancer causing; and 33 percent see chemical plant water pollution as a cancer cause. Thirty-three percent see the industry as doing especially poorly in providing enough information to consumers; only 15 percent see the chemical industry as socially responsible.

According to one leading advertising professional, "15% of any sample are mavericks who like to take the opposite side of any questions. So there is a fair chance that no one really saw the industry as really responsible." Half the public say they want strong government regulation of the chemical industry. And this is in spite of the public's bias against further government involvement in most other things.

Faced with these findings, industry executives realized that such a negative image had adverse effects on its public image, as well as on relations with government, employees, and the financial community. Inherent in this objective was a desire to reduce the public pressure for restrictive legislation. Therefore, what was required from the industry was a new approach to help people understand what the industry was doing to protect them from the health and safety risks of chemicals. What was most needed was a dialogue between the public and the chemical industry to create an acceptable balance between risk and benefits.

With much research data in hand, the CMA launched a Chemical Industry Communications Action Program (ChemCAP), now known as the CMA Communications Program, which was to complement CMA's comprehensive public relations activities. CMA's advocacy advertising is a major element of this program. The objective of the advertising program, like the overall program, is to increase recognition that the chemical industry is committed to doing a responsible job to protect the public from the health and safety risks of chemicals.

A major issue for analysis is: How does the desirability of undertaking industrywide advocacy campaigns compare with the desirability of individual corporations sponsoring their own campaigns? Are there specific issues that are best addressed through an industrywide campaign, as opposed to individual corporate campaigns? What are the long-term effects of an industrywide campaign as opposed to those of individual corporate campaigns? Furthermore, is there a danger that industrywide campaigns are likely to deteriorate to the least offensive or controversial level of issue discussion, thereby stifling creativity and making such campaigns bland and boring?

Another question pertains to the use of benchmark studies in selecting issues and media themes. It is always possible to develop benchmark studies that can provide the sponsor with answers that he or she is looking for in determining which issues are critical and, therefore, which issues need to be addressed. A tunnel vision—especially when an industry group is facing public hostility—is likely to ignore the issues that may be underlying the public hostility but are not regarded, or even visualized, by the sponsor as such and are therefore excluded from the study. Second, a poorly conceived study may provide erroneous answers as to copy themes and media approaches and thereby severely limit the effectiveness of a campaign based on such a study.

THE ADVERTISING CAMPAIGN

Since the CMA program did not have the resources to cover the entire population, certain key groups of individuals that most intimately effect public attitudes and the public policy formation process became priority target audiences. These included politically active individuals, government representatives, educators, communicators, and "plan neighbors"—those living in areas of major chemical plant concentration. Active individuals were defined as the estimated 14 million people who participated in two or more public actions (such as writing to elected officials or playing leadership roles in local civic or political organizations) other than voting within the past year.

The campaign was developed by the Brouillard Communications Division of the J. Walter Thompson advertising agency. It was designed for the print media and included "thought leader" magazines and major newspapers in Washington, DC, and New York. These were: *Time, Newsweek, U.S. News & World Report, Harper's, Atlantic, Smithsonian, The New Yorker, Psychology Today, Natural History,* the *New York Times,* the *Washington Post,* and *Star.* There have been some adjustments in this media schedule from year to year.

Campaign Budget

The advertising expenditures for 1980–81 were slightly over $3 million. They were reduced to $2.52 million for 1981–82 and $2.25 million for 1982–83.

Copy Themes

The first phase (1980–81) of advertising—a *Scientific American* print campaign—presented the five areas of concern in such a way as to display the chemical industry as one of high technology and scientific innovations. The first ad dealt with the issue of managing chemical wastes. The second dealt with improving chemical product safety, and the third discussed the issue of worker safety. Although these ads proved to be persuasive and able to communicate a message, they had a low stopping power. The human interest format was adopted when research by Brouillard Communications showed the personalized advertisements to be more effective.

The second phase (1982) was aimed at showing that chemical industry engineers and scientists are just like other citizens, with normal family concerns. It emphasized that these scientists are responsible citizens and concerned about the environment and it pointed out that they would not be working for the chemical industry if they did not believe the industry was concerned with producing safe products and also protecting the environment. It was felt that a scientist-employee as a spokesperson would have better public credibility than a professional model, well-known public figure, or corporate executive.

In both phases, the two ad insertions were made both in single-page and double-page formats. The copy themes and layouts were designed to show audiences that the chemical industry, in fact, was doing a lot to protect the public from risks associated with chemicals.

MEASURING AD CAMPAIGN EFFECTIVENESS

CMA undertook two tracking studies in 1981 and 1982 to measure the effectiveness of the ad campaign. The studies were conducted by Cambridge Research Associates. Most of the questions asked in the 1981 and 1982 questionnaires were the same as those asked in the 1980 benchmark survey. Interviews were conducted with 900 politically active individuals and 200 "neighbors." The first tracking study to measure the impact of the CMA advertising campaign took place during January-February 1981. Four principal topics were discussed in this survey.

- What is the present image of the chemical industry?
- Have attitudes toward the chemical industry in the target audience (politically actives) changed in the last year?
- How aware of the CMA advertising campaign are the target audiences?
- How well is the CMA advertising campaign working?

The 1981 Study

The Image of the Chemical Industry. A majority of people in the study felt that chemical waste was still the major problem related to the chemical industry. At the time of the benchmark survey and the 1981 tracking study, the degree of personal concern over chemical waste had increased dramatically between the two surveys. Overall, the chemical industry continues to be seen as paying too little attention to this problem.

The Attitude of the Public. Data were analyzed for two separate groups: opinion leaders and politically active individuals, and the chemical industry neighbors. Within the first group, educators were found to be most positive toward the industry, but this group was also less homogeneous. Some members of this group felt that the industry was very concerned about the average person's welfare, whereas others asserted that this was not so, thereby joining the majority of the public.

In measuring the chemical industry's favorability and perceived truthfulness, the industry's position was found "not really good" among the six industries tested: oil, nuclear energy, chemical, retail, banking, and insurance.

Awareness of CMA Advertising Campaign. The tracking study was undertaken by Cambridge Reports. Its major findings were that those who saw the ads found them believable: 85 percent of the "politically active individuals" and 87 percent of the "neighbors" found them very or somewhat believable. Attitudes of those in the sample who had been exposed to the industry messages improved significantly. Regular readers of *Time* and *Newsweek* (where the industry campaign was running) were significantly more aware than nonreaders of "the chemical industry's effort to inform the public of its actions to reduce public risk."

There were also some discouraging findings: 60 percent of those interviewed admitted that they were not aware of any industry efforts; of 40 percent of those who claimed awareness of any industry effort to inform them, about one in four—or 10 percent of the total—claimed to have seen any industry print advertising on what was being done to reduce risk. When asked about the sponsorship of the advertising, fewer than 10 percent of the politically active individuals named

any individual company. And only 1 percent of the politically active individuals said they were aware of ad sponsorship by America's chemical industry.

Effectiveness of the Campaign. The communications committee of the CMA concluded that attitudes toward the chemical industry had not changed significantly since 1980. There was no significant level of identification of the CMA advertising campaign. (According to CMA, this was not a campaign objective.) There did appear to be somewhat more awareness of messages in the CMA advertisements than of CMA's sponsorship of those messages. Those aware of CMA messages held more favorable views toward the chemical industry than those who were not aware. Clearly, very little, if anything, was accomplished. One might, however, speculate that the 1981 figures might have been worse if the industry advertising had not taken place, or that the media weight was too low to make a statistically significant impact.

There was only a slight increase in the awareness of CMA communication efforts, but there were some positive results:

- The percentages of chemical industry neighbors and politically active individuals who wanted information about waste disposal has doubled since the previous year.
- The percentage of people feeling that the chemical industry was concerned rather than unconcerned had grown.
- Worker safety and product safety were seen by the largest percentages of politically active individuals, chemical industry neighbors, and educators as areas where efforts at improvement had been displayed.

John Elliott, former chairman of the board of Ogilvy & Mather, had the following observations to make concerning CMA's advocacy campaign:

O&M asked Gallup & Robinson to do a computer run of 2,000 corporate advertisements in 1979 and 1980, comparing them on the basis of recall and persuasiveness with the norm for all product advertising. It was found that: Giving all product advertising an index of 100, on the basis of recall and persuasiveness, all corporate advertising got a rating of 81, and institutional/advocacy advertising a rating of 62. The index value of the chemical industry's corporate advertising was 63, compared with the index value of 81 for all corporate advertising.

In Elliott's opinion, by far the most important reason for the slow progress of the chemical industry's campaign was that it was grossly underfunded. He felt that while chemical companies were separately spending millions of dollars in advertising, this effort was largely wasted because it was not well coordinated. He felt that this very modest effort on the part of the chemical industry might be seen on the part of the public as "secretiveness" and as evidence that the industry didn't take the problems seriously and wasn't doing anything about them. Even more of the public might come to the conclusion that others (meaning the government) would have to be given the responsibility to fix things. Elliott comments:

All the hundreds of millions the industry has already spent to control pollution, to reduce risks, won't count a dime if the public isn't aware of it, or if the public sees it as a reaction to laws made necessary by irresponsible engineering and operations.

Elliott also felt that the chemical industry should bring its messages to the general public, not just to the so-called politically active individuals and influentials:

I think there is a myth about thought-leaders. The theory goes that if you get your message to them, they'll lead public opinion. It has been repeated so often that a lot of people accept it. But I can't remember an example of the theory working in advertising. It is the general public—all of us—who are besieged daily by front-page stories of spills, leakages, fires, toxic reactions, etc. Elected officials have an inordinate interest in numbers of votes. It is the general public who are the thought-

leaders, the influentials who influence the legislators.

The 1982 Study

The second survey revealed that, in general, the communications objectives of the CMA campaign were being met, in that those who had seen the industry's communications were more likely than those who had not to concur with messages presented in the communications. However, the communications were reaching a limited audience, and current results showed that this audience had not increased over the past year. As a result, overall public attitudes and perceptions of the chemical industry showed little change over recent years, and much of the impact of the communications was "hidden" when evaluated in terms of aggregate results.

The tracking study showed that in many aspects, the CMA communications program had mixed results.

- The ads were reaching a stagnant limited audience; there was no appreciable increase in reach from last year. It should, however, be kept in mind that the 1981–82 campaign was based on a funding level lower than that of 1980–81.
- The awareness of messages communicating the industry's efforts to reduce the risk of potentially hazardous chemicals had dropped 10 points among persons in all groups except politically active individuals, the main target audience. Among the people who could remember the ads, the reactions to the industry's advertising were positive in terms of both the believability and the importance of those ads. At least seven out of ten persons from all groups sampled stated that the ads were believable rather than not believable. More than eight out of ten politically active individuals who remembered the ads described them as believable.
- One of the more interesting results was that people who had been exposed to the communication campaign held different opinions of the chemical industry than those who had not been exposed. However, as one would expect, responses from individuals in each of the

three groups were less likely to show difference of opinion on questions that were not related to the advertising messages. Consequently, there were not differences between the views of people in each of these groups when asked about the general favorability of their opinions on the chemical industry, their impressions of the chemical industry's truthfulness, and their personal levels of concern about each of the issues discussed in the advertising.

The most widespread endorsement of the advertising credibility came from the chemical industry's neighbors. More than nine out of ten persons in this group said the ads were either very or somewhat believable. The previous year, reactions to the industry's advertising were equally positive among persons in all groups questioned. In determining the impact of CMA's advertisements, the survey used a conservative and narrow definition of opportunity of exposure (Tables 1–3).

Public opinions and perceptions of the chemical industry often differ between the respondents who were probably exposed and aware of the communications and those who were probably not exposed or were unaware of the communications. The most consistent differences between individuals in each of these groups were overperceptions of the chemical industry's concern and the industry's efforts on each of the five issues discussed in the advertisements. Since the advertising focused specifically on the industry's concern about and efforts on each of these issues, these consistent differences of opinion between groups are confirmations that the advertising is having an impact. However, responses from individuals in each of these groups were less likely to show differences of opinion on questions that related less to the advertising messages.

The greatest differences between those who were probably exposed and aware of the communications and those who were not exposed or aware of the communications were overperceptions of the chemical industry's concern about each of the five issues discussed in the advertising. In general, politically active individuals who were probably exposed and aware of the communications were currently 7-to-18 percentage points more likely than their counterparts to believe that the chemical industry was concerned rather than unconcerned about each of the five key issues. In 1982, the widest margin separating individuals in each of these groups was on the issue of chemical waste disposal. In 1981, perceptions of the industry's concern with these issues differed on four of the five issues, the exception being the industry's concern with the transportation of chemicals.

The 1982 results showed equally consistent differences between the perceptions of persons in both groups when asked about the industry efforts at solving the problems with each of the five issues. In 1982, those individuals who were probably exposed and aware

TABLE 1. Changes in Perceptions of the Industry: Personal Concern for Waste Disposal

	1982		1981	
	Exposed	*Unexposed*	*Exposed*	*Unexposed*
Concerned (very/ somewhat)	98%	94%	96%	94%
Not concerned at all (not very/not at all)	2	6	3	6

Note: This question measures the importance of one of the five designated areas of what the chemical industry is doing to manage chemicals. The response confirms that waste disposal continues to be the most important activity area and that placing the most communications emphasis on this area is warranted. Second, any preexisting difference in the attitudes of exposed and not exposed groups is negligible. This means that such a topic is of major importance to people, whether or not they are likely to be readers of our communications.

TABLE 2. Changes in Perceptions of the Industry: Industry Effort on Waste Disposal

	1982		1981	
	Exposed	*Unexposed*	*Exposed*	*Unexposed*
Effort (a lot of/some)	72%	59%	66%	59%
No effort (only a little/ hardly any)	27	38	32	35

Note: Those exposed have more favorable opinions as to what the industry may actually be doing to manage hazardous waste disposal.

of the communications were 6 to 13 percentage points more likely than their counterparts to believe that the chemical industry was making an effort rather than no effort with all five issues. Once again, the greatest difference between individuals in each group was in their perceptions of the industry's effort with waste disposal.

Perceptions of the chemical industry's concern about the average person's welfare also differed between individuals in both groups. The group of individuals with the opportunity for exposure and who were aware of the communications were 9 points more likely than the group who were neither exposed nor aware of the communications to view the chemical industry as concerned rather than not concerned about the average person's welfare.

There was no sizable difference between both groups on overall opinions of the chemical industry, however. The absence of a difference between both groups on more general questions about the industry, and the consistent differences on questions specifically relating to issues discussed in the communications, provide some evidence as to what kind of impact the campaign was having. These findings suggest that those who were exposed to the communications were accepting the specific messages in the campaign. However, this acceptance of the specific messages was not yet being transformed into a general favorability toward the chemical industry.

THE IMAGE OF THE CHEMICAL INDUSTRY IN CONTEXT

Although the communications campaign appears to have had an impact on those exposed to the communications, most of this impact cannot be noticed when we examine the overall attitudes and perceptions of the chemical industry.

Out of a field of six major American industries, the chemical industry continues to receive the fifth most favorable rating overall from politically active individuals.

TABLE 3. Changes in Perceptions of the Industry: Industry Efforts to Reduce Pollution

	1982		1981	
	Exposed	*Unexposed*	*Exposed*	*Unexposed*
Effort (a lot of/some)	77%	70%	78%	70%
No effort (only a little/ hardly any)	21	27	21	24

Note: The activity area of general air and water pollution is second in importance (after waste disposal) to our sample, again confirming previous hypotheses. For this reason, recommendations were made to put approximately 2/3 of the advertising weight behind waste disposal and approximately 1/4 behind the area of air and water pollution. This chart reflects those proportions of communications effort. Once again, we see a favorable difference between those exposed and not exposed. The differences, however, are less dramatic, as one might expect.

Despite this persistently low ranking of the chemical industry, the actual numbers of favorable and unfavorable ratings given by politically active individuals show a slight improvement over the previous year's ratings. Currently, more than two-fifths (43 percent) of all politically active individuals hold a favorable, rather than unfavorable, opinion of the chemical industry.

The industry neighbors were also most likely to perceive the industry as least concerned about pollution and waste disposal. Perceptions of the chemical industry's concern about both issues had changed little since 1980. For all three years, the fewest chemical industry neighbors (42 percent) felt the industry was concerned about waste disposal, while a moderately larger percentage (52 percent) felt the industry was concerned about air and water pollution.

PERCEPTIONS OF INDUSTRY EFFORT

Of the five issues, the chemical industry was seen by the fewest politically active individuals (63 %) as making an effort to reduce the risks associated with waste disposal. For the third year in a row, more than one out of every three politically active individuals felt the industry had made only a little or hardly any effort on waste disposal. Perceptions of the chemical industry's efforts with air an water pollution were more favorable to the industry, however. The efforts with air and water pollution ranked third out of the five issue areas examined. The third largest percentage of politically active individuals (72 percent) stated that the chemical industry was making either a lot of effort or some effort to reduce the risks of air and water pollution.

The percentage of politically active individuals neither exposed nor aware of the communications who believed the chemical industry was making only a little effort or no effort at all with waste disposal had grown slightly, from 35 to 38 percent, over the past year. Meanwhile, those individuals exposed to and aware of the communications believing the industry was making only a little effort or not effort at all had dropped by 5 points, from 32 to 27 percent. What these contrary trends suggest is that those not exposed to the communications are viewing the industry's efforts with waste disposal in increasingly negative terms, while those exposed to the communications are viewing the industry's efforts in increasingly positive terms.

NOTES

1. John Elliott, Jr., former chairman of the board, Ogilvy & Mather, Inc., "Why Don't You Speak for Yourself, John?" Keynote address. "Issue Advertising: How to Make It Work on Television." Sponsored by AAAA, ANA, PRSA, PUCa, TVB, New York, September 15, 1981.
2. "CMA—What It Is, What It Does." Chemical Manufacturers Association, Washington, DC, October 1981, p. 1.
3. *Ibid.*, p. 2.
4. James N. Sites, "Changing Your Image: The Story of How the Chemical Manufacturers Association Mobilized Its Members to Win Public Support." *Association Management* (March 1981), p. 48.
5. Sites, "Changing Your Image," p. 49.

REFERENCES

Birnbaum, Alex, and Steven E. Stegner. "Source Credibility in Social Judgment: Bias, Expertise, and the Judge's Point of View." *Journal of Personality and Social Psychology*, 37 (1979), pp. 48–74.

Botein, Michael, and David M. Rice, *Network Television and the Public Interest*. Lexington, MA: D.C. Heath, 1980.

"Crooks, Conmen and Clowns: Businessmen in TV Entertainment " (1981).

Current Company Practices in the Use of Corporate Advertising, 1981: ANA Survey Report. New York: Association of National Advertisers, 1982.

Dardenne, Peggy. "Cost of Corporate Advertising." *Public Relations Journal: 1980–1984*, yearly survey published in November of each year.

Hass, R. Glen, and Darwyn E. Linder, "Counterargument: Availability and the Effects of Message Structure on Persuasion." *Journal of Personality and Social Psychology*, 23 (1972), pp. 219–33.

Jaccard, James. "Toward Theories of Persuasion and Belief Change." *Journal of Personality and Social Psychology*, 39 (1980), pp. 752–66.

Kaplan, Stuart J., and Harry W. Sharp, Jr., "The Effect of Responsibility Attributions on Message Source Evaluation." *Speech Monographs*, 41 (November 1974), pp. 364–70.

Ludlum, Charles E., "Abatement of Corporate Image Environmental Advertising," *Ecology Law Quarterly*, 4 (1974), pp. 247–78; "Notes: Freedom of Expression in a Commercial Context." *Harvard Law Review*, 78 (1965) p. 674; "Developments in the Law, Deceptive Advertising." *Harvard Law Review*, 80 (1967), p. 1004.

Sethi, S. Prakash, *Advocacy Advertising and Large Corporations*. Lexington, MA: D.C. Heath, 1977.

_____, Testimony in "IRS Administration of Tax Laws Relating to Lobbying (Part 1)," *Hearings before a Subcommittee of the Committee on Government Operations, House of Representatives*, 95th Congress, 2nd Session, July 18, 1978, pp. 381–455.

Smith, Nelson, and Leonard J. Theberge (eds.). *Energy Coverage—Media Panic*. New York: Longman, 1983.

Watson, Francis W., Jr., *The Alternative Media: Dismantling Two Centuries of Progress*. Rockford, IL: The Rockford College Institute, 1979.

THE NATIONAL RIFLE ASSOCIATION
AND GUN CONTROL

*Lobbying activities and their influence
on government decision making*

The debate over gun control in the United States has repeatedly been punctuated by dramatic tragedies that have both shocked and outraged the nation. Witness the assassinations of President Kennedy in 1963, and of Martin Luther King and Robert Kennedy in 1968, as well as the attacks on President Ford and President Reagan in 1975 and 1981. Add in the massacre of 5 children in a Stockton, California, schoolyard in 1989, and other attacks upon innocent people in their places of work, at restaurants such as Luby's Cafeteria in Killeen, Texas, where 23 people were gunned down in 1991, and on the Long Island Railroad where Colin Ferguson gunned down unsuspecting passengers in 1993. These incidents, coupled with the staggering statistics on the use of guns in violent crimes, where guns figured in 69% of murders, 42% of robberies, and 25% of aggravated assaults in 1993, have led the public to clamor for more regulations and control without banning guns altogether. (See Table 1.)

The complexity of the issue has been ratcheted up another notch in recent years, with the violent flame–out of the Branch Davidian compound in 1993 and the detonation of the Federal Building in Oklahoma city in 1995. These events, rightly or not, have served to broaden the issue of gun control to include the role of private militia in modern-day America in the face of the threat to freedom posed by the allegedly intrusive policies of the Bureau of Alcohol, Firearms and Tobacco (BAFT).

Paradoxically, guns in the United States are seen as: (1) the weapon of choice at the root of social violence that must be rigorously controlled, and, (2) as the only reliable means private citizens and interest groups (including militia) have to safeguard their freedom, protect their property and be secure in their homes.

Such a contradictory culture of guns is deeply embedded in American history. In the South, the Midwest and the West, and in many rural areas throughout the country, it is commonplace for people to grow up with guns and a culture of hunting. Indeed, in its 125-year history, the National Rifle Association has primarily been focused on gun safety, marksmanship competitions, and hunting.[1] In America's large urban centers, however, guns in the wrong hands are primarily seen as a threat to human safety that must be faced every time one steps out the door and goes about the ordinary tasks of day-to-day life.

America's contradictory gun culture, therefore, comprises many philosophical as well as psychosocial components. Chief among them are:

1. guns as either a means of protection of life, liberty, and property or as a major threat to all three.

2. the "hunting and outdoor life" orientation of gun owners vs. the paramilitary groups and militia.
3. the proper role of the federal government and its agencies in the lives of ordinary citizens.

It is no surprise that the patchwork of over 20,000 gun regulations at every level of government across the country manifests the contradictions of American culture. As an example, witness the response of two communities to the assassination attempt upon President Reagan in 1981.

In 1981, President Reagan was the object of an assassination attempt at the hands of John Hinckley, who, weeks before, had easily purchased a handgun in a Dallas pawnshop. The White House press secretary, James S. Brady, was seriously wounded in the head and remains disabled to this day. Once again, the nation faced its paradoxical myth of the frontier, which somehow combines liberty with license, personal safety with the menacing of others.

Reaction was swift on all sides. Two communities—Morton Grove, Illinois, and Kennesaw, Georgia—came to symbolize the polarization gripping the nation. Morton Grove passed the nation's first ordinance banning both the sale and the possession of handguns. This inflamed passions in Kennesaw, some 600 miles to the southeast. The officials there passed an ordinance of their own: provided that they were neither lame nor mentally impaired, the heads of all households were to be required, under penalty of law, to keep a working gun in their residences.[2]

Since then the political battle has been raging on local, state and federal levels. Lobbying groups such as Handgun Control, Inc., (which was founded in 1974 by Peter Shields of Delaware, following the murder of his 23-year-old son in California) call for strict federal legislation, which would override any state or local ordinances.[3]

The National Rifle Association (which was founded in 1871) vehemently opposes federal gun control.[4] At the same time, its

TABLE 1. Public Opinion Regarding Making Handgun Legislation More Strict, and Banning the Possession of Handguns by the Ordinary Citizen

| Year | Strictness of the Laws | | | |
	% Favoring More Strict	% Favoring Less Strict	% for Status Quo	% with No Opinion
1993	70	4	24	2
1991	68	5	25	2
1990	78	2	17	3
1987	60	5	28	7
1986	60	8	30	2
1983	59	4	31	6
1980	59	6	29	6

| Year | Should the U.S Ban Handguns for Ordinary Citizens? | | |
	% Yes	% No	% No Opinion
1993	48	51	1
1991	46	53	1
1990	47	52	1
1989	47	51	1
1985	44	55	1
1983	40	58	2
1980	45	53	2
1968	50	50	—

SOURCE: Gallup Poll, 1994, Survey No. GO 42202501.

members fear that local ordinances may well sweep across the nation. It has campaigned in 17 states for laws preempting rights of municipalities to enact gun control measures. Nowhere was it more successful than in Florida, where the state government passed a law in 1987, which would grant virtually anyone a permit to carry a hidden pistol, while guns in plain view carried no restrictions at all. The state has issued 266,710 right-to-carry permits since the law went into effect. Its experience has strengthened those who argue for easy access. From 1987 to 1992 handgun-related homicides in Florida dropped by 29%, from 5.0 to 3.6 per 100,000.[5]

On the other side, the State of Maryland in May 1988 passed a law banning the sale of pistols, which are easily concealed, unsafe, or poorly made. The law set up a special board to determine which pistols should be banned. The law was unsuccessfully challenged in a 1988 statewide referendum.[6]

On the national level, the two sides locked horns over the proposed McClure-Vollmer Act of 1985. This act, which passed the Senate easily without public hearings, would have gutted the 1968 Gun Control Act. It was eventually defeated. The battle continued into 1988 when antigun proponents succeeded in getting through the Senate a bill proposed by Howard Metzenbaum (D-Ohio), which would have required a seven-day waiting period (for a background check) in purchasing a handgun. When a similar measure was proposed in the House by Edward Feighan of Ohio in the summer of 1988, it was eventually defeated by a vote of 228,182. Neither side can work its will.[7]

It would appear that the nation, Congress, the presidency, and the NRA keep going through cycles of high activity after a national crisis (such as the assassination of President Kennedy), followed by a weak gun control bill, if any, and then business as usual, where the NRA largely has its way. President Johnson's success in getting a gun control law, albeit a weak one, could appear from hindsight as no victory at all, because the law has been poorly enforced by the Bureau of Alcohol, Tobacco, and Firearms (ATF), and there have been continuous NRA efforts to further weaken the law.

The unparalleled congressional nonresponse to consistent and overwhelming public support for gun control legislation is the achievement of the "gun lobby," spearheaded by the National Rifle Association. The success of the gun lobby is not due to a dearth of proposals by the forces favoring gun control legislation. There has been a steady flow of bills at the federal, state, and local levels with, as might be expected, increased activity following actual or attempted assassinations of public figures. Every year, numerous gun control bills are introduced in Congress. However, with a few minor exceptions (the NRA calls them "major setbacks"), none of these bills is enacted. Public opinion polls taken since 1934, the height of the Prohibition-sparked gangster era, have shown that an over-whelming majority of the American public supports some kind of restriction on the sale and possession of guns.[8]

What emerges from these surveys is that over the past decades, a solid 2/3 of the public favors stricter legislation regarding the sales of firearms, but a majority has never favored limiting the possession of firearms to police or other "authorized persons." (See Table 1.)

The only contrary information to date emerged in a 1979 poll of 1,500 respondents conducted by Decision Making Information (DMI), a California-based polling firm sponsored by the National Rifle Association.[9]

Official gun control supporters include the National Riot and National Crime Commission, the American Bar Association, the National Council on Crime and Delinquency, the General Association of Women's Clubs, Women's Clubs of America, the National Association of Sheriffs, the American Civil Liberties Union, the AFL-CIO, the United Auto Workers, Americans for Democratic Action, and the Leadership Conference on Civil Rights (with forty affiliate organizations).

ISSUES FOR ANALYSIS

The opposition to gun control legislation includes some libertarian groups, conservation groups, and right-wing extremists. It is, however, almost entirely focused on the National Rifle Association, which has proven to be a most effective lobbying agent.

The success of the NRA and its allies raises a number of questions about its role in the legislative process:

1. Is the NRA, as it claims, protecting the constitutionally guaranteed freedom of millions of men, women, and children to keep and bear arms in the interests of sports, liberty, and the American way of life? Or is it working to protect special interests?
2. Does the NRA's ability to prevent the enactment of legislation signal the strength of a system that enables citizens to protect their rights? Or does it point out the vulnerability of a system that can be virtually paralyzed by a small but vocal and organized minority protecting its privilege against the contrary demands of public opinion, the public interest, and the general welfare?
3. In either case, is it acceptable for any special interest group to ensure that Congress does not act contrary to the group's own view of public welfare? Or is it Congress's responsibility to regulate the activities of such groups to ensure that their limited definitions of the public interest do not completely override broader and more generally accepted ones?
4. Where does the proper compromise lie between individual rights and liberties and collective or societal necessity? And is such a compromise either possible or in the public interest?

THE HISTORY OF REGULATION

State and Local Regulation

Although legislation restricting a citizen's right to carry arms in public predates nationhood (Massachusetts, for example, enacted such a law in 1692), the concept of legislation to control the purchase and ownership of guns did not appear in this country until 1911. At that time, New York enacted its still-controversial Sullivan Law, which requires a license to purchase or own a handgun or other concealable weapon. The other 2,000 or so state laws dealing with the manufacture, sale, and use of firearms, which existed as of 1988, are less effective in controlling or recording the rapidly proliferating possession of guns by the general public. In the past decades, a number of states have passed more restrictive gun legislation.[10]

A summary of state legislation as of 1985 is presented in Table 2. As of 1984, only 6 states required registration and 13 required a permit to purchase a handgun. Twenty states imposed a waiting period. Only 18 states required a license to carry a handgun openly, while 33 required a license if it was carried concealed.

In the decade since 1985, there has been a growing movement on the part of many states to further relax restrictions upon ordinary citizens to carry concealed weapons. As of early 1995, some twenty states were on the books with what are termed "liberal permit laws." More liberal legislation was pending in 14 states, leaving only 16 states with what is called "restrictive legislation." These included Nevada and Colorado in the West, Nebraska and Iowa in the Mid West, Louisiana and Kentucky in the South, with the rest being in the Northeast."[11]

To counter the lack of effective control at the state level, various municipalities have enacted their own, more stringent regulations. Some local communities have historically had requirements covering such areas as dealer registration, purchase permits, waiting periods, permits for possession, regulations on indiscriminate firing of guns, and in some cities the registration of all handguns. In the end, state and local legislation manifests a very wide spectrum of attitudes and initiatives. As of 1991, the majority of states still had no waiting period, no required permit to purchase, as well as no required registration of the firearms, licensing of the owner, or permit to carry.[12]

TABLE 2. Statutory Restrictions on the Purchase, Carrying, and Ownership of Handguns, by State, as of July 1985

State	Purchase				Carrying				Ownership	
	Application and waiting period	License or permit to purchase	Registration	Record of sales sent to state or local government	Carrying openly prohibited	Carrying concealed prohibited	License to carry openly	License to carry concealed	Owner licensing or identification card	Constitutional provision
Alabama	✔			✔			✔a	✔		✔
Alaska						✔				✔
Arizona						✔				✔
Arkansas					✔b	✔b				✔
California	✔			✔		✔		✔		
Colorado						✔		✔		✔
Connecticut	✔			✔			✔	✔		✔
Delaware							✔	✔		
Florida	✔c	✔c	✔c	✔c			✔	✔		✔
Georgia							✔	✔		✔
Hawaii	✔	✔	✔	✔			✔	✔		✔
Idaho							✔	✔		✔
Illinois	✔	✔	✔d,c	✔c	✔f		✔		✔g	✔
Indiana	✔			✔			✔	✔		✔
Iowa		✔		✔			✔	✔		
Kansas	✔c	✔c	✔c					✔	✔	
Kentucky						✔				✔
Louisiana		✔h				✔		✔		✔
Maine						✔		✔		✔
Maryland	✔			✔			✔	✔		✔
Massachusetts		✔		✔			✔	✔	✔	✔
Michigan		✔	✔i	✔			✔a	✔		✔
Minnesota	✔	✔	✔	✔			✔	✔		
Mississippi			✔			✔				✔
Missouri		✔		✔		✔				✔
Montana						✔		✔		✔
Nebraska						✔				
Nevada						✔j		✔		✔
New Hampshire						✔		✔		✔
New Jersey	✔	✔		✔			✔	✔	✔	
New Mexico						✔				✔
New York		✔	✔	✔			✔	✔	✔	
North Carolina		✔		✔			✔			✔
North Dakota				✔	✔f			✔		✔
Ohio	✔c	✔k		✔k		✔				✔
Oklahoma				✔f		✔				✔
Oregon	✔			✔		✔		✔		✔
Pennsylvania	✔			✔			✔a	✔		✔
Rhode Island	✔			✔			✔	✔		✔
South Carolina				✔			✔	✔		✔
South Dakota	✔			✔				✔		✔
Tennessee	✔			✔	✔b	✔b				✔
Texas					✔	✔				✔
Utah					✔f	✔		✔		✔
Vermont					✔l	✔l				✔
Virginia	✔c	✔c						✔		✔
Washington	✔			✔			✔a,f	✔		✔
West Virginia				✔			✔	✔		✔m
Wisconsin	✔					✔				✔
Wyoming						✔		✔		✔
District of Columbia		✔e	✔e		✔e	✔e			✔e	

aLicense to carry in a vehicle either openly or concealed.
bArkansas prohibits carrying "with a purpose to employ it as a weapon against a person." Tennessee prohibits carrying "with the intent to go armed."
(continued on next page)

FEDERAL REGULATION

Congress enacted two minor pieces of legislation during the 1920s; a 1924 excise tax on gun and ammunition sales, and a 1928 prohibition, with some exceptions, of handgun shipments by mail (avoided by express shipment). These attempts at federal regulation did not come to grips with the issue of controlling the purchase and possession of guns. The attention of an increasingly crime-conscious nation came into abrupt focus with the February 15, 1933, attempted assassination of president-elect Franklin D. Roosevelt. In a pattern that was to become fearfully familiar in the ensuing forty years, national shock was soon translated into stringent gun control demands. During 1933, twelve gun control bills were introduced in Congress—seven in the House, five in the Senate. These laws, as originally proposed, required record keeping at the time of sale of small, concealable handguns, such as pistols and revolvers, as well as such "gangster" weapons as machine guns, silencers, sawed-off shotguns, and rifles. The penalty for illegal possession was to be up to five years in prison. The intent of the law was to discourage weapons use and to afford another device for arresting gangsters. The NRA reacted strongly, with the result that pistols, revolvers, handguns, and semi-automatic rifles were eliminated from the list of weapons. The final version of the law, enacted over the opposition of the NRA was the National Firearms Act of 1934. This law, which excludes handguns, provides for a prohibitive tax on the manufacture, sale, or transfer of machine guns and other fully automatic weapons, sawed-off shotguns and rifles, mufflers, and silencers. Although useless in controlling the flow of handguns to the general public, the act did eliminate the "smoking tommy gun" as the symbol of organized crime and ended much of the more open underworld warfare.

The Federal Firearms Act, a second bill enacted in 1938, makes the interstate shipment of firearms a criminal offense if a dealer knows or has reasonable cause to believe that the recipient is a criminal. Since it is one thing to prove that a gun was shipped to a convicted felon, but quite another thing to prove that the dealer knew the recipient was a felon, the law was almost ineffectual. This was, with a few minor exceptions (such as the Federal Aviation Act of 1958, which prohibited carrying weapons on an airplane), the state of federal gun control laws until 1968.

Table 2 (Continued)

cCertain cities or counties
dChicago only.
eApplies only to preregistered firearms. No new handguns can be brought into the city.
fLoaded.
gHandguns prohibited in Evanston, Oak Park, and Morton Grove.
hNew Orleans only.
iHandguns must be presented to the city chief of police or county sheriff to obtain a certificate of inspection.
jPermission to carry concealed may be granted by county sheriff on written application.
kSome municipalities control the possession, sale, transfer, or carrying of handguns, e.g., Cleveland and Columbus require a police permit for
   purchase; Toledo requires a handgun owner's identification; Cincinnati requires application for purchase.
lProhibits carrying a firearm "with the intent or purpose of injuring another."
mConstitutional provision to be on November, 1986, ballot.
NOTE: These data were compiled by the National Rifle Association's Institute for Legislative Action. In addition to state laws, the purchase, sale,
   and in certain circumstances, the possession and interstate transportation of firearms are regulated by the Federal Gun Control Act of
   1968 and Title VII of the Omnibus Crime Control and Safe Streets Act. Also, cities and localities may have their own firearms ordinances
   in addition to federal and state laws. State firearms laws are subject to frequent change. State and local statutes and ordinances, as well
   as local law enforcement authorities, should be consulted for full text and meaning of statutory provisions.
Constitutional provision can be defined by citing Article 1, Section 15 of the Connecticut State constitution as an example of the basic features
contained in the constitutions of many states. It reads: "Every citizen has a right to bear arms in defense of himself and the State."
SOURCE: Table provided by the National Rifle Association, Institute for Legislative Action.

The Gun Control Act of 1968.[13] The assassinations of Martin Luther King, Jr., in April of that year and of Senator Robert Kennedy in June, finally broke the resistance of Congress. It had not acted following the deaths of President John F. Kennedy, Malcolm X, George Lincoln Rockwell, and Medgar Evers. On June 7, 1968, the day after Senator Robert Kennedy's death, the House passed the 1968 Omnibus Crime Bill, Title IV, which contained restrictions on the sale and possession of handguns.[14] The bill originally covered rifles and shotguns as well, but this coverage was deleted in the Senate, which had earlier passed the bill. In the interest of capitalizing on the national shock of Kennedy's death, President Johnson urged immediate passage of this bill as a first step but not a final solution. When he signed it on June 20, he called on Congress to take more decisive action: "We must go further and stop mail order murder by rifle and shotgun . . . What in the name of conscience will it take to pass a truly effective gun control law?"[15]

Congress complied, and in October, President Johnson signed the second major federal gun control legislation of the last three decades. The Gun Control Act of 1968 was a compromise bill whose passage was made possible by concessions to those who were opposed to further federal controls and those who wanted extensive further involvement. The main objectives of the act were these:

1. Eliminating the interstate traffic in firearms and ammunition that had previously frustrated state and local efforts to license, register, or restrict ownership of guns.
2. Denying access to firearms to certain congressionally defined groups, including minors, convicted felons, and persons who had been adjudicated as mental defectives or committed to mental institutions.
3. Ending the importation of all surplus military firearms and all other guns unless certified by the secretary of the treasury as "particularly suitable for sporting purposes."

The act also extended the coverage and relative prohibitive taxes to "destructive devices" first imposed in the 1934 Act, and mandated additional penalties for persons convicted of committing federal crimes with firearms.

Interstate Traffic

Interstate traffic in firearms was prohibited except by federally licensed dealers. It was also declared unlawful for any unlicensed person to engage in the manufacture and sale of firearms, regardless of whether or not such a business involved interstate commerce. Federal licenses were also subjected to minimum standards established by the Treasury Department. The act also provided for criminal penalties for law violations.

A dealer selling firearms was required to seek identification from the purchaser establishing that he or she was not an out-of-state purchaser, and to keep such records for inspection by the Bureau of Alcohol, Tobacco and Firearms. Any violation of the law would require either a falsification of documents on the part of the purchaser or willful violation by the dealer. The system of recordkeeping was kept deliberately highly decentralized by the Treasury with the concurrence of Congress, to avoid any potential charge of "gun registration," even though it made problems of detection of any law violation and enforcement extremely expensive.

Denial of Access

The 1968 act expanded the categories of persons named in the Federal Firearms Act of 1938 who were banned from owning firearms or ammunition. Federal licensees were banned from the knowing transfer of guns or ammunition to:

1. Minors (under 18 for shotguns and rifles; under 21 for handguns);
2. Persons convicted of a state or federal felony, as well as the fugitives and defendants under indictment covered by the Federal Firearms Act;
3. Adjudicated mental defectives and any person who had been committed to a mental institution;

4. Persons who are unlawful users of or "addicted to marijuana or any depressant or stimulant drug . . . or narcotic drug."

The purpose of these prohibitions was to deny access to guns and ammunition to these defined special risk groups or, failing that, to punish possession of a firearm as a federal offense, whether or not the possession was in violation of local law.

Limitation of Imports

The act banned importation of any firearm or ammunition into the United States except when specifically certified by the secretary of the treasury as particularly suitable for sporting purposes. The primary aim of this provision was to ban the import of cheap guns called "Saturday Night Specials." Testimony before Congress would suggest that the cheap imported guns were considered unsafe and were associated with easy availability to a specific class of people regarded as violence-prone.

Since 1968, many new bills have been introduced in Congress each year to both ease and tighten various provisions of the 1968 law. The most significant of these are the McClure-Vollmer Act of 1985, the 1988 Feighan-Metzenbaum legislation, and the 1993 Brady Bill. The provisions of the 1985 and 1988 legislation represent a list that by now has become familiar. The issues are:

- a mandatory waiting period and background check for handgun purchasers
- a mandatory jail sentence for using a handgun in the commission of a crime
- requiring a license-to-carry law to carry a handgun outside one's home or place of business
- federal licensing of individuals who make occasional sales, such as pawnbrokers and other part-time dealers
- prohibition of mail-order sales
- prohibition of interstate handgun sales
- regulation of sales from private collections
- allowing BATF to make surprise inspections
- tighter regulation of "Saturday Night Specials" and UZI-type assault weapons

- ban on manufacture and sale of plastic handguns

The Brady Bill

Not much happened in the way of meaningful legislation until what came to be known as the Brady Bill was signed into law by President Clinton in 1993. Named after President Reagan's press secretary, James Brady, who was wounded in 1981, the Brady Bill provides for a five-day waiting period for handgun purchases. Attendant legislation also provided for a ban on semiautomatic assault weapons. In 1995, the new Republican controlled Congress threatened to repeal such measures. With the bombing of the Federal Building in Oklahoma City, however, the attempts to repeal were put on hold. Supporters claim that the Brady Bill has had some beneficial effects. In a 1995 study, it was found that the Brady Bill background-check provision led to the denial of a gun permit to some 45,000 convicted felons, roughly 2 to 3.5% of all applicants for handguns.[16]

However, gun sales are not as well regulated as they might seem. Another study of private gun sales at unregulated flea markets suggests "anyone can buy easily with no questions asked."[17] There is no doubt that gun regulations are very porous. *The Economist* magazine reports:[18]

> Every ten seconds a gun is made in America; every nine seconds one is imported, adding over 6 [million] guns annually to the estimated 212 [million] already in private circulation, nearly one per citizen.

The same article continues to outline the main players in the gun trade: some 1,200 gun makers, most of whom represent small concerns, and 284,000 licensed gun dealers. Of these, nearly half were pawnbrokers and only 20,000 sold out of proper stores. Citing a Department of Justice study [p.24], it is estimated that 27% of felons get their guns over the counter, while 31% get them from family and friends, leaving 42% to obtain them "by other means," usually theft. Of the 212 million guns in circulation, 67 million are handguns.

THE ARGUMENTS: PRO AND CON

For over four decades, those on both sides of the gun control debate have held firm positions. In the aggregate there are three sets of arguments: constitutional, crime, and public health.

The Constitutional Argument

Many critics of proposed handgun control legislation see it as an attack on civil rights. An official NRA study puts it this way:[19] "Today grave dangers and assaults from many directions threaten all the individual rights of the people. The most fierce assault is the erosion of rights by legal process, a procedure most dangerous because it is so effective."

Article II of the Bill of rights (the Second Amendment to the Constitution) states: "A well regulated militia, being necessary to the security of a free State, the right of the people to keep and bear Arms, shall not be infringed."

The NRA interprets this statement literally. According to the statement of policy of the National Rifle Association:[20]

> The NRA is opposed to the registration on any level of government of the ownership of rifles, shotguns, pistols or revolvers for any purpose whatever. Regardless of professed intent, there can be only one outcome of registration, and that is to make possible the seizure of such weapons by political authorities, or by persons seeking to overthrow the government by force. Registration will not keep guns out of the hands of undesirable persons, and few people seriously claim that it will.

Supreme Court cases have established two conceptual interpretations of the Second Amendment. In *United States* v. *Miller*, 306 U.S. 174, 178 (1939), the Supreme Court upheld the conviction of two men who transported in interstate commerce a shotgun, which came within the definition of a firearm under the National Firearms Act of 1934 and was not registered as required by the act nor covered by a stamp-affixed order. The act was challenged on constitutional grounds. The Court found that the Second Amendment did not guarantee the keeping and bearing of any weapon not having a reasonable relationship to the preservation or efficiency of a well-regulated militia. The court stated that the obvious purpose of the amendment was to ensure the continuation and render possible the effectiveness of the militia subjected to call and organization by Congress under Article I, section 8, clause 15 and 16 of the Constitution and the amendment must be interpreted and applied with that end in view.

In *Presser* v. *Illinois*, 116 U.S. 252 (1886), the Supreme Court upheld an Illinois state law that forbade drilling or parading with arms in cities and towns unless authorized by law. The Supreme Court defined the well-regulated militia as a governmentally controlled body rather than a privately organized army, and this is the definition generally accepted today. It guarantees a collective right to keep and bear arms in order to preserve a militia. A question arises as to the type of arms included with the protection of the provision.

The majority of state cases follow the doctrine expressed in *Commonwealth* v. *Murphy*, 44 N.E. 138 (Mass. 1896) that "it has been almost universally held that the legislature may regulate and limit the mode of carrying arms." Therefore, a state statute regulating or sometimes prohibiting the carrying of enumerated weapons is not in opposition to the Second Amendment or its counterpart in a state constitution. No infringement would bear upon the amendment with acts barring deadly weapons or requiring licenses.

The NRA has also emphasized the relevance of the First and Fourth Amendments in interpreting the Second Amendment. Critics of the NRA interpretation of the Second Amendment right to bear arms interpret the term "people" collectively. However, such a restrictive reading of the First Amendment right of assembly or the Fourth Amendment "right of the people to be secure in their persons, houses, papers and effects, against unreasonable searches and seizures" would surely be an erosion of individual rights, which those amendments have traditionally been construed to protect. The context suggests that the Second Amendment be interpreted individually, rather than merely collectively.[21]

The Supreme Court, however, has struck down one provision of the 1934 law on constitutional grounds. In 1968, the Court declared unconstitutional a portion of the law's registration system. The Court's decision was, however, based on the Fifth Amendment, not the Second; the Court held that the registration system in effect required persons to testify against themselves.[22]

Gun control proponents hold that the federal government has full power, under the Constitution, to control firearms in the United States. The power of Congress to regulate firearms under the taxing and commerce clause is clear. Recent Supreme Court decisions have reaffirmed congressional power to enact a broad range of regulatory legislation under the taxing provisions of the National Firearms Act as a legitimate exercise of the United States Congress's power to tax. If Congress were to find that sale and possession of firearms affects interstate commerce or should be taxed, it may take whatever regulatory steps it desires.

The NRA has continued to maintain that the right to possess arms, including shotguns and rifles for sports, in the interest of a prepared citizenry is fundamental to Americans. The NRA further insists that this liberty, far from being a privilege, is a necessity for the protection of the nation from its enemies, both foreign and domestic. The NRA has not wavered from its position stated over thirty years ago in *The American Rifleman:*[23]

> Fighting in the next major war will not be confined to the battlefield alone. It is inevitable that our homeland will be attacked. . . . More than ever, the individual soldier and the individual citizen will be forced to rely on the weapon with which he is armed, and on his ability to use it effectively, if he is to survive.

The Crime Argument

The crime argument is related to the number of guns available in the United States, the lack of adequate controls to prevent acquisition by unauthorized persons, the number of crimes committed with handguns, the number of homicides involving handguns, and the potential deaths and injuries that could possibly be eliminated with better handgun controls. There are numerous controversies over the correct interpretation of statistics. Both sides employ unverifiable rhetoric: "less crimes are committed because the intended victims had guns to use for self-defense and, thereby, frightened away criminals," or "crimes would surely be less if guns were not so easily available." The use of such rhetorical devices suggests that the statistical evidence is itself ambiguous.

Advocates make three arguments in favor of gun control. First is the danger-of-proliferation approach—that is, more guns lead to more crimes and killings using guns. The second related argument is the use of guns by citizens in noncriminal situations; the third is the "weapons sickness" approach—that is, that mere possession alters consciousness, predisposing the owner to violence.

During the decade 1983–1992, total crime increased by 19.2%. Although property crime decreased by 15.3%, violent crime increased during the decade by 53.6%. The high growth categories were clearly forcible rape (up by 38.2%) and aggravated assault (up by 72.5%). Robbery was up by 32.8% and murder by 23.0%. Metropolitan area rates (6,272 per

100,000 population) were consistently above other cities (5,317/100,000) and far above rural rates of 2,025 per 1,000,000 population. These figures are relevant to the regional strength of the pro- and anti-gun lobbies, especially as manifested in congressional votes.

Firearms figured in 69.2% of murders, 42.4% of robberies and 25.0% of aggravated assaults (Table 3); firearms usage in these crimes actually increased over the previous decade, when (in 1985) they averaged 59.1% of murders, 34.3% of robberies, and 21.3% of aggravated assaults. These figures reveal a shift back towards the higher levels of 1975 when firearms figured in 65.8% of murders, 24.9% of aggravated assaults, and 44.8% of robberies. With such swings, it is difficult to ascertain whether there is a central long-term tendency towards increase or decrease. What appears incontestible, however, is that 2 out of every 3 murders, 1 out of every 3 robberies and 1 out of every 4 aggravated assaults involves firearms.

What sense is to be made of such trends, especially when gun control advocates imply that the number of handguns in circulation has actually increased? The NRA contends there is little connection between "carry laws" and crime rates. The NRA argues that crimes rates are actually lower in areas where gun legislation is the least restrictive.[24] In 1992, the crime rates in large metropolitan areas, which tend to be more restrictive, were 6,272 per 100,00 inhabitants for all crimes, with a rate of 871 violent crimes per 100,000 inhabitants. In rural areas, by contrast, over-all crime rates stood at 2,026 per 100,000 and

220 per 100,000 respectively.[25] The least restrictive areas are more rural where crime rates are *socioculturally* lower and where, therefore, there is little social impetus to be restrictive. At the very least the NRA contends that "carry laws" are not the determining variable in crime rates. Clearly, analysts must give more attention to determining all the relevant indicators in the origins of crime. While the ability to have a gun may not cause crime to be committed, in areas where, for whatever reasons, high crime rates are prevalent, it is dangerous to the public to have guns available as the weapon of choice.

James D. Wright, who formerly was a very strong proponent of gun control, has come to rethink the issue:[26]

> As far as I can tell, the arguments in favor of "stricter gun control" fail nearly every empirical test, although in many cases, I hasten to add, the "failure" is simply that the appropriate research is not available.

The analysis of the issue has clearly suffered from the "single variable approach" adopted by both sides. In this regard, Wright may be correct in calling for "appropriate research." Furthermore, the NRA would still have to assess whether the rate of gun-related crime that does exist might actually be lessened by appropriate legislation. The needed comparison is not between low crime/less restrictive areas and high crime/more restrictive areas but between high crime/nonrestrictive and high crime/restrictive areas.

People question whether accurate data are available on the number of handguns and other firearms in the possession of civilians in the United States. A survey of gun ownership over the 1974–1993 period suggests that, overall, gun ownership has run from a high of 48% to a low of 40%. In 1993, roughly 1 in 4 Americans owned a pistol. There are significant differences according to sex, education, race, and political outlook. [27]

In another survey of motives for firearm ownership, 65% (of the 42% who said they

TABLE 3. The Use of Firearms in Selected Crimes, 1993

Crime	Percent
Murder	69.2
Robbery	42.4
Assault	25.0

Source: U. S. Department of Commerce, *Statistical Abstract of the United States, 1994*, Washington, DC.

were gun owners) said it was for recreation, 20% for protection, 12% for both equally and 2% expressed no opinion.[28] In all, 37% link gun ownership to protection. Overall, one might expect that such figures would vary considerably from region to region.

Handgun production in the U. S. has hovered around 2 million over the past decades and together with imports, the new supplies on the market can range from 4 to 6 million pieces. The United States is the only industrialized nation that does not have strict firearms regulation on a national basis. In Britain, for example, the purchaser of any gun, even for hunting, must obtain a permit, and all sales are registered with the police. France and Italy have similar regulations, and background investigations of would-be gun purchasers in those countries may take up to six weeks. Spain imposed the additional restriction that only fifty rounds of ammunition may be purchased at one time. In West Germany, well-reputed and trustworthy citizens may own handguns only upon showing a specific need for personal protection, such as dangerous occupations or living quarters, and permits are required for purchase and carrying. Opponents of controls frequently point to Switzerland as an example of a country where gun ownership is universal. Virtually every male of military age is required to keep his military equipment in his home, including weapons and ammunition. Pro-control advocates counter that each of these guns is registered and every round of ammunition for them must be accounted for. The purchase and ownership of nonmilitary weapons is as strictly regulated in Switzerland as in other European countries. These countries, all with stricter firearms controls than the United States, also have a much lower fatality rate than does this country, as shown in Table 4.

It truly is difficult to know what to make of such statistics. The suicide rates in all of these other countries dwarf those of the United States. Is one to conclude that in the U. S. one shoots one's neighbor while in these other countries one shoots oneself!

Those who try to be objective observers suggest that many of these arguments are contrived, based on abuse or misuse of statistics, and are advanced to support a predetermined position. Blackman explicitly raises the criticism that such comparisons are too facile and neglect the other determinants of the homicide rate—notably, cultural differences and different modes of law enforcement.[29]

A second argument advanced by the NRA is that even if gun control laws were relevant to crime statistics (which they deny), they could not be enforced anyway. The result would be that law-abiding citizens

TABLE 4. Guns, Homicides, and Suicides

Country	% Households with Guns	Homocides with Guns per million	Homocides without Guns per million	Suicides with Guns per millions	Suicides without Guns per million
United States	48.9	44.6	31.3	73	51
Switzerland	32.6	4.0	7.7	57.4	187.1
Canada	30.8	8.4	17.6	44.4	95.0
Finland	25.5	5.5	23.1		
Australia	20.1	6.6	12.9	34.2	81.6
Belgium	16.8	8.7	9.8	24.5	207.0
Germany	9.2	14.8 [not broken out by weapon]		13.8	189.9

Source: Erik Eckholm, 1992, "A Basic Issue: Whose Hands Should Guns Be Kept Out Of?, *New York Times*, April 3, 1992, pp. A1, A15, citing studies covering the mid-1980s.

would be at a serious disadvantage in facing the criminal element, which could care less about regulations. Given the fact that there are between 50 and 100 million handguns in the country, the NRA asks how we are supposed to cope with the problem of enforcement when even a small minority refuses to comply. Even if a majority of owners were willing to give up their guns, the owners of the several thousand handguns involved in murders are unlikely to do so. Thus, enforcement of the laws would have to exceed 99 percent effectiveness before even one murderer would be disarmed.[30]

Suppose, for the sake of argument, says the NRA, that between 10 and 25 percent of handgun owners refuse to comply with any law pertaining to handgun registration or confiscation, a not unrealistic presumption, what would be the alternative? It could mean massive police searches, violation of individual privacy, and tremendous cost of enforcement with dubious benefits.

PUBLIC HEALTH

In recent literature, much more attention is being given to guns as a public health hazard. The overall data indicate that accidents caused by firearms declined from 1.2% in 1970 to 0.9% in 1980 and 0.6% in 1990. The gross number of persons involved declined from 2,406 to 1,695 in 1980 and to 1,441 in 1990. Handgun Control, Inc., has focused on the family tragedies involved, especially in the cases of violent family situations and suicide. 1983 Gallup polls suggested that 26% of respondents polled felt that stricter gun laws would reduce deaths due to family arguments "a great deal," while 28% said "quite a lot," 25% said "not very much," and only 18% "not at all." When asked the same question regarding accidental deaths, the responses were practically identical.[31] To take the example of those aged 30–34 years, in 1991 the incidence of accidental firearm mortality for men was 0.8/100,000 for white males and 1.2/100,000 for black. For women the rates

were 0.1/100,000 for both blacks and whites. Suicide rates were higher: 14.9/100,000 for while males and 2.8/100,000 for white females. And correspondingly, 10.5/100,000 for black males and 0.7/100,000 for black females. The breakdown for other ages groups is similar, although the accident rate is higher among 15–19 year olds.[32] The NRA questions whether gun control would actually resolve those problems. The tragedy remains nonetheless and the question is whether public policy is called for to prevent such accidents or self-inflicted harm.

Power and Justice: The Morality of Strategies and Tactics

In a democratic society, laws invariably reflect lawmakers' perceptions of the long-run public interest—perceptions often tempered by lobbyists for special interests. Therefore, the fate of gun control efforts must be analyzed not only from the rationale of various sociopolitical, legal, or economic arguments pertaining to society overall, but also based on the strengths, weakness, and influence of vested interests, most notably here the NRA.

The gun lobby, spearheaded by the National Rifle Association, includes manufacturers of guns and related equipment (including clothing), sportsmen, target shooters, conservation groups, and right–wing extremist groups.

THE NATIONAL RIFLE ASSOCIATION (NRA)

The National Rifle Association was organized in 1871 by a few National Guard officers to enhance the peaceful and safe use of firearms. It gained tax exemption at its founding and is not a registered lobby group, since only a small part of its funds go to legislative work. During the 1970s, membership was around 1 million but by 1986 it had risen to 3.1 million. It edged toward 3.5 million in the early 1990s, but seems to have fallen back since to about

3.2 million. The NRA seems to attract two groups of constituents: the sports-minded (hunting, marksmanship) and the paramilitary. As the organization grew and broadened its membership, its goals also broadened. Its restated aims are: To promote social welfare and public safety, law and order, and the national defense; to educate and train citizens of good repute in the sale and efficient handling of small arms and in the technique of design, production, and group instruction; to increase the knowledge of small arms and promote efficiency in the use of such arms on the part of members of law enforcement agencies, of the armed forces, and of citizens who would be subject to service in the event of war; and generally to encourage the lawful ownership and use of small arms by citizens of good repute. In pursuit of these goals, the NRA sponsors firearms safety and marksmanship courses, as well as thousands of shooting matches each year. It also selects the rifle and pistol teams that represent the United States in the Olympics and other international competitions.

The clearest self-portrait by the NRA is provided in an article by Paul Blackman and Richard Gardiner.[33] In the 1990s the NRA has been beset by ideological struggles from within.[34] The most serious differences are between the paramilitary wing and the hunting/recreational wing. In a 1992 survey, 27% of the public was favorable to the NRA, as were 42% of gun owners. Of those two groups, 25% and 12%, respectively, were unfavorable and 16% and 15% were undecided. In each case, a full 35% and 30% of respondents said they "had not heard enough" and could not form an opinion.[35] Support among traditional supporters deepened with the involvement of the NRA in the congressional hearings on Waco and its criticism of BATF agents as "jack-booted thugs."[36]

The main tactic employed by the NRA is to exhort members to write their senators and representatives and register their opposition to any pending gun control legislation. Members are reached via two channels: the well-edited and widely circulated *American Rifleman*, the official organ of the NRA sent free to all dues-paying members; and legislative bulletins sent to members in localities considering firearms legislation. Other tactics include editorials in the *American Rifleman* and assistance in the election or defeat of candidates based on their gun control position. The *American Rifleman*, besides carrying articles of interest to the gun enthusiast, fills two important and related functions for the NRA: it provides a major revenue source through advertising sales (11% of its 1987 $71.1 million income); the balance of income is principally derived from $20 membership dues assessed of each of the 3.1 million members.[37] In a monthly column called "What the Lawmakers Are Doing," the magazine carries "a concise bill-by-bill summary of firearms proposals and legislative action at both the federal and state levels." Other magazines carrying the NRA message are *Field and Stream*, *Outdoor Life*, and *Sports Afield*. The NRA denies that it is simply obstructionist:[38]

"Our critics and adversaries often proclaim by word of mouth and on the printed page that the NRA is for minimum firearms controls or no gun regulation at all. This is, of course, completely untrue," said the late executive vice–president Franklin Orth. But the NRA "looks on the vast majority of bills for firearms legislation as the misdirected efforts of social reformers, do–gooders and/or the completely uninformed who would accomplish miracles by the passage of another law." In its opposition to the 1968 gun control law, Frank C. Daniel, the NRA's secretary, explained that the organization had been unable to support a specific bill, because no one had been able to come up with a definition of a Saturday Night Special that was agreeable to the organization.

While the NRA may have been more "approachable" even a decade ago, critics maintain that an internal power struggle has seen hard–liners come out on top. Some suggest that the theme of the present leadership is to take no conciliatory stances. This was evident in congressional hearings on

"Firearms That Can Escape Detection and Armor Piercing Ammunition and the Criminal Misuse and Availability of Machine-guns and Silencers."[39] The NRA has turned on former supporters, such as governor Cecil Andrus of Idaho who favors legislation against armor piercing bullets, labelling him a "lap dog for the national gun control movement."[40]

THE GUN INDUSTRY

In addition, critics question the NRA's links to the gun manufacturing industry. According to the *Wall Street Journal*:[41]

> Gun manufacturers play an important part in bankrolling the thus–far largely successful fight to minimize gun legislation. Money from gun makers and sellers, either through outright subsidy or indirectly in the form of advertising in membership journals and the like, helps finance such leaders in the antigun fight as the National Rifle Association and the National Shooting Sports Foundation.

In 1986 the small arms (under 30 mm) industry shipped $918 million in ammunition and $1,030 million in small arms. The industry employed 20.7 thousand workers and met a payroll of $531.3 million.[42] While by no means one of the largest industries in the U. S. it does have clout.

The split in NRA ranks that has developed over the past ten years with respect to semi-automatic weapons, armor-piercing bullets, and the sponsoring of local militia, has left the firearms industry in a quandary. While it looks favorably upon, and wishes to vigorously maintain, its markets in hunting, sports shooting, and personal security areas, it is not all that comfortable with the hard-line paramilitary groups, much less criminals, if for no other reason than trying to maintain a positive public image.

The industry exerts considerable economic clout and generates important advertising revenues for the NRA. Industry group representatives include the National Shooting Sports Foundation (NSSF), founded in 1961, and the Sporting Arms and Ammunition Manufacturers' Institute (SAAMI), founded in 1926. While neither group has favored gun control legislation they have been historically more conciliatory than the recent hard-line NRA stances.

CONSERVATION GROUPS

Conservation groups make strange bedfellows with gun control opponents. Hunting is, however, part of the conservation strategy for managing the ratio of wildlife to resources. Also, conservation groups depend heavily on the financial support of the firearms and ammunitions industry. Furthermore, a sizeable portion of the federal funds earmarked for wildlife and conservation are directly related to gun and ammunition manufacturing. Under the Pittman-Robertson Act (the Federal Aid in Wildlife Restoration Act) of 1937, which was supported by the gun industry, an 11 % excise tax on the manufacture of sporting arms and ammunition is used for aiding state fish and game agencies. In 1987, the excise taxes brought in by firearms broke down as follows: $26,261,000 from a 10% tax on pistols and revolvers; $42,182,000 from an 11% tax on firearms; and $34,978,000 from an 11% tax on shells and cartridges.[43]

Further cementing the relationship between conservation activities and anticontrol sentiment is the fact that hunting license revenues are also applied to state and local wildlife programs. According to a 1987 publication of the Fish and Wildlife Service (commemorating the fiftieth anniversary of the Pittman-Robertson Act), revenues from the firearms industry have been instrumental in restoring America's wildlife.[44]

In addition, the Virginia Commission of Game and Inland Fisheries wrote to a congressional subcommittee in 1968 in opposition to controls, stating that if it became more difficult legally to obtain, possess, transport, and use firearms for legitimate purposes, there would be less and less participation in hunting and other shooting sports. Since hunting licenses and taxes on sporting arms and ammunition support virtually all government programs for wildlife protection and management, the wildlife resources of the nation would be endangered to the same degree that interesting shooting sports would wane. Not all conservationists share in the gun industry's financial support or in the concept of managing wildlife for the benefit of hunting activities. But the National Wildlife Federation and the Wildlife Management Institute, two of the largest beneficiaries of industry support, were created with the help of the industry and have numerous industry representatives as officers and directors. The president of the World Wildlife Fund's American chapter and the honorary president of World Wild-life, C.R. Gutermuth, was the second ranking officer of NRA. John Olin, retired chairman of Olin Corporation (a manufacturer of arms and ammunition), is a director of World Wildlife. Thomas Kimball, executive director of the National Wildlife Federation, testified in 1968:[45] "The reason a wildlife conservation organization such as ours is interested in gun legislation revolves around the fact that hunters contribute materially to the wildlife management programs of this country through their license fees, and that they are quite interested in seeing that legislation that is considered by the Congress does not materially and adversely affect this interest . . . ."

For this reason, the federation is vitally interested in preventing any unnecessary discouragement of law-abiding citizens desiring to purchase, possess, and transport arms for hunting purposes, while at the same time anxious to be helpful in reducing the crime rate.

LAX ENFORCEMENT: FRIENDS IN HIGH PLACES

More important to the NRA agenda have been links to the Treasury and State Departments as well as to the Justice Department and law enforcement agencies. Up until the NRA's championing of semi-automatic weapons and armor-piercing bullets and the recent Waco disaster and the bombing of the Oklahoma Federal Building, the relations between the NRA and these groups that oversee enforcement of gun control laws were thought to be very strong.

Historically, the loopholes in the gun control laws have been more than matched by the lax attitude of the federal bureaucracy charged with the responsibility of enforcing federal laws. For example, although the authority existed under the 1930 and 1934 laws, the Treasury Department did not collect any figures on the production of different types of guns in the United States. In 1968, the only figures available were those collected by the Bureau of the Census for 1963. The State and Treasury departments have not done enough to execute the gun control laws of which they are the chief custodians. Specifically, this is the fault of particular bureaucrats. More generally, it is a reflection of governmental nonchalance toward gun control measures. The pervasive attitude is summed up in Acting Assistant Secretary William Dickey's comment that "there was no requirement" for his office to collect information legitimately requested by a senator and that he didn't intend to collect it. For more than thirty years, bureaucratic neglect of gun control duties has increased on two fronts: gun dealer supervision and State Department attitude toward gun imports. The attitude toward the importation of guns seems to be reflected in the words of John Sipes, director of the Office of Munitions Control (OMC) of the State Department. He admitted that his agency was authorized to keep out arms it felt to be detrimental to the security of the United States, but held it did not have the authority to ban firearms for which there is legitimate commercial market, just because there is the possibility that these guns may end up in the hands of dangerous people. Sipes's statement demonstrates that Congress's interest in passing the Mutual Security Act was only in how to unload millions of dollars worth of United States arms and ammunition onto other countries.

As of early 1995, there were many signs that this alliance was splitting up. In the Waco hearings and in the investigation of the bombing of the Federal Building in Oklahoma City, the militia wing of the NRA has shown itself to be quite hostile to federal powers, in general, and to the Bureau of ATF, in particular. Actually, the alliance began to become unglued during the debate over armor-piercing bullets and [plastic] guns that can escape detection. This drove a wedge between the NRA and law enforcement agencies at all levels of government.

In early 1989, a person brandishing a semi–automatic weapon mowed down children in a schoolyard in Stockton, California. Following that tragedy there was a renewed impetus to ban such weapons "whose only purpose was to kill another human being." Los Angeles Police Chief Daryl Gates testified in favor of strict legislation on behalf of law enforcement officers across the country saying, "I don't want that gun on the street." The NRA, of course, opposed the new legislation. They were joined in their opposition by President George Bush:[46]

Look, if you're suggesting that every pistol that can do that [referring to a recent shooting in the Washington area] or every rifle [referring to the Stockton massacre] should be banned, I would strongly oppose that. I would strongly go after the criminals who use these guns. But I am not about to suggest that a semi-automated *hunting rifle* should be banned. Absolutely not. (emphasis added).

By 1995, George Bush resigned his membership in the NRA in protest of NRA attacks upon BATF and FBI agents as well as other law enforcement officers.

EXTREMIST GROUPS

One final component, and probably the least savory, of the lobby must be mentioned. Various extremist and paramilitary groups and militia, such as the Minutemen, Klu Klux Klan, Breakthrough, and Revolutionary Action Movement, have more of an ideological than an economic interest in protecting their right to own guns. These groups frequently form or join organizations that, through NRA affiliation, are eligible for special discount rates on surplus military weapons and ammunition. The NRA repudiates these groups and does not knowingly allow them to join the association, but it lacks screening procedures to identify individuals.

NOTES

1. John J. Fialka, "NRA's Latest Campaign Seeks to Recruit Women and Project New Image as Crime-Fighting Group." *Wall Street Journal* (May 22, 1995) p. A14.
2. William E. Schmidt, "Pressure for Gun Control Rises and Falls, but Ardor for Arms Seems Constant." *New York Times* (October 25, 1987), p. E5.
3. Margaret Dicanio, "Gun Control: Advocates," in *Encyclopedia of Violence: Origins, Attitudes, Consequences.* New York, NY, Facts on File, 1993, p. 112.
4. *Ibid.,* "Gun Control: Opponents," pp. 114–16.
5. Sam Hoe Verhovek, "States Seek to Let Citizens Carry Concealed Weapons." *New York Times* (March 6, 1995), pp. A1, B8.
6. George Volsky, "Guns in Florida: This Week It Suddenly Becomes a Lot Easier to Be Legal." *New York Times* (September 27, 1987), p. 26.
   New York Times, "New Law In Maryland Bans Sale and Manufacture of Some Pistols" (May 24, 1988), p. 27.
   New York Times, "Maryland Gun Ban Is Hotly Debated" (October 9, 1988), p. 35.
7. Address by Sarah Brady to the National

Press Club, Washington, DC, September 29, 1988. *Congressional Quarterly Weekly Report,* "NRA Shows It Still Has What It Takes . . . to Overcome Gun Control Advocates" (September 17, 1988), pp. 2564–2565. NRA, "Criminals Don't Wait; Why Should You?— the Case Against Waiting Periods," Washington, DC., January, 1987.

8. U.S. Department of Justice, Bureau of Justice Statistics, *Sourcebook of Criminal Justice Statistics—1985,* Washington, DC., 1986, pp. 195–201. James D. Wright, "Second Thoughts about Gun Control." *The Public Interest,* no. 91 (Spring 1988), pp. 34–35. *Newsweek,* "A Goetz Backlash?" (March 11, 1985), pp. 50–53. Howard Schusser and Stanley Presser, "Attitude Measurement and the Gun Control Paradox." *Public Opinion Quarterly,* 41 (Winter 1977–78), p. 427.

9. A. O. Sulzberger, Jr., "Rifle Association Poll Says Majority Oppose More Gun Legislation." *New York Times* (March 10, 1979), p. 25. NRA, "Ten Myths about Gun Control." Washington, DC., (March 1985), pp. 1–4. Don B. Kates, "Reflections on the Relevancy of Gun Controls." *Criminal Law Bulletin,* 93 (March/April 1977), pp. 119–24.

10. Wright, "Second Thoughts about Gun Control," *Public Interest,* no. 91, (Spring, 1988), pp. 24–25.

11. Sam Howe Verhovek, "States Seek to Let Citizens Carry Concealed Weapons." *New York Times* (March 6, 1995), pp. A1, B8.

12. *Congressional Quarterly Editorial Research Reports,* "Reassessing the Nation's Gun Laws," (March 22, 1991), no. 11, p. 160.

13. Gun Control Act of 1968, U.S.C. Sec. 925(d) (3) (1970).

14. D. S. Greene, "Gun Control," *Congressional Quarterly Editorial Research Reports,* November 13, 1987, pp. 594–95.

15. *New York Times,* "Transcript of Johnson's Statement On Signing Crime and Safety Bill," (June 20, 1968), p. 23.

16. Fox Butterfield, "Brady Law Halts Permits for 45,000." *New York Times* (March 12, 1995), p. 23.

17. Erik Larson, "Brisk Sales: Private Gun Sales Go Unregulated at Shows and at Flea Markets," *Wall Street Journal* (July 12, 1994), pp. A1, A6.

18. *The Economist,* "Home on the Range: Gun Control Does Not Work in America, Because It

Barely Exists." March 26, 1994, pp. 23–24, 28.

19. David I. Caplan, "Constitutional Rights in Jeopardy," National Rifle Association, Washington DC, (December 1986).

20. Appendix V, "Statement of Policy of the National Rifle Association," cited in Carl Bakal, *The Right to Bear Arms,* New York, McGraw Hill, 1966.

21. Caplan, "Constitutional Rights," pp. 1–9.

22. *Haynes v. U.S.,* 390 U.S. 85, 98 (1968).

23. *American Rifleman,* May 1957, p. 12ff.

24. Paul H. Blackman, *Firearms and Violence, 1974–84.* NRA Institute for Legislative Action, Washington, DC, (July 1985).

25. U.S. Department of Commerce, *Statistical Abstract of the United States, 1994,* Table 302, Washington, DC, U. S. Government Printing Office, 1995, citing Federal Bureau of Investigation, *Crime in the United States, 1994.*

26. Wright, "Second Thoughts," p. 35. Cited in U.S. Department of Justice, *Sourcebook—1985* p. 194, based on a January 11–16, 1985 ABC News *Washington Post* poll.

27. *Statistical Abstract,* 1994, Table 409.

28. Blackman, *Firearms* p. 19ff.

29. Jeffrey H. Boyd and Eve K. Mosciki, "Firearms and Youth Suicide." *American Journal of Public Health* (October 2, 1986), pp. 1240–42.

30. Paul H. Blackman and Richard E. Gardiner, *The N.R.A. and Criminal Justice Policy: The Effectiveness of the National Rifle Association as a Public Interest Group,* National Rifle Association Institute for Legislative Action, Washington, DC, November 1986.

31. Arthur L. Kellermann and Donald T. Reay, "Protection or Peril? An Analysis of Firearm Related Deaths In The Home." *The New England Journal of Medicine* (June 12, 1986), pp. 1557–60. Garen J. Wintemute, Stephen P. Teret, and Jess F. Kraus, "The Epidemiology of Firearm Deaths among Residents of California." *The Western Journal of Medicine* (March 1987), pp. 374–77; U.S. Department of Justice, *Sourcebook—1985,* pp. 201–02.

32. U.S. Department of Commerce, *Statistical Abstract of the United States, 1994,* Table 137, Washington, DC, U. S. Government Printing Office, 1995, citing U.S. National Center for Health Statistics, *Advance Data from Vital and Health Statistics.*

33. Blackman and Gardiner, *The N.R.A.;* Steven A. Holmes, "Rifle Lobby Torn by Dissidents

and Capitol Defectors." *New York Times* (March 27, 1991), p. 20; Erik Larson, "Hard Liner Prevails as Neal Knox Gains Control over NRA." *Wall Street Journal* (October 26, 1993), pp. A1, A5.

34. Paul Weiss, "A Hoplophobe among the Bunnies." *New York Times Magazine* (September 11, 1994), pp. 65–71, 84, 86, 100.

35. Neil A. Lewis, "NRA Meets Call for Gun Control with a Muzzle." *New York Times* (March 12, 1992), pp. A1, D22.

36. Jane Fritsch, "N.R.A. Criticized for Its Aggressive Tactics." *New York Times* (July 30, 1995), p. 20.

37. Jeffrey H. Birnbaum, "Surprise Setback—Mighty Gun Lobby Loses Its Invincibility by Taking Hard Line." *Wall Street Journal* (May 24, 1988), pp. 1, 25. Blackman and Gardiner, *The NRA*, p. 2

38. Robert Sherill, "Lobby on Target." *New York Times Magazine*, (October 15, 1967), p. 112.

39. Committee on the Judiciary, Subcommittee on Crime, *Hearings on Armor Piercing Ammunition and the Criminal Misuse and Availability of Machine guns and Silencers*, (May 17 and 24 and June 27, 1994) 98th Congress, 2nd Session.

   Committee on the Judiciary, Subcommittee on Crime, *Hearings on Firearms That Can Escape Detection* (May 15, 1986), 99th Congress, 2nd Session.

40. Sarah Brady, Address to the National Press Club, (September 29, 1988). *New York Times*, "Rifle Association Power Struggle Pits Board against Conservatives," (January 28, 1987), p. D26.

Peter Wiley, "Idaho Feud Finds NRA under Fire." *Wall Street Journal* (December 21, 1987), p. 20.

Business Week, "The NRA Shoots Itself In The Foot—Extremism Is Souring Lawmakers," (May 16, 1988) pp. 44–45.

41. David Gumpert, "The Gun: To the Arms Industry, Control Controversy Is a Business Problem." *Wall Street Journal* (May 21, 1972), p. 21.

42. U.S. Department of Congress, Bureau of the Census, *1986 Annual Survey of Manufacturers*, "Statistics for Industry Groups and Industries," pp. I–18, I–19, Washington DC, (1987).

43. Internal Revenue Service, Public Affairs Division, "Internal Revenue Report of Excise Taxes," News Release IR-88-22 (April 11, 1988).

44. United States Fish and Wildlife Services, *Restoring America's Wildlife, 1937–1987*, Washington, DC, (1987).

45. U.S. Congress, Senate Committee on the Judiciary, Subcommittee to Investigate Juvenile Delinquency, *Hearings on Federal Firearms Legislation*, June 26, 27, 28 and July 8, 9, 10, 1968, pp. 599–40.

46. Gerald M. Boyd, "Bush Opposes Ban on Assault Firearms but Backs State Role." *New York Times*, (February 17, 1989), pp. A1. Robert Reinhold, "Effort to Ban Assault Rifles Gains Momentum." *New York Times* (January 28, 1989), pp. 1, 9.

WARNER-LAMBERT COMPANY

*Personal criminal liability of senior executives
for accidents causing workers' death and injury*

At 2:40 A.M. on Sunday, November 21, 1976, a large section of a five-story manufacturing plant owned and operated by the American Chicle Division (ACD) of the Warner-Lambert Corporation (W-L) was destroyed by an explosion and fire that reached 1000° F. The explosion originated in and involved the Freshen-Up gum department on the fourth floor. One hundred and eighteen employees were working on the morning shift at the time of the explosion. Fifty-four received burns or other injuries; many required extended hospitalization. Six employees died as a direct consequence of the second-and-third degree burns over most of their bodies and from related complications.[1]

On August 1, 1977, the Grand Jury for Queens County returned a twelve-count indictment (six counts of manslaughter in the second degree and six counts of criminally negligent homicide) against two corporations, the Warner-Lambert Company (American Chicle Division) and against four individuals, all of whom were corporate officers of Warner-Lambert Company. All five respondents entered pleas of not guilty on August 18, 1977, and subsequently argued that there was insufficient evidence to support the grand jury indictment. The trial court, the Supreme Court of the State of New York for the County of Queens, agreed with the respondents and on February 15, 1978 dismissed the indictments. After considering further arguments by the district attorney of Queens County, the trial court reaffirmed its dismissal of the indictments on July 26, 1978. The district attorney appealed to the Appellate Division, Second Judicial Department. On July 9, 1979, the Appellate Division reversed the order of the trial court, reinstated the indictments, and directed that the trial proceed.[2]

ISSUES FOR ANALYSIS

The Warner-Lambert indictments present a number of crucial issues in the area of corporate liability and the susceptibility of corporations and executives to criminal sanctions for failure to provide a safe working environment.

1. What are the *standards* by which one might judge hazardous or unsafe conditions in the workplace? Should safety standards be based on *known* dangers, or dangers that should have been *anticipated*? What are the relevant criteria for determining that due diligence was exercised by responsible executives to protect workers from previously unknown dangers?
2. Could the explosion at the American Chicle Company have been prevented through effective communication, reporting, and control mechanisms within the corporate hierarchy? The record shows that Warner-Lambert plant

management took numerous measures to keep the plant safe and dust-free while at the same time urging the Warner-Lambert head office people to install a comprehensive exhaust system. How should the decision-making delegation of authority and communication be made more effective to prevent similar situations from occurring in the future?

3. Is it possible that the company kept postponing the installation of exhaust equipment or making other changes in the plant in order to meet the tremendous demand for the product? Did the company compromise on safety to protect large sales and profits that were being generated by Freshen-Up chewing gum?

4. What are the appropriate conditions and safeguards under which a corporation and one or more of its executives may be charged with the crime of causing death or injury to their employees?

5. To what extent are the law courts a proper societal mechanism to determine whether a safe working environment has been provided and, if it has not, who within the corporate structure should be held responsible?

6. What is the responsibility of workers, union organizations, and government agencies?

7. What else might be done in the legislative arena or other societal mechanisms to increase the degree of care and responsibility that managements must assume for worker health and safety?

THE RESPONDENTS: WARNER-LAMBERT

The Warner-Lambert Company doing business under the name of Warner-Lambert Company and the American Chicle Division, maintained a manufacturing plant at 3030 Thompson Avenue, Long Island City, Queens County, New York. Several products were manufactured at this facility, including Freshen-Up® chewing gum.

Arthur Kraft was Warner-Lambert's vice-president in charge of manufacturing, with offices at Warner-Lambert's corporate headquarters in Morris Plains, New Jersey. Ed

Harris was director of corporate safety and security for Warner-Lambert, with an office at the corporate headquarters in Morris Plains. While both men visited the Long Island plant on occasion, neither official was responsible for the day-to-day operations of the plant.[3]

James O'Mahoney was plant manager of the manufacturing facility in Long Island City where the explosion occurred. His offices were located on the fifth floor of the Thompson Avenue plant, and he was involved in day-to-day operations. John O'Rourke was the plant engineer at the Long Island City facility, with an office in that building. He worked in the Freshen-Up department on an almost daily basis.[4]

The Introduction of Freshen-Up Gum into the American Market

In the latter part of 1969, the Research and Development Department at Warner-Lambert's Long Island City factory began a market project to introduce a new chewing gum product. Subsequently sold as Freshen-Up gum, it was unique because of its flavored liquid or jelly- filled center. The product had been previously introduced and successfully marketed in both Europe and Asia, By 1972, experimentation and development had proved so encouraging that Warner-Lambert decided to go into limited production A pilot, or prototype, manufacturing operation was established on the first floor to support limited production for the purpose of testing consumer interest and marketing potential.

Consumer reaction to Freshen-Up gum was extremely favorable, leading Warner-Lambert to set up full-scale production under the aegis of its manufacturing division in September 1974. The company invested $10 million in manufacturing equipment and expanded operations to include six processing lines on the fourth floor of the Long Island City plant operating twenty-four hours a day, six days a week. The Freshen-Up department became fully operational in December 1975.

By the fall of 1976, production had risen to some two million packages of gum per day. At a price of 20 cents per package, Freshen-Up generated retail sales of over $400,000 per day. The new product sold better than any other chewing gum on the market, and Warner-Lambert found it could sell all that it could produce. Freshen-Up was given priority status over such other well-known items produced by Warner-Lambert as Chiclets, Dentyne, Trident, Dynamints, and Certs. Efforts were made to reduce all downtime. Supervisory personnel were promised bonuses for increased productivity.[5]

EVENTS PRECEDING THE EXPLOSION

The Warner-Lambert case really began in February 1975. The Freshen-Up operation at that time was still located on the first floor of the Long Island City plant and the six processing lines on the fourth floor had not yet become operational.

The Freshen-Up Manufacturing Process

The manufacturing process developed by the corporation provided for slabs of a basic gum product to be introduced into the processing line through a hopper located above a batch-forming complex called the extructor/extruder. As the gum passed out of the extruder in the form of a "rope" approximately two inches in diameter, its center was injected with a variably flavored liquid or jelly filling. The product was then moved through a rope sizer wherein the gum strip was further reduced in diameter to a workable one-half inch. On leaving the sizer, the gum rope was drawn through an open transition plate. At this point, among others, a powdered lubricant or metallic and organic compound known as magnesium stearate (MS) was applied to prevent sticking.

The product was then introduced into a tablet-forming machine called the Uniplast.

The gum rope passed into a rotating die head, furnished with plungers and guiding cams, for the stamping and formation of 38 separate pieces of liquid-filled gum, each approximately 3/8 of an inch in thickness and 5/8 of an inch square. To facilitate release of the tablets and prevent adherence of the gum to the dies, the latter was sprayed with a cooling agent known as liquid nitrogen (LN_2), which produced temperatures in and around the machinery sufficiently cold to form ice on the die head and base. (A temperature of -320°F exists at the point of LN_2 emission, compared with the freezing of water at +32°F.) On leaving the Uniplast, the newly formed gum pieces were conveyed into a cooling tunnel. From there, they moved to an adjacent wrapping section for other processing and packaging.

The district attorney contended that the uniplast machine, the centerpiece of the processing line, was designed by a German concern for the manufacture of hard candy at warm or room temperatures. This contention was based on the manufacturer's brochure and supported by testimony of the manufacturer's representative. It was not designed for gum production in the kind of extreme cold and dust environment created in the manufacture of Freshen-Up gum. The Uniplast machine was made of cast iron and other brittle, low-alloy metals not suitable for use under the extreme cold conditions produced by the application of liquid nitrogen. Nor was the machinery made to operate in a continuously cold environment twenty-four hours a day, six days a week. The district attorney argued that this extremely cold environment induced embrittlement or structural weakness of the metals and caused them to lose ductility, or the capacity to withstand fracture, when subjected to impact or temperature changes. The machine's motor was also not sealed to prevent electrical spark or arc emission or to prevent the entry of dust—features necessary in any process that generates industrial dust. The machines used in the production of Freshen-Up gum were specifically modified and adapted by Warner-Lambert to produce Freshen-Up gum. In the opinion of the district attorney, they were not suitable for the manufacturing process established by Warner-Lambert.[6]

The 1975 Pilot Project

As early as February 1975 , while the Freshen-Up operation was still located on the first floor of the Long Island City plant, an employee observed a small flash explosion of magnesium stearate produced from an electrical extension cord lying on the floor. When he reported the incident to the assistant production manager, he was told: ". . . yeah, well, it's one of the problems we have to work out." Based on what he had seen, the employee made an entry in a corporate journal, as required under company rules, recommending that the use of magnesium stearate be discontinued.[7]

Anticipating similar problems with the move upstairs, another employee made an inquiry and was led to believe that effective dust- collecting equipment would be provided in the new fourth-floor department. Warner-Lambert disputed the veracity of these statements, contending that the employee was only a college intern on the payroll for a total of six months. According to the employee's grand jury testimony, there was no explosion but "sort of a white flash, like similar to a small flashbulb going off." This occurred when another employee kicked a household electrical cord being used to operate a 1/4-inch drill with a brush on it to clean out the die punches. The corporate journal was, in reality, the employee's own log book. The facts of this particular incident were not officially recorded and the employee made only a vague reference to eliminating MS.[8]

The grand jury investigation, however, showed that the problem of MS dust was becoming serious. In June 1975, Warner-Lambert's manager of safety and fire protection, who worked directly under the supervi-

sion of Ed Harris, dispatched Warner-Lambert's own industrial hygienist to the Freshen-Up department for the purpose of determining employee exposure to MS dust and making appropriate recommendations. The manufacture of Freshen-Up utilized large quantities of MS, raising concern regarding the "nuisance level" of the dust and the health problems that might arise from the workers' exposure to the dust, as opposed to an explosion hazard. The industrial hygienist issued a report in March 1976 recommending: (a) use of local exhaust systems; (b) substituting a vacuum unit for compressed air in the cleaning of machinery; (c) vacuuming, not sweeping, the floors; and (d) issuance of face masks until the above controls could be instituted by plant engineers. The face masks were issued, but the other recommendations were never implemented. Notwithstanding, Ed Harris concluded in an analysis around December 1975, that the concentration of ambient MS was *not* sufficient to create a dust explosion. It should be noted that the hygienist's survey (the basis of Harris's conclusion) was conducted at a time (November 1975) when only three processing lines were in operation on the plant's fourth floor.[9]

The Fourth-Floor Manufacturing Operation

In August 1975, the Freshen-Up project moved to the fourth floor of the plant and Warner-Lambert put the six production lines in operation. In establishing operations on the fourth floor, the electrical contractors who were installing power lines and control panels were never informed that the operations would involve a combustible dust or that the equipment had to comply with standards and regulations for "hazardous locations" as set forth in the national and New York City electrical codes. Instead, emphasis was placed on establishing a production line that would satisfy the city health department regulations affecting food processing plants. The company's own electrician, who was aware of the amount of MS dust being generated on the first floor during the pilot project, specifically asked the plant engineer, John O'Rourke, whether he wanted a "dust-proof" installation. He was told "no" because "there will be no dust."[10]

In October 1975, Warner-Lambert's manager of safety and fire protection, who worked directly for Ed Harris, submitted a report to Warner-Lambert's Rockford, Illinois plant warning of the explosive nature of MS and the proper venting ratios to be used to protect plant equipment in the event of an explosion. In November 1975, the corporation's own industrial hygienist again recommended major changes in the fourth-floor venting system to minimize workers' exposure to MS dust. Warner-Lambert contended that this inspection clearly established, apart from the issue of a worker health hazard, that the nuisance level of dust from the standpoint of employee health was, at most, one-one-thousandth of the lowest level at which the dust would explode. Therefore, no fire or explosive hazard was present.

On February 24, 1976, Factory Mutual, a loss-prevention consultant employed by Warner-Lambert's insurance carrier (Arkwright-Boston Company) made an inspection of the Freshen-Up department. It determined that "the magnesium stearate dust in the fourth story Freshen-Up gum manufacturing area presents a serious explosion hazard." The consultant recommended the installation of a central vacuum cleaning system, removal of accumulated dust, and modification of all electrical equipment to conform to national electric code standards for "dusty locations." The implementation of these measures was necessary "to prevent a serious dust explosion." The consultant's findings and advice were relayed to the plant engineer, John O'Rourke, who assured the Factory Mutual consultant that Warner-Lambert would comply with the recommendations. The inspector's report also indicated that Harris' prior determination of no

explosion hazard was based on dated information and was no longer valid. A written version of the report and advice was sent to the Warner-Lambert safety director, Ed Harris. When no reply was received, a follow-up letter was sent to Harris in June 1976, emphasizing once more "the possibility of a dust explosion due to the use of magnesium stearate powder.[11]

In April 1976, the New York City Fire Department inspected the Freshen-Up department. According to Warner-Lambert, the New York City Fire Department did not report any explosive conditions whatsoever or indicate the need for any action on the part of the corporation. The following month, a compliance officer from the Occupational and Safety Health Administration of the U.S. Department of Labor visited the plant. According to Warner-Lambert, the OSHA inspection established that the airborne dust was below the nuisance level of 15 mg/m; OSHA's only recommendation was to have a class A fire extinguisher on hand. The district attorney for Queens County disagreed with this factual summation and contended that the OSHA inspector discussed personally with defendants O'Rourke and O'Mahoney the dust problem and the need to eliminate its source. On May 5, 1976, the plant's chief engineer also gave the same defendants a written report that MS use "continues to be our greatest problem.[12] It should be noted that New York State, for budgetary reasons, lets OSHA handle inspection chores. But OSHA had no comprehensive standards against explosion hazards, while the New York State labor law did.

On May 25, 1976, a formal proposal for the purchase of a central dust-removal system, at a nominal cost of $33,000, was submitted to O'Mahoney for transmittal to corporate headquarters. Also submitted was a separate capital expenditure request covering the proposed exhaust system. The request apparently met with initial rejection from the corporation's engineering division (headed by Joe Zagvali) as a short-term solution. The executives at the plant were very unhappy with this approach. The manager of the Freshen-Up Department, in a memo to O'Mahoney (with a copy to O'Rourke) put the matter bluntly by saying: "[while] Joe Zagvali . . . re-invent(s) the wheel . . . an expenditure of $35,000 [sic] is a small price to pay to get out of the problems we now have and to show our good faith to our employees who are putting up with a very unpleasant environment."[13]

Warner-Lambert continued to conduct dust tests in June of 1976 for the purpose of determining the nuisance level of the dust in the department. According to Warner-Lambert, these tests established that the density of airborne dust was well below the lower explosive limit. On July 7, a meeting was held at corporate headquarters for the purpose of considering the capital expense request of $33,000 to purchase a central dust-removal system. Present at this meeting were defendants Kraft and O'Rourke, among others. The purchase request was determined to be "a waste of good money" and was therefore rejected. A decision was made to embark on a long-range solution to eliminate the use of MS altogether from the Freshen-Up production process. Arthur Kraft endorsed the decision. The topic of dust collection systems for the Freshen-Up gum operation was never again considered by top corporate management prior to the explosion. On July 13, 1976, the corporation's manager of safety and fire protection sent a brief note to O'Mahoney notifying him that the insurance carrier's February 1976 recommendation to eliminate the dust hazard would not be followed.[14]

On August 10, 1976, O'Mahoney sent a memorandum to his staff recommending measures to cut down the use of MS because it was a "major problem—having a deleterious effect on employee health and safety." During the first two weeks of August 1976—the conventional period when plant operations shut down every year and everyone takes vacation—the entire department was cleaned and dust accumulations eliminated.

Along with the August 10 memorandum, eleven "strict" procedures were promulgated concerning control procedures upon reopening of the department. These steps included tighter control over the amount of MS used in each shift, improved cleanup, and strict disciplinary measures for failure to conform with the guidelines. Coarser-grade MS was utilized so that ambient dust levels would remain reduced. The cooling tunnel on processing line A was modified so that MS could be eliminated from the process altogether. Warner-Lambert later argued that these cleaning procedures and the decision to modify all the cooling tunnels to run without MS obviated the necessity for the installation of either a dust-collection or vacuum system as recommended on May 25, 1976.[15]

On September 16, 1976, a second loss-prevention report was filed with the respondents based on an inspection made by a representative of the insurance carrier, Factory Mutual. Warner-Lambert contended that this report established that "the present dust concentration is well below the lower explosive limits." Thus, at the time of the accident, no risk of any kind—possible or probable—could have been perceived by anyone familiar with the circumstances at the plant.

On November 15, 1976, the plant's chief engineer notified O'Mahoney and O'Rourke that the coarser grade of MS was still fouling up the fourth floor air conditioning system and that the concentration of ambient MS dust in the Freshen-Up department was substantial. Although work had begun to modify one of the processing lines to eliminate MS use (at a cost of some $40,000), no decision had been made to modify the other five lines. In fact, by the Fall of 1976, public demand for Freshen-Up gum had forced production up to 2 million packages of gum per day and six processing lines operating twenty-four hours a day, six days a week. At 2:40 A.M. on Sunday, November 21, 1976, the Freshen-Up operating came to a halt with an explosion that resulted in the death of six employees and injuries to forty-eight others. A large section of Warner-Lambert's five-story manufacturing plant was devastated.

THE CAUSES OF THE EXPLOSION

The cause or causes of the explosion are a matter of controversy, and two versions have emerged: one offered by Warner-Lambert and its experts, and the other by the Queens County district attorney and his experts.

The District Attorney's Version[16]

According to the district attorney, the deaths, injuries, and physical damage resulted from the explosion of a heavy concentration of ambient MS dust present in the Freshen-Up department during the early morning hours of November 21, 1976. Testimony was offered to the grand jury by employees as to the existence of a foglike atmosphere just prior to the explosion. A substantial residue of MS dust in the area involved was also reported after the explosion. The windows on the fourth floor and elsewhere in the plant had been blown out and then in, as the explosive pressure first vented itself out, creating a vacuum into which air from outside the building was then drawn. Broken glass and other damaged items from the plant's fourth floor were strewn all over the street and on the roofs of adjacent buildings, which were themselves damaged by flying debris and the force of the explosion. The Freshen-Up department was found to be in a shambles, with the interior walls pushed down, machinery and fixtures displaced, shattered, and twisted; and small pockets of fire in existence among the materials. These are all characteristics of a dust explosion. The ceilings, walls, and overhead areas showed charring or scorching, indicating not general fire damage, but the burning of ambient MS dust.

The district attorney contended that a dust explosion results when sufficient quantities of a combustible material, pulverized in a finely subdivided state and suspended in a confined atmosphere, are ignited. The ignition is followed by the rapid propagation of flame (as the ambient material is consumed), intense heat, expansion of the air pressure, and finally, a bursting effect. An explosion will occur when there are three essential elements: (1) a combustible fuel, (2) oxygen from the air, and (3) ignition sufficient to initiate combustion and reaction among the dust particles. Although MS dust in a settled state will burn, it is not regarded as "explosive" unless it is dispersed in the air in heavy enough concentrations. It is then rated as a "severe," "strong," or "very strong" explosive hazard. At the time of the explosion in question, the Freshen-Up gum department was using approximately 500 pounds of MS per day, six days a week, or about a ton-and-a-half per week. A minimum of 25 pounds of MS was allotted to and used by each of the six processing lines per eight-hour shift, with more being used merely upon request.

The powdered MS lubricant was applied by hand (by throwing), by can, or by dumping all along the processing line constantly and in large quantities. This sanctioned method of use caused or contributed to the ever-present "fog" or "mist" of ambient MS dust in the department. Thick quantities settled in and around the machinery and over all the flat surfaces, including the overhead areas. The dust condition reached a point where employees were forced to wear (and were observed wearing) the face masks and goggles to protect their eyes and breathing passages. Just prior to the explosion, several processing lines were still in operation, and many engaged in the weekly duty of general cleanup. MS dust was removed from overhead areas and machinery by knocking the dust from overhead areas with brooms and air hoses and sweeping the dust from one end of the department to the other. One employee, standing very close to one of the Uniplast machines, observed a "sparkle" or "spark" in the area of one of the processing lines. According, to the employee, "the next thing I knew a big boom, that was the fire."

Other employees positioned farther away thought they heard two explosions almost simultaneously and that with the second, "just everything caught on fire."[17]

According to the district attorney's experts, there was low-order detonation at the base of the D assembly line Uniplast machine, followed by a major dust explosion. The ignition or primary detonation was attributed to a mechanical sparking or heat-induced breakup of the parts of the Uniplast equipment on line D. The use of LN_2 had completely iced the rotating die head, which then jammed. The equipment, because it was not made to be used with liquid nitrogen, lost its ductility and became extremely brittle. The machine, operating under a tremendous strain just prior to explosion because of the jammed rotating die head, overloaded the motor as it drew more electrical current to meet the resistance of the slowed-up gears. The machinery began to break apart due to the vibration or slippage of the components. The resulting heated metal, mechanical sparking, or friction ignited the settled or ambient MS dust at the base of the Uniplast equipment, causing a violent reaction or detonation in what may have been an oxygen-enriched atmosphere containing ambient MS dust in sufficient quantities for an explosion.

Warner-Lambert's Version[18]

Warner-Lambert contended that liquid nitrogen is basically noncombustible and vaporizes quickly without dangerous effects when exposed to room temperatures. Because of its inherent stability, it is often used in fire extinguishers. MS, in bulk, inert, or settled form, does not create an explosive risk. If ignition is applied, it will only burn or smolder. If it is dispersed into the air at or above the lower explosive level (LEL), it will create a serious risk of explosion if ignited. Warner-Lambert contended that minimum combustible densities of cornstarch, flour dust, peanut hulls, and powdered sugar create a greater danger of explosion than MS dust.

In addition to the lower explosive level, there is also a "nuisance" level of dust established by the Office of Safety and Health Administration. This level identifies the point at which exposure to dust will cause irritation and difficulty in breathing. Warner-Lambert argued that the "nuisance" level for MS is one-three-thousandths of the LEL, and that since the nuisance level was one-three-thousandths of the lower explosive level for MS dust, there was an insufficient concentration of ambient MS dust in the air to support an explosion. If there had been a sufficient concentration, it would have been humanly impossible for employees to work in the area without continuous respiratory assistance. Since the Freshen-Up department was in full production and the three shifts operated six days a week, despite whatever subjective testimony there may have been that conditions were "foggy" or "cloudy," the objective fact was that production workers did function with ease and in so doing established clearly that the MS dust in the air was below the lower explosive level.

Warner-Lambert's experts contended that there was a powerful primary detonation caused by a cryogenic phenomenon called liquefaction. This phenomenon results when volatile liquid oxygen is formed due to the exposure of the atmosphere at the base of the Uniplast machine to extremely cold, but otherwise harmless, liquid nitrogen. This detonation then ignited settled MS dust at the bore of the Uniplast machine. The crucial point made by the experts for Warner-Lambert was that the explosion did not involve the two alleged "hazardous" elements, MS or liquid nitrogen. But for the unforeseen cryogenic phenomenon involving liquid nitrogen, the quantity of MS at the base of the Uniplast equipment actually presented no risk of fire or explosion. Warner-Lambert's experts further testified that the creation of volatile liquid oxygen from the use of stable liquid nitrogen could not reasonably have been foreseen. Liquification is not regarded as a credible hazard in the use of liquid nitrogen. Warner-Lambert's supplier of liquid nitrogen, its insurance carrier, and the various governmental agencies such as the New York City Fire Department and OSHA, never indicated, suggested, or warned of any risk associated with the use of liquid nitrogen. Consequently, the explosion and the resulting deaths occurred as a result of a hazard that could not have been foreseen by Warner-Lambert, thus clearly indicating Warner- Lambert's lack of responsibility for the incident.

THE LEGAL ISSUES AND LEGAL PROCEEDINGS

The respondents in this matter were charged with: (1) manslaughter in the second degree, and (2) criminally negligent homicide. Under the Penal Law of the State of New York, Section 125.15, Subdivision 1, a person is guilty of manslaughter in the second degree when he "recklessly causes the death of another person." Subdivision 3 of the Penal Law, Section 15.05, defines "recklessly" as follows:

> A person acts recklessly with respect to a result or to a circumstance described by a statute defining an offense when he is aware of and consciously disregards the substantial and unjustifiable risk that such results will occur or that such circumstance exists. The risk must be of such a nature and degree that disregard thereof constitutes a gross deviation from the standard of conduct that a reasonable person would observe in the situation.

Therefore, to establish manslaughter in the second degree, the prosecution must prove beyond a reasonable doubt that: (1) the defendants, by their actions, created a substantial risk of death; (2) they were aware of this risk; (3) the defendants consciously disregarded this substantial and unjustifiable risk; and (4) that the risk itself must be of such a nature and degree that disregard there-of

would constitute (a) a gross deviation, (b) from the standard of conduct, (c) that a reasonable person would observe in the situation. (This is the burden of proof required at the trial, not during a grand jury proceeding.)

Under the New York Penal Law, Section 125.10, a person is guilty of criminally negligent homicide when with criminal negligence he causes the death of another person. Subdivision 4, Penal Law, Section 15.05, defines "criminal negligence" as follows:

> A person acts with criminal negligence with respect to a result or to a circumstance described by statute defining an offense when he fails to perceive that a substantial and unjustifiable risk that such result will occur or that such circumstances exist. The risk must be of such nature and degree that the failure to perceive it constitutes a gross deviation from the standard of care that a reasonable person would observe in the situation.

The distinction between criminal and negligent homicide in manslaughter in the second degree lies in their differing mental states. The reckless offender (manslaughter, second degree) is aware of the risk and consciously disregards it; the criminally negligent offender is not aware of the risk created and hence cannot be guilty of consciously disregarding it. The criminally negligent offender's liability rises from a culpable failure to perceive the risk. This culpability is appreciably greater than that required for ordinary civil negligence by reason of the substantial and unjustifiable character of the risk involved and the factor of gross deviation required from the ordinary standard here.

In order to establish criminally negligent homicide, the district attorney must prove beyond a reasonable doubt: (1) a culpable failure to perceive, (2) a substantial and justifiable risk, and (3) that the failure to perceive the risk was so flagrant as to be deemed a gross deviation from the standard of care a reasonable person would observe. (Decisions by the courts of New York have defined the conduct prescribed by these provisions as that involving a "flagrant disregard of a known risk of death to others, which risk is both substantial and unjustifiable.")[19]

The trial court dismissed the indictment on the ground that the evidence presented to the grand jury was legally insufficient to establish either manslaughter in the second degree or the lesser offense of criminally negligent homicide.

THE CASE BEFORE THE APPELLATE DIVISION OF THE NEW YORK SUPREME COURT

The district attorney appealed the decision of the trial judge. The prosecution contended that there was absolutely no question—a matter of considerable proof—that the deaths, injuries, and physical damage resulted directly from the explosion of a heavy concentration of ambient magnesium stearate dust (both preexistent and explosion-generated) present during the early morning hours of November 21, 1976. Among other things, the pattern and extent of damage, and the nature of injuries received, bore this out. Even though use of MS was cut down after the August 1976 cleanup, allotments over a ton-and-a-half per week were excessive and still fell within the explosive-use range. While there was a continuous stream of corporate memoranda regarding the dust problem and cleanup methods, the old procedures remained intact. No type of dust removal equipment was ever installed or purchased, including portable vacuum cleaners. The only cleanup tools available to workers were air hoses and brooms. No changes in electrical equipment or wiring were made to eliminate potential ignition sources. The use of LN_2, with its tendency to embrittle metal, was also unchanged. Even after receipt of advice as to the existence of a definite explosion hazard, no measures were ever implemented to inform the employees of the fact and instruct them on work safety measures.[20]

Based on the grand jury testimony and the exhibits admitted as evidence, there appears to be no escape from the conclusion that the defendants, each and all, were "aware of . . . a substantial and unjustifiable risk" of death. Hence the charges of manslaughter in the second degree. But it is possible to find from the facts that the acts of omission and commission amounted alternatively or also to criminally negligent homicide, and not just recklessness—that is, some or all of the defendants perhaps did not realize the risk involved. The same proof actually supports both charges, distinguished by the degree or state of mental culpability.[21]

The defendants created and tolerated a substantial and unjustifiable risk of death (through dust explosion) in just about every phase and facet of the Freshen-Up department, to the extent that the department became ripe for the explosion, awaiting only a source of substantial ignition. But more than that, they ignored, disregarded, or rejected every warning, every rule, and every piece of advice solicited from those whose only concern was what is best for the company and its employees. After an investment of $10 million, the cost of a dust exhaust system at a mere $33,000 became "a waste of money" where lives, property, and the future of a highly profitable operation were at stake. That is what the evidence established, and it constituted a gross deviation from the standard of conduct or care a reasonable person would have observed in the situation.[22]

Warner-Lambert's Brief

The W-L brief argued that although the evidence before the grand jury showed the explosion in the case involved magnesium stearate dust, MS was not the cause of the explosion. "The evidence is clear and uncontroverted that MS can only explode when it is airborne in a well-defined concentration called the lower explosive limit (LEL)."[23] The brief contended:

> The unanimous testimony of the expert was that the cause of the explosion which killed the employees was a primary detonation at the base of one of the production machines. The experts also agreed that the cause of this primary detonation was not and could not have been an MS dust explosion, but rather most likely was the result of a freak cryogenic phenomenon called "liquefaction" . . . . There was absolutely no evidence presented before the Grand Jury which tended to show that any defendant-respondent was aware of the possibility, let alone a substantial risk, of liquefaction.[24]

According to W-L, the central fact that emerges from an objective reading of the evidence before the grand jury is that the explosion at the plant resulted from a cryogenic phenomenon that was unforeseen and unforeseeable. That conclusion, according to W-L, does not depend on weighing conflicting evidence or assessing the credibility of divergent testimony. Rather, it stems from the consistent and undisputed testimony of all the witnesses before the grand jury who analyzed the complex chain of events that caused the explosion.[25]

The W-L brief pointed out that none of the outside institutions involved with W-L in this case (the governmental agencies which regularly inspected the plant, the LN_2 suppliers, the production machinery suppliers, and W-L's insurer), ever warned W-L of any risks associated with the use of LN_2.

Thus, "to hold Warner-Lambert criminally liable under such circumstances is manifestly unsupportable in view of the essential element of the crimes, alleged, i.e., that Warner-Lambert acted in a manner grossly deviant from a standard of reasonable care."[26] W-L also contended that it had made continuous and successful efforts at reducing the dust levels and controlling MS use. According to W-L, following the explosion,

representatives of OSHA, the National Bureau of Standards, the Mining Enforcement and Safety Administration of the United States Department of the Interior, the New York City Fire Department, and others investigated the explosion to determine its cause. "Although the testimony involved complex technical matters, there was substantial agreement among the experts as to the unique chain of circumstances which resulted in the explosion."[27]

The brief argued that evidence provided by the people was circumstantial. While W-L's objective tests showed dust levels to be at most, "one-one thousandths of the LEL," the prosecution relied on workers' "subjective" testimony of foglike conditions in the processing plant. The testimony also showed that on the day of the accident the Freshen-Up area "was as clear as this jury room" and that "only forty-five minutes before the accident—after clean-up was in progress—there was no visible dust and everything seemed normal.[28] According to the W-L brief, the prosecution's presentation of the causes of the accident was a collection of theories and not incontrovertible facts. For example, the notion that machinery might have failed because it was not designed to work under the extremely cold temperatures was based on the testimony of an expert who stated that he was "dancing a little bit" in stating that "possibly the machinery may have broken apart. . . . There's really no way of actually telling."[29] This expert performed no metallurgical tests on the equipment, and therefore his speculation was incompetent and inadmissible. Furthermore, there was no evidence to show that defendants-respondents were or should have been in any way aware that liquid nitrogen might cause the Uniplast to become brittle. Since the cause of explosion could only be established by circumstantial evidence, it must be shown that the evidence established that cause to a "moral certainty"—that is, it must exclude any reasonable hypothesis of causation under which defendants would not be criminally responsible. W-L contended that the state's case failed to establish to a moral certainty an essential element of the crime charged.

Briefs of James O'Mahoney, John O'Rourke, Arthur Kraft, and Ed Harris

At the time of the accident, O'Mahoney and O'Rourke were the plant manager and plant engineer, respectively, of the American Chicle facility. They both argued that all the evidence before the grand jury demonstrated they were extremely conscious of the situation about the dust problem at the Freshen-Up plant and took vigorous steps which resulted in bringing the dust level considerably below LEL.[30] In support of these efforts, the brief cited extracts from the opinion of the lower court which completely absolved O'Mahoney and O'Rourke of any wrongful acts and instead commended them for the diligent discharge of their duties.

At the time of the accident, Arthur Kraft and Ed Harris were vice- president in charge of manufacturing and director of corporate safety and security, respectively, of the American Chicle's parent, Warner-Lambert Company. Their brief contended that evidence against them was very sparse and that their names were mentioned only a few times in the course of the lengthy grand jury proceeding. After summarizing the essential facts of the case in a manner similar to that of other defendant-respondents, Kraft and Harris cited the lower court opinion that there was no adequate proof to "establish any criminal liability associated with their explosion.[31]

On March 8, 1979, the Appellate Division of the New York Supreme Court reversed the lower court's decision and ordered the matter to trial so that a jury could determine whether or not the elements of criminally negligent homicide or the more serious offense of manslaughter in the second degree had been established beyond a reasonable doubt by the district attorney.

The Next Legal Step: The Court of Appeals of the State of New York

Warner-Lambert and the four defendants appealed the decision of the Appellate Division to the highest court in New York State, i.e., the Court of Appeals of the State of New York. The petitioners asked the court to dismiss the indictments for second-degree manslaughter and criminally negligent homicide. The court agreed with the petitioners and on November 20, 1980, dismissed the indictments on grounds that "there was not legally sufficient evidence in this case on the premise of which any jury could permissibly have imposed criminal liability on any of these defendants.[32]

The victims and their families also filed a number of civil lawsuits for damages against Warner-Lambert, various suppliers of chemicals and machinery, and cleaning companies.

These suits were all combined and were settled by the different parties. The judgment, which was approved by the court on October 3, 1984, involved more than $16 million. Warner-Lambert would pay $11 million; $500,000 each would be collected from Hamac-Hansella, a West German machinery manufacturer; Petrochemicals, Ft. Worth, Texas; and Liquid Carbonics, Belleville, New Jersey. Additional payments ranging from $10,000 to $200,000 were made by 12 other defendants.[33]

The chicle factory itself was closed in late 1981. Warner-Lambert transferred the production to its more modern and efficient plants in Rockford, Illinois and Anaheim, California, where there was excess capacity. The company, however, made considerable efforts to help employees cushion the shock of the plant closing. At a total cost of over $7 million, W-L provided severance benefits plus employee benefits, such as health insurance. Employees were offered jobs at the company's other locations, with the company picking up relocation costs. W-L also provided assistance in job search, resume typing, and services of an outplacement firm. Most of the employees appeared to have agreed with the findings of the court that the danger of explosion at the plant could not have been foreseen. During the shutdown after the explosion, many of them had petitioned the New York City administration to allow the plant to be reopened.[34]

NOTES

1. Appellant's Brief, *The People of the State of New York* v. *Warner-Lambert Company, et al.* Indictment No. 915–77, filed September 1978 by the district attorney, Queens County (hereafter cited as *DA Brief*), p. 4; Record on Appeal, Volume I, *The People of the State of New York* v. *Warner-Lambert Company, et al.* Indictment No. 915–77 (hereafter cited as *Record*), pp. 12, 128, 144; *DA Brief*, pp. 3; 4; Brief of Defendant-Respondent Warner-Lambert Company, *The People of the State of New York* v. *Warner-Lambert Company, et al.* Indictment No. 915–77, filed September 1978 by attorneys for Warner-Lambert Company (hereafter *W-L Brief*), p. 5; Opinion of the Appellate Division, Supreme Court, Second Judicial Department, July 9, 1979, *The People of the State of New York* v. *Warner-Lambert Company, et al* (hereafter *Opinion*), pp. 2, 3.
2. *Record*, pp. 1, 2; *DA Brief*, pp. 1, 2; *W-L Brief*, pp. 1–3; *Opinion*, p. 2.
3. *Record*, p. 37; Brief of Defendants-Respondents, Arthur Kraft and Ed Harris, *The People of the State of New York* v. *Warner-Lambert Company, et al.*, filed December 11, 1978, by attorneys for Kraft and Harris (hereafter *Kraft Brief*), p. 8; *Opinion*, p. 3.
4. *Record*, p. 37; Brief of Defendants-Respondents, James O'Mahoney and John O'Rourke, *The People of the State of New York* v. *Warner-Lambert Company, et al.*, filed December 1978 by attorneys for O'Mahoney and O'Rourke (hereafter *O'Mahoney Brief*), p. 5; *Opinion*, p. 3.
5. *Record*, pp. 13, 102; *DA Brief*, p. 7.
6. *Record*, pp. 14, 14; *DA Brief*, pp. 5–7; *Opinion*, pp. 3, 4.
7. *DA Brief*, p. 17.
8. *W-L Brief*, pp. 24, 25.
9. *DA Brief*, pp. 21, 22; Court of Appeals, State of New York, Respondent against Warner-Lambert Company, et al., Defendant, Appellants, filed March 1980, p. 21.
10. *Record*, p. 13; *DA Brief*, pp. 17, 18; *Opinion*, p. 5.
11. *Record*, pp. 100,140; *DA Brief*, pp. 20, 23; *Opinion*, p. 7.
12. *Record*, p. 91.
13. Cited in *Respondent's Briefs* (State of New York), March 1980, p. 24.
14. *DA Brief*, p. 25.
15. *Ibid.*, pp. 25,26; *Record*, p. 102.
16. *DA Brief*, pp. 8–14.
17. *Ibid.*, pp. 12, 13.
18. *Record*, pp. 15–17, 87–90, 96, 97, 129–133, 145–149.
19. *People* v. *Montanez*, 41 N.Y., 2nd 53, 390 N.Y.S., 2nd 861, 359 N.E. 2nd 371 (1971), cited in *W-L Brief*, p. 8.
20. *DA Brief*, pp. 27–28, 35, 36.
21. *Respondent's Brief* (State of New York), pp. 26–28.
22. *Ibid.*
23. *W-L Brief*, p. 3.
24. *Ibid.*
25. Court of Appeals, State of New York, *The People of New York* v. *Warner-Lambert Company*, November 29, 1979, Brief of Defendant-Appellant Warner-Lambert Company, p. 4.
26. *W-L Brief*, p. 4.
27. Cited in Brief of Defendant-Appellant Warner-Lambert Company, pp. 19, 20.
28. *W-L Brief*, p. 11.
29. *W-L Brief*, p. 19.
30. *O'Mahoney Brief*, pp. 9–10, 12–14.
31. *Kraft Brief*, p. 15.
32. Record on Appeal, *The People of the State of New York* v. *Warner-Lambert Company, et al.* (Hereafter cited as *Record*). Court of Appeals of New York, Nov. 20, 1980. 434 New York Supplement, 2nd series, pp. 159–165 cite 51, N.Y. 2d, 295.
33. *Martinez* v. *Warner-Lambert*, 16062/79, cited in *New York Law Journal*, pvd. 192, no. 66 (October 3, 1984), pp. 1, 30.
34. Sandra Salmans, "Chicle Closing: Family Sorrow." *New York Times* (April 25, 1981), pp. 19, 21.

REFERENCES

American Bar Association. *American Bar Association Standards Relating to the Administration of Criminal Justice: Sentencing Alternatives and Procedures. Second Tentative Draft. American Bar Association Standards of Criminal Justice,* Washington, DC (Summer 1979).

Bequelle, Assefa. "The Cost and Benefits of Protecting and Saving Lives at Work: Some Issues." *International Labour Review,* vol. 123, (January–February 1984), p.1.

Coffee, John, Jr., Corporate Crime and Punishment: A Non-Chicago View of the Economics of Criminal Sanction. *American Criminal Law Review,* 17 (1980), pp. 471–85.

_____. "Making the Punishment Fit the Corporation. The Problem of Finding an Optimal Corporation Criminal Sanction." *Northern Illinois University Law Review,* (1980), pp. 78–89.

Comments: Criminal Sanction for Corporate Illegality." *The Journal of Criminal Law and Criminology,* 69, 1 (Spring, 1978), pp. 15–24.

Conyers, John, Jr., "Corporate and White-Collar Crime: A View by the Chairman of the House Subcommittee on Crime." *American Criminal Law Review,* 17,3 (Winter 1980), p. 287.

"Developments in the Law—Corporate Crime: Regulating Corporate Behavior through Criminal Sanction." *Harvard Law Review,* 92 (April 1979), p. 1227.

Fletcher, George P., "The Theory of Criminal Negligence: A Comparative Analysis." *University of Pennsylvania,* 119, 3 (January 1971), p. 401.

"Hyatt Hotel Engineers Cited for 'Negligence.'" *Engineering News Record* (February 9, 1984), p. 14.

McAdams, Tony, and Robert C. Miljus, "Growing Criminal Liability of Executive." *Harvard Business Review* (March–April 1977), pp. 36–40.

Nielson, Richard P., "Should Executives Be Jailed for Consumer and Employees Health Violations?" *The Journal of Consumer Affairs* (Summer 1979), pp. 128–134.

Orland, Leonard, "Reflections on Corporate Crime: Law in Search of Theory and Leadership." *American Criminal Law Review,* 17,4 (Spring 1978), pp. 501–20.

Sethi, S. Prakash, "Corporate Law Violations and Illegality." *Journal of Criminal law and Executive Liability. Testimony on H.R. 4973 before the Subcommittee on Crime of the House Judiciary Committee* (December 13, 1979).

_____. "Liability without Fault? The Corporate Executive as an Unwitting Criminal." *Employee Relations Law Journal* (Autumn 1978), p. 185.

"Toward a Rational Theory of Criminal Liability for the Corporate Executive." *The Journal of Criminal Law and Criminology,* 69, 1 (Spring 1978), p. 75.

Weinfeld, Sharon R., "Criminal Liability of Corporate Managers for Deaths of Their Employees: People v. Warner-Lambert Co." *Albany Law Review* (Winter 1978), pp. 655–85.

"Why More Corporations May Be Charged With Manslaughter." *Business Week* (February 27, 1984), p. 62.

IOWA BEEF PROCESSORS, INC. (IBP, INC.)

*Unsafe working conditions and
labor practices in the meat industry*

Janet Henrich was 18 when she went to work at IBP, Inc.'s (formerly known as Iowa Beef Processors, Inc.) hog slaughter plant in Storm Lake, Iowa. She had been working about a week—three days on a pork butt skinner—when the machine with tooth rollers and a fixed blade grabbed her gloved right hand and pulled it through, skinning it like another piece of meat. She severed four tendons and damaged nerves in her hand and fingers. There was no safety switch. As Janet went to the hospital, the machine was hosed off and work continued. The Union and workers claim such incidents are not uncommon.[1] In fact, they maintain that unhealthy and dangerous working conditions are endemic to the entire meat packing industry of which IBP, the largest company, is also the prime example.

The industry has had a sorry record of worker safety from its early days, and if the current industry injury rates are any indication, the situation has not changed substantially when compared with improvements in other industries.

In 1906 Upton Sinclair stunned the public when he published *The Jungle*,[2] which exposed the brutal working conditions of the Chicago slaughterhouses. Now over eighty years later, the meatpacking industry remains one of the most hazardous occupations in the country. From the setting of *The Jungle* until now, a meatpacking house has been a grim place to work. The atmosphere of the workplace hearkens back to an earlier period of the industrial revolution, as chronicled, for example, in *Hard Times*,[3] by Charles Dickens. In the meatpacking plant, the worker seems to be an "appendage of the machine."

THE MEATPACKING INDUSTRY

The meatpacking industry employs about 100,000 people. This is one of the most dangerous industries in the entire economy, as even meat industry analysts attest.[4] At 26.3 injuries per 100 full-time workers, it ranked fourth in 1985 behind manufacturers of structural wood members (28.3), sawmill operations (27.8), and mobile home manufacturers (27.3). These rates, as well as others in the 20-plus range, reflect the nature of the industries in which they occur: industries characterized by hard physical labor involving tools that can do bodily harm if not used properly.

At one end of the meatpacking plant are the yards full of livestock ready to be slaughtered. At the other end, processed meats emerge cut up and boxed ready for market.

233

The technology of the industry has changed considerably since Lewis wrote his novel. Yet meat processing follows basically an assembly line process. A job in the meatpacking industry does not demand great skills, but it does call for vigilance and attention.[5] Any momentary lapse can result in serious injury. An overwhelming majority of workers perform monotonous repetitive-motion jobs at their assigned stations on the assembly line. Depending on where people are stationed the temperatures may be extremely hot or cold. Workers often stand shoulder to shoulder, plying their trade with power saws, specialty knives, and machines such as slicers. Both grease and blood from the animals tend to make floors and tools slippery. The tools and conditions spell a formula for accidents. Workers are especially accident prone when they experience fatigue. Working conditions combine a constant roar from machinery, a strong stench from open bladders and stomachs, and monotony that sets in when people perform the same tasks—often simply cutting the same part from a carcass moving by on an overhanging conveyor— hour after hour. A person may perform the same cuts a thousand times an hour. There is constant pressure to keep pace with the conveyor belt. The work force is comprised largely of inexperienced and unskilled workers due to low comparative wages and high turnover rates. This worker inexperience, when combined with unsafe machinery and hazardous working conditions, creates fatigue and lapses of attention. These factors contribute to the high accident rates prevailing in the industry.

At the same time, there is intense competition in the industry.[6] Most meatpackers are straining themselves to implement low-cost production strategies. On the one hand, they introduce more automation. On the other hand, the supply of labor is greater than demand, with the result that the bargaining power of unions is weakened as they themselves fight for survival. Furthermore, worker health and safety regulations are either often weak or poorly enforced.

IBP AND THE OCCUPATIONAL SAFETY AND HEALTH ADMINISTRATION (OSHA)

On July 21, 1987, the Occupational Safety and Health Administration, a branch of the Labor Department, proposed a $2.59 million fine against IBP, Inc., the nation's largest meat packing company.[7] This investigation followed from a complaint filed against IBP by the IBP workers' union, the United Food and Commercial Workers Union (UFCW).[8]

The charges were that IBP failed to report 1,038 job-related injuries and illnesses at its plant in Dakota City, Nebraska, from January 1985 through December 1986. In announcing the action, Assistant Labor Secretary John A. Pendergrass said, "This case is the worst example of underreporting injuries and illnesses to workers ever encountered by OSHA in its sixteen-year history." Under the law, such fines take effect in fifteen days unless contested.

Mr. Gary Mickleson, a spokesman for IBP, provided the initial company response: "We did not wilfully violate OSHA's record-keeping requirements and we will not pay the proposed penalties. We wish to have and will have an opportunity to show our side of the story."

ISSUES FOR ANALYSIS

The IBP's case raises a number of issues for discussion. They pertain to the nature of the industry, including: its competitive character; the organizational characteristics, corporate culture, and management attitudes at IBP; the composition of the work force and the attitudes of the union; the adequacy of the regulatory and enforcement procedures; and society's perception of the problem and its willingness to take appropriate measures to correct it. In particular:

1. What are some of the dimensions where improvements can be made to make the meat-

packing industry safer for workers, and efficient for employers? To what extent have these measures been taken by IBP and the meatpacking industry, and what additional efforts are called for?

2. What has been the attitude of management in the meatpacking industry regarding working conditions? Have they been reactive or proactive, and why?

3. How would one evaluate the management attitude and performance of IBP both prior to the OSHA investigation and subsequent to the filing of the complaint by the United Food and Commercial Workers Union (CFCW)? In case we find the management performance lacking, what measures could be suggested to induce/compel managers to pay more attention to worker safety?

4. How effective have the unions been in protecting the workers? What are the sources of either their successes or failures? Do we need any changes in the way meatpacking workers are organized and represented to help them better protect their lives and limbs, and their other rights?

5. What should be our assessment of the performance of OSHA in this case as well as other situations within the framework of its operational philosophy and enforcement procedures? Is this performance satisfactory? If not, what are some of the factors that might account for OSHA's failure in protecting workers from unsafe working conditions?

6. What sort of regulations are called for both with respect to prevention of injury, on the one hand, and compensation, on the other?

7. What changes in the external sociopolitical environment have had a strong bearing on the corporate, union and government policies in this particular case?

IBP, INC.

IBP, Inc. is a subsidiary of Occidental Petroleum and lists sales of $6.82 billion a year. Occidental acquired IBP in 1981 for $795 million. In 1980 IBP had profits of $53 million on sales of $4.6 billion. On the day before the OSHA announcement, Occidental was reported ready to sell some forty percent of IBP for an estimated $600 million.[9]

TABLE 1. IBP Sales and Operating Earnings

Year	Sales ($ billion)	Earnings ($ million)
1985	6.5	144.6
1984	6.6	108.2
1983	6.1	120.4
1982	5.0	127.9
1981	5.0	104.8

In 1986 IBP and two small unrelated units that comprise Occidental's Agribusiness Division earned $58.8 million, or 6% of the company's operating profits of $963 million. The sale had been rumored since 1984 and was not directly linked to the OSHA complaint.

IBP employs 18,000 workers (roughly 18% of the industry work force) in 10 beef plants and 4 pork plants located in 8 states. About half of the company's processing capacity is located close to supplies in the upper Midwest. In 1986, IBP processed 7.9 million cattle and 4.4 million hogs, a record for the company.

IBP is a giant in the meatpacking industry. Unions, and even consumer groups and public officials, have charged it with being ruthless and striving to attain and exercise monopoly power, with all the excesses that such power entails. IBP is a giant and accounted for 45% ($6.5 billion) of Occidental Petroleum's 1985 sales of $14.5 billion. From 1985 to 1988 it experienced healthy growth in both sales and earnings as shown in Table 1.

THE COMPLAINT AGAINST IBP— THE UNITED FOOD AND COMMERCIAL WORKERS UNION'S (UFCW) POSITION

In filing its complaint against IBP, The UFCW alleged that IBP kept a fraudulent set of books regarding job safety with the intent of deceiving OSHA and forestalling plant inspections. This complaint led to the $2.46 million fine assessed against IBP by OSHA.[10] The complaint was filed against a background of bad relations between the union and the corporation. In what follows, we detail the union view of the struggle.[11] The union sees IBP's management as concerned only with the bottom line. This goal is so paramount that they will trade workers' safety to enhance it. Furthermore, they see the company as embarked on a strategy of union busting. The twin issues of worker safety and union busting frame the debate. The struggle at Dakota City began as follows (*IBP Dakota*, p.1):

> On December 14, 1986, IBP gave their Dakota City employees an early Christmas present— IBP locked the workers out. This heartless action came after UFCW Local 222 members rejected IBP's so called "last-best-final proposal" 2,250 to 50. And while the membership soundly rejected the company's proposal, they offered to work without a contract while the parties continued to negotiate, which IBP rejected out of hand.
>
> Struggle is no stranger to the IBP Dakota City workers—the 1986 Christmas lockout is the fifth time in seventeen years that Local 222 members have had to struggle on the picket line against IBP's ruthless tactics and greed. In fact, IBP's labor policies are as bloody as the cattle slaughtering business of which IBP is the undisputed king: 1969—seven and one-half month strike, 1972—eight month lockout, 1977-78—fifteen month strike, 1982—four-month strike. All tallied, IBP Dakota City workers have struggled on the picket line for economic justice, worker dignity and a safe place to work for an aggregated three of the last seventeen years. Their plight is no way the result of their lack of militance or resolve.

The General Picture

The above setting serves as a symbol of a whole set of grievances (*IBP Dakota*, p. 1):

- How the world's largest and one of the most profitable beef packers uses its size, power, and ruthless tactics to smash competition and destroy industry wages, benefits, and working conditions.
- How for the fifth time in seventeen years the IBP Dakota City workers have been forced to

the picket line to struggle against the savage attacks of IBP.
- How workers employed by the world's largest beef packer have not had a general increase in five years and, under the company's current proposal, would not receive a wage increase for another four years making it almost a decade without any kind of wage increase whatsoever.
- How many of the new IBP workers earn just $21.50 a week above the U.S. poverty line and qualify for food stamps and other welfare assistance. All of this while being employed for a company that had an operating income of $144 million in 1985.
- How workers risk life and limb daily to labor away in an industry that the U.S. Department of Labor classifies as one of the most dangerous occupations in the nation.
- How workers at the IBP Dakota City plant work in one of the most unsafe meat packing plants in the country that in 1985 had an injury and illness rate that is 23 percent higher than the outrageously dangerous industry average.

Attack on Workers by Corporate America

Clearly, the union sees IBP as out to bust the union. It is clear from Mr. Peterson's testimony (in the following section) that IBP thinks the union is recalcitrant and the cause of trouble at Dakota City. The UFCW sees the union movement as the target of an all out corporate attack. It notes that since 1973 the average weekly earnings of middle-income families have declined by 14.3% in real terms (pp. 7–10). Union analysis concludes (p. 2):

> Without question, the economic plight of U.S. workers is the direct result of a savage attack by Corporate America on worker's wages, benefits and working conditions. Furthermore, such an assault is compounded by the Reagan administration's anti-union policies and its cozy relationship with the wealthy and powerful of this nation. The tools of destruction utilized by the corporate community entail forced wage concessions with threats of plant closings, capital flight to low

wage markets, Chapter 11 bankruptcy ploys, corporate spin-offs and subcontracting arrangements. Tactics that cut across all industries and negatively impact tens of millions of American workers.

In the Union view, corporate greed and hardheartedness are the main problem. The UFCW is not attacking IBP alone. In an August 1987 study, it also turned its guns on another giant meatpacker, John Morrell, in a report entitled, "The John Morrell Workers' Struggle."[12]

Wages

As far as the Union is concerned, wages are as important as the job safety issue. The general wage picture is as follows (pp. 7–10):

Currently, the IBP Dakota City workers who are not on a starting wage rate receive a base labor rate of $8.20 an hour in the slaughter division and $7.90 an hour in the processing division. Based on a 40-hour workweek, which many weeks the workers do not receive, their annual income falls below the "low-family budget" of $17,567 as of October 1, 1986, according to the Bureau of Labor Statistics information (and updated by the AFL-CIO Economic Research Department).

Some 15% of IBP's total work force is employed at Dakota City, the principal location of the union's complaint, making it the largest plant workforce. Table 2 provides a listing of IBP's beef and pork plants in the United States.

To complicate the matter, the IBP Dakota City workers did not have a general increase in the five years from 1981 to 1986. The IBP proposal to the union, which was rejected by the membership by a vote of 2,250 to 50, called for a four year wage freeze extending to 1990. In addition, the IBP 1986 proposal called for a permanent two-tier wage structure for new workers. This would mean that after 30 months on starting rates, this new category of workers would still work for $0.68 an hour less in slaughter and $0.47 an hour less in pro-

TABLE 2. IBP Plant Locations in the United States

Federal Inspection No.	Plant Location	Number of Workers
245c	Dakota City, NE	2,800
245	Denison, IA	240
292A	Luverne, MN	150
245B	West Point, NE	200
245D	Emporia, KS	2,000
278	Garden City, KS	950
245E	Amarillo, TX	1,700
9268	Pasco, WA	n/a
245G	Boise, ID	250
245J	Joslin, IL	1,500
2923	Madison, NE*	250
244	Storm Lake, IA	750
244L	Columbus Junction, IA	200
244C	Council Bluffs, IA	350

*subcontractor for Conagra

cessing, standing side by side of workers doing the same work (*IBP Dakota*, p.9). IBP reportedly also wanted other concessions regarding overtime, reduced wage rates for certain job classifications, and greater worker contributions to their monthly health insurance premiums. The union also claimed that from 1983 to 1986, IBP extracted a $1.07-per-hour wage cut, which represented an annual loss of $2,225.60 for each worker, or a total three-year wage loss of $6,676.80 per worker. The Union maintained that IBP's profit picture (presented above) did not warrant such action.

To drive its point home, the UFCW claimed the IBP wage rates had barely kept a worker with a family above the poverty line. According to UFCW, under the old labor agreement, new workers were required to work for one year at $2.00 under the base labor rate, which placed their hourly rate at $6.20 for slaughter workers and $5.90 for processing workers. Based on a 36-hour work week, a worker with a family qualified for food stamps. Many IBP workers had been receiving food stamps while working full time because their wages were so low. Because of a massive work force turnover (100%-plus per year), it was estimated that over 40% of the 2,800 workers at the Dakota

City plant were new hires working at the starting rate. A new worker employed at the IBP processing division working a 40-hour work week earned just $21.50 a week above the U.S. poverty line.

The union also specifically countered the IBP position that it had to cut labor costs in order to be competitive in the industry (*IBP Dakota*, pp. 18–20). It asserted that the company's position was self-serving, for it ignored the fact that it was IBP who drove down wages in the first place and for all practical purposes IBP was the wage pacesetter. The company was paying what the market would bear. The union contended that the wage rate did not reflect "just" compensation either with respect to the hazard involved, the cost of living, or the company's profit picture. The union's position was that wage rates in the meatpacking industry were what IBP made them. IBP's competitive strategy is described by the Union as follows (*IBP Dakota*, pp. 19ff):

> During the 1960s, into the mid 1970s, Armour, Swift, Wilson, John Morrell and many independents paid the prevailing national wage rate to their beef workers. When IBP first came into the industry in 1961 and expanded into the mid 1970s, IBP maintained they were going to be a low cost producer, which translated into being a low wage operator. IBP forced its employees to work at $2.00 and $3.00 an hour less than what IBP's competitors paid their employees.
>
> As a result of such a labor cost advantage, IBP could pay more for live cattle, which took the raw product away from competitors or forced them to match IBP's bids on top of a higher labor cost which squeezed profit margins. On the other end of the business, IBP could sell their products cheaper to the retailers which took the marketplace away from competition, or forced them to sell their products at a loss in trying to compete with IBP's low wage operation.
>
> Now this all sounds fine for the livestock producers and the consumers, except for one overlooked fact. IBP drove Wilson, Swift, Armour and several independents out of the beef business. As studies would later show, with such big operators out of the business,

with thousands of jobs lost and communities devastated, IBP was dictating prices to be paid for livestock and those prices were much lower than when there was still competition, for example, say in the Southwest part of the United States. And again studies showed consumers did not realize any savings in the price of beef at the retail meat counter. No one—workers, communities, livestock producers or consumers—derives any benefit from IBP's domination of the industry.

IBP'S ABUSE OF MARKET POWER

The UFCW maintains that the way IBP deals with labor reveals a pattern of using its size and power to beat down all of the people it deals with: customers, competitors, suppliers, and the communities that vie with one another to land one of its plants. For example, IBP has been accused in federal court by the Bohack retail chain of illegal price discrimination. Two New York juries, in 1981 and 1982, agreed with Bohack. IBP has also been the subject of antitrust suits, brought by Cattle Feeders, now awaiting trial in federal court in Texas. IBP has also been the subject, through its domination of the market, of investigations by the Department of Agriculture, the U.S. House of Representatives' Small Business Committee, and the Justice Department to shed light on its marketing practices. One of these investigations revealed through the disclosure of an internal document that IBP was withholding Grade 2 and 3 carcasses from the market, in order to "hasten the conversion of chain stores from carcass beef to boxed beef," which had higher profit margins for IBP.

The union also sees IBP as a burden on local communities. It wrings concessions from local communities in terms of water treatment facilities and tax breaks and other subsidies. At the same time, it squeezes wages so that these communities are denied the anticipated spending of employees. The union contends that at Dakota City, "wages are low enough that some employees who work full time are still eligible for welfare and food stamps" (*IBP Dakota*, p. 6).

WORK-RELATED INJURIES IN THE MEAT PACKING INDUSTRY

The UFCW complaint underscores the fact that the meatpacking industry is one of the most dangerous in the country. Citing statistics for 1985, the Union says that there were 30.4 work-related injuries and illnesses for every 100 workers in meatpacking; of these 15.1 of the injuries (per 100) led to time away from work. It is, however, important to evaluate the job-related injury figures in the meatpacking and other industries in a proper context.

According to the American Meat Institute, the industry's trade and lobbying group, because of the nature of meatpacking and other industries where injury incidence rates are high, and because these industries are very different from what workers in the service and information sector are used to, it is perhaps best to focus on what is being done to reduce injuries rather than concentrating on the rates themselves. In this way, say the industry groups, we can see the progress that has been made to date.

The injury incidence rate in meatpacking has declined by 23% since 1979. This reduction has been larger than those for all food manufacturing (down 18%) and all manufacturing as a whole (down 22%). In human terms, the reduction in meatpacking injuries translates to 16,000 to 17,000 fewer workers hurt on the job today than in 1979. Still, there is room to improve and the industry continues to move in that direction.[13] (See Exhibits 1–4 and Table 1).

WORK-RELATED INJURIES AT IBP

The union's assessment of IBP is severe (*IBP Dakota*, pp. 11–17). According to IBP's own official records filed with OSHA, for the year 1985, "IBP may be the worst of the worst." For 1985, IBP listed 1,049 illnesses and injuries requiring more than just first aid. Of these, 649 involved lost workdays. Since there were approximately 2,800 workers at IBP's Dakota City plant, this worked out to

an illness and injury rate of 37 per 100 workers, which was 23 percent higher than the already outrageous industry average. The horrendous safety problem at the IBP Dakota City plant, according to the union, was the result of a number of factors: excessive chain speeds, work force turnover, improper training, and production receiving priority over worker's safety.

First, IBP workers labor with one of the fastest meat packing line speeds in the world. On a normal two shift workday, 3,200 cattle are slaughtered and 5,600 slaughtered cattle are disassembled and put into boxes. The working conditions are cramped, with lines of people working side by side with approximately 48 inches of workspace wielding razor sharp knives and power tools, frantically trying to keep up with a relentless chain bringing production to their work station. Most workers toil away in numbing cold temperatures of 30 to 35 degrees, standing in blood and animal fat which creates a dangerously slippery floor.

Second, IBP has programmed into its system of operation a workforce turnover that is close to 100 percent a year. The IBP Dakota City plant employs approximately 2,800 workers. Such turnover translates into a constant flow of new workers at the work stations every day. This in an of itself is a dangerously intolerable situation where large numbers of inexperienced workers are placed on a fast moving chain, crowded with workers using razor-sharp knives, trying to meet IBP's production quota demand.

Third, all too often, IBP provides little meaningful training for new workers. The worker turnover is so great and IBP's production demands take priority over all else, that new workers are thrown into the system with little training of even the basics of how to maintain their equipment, not to mention, the damages that lurk on the line to body and limb. New workers have to rely on older workers, who are already overworked with excess chain speeds and unqualified help, for tips on how to do the job, the proper maintenance of equipment and safety procedures. This procedure creates dangerous working conditions for new and older workers alike.

Fourth, production at IBP takes priority over all else. A battalion of foremen hyped up by the corporate office to meet staggering production quotas create pressure-cooker working conditions for the workers. Even though meat packing is one of the most unsafe occupations in the country and IBP is worse than the industry average, production, not safety, is the daily drumbeat coming for IBP.

There were numerous injuries in a three-month period, between May and July of 1985, there were over 1,800 visits to one nurse's station which didn't even cover the whole plant. (And the workers don't just run to the nurse for every scratch and fall.) The chain is moving so fast that they can only break away when the are really in trouble and only with the foreman's approval.

The union report goes on to illustrate each of these points with individual examples of people who have had accidents and it indicates how easily it could have been avoided.

UNION'S LACK OF BARGAINING POWER AND INABILITY TO PROTECT WORKERS

The union felt that industry concentration on the one hand, and changing worker demographics on the other, had seriously impacted its ability to protect workers. Thus, despite the fact that the Dakota City workers rejected

EXHIBIT 1. Injuries and Rate of Incidence in Meatpacking

INJURY INCIDENCE RATE, EMPLOYEE NUMBERS AND ESTIMATED INJURIES[a]

	1979	1980	1981	1982	1983	1984	1985
Injury incidence rate (per 100 employees)	34.2	31.0	29.7	27.7	27.4	29.0	26.3
Employees (thousands)	162.6	161.4	155.2	146.9	143.4	146.7	148.5
Injuries[a] (thousands)	55.6	50.0	46.1	40.7	39.3	42.5	38.9

[a]Incidence rate multiplied by employees.
SOURCE: "Update on Injuries." Memo from Jene Knutson to Manly Molpas, the American Meat Institute, Washington, DC, July 28, 1987.

EXHIBIT 2. Index of Incidence of Occupational Injuries

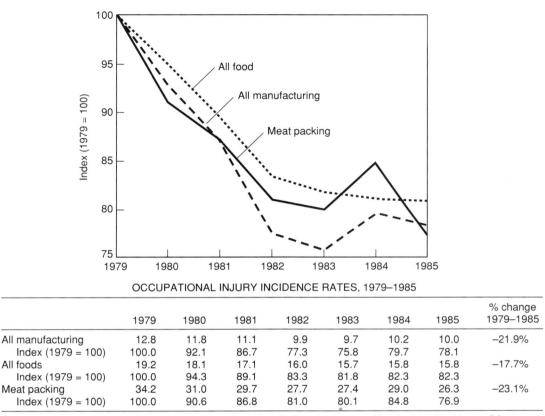

OCCUPATIONAL INJURY INCIDENCE RATES, 1979–1985

	1979	1980	1981	1982	1983	1984	1985	% change 1979–1985
All manufacturing	12.8	11.8	11.1	9.9	9.7	10.2	10.0	−21.9%
Index (1979 = 100)	100.0	92.1	86.7	77.3	75.8	79.7	78.1	
All foods	19.2	18.1	17.1	16.0	15.7	15.8	15.8	−17.7%
Index (1979 = 100)	100.0	94.3	89.1	83.3	81.8	82.3	82.3	
Meat packing	34.2	31.0	29.7	27.7	27.4	29.0	26.3	−23.1%
Index (1979 = 100)	100.0	90.6	86.8	81.0	80.1	84.8	76.9	

SOURCE: "Update on Injuries." Memo from Jene Knutson to Manly Molpas, the American Meat Institute, Washington, DC, July 28, 1987.

the company offer by the overwhelming vote of 2,250 to 50 (out of 2,800 workers), the Union was unable to force IBP to renegotiate. Part of the explanation is to be found in the ready availability of unorganized workers.[14] According to CFCW, there is a new breed of packinghouse worker who is very difficult to organize.[15] The twin problems confronted by the union and the workers are the new breed of modern plants and the system of turnover among workers. Turnover is considered profitable for these companies. It affects every aspect of the workers' lives and it also defeats unions. The new generation of workers is generally young (between the ages of 18 and 25) and female. These individuals are often mothers of very young children; many are Mexicans or Southeast Asians.

The system that these employers have created is designed to increase employee turnover. The companies don't want these employees to stay. Employees with more seniority cost them more money. These companies bank on turnover and, according to UFCW, view it as a profit enhancer. Turnover rates of 500 percent per year are not uncommon. Employees are at the very low entry level. These companies' health insurance

EXHIBIT 3. Injuries and Illnesses and Rate of Incidence in Meatpacking

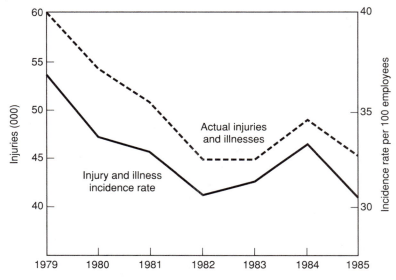

INJURY AND ILLNESS INCIDENCE RATE, EMPLOYEE NUMBERS, AND ESTIMATED INJURIES AND ILLNESSES[a]

	1979	1980	1981	1982	1983	1984	1985
Injury incidence rate (per 100 employees)	36.9	33.5	32.8	30.7	31.4	33.4	30.4
Employees (thousands)	162.6	161.4	155.2	146.9	143.4	146.7	148.5
Injuries and illnesses (thousands)	60.0	54.1	50.9	45.1	45.0	49.0	45.1

[a]Incidence rate multiplied by employees.
SOURCE: "Update on Injuries." Memo from Jene Knutson to Manly Molpas, the American Meat Institute, Washington, DC, July 28, 1987.

costs are negligible because most of the work force does not have the required six months seniority to be eligible for coverage. There are also certain tax incentives available to employers who hire more of a particular category of employees. Furthermore, the constant turnover apparently does not affect production, nor result in sufficient losses to counter the obvious economic incentives in favor of turnover.

Most importantly, for union organizing, the system of turnover prevents employees from becoming knowledgeable and more sophisticated because they are simply not there long enough. In studies of worker populations, it was found that these workers had no ties with their community. Their relations with the community were hostile. They were ostracized. They put a strain on the community resources. The hospitals were reluctant to treat indigents. The schools disliked teaching English to non-English speaking children. Police enforced the criminal laws more restrictively against the workers. These were not the type of people that small towns wanted to have around. In short, according to UFCW, the workers in the IBP plants were working under subhuman conditions, living in a system fostered by tax incentives, and facing a hostile and indifferent local community.[16]

EXHIBIT 4. Index of Incidence of Occupational Injuries and Illnesses

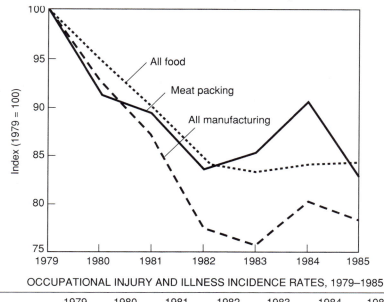

OCCUPATIONAL INJURY AND ILLNESS INCIDENCE RATES, 1979–1985

	1979	1980	1981	1982	1983	1984	1985	% change 1979–1985
All manufacturing	13.3	12.2	11.5	10.2	10.0	10.6	10.4	−21.8%
Index (1979 = 100)	100.0	91.7	86.5	76.7	75.2	79.7	78.2	
All foods	19.9	18.7	17.8	16.7	16.5	16.7	16.7	−16.1%
Index (1979 = 100)	100.0	94.0	89.4	83.9	82.9	83.9	83.9	
Meat packing	36.9	33.5	32.8	30.7	31.4	33.4	30.4	−17.6%
Index (1979 = 100)	100.0	90.8	88.9	83.2	85.1	90.5	82.4	

SOURCE: "Update on Injuries." Memo from Jene Knutson to Manly Molpas, the American Meat Institute, Washington, DC, July 28, 1987.

IBP AND THE MEATPACKING INDUSTRY'S RESPONSE

In May of 1987, the Subcommittee on Employment and Housing of the U. S. House of Representatives Government Operations Committee held hearings on safety in the meat industry. Testimony was provided by C. Manly Molpas,[17] president of the American Meat Institute, and Robert L. Peterson, chairman and chief executive officer of IBP, Inc.[18]

Mr. Molpas underscored the commitment of the meat industry to safety. He went on to define safety in two ways. The first aspect of safety he underlined was the provi-

sion of safe products for the consumer. He went on to say:

Toward this end, we work on a daily basis with USDA inspectors who administer the most intensive health-related regulatory program in government. All livestock is subject to veterinary examination by USDA both before and after slaughter. Our plant sanitation is monitored on a daily basis, including a pre-operational check by an inspector before each shift begins. This comprehensive regulatory scheme even extends to areas such as blueprints, equipment and labeling materials, all of which must be approved by USDA prior to their use. We are extremely proud of the track record that comes out of this partnership, with the result being the American consumer enjoys the world's safest supply of meat products.

Mr. Molpas listed in detail the concrete measures the American Meat Institute had taken to achieve the goals of safety in the workplace. First, the AMI had been a cosponsor in conjunction with the National Safety Council and Georgia Tech University of an annual meat industry safety workshop. In addition, the AMI had sponsored a number of seminars and workshops that dealt with the reduction of accidents, improving loss prevention, and implementing OSHA's work hazard communication standards.

Mr. Molpas then went on to stress the interrelation between product safety and safety in the workplace:

> Our employees work with live animals, heavy machinery, knives and a variety of other cutting and trimming implements. In such an environment, it is imperative to maintain a constant on-going focus on human safety. First and foremost, this must be done in order to eliminate unnecessary human suffering. Second, good safety is good business. Accidents and injuries impose impediments to productivity and efficiency and add significant costs to businesses that have traditionally operated with low profit margins. (Peterson, p.2)

According to Molpas, the Bureau of Labor Statistics reports that meatpacking plants (SIC Code 2011) have reduced their injury incidence rates by 23% during the period from 1979 to 1985.

These same statistics show that the combined injury and illness figures for the meatpacking industry dropped a total of 9% in a single year from 1984 to 1985. The industry affirmed that it was not content with past successes. In February 1987, the AMI board of directors approved as a priority objective the establishment of a broader industrywide safety program. The board subsequently appointed an industrywide task force with

the initial task of publishing and distributing an ergonomics handbook for the meat industry, the development of a national safety seminar, and the sponsorship of a meat-industry safety ward program in conjunction with the National Safety Council.

Molpas then addressed the issue of OSHA's record-keeping requirement. (Peterson, p. 4ff) He noted that, given the nature of the meatpacking business, all meat companies were forced to operate at rates that kept them in the high-hazard category under OSHA's inspection targeting program. He denied that companies intentionally misreported in order to avoid OSHA inspections. Rather, he suggested that reporting requirements should be more clearly written, simple, and easily understood. Otherwise, the policy would not work properly.

As an example, he pointed out that OSHA felt it necessary to issue an 84-page booklet to explain how to fill out Reporting Form 200. He cited a number of ambiguities in the regulations regarding "repetitive motion trauma." That problem is surely not as easy to document as, for example, a broken arm or a cut. Spotting "repetitive motion trauma" is like spotting fatigue before the consequences of fatigue—for example, an accident ensuing from a lapse of attention—happen. On this basis, Mr. Molpas emphasized what he called a critical distinction between a conscious attempt to circumvent the law and an honest difference in judgment. Molpas did not, however, adopt a stonewalling posture. He expressed a desire to move beyond simply criticizing the present program and to make efforts to improve upon it and maximize compliance within the industry. He mentioned the following three areas for further exploration (Peterson, pp. 7–8):

1. Initiation of a comprehensive program to identify and clarify the areas of ambiguity in OSHA reporting requirements that may be unique to our industry.
2. Institution of a broad-based industry information and training program, utilizing out-

side experts as appropriate, in order to assure the broadest possible understanding and application of record-keeping requirements.
3. A broad review of injury and illness data relating to our industry to determine whether the current information base is adequate.

In his testimony, Peterson, the chairman and CEO of IBP, Inc., noted that since he had joined IBP as a cattle buyer in 1961, the economies of mass production had revolutionized the industry (Peterson, p. 1):

Today, beef and pork are processed at packing plants through a labor intensive production process. After slaughtering, the livestock are put on a line where they are processed by workers who stand at work stations and make various cuts on the meat with sharp knives as it passes along the disassembly line. These pieces of meat are then vacuum packed and boxed in sturdy corrugated containers and shipped to various wholesale and retail customers throughout the United States.

There are many benefits from this modernization process. Locating plants near major livestock production centers lowers the transportation costs and reduces shipping damage. Mass production allows us to take advantage of scale economies. In addition, boxed meat is easier to ship over long distances, has a longer product life, and is more sanitary for shipping and storage. The bottom line is that these changes keep costs lower and ensure that consumers get more value for their dollar. In fact, meat processing is one of the few labor intensive industries in which the vast majority of jobs has remained here on our shores.

After six years devoted exclusively to meat slaughtering, IBP began meat processing operations in 1967 with the construction of the Dakota City plant. . .

Peterson saw IBP as an industry leader. Of IBP's 14 plants, only the Dakota City plant was represented by the United Food and Commercial Workers Union (UFCW). Peterson then went on to say: "We are currently involved in a bitter strike at this plant, our fifth in five negotiations. Two of our other large operations have contracts with another major union and have never experienced a labor dispute." (Peterson, pp. 3–4).

Peterson directly countered the testimony of UFCW witness or before the subcommittee. He denied that meat processing plants were unclean and unsafe, noting that they were subject to frequent and unannounced OSHA inspections. In addition, he said that 200 inspectors from the Department of Agriculture were constantly making inspections to ensure the plants and equipment are clean and that the meat is processed under stringent sanitary conditions. He also asserted that many of the UFCW claims were demonstrably untrue (Peterson, pp.4–5):

- Contrary to what the UFCW said, most workers do not work in 20 to 30 degree temperatures on the processing floor. In fact only three percent of our employees—those who work in the meat coolers—face these temperatures, and these people are issued special clothing for their protection.
- Contrary to what the UFCW claimed, "most workers" are not forced to stand in blood. This condition is applicable only to the three to five workers per shift directly involved in the slaughter of the animals and affects less than 0.4 percent of the workforce.
- Contrary to what the UFCW claimed, our floors are not "treacherously slippery." In 1985 and 1986 we spread over two million pounds of salt on our floors to keep them as safe as possible. In Dakota City alone, 36 individuals are continuously cleaning the floors to remove all debris and eliminate slippery conditions. We have spent well over $1 million in 1985 and 1986 to keep our floors clean and reduce the chance of slipping.

Peterson then went on to affirm IBP's commitment to safety in the workplace. He contended that it was good human relations. Safety was also sound economics. Every worker's compensation payment, every work stoppage due to an injury, every lost work day or light-duty day has an impact on the bottom line. (Peterson, p. 6).

Peterson insisted that IBP management was not indifferent to safety considerations. He indicated that IBP had adopted ten specific measures to maximize workplace safety: (1) safety equipment; (2) executive safety committee; (3) human resources policy; (4) corporate safety department and safety coordinators; (5) safety committees; (6) safety training for new workers; (7) safety training observation program (S.T.O.P.); (8) supervisor's daily safety inspection; (9) facility safety inspection; and (10) accident investigation regarding safety equipment. (pp. 6–13)

According to Peterson, "IBP employees are issued, at company expense, and are required to wear extensive personal protective equipment . . . To train workers in the use of safety equipment, the appropriate office has been provided with a training video, which both instructs workers on the safe use of knives and demonstrates the use of proper safety equipment. (Peterson, p. 7)

Though there are others, these 10 policies represent the core of IBP's safety policy. Peterson claims that the results of the policy have been good. In support, he cites the declining number of worker's compensation claims (Peterson, p. 13):

I am pleased to report that over the last several years, IBP's worker's compensation claim rate has dropped dramatically. According to figures supplied by our worker's compensation adjusters, total claims filed has declined in each of the last four years—despite the fact that total manhours has increased. The percentage of total worker claims filed per 200,000 manhours (the same standard used by OSHA) has declined by approximately two-thirds since 1983. The totals are as follows:

Year	Total Claims	Total Manhours	Claims per 200,000 Manhours
1983	7,942	25,906,000	61
1984	6,588	26,614,000	50
1985	5,188	30,235,000	34
1986	3,546	33,397,000	21

Mr. Peterson also accused the UFCW of being uncooperative.

We have actively sought UFCW cooperation in these efforts, but often the union has been a roadblock to mandatory use of safety equipment. For example, during the term of the recently expired collective bargaining agreement the UFCW filed eight grievances resisting safety gear requirements we established at Dakota City after safety studies led us to conclude that they were necessary. (Peterson, p. 7)

Our Dakota City plant, which the UFCW criticized so severely in your last hearing on this issue, has four Safety Committees—each with UFCW representatives on it. It is unfortunate that many of the alleged safety problems the union described in its earlier testimony never were bought to our attention at Dakota City Safety Committee meetings. (Peterson, p. 10)

In the final part of his testimony, Peterson discussed IBP's compliance with OSHA's recordkeeping requirements. (Peterson, pp. 14–20) Labelling the allegations levelled by UFCW as "sensational and blatantly untrue," he denied that IBP ever kept two sets for safety books in order to deliberately deceive OSHA and, thereby, avoid inspections. He stated that IBP kept detailed records of injuries and illness as well as medical history. The records were kept in various forms because reporting requirements differed for different regulations.

He insisted that contrary to the union's claims, there was nothing sinister or suspicious in any of this record keeping. And, most importantly, there was no effort to mislead OSHA. In fact, the extraneous entries made it extremely easy when OSHA inspectors conducted inspections in 1985 and 1986 to determine whether any dispensary visit constituted a recordable entry for OSHA purposes. Moreover, in 1987, when OSHA inspectors examined the revised log as part of their current record-keeping examination, IBP also provided them with the comprehensive dispensary log. Thus, at no time was the revised log used to hide any visits by Dakota City workers to our medical dispensaries.

Peterson attributed much of the confusion to the ambiguity of OSHA's regulations. He cited testimony by other witnesses at the earlier hearing, and also the Bureau of Labor Statistics ("BLS") guidelines, showing that OSHA rules and guidelines were not precise. They required frequent interpretation and many good-faith judgment calls.

> That review is underway. While the final results are not yet available, it is clear that some changes to our OSHA No. 200 records for prior years will be needed to bring IBP into complete compliance with OSHA's new guidelines. It is also likely that our recordable injuries for the years 1982–86 will increase, in part because of our instructions to make sure that we call the close ones in favor of recording.

Finally, Peterson charged that a complaint with OSHA on January 22, 1987, was part of what the union's "corporate campaign" against IBP. As a result, OSHA began an investigation and Peterson affirmed that IBP Was cooperating. He affirmed that IBP is committed to improving its own performance.

IBP CHANGES ITS COURSE

Subsequent to the initial OSHA fine, IBP started on a plan to modernize its Dakota facility and also adopted a more conciliatory stance toward the union. UFCW had launched a major publicity campaign highlighting IBP's unsafe working conditions, while at the same time displaying a willingness to work with IBP. The congressional hearing further intensified the negative public image of IBP, which was heightened when OSHA refused to accept IBP's modernization plan and hit IBP with another fine of $3 million, making it a total of $5.6 million—the agency's largest fine ever.

In a major change of stance, IBP voluntarily recognized the union (UFCW) at its Joslin, Illinois plant where it had been resisting the union's efforts toward worker organization. This was a major turnaround and, as a result, put the union on a growth path. It plans to launch more organizational drives at other nonunion packers. Finally, there is peace at IBP. Whether it will be a lasting peace, only time will tell.[19]

NOTES

1. Gene Erb, "Newspaper Finds 'Injury Epidemic' at Storm Lake." *No Bull Sheet* (September 1987), p. 4.
2. Upton Sinclair, *The Jungle.* Cambridge, MA:, R. Bentley, 1946.
3. Charles Dickens, *Hard Times.* New York: Hearst's International Library Co., 1968.
4. Alan Pezaro, *Critical Review Analysis for Injury Related Research in the Meatpacking Industry (SIC 2011).* Washington, DC; American Meat Institute (January 1984).
5. William Glaberson, "Misery on the Meatpacking Line." *New York Times* (June 14, 1987), pp. F1, F8.
6. William Robins, "A Meatpacker Cartel Up Ahead?" *New York Times* (May 29, 1988) p. F4.
7. Philip Shabecoff, "OSHA Seeks $2.59 Million Fine for Meatpacker's Injury Reports." *New York Times* (July 22, 1987), pp. A1, A20.
8. *Ibid.*
9. Andrea Adelson, "Occidental Hints at IBP Sale." *New York Times* (July 21, 1987), pp. D1, D17.
10. Shabecoff, "OSHA Seeks Fine."
11. United Food and Commercial Workers International Union, *IBP Dakota City Workers' Struggle*, Washington, DC: and Sioux City, IA, (January 1987).
12. *Ibid.*
13. "Update on Injuries." Memo from Jene Knutson to Manly Molpas, The American Meat Institute, Washington, DC, July 28, 1987.
14. United Food and Commercial Workers International Union, *The John Morrell Workers' Struggle*, Washington, DC, (August 1987).
15. *Ibid.*

16. United Food and Commercial Workers International Union, *General Report: 1986 National Packinghouse Strategy and Policy Conference, Washington, DC, (April 10, 1987).*

17. C. Manley Molpas, "Testimony Regarding Safety in the Workplace before the House Government Operations Committee, Subcommittee on Employment and Housing, U. S. House of Representatives,"

American Meat institute, Washington, DC, (May 6, 1987).

18. Robert L. Peterson, "Testimony before the Subcommittee on Housing and Employment, House Government Operations Committee," American Meat Institute, Washington, DC, (May 6, 1987).

19. "How OSHA Helped Organize the Meatpackers." Business Week (August 29, 1988), p. 82.

FILM RECOVERY SYSTEMS, INC.

*The extent of officers' culpability for serious harm, and even
death of workers, due to unsafe working conditions*

On June 14, 1985, Judge Ronald J.P. Banks, sitting on a nonjury trial, convicted three executives of National Film Recovery Systems, a small firm then based in Elk Grove, Illinois, of murder in the death of one employee, Stefan Golab, 61, a Polish immigrant who had been on the job for only two months.

In Illinois, murder is the first degree of homicide, higher than voluntary manslaughter cases. Defendants are often charged with killing someone by acting with a reckless lack of caution. According to the Illinois Criminal Code, the act of murder is defined as: "A person, who kills an individual without lawful justification, commits murder if performing such acts creates a strong probability of death or great bodily harm to the individual or another."[1] (*The People of the State of Illinois* v. *Film Recovery Systems, et.al*, Circuit Court of Cook County, Fourth Municipal Division, No. 83–11001 and No. 94–5064, June 14, 1985.)

The Film Recovery Case is a landmark in that it marks the first time corporate officials have been found guilty in a job-related death. There have been other cases where corporations and their executives have been charged with manslaughter. However, more often than not, it is the corporation that ends up paying the fines, and the executives get off with a slap on their wrists.[2]

The victim, Stefan Golab, left his native Poland in November 1981 to start a new life in the United States. On December 26, 1982, he began work as a laborer for Film Recovery systems, which operated to recover silver from used photographic film. He was on the job barely two months when on February 10, 1983 he met his death.[3] On that day, Golab arrived for work as usual at 7:00 AM and began working with a Polish co–worker, Roman Guzoski, around the cyanide-filled vats. After pumping cyanide solution into the tanks at 9:30 he went over to disconnect a pump. Upon moving a few steps he slumped against the wall. His co-workers told him to leave the area. He did so, going to the locker area and (later) to the lunchroom. Shortly thereafter he slumped over in his chair. His co-workers gathered around to help. Emergency aid was summoned but to no avail. Upon arrival at Alexian Brothers Hospital at 10:50 Stefan Golab was pronounced dead.

A grand jury, convened in October 1983, indicted the companies involved—Metallic Marketing Inc. (MMI), Film Recovery Systems Inc. (FRS), and B. R. McKay and Sons. On November 21, they reached the consensus that the companies were guilty of involuntary manslaughter. The same grand jury found the corporate management (Steven O'Neil, president of FRS; Gerald Pett, vice-president of FRS; Charles Kirschbaum, plant manager at Elk Grove; Daniel Rodriguez, job supervisor at Elk Grove, and

249

Michael MacKay, a Director of FRS whose company, B. R. MacKay and Sons, owned half of FRS) with twenty violations of the reckless conduct statute. On May 1, 1984 another grand jury (which was convened in April) indicted these same individuals for murder because they knowingly caused the death of Stefan Golab by exposing him to unsafe working conditions in the FRS work environment.[4]

ISSUES FOR ANALYSIS

1. Under what conditions, if any, should the top managers of a company or a plant be held responsible for the death of, or serious injury to, workers? Were these conditions met in the Film Recovery case?
2. What are the minimum conditions of "adequacy of care" that must be met before managers or plant supervisors could be charged with criminal behavior against the person or workers?
3. In the case of a corporate policy or practice causing harm to others, who should ultimately be held responsible: the owners (shareholders); the board of directors; top, middle, or low management? Alternately, how should responsibility be apportioned among these groups?
4. What is the responsibility of the workers themselves to see to it that their working environment is safe?
5. What is the responsibility of public agencies such as OSHA to see to it that the work environment is without serious problems?
6. Are there specific industry/company/management characteristics that make some firms more prone to reckless disregard of worker safety? If so, what might these conditions be? In particular, are smaller companies more prone to engaging in such criminal behavior as compared to larger companies?
7. Is the behavior of Film Recovery Systems' managers an aberration or is it symptomatic of conditions that are more prevalent in plant operations in the United States?
8. What are some of the changes that one might make in organization structure and manager behavior to minimize the occurrence of incidents such as that of Film Recovery Systems?

9. What are the moral/ethical dimensions of the managers' behavior in this case? How are they different from standards of legal culpability? How one might go about inducing higher moral and ethical standards among plant managers charged with protecting the lives and health of their workers?

FILM RECOVERY SYSTEMS, INC.— THE COMPANY PROFILE

Film Recovery Systems (FMS) was formed in late 1979, to extract silver from used film. It was founded by Steven O'Neil together with Michael MacKay and Alvin Tolin, whom O'Neil met at a meeting of the Radiological Society of North America. He was twenty-five years old at the time. He had studied commercial photography at Colorado Mountain College for two years, leaving in 1974. He immediately went to work for RKS Future Industries, a silver recycling firm in Denver. While there, he learned the cyanide-wash system. In this process, sodium cyanide was diluted into a caustic solution, which went into holding tanks of around 1,000 gallons. The mixture of sodium cyanide in the solution registered as a 2% cyanide solution. Used film was then granulated and placed in the holding tanks. The solution extracted silver from the film product. After that, the cyanide solution and the extracted silver were drained from the holding tanks into electronically charged 125-gallon plating tanks. The extracted silver would adhere to the plates. Later, the plates were removed from the tanks and the workers scraped the silver from them. The company then shipped the silver to refineries for processing. Workers would also remove the remnants of granulated film product from the holding tanks by climbing into them and shoveling the film residue out. The silver removal process took about three days.[5]

O'Neil worked at RKS full-time until 1977, at various positions both inside and outside the plant. This work experience proved to be important to his case, for he claimed that during these three years he suffered no injury or illnesses.[6] O'Neil then moved to Chicago, where he worked as a trader who purchased used film and then subsequently sold it to processors. In so doing, he traveled extensively. As a result, he met Bob Fields of Drum Silver Company in Norman, Oklahoma. Fields agreed to buy film product from O'Neil. He had modified the cyanide wash system by installing a vacuum system to remove remnant film product from the holding tanks—a safer system.

In late 1977 and early 1978, O'Neil formed Metal Marketing Systems, Inc., (MMI) with two other individuals. MMI continued the film purchase and resale business. But by late 1978, a dispute arose with Drum Silver. In a settlement, MMI received money and one–half of Drum's plant equipment, which it proceeded to install in Wheeling, Illinois. O'Neil was intimately involved in plant operations at Wheeling. He also modified the evacuation system in such a way as to prevent workers from coming into contact with the cyanide solution. Again, he was to claim he never suffered any injury or illness.[7]

When FRS was formed, it acquired MMI's Wheeling plant and entered into a noncompetition pact where MMI would confine its operations to Florida. In return MMI obtained 51% of FRS stock; O'Neil himself owned 51% of MMI. The Elk Grove plant opened in 1980. All went well. The plant expanded from 80 tanks in 1980 to 120 in 1981 and 140 in 1982. According to the defendants, additional ventilation fans were installed. Only two-thirds of the vats were used at one time, half for holding and half for plating. Both of these points were important in estimating the degree of toxicity in the air.[8]

It was in this work environment that Stefan Golab collapsed and died.

FACTS OF THE CASE

During the nonjury trial, the defendants and the prosecution presented the work environment in FRS plant in totally different terms; the former asserting that it was safe within the context of the essentially hazardous nature of the chemicals being handled at the plant. The defendants also contended that any infractions of safety regulations were at best minor, and that, in many cases, workers' discomfort arose out of their disregard for properly following safety regulations. And in any case, the events and circumstances surrounding them in no way justified the charges for which they were indicted.

Stefan Golab

According to the defendants, Stefan Golab had a history of heart problems, including evidence of an earlier heart attack. When he began working at FRS, he smoked cigarettes and suffered from a heart condition, which included an enlarged heart and a 50% blockage in the two major arteries to the heart. He last visited a doctor before coming to the United States from Poland in November 1981. Thus, FRS was unaware of Golab's physical condition.[9] On the day of his collapse at the plant, all signs indicated a heart attack. When paramedics arrived at the plant to provide emergency medical aid, Golab lay in the company's parking lot. His face was grayish blue in color. He already had convulsed and foamed at the mouth, all symptoms of a heart attack victim. As a consequence, the paramedics administered life-support procedures. They were of no avail.

The next day, the Cook County Medical Examiner performed an autopsy on Golab. He found that Golab suffered from a heart condition, including pulmonary edema (fluid in the lungs), coronary atherosclerosis (artery blockage), and hyperthrophy (thickening) of the heart's left ventricle. He concluded that the condition could cause death. Based on these findings, the medical examiner reported to an Elk Grove village police investigator on February 12, 1983 that he saw no indication during the autopsy that Golab died of anything other than a heart attack. However, he reserved providing a definitive cause of death until he received the results of toxicological laboratory tests on Golab's blood and other bodily specimens. On May 6, 1983, after receiving a toxicological laboratory report dated March 17, 1983, the medical examiner ruled that Golab died from acute cyanide poisoning through the inhalation of cyanide fumes in the plant air at FRS.[10] In all, two medical examiners and two toxicologists were called in to discern the cause of death. They came up with a split verdict. One medical examiner and one toxicologist found that Golab died of heart failure; the others cited cyanide poisoning. Contrary to the defendant's assertion that Golab died of heart failure, the prosecution claimed that Golab suffered a fatal cyanide blood concentration.

The preceding events led to the indictments against the defendants for murder, involuntary manslaughter, and reckless conduct. The murder indictment alleged that the individual defendants (who as "officers and high managerial agents" operrated FRS, a business engaged in the use of cyanide in its industrial process) hired Golab as an employee of FRS without informing him of the company's use of cyanide and of safety procedures pertaining to the use of cyanide and failling to provide necessary safety equipment and adequate storage facilities for cyanide. As a consequence of these acts, the indictment alleged that the individual defendants, knowing that the hazards and dangers of cyanide created a strong probability of death or great bodily harm, caused Golab's death on February 10, 1983.

The involuntary manslaughter indictment charged only the corporate defendants. It alleged that the corporate defendants, while engaged in the silver recovery business, unintentionally killed Golab through acts authorized and commanded by the individual defendants named in the murder indictment. According to the involuntary manslaughter charge, the individuals acted recklessly in their capacities as "officers, board of directors

and high managerial agents" and "within the scope of their employment" with the corporate defendants.[11]

Twenty reckless conduct charges accompanied the involuntary manslaughter charge.[12] However, these charges named both the corporate defendants and the individual defendants, "acting within the scope of their employment as officers, board of directors, high managerial agents and employees" of the corporate defendants, and related to various employees of the corporate defendants other than Golab, who purportedly sustained injuries as a result of toxic exposure to cyanide in the work environment. Specifically, the reckless conduct charges alleged that the defendants, acting in a reckless manner, hired the named employees without disclosing the use and attendant dangers of cyanide in the workplace and failed to provide necessary safety equipment and adequate storage facilities for cyanide. As a result, the employees purportedly sustained injuries which occurred both before and after Golab's death.

Significantly, the indictments charged as defendants the corporations engaged in business in interstate commerce and individuals who, in their capacity as corporate officials, acted within the scope of their employment. The indictments also named employees as victims of injuries purportedly sustained during working hours on the business premises. In addition, the indictments described the employee injuries as arising from the toxic exposure to a chemical used in the normal industrial process of the corporations. In short, the charges related to working conditions provided employees by employers and employee injuries purportedly arising from those conditions.

The Labor Safety Record in the FRS Plant at Elk Grove

The labor force at Elk Grove was largely composed of illegal immigrants of both Mexican and Polish origin. In all, there were some 89

Hispanic and 15 Polish employees. According to the defendants' own admission, most of the plant workers neither spoke nor read English. The defendants also claimed that the workers were neither underpaid nor mistreated.[13] Indeed, many of the workers sought jobs at FRS for their relatives and friends. Many of the workers never missed work.

The plant, nevertheless, had a high odor threshold and a history of minor health problems: eye irritation, headaches, dizziness, and nausea. However, only one or two employees incurred injuries that required subsequent medical attention. When workers complained about feeling sick, they were generally told (by Rodriguez and Kirschbaum) to go outside for some fresh air. Cloth gloves and cloth face masks were generally available at the plant. Some workers also wore rubber boots, rubber gloves, and rubber aprons. Though this safety equipment was available, many of the workers refused to wear it. According to the defendants' brief, on many occasions some workers refused to comply with specific requests to wear the safety equipment. FRS also purchased face shields, eye goggles, earphones, and hard hats. Moreover, the plant contained at least one oxygen tank and several gas masks.

FRS had at least nine ceiling exhaust fans that rotated the air in the plant three times per minute. The plant also had cyanide air-test kits, two cyanide antidote kits, eye washes, deluge showers, and fire extinguishers. FRS regularly stocked the medicine cabinet with pain pills and other first aid equipment.[14] When FRS first opened its Elk Grove Village facility in 1980, an employee was tested for cyanide exposure twice a week for approximately a year. On one occasion, he received a hazardous cyanide reading directly over the plating tanks while they were operating. Thereafter, the company prohibited workers from working over those tanks while they were in operation. Following 1980, the same employee measured cyanide levels in the plant on a regular basis at least

until October 1982. The highest reading obtained as a result of these tests reflected levels within applicable standards promulgated under the Occupational Safety and Health Act. The employee communicated the readings to defendant O'Neil. After October 1982, defendant Kirschbaum measured air quality in the plant on four or five occasions. Like the earlier readings, these tests reflected permissible levels of cyanide fumes in the plant environment.

The workers painted a far more grim picture of safety conditions and many of them later filed suit. Golab's friend and co-worker, Roman Guzoski, also testified that Golab had felt so ill before that he was actually seeking a job transfer.[15]

Workers were not told specifically that they were dealing with cyanide, although the cyanide drums contained the skull-and-crossbones symbol. The word "poison" was printed in bold red letters on the walls of the plant in both English and Spanish.

Inspections by Government Agencies and the Insurance Carrier

From 1980 through 1983, governmental agencies and a private insurance company made numerous inspections of the plant. In November 1982, an inspector from the Occupational Safety and Health Administration came to the plant and, after reviewing company records relating to worker injuries, determined that no follow-up investigation was required. There were eight or more inspections by the Metropolitan Sanitary District between 1981 and 1983. Although odor was detected, the inspectors never reported any violations concerning improper waste discharge or pollution problems. Similarly, inspections by the Elk Grove Village Fire Department during 1980 and 1981 did not indicate any ventilation problems.

In addition to governmental inspections, FRS' insurance company regularly inspected the FRS plant. Thus, when FRS first sought insurance coverage in 1980, the insurance company sent an industrial hygienist to inspect the plant. After the inspection, FRS obtained insurance. Thereafter, the insurance company conducted thorough yearly inspections covering all aspects of the plant's operation. On each occasion, the insurance company made recommendations and the FRS company always obtained insurance coverage after the inspections. Indeed, the insurance company characterized FRS as a fair insurance risk.

After the fact of Golab's death, OSHA carried out an inspection. As a consequence, on March 11, 1983, the Occupational Safety and Health Administration issued citations against FRS for using unapproved respirators; having no training program regarding cyanide exposure and the use of respirators; using inappropriate gloves and provided no emergency eyewash, protective eye gear or antidote for cyanide poisoning. OSHA proposed fines of $4,850. Judge Josephine O'Brian later settled the issue with FRS for a sum of $2,425. (She defended the sum saying FRS was in dire financial straits).[16] In their appeal, the defendants questioned the validity of the OSHA inspection. OSHA apparently tested the plant at *full capacity* conditions and thus overestimated the toxicity of the environment; the plant normally ran at two thirds capacity.[17]

The Corporate Involvement of the Individual Defendants

FRS employed the individual defendants in markedly different capacities. Steven O'Neil was the president of FRS. His defense tried to distance him from day-to-day operations.[18] While the plant was getting underway in 1980, he was present continuously. Thereafter, he worked off–site, procuring film for processing and marketing the retrieved silver. In 1981 he visited the plant twice a week for two-to three-hour periods; in 1982, his total annual visits declined to about twenty. In 1983, he stopped visiting the plant, devoting himself entirely to off–site duties. No one in the plant had much contact with him, especially after 1980. In his absence, Gerald Pett, Fred Kopp (who was not indicted), or Charles Kirschbaum ran the plant. The judge acquitted Pett, so the onus fell on Kirschbaum.

Kirschbaum, who had two years experience with another silver extraction firm, joined FRS in July 1981. His defense portrayed him as follows.[19] His responsibility was to monitor film product from the time it was received until it was processed; he also supervised the workers. He himself was on the plant floor six to eight hours a day; he never wore safety equipment and suffered no adverse effects. He did try, however, to get workers to use such equipment, but with little success—even claiming to have fired some who resisted. From July 1981 to the summer of 1982, Kirschbaum monitored the production process and supervised the workers to assure that they were performing their jobs correctly. In September 1982, he moved his office to a newly acquired building located adjacent to the plant building. However, during all this period, he was in the plant area six to eight hours a day, six days a week, and never wore anything on his face when he was in the plant.

As part of his duties and pursuant to company policy, Kirschbaum attempted to get workers to wear rubber boots, rubber gloves, rubber aprons, and eye goggles. However, some workers did not like to wear the equipment. As a result, Kirschbaum fired some workers who refused to wear the equipment. Kirschbaum took order from Fred Kopp, Gerald Pett, Steve O'Neil, and B.R. Mackay in Salt Lake City.

Daniel Rodriguez was something of a shop floor manager. In his defense, he denied being a foreman.[20] He came to the United States in 1979 and went to work at FRS in 1980 on the recommendation of another Mexican worker. Rodriguez worked full time on the floor doing all jobs. He knew that he was working with poison, as did all the other workers, but he did not know exactly what cyanide was. He observed that workers were getting sick and (together with Kirschbaum and Kopp) advised them to wear safety equipment. He frequently acted as interpreter for the Spanish workers.

Decision of the Lower Court

In rendering his decision, Judge Banks observed that he had reviewed and taken into consideration the oral testimony given by the defendants, plus a review of all exhibits that were presented; also, weighing the credibility of all the witnesses who appeared before the court. Even more important, he stated: "During my deliberations and evaluations of all the evidence, let it be known that I never forgot the most important concept in criminal law, that being the defendants are presumed innocent and that it is the burden of the State that they must prove guilt beyond a reasonable doubt."[21]

Judge Banks had earlier acquitted Pett of all charges and acquitted the other defendants of six reckless conduct charges. This took place on May 14, 1985 at the close of the prosecution's direct case.

Thus, on June 14, 1985, at the close of all the evidence and after argument of counsel, Judge Banks found the remaining individual defendants guilty of murder and fourteen counts of reckless conduct. He also found the corporate defendants guilty of involuntary manslaughter and the fourteen reckless conduct charges.

On July 1, 1985 Judge Banks sentenced the individual defendants to 25 years in the custody of the Illinois Department of Corrections and fined them $10,000 each on the murder conviction. In addition, he sentenced them to a concurrent period of 364 days in the custody of the Illinois Department of Corrections on the reckless conduct convictions. With respect to the corporate defendants, Judge Banks fined them $10,000 each on the involuntary manslaughter conviction and $14,000 each for the reckless conduct convictions.

MacKay's indictment was tied to the fact that he was a majority owner. Furthermore, a month before Golab's death, his company, B. R. MacKay and Sons, went through the motions of taking over FRS because of unpaid debts. Both O'Neil and MacKay claimed the other was "in charge" at the time of death. (It is interesting to note that MacKay never faced trial. The governor of Utah refused the State of Illinois' request to extradite him.)

On February 6, 1984, Governor Scott M. Matheson of Utah, describing Mr. MacKay, a Salt Lake City businessman, as "an exemplary citizen," refused to extradite him to Illinois to face murder and other related criminal charges. Among his reasons, he cited the "unique and sensational" nature of the charges and publicity in the news media that made him "very concerned" about Mr. MacKay's "chances for a fair trial in Illinois." That led Gov. James R. Thompson of Illinois to retort: "The pretrial publicity, while novel for Utah, was not novel for the state of Illinois. Maybe Utah's sensibilities are more easily shocked."

Mr. Daley, son of the former Mayor, accused Governor Matheson of "abusing his responsibility to justice and law enforcement." That brought a response from one of Mr. MacKay's attorneys, David K. Watkiss, who said, "What the hell does Mr. Daley know about law and order?"[22]

Governor Matheson refused Illinois' request for extradition a second time later that year, arguing that Illinois couldn't directly link Mr. MacKay to the death. On June 16, 1985, the new governor of Utah, Norman H. Bangster, refused a third request from Illinois to extradite Mr. MacKay, ruling that the facts in the case hadn't changed since former Gov. Matheson denied the original request. He also added: "The case represents an unprecedented attempt to expand the liability of a corporate official for consequences which are not demonstrably connected to the official's knowledge or actions."[23]

Defendants Appeal the Lower Court's Verdict

In their appeal of Judge Bank's decision, the defendants raised the following issues pertaining to interpretation of evidence and applicability of pertinent laws.

1. The state of Illinois was wrong to apply its criminal laws to regulate working conditions provided for employees in the industrial workplace by employers engaged in business in interstate commerce. The federal law pertaining to industrial work environment, i.e., the Occupational Safety and Health Act of 1970, 29 U.S.C. S651 et. seg. preempts state laws.
2. The due process rights of defendants requires that prosecution must prove violation of applicable occupational safety and health standards before convicting employers and their officers and agents of state law crimes for alleged injuries sustained by employees from unsafe working conditions in the industrial workplace.
3. The evidence does not support defendants' convictions for state law crimes arising from injuries allegedly sustained by employees from unsafe working conditions in the industrial workplace where the evidence failed to establish the existence of a dangerous work environment, the requisite mental states for the defendants, and the cause of death of an employee who died at the workplace.
4. The murder findings against the individual defendants were inconsistent with the voluntary manslaughter findings against the corporate defendants where both the individual and corporate defendants were charged and convicted because of the acts and statements of the individual defendants, acting in their capacity as officers and high managerial agents of the corporate defendants.
5. The murder findings against the individual defendants were inconsistent with the reckless conduct findings against the same defendants.

In the interview, the attorney who represented Steven O'Neil, FRS, and MMI maintained that the preemption argument was the cornerstone of the defense. Briefly stated, the preemption doctrine strikes the distribution of federal and state power in our federal system of government. It grants the federal government, in the exercise of a constitutionally granted power, the ability to completely occupy a particular field or activity to the exclusion of all state action. In short, the defense maintains that: (1) Illinois law is not relevant, and (2) the defendants broke no federal law.

The preemption doctrine provided the foundation of the defense. The defendants' explanation of this doctrine follows:[24]

"The preemption doctrine strikes the distribution of federal and state power in our federal system of government. It grants the federal government, in the exercise of a constitutionally granted power, the ability to completely occupy a particular field or activity to the exclusion of all state action. Whether the federal government preempts a given area depends solely upon the congressional intent underlying a particular enactment. As a consequence, federal preemption becomes largely a matter of statutory construction. Once Congress expresses a preemptive intent, however, no state action, either through conflicting with the actual congressional enactment or intruding upon a field that Congress validly reserved to federal control, will stand. Though controversial at its inception in the early nineteenth century, the preemption doctrine now stands as an established principle of law without exception or challenge, which all courts, federal or state, must enforce. (p. 24)

. . . The Occupational Safety And Health Act Congress, pursuant to its constitutionally authorized power to regulate interstate commerce and provide for the general welfare, enacted OSHA in 1970 "to assure so far as possible every working man and woman in the Nation safe and healthful working conditions and to preserve our human resources." 29 U.S.C. S665 (b) (5). Once promulgated, the statute intended the standards to provide guidelines for employer administration of the workplace and to define acceptable working conditions. Indeed, the statute directs that enacted standards, "whenever practicable. . . shall be expressed in terms of objective criteria and of the performance desired." 29 U.S.C. S655(b)(5) (pp. 31–32)

... Central to OSHA is the primacy accorded to the standards established by the Secretary of Labor to regulate the work environment. First, OSHA standards apply without exception to all employers engaged in business in interstate commerce and thei r employees. Compliance is mandatory (p. 35)

Moreover, though the states are permitted a role in the field of occupational safety and health, OSHA permits independent state action only in carefully circumscribed situations. Section 667(a) of OSHA provides that where no federal standard is in effect as to a given occupational safety or health issue, federal law does not prevent a state agency or court from asserting jurisdiction over that issue under state law. 29 U.S.C. S667(a). If, however, a federal standard exists as to a given health and safety issue, the only manner in which a state may attempt to exercise jurisdiction over that issue is to submit an enforcement plan to the United States Secretary of Labor for approval. Section 667(b) of OSHA states in material part: Any State which, at any time, desires to assume responsibility for development and enforcement therein of occupational safety and health standards relating to any occupational safety or health issue with respect to which a federal standard has been promulgated . . . shall submit a state plan for the development of such standards and their enforcement. 29 U.S.C. S667(b). When a plan is submitted, the submitting state continues to be barred from acting within the occupational safety and health field until the Secretary of Labor approves the plan. The requirements for approval are stringent. Among other things, the plan must:

1. Designate a state agency responsible for the administration of the plan;
2. Provide for the development and adoption of standards that are at least as effective as comparable OSHA standards and;
3. . . . with assurances that the state will devote adequate funds to the administration and enforcement of such standards.

29 U.S.C. S667(c)(1), (2), (4) and (5). Thus, OSHA premises the acceptance of a state plan and the ensuing state regulatory action in the field of occupational safety and health, on the adoption of (1) published standards "at least as effective as" their OSHA counterparts and (2) an effective and adequately funded enforcement program.

... In order to obtain approval of such standards, the submitting state must show that there are compelling local circumstances justifying such differences and that the different standards will not impose an undue burden on interstate commerce. 29 U.S.C. S667(c)(2). In short, the more stringent state standards must be compelled by local conditions and cannot impose an undue burden on interstate commerce. Otherwise, OSHA will preempt their application in the work environment. Finally, OSHA requires a state plan to provide for a procedure of granting variances which correspond to variances granted by the Secretary of Labor under federal standards.

Succinctly, OSHA provides an express preemption provision where Congress preempted state regulation in the field of occupational safety and health with respect to issues for which federal standards exist and then delegated to the Secretary of Labor the discretion to allow state participation in the regulated field after the state meets certain statutory prerequisites." (pp. 35–36)

Epilogue

In January of 1990, the state appellate court overturned the lower court decision of 1985.[25] The appellate court raised the issue of whether it was sensible to find the defendants guilty of both murder and reckless conduct, a charge logically linked to manslaughter. While the court found that the evidence could have sustained a conviction on either grounds, it was legally inconsistent to find the defendants guilty of both.

The case was then in abeyance. The reason is that the court in the National Film Recovery case was awaiting an Illinois Supreme Court decision in a similar case brought against Chicago Magnetic Wire Corp. The management of that corporation was indicted in 1984 for aggravated battery and reckless assault in the injury of its employees. The case against Chicago Magnetic Wire reached a milestone when, on February 2, 1989, the Illinois State Supreme Court ruled that OSHA does not bar states from prosecuting corporate officials.[26] This decision is a landmark and opened the way for similar actions against corporate executives by other states, where some eight actions were pending in early 1989.

The Chicago Magnetic Wire Corporation case was finally settled in April 1991, when an Illinois judge acquitted the five executives involved.[27] The attempt to convict corporate executives, while allowable under the 1989 State Supreme Court ruling, was unsuccessful. The acquittal of the executives left the legal world pondering how best to approach worker safety issues as they relate to executive personal liability. The acquittal of the Chicago Magnetic Wire executives did, however, set the stage for a final resolution of the Film Recovery Systems case in terms of executive personal liability for manslaughter.

It took another 2 years to be sorted out. However, on September 7, 1993, the former president, Stephen O'Neil, and Daniel Rodriquez, the job supervisor at the Elk Grove plant, pleaded guilty to involuntary manslaughter.[28] O'Neil was sentenced to 3 years in prison and Rodriquez received 30 months of felony probation, 4 months of home confinement, and 500 hours of community service. Three days later, Charles Kirschbaum, the plant manager at Elk Grove, also pleaded guilty to involuntary manslaughter and received a sentence of 2 years in prison.[29]

Gerald Pett, the vice–president of FRS, had been acquitted during the 1985 trial. The fate of Charles MacKay, a member of the Film Recovery Board and also president of its parent firm, remains unresolved. He is a prominent Salt Lake City businessman and Utah officials have opposed attempts to extradite him to Illinois. He has never been either exonerated or sentenced.

In the meantime, Film Recovery Systems, Inc., has gone out of business.

NOTES

1. *The People of the State of Illinois* v. *Film Recovery Systems, et al.*, Circuit Court of Cook County, Fourth Municipal Division, No. 83-11001 and No. 94-5064, June 14, 1985.
2. Steven Greenhouse, "3 Executives Convicted of Murder for Unsafe Workplace Conditions." *New York Times* (June 15, 1985), pp. 1, 29; Mary Breasted, "4 Are Indicted in Fire Fatal to 6 at Chicle Plant." *New York Times* (July 23, 1977), p. 1; Donald Janson, "Great Adventure Owners Cleared of Criminal Charges in Fatal Fire." *New York Times* (July 21, 1985), p. 1; David R. Spiegel, "The Liability of Corporate Officers." *ABA Journal, The Lawyer's Magazine*, 71 (November, 1985), pp. 48–52.;
3. *People of the State of Illinois* vs. *Steven O'Neil, et.al.*, Appellate Court of Illinois, First Judicial District, # 85–1853,1854,1855, 1952,1953 Consolidated, Brief of Appellants, May 10, 1986, pp.xiii–xv. (All future references to this source in this text will hereinafter be referred to as *Appellants' Brief* followed by appropriate page number.)
4. *Appellants' Brief*, p. xiii; E. R. Shipp, "Workplace Death Prompts a Dispute: 5 Executives Are Accused of Murder—Utah Governor Will Not Extradite One." *New York Times* (February 20, 1984), p. A9; The April 1984 Grand Jury of the Circuit Court of Cook County, May, 1, 1984, pp. 1–2.
5. *Apellants' Brief*, pp. 6ff.
6. *Ibid.*, p. 7ff.
7. *Ibid.*, pp. 8–9.
8. *Ibid.*, pp. 9–10.
9. *Ibid.*, p. 1.
10. *Ibid.*, pp. 2–3.
11. *Ibid.*, pp. 4–5.
12. *Ibid.*, pp. 10–11.
13. Ray Gibson, "Murder Trial Set for Execs of Factory." *Chicago Tribune* (April 14, 1985), pp. 1–2.
14. *Appellants' Brief*, pp. 10–12.
15. Debbe Nelson, "Foul Haze Veiled Factory

Death," *Daily Herald* (April 16, 1985), pp. 1, 3; Debbe Nelson, "Victim Sought Job Transfer—Cyanide Work Made Him Sick," *Daily Herald* (April 17, 1985), pp. 1, 3.

16. Patrick Owens, "Death of Worker Puts Factory Safety on Trial." *Newsday* (June 6, 1985), pp. 30–31.
17. *Appellants' Brief*, p. 15ff.
18. *Ibid.*, pp. 16–17.
19. *Ibid.*, pp. 17–19.
20. *Ibid.*, pp. 19–20.
21. Decision of Judge Banks, pp. 5–6; *Appellants' Brief*, pp. 21–25; Jackie Koszcuk, "Judge Frees One Exec in Cyanide Trial." *Daily Herald* (May 15, 1985), p. 1.
22. E. R. Shipp, "Workplace Death," p. A9.
23. *Wall Street Journal*, "Illinois Extradition Bid for Utah Man Is Rejected." (June 17, 1985), p. 4.
24. *Appellants' Brief*, pp. 24, 31–32, 35–37.
25. William Presecky, "2 Bosses Guilty in Death of Employee in '83." *Chicago Tribune* (September 8, 1993), sec. 2, p. 4.
26. Susan B. Garland, "The Safety Ruling Could Be Hazardous to Employers' Health." *Business Week* (February 20, 1989), p. 34.
Bill Richards, "Corporate Officials Ordered to Face Criminal Trial for Worker Injuries." *Wall Street Journal* (February 3, 1989), p. 86.
27. Ann Hagedorn and Ellen Joan Pollock, "Executives Acquitted in Work–Injury." *Wall Street Journal* (April 26, 1991), p. B4.
28. William Presecky, "2 Bosses Guilty," p. 4.
29. William Presecky, "3rd Exec Pleads Guilty in 1983 Death." *Chicago Tribune* (September 10, 1993), sec. 2, p. 2.

C. ITOH & CO. (AMERICA), INC. AND SUMITOMO CORPORATION OF AMERICA

Conflicts between the personnel policies of foreign multinational corporations (MNCs) in the United States and application of U.S. civil rights laws

One manifestation of the decline in America's once-vaunted international competitiveness and manufacturing strength has been the enormous growth of imports from foreign nations. Foreign products and brand names like Sony, Matsushita, Phillips, and Braun have become household words. While American consumers and even industrial companies increasingly seem to prefer foreign goods because of their perceived quality and price advantages over U.S.-made goods, U.S. manufacturers have been losing ground not only at home but also abroad. The result has been massive. In 1987 the United States international trade deficit totalled a whopping $171 billion. [1]

These large trade deficits have had to be paid for through borrowing from foreigners and also through selling U.S. assets to foreign investors. Thus, the United States has moved from a positive net investment position in the early 1980s to a negative international investment status in the latter part of the decade. (See Figure 1.) While the U.S. creditor position was a negative $402 billion in 1987, Japan's creditor status was a positive $260 billion. (See Figure 2.) Although the number of investments in the U.S. was slightly less in 1987 than in 1980 (Figure 3), the net dollar value was greater. Of 1,051 foreign investments in the U.S. in 1987, Japan led the way with 351. (See Figure 4.)

In this they have been bolstered by the declining price of the U.S. dollar in terms of their own currencies, and a decline in the price of U.S. companies because of their poor profits and the tight financial squeeze they have experienced as they have been losing in the global competition. Of the 351 Japanese investments in 1986, 68 were acquisitions, 58 new ventures, 31 joint ventures, 23 plant construction, and 5 equity investments. The other 104 went to branches, agencies, warehouses, offices, and so forth. [2]

The increased presence of foreign multinationals in the U.S. as employers has raised a host of operational problems (for example, treatment of minorities and job discipline issues) for the U.S. workers and society-at-large. [3] In an ironical twist of circumstances, foreigners are accused of being like the "Ugly Americans" of an earlier era when American companies were chastised for acting arrogantly abroad and being insensitive to local cultures and sensibilities. Foreign multinationals bring with them their own unique set of management and personnel policies developed and perfected in their respective homelands, just as the U.S. multinationals took their management systems and applied them to their overseas operations. In one sense, it is not unnatural to do so because the foreign MNC is both comfortable with them and feels them to be superior to local policies and, thereby, finds in them a source of competitive advantage. Of course, enlightened employers would want to adapt their management and personnel policies to conform to local laws

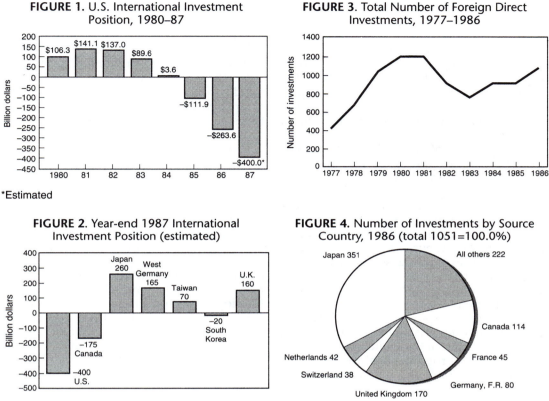

FIGURE 1. U.S. International Investment Position, 1980–87

*Estimated

FIGURE 2. Year-end 1987 International Investment Position (estimated)

FIGURE 3. Total Number of Foreign Direct Investments, 1977–1986

FIGURE 4. Number of Investments by Source Country, 1986 (total 1051=100.0%)

SOURCE: U.S. Department of Commerce, International Trade Administration, *Foreign Direct Investment in the United States, 1986 Transactions.* Washington, D.C.: U.S. Government Printing Office, 1987, pp. 4-5; and *United States Trade: Performance in 1987.* Washington, D.C.: U.S. Government Printing Office, 1988, pp. 8-9.

and mores. However, this is not always possible because of the conflicting intents and social objectives that underlie specific laws and a foreign MNC's operational policies. These may make strict compliance with local (U.S.) laws almost impossible except at the cost of abandoning or radically altering the FMNCs' unique practices and thereby losing their inherent "superiority." From the vantage point of the foreign MNC, its losses will serve only "to the benefit of its American workers."

Nowhere is this dilemma more profoundly illustrated than in the case of the Japanese and other Asia-based companies, on the one hand, and the compliance with U.S. civil rights laws in their personnel poli-

cies, on the other hand. Because of their almost monoracial national make-up and their highly distinctive cultural traits, their societies have evolved management systems that are quite dissimilar to those practiced by companies based in industrialized Western Europe and the United States. These companies also strongly believe that their superior manufacturing systems could not be separated from their distinctive management and personnel policies, and that to do so in any substantial degree would jeopardize the inherent soundness of their management infrastructure.

At the same time, U.S. civil rights laws reflect a strong desire to correct an historical wrong. They also represent a fundamental American belief in the equality of opportunity and elimination of injustice. Moreover, their scope is currently being widened to cope with changing societal needs and to protect individuals from new sources of discrimination as they emerge. Thus, any perceived violation of these laws evokes not only a legal but aslo a strong emotional response.

The frontiers of the Civil Rights laws and their expanded application are constantly being tested in issues such as reverse discrimination, on one hand, and the desire to have American multinationals operating overseas (in South Africa, for example) implement the intent of the law, on the other hand.[4] The latest, but certainly not the last, twist to the expanding scope of the civil rights statutes is the case of American employees suing Japanese multinationals for discrimination.

The two cases presented here illustrate a plethora of issues arising out of the working of foreign MNCs in the United States. These cases were brought against C. Itoh Corporation by its management-level employees who were U.S. citizens, and against Sumitomo Corporation of America, by the female American employees working in clerical positions. Although these cases deal with Japanese companies, they are atypical only in terms of the scope of their coverage and not necessarily in terms of the types of problems encountered. As a matter of fact, the U.S. Equal Opportunities Commission has become quite active in this area and is currently in various stages of investigation or litigation involving a number of foreign companies based both in Western European and Pacific Basin countries.

On February 21, 1975, three white American executives filed charges against the U.S. affiliate of C. Itoh (*Spiess et al.* v. *C. Itoh & Company* (America), (Inc.), alleging job discrimination because of their race and national origin.[5] The plaintiffs, Michael E. Spiess, Jack K. Hardy, and Benjamin

Rountree, were all American citizens and white Caucasians of non-Japanese national origin. Spiess had worked for Itoh since January 10, 1972, Hardy since September 22, 1969, and Rountree from June 12, 1970, until September 30, 1973. The plaintiffs performed middle-management duties. At the time their complaint was filed, all worked in Itoh's Houston offices. The suit was settled out of court in September, 1985. As part of the settlement, and at the insistence of C. Itoh, it was agreed that the terms of the settlement would not be disclosed in public by the plaintiffs.

In the Sumitomo case, twelve present and former female employees working as secretaries filed charges of national origin and sex discrimination.[6] On November 21, 1977, they sued as individuals and as representatives of a class, charging Sumitomo with unlawful sex and national origin discrimination in employment under the Equal Employment Opportunity Act of 1964, 42 U.S.C. 2000 et. seq. (Title VII), 42 U.S.C. 1981, and the Thirteenth Amendment to the Constitution. Compensatory and punitive damages were sought. The twelve plaintiffs were all employed in Sumitomo's New York office in clerical or secretarial positions: The Sumitomo case was settled out of court in a consent decree in February 1987.[7]

These cases are unusual and without any legal precedent. Therefore, the court decisions at various stages of litigation as well as the nature and scope of settlements ultimately reached would have a significant impact on the personnel practices of multinational corporations in the United States and abroad. Multinational corporations (MNCs) must contend with two factors in their overseas personnel policies and practices. One, they must conform to the local laws and customs that define the industrial relations of the foreign (host) country where their operations are located. Two, they must pay competitive wages and benefits to employees from the country of headquarters (home country) to persuade them to work in an overseas location. MNCs have been able to accomplish both objectives through a dual personnel policy by which all host-country employees are treated in accordance with the local employment laws. Employees from the MNC's home office are treated according to the laws and competitive conditions prevailing in the home country.

ISSUES FOR ANALYSIS

The issues involved are by no means simple, either as to fact or as to law.

1. Should a foreign multinational have a right to bring its own people (foreign nationals) into the United States for specific management jobs or must it hire local people in the U.S. if similarly qualified people are available?
2. The comparative similarity of candidate qualifications and the job functions may be more apparent than real. A foreign multinational may have a different management philosophy and operational style, which are the product of the particular sociocultural milieu of the home country and people. This difference in management philosophy and operating style may make it difficult, if not impossible, for any direct comparisons of job specifications or individual qualifications as to suitability for certain jobs. What criteria can be used for comparing job performance and individual qualifications under those circumstances?
3. When a foreign multinational uses its own people for certain jobs with its U.S. affiliate because it considers those jobs "highly sensitive" and important not only in terms of its U.S. operations, but also in terms of its overall global operations, how must it justify those decisions to avoid charges of job discrimination?
4. A foreign multinational may have a psychological predisposition to hire its own people for certain top management jobs in its U.S. and other overseas operations. Should this be considered a prerogative of the owners, or should it be considered a job restriction based on national origin?
5. The civil rights laws were essentially a societal response to a dramatic change in the national climate as regards domestic discrimination by U.S. firms against blacks. In many instances, expatriate personnel of foreign multinationals are members of a racial, color, or national-origin minority group by statutory definition. Considering these factors, should foreign multinationals doing business in the United States be subject to the civil rights laws in their employment practices?
6. Foreign multinationals are entitled to operate in the United States under treaties of friendship, commerce, and navigation that carefully define the rights each nation will render to the nationals and products of the other. Distinctions are made in many of the treaty provisions between U.S. subsidiaries of foreign firms incorporated under U.S. laws and branch offices of foreign multinationals. Essential to the successful operation of a multinational is the ability to use nationals from the home country of the parent firm for "sensitive" positions, a right recognized by treaty. Do these treaties permitting such commercial activities exempt or qualify the applicability of the civil rights laws to foreign multinationals?
7. Not all discrimination is prohibited under the civil rights laws; discrimination resulting from a *bona fide occupational qualification* (BFOQ) is permitted. Do expatriate personnel job positions constitute a bona fide occupational qualification? Are there other exemptions by which expatriate employment practices can be legally justified?
8. If U.S. affiliates of foreign multinationals are subject to U.S. civil rights laws, what changes in expatriate employment policies and practices are required to achieve compliance with the laws?

BACKGROUND TO THE U.S. CIVIL RIGHTS LAWS

The Civil Rights Act of 1866 and, particularly, the Civil Rights Act of 1964, Title VII, were designed primarily to protect minority groups in the United States from job discrimination.[8] As should be the case, these laws were passed specifically to satisfy societal needs and circumstances unique to the United States.[9]

At the time the 1964 act was passed, there was little question about what groups needed the most protection.[10] The legal scope and enforcement effort was gradually expanded to other groups that faced job discrimination—Hispanic Americans, women, and the aged. It also became apparent that discrimination may result not only from intentional discriminatory acts, but also from business practices that have unintentional discriminatory consequences.[11] In addition, eradication of discrimination arising out of historical antecedents and past practices may not be instant because of a paucity of qualified candidates in the minority groups. Thus, remedial attention was focused on affirmative action plans and "good-faith" efforts on the part of employers.[12]

THE CASE AGAINST ITOH: PLAINTIFF'S ALLEGATIONS

On February 21, 1975, three white male executives of C. Itoh (America), Inc., sued as individuals and as representatives of a class, charging Itoh with unlawful deprivation of civil rights of the plaintiffs and others similarly situated.[13] The civil action was brought under 42 U.S.C. Section 1981 (1974), formerly the Civil Rights Act of 1866 (hereafter Section 1981), and Title VII of the Civil Rights Act of 1964, as amended, 42 U.S.C. Section 2000e (1974) et seq. (hereafter Title VII). Compensatory damages of $8 million and punitive damages of $5 million were sought. The plaintiffs in the Itoh case alleged that except for participation in the management of defendant (Itoh), from which they had been unlawfully excluded, they performed the same types and quality of work as did certain of Itoh's nonsecretarial employees who were of Japanese national origin. In many instances, primarily involving negotiations and servicing of major contracts with U.S. corporations and various agencies of the U.S. government, plaintiffs contended that their understanding of American business

and social practices enabled them to outperform their Japanese counterparts. Yet, despite their accomplishments, the plaintiffs charged that defendant Itoh discriminated, intentionally and otherwise, against them and in favor of employees of Japanese national origin with respect to compensation, terms, conditions, and privileges of employment.[14]

They alleged that this discrimination, in direct violation of Title VII, included, but was not limited to, the following practices:

1. Paying monthly salaries to the Japanese at least 20% greater than the monthly salaries paid to the non-Japanese.
2. Paying midyear summer bonuses in excess of $4,000 to Japanese employees but not making such payments to the non-Japanese.
3. Paying year-end bonuses to the Japanese substantially greater than those paid to the non-Japanese.
4. Providing direct reimbursement of substantially all medical and dental expenses, in excess of that provided by insurance, to Japanese but not to non-Japanese employees.
5. Paying personal automobile insurance premiums for Japanese but not for non-Japanese employees.
6. Providing loans to Japanese employees to enable them to purchase automobiles, homes, and speculative securities for their personal accounts, but not making any such funds available to non-Japanese employees.
7. Providing automatic pay increases of up to 50% of monthly compensation based upon marital status and size of family to Japanese but not to non-Japanese employees.
8. Providing to each Japanese employee but not to non-Japanese employees a subsidy for the rental of personal living quarters in amounts equal to one-half of the excess of such rental payments over 20% of monthly net salary.
9. Unlawfully segregating and classifying its employees according to whether they are of Japanese or non-Japanese national origin, as demonstrated by the initials "J" (standing for "Japanese") and "A" (standing for "American") appearing after each employee's name on the monthly payroll records.
10. Limiting the employment opportunities of its non-Japanese employees by refusing to promote them to managerial positions.

11. Regularly holding evening staff meetings to discuss and plan management policies which only the Japanese employees were permitted to attend.

The plaintiffs further charged that these discriminatory employment practices were in existence during the entire tenure of their employment and continued thereafter. Plaintiffs also insisted that these discriminatory employment practices remained a closely guarded secret among Itoh's Japanese employees until one employee unintentionally indicated the existence of these practices to Hardy. At no time before the plaintiffs accepted the Itoh job offers did any representative of Itoh inform them of these practices. To the contrary, plaintiffs, as intelligent and capable American businesspeople, were induced to work for Itoh by company representations that it treated its employees with fairness and impartiality and that positions of management and responsibility could be attained by dedication and hard work, regardless of one's national origin. The plaintiffs were thus induced to spend what could otherwise have been some of the most personally and financially rewarding years of their lives working for Itoh. Furthermore, Itoh allegedly refused to train its non-Japanese employees for higher management-level positions. Itoh evaluated its employees on the basis of a double standard, one for Japanese and another for non-Japanese, which effectively precluded non-Japanese employees from attaining management positions. The plaintiffs contended that had they known of these discriminatory employment practices, they would never have accepted jobs with Itoh.

Rountree left Itoh's employment shortly after the civil action was filed. Spiess and Hardy were notified on December 30, 1975, that Itoh was terminating their employment as of January 9, 1976. Itoh's reason was that Spiess and Hardy had removed from company files certain documents designated as confidential information not to be removed without permission from company officials.

Spiess and Hardy alleged that Itoh had engaged in "retaliatory firing" in violation of their civil rights. They sought a temporary restraining order, contending that the documents in question were furnished only to plaintiff's counsel to be used in furtherance of their Title VII suit.

The district court refused to grant the temporary restraining order. An employee, the court held, may not engage in unlawful or unethical conduct under the guise of promoting the public interest favoring nondiscriminatory employment practices. Nor would the court contenance the "theft" of confidential data based on an attorney-client relationship rationale, since the plaintiff's counsel could have sought the documents in question through discovery. The court concluded: "Judicially protecting an employee's assistance and participation equitably is one thing; protecting the taking of documents unauthorizedly is another."[15]

THE CASE AGAINST SUMITOMO PLAINTIFFS' ALLEGATIONS

The plaintiffs in the Sumitomo case alleged that Sumitomo was guilty of national origin and sex discrimination by denying women promotions to executive, managerial, and sales positions in favor of Japanese males.[16] According to the complaint:

> Plaintiffs bring this as a class action to 23(a) and (b)(2), of the Federal Rules of Civil Procedure, on their own behalf and on behalf of all women who have worked for the defendant, are working for the defendant, have left employment of the defendant because of its discriminatory policies, or may seek employment with the defendant. The members of this class, or classes, are discriminated against in ways which deprive them or have deprived them of equal employment opportunities by reason of their sex, and/or nationality.

The specific cause of action was that Sumitomo Corporation of America (SCOA) restricted the plaintiffs to clerical jobs and refused to train or promote them to executive, managerial, and/or sales positions on the basis of both sex and racial discrimination. At the time the suit was filed, the plaintiffs alleged that Sumitomo had no women employees above the clerical level, and no training programs in the U.S. to qualify women (or American males) for higher-level jobs. The plaintiffs also alleged that even though they may have had as much education, and were doing the same work, they were denied promotion to higher-level jobs held by Japanese males. In the words of Lisa Avigliano: "You just knew you weren't going to get anywhere. I was doing the same job as most of the Japanese men, but I knew it was useless to think I could have the same opportunities, even though I had as much education. All the women were in clerical jobs. I think they really honestly thought women were inferior."[17]

THE COMPANIES: C. ITOH & CO. INC. AND SUMITOMO CORPORATION OF AMERICA

C. Itoh & Company (America), Inc., is a wholly owned subsidiary of C. Itoh & Company, Ltd. of Japan, which in 1988 had total trading transactions of $123.97 billion, gross trading profits of $2.2 billion, and net profit of $202 million. It is the leading integrated trading company (*sogo sosha*) "with a fully integrated worldwide network of 187 offices in 85 nations, including 41 in Japan, 585 affiliated companies, and over 10,000 employees located throughout the world."[18] It trades in many areas including communications, textiles, machinery and construction, metals and ore, food and agriculture, forest products, energy and chemicals, and general merchandise. C. Itoh and Co. (America) Inc. is a flagship subsidiary of the parent and is a general trading company. Although separate financial statements are not issued, it does business of several billion dollars a year, of which approximately 65% constitutes exports from the U.S. to Japan and other countries, and 35% involves imports from Japan and other countries. Itoh (America) and the parent company deal in some 50,000 commodities. Itoh (Japan) maintains locally incorporated companies in 12 major countries in the world and also branches and representative offices in more than 100 principal cities in Japan and overseas.

According to a company brochure, Itoh (Japan) has "a positive attitude on capital and trade liberalization in Japan." The company states its management philosophy thus:

> The general trading companies fulfill all round and diversified functions for the promotion of trade, efficiency of distribution and performance of various development projects. In line with the rapid changes of circumstances at home and abroad and in accordance with the new demands of society, C. Itoh will become increasingly dynamic in its functions. Recently, the social and economic environment has become subject to rapid changes on an international scale, and all the peoples of the world have come to expect their share of the world's riches. Therefore, C. Itoh has become very much aware of its mission and the role which it must perform with regard to changes of social and economic environment, and is also very much aware of the need for social responsibility in business activities. C. Itoh earnestly desires to contribute to the betterment of social welfare with due regard to international activities, on the basis of its desire for international cooperation. C. Itoh strives to foster the harmonious development of the world and betterment of the quality of life of its inhabitants.

Sumitomo Corporation of America is a subsidiary of Sumitomo Corporation (Japan), a member of the Sumitomo Group, which is similar in structure and operation to C. Itoh. In 1987, the parent company's gross trading volume stood at $89.4 billion. Gross profits were $1.4 billion and net profits $201,527 million.[19]

Both companies are "integrated general trading companies (*sogo sosha*)." Sumitomo put its overall business philosophy this way:[20]

A business principle of Sumitomo Corporation of America is that the interests of people and society should be placed before that of individual enterprises. Increasingly, American industry strives to accommodate public interest and we are uniquely equipped to cooperate, because we are long experienced at combining public and business interests for the benefit of both.

Sogo sosha possess vast communications networks that span the world, collecting and transmitting data on day to day commodity prices, markets, areas of surplus and storage, and everything that bears on trade. But a *sogo sosha*'s undertakings may spread beyond trade and distribution of goods to financing, engineering and construction, to transportation and natural resources development...

Sogo sosha differ from other companies in that they are supply/demand oriented and work to solve such problems. When a demand for goods and services is identified, *sogo sosha* immediately look for a way to satisfy it.

Japanese trading companies are already a big factor among the Japanese businesses operating in the United States. During 1981, American subsidiaries of Japan's *sogo sosha* accounted for close to 10% of total trade.

According to brochures and interviews with representatives of both companies, they claim to contribute to United States trade and investment in three ways:

1. As a conduit through which American capital goods, coal and minerals, wood pulp, grain, raw cotton, chemicals, construction machinery, scrap metal, computers, aircraft, and foodstuffs flow to Japan and other nations.
2. As a supplier to the American market of industrial and consumer goods—textiles, steel, electronic equipment, footwear, radio and television sets, phonographs, plywood,

foodstuffs, bicycles, automobiles—produced in Japan and other countries.
3. As an active partner or as the creator, sponsor, and organizer of joint ventures and licensing arrangements in the United States, Japan, and elsewhere for American companies.

Organizational Structure: Parent-Subsidiary Relationships

Corporate organizational charts are provided as Exhibits 1, 2, and 3 on pp. 268-69. We use C. Itoh to clarify the general picture. The point of organizational authority proved to be very important, as is the geographic place of incorporation.

For C. Itoh, the hierarchy of authority begins with the board of directors (*yakuin*) and continues through the president (*sochihainin*); executive vice-president (*sochihainin daiko*); managers of divisions (*bucho*), who are considered vice-presidents; in some cases, assistant managers of divisions (*buchodaiko*); managers of departments (*kacho*); in some cases, assistant managers of departments (*kachodairi*); supervisors (*kakaricho*); in some cases, assistant supervisors (*kakaricho daiko*); and finally, the section members, the low-level employees, plus secretaries, clerks, and porters. This is in addition to various staff departments commonly found in any large business organization.

The relationship between Itoh (America) and Itoh (Japan) is that of a subordinate-superior. Decisions regarding management staff, (particularly top management and Japanese staff) rests almost exclusively with Itoh (Japan). In choosing an executive vice-president to serve as "the right hand or left hand" of the president of Itoh (America), the board of directors has authority, theoretically, to approve a candidate. In reality, the candidate is selected by and sent from Itoh (Japan).[21] Thus, even though a business unit may be incorporated in the United States—as both SCOA and Itoh America are—real organizational authority rests with Japan.

EXHIBIT 1. Organizational Chart of C. Itoh & Company (America), Inc.

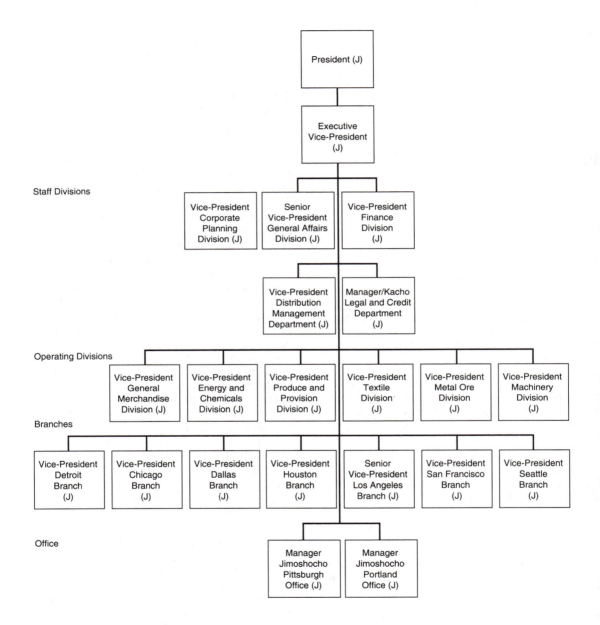

Staff Divisions

Operating Divisions

Branches

Office

President (J)

Executive Vice-President (J)

Vice-President Corporate Planning Division (J)

Senior Vice-President General Affairs Division (J)

Vice-President Finance Division (J)

Vice-President Distribution Management Department (J)

Manager/Kacho Legal and Credit Department (J)

Vice-President General Merchandise Division (J)

Vice-President Energy and Chemicals Division (J)

Vice-President Produce and Provision Division (J)

Vice-President Textile Division (J)

Vice-President Metal Ore Division (J)

Vice-President Machinery Division (J)

Vice-President Detroit Branch (J)

Vice-President Chicago Branch (J)

Vice-President Dallas Branch (J)

Vice-President Houston Branch (J)

Senior Vice-President Los Angeles Branch (J)

Vice-President San Francisco Branch (J)

Vice-President Seattle Branch (J)

Manager Jimoshocho Pittsburgh Office (J)

Manager Jimoshocho Portland Office (J)

EXHIBIT 2. Organizational Chart of a Typical Staff Division

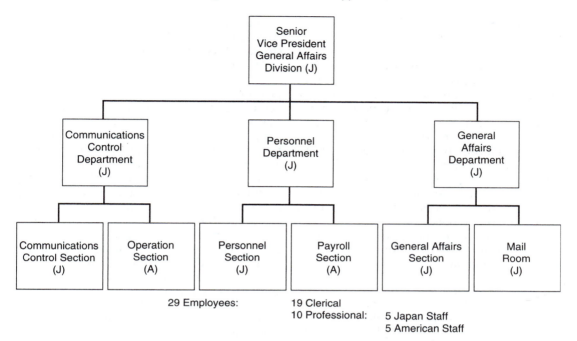

29 Employees: 19 Clerical
10 Professional: 5 Japan Staff
5 American Staff

EXHIBIT 3. Organizational Chart of a Typical Operating Division

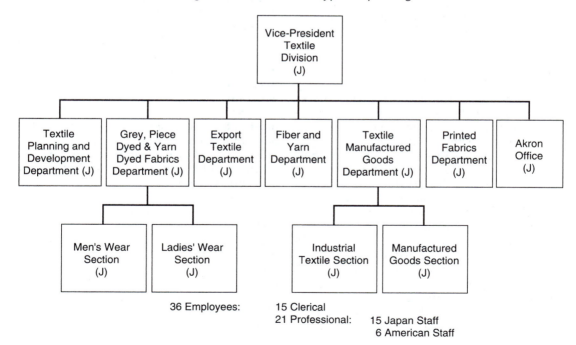

36 Employees: 15 Clerical
21 Professional: 15 Japan Staff
6 American Staff

EMPLOYMENT AND OTHER PERSONNEL POLICIES

Although indigenization of employees has increased significantly in the last decade, expatriates continue to play an important role in overseas operations, especially with the continuing increase in international trade and the liberalization of investment policies by most nations. Both companies claim to have a flexible personnel policy, which is determined in light of perceived competitive advantage, given the nature of the business itself. It is these factors, not discrimination, which determine policy.

Itoh had a stated policy of nondiscrimination set forth in the American staff's employee's manual.[22]

> It is the policy of C. Itoh & Company (America), Inc., and its subsidiaries that all applicants for employment are considered only on the basis of merit, without discrimination because of race, creed, national origin, age or sex. Our employment practices ensure equal treatment to all employees without distinction in pay or opportunity because of an employee's color, religion, national origin, age or sex.

The "Job" and "Tasks"

In an interview, Sumitomo representatives explained how their historical personnel policies were in part a function of the nature of the business of being a trading company.[23] Beginning in the 1960s, the nature of their trading was primarily marketing Japanese goods in the USA. The products were easy to sell because of high quality and low price. It was also easy to find American outlets to market them. The key strategic relation, therefore, was with the supplier, who was Japanese. As far as SCOA was concerned, the key persons in their operations were the "rotating staff," who were Japanese. It is, in fact, their *expertise* the suppliers were buying.

The primary "job" of rotating staff amounted to responsibility for a customer's account or project to satisfy the supplier by channeling goods to markets. "Job" understood in this sense could entail any number of "tasks,"—in other words, whatever was necessary to handle the project. Secondary positions were filled by "support staff," the key word being support. In the SCOA offices, they were called secretaries; in fact, they were supposed to do anything required to support the work of the rotating staff. This included administrative tasks such as customs clearance and documentation, communicating with customers, handling minor complaints, as well as performing clerical tasks.

Difficulties arose at SCOA when the support staff personnel realized that they were doing many of the same "tasks" as rotating staff and yet did not have the same career or job opportunities. According to SCOA representatives, it was not unusual for rotating staff to negotiate a deal and come back and type up the documentation attendant to it—it would all be the "same job." The secretaries' impression that they were doing the same job was further underlined by the physical organization of a typical Japanese office, where everyone sits in one open room. In the American office, a secretary understands that he or she does not do, nor does he or she have the ability to do, what the boss does. Furthermore, in the U.S., a secretary generally has a good grasp of the boss' business. Such was not the case at SCOA, where most of the real business was handled internally in Japanese. Thus, as far as "tasks" go, there was a clear overlap between what the rotating and support staff did. But for the Japanese, the job responsibilities were clearly distinct.

However, Itoh also made a fundamental distinction between their "Japan staff" and "American staff." "Japan staff" were employees sent by the parent company to work in the United States. "American staff" were all other employees and included workers of Chinese and Korean origin. "American staff" also included Japanese who were born and raised in the United States. Although of

"Japanese national origin," as that term is used in the civil rights laws, they were not considered Japan staff by Itoh. According to the testimony of Sadao Nishitomi, secretary and EEO coordinator of Itoh (America), taken during the course of depositions by the plaintiff's attorney in September 1975, this staff distinction appeared on payroll records.[24] When asked how far up in the ranks of C. Itoh (America) a member of the American staff could climb, Sadao Nishitomi, the EEO coordinator for Itoh (America), responded: "As far as I understand it, any employee can climb up in rank, all the way up, excepting for the position of president."[25]

The testimony of Sadao Nishitomi, was to the point. He indicated that Japan staff were favored over American staff in management positions because Japan staff were believed to possess *shosha*. Literally translated as "intensive industry knowledge" or "moving think tank," *shosha* describes an individual with extensive knowledge about an industry. Such a person possesses the ability to collect relevant information, analyze this information, and apply the results to a business transaction on a higher level. Mr. Nishitomo testified that, while the American staff could, "with good effort on their part," acquire this capability, there were very few who had that capacity. When asked how an American could acquire *shosha*, Mr. Nishitomi responded that the American would have to apply for a position with Itoh (Japan), after overcoming very stiff employment competition, and work up the employment ladder with Itoh (Japan).[26]

In filing the lawsuit, C. Itoh's American managerial employees contended that training courses for Americans to develop *shosha* were not available, and Americans were not transferred to Japan with the parent company for experience. Although Japanese-language training through the Berlitz schools was subsidized for all employees by Itoh (America), no formal notification of the availability of the program was circulated to the American staff.

Itoh (America)'s stated nondiscriminatory policy notwithstanding, there was no established procedure or criteria by which management staff were selected to head departments or fill other supervisory positions. The result, as demonstrated through Nishitomi's testimony, was a general systematic exclusion of Americans from higher managerial positions. Nishitomi himself had never chosen an American manager. Only one American in the Itoh (America) organization served at the level of vice-president or above, and this title was largely illusory, since the employee functioned only as *shitencho daiko*, or assistant manager of a branch office. After some years of service, the employee was still performing the same job and exercised the same authority as he did when first employed by Itoh (America). Significantly, his position as vice-president did not appear on a formal list of the executive officers of Itoh (America).

The disadvantages under which American staff operated in rising to managerial positions is demonstrated by the appointment of Mr. Ogata, formerly with Itoh (Japan), as *kacho* or department manager of the personnel department.[27] Prior to his appointment in February 1975, Ogata was with Itoh (Japan). Because the *kakaricho* of the personnel department related to both Japan and American staff, Itoh (America) felt the position should be filled by a Japan staff member. Testimony by Nishitomi established that while Ogata lacked knowledge about American personnel matters, this deficiency could be overcome by appointing a knowledgeable American staff member to assist him. Conversely, there was a reluctance to appoint an American staff member as *kacho* and give him a knowledgeable Japan staff member to compensate for a lack of expertise in Japanese personnel matters. Thus, if a Japanese candidate with suitable qualifications could not be found within the Itoh (America) organization, a request was made to the personnel department of the parent company for some Japanese candidates who might be transferred to the U.S. Recruitment from outside the organization was not even considered.

It was not at all unusual for a Japanese to hold a number of unrelated functional positions within the Itoh organization until a certain position could be filled by the parent company. Nishitomi's many "hats"—secretary of Itoh (America), manager of the general affairs division, manager of the communication control department, and EEO coordinator—illustrate this tendency. Nor did it appear to be essential that Japanese staff members have special training in the activities they were managing. Thus, American staff members may have had better credentials than the Japan staff persons. However, since the Japan staff persons were considered to be on twenty-four-hour duty (while the Americans worked between designated hours), Itoh felt that the nature of the Japan staff's work was different.

At Itoh, an essential difference between Japan staff and American managerial staff resulted from special skills "not able to be acquired in the United States." Nishitomi testified that Japan staff were ". . . mostly engaged in the transaction or the business transaction within Japan which would require in-depth knowledge of customs and habits of business transactions in Japan, which would not be too easy for American staff to acquire. . . ." The converse, however, is not necessarily true. American staff were not assumed to have a "correspondingly greater knowledge of American business practices and companies than members of the Japan staff" when doing business in the United States. As Nishitomi testified, ". . . those who are back in Japan might have a long-standing business relationship with foreign countries and they might have knowledge of foreign countries from that way, as well . . . ."[28]

Career Path

Both Sumitomo and Itoh had a more complicated personnel policy than the model described above. In understanding the difference between the treatment of Japan staff and American staff, it is important to recognize the distinction that exists in the Japanese management system between "status levels" and "functional authority."[29]

Functional authority is a familiar concept for American managers and describes the typical chain of command found in organization charts. It is based on a job description in terms of specific tasks each person is to perform. Each position on the chart has certain assigned job responsibilities in terms of functions. Distinctions are drawn between line and staff functions. Hierarchical relationships between members of the organization, the degree of authority within the organizational structure, and compensation are all determined by the functional position of the individual within the organization.

"Status" is a Japanese concept and reflects an individual's standing in the organization based on such factors as length of service (seniority) and level of achievement or accomplishment. A correlation between status and functional position is not necessary. Status is best described as similar to an attitudinal response that American firms may informally display toward an "old and trusted" employee who is given supervisory responsibilities, special assignments, and additional compensation because of "long and faithful service" to the company that may not be reflected in the actual functional job position occupied by the employee. The concept of status is a formalized, organizational response to the traditional Japanese system of lifetime employment. Once an individual is employed, he or she remains with the firm until retirement age is reached unless employment is terminated for breach of company rules and regulations.

Itoh (America), like its parent, has eight status levels, ranging from *sankyu* to *sanyo* (see Appendix, Glossary of Japanese Terms). *Sankyu* is the lowest level and is assigned to an employee who has just graduated from college and joined the Itoh (Japan) staff. This position is that of a recruit or, in the words of Sadao Nishitomi, a private in a military organization.[30] *Sanyo* is the top level awarded to employees who have been with Itoh (Japan) for a number of years and contributed to the firm's welfare through loyal and dedicated service. This position can best be described as that of a commissioned officer. Though it is possible that a person of higher status may report to a person of lower status because of a difference in funtional authority, Itoh makes an effort to avoid this kind of conflict. Thus, individual positions exist in Itoh (America) with no fuctional titles, and individuals occupying those jobs perform managerial functions. A Japan staff member will rarely be in a subordinate position reporting to an American staff member, a policy that minimizes the inherent potential conflict between status and function.

Compensation

Itoh's management system resulted in a dual personnel compensation and promotion system, one for the Japan staff and one for the American staff, each with its own employee operating manual. This dualism did not apply in the Sumitomo case for, as the plaintiffs alleged, they were confined to a clerical level and precluded from management. But, taking the dual management tracks at C. Itoh, Japanese staff were paid primarily on the basis of status and Americans on the basis of functional authority. The result was a notable difference in pay and benefits.

An American worker started at a salary level substantially lower than that of a Japanese at the same functional level. Americans were paid a gross salary; Japan staff were guaranteed a net salary. Itoh therefore followed a practice of "grossing up" for its Japan staff. All taxes—federal, state, and local—were estimated and that amount added to the Japanese staff's salary so that the employee would receive the guaranteed net. In addition, midyear bonuses were paid to Japanese staff, but not to the American

staff. The amount of the midyear bonus was determined by Itoh (Japan) but charged against the accounts of Itoh (America).

Medical insurance was available for both American staff and Japanese staff. However, the Japanese staff was immediatly eligible for benefits, while the American staff had to first satisfy a three-month eligibility requirement before benefits could be received.

Until March 31, 1974, Itoh sponsored a program of rental subsidies for the Japanese staff only. Although that program was discontinued, the Japanese staff still had available to them a lease termination subsidy not open to the American staff. Automobile purchase and vehicle insurance were subsidized by Itoh (America) only for its Japanese staff. While loans were available to all Itoh employees, only the Japanese staff was officially notified of the availability of assistance.

The Japanese staff also received a family allowance—30% of the base salary for the wife, 10% for each child of school age and above, and 5% for each child under school age, not to exceed 50% of the base salary. The allowance was paid, if necessary, directly to the family member who remained in Japan. Thus, Itoh (Japan) would pay an allowance in yen to children of Japan staff attending college in Japan. Itoh (Japan) would then charge Itoh (America) for the amount of this allowance in dollars to be included in the salary of the employee. The allowance paid by the parent company appeared on the withholding tax statement furnished to the employee by Itoh (America) for income tax purposes. This family allowance was not available to American staff, since their salaries were paid "according to what is practiced generally in the U.S. business environment," based upon the assumption that the American staff employee has taken into consideration the amount needed as a family allowance.

ITOH'S AND SUMITOMO'S DEFENSE

The civil action against Itoh began in the U.S. District Court at Houston (where the plaintiffs won), and was appealed to the Fifth Circuit Court of Appeals (where they lost 2 to 1). The Supreme Court did not hear the Itoh case, for in the meantime the Court agreed to hear the Sumitomo case, which had been brought two years after the Itoh case but which moved more quickly through the court system.

Both Itoh and Sumitomo initially moved for dismissal and lost. Itoh mounted a two-pronged defense. The company first questioned the right of the plaintiffs to bring suit under Title VII of the Civil Rights Act. Secondly, it claimed that Itoh was protected by the Treaty of Friendship concluded by the United States and Japan in 1953.

Itoh's interpretation of civil rights laws led it to challenge the plaintiff's standing to sue.[31] Itoh filed a motion to dismiss on March 6, 1975, in which it contended that the plaintiffs, as white citizens, were not protected by Section 1981 of Title VII. Section 1981 provides: "All persons within the jurisdiction of the United States shall have the same rights . . . to the full and equal benefit of all laws . . . as is enjoyed by white citizens . . . ."

Itoh argued that since the standard set forth in Section 1981 is rights "enjoyed by white citizens," only nonwhites have standing to sue under Section 1981 and Title VII. Itoh claimed that the plaintiffs, by the clear and unequivocal terms of Section 1981, must demonstrate as whites that they had been denied the same rights given by Itoh to its other white employees. Since Itoh treated all its white employees equally, which means its American staff, the plaintiffs failed to satisfy the statutory burden imposed under Section 1981. The motion was denied by the district court on January 29, 1976, since the statute eradicates "all social discrimination in the enumerated rights rather than merely [elevating] nonwhite citizens above white citizens to a privileged legal status because of race." The cutting edge of Section 1981, the judge held, was "protection against discrimination on the basis of race, not protection against discrimination by numerical majorities."[32]

Five months later, the Supreme Court would rule in the McDonald case that both Section 1981 and Title VII prohibit racial discrimination in private employment against white persons as well as nonwhite.[33]

> . . . we cannot accept the view that the terms of Section 1981 exclude its application to racial discrimination against white persons. On the contrary, the statute explicitly applies to "all persons.". . . While a mechanical reading of the phrase "as is enjoyed by white citizens" would seem to lend support to respondents' reading of the statute, we have previously described this phrase simply as emphasizing "the racial character of the rights being protected."

The second legal defense raised by Itoh (America), in a motion to dismiss filed on May 10, 1978, was that Itoh's employment practices were "immunized" under the terms of the U.S.-Japan Treaty of Friendship, Commerce and Navigation. Sumitomo also employed this defense.[34]

Itoh argued that the effect of the U.S.-Japan Treaty was to create an absolute right on the part of American and Japanese firms to employ in each other's countries managerial and specialized personnel of their choice to the exclusion of nationals of their host country. Since the treaty predates Title VII and the reenactment of Section 1981, and since the legislative history of both acts is devoid of any reference to treaty commitments, the treaty thus "immunizes" Itoh from the impact of Section 1981 and Title VII to the extent that Itoh discriminates in favor of its nationals. Accordingly, Itoh contended that the plaintiffs have not stated a cause of action upon which relief can be granted.

Sumitomo's Defense

Sumitomo followed a similar tack.[35] Dismissal was sought by Sumitomo pursuant to F.R.Civ. P. 12(b)(6) on the ground that the 1953 Treaty of Friendship, Commerce and Navigation between the United States and

Japan . . . exempts Japanese trading companies and their wholly owned subsidiaries incorporated in the United States from the application of Title VII.[36] The chronology of events in the Sumitomo legal proceedings was as follows: In December 1976, SCOA was charged by the EEOC; in September 1977, it brought the Treaty Argument and in December of that year it was faced with a class-action lawsuit. In May 1978, the company filed a motion to dismiss, which was denied in June the following year. In May 1980, the second circuit agreed to hear the case and in January 1981 it gave its judgment. In June 1981, Sumitomo appealed to the Supreme Court. The Court accepted to hear the case in November 1981, and the hearing took place in April 1982, with a decision handed down in June 1982. In February 1982, the plaintiffs filed a motion for class certification and by August 1982, Sumitomo filed for dismissal. Class certification was granted in November 1984. In January 1986, settlement talks started. An agreement was reached in January 1987, the Court approved it in March, and it became effective in June 1987.

The "treaty" defense argument in the Sumitomo case was decided by the Supreme Court on June 15, 1982. The attorney for the Itoh plaintiffs pointed out in an interview that the Supreme Court opinion borrowed significantly from Judge Reveally, who was the dissenting judge in the Houston Fifth Circuit Court of Appeals. The essence of the argument is that the "nationality" of a corporation depends on where it is incorporated. For the Court's purposes, Sumitomo was an American corporation. Chief Justice Burger stated, in part:[37]

> The purpose of the treaties was not to give foreign corporations greater rights than domestic companies, but instead to assure them the right to conduct business on an equal basis without suffering discrimination based on their alienage."

And, because the company is a subsidiary incorporated in the State of New York:

We are persuaded, as both signatories agree, that under the literal language of Article XXII(3) of the Treaty, Sumitomo is a company of the United States: we discern no reason to depart from the plain meaning of the Treaty language. Accordingly, we hold that Sumitomo is not a company of Japan and is thus not covered by Article VIII(1) of the Treaty.

The Supreme Court thus reached an extremely limited decision and left many questions unanswered. Moreover, it explicitly did not rule on a line of defense which, by implication, may have been the most fruitful for both Itoh and Sumitomo to employ: the bona fide occupational qualification (BFOQ). In a footnote to the decision, Chief Justice Burger explicitly addressed this issue when he stated:

> We express no view as to whether Japanese citizenship may be a bona fide occupational qualification for certain positions at Sumitomo or as to whether a business necessity defense may be available. . . . Whether Sumitomo can support its assertion of a bona fide occupational qualification or a business necessity defense is not before us.

Itoh saw that its prospects for victory under the treaty defense were limited indeed. Sometime after the Supreme Court decision, it moved to settle. By September 1985, it had concluded a confidential settlement with the plaintiffs.

Sumitomo's problem was a bit more complex. The plaintiffs' suit against it was certified as a class action suit. After the Supreme Court decision, Sumitomo had a change of strategy and was bent on settling, as manifested by the fact that it changed its legal counsel. The company declined to pursue the case in court on the question of bone fide occupational qualifications and eventually entered into a consent decree effective March 30, 1987. In declining to pursue the case further, company representatives cited transaction costs, the adverse effects on company image and on the morale of personnel, and the fact that the nature of the business had changed sufficiently to call for a new personnel policy anyway. (In fact, company representatives maintained that, had litigation not been pending, they would have initiated new policies in many of the areas of complaint much sooner).

Sumitomo described the conditions of the consent decree in a press release to announce the settlement:[38]

The settlement agreement contains various monetary provisions, good faith staffing goals and objectives, a job titling and compensation program, career development actions, a process for the resolution of any dispute by a court-appointed special master and customary monitoring and reporting provisions. Sumitomo Corporation of America will make all career development programs available to all personnel at its cost. It has agreed to dedicate $1 million for participation in various employee programs by female employees. The agreement runs for three years. . . . In the settlement, the company did not admit to any violations of law nor did the court make any such findings. Throughout the case SCOA consistently and emphatically denied allegations of discrimination on the basis of sex, national origin or race. Agreed-on goals, which are not quotas, in the agreement provide that the company will make a good faith effort to ensure that female employees hold 23 to 25 percent of the management and sales jobs at the company, including some senior management and senior sales positions, by the end of the three-year period.

Under the terms of the decree, Sumitomo retains the right to determine all employees' qualifications for promotion. This point seems to affirm that, indeed, there is something of substance to BFOQs. The consent decree emphasizes training programs to improve the qualifications of female employees.

NOTES

1. United States Department of Commerce, International Trade Administration, *United States Trade: Performance in 1987*. Washington, DC, U.S. Government Printing Office, 1988, pp. 11-13.
2. United States Department of Commerce, International Trade Administration, *Foreign Direct Investment in the United States: 1986 Transactions*, Washington, DC, U.S. Government Printing Office, 1987, p. 25.
3. Jacob M. Schlesinger, "Fleeing Factories." *Wall Street Journal* (April 12, 1988), p. 1.
4. Section 1981 explicitly applies to "all persons" including white persons. The phrase "as enjoyed by white citizens" simply emphasizes the racial character of the rights being protected. *McDonald v. Santa Fe Trail Transportation Company* 427 U.S. 273.96 S. Ct. 2574 (1976); see also *Regents of University of California v. Bakke*, U.S. 98 S. Ct. 2574 (1978).
5. *Michael E. Speiss, Jack K. Hardy, and Benjamin F. Rountree v. C. Itoh and Co. (America)*. Civil Action No. 75-H-267, United States District Court for the Southern District of Texas Houston Division.
6. *Lisa M. Avigliano, et al., v. Sumitomo Shoji America, Inc.*, 77 Civ. 5461, United States District Court, Southern District of New York.
7. 77 Civ. 5641, 82 Civ. 4390—consent decrees in full settlement of civil actions.
8. 42 U.S.C. Section 1981 (1974) and 42 U.S.C. Section 2000 (1974).
9. Debate by Senator Hubert H. Humphrey, reported in *Statuary History*, p. 1236. Therefore, the initial enforcement thrust on the part of the Equal Employment Opportunity Commission (EEOC) and the courts was directed to the protection of black minorities.
10. The first case to be considered by the Supreme Court involved a refusal of a Georgia motel to rent rooms to blacks. A bare five months after enactment of the 1964 Civil Rights Act, the Supreme Court upheld the constitutionality of the act, specifically Title II dealing with discrimination in public accommodations, *Heart of Atlanta Motel v. United States*. 379 U.S. 241M 85 S, CT. (1964).
11. The current emphasis on sex discrimination is illustrated by many recent court decisions,

including *Webster* v. *Secretary of Health Education & Welfare*, 43 F. Supp 127 C.N.Y. (1976), reversed on other grounds 430 U.S. 313 97 S Ct. 1192, striking down differences in Social Security payments paid to men and women; see also the Age Discrimination in Employment Act of 1967, 29 U.S.C. Section 623.

12. Title VII proscribes not only overt discrimination but also practices that are fair in form but discriminatory in operation without regard for intent or motivation; *Griggs* v. *Duke Power Co.*, 401 U.S. 424, 91 S. CT. 849 (1971). *Albermarle Paper Co.* v. *Moody*, 422 U.S. 405, 95 S. CT. 2362 (1975).

13. Courts have broad remedial powers not only to issue injunctions but also to order such affirmative action as may be appropriate to remedy unlawful employment practices. *Alexander* v. *Gardner-Denver Co.* 415 U.S. 36.94 S CT. 1011 (1974) and *Franks* v. *Bowman Transportation Co., Inc.* 424 U.S. 747.96 S, CT. 1251 (1976).

14. Michael E. Speiss, et. al. cited in note 5.

15. U.S. District Court for the Southern District of Texas Houston Division, Court's memorandum and Order, filed January 9, 1976, Court's Memorandum and Order, filed September 2, 1977.

16. *Avigliano, et al.* v. S*umitomo Shoji America, Inc.*, USDC SNY, No. 77 Civ. 5641, 1977.

17. Tamar Lewin, "A Complex Sex Bias Case." *New York Times* (April 4, 1982), pp. D1, D6.

18. C. Itoh and Co., Ltd., *Annual Report*, 1988; pp. 1, 20ff.

19. Sumitomo Corporation, *Annual Report*, 1987; pp. 1, 30-31.

20. Sumitomo Corporation, *Sumitomo Corporation of America*, annual brochure, p. 21.

21. Deposition of Sadao Nishitomo, secretary and EEO coordinator at Itoh America, taken at the offices of C. Itoh and Co., New York, NY, by the plaintiff's attorneys during the period September 10-26, 1975, pp. 571-578; 594-95.

22. Cited in S. Prakash Sethi, Nobuaki Namiki, and Carl L. Swanson, *The False Promises of the Japanese Miracle*. Boston, MA: Pitman Publishing Co., Inc., 1984, p. 68.

23. Sumitomo Corporation, Interview with Professor Sethi, September 1987.

24. Nishitomo, *Deposition*, pp. 633-58.

25. *Ibid.*

26. *Ibid.*, pp. 433-36; 453-55; 697-702.

27. *Ibid.*, pp. 643-653.

28. *Ibid.*, pp. 590-91.

29. *Ibid.*, pp. 184-87.

30. *Ibid.*, pp. 172, 184.

31. *Ibid.*, pp. 143-45; 249-50; 257-58; 272-77; 286-92; 304-18; 356-67.

32. U.S. District Court for the Southern District of Texas, "Memorandum and Opinion," January 29, 1976, cited in *Lexis Nexis*, pp. 13-14, 22.

33. *Ibid.*, pp. 22-31.

34. *Ibid.*, pp. 27-30.

35. U.S. District Court for the Southern District of Texas Houston Division, "Opinion, March 1, 1979," cited in *Lexis Nexis*, pp. 4-12; "Order, April 10, 1979," cited in *Lexis Nexis*, pp. 1-3.

36. Sumitomo Corporation, interview, September 1987.

37. Supreme Court of the United States, Nos. 80-2070 and 81-24, "Opinion," by Chief Justice Burger, June 15, 1982, p. 13.

38. Hill and Knowlton, Inc., "News Release for Sumitomo Corporation of America," February 24, 1987; April 6, 1987. U. S. District Court Southern District of New York, *Consent Decree In Full Settlement of Civil Actions, 77 Civ. 5641 (CHT); 82 Civ. 4930 (CHT)* .

Glossary of Japanese Terms follows on page 278

APPENDIX Glossary of Japanese Terms with English Equivalents

JAPANESE TERMS AS USED BY ITOH[a]	ENGLISH EQUIVALENTS AND/OR EXPLANATIONS
Organizational Titles	
yakuin	Member of the board of directors
sōshihainin	President
sōshihainin daikō	Executive vice-president
buchō	Division manager (vice-president)
shitenchō (equivalent to *buchō*)	Branch office manager (equivalent to vice-president)
buchō daikō	Assistant division or department manager (equivalent to assistant vice-president)
shitenchō daikō (equivalent to buchō daikō)	Assistant branch office manager (equivalent to assistant vice-president)
kachō	Department manager/section chief
kachō dairi	Assistant department manager/section chief
jimushochō	Manager of a subbranch office
kakarichō	Assistant section manager or supervisor
kakarichō daikō	Assistant supervisor
SM	Section members (low-level employees within a section, excluding secretaries, clerks, and porters)
daikō (the term *dairi* was used prior to April 1, 1975)	Assistant
Status Levels—Old and New Systems	
Old System (before April 1, 1975):	
sanyo	Head
ittōshain	Level 1
nittōshain	Level 2
santōshain	Level 3
yontōshain	Level 4
gotōshain	Level 5
New System (effective April 1, 1975):	
sanyo	Head
buchō-yaku	Chief (equivalent in military hierarchy to a commissioned officer)
buchō-ho	Assistant chief (commissioned officer status)
kachō-yaku	Manager (equivalent in military hierarchy to noncommissioned officer)
kachō-ho	Assistant manager (noncommissioned officer status)
ikkyu	First grade status (equivalent in military hierarchy to enlisted personnel—i.e., corporal)
nikyu	Second grade status (private first class)
sankyu	Third grade status (recruit right out of college)
Miscellaneous Terms	
Dowa Kaijō Kasai Hoken	Marine Fire and Casualty Insurance Company in Japan
gyōmuhonbu	Administrative and coordinating division of C. Itoh Japan
hikitsugi-sho	Document verifying transfer of authority upon resignation
honbusho	A unit consisting of several divisions
jimusho	Office
ka	Departments (sections under the old status system)
kaigaisojatsu-bu	Overseas department

JAPANESE TERMS AS USED BY ITOH[a]	ENGLISH EQUIVALENTS AND/OR EXPLANATIONS
kaigaitenshukansha	Emergency expense approved by the manager of an overseas branch office
kanrishoku-kyū	Management positions
kanrishoku	All status levels above *kachō-ho* that allow employees to receive certain allowances
karibaraikanjō	Suspense account—an account for purchases of items that do not bear a clear purpose
kyuyogakari	Personnel in charge of payrolls
naiki	Company regulation—policy giving guidance as to whether a loan will be extended
saigaihukyūhi	Repair expense for damages related to the employee's property
sangokukan	Third country transaction—transaction with countries other than Japan and the United States
shiten	Branch officed
shosha	In Japan, the term usually refers to a "general trading company." Itoh management uses the term to designate knowledge-intensive industry—ability to look at an entire industry, absence of a narrow perspective, "moving think tank."
shōyo	Bonuses
sōgokaihatsubu	Project development department
sōmubu	General affairs division—department that pays salaries
torishimariyaku	A level of employment above *sanyo*—equivalent to members of the board of directors, or *yakuin*
ukewatashi	Delivery of general machinery
zaimubu	Finance department
zaikinkyū	Overseas base salary—base salary plus family allowances

[a]Other Japanese companies may use slightly different titles.

COMPARABLE WORTH

*A new approach to eliminating sex-based wage
inequities in employment*

The doctrine of comparable worth holds "that if individuals of different sexes have jobs that differ in duties yet are comparable in worth, the jobs should be paid the same regardless of external market value."[1]

Although very recent in its origin, this doctrine has been gaining rapid ground in public awareness. It has especially strong emotional appeal to the women's movement, segments of organized labor, and population groups who view it as an important tool with which to fight job discrimination and wage inequities suffered by women. The issue of comparable worth has been a key issue of the 1980s and 1990s. In an introduction to one of the best surveys of the issue, Helen Remick, director of the Office for Affirmative Action at the University of Washington, says: "Comparable worth addresses the sex difference in compensation that cannot otherwise be explained; when we advocate comparable worth, we mean that wages should be based on the worth of the work, not upon the sex of the person doing it."[2] As an issue, comparable worth rides in the wake of a profound sociocultural change that occupies the forefront of public debate in the "modernized" Western world: are women truly the equals of men? This is an idea that is not well established in the West and hardly rates mention in traditional societies. Comparable worth, nonetheless, is a policy that is rooted in the new thinking. In its present state it remains exploratory and unfinished.

The notion of comparable worth, however, is surrounded by intense controversy encompassing the validity of the concept itself, difficulties in its measurement and application, and its potential consequences for growth in the U.S. economy and employment as well as the global competitiveness of American business. Although the methodological and process-related issues are quite serious, they can eventually be resolved. But there remains the most fundamental question posed by the comparable worth doctrine. To wit, comparable worth strikes at the very core of market economy by asserting that wages should be determined administratively, largely without regard to factors of supply and demand and market pricing. In the process, it may create an entire array of new inequities and market dysfunctioning while attempting to eradicate one set of inequities.

The debate on the issue, however, has only just begun and the intellectual arguments are likely to rage for quite some time. The issue is gaining greater immediacy and is being looked at rather closely as more and more women enter the work force. To date, 17 states have passed legislation that tries to deal with the issue.[3] Thirteen states use the term "comparable worth" directly in their legislation. Representative Olympia Snowe of the Joint Economic Committee further states that "The lack of pay equity for the women of this country is the most urgent problem facing women in the labor force."[4] While these arguments would provide shape and substance to the future debate, eventual solutions must emerge in the political and legal arena. For eventually it is the political will of the people expressed through a democratic system that can alter the distributive effects of the market economy.

COMPARABLE WORTH: THE FIRST VICTORY

The proponents of comparable worth achieved their first significant victory in a case filed by the American Federation of State, County and Municipal Employees (AFSCME) against the State of Washington. On December 14, 1983, an employer, the State of Washington, was for the first time found guilty of discrimination under Title VII for personnel policy disparities in functionally unrelated jobs. The case grew out of a 1974 survey of state personnel which revealed massive pay discrimination against women. The court's judgment culminated ten years of debate and it assumed national significance.[5]

The antecedents of this case, however, were building up through the legal system, where the concept of job discrimination was being litigated and refined in terms of bona fide occupational qualifications (BFOQ), disparate treatment, and disparate impact. An important precedent was set in *County of Washington* v. *Gunther*, decided in 1981, wherein the United States Supreme Court resolved the threshold legal issue of whether sex-based wage discrimination claims can be brought under Title VII without satisfying the equal work standard of the Equal Pay Act. In a significant but narrowly written opinion, the Supreme Court ruled that compensation discrimination claims brought under Title VII are not restricted to claims for equal pay for "substantially equal" work.[6]

The Gunther case set a precedent for the *AFSCME* v. *the State of Washington* case.[7] In this case, the County of Washington's market study showed that female jail matrons, based on relative skills, effort, responsibility, and working conditions, should have received 95% of what male jail guards received in pay. The county, however, only paid the matrons 70% of the amount paid to guards. Four female matrons filed a suit claiming they were paid less than their evaluated worth. The United States Supreme Court decided that "a claim of intentional wage discrimination can be brought under Title VII even when jobs are not considered substantially equal under the Equal Pay Act."[8]

The *Gunther* decision represented a crucial first step toward development of the concept of comparable worth as a means of achieving pay equity through litigation. *Gunther* established that women may challenge systematic sex-based wage discrimination under Title VII without the necessity of showing that the employer had hired male workers at higher wages to perform substantially equal work.[9] The Supreme Court indicated that Title VII should be interpreted more broadly and that claims under it are not restricted to equal pay for substantially equal work. Instead, they cover the entire spectrum of sex-based employment discrimination practices.

Although this case did set precedents for future claims, the court at this point stressed the narrowness of its ruling. These jobs were only slightly different, not unrelated. The court did not lay down any guidelines or conditions for future claims. However, the ruling did give precedence for future claimants that decisions would be different when brought under the Equal Pay Act versus Title VII.

ISSUES FOR ANALYSIS

1. How substantive are the intellectual, legal, and operational arguments made by the proponents and opponents in the *AFSCME* v. *The State of Washington* case? To what extent and along what dimensions are the merits of opposing arguments relevant in other situations?
2. What does "worth" mean in the context of the employers' options and those of employees? Should an employer be forced to pay more for a job if it employs predominantly female

workers? If the logic of the argument of comparable worth is to be held across-the-board, why should it not be argued in favor of other job classifications that are predominantly occupied by blacks, Hispanics, or other identifiable disadvantaged groups?

3. What are some of the measurement problems that arise in evaluating jobs that are functionally distinct? How can they be evaluated so as to determine their relative worth?

4. What administrative mechanisms can be used in comparing the relative worth of different jobs? What are the limitations and biases built into these systems?

5. What proof is needed to show discrimination in the case of functionally unrelated jobs? Does the fact that employers' self-studies on this issue have been used against them in suits discourage employers from doing such studies?

6. How might one evaluate the role of unions in fighting for "comparable worth" for female employees? Is it a concern for "pay equity" or is it another device to protect union members from market and competitive pressures?

7. Is the issue of social equality of women being improperly confused with the pay equity issue or are the two the same?

8. To what extent are market wage rates biased by cultural factors and, therefore, do not simply respond to the scarcity of valuable skills? Is an administratively determined wage rate for comparable worth the best approach to it? If not, how might the wages for different jobs be made more responsive to the market?

9. What are some of the possible costs to the economy, and the implications for the labor market, if the doctrine of comparable worth is accepted and/or legislated?

AFSCME V. STATE OF WASHINGTON

The State of Washington has two systems of classified service. One is the civil service, and the other is higher education. Each of these systems has a personnel board, which is responsible for any changes in the classification of jobs within the system. All jobs are classified, and those having the same classification receive the same pay. Pay rates must

also be comparative to the rates of other private and public institutions. To determine this comparability, the state does salary surveys of specific benchmark positions every two years. Once rates are formulated by the personnel boards, they are adopted in open hearings; the governor uses them in the state budget; and the state legislature appropriates the required funds.

AFSCME International, or the American Federation of State, County, and Municipal Employees, is the largest union of public employees. Of its 1 million members, 400,000 are women. Half of these women perform clerical jobs; the remaining women are found in other traditionally female occupations.[10] One third of their local presidents and 45% of local union officers were women in 1982.[11]

In 1974, at AFSCME's urging, the Governor of Washington State at that time, Daniel J. Evans, asked that the two personnel boards do an internal study of the disparities between female-dominated jobs, and male-dominated jobs. Both boards did a small study, and following this, the governor had the two boards meet together with an outside consultant, Norman D. Willis, and conduct a much larger study.

The Willis study evaluated jobs based on four factors: skills/knowledge; mental demands; accountability; and working conditions. They studied those jobs that were 70% or more female versus those jobs that were 70% or more male-dominated. The study's major conclusion was that those jobs that were equal according to the factors, but were female-dominated, paid on the average 20% less than male-dominated jobs.

In 1976, Governor Evans put just over $7 million into the budget to start to correct these disparities. Soon after, he left office, and the newly elected governor withdrew the money. Four more studies were done from 1974–1982 with basically the same results. AFSCME asked both the new governor and his successor to replace the money in the budget. The Willis Plan was never instituted, partially due to financial considerations involved. So, in 1981, nine AFSCME members filed charges of discrimination with the Equal Employment Opportunity Commission on behalf of all workers employed in female-dominated jobs. In 1982, when the EEOC did not respond to the claim, AFSCME filed a suit.

Just prior to the trial in 1983, the state legislature voted to modify the classification process to include not only market ratings, but also increases to obtain comparable worth. The state maintained that the disparities were not illegal, just unfair. Both of the personnel boards were to set up ten-year comparable worth schedules to be started between 1983 and 1985, and completed by June 1993. The legislature defined comparable as being jobs similar in responsibilities, judgements, knowledge, skills, and working conditions.

Even with this step toward the goal of pay equity, criticism remained. The Engrossed House Bill No. 1079 gave one-and-a-half million dollars to this end. There were, however, no specifics on how to accomplish this goal, just time limits on its completion. Secondly, the money appropriated worked out to be only $100 per person with respect to the 15,000 to 20,000 people employed in those jobs. Critics maintained that it would take 80 to 90 years to accomplish pay equity at that rate. And so the trial ensued.

AFSCME went to trial on behalf of all individuals who were employed in jobs comprised of 70% or more females as of November 20, 1980. AFSCME based its suit on four claims:

1. The studies done had shown disparities of 20% differences in income. In 1983, this disparity had even increased. Disparities were also found in closely related jobs such as barber and beautician. In addition, these studies showed that even entry-level jobs which required the same qualifications were paid differently depending on the sex of the employee. Positions filled by men, which required no high school education, were paid approximately 10% more than female positions requiring no high school. Male jobs which required a high school degree paid about 22% more, and jobs requiring one year of college paid men 19% more.[12]

2. The state failed to act promptly to correct the disparity, and even when it did, in 1983, the action was inadequate.

3. The state had a history of sex-segregating jobs. Employment ads placed in newspapers were put in columns labeled "men" and "women" from the 1950s to 1973. The state also had "protective" laws prohibiting women from certain jobs.

4. Statements were made by public officials and administrators on the "problem" and efforts to correct it. In addition, there were personnel boards reports, and the governor's Affirmative Action Committee's statements concerning the situation.

The State defenses included:

1. The system used was legal as well as nondiscriminatory. Salaries were based on a fair, legitimate system, and provided the most for the tax payers' dollars. Changing the system could alter the state's ability to recruit and keep workers. Changing would also seriously disrupt the labor force.

2. The studies that were undertaken were only informational studies used by the state to look into the idea. Before the results of these studies could be implemented, the validity, feasibility, and implications had to be considered.

At the trial, Judge Tanner allowed only two of the fourteen witnesses on behalf of the state to testify. He did not accept any of the state arguments about possible flaws in the study. The judge found that the state had acted in bad faith, and should have known the legal implications of the studies when it began to conduct them. In addition, he felt the evidence proved, "pervasive and intentional discrimination."[13]

When claiming discrimination, there are two avenues of proof: disparate treatment and disparate (adverse) impact. Disparate treatment holds that the employer intentionally discriminated against its employees.

Disparate impact states that just because an employer does nothing, and the practice is discriminatory, even without intent, the employer is liable. AFSCME sought relief under both disparate treatment and disparate impact. The state argued that in all previous cases of comparable worth, primarily *Gunther v. County of Washington,* proof of intent was required. Therefore, AFSCME could not claim disparate impact. The court "held that the plaintiffs in fact had established a prima facie case of discrimination under either a disparate impact or disparate treatment theory using direct or indirect evidence."[14]

Even the award made by the judge proved quite controversial. Through previous cases, the Supreme Court had set precedents for the District Court in determining relief. The guidelines concerned: the extent to which an award would be economically damaging to the defendants; any adverse effects the award could have on the economy or any innocent third parties; and lastly, whether the defendants had reasonable time with which to correct their wrongdoings. The judge found these guides to be irrelevant to this case and ordered the following:

1. All practices of discrimination will be stopped;
2. All plaintiffs will be paid the amount they are due under a plan adopted as of May 1983;
3. Further evaluation studies will be conducted listing completely all employees who are entitled to back pay;
4. The court will appoint a master who will have broad access to state buildings and files and will report back in 90 days on the extent of progress in implementing the plan;
5. The state will pay for the master's fees.

Estimates are that this case will cost the state anywhere from $500 million to $1 billion dollars. Two-thirds of this amount is back pay the state might have avoided had it shown greater and quicker action concerning the controversy. Had it taken such action, the state could have used as little as 2% of its budget to bring pay equity.[15]

THE CONTROVERSY CONTINUES: ARGUMENTS FOR AND AGAINST COMPARABLE WORTH

The proponents of comparable worth doctrine start by asserting the fact that women have historically earned less and continue to do so compared to men in general, and also in particular where two jobs require essentially similar levels of competence and skill and may be of equal value to the employer. They also point out that occupational categories such as teachers and nurses where women predominate tend to have lower wages. Moreover, when a particular job category or occupation starts having more women workers, the average level of wages has a distinct tendency to fall when compared to previous levels and also in relation to other job categories that have been historically used in wage rate comparisons.

In 1939, women earned 63¢ for every dollar that a man earned. In 1950, the figure dropped to 62¢, and has not changed since.[16] Emphasis is specifically given to female-dominated occupations, which typically earn significantly lower wages than male-dominated occupations. (See Table 1.)

The issue is complicated by the fact that society categorizes certain types of jobs and professions by sex. For example, 81% of clerical workers, 96% of nurses, and 82% of elementary school teachers are women. These are also the occupations that are typically found at the lower end of the pay structure. On the average, a secretary earns $4,000 less per year than a truck driver. Not only are women paid less, but evidence has been offered that women are also generally employed by lower-paying firms.

The proponents of comparable worth also reject the two arguments made most often by their critics: the market pricing of a job's relative worth, and the difficulty in determining alternative pricing mechanisms that would overcome the alleged market pricing deficiencies and provide a more efficient and socially equitable criterion for

TABLE 1. The Wage Gap

	Figures for full-time workers in selected occupations			
	Women as percent of all workers		Earnings ratio, female to male	
	1979	1986	1979	1986
Accountants and auditors	34%	45%	0.60	0.72
Computer programmers	28	40	0.80	0.81
Computer systems analysts	20	30	0.79	0.83
Lawyers	10	15	0.55	0.63
Managers and administrators	22	29	0.51	0.61
Sales of business services	28	34	0.58	0.79
Teachers, elementary school	61	82	0.82	0.95

SOURCE: Robert Pear, "Women Reduce Lag in Earnings but Disparities with Men Remain" *New York Times* (September 4, 1987), p. A13.

determining the wage base for various jobs and occupational categories.

Market pricing, in its simplest form, assumes that a job is worth as much as an employer is willing to pay for and an employee is willing to work for. Thus, an employee performing exactly the same work may accept lower wages when there are too many people competing for work, and may demand and receive higher wages when jobs go begging and not enough people are available to take them. If the workers demand too high a price for their services, the employers would hire fewer workers to do only the most valuable or profitable work; find substitution for workers, i.e., become more capital intensive; or, go out of business. In all these cases, the effect would be to reduce the demand for labor to a point where at a given wage rate the demand and supply for workers balances out. Conversely, if employers offer wages that are too low compared to the alternatives available to workers, the workers would be inclined to leave that occupation; fewer new workers would enter that occupation; and employers in other businesses would tempt these workers to come to work for them at higher wages. In all these cases, the effect would be to reduce the supply of workers so that employers would be forced to raise wages to a level where they could get the number of workers they need. Thus, employers use the market to determine what is the

going rate for a particular job on the basis of actual supply and demand of workers for that job. It entails a survey of various occupations and the job classifications within them. Basically, wages are based on what everyone else is paying. Those trying to validate market ratings as a measure of job worth propose that the law of supply and demand will ensure that a job is paid what it is worth.

Opponents argue this may not be the case for women, and use the example of the recent shortage of nurses. Based on the increased demand, and decreased supply, their wages should have risen considerably, yet this did not occur to any significant degree. "Many compensation professionals feel that the market truly does not reflect the internal worth of jobs"[17] and that, in effect, the market both embodies and prolongs discrimination.

The market theory also assumes that the labor market is freely competitive. This is a critical assumption that may be flawed.[18] Consider the following :

1. Because of the necessary skills and training, people are not free to change jobs at will.
2. Because of family or other considerations, restrictions exist geographically.
3. Information is not openly accessible; therefore, much of the information an individual does possess is inadequate.
4. Institutional structures such as seniority, rather than merit, inhibit pure competition.

5. Employers often fill vacancies internally rather than on the open market.
6. Supply and demand of the labor force is influenced by other institutions such as unions and government.

The second method of job evaluation is to determine a job's internal worth. The Committee on Women's Employment and Related Social Issues concluded that job evaluation systems hold much promise as an equitable, consistent method of evaluating a job's intrinsic value. "Women are concentrated in low paying jobs, not solely out of choice—though choice may play some role—and not because these jobs would be low paying regardless of who did them but rather as the result of earlier traditions of discrimination that have become institutionalized—as well as, possible current intentional discrimination."[19] Using this method, an employer ranks jobs on the basis of several factors that are taken as representative of a job's worth. Those jobs that have equal total points should be paid the same wage.

In reviewing the study that underpinned the *AFSCME* v. *State of Washington* case, Helen Remick writes:

> Examples bring the issue to life. A Food Service Worker I at 93 points, earned an average salary of $472 per month, while a Delivery Truck Driver I, at 94 points, earned $792; a V Clerical Supervisor III, at 305 points, earned an average of $794. A Nurse Practitioner II, at 385 points, had average earnings of $832, the same as those of a Boiler Operator with only 144 points. A Homemaker I, with 198 points and an average salary of $462, had the lowest earnings of all evaluated jobs.[20]

Obviously, the methodology used in assigning points is a very hotly disputed issue. Although the job evaluation idea may hold promise, it needs development. First, current systems in use do not reflect the advances in social science measurement techniques that could greatly enhance validity. Secondly, many job evaluation systems incorporate market rates which, as mentioned previously, may be discriminating in themselves. Thirdly, the system must be used firmwide, and often different systems are used for different classifications or levels within an organization.

Judy Fulgham has proposed some guidelines for conducting a job evaluation.[21] She gives considerable attention to both defining the evaluation tools as well as to the organizational interaction of the parties involved. Her work is most helpful in pointing out some of the pitfalls to be expected.

ARGUMENTS FOR COMPARABLE WORTH

The notion of comparable worth has been strongly criticized by a number of scholars and public and private institutions on grounds that it is inherently flawed as logic; that it would introduce more politics and ideology into the wage determination system and thus make it more, and not less, equitable; and that it would be an administrative nightmare.

The chairman of the U.S. Civil Rights Commission calls comparable worth "the looniest idea since Looney Tunes."[22] The Commission, in an early policy statement, by a 5-2 vote, had rejected the comparable worth concept as a remedy for sex bias in the workplace. It went so far as to urge that Congress and federal enforcement agencies oppose the notion of equal pay for men and women employed in different jobs of comparable value. "Implementation of the unsound and misplaced concept of comparable worth would be a serious error." The latest policy statement, an outgrowth of hearings the panel held in June 1985, supported the Reagan Administration's opposition to the comparable worth concept. In its statement, the Commission contended that salary differences between men and women were often caused by factors other than discrimination, such as unequal educational backgrounds and skills. It also suggested that the evaluation studies frequently used to implement the comparable-worth concept "are inherently subjective" and don't prove wage bias. Civil rights laws don't prevent employers "from relying on market factors" to set pay, the statement adds. Speaking for the Commission, Morris Abram, it's vice president, stated that the comparable-worth concept would amount "to permanent government wage control over a substantial, if not the majority, of the working population and I don't think this country is ready for it.[23]

Furthermore, in a case dealing with alleged sex discrimination, the Equal Employment Opportunities Commission (EEOC) held that the payment of lower wages to employees in the female-dominated administrative branch than to those in the male-dominated maintenance branch of an employer's operations did not amount to unlawful sex discrimination, especially where there was no evidence that employees were assigned on the basis of sex or that there were barriers to movement between the job categories. Further, there is no statutory basis for a claim of increased wages based on a comparison of the intrinsic worth of jobs in one category with that of other jobs in the same organization.[24]

Similar views were also expressed by the Appeals Court judges in their decision rejecting AFSCME's claims in reversing the lower court's decision against the State of Washington. The Appeals Court stated that "Neither law nor logic deems the free market a suspect enterprise" in overturning a decision that required the State of Washington to pay 15,500 mostly female workers as much as $1 billion in damages.[25]

The critics of comparable worth argue that despite its deficiencies, market-based pricing of human labor still offers the most efficient and equitable system and that any other system would lead to inefficiencies and would be inherently more inequitable. The rationale for a market-based wage goes somewhat along the following lines:

To begin with, the determination of the worth of anything is individual and relative. It is individual in that values differ among individuals, resulting in different assessments of the worth of any object of exchange. Were this not so, no exchange of goods or services would occur; the purchaser in any exchange must judge the object of exchange as worth more than does the supplier of the object. Judgments of worth are also relative; they reflect the comparison between the anticipated outcomes of one exchange and the most attractive alternative to that exchange. The market concept as elaborated in economic theory provides a potential mechanism for identifying some common measure of value of exchanges. Individual buyers and sellers seek out beneficial exchanges, and the various rates of exchange observed in the market influence the valuations of opportunity cost of both buyers and sellers. Alternative rates of exchange available in the market represent to both buyers and sellers an element of what is foregone when entering into any specific exchange. Another major element of opportunity cost is the valuation of nonmarket uses such as work in the home or leisure. Both alternative wage rates in the labor market and personal valuation of time spent homemaking or skiing influence the opportunity cost to the worker of accepting a specific wage and employment offer.[26]

In the competitive market, the actions of both buyers and sellers seeking their personal advantage tend to converge upon a single rate of exchange, a market rate at which all who wish to buy and sell are accommodated. In a similar manner, a market wage is generated through the actions of buyers and sellers in a competitive labor market. Each employer and employee considers alternatives and the opportunity cost associated with each, and enters into exchanges of work and wages that are considered worthwhile. Alternatives available to the employer include hiring other persons with greater or lesser potential productivity, losing production and sales, subcontracting to other employers, and making technological substitutions for labor. Alternatives available to the employee include other job opportunities, investment in education and training, nonmarket work in the home, and consumption or leisure. Only exchanges judged worthwhile by both parties are consummated, and the rates of exchange converge upon a common-market wage rate through competitive action. The market wage rate is, therefore, the best available measure of job worth, reflecting as it does the collective valuations of worth by employers and employees.

In theory, a market wage is associated with each job or occupation, and the wage differential between any two occupations reflects the collective judgments of relative worth of these occupations by employers and employees. One occupation is paid more than another as necessary to attract the desired number of applicants and to the extent that it is viewed as more productive of value to the employer. It is this structure of wage differentials obtained in a competitive labor market that reflects the relative worth of different occupations. Furthermore, the structure of wage differentials can be expected to change as labor demands and supplies change as a result of employers and employees altering their valuations of different jobs.[27]

The worst part of the comparable worth concept is that it tends to perpetuate job rigidities and thus condemns women to the same "undesirable" jobs that they seek to get out of. To the extent that no overt or covert discrimination is involved, wages in occupations with excess supply over demand would tend to be more depressed than the prevailing wages in other occupations. And should women, or any other identifiable group, be concentrated in that particular occupation, it would, as a group, receive lower wages. Suppose, for the sake of argument, we decide that primary school teachers who are predominantly women, and who are also underpaid, should receive higher wages. In the

absence of any restriction to job mobility based on sex, the more competent among these women would move to other jobs leaving those who, for one reason or another, are unmovable. In some cases, these reasons are personal; this is an individual choice and nothing needs to be done. However, in other cases, employees are staying because they cannot find better, more highly paid jobs. Thus, employers would be forced to upgrade jobs and attract better people or they would receive poor performance.

If we were to raise the wages of these people that are above the market rate, it would have the effect of keeping people in these jobs when they would have been more productive elsewhere. It would also pay the less efficient people more money since they have no incentive to move. Finally, it would attract more people to these jobs, when, in fact, the demand for their services would be declining, for the employers would constantly be seeking alternative ways to accomplish these tasks and thereby avoid paying above-market wages.

Although couched in male vs. female, and primarily white-collar terms, the issue of comparable worth pervades examination of every kind of wage differential. Basically, the issue of comparable worth relates to the determination of relative worth of any two jobs or occupations. Most pilots are men. Most typists are women. In the name of fairness, as proponents of comparable worth see it, employers should raise the salaries of typists. The private-sector implications are obvious. If it is discriminatory for the federal government to pay a female typist less than a male pilot, isn't it true for American Airlines as well? And wouldn't it be up to the federal government to ensure that such discriminatory practices are rectified? It is also argued that any implementation of a comparable-worth plan would not so much pit women against men as blue-collar workers against white-collar workers. Most comparable-worth studies favor white-collar occupations over blue-collar occupations, assessing points for degrees and credentials while ignoring such factors as working conditions and market demand. To comparable-worth advocates, it doesn't seem fair that a truck driver with no high school degree could earn more than a systems analyst with a college education.[28]

George F. Will, the noted conservative syndicated columnist criticizes comparable worth in terms of an ideological play by the liberal left in America. He argues that "comparable worth might have the retrograde effect of reinforcing a 'pink collar' ghetto of jobs considered women's work. Advocates of comparable worth say comparable jobs are of comparable worth to employers. Advocates are not content to let employers say what that worth is."[29]

Will outlines four criteria by which advocates of comparable worth would ascertain that "worth" of a job. One is the amount of "knowledge and skills" required, meaning the "total amount of information or dexterity" involved. It requires an assessment of the comparable "worths" of mental and manual capabilities—of information relative to dexterity. The second criterion is "mental demands." However, he argues that the distinction between mental demands and knowledge is at best arbitrary and at worst subjective, i.e., nonscientific. Rather than paying more for jobs making high mental demands, he suggests (albeit facetiously), that "a job that is dull because it is simple and repetitive should be considered a job that makes especially difficult mental demands. A dull job can be difficult because attention and zest are difficult to maintain." A third criterion is "accountability," meaning the amount of supervision the job involves. A fourth criterion is "working conditions." However, supervision could be a pleasure and not necessarily a chore. Similarly, a job performed outside would, presumably, get special "worth points" because working outside is less pleasant than working inside. Unless, of course, the worker prefers working outside. But, then, who asked the worker? It is the

manufacturers of criteria—the social scientists formulating formulas—who will be asked.[30]

Finally, Will alludes to the ideological leanings of the proponents of comparable worth and observes:

> Comparable-worth look like part of the not-very-hidden agenda of the left. It serves the goal of giving control of almost everything—in this case, everyone's wages or salary—to a small priestly class of "experts." Computing the comparable worth of every activity would inevitably be the work—the profitable work—of a particular class. Comparable worth would be a jobs program for an articulate, theorizing class of intellectuals.

And not surprisingly, that formula gives special value—extra "worth points"—to the kind of work done by the kind of person who devises such formulas, work involving "knowledge" skills. Surprise! The formula enhances the economic value of formula makers. And, of course, it lowers the relative "worth," moral and monetary, of the labor performed by the neediest women.

When society's least pleasant work is considered, someone might ask a really radical question: should not nurses be paid more than doctors? Doctors have the psychic income of intellectual stimulation and social prestige. Nurses have bedpans and subordination. Surely nurses should have more money. Michael Walzer, a political philosopher, goes a step farther: perhaps citizens should be conscripted to collect the garbage.

Onerous Jobs: There are other jobs that must be done but are onerous. Garbage collection is one. Caring for the very aged is another. Such jobs often are filled by people of whom Walzer says, felicitously, this: "When they were growing up, they dreamed of doing something else." Anything else. Walzer argues that "negative" but necessary jobs should not be allotted by economic forces to "negative" categories of people such as the poor or recent immigrants. Walzer is not saying that collecting the garbage is work without dignity. He says the physical nature of such unpleasant work cannot be changed, but its moral nature can be. It can be accorded due dignity by distributing it as a duty of citizenship, rather than leaving it for those at the bottom of society's status system.[31]

LEGISLATION: THE EQUAL PAY ACT AND TITLE VII

There are two major pieces of legislation that govern pay equity. The first of these is the Equal Pay Act of 1963 (29 U.S.C. 206[d]), which is an amendment to the Fair Labor Standards Act of 1938. This act guarantees that employees of different sexes doing the same job are required to receive equal pay.[32]

There are four factors that determine job similarity. First, skill that includes experience, training, education and ability. Secondly, effort, which can be both physical and mental. Third is responsibility, or how much accountability is required to do the job. And, fourth, the working conditions of the employee. If these four conditions are equal, and there is disparity in pay, then discrimination may be evident.

However, there are four defenses that can excuse an employer from liability under the Equal Pay Act. These are: (1) disparity due to seniority; (2) disparity due to merit; (3) disparity due to differences in productivity in which earnings are distributed based on quantity or quality of output (an example of this would be a salary based on commission according to sales volume); and (4) disparity due to any factor other than sex.

To use these defenses, the systems must be formalized and used in a sex-blind manner. Title VII of the Civil Rights Act of 1964 (42 U.S.C. 2000E) is the second major piece of legislation dealing with pay equity. Title VII makes it unlawful to discriminate in hiring, job classifications, promotion, compensation, fringe benefits, discharge, and any other terms of employment.

The Bennett Amendment (section 703(h)) of Title VII incorporates the provisions of the Equal Pay Act into Title VII. This amendment has caused considerable controversy. Two interpretations of its meaning have been expressed. The first interpretation stresses that in order for wage discrimination to be tried under Title VII, it must satisfy the conditions of equal work as in the Equal Pay Act. The second interpretation holds that only the four exceptions or defenses are incorporated into Title VII. This distinction is a major one for the issue of comparable worth. The way in which the courts interpret the Bennett Amendment has significant impact on the decisions of future comparable worth cases.

NOTES

1. Elizabeth Cooper and Gerald V. Barrett, "Equal Pay and Gender Implications of Court Cases for Personnel Practices." *Academy of Management Review*, 9 (January 1984) pp. 84–92; and *Wall Street Journal*, "Pay Equity, Born in Public Sector, Emerges as an Issue in Private Firms," (July 8, 1985), p. 15.
2. Helen Remick, ed., *Comparable Worth and Wage Discrimination*. Philadelphia, PA: Temple University Press, 1984, p. x.
3. Judy B. Fulgham, "The Employer's Liabilities under Comparable Worth." *Personnel Journal*, 62 (May, 1983), pp. 396–419.
4. U.S. Congress, Joint Economic Committee, *Hearing on Women in the Workforce: Pay Equity*, 98th Congress, Second Session, 1984, p. 2.
5. Gary R. Siniscalso and Cynthia L. Remmers, "Comparable Worth In the Aftermath of AFSCME vs. State of Washington." *Employee Relations Law Journal*, 10 (Summer, 1984), pp. 6–29.
6. Mary Heen, "A Review of Federal Court Decisions under Title VII of the Civil Rights Act of 1964." In H. Remick, *Comparable Worth*, p. 198.

7. Barbara R. Bergman and Mary W. Gray, "Economic Models as a Means of Calculating Legal Compensation Claims." In H. Remick, *Comparable Worth*, pp. 155–172; Heen, "Review," pp. 197–202, 212–13.
8. Gary R. Siniscalso and Cynthia L. Remmers, "Comparable Worth." *Employee Relations Law Journal*, 9 (Winter, 1983–1984), pp. 496–99.
9. Heen, in H. Remick, ed., *Comparable Worth*, p. 1984.
10. *Ibid.*, p. 4.
11. Committee on Post Office and Civil Service, U.S. House of Representatives, *Hearing on Federal Pay Equity Act of 1984*, 98th Congress, 2nd Session, 1984, p. 63.
12. Committee on Post Office and Civil Service, *Hearing* (1984), p. 204.
13. *Ibid.*, p. 134.
14. Siniscalso and Remmers, "Comparable Worth" (1983/1984), p. 497.
15. Siniscalso and Remmers, "Comparable Worth" (1984), p. 13.
16. Committee on Post Office And Civil Service, *Hearing* (1983), p. 204.
17. Committee On Post Office and Civil Service, U. S. House of Representatives, *Joint Hearing On Pay Equity: Equal Pay for Work of Comparable Value*, 97th Congress, 2nd Session, 1983, pp. 1–2; and Robert Pear, "Women Reduce Lag in Earnings but Disparities with Men Remain." *New York Times* (September 4, 1987), pp. A1, A13.
18. Fulgham, "Employer's Liabililties," p. 404.
19. Joint Economic Committee, *Hearing on Women*, pp. 12–14; Thomas A. Mahoney, "Market Wages and Comparable Worth."

20. Joint Economic Committee Report, Supra note 9, p. 5.
21. Remick, *Comparable Worth*, p. 103.
22. Judy B. Fulgham, "The New Balancing Act: A Comparable Worth Study." *Personnel Journal*, 63 (January 1984), pp. 32–38.
23. "Business and the Law—States Leading on Pay Equity." *New York Times* (June 22, 1987), p. D2.
24. Joann S. Lubin, "Use of Comparable-Worth Idea to Fight Job Sex Bias Opposed by Rights Panel." *Wall Street Journal* (April 12, 1985), p. 60.
25. EEOC, Decision No. 85–8, June 17, 1985, as reissued July 12, 1985. Commerce Clearing House (1985), pp. 7044–48.
26. David L. Kirp, "Comparable Worth Debate Lives on—Courts Not the Place to Set Job Values and Pay," and Michael Evan Gold, "Federal Court Decision Blind to New Realities." *Sunday Press*, Binghamton, NY, (September 15, 1988), pp. 1, 4E.
27. Thomas A. Mahoney, "Market Wages and Comparable Worth." *ILR Report* (Spring 1982), pp. 15–19.
28. *Ibid.*, p. 56.
29. Dick Armey, "Comparable-Worth: A Bad Idea That Won't Die." *Wall Street Journal* (September 26, 1988), p. 26.
30. U.S. Supreme Court, 29 U.S.C. 206[d], June 1988.
31. *Ibid.*
32. *Ibid.*

19. *ILR Report*, Cornell University (Spring, 1982), pp. 15–19.

UNITED AIRLINES, INC.

*A case of age discrimination or a concern
for the safety of the flying public*

The United States has been in the forefront of nations protecting the rights of its citizens against discrimination in places of work, pleasure, and habitation, i.e., in all walks of life. Enshrined in various civil rights laws, American citizens are protected from discrimination based on sex, race, national origin, age or other disabilities that are not directly related to the specific performance of tasks at hand, do not adversely affect job performance, or do not threaten public safety.

The primary intent of these laws has been to protect individuals from arbitrary and capricious behavior on the part of other individuals or institutions, i.e., employers in cases of jobs, builders and landlords in cases of home ownership and rentals, owners of restaurants and other places of entertainment in cases of leisure time activities. Discrimination, however, can and does take place even where it is not motivated by racial or other prejudicial motives. This situation arises when an individual is denied certain rights because he/she falls into a general class that may have a high statistical propensity to fail expected standards of performance. Thus, women as a group may be required to pay higher life insurance premiums than men because women *as a class* live longer and thus require annuity payments for a longer time span than men *as a group* of comparable age. Similarly, young unmarried

men under age 26 are charged higher car insurance premiums than women of similar age and marital status because men in this group *as a class* are involved in more accidents than women. In all these cases, two issues remain paramount. The first issue is that all group-based discrimination affects individual rights. It is immaterial whether the impact is derived as a consequence of prejudice or society's inability to isolate individuals from within a particular group where such a group may generally be more prone to engage in activities that are perceived harmful to the legitimate interests of those imposing discriminatory behavior on others. In the United States, public opinion, political and legislative action, and legal proceedings have consistently eroded such barriers to individual rights based on some group or class characteristic. Thus as a matter of public policy, group-based discrimination has been effectively outlawed even where it can be shown that to do so would adversely affect those who are not part of such a group.

Age-based discrimination raises similar and even more thorny issues. Age as a criterion has long been used as a determining factor for suitability in employment where a job is perceived to require certain physical attributes that are considered necessary to perform the job satisfactorily, to protect the individual involved, or, in the interest of public safety.

The rationale is that a person's responses/reflexes deteriorate with age. Since individual rates of deterioration are hard to determine, it is better, in the interest of individual protection, the employer's right to satisfactory job performance, and public safety where such is the case, to require an employee to retire involuntarily from the job.

There are, however, other reasons based on history and tradition that enforce conditions of involuntary removal from a job at a predefined age. These may have to do with a society's desire to allow its senior citizens to enjoy their golden years in relaxation through accumulated pension and other retirement benefits, to create opportunities for younger generations to move up, and to minimize discriminatory actions against individual workers by imposing generally uniform conditions of retirement on all workers. Moreover, these conditions have had the force of custom as well as law and employment contracts.

The issue, therefore, is not that of age-based job discrimination per se but that of balancing competing interests of employers, employees, and society-at-large in a manner that is fair and equitable to the individuals and institutions involved on the one hand and society on the other hand. The issue has become even more important in the United States because this country's population, as that of most other industrially advanced countries, is becoming gradually older. This has come about because of a declining birth rate, improvement in medical and health care technologies, and increases in life expectancy. The latter two factors have made it possible for most people to live longer and remain healthier well into their seventies and even later years. The United States is currently in the midst of a major demographic change. By the year 2010, 25% of the population is projected to be age 55 or older. People in this category numbered 47.4 million in the 1980 census. They are estimated to reach 58.8 million in the year 2000 and 74.1 million in 2010.[1] At the same time, while the number of young workers entering the work force stood at 3 million in the early 1970s, it has now fallen to 1.3 million per year.[2]

The case of United Airlines and certain of its pilots and flight engineers amply demonstrates the nature of these conflicting claims. It also shows the process by which these claims may be balanced to arrive at more equitable and socially desirable solutions. Equally important, it suggests that such a balancing of interests need not be permanent and irreversible. In fact, changes in the technology of specific jobs, improvement in medical and health care, and advances in diagnostical and statistical evaluation techniques may allow the society to discard older group-based measures in favor of conditions that apply to specific individuals.

THE CASES OF AGE DISCRIMINATION AGAINST UNITED AIRLINES

On January 31, 1979, a number of flight engineers filed an age discrimination action against United Airlines and the Air Line Pilots Association challenging United's policy of retiring all flight engineers at age 60. Another action was filed by certain of United's pilots because of the airline's refusal to allow the pilots to transfer to flight engineer's position when they reached age 60. The action was joined by the Equal Employment Opportunity Commission. The combined cases became known as "*Gerry V. Monroe and Lee E. Higman, et al., and Equal Employment Opportunity Commission* v. *United Air Lines Inc., and Air Line Pilots Association International.*"[3] The plaintiffs asserted that United's policy of involuntary retirement at 60 was in contravention of the Age Discrimination in Employment Act of 1967 (ADEA) in that the mere fact of age could not be shown as a bona fide occupational qualification (BFOQ) that could be considered "reasonably necessary" for satisfactory job performance. United, in its defense, argued that a flight engineer's age (second officer) indeed met the criterion of "reasonably necessary" for the safe operation of the aircraft. It further argued that it was impractical to screen out, through vigorous periodical medical examinations, individual officers who could become incapacitated or otherwise become unable to perform their duties during the period between regularly scheduled medical examinations. In the case of the pilots, United argued that it was the company policy and the binding union agreement that disallowed pilots from down-bidding for jobs, regardless of age, except in very specific, clearly defined, and contractually agreed circumstances between the company and the air line pilots association.

ISSUES FOR ANALYSIS

1. How are the rights of employees affected in hiring people based on age? Under what conditions should these criteria be considered reasonable and where they might be considered contrary to public interest?
2. Under what circumstances may employers be allowed to discriminate among employees based on age for purposes of promotion and retention?
3. Where issues of public safety and social policy are raised, how might the balancing of rights be achieved as between the employees, employers, and society-at-large?
4. In addition to airline pilots, what other job categories raise substantive issues of public safety based on an employee's age, health, and medical fitness?
5. Age-based hiring, promotion, and retention issues have serious economic implications for certain employers as well as general social concerns. Under conditions of economic downturn or severe market competition, an employer may be under tremendous pressure to reduce costs or face business failure. Other things being equal, older employees with longer tenure on the job command higher wages that may not necessarily be associated, on a one-to-one basis, with increased productivity. Thus it would be economically prudent for the employer to effect savings in labor

costs by laying off older employees. It would also allow the company to retain younger workers who may be in a more vulnerable economic position and thus less able to survive extended periods of unemployment. Under what circumstances may it be legally or morally justified to retain younger employees at the expense of older workers?
6. How are the issues raised in items 1 through 5 related to the United Airlines case and the relative arguments made by the airline, the pilots and the flight engineers, the Air Line Pilots Association, and the Equal Employment Opportunity Commission? Are the lower court's verdict and the decision of the Appeals Court reasonable and fair based on your analysis of the facts of the case and your understanding of the concepts of equity and fairness as applied to different parties in the case?
7. Where age-based hiring and promotion criteria become necessary, how might the employers, and society-at-large, help those who become the unintended victims of these standards? What measures, if any, can be taken to help those who, because of age, might be unable to perform satisfactorily in their current jobs, but are otherwise healthy, anxious to work, and need employment to survive and maintain their standard of living?

OLD AGE AND EMPLOYMENT PRACTICES: SOCIAL AND LEGAL FRAMEWORK

It has long been assumed in Western countries that people would retire at age 65. This arbitrary age was apparently selected in 1889 by Otto Von Bismarck, Chancellor of the German Republic.[4] Bismarck was establishing the first formal national old-age pension program. He himself was 74 at the time. There do not appear to be documented scientific or health reasons which prompted him to choose that age. Be that as it may, it was not long before other Western countries followed suit.

The United States opted for the retirement age of 65 with the passage of the Social Security Act of 1935. The choice of that plateau by Congress also appears to have been arbitrary.[5] There were a number of different motivations surrounding the law. One was to make room for younger workers.[6] Another was the desire to create an independently financed retirement system based upon employee contributions, which would also be free of the political process.[7] In Japan, the mandatory retirement age has been 55 years for a long time and has only recently been raised to 58 years. Japanese life expectancy, on the other hand, has been rising steadily and now exceeds 72 years for males and 74 years for females. In contrast to most Western countries, Japanese social security payments do not start until age 60 and retirement benefits are generally meager compared to Western standards. Thus, Japan alone among all the industrially advanced countries has more people over the age of 60 who work full-time out of necessity rather than choice. In large parts of the Third World, 55 is still the age at which mandatory retirement takes place.

Elderly Americans have become a very potent political force, represented by powerful lobbying groups. Largely due to their efforts, several important pieces of legislation were passed. First came the Age Discrimination in Employment Act (ADEA) of 1967. This act outlawed discrimination based upon age with respect to workers who were between 40 and 65. It applied to all establishments employing 25 persons or more and also included the policies of employment agencies and labor unions.[8] It became unlawful for an employer to take any personnel action—including hiring, promotions, demotions, or firing—because of an individual's age. Personnel actions which proved to be adverse to older workers had to be justified in terms of a "bona fide occupational qualification (BFOQ)." The BFOQ clause specified that actions be based on "reasonable factors other than age."

The Federal Aviation Administration (FAA) has implemented the "Age 60 Rule" under the Federal Aviation Act of 1958. This rule prohibits the airlines from employing pilots who are over age 60. Prior to the United case, the FAA was sued some eight times between 1959 and 1978, but in each case the courts upheld the age 60 rule. The rule became the subject of Congressional Hearings in July of 1979 and was further put in jeopardy by 1975 and 1978 amendments to the Age Discrimination in Employment Act of 1967, which raised the mandatory retirement age to 70.[9]

The BFOQ has been the subject of considerable, and often contentious, debate. Employers have increasingly sought to use it to defend certain employment practices, including age-based differential treatment of employees. At the same time, employees have consistently and increasingly challenged BFOQ exceptions in employment practices by forcing employers to defend their practices on specific grounds of performance standards. In the case of airlines, BFOQ was unsuccessfully used to limit flight attendant jobs to female employees and to ground female employees in the event of marriage or pregnancy. The intensity of legal conflicts and court cases led Congress to amend the ADEA in 1975 by deleting the vague term "reasonable." In 1978, further amendments extended protection from age discrimination to age 70 and expanded coverage both to private industry employees as well as to those in state and local governments.[10]

In January 1987, H.R. 4154 was approved. It further extended protection to workers over the age of 70 and eliminated mandatory retirement at age 70. In approving this measure, Congress included a seven-year exemption with respect to public safety and welfare employees such as police and prison guards, as well as college professors. During this period, the EEOC and the Department of Labor are charged with the responsibility of conducting studies to see if reliable tests of physical and mental fitness of older employees may be devised. The elderly have thus won the right to work as long as they are willing and able.[11] Employees also have the right to a jury trial should they choose one and, if victorious, they are entitled to double damages in cases of willful violations of the ADEA.

THE LEGAL FRAMEWORK

The law provides two avenues through which a person can establish the fact of discrimination, i.e., disparate treatment and disparate impact. Under the disparate treatment doctrine, a person must show that the discrimination was intentional, i.e., the employer purposefully applied terms or conditions of employment that led to less favorable employment consequences for older workers. Evidence of discrimination can be either direct or indirect. Direct evidence in ADEA cases includes organizational policies or procedures where the employer can be shown to be treating older workers differently, such as mandatory retirement policies or the refusal to hire individuals over a certain age. Indirect evidence suggests a showing of intent by inference.

Statistical evidence is also used to demonstrate discriminatory intent on the part of an employer under ADEA's disparate treatment doctrine. For example, statistical disparities establishing that those treated less favorably are significantly older than those treated favorably are often used to help establish an employer's discriminating motivation. However, there are several reasons why statistical proof is not conclusive in ADEA cases. First, natural occurrences may better explain the statistical discrepancies where age is the implied discriminating variable. Also, age discrimination is often based on assumptions about the effects of age on ability and efficiency. Thus, the possibility of a justifiable relationship between age and reduced performance renders age-related statistical disparities inconclusive. Courts hearing age discrimination cases typically require large statistical discrepancies.

Therefore, statistical evidence is more helpful in establishing a claim of age discrimination when it is combined with other evidence.[12]

Under the disparate impact doctrine, it is only necessary to show that the employment practices in question have a differential effect on older workers regardless of employer motivation. For example, if the plaintiffs in an ADEA suit were able to show a statistically significant difference between the number of old and young employees laid off during a reduction-in-force, this would be sufficient for a prima facie showing under the requirements of the disparate impact doctrine. Also, "Employment criteria that are age neutral on their face but which nevertheless have a disparate impact on members of the protected group must be justified as a business necessity."[13] There are of course defenses against these claims. Not every personnel decision that had negative consequences for older workers is a violation of the ADEA, however. It is not unlawful for employers to base personnel decisions on age "where age is a bona fide occupational qualification (BFOQ) reasonably necessary to the normal operation of the particular business" (29 U.S.C. s623 [f][1]). Employers are also protected against personnel decisions that result in age differentials where the decisions are based on reasonable factors of age (FOA), (i.e., seniority systems or discharge or discipline of an employee for good cause).

Employers raising the BFOQ defense admit their personnel decisions were made on the basis of age but seek to justify them by showing that those decisions were reasonably necessary to normal business operations. When treated as a BFOQ, age is commonly used as a generalization about the ability level of all older workers. For example, a BFOQ defense might be based on a showing that all workers below a certain age would be more effective than those above that age limit. This is called a factual showing. Another possible defense is to show that it was impossible or impractical to make such decisions based on individual evaluations.

For instance, an airline that could not make a factual showing might be able to justify a BFOQ by showing there was no accurate or efficient way to determine which of its pilots ought to retire except by reference to age. The test case was provided by *Usery* v. *Tamiami Trail Tours, Inc.*, 531 F.2d 224 (5th Cir. 1976). According to Rosenblum:

> Under the so-called *Tamiami* test, the age-based classification (1) must be reasonably necessary to the essence of the employer's business, and (2) the employer must have reasonable cause, i.e., *a factual basis* for believing either (a) that *all* or *substantially all* persons within the excluded class would be *unable to perform safely and efficiently* the duties of the job or (b) that it is *impossible or impractical* to deal with persons over the age limit on an individualized basis (emphasis in the original).[14]

Safety-related businesses using the BFPQ defense present a special problem for the courts. Any increase in the risk to others resulting from the abandonment of age-related employment criteria has come to be viewed as an important legal consideration.[15]

An employer who raises the FOA (factor of age) defense asserts that its actions were "reasonable" and based on some factor other than age. The defendant's only legal burden is to articulate clearly the specific nature of the FOA.

Employers can use two broad categories of defenses to refute charges of age discrimination. These are: noneconomic and economic considerations. Included among those not directly related to economic considerations are violations of company policy, uncooperativeness, poor performance, lack of confidence in an employee's ability, and lack of training. Defenses directly related to economic considerations include reductions-in-force and other cost-cutting gestures as well as other personnel decisions directly made on the basis of employment costs. Thus, it would be appropriate under the ADEA for an employer to terminate all employees whose compensation was more than a prescribed amount, even though the practice would result in the discharge of a greater number of older workers.[16]

Since ADEA cases are often resolved based on research evidence that examines the relationship between age and organizational variables, it is important to appreciate the role of research in investigative efforts in ADEA-related cases. Furthermore, since age-related research findings are not uniform and methodologies suspect, caution should be exercised when using the results of age-related research to justify relationships between age and important organizational variables.[17]

THE FLIGHT ENGINEERS' AND PILOTS' CASE: ARGUMENTS IN SUPPORT OF CHARGES OF AGE DISCRIMINATION

On January 31, 1979, the three named *Monroe* plaintiffs, who served as flight engineers, brought suit claiming that their forced retirement at age 60 violated the Age Discrimination in Employment Act of 1967, as amended (29 U.S.C. sec. 621 et seq.). The *Higman* plaintiffs, who were captains seeking to transfer to flight engineer positions at age 60, filed their complaint on April 18, 1979. During the course of the proceedings, many additional pilots and flight engineers joined the complaint, bringing the number of individual plaintiffs to 112.[18]

The individual plaintiffs brought suit claiming that their forced retirement at age 60 violated the ADEA. Two groups of plaintiffs were suing. The *Monroe* plaintiffs were suing as flight engineers at the time of their involuntary retirement and sought to continue in that position beyond their sixtieth birthdays. The *Higman* plaintiffs served as captains, copilots, flight instructors, or flight management pilots until age 60, the age at which Federal Aviation Administration (FAA) regulations require that they cease to serve as pilots on commercial flights. They sought to transfer to the position of flight engineer, for which the FAA imposes no age requirement. The Equal Employment Opportunity Commission (EEOC) intervened in this action seeking an injunction to prohibit United from continuing these age-based policies. The EEOC alleged that United had violated the ADEA by denying plaintiffs and other employees the opportunity to work as flight engineers solely because of their age (60).[19]

All the plaintiffs were seeking either to continue in or transfer to the flight engineer position at age 60. All were fully qualified in terms of medical qualifications and airman proficiency up to their sixtieth birthdays, when they were forced to retire by United. United, however, refused to permit them to continue their employment, citing a company policy prohibiting any flight engineer to work past his or her sixtieth birthday. (*Plaintiffs' Brief*, pp. 4–7)

In 1975, United Airlines performed a detailed study of the effect of incapacitation of the flight engineer on flight safety and concluded that such incapacitation did not interfere with the safe operation of the flight. Consistent with the findings of this study, United had, on numerous occasions, permitted individuals recently recovered from serious medical conditions to return to flight duties but limited them to the position of flight engineer.

United has an elaborate and very sophisticated system of testing the current proficiency of its flight crew, including its flight engineers. All of United flight-deck crew members pass through a training center once a year for proficiency training and checking conducted by United flight instructors and check pilots. During these sessions, the flight engineer's performance is evaluated using a computerized flight simulator. Thus, even United's vice-president for flight standards and training admitted that United's system of proficiency checking provided an objective measure of the proficiency of the flight crew

member that is effective regardless of the age of the individual tested. (*Plaintiffs' Brief*, pp. 10–14)

In addition, United's flight engineers are not permitted to continue in duty status unless they pass two physical examinations per year. (One is administered by the FAA and the other by United.) Therefore, United doctors have a longitudinal medical history detailing any significant changes or patterns in the health of each individual. United doctors have admitted that these tests are effective in screening crew members of all ages, including those aged 59. They also admit that as far as they were aware, all of their medical procedures could be used to test flight engineers over age 60.

All experts agree, even those from United, that there is enormous variability in aging between individuals. There is no age at which aging begins or accelerates. Therefore, from a medical point of view, age 60 has no special significance in the aging process. A deterioration in function is caused by specific, identifiable diseases and not by the aging process itself. Thus, conditions that could impair a flight engineer's ability to perform his or her job duties are capable of detection through medical and performance testing. (*Plaintiffs' Brief*, pp. 14–18) For many years United had used tests to assess, on an individual basis, the ability of pilots and flight engineers to perform their jobs safely and efficiently. The FAA and United have permitted numerous pilots to return to flight duty following serious ailments provided they can first pass appropriate medical and psychological tests. Since these tests can be used to evaluate individuals regardless of age, an upper age limit of 60 for employment for United flight engineers is not reasonably necessary for safety. (*Plaintiffs' Brief*, pp. 21–23)

In 1960, the FAA adopted the age-60 rule. The FAA repeatedly ruled, however, that this regulation was not applicable to flight engineers and that no other FAA regulation required that a flight engineer be below age 60. Therefore, United's only reason for enforcing the age-60 rule for flight engineers was that such employment was contrary to the terms of their pension plan. However, in 1978, Congress amended the ADEA to eliminate the "pension plan" exception and prohibit involuntary retirement based on age. For United to continue this practice, it would have to prove that age was a BFOQ reasonably necessary to the normal operation of its business. United did not present any evidence that they had conducted studies or prepared any reports in 1978 to evaluate whether their policy with respect to flight engineers was necessary for safety. Thus, it must be concluded that United is in violation of the ADEA. (*Plaintiffs' Brief*, pp. 26–28)

The *Higman* plaintiffs were captains who wanted to "downbid" to flight engineers. The collective bargaining agreement did contain certain restrictions on "downbidding" by the captains. In general, crew members were limited to bidding up to higher-ranking positions or to higher-status equipment. However, downbidding was permitted where a pilot wished to bid onto a higher-status plane as a second officer. In fact, a very substantial number of pilots had been permitted to downbid over the last ten years. United never gave any serious consideration to the request of age-60 pilots to downbid to second officer positions when they became unable, solely because of the FAA rule, to continue in their positions as captains. Although United permitted downbidding in all situations ranging from reductions-in-force to performance failure, they would not permit a captain to downbid. United could not show that there was even one other instance, aside from pilots affected by the age 60 rule, where a pilot who became unable to continue in his present position was denied the opportunity to downbid to a position he could hold. (*Plaintiffs' Brief*, pp. 33–33A)

There is no dispute in this case that United refused to allow flight engineers to work past their sixtieth birthdays. Such an age-based employment policy is a prima facie violation of the ADEA. Thus, it is United's burden to prove that its policy of barring all persons over the age of 60 from the flight engineer's position is a BFOQ reasonably necessary for the safe transportation of passengers, and that fitness could not be determined on an individual basis. As to the reasonable necessity of United's policy, there is no evidence showing that the flight engineer's position was critical to safety. The flight engineer has no responsibilities for flying the plane or manipulating the flight control. In fact, United does not consider it necessary to use a flight engineer at all on two of its jets. This is why the FAA has never imposed any age limitation for the position of flight engineer.

As to the inability to determine fitness of a person on an individual basis, even United admits that their systems are fully capable of identifying unfit crew members at all ages through age 59. They also know of no procedure that becomes ineffective beyond age 60. United's capacity to test fitness on an individualized basis is underscored by its well-established policy of permitting crew members to return to flight duties following serious illness provided that they pass appropriate medical tests. There is no explanation why United could not perform similar tests or determine whether otherwise healthy 60-year-olds were experiencing any loss of function. (*Plaintiffs' Brief*, pp. 35–40)

Moreover, United's ability to detect deterioration in function is not limited to its periodic medical exams and performance evaluations. The flight engineer does not work in isolation. His job requires him continuously to interact with other individuals. Several times on every flight, the captain, copilot, and flight engineer check their instrument panels by calling out challenges and responses to each other. Any deterioration in cognitive function would be apparent to the flight engineer's co-workers. Thus, there is ample evidence for a jury to conclude that United's requirement that flight engineers retire at 60 was not reasonably related to, nor necessary for, the safe transportation of passengers, and that individualized testing of fitness was possible. (*Plaintiffs' Brief*, pp. 40–41).

United's refusal to permit pilots affected by the FAA age 60 rule to downbid, while permitting downbidding by pilots displaced from their positions for non-age related reasons, constitutes disparate treatment. The ADEA makes it unlawful for an employer to treat employees differently on account of their age. The evidence previously stated demonstrated that the plaintiffs were indeed treated differently because of their age, and that age was a determining factor in the rejection of their transfer requests. United could not demonstrate that there was even one circumstance, other than disqualification by the FAA age 60 rule, where the airline had refused to permit downbidding by a pilot displaced from his or her current job. There is no nondiscriminatory, age-neutral reason for this difference in treatment. Therefore, one must conclude that pilots over age 60 were discriminated against on account of their age. (*Plaintiffs' Brief*, pp. 65–68)

The FAA age 60 rule does not require retirement at age 60; it merely requires that pilots cease to occupy captain or copilot positions at that age. The FAA rule presents no bar to pilots transferring to flight engineer positions at age 60. Although the ADEA does not require that older workers be afforded special working conditions in order to allow them to remain employed, it does require that older workers be granted the same opportunity as younger employees to transfer to other jobs when they are forced to vacate their current positions. Therefore, since age 60 pilots were denied the right accorded to younger employees to transfer to lower status positions when displaced from their pilot jobs, United violated the ADEA by engaging in disparate treatment on account of age. (*Plaintiffs' Brief*, pp. 70–73)

UNITED'S DEFENSE

Since the plaintiffs' action involved the collectively bargained agreements between United and the Airline Pilots Association (ALPA), United counterclaimed against the ALPA. United claimed that it had the lawful right to require all crew members to retire at age 60. For over 30 years, United, for publicly asserted reasons of safety, had a policy of requiring flight engineers to retire at 60. It asserted a bona fide occupational qualification (BFOQ) defense permitted under the ADEA to all the plaintiffs. As to the *Higman* plaintiffs, it also asserted defenses based on age-neutral terms of the ALPA-United collective bargaining agreement.[20] In the 1950s, United adopted a retirement policy requiring each cockpit member to retire at age 60.

In 1960, the FAA adopted its own rule prohibiting captains and copilots from serving after age 60 because of the inability of medical science to predict declining function on an individual basis. In addition, in 1981, the National Institute of Aging concluded as part of a congressionally mandated inquiry, that the FAA rule should not be changed since the decline in pilot functions cannot be accurately predicted or measured. Furthermore, United cannot predict or detect conditions that result in medical groundings after the annual extensive examination. In the five-year period from 1976 to 1981, United medically grounded 209 flight officers. Only 53 individuals with medical problems were detected in the annual examination. Stated another way, 146 of the 209 were not discovered. The medical condition developed after the detailed examination given by United Airlines. (*Defense Brief*, pp. 5–9)

The inability of medical science to predict an individual's reaction to say, stress, is illustrated in United's attempt to follow FAA "exemption" policies. The FAA identifies certain illnesses or medical conditions that require grounding. With changed scientific procedures, including sophisticated stress tests, the FAA adopted an exemption practice in which a grounded pilot who had presumably recovered could subject himself to expert professional physical examination to seek reinstatement from the medical grounding. United allowed 20 such pilots who were granted exemptions after the most extensive physical examination available to return to the cockpit. However, many members of the test group, far from having recovered, had recurrent serious difficulties resulting in subsequent grounding. In short, United's experience was that the supposed ability to predict, on an individual basis, was invalid. (*Defense Brief*, p. 11)

Barring Flight Engineers to Work beyond Age 50 Met the BFOQ Criteria

A BFOQ was established if United's age policy was reasonably related to safety and if, further, the evidence demonstrated that a blanket rule must be used because of the inability to rely on individualized analysis. United contended that the facts of the case and its actions proved that it was so in the present case. As to the duties of the flight engineer, United contended they were crucial to the safety of the plane. It was important in this respect to look at flight handbooks of various planes. The "Irregular Procedures" and "Emergency Procedures" portions of these handbooks are significant in this case. The B–747 handbook specifies about 15 emergencies that require the flight engineer to respond appropriately and 50 emergencies where he has very specific duties. In the DC–10 handbook, there are about 22 emergency procedures. Every witness on the subject had stated that if the flight engineer was unable to perform his duties properly, it could have an adverse impact on safety. This assertion was in direct conflict with the plaintiffs' claim that the flight engineer did not contribute to safety. (*Defense Brief*, p. 21)

United, therefore, contended that its 1950 policy, which required all crew members to retire at age 60, was, therefore, lawful. It was "reasonably related" to the essential operation of its business. Furthermore, it was impossible or impractical to decide who should retire through individual analysis.

United asserted that its policy met the BFOQ criteria, which required a two-step order of proof. First, the rule must be reasonably related to the defendant's business. The essence of United's business is safe transportation. Second, it must be determined that the defendant cannot handle the retirement issue by individual or case-by-case review. Every witness who had been asked to comment on the importance of the flight engineer conceded that the flight engineer performed duties that were necessary to safety. A sampling of National Transportation Safety Board (NTSB) reports on the causes of major accidents also disclosed that the failure to perform flight engineer duties had been responsible for some major accidents.

In addition, the courts in a number of cases have held that flight attendants with limited safety duties, under the BFOQ defense exception in Title VII, may require those who become pregnant to take involuntary leaves of absence. If the law treats flight attendants in this manner, surely a B–747 flight engineer who has very specific duties in about 50 emergency situations and which, if not performed properly, could lead to disaster, has an adequate legal relationship to safety. Passenger safety is the essence of United's business. Congress has mandated that United must operate its business with the highest possible degree of care. Thus, safe is not sufficient, rather, the safest possible air transportation is the ultimate goal. (*Defense Brief*, pp. 25–30)

Contractual Obligations under the Collective Bargaining Agreement

The application of the age 60 policy was based in part on the fact that all cockpit crew members were pilots under the collective bargaining agreement. The simple fact was that the contract provision against downbidding impacted equally on all crew members regardless of age. The bona fide seniority system established by United's collective bargaining contract was, as a matter of law, a valid defense calling for judgment against the *Higman* plaintiffs. *Higman* plaintiffs alleged that they retained sufficient seniority to be employed as flight engineers. United denied this, pleading that contract provisions barred plaintiffs' transfer to the flight engineer positions. (*Defense Brief*, pp. 33–37)

Prior to 1978, United's age policy was expressly sanctioned by the ADEA, as part of its pension plan. Congress withdrew this exemption. The key issue, therefore, was United's decision in 1978 to continue and reaffirm a medical policy that was established in 1950 before there was an ADEA. The evidence provided by United's Medical Department was not contradicted at the trial. Among other things, it showed that as of the end of 1978, over 50% of medical groundings were unanticipated. It would be inconceivable that United, with the finest medical department in the industry, would not detect and remove from flight those hundreds of cases at the time of the examination if techniques for such detection were available. In short, United contended that it could not predict and, therefore, control through individual testing, such unanticipated occurrences. Furthermore, the FAA rule, while limited to two crew members, was based on the inability to predict psychological and physical failure. Thus, there should be a judgment for the defense since there was no evidence to consider contradicting United's strong medical case. (*Defense Brief*, pp. 51–53)

Stated again, in 1978 the Congress amended the ADEA to bar the use of retirement plans or seniority systems to require involuntary retirement because of age. However, Congress did not amend the ADEA as it applied to promotion and trans-

fer opportunities affected by terms of a bona fide seniority system. In the absence of United's age 60 policy, the eligibility and bidding rule applicable to all United pilots would not have allowed captains, at age 39 or 69, to transfer to flight engineer positions without extraordinary circumstances not applicable to plaintiffs. In 1978, Congress did not intend to require that employees disqualified from continuing in a position subject to a BFOQ be given the statutory right to transfer to positions not subject to a BFOQ. Lack of seniority rights, not age, caused plaintiffs to be denied transfers to flight engineer positions. Whether or not the age 60 policy precluded service by flight engineers after 60, *Higman* plaintiffs would have been denied transfers to flight engineer positions in observance of the terms of a bona fide seniority system, which is not a subterfuge to evade the purposes of the ADEA. (*Defense Brief*, pp. 67–68)

Furthermore, a court has held (in *United Airlines, Inc.* v. *McMann* 434 U.S. at 203) that a retirement plan provision established prior to the enactment of the ADEA, and maintained without material changes thereafter, could not be considered a subterfuge to evade the purposes of the ADEA. The seniority system, as it existed in the 1965–1966 pilot agreement, limited bidding rights in the same manner as subsequent agreements, except for post-1967 modifications, which allowed greater use of length of service. Therefore, plaintiffs were in no worse position under any agreement negotiated after 1967 than they were under the 1965–1966 agreement. The challenged provisions of the seniority system had not been materially modified since the enactment of the ADEA. Therefore, the failure to amend the seniority system could not be deemed to constitute a subterfuge. (*Defense Brief*, pp. 53 and 67) United, therefore, asserted that it had not violated the ADEA by engaging in disparate treatment and that the company's policy was reasonable and not in violation of the ADEA.

LEGAL PROCEEDINGS:
OUTCOME OF THE LAWSUIT

On September 29, 1982, the jury in a district court returned a verdict for the plaintiffs. It also found that United's violation of the ADEA Act was willful. Based on the finding of willfulness, the district court doubled the damages awarded by the jury. In four following decisions in 1983, the district court issued rulings to force compliance with the jury decision by the defendants. On January 6, 1984, United and other defendants appealed to the Seventh Circuit of the United States Court of Appeals (736 F.2d394 [1984]). In its appeal, United claimed that the district court had erroneously instructed the jury in several crucial respects, thereby denying United its right to proper defense. In particular, United argued that the trial court should not have denied the airline a method of establishing its defense of BFOQ to which it was entitled. United also claimed that the trial court erroneously instructed the jury on the role of pretext in evaluating the airline's claims; and,

that the airline was not entitled to judgment notwithstanding the verdict with respect to the claim of one career second officer on the ground that the officer's retirement was required by the terms of the airline's bona fide retirement plan.

In proceedings that dragged on until August 10, 1984, the Appeals Court reversed the lower court verdict. The Appeals Court agreed with United's contention that the lower court had erred against United in denying its lawful defense. On February 25, 1985, the United States Supreme Court refused to hear a further appeal (No. 84–916; No. 84–958, 470 U.S.).

In the end, the age 60 rule remains in effect, albeit ambiguously. At the same time, general practice allows pilots to downgrade to the flight engineer job (to which the age 60 rule does not apply). In 1985, United Airlines agreed to pay some $11 million in damages to over 100 pilots in the "job downgrading" issue. Pan Am Airways fought a similar issue through courts from 1981 to 1988 with essentially the same results.[21]

NOTES

1. Robert Clark, *Reversing the Trend Towards Early Retirement*, Washington, DC: American Enterprise Institute, 1981.
2. Alan Halcrow, "Age Old Problem of Discrimination." *Personnel Journal* (April 1985), p. 11.
3. 736 *Federal Reporter* 2nd Series, p. 394.
4. V. Louviere, "The Fight over Mandatory Retirement: How Old Is Old?" *Nation's Business* (March 1978), pp. 48–54.
5. J. Roger O'Meara, "Retirement." *Across the Board* (January 1977), pp. 4–8.
6. R. N. Butler, "The Relation of Extended Life to Extended Employment Since the Passage of Social Security in 1935." *Health and Society*, 61 (1983), pp. 420–29.
7. Barnet N. Berin, "From the Penny Express to the Pension Express." *Across the Board* (June 1978), pp. 42–47, 50–53.
8. Stanley Yolles, *The Aging Employee*. New York: Human Sciences Press, Inc., 1984; U.S. Government Printing Office, *Laws Of 90th Congress, 1st. Session*, "Age Discrimination in Employment Act of 1967," (Public Law 90–202; 81 Stat. 602), pp. 658–65.
9. United States House of Representatives, Subcommittee on Aviation of the Committee on Public Works and Transportation, *To Eliminate Age Limitations Presently Imposed on Certain Pilots of Aircraft*, Hearings, 96th Congress, 1st Session (July 18–19, 1979). Washington, DC: U.S. Government Printing Office, pp. 5–10.
10. Robert MacDonald, *Mandatory Retirement and the Law*, Washington, DC: American Enterprise Institute, 1978.
11. Stephen Cabot, "Living with the New Amendments to the Age Discrimination in Employment Act." *Personnel Administrator*, 31, no. 12 (January 1987), p. 53.

12. Robert H. Faley, Lawrence S. Kleiman, and Mark L. Lengnick-Hall, "Age Discrimination and Personnel Psychology: A Review and Synthesis of the Legal Literature with Implications for Future Research." *Personnel Psychology*, 37 (1984), pp. 329-31.

13. Equal Employment Opportunity Commission, "Final Interpretations: Age Discrimination in Employment Act." *Federal Register*, 46, no. 188, pp. 47724–47728.

14. Marc Rosenblum, "The Role and Influence of Technology on Enforcement of the Age Discrimination in Employment Act of 1967." *Aging And Work* (Fall 1983), p. 305.

15. Faley et al., *"Age Discrimination,"* pp. 332–35.

16. *Ibid.*, pp. 335–37.

17. *Ibid.*, pp. 343–45.

18. *Gerry W. Monroe and Lee F. Higman, et al., Plaintiffs-Appellees and Equal Employment Opportunity Commission, Intervening Plaintiff-Appellee* v. *United Airlines, Inc., and Airline Pilots Association,* Defendants-Appellants, United States Court of Appeals, Seventh Circuit, August 10, 1984, 736 *Federal Reporter*, 2nd Series, p. 394.

19. "Brief for Appellees Gerry W. Monroe and Lee F. Higman, et al., and the Equal Opportunity Employment Commission," submitted to the United States Court of Appeals, Seventh Circuit (October 28, 1983). (Hereafter cited as *Plaintiffs' Brief*.)

20. "Brief and Appendix for Appellants United Airlines, Inc., Airline Pilots Association International," submitted to the United States Court of Appeals, Seventh Circuit (April 1984). (Hereafter cited as *Defense Brief*.)

21. Katherine Bishop, "Pan Am to Pay Retired Pilots in Age Bias Suit." *New York Times* (February 4, 1988), p. a18.

SEARS ROEBUCK AND CO. v.
EQUAL EMPLOYMENT OPPORTUNITY COMMISSION

Employment discrimination and affirmative action

Equal opportunity and its concommitant, affirmative action, have been the bulwark of antidiscrimination policies of the civil rights movement during the last 30+ years. They have manifested themselves in a number of laws, court decisions, and government policies. They have influenced virtually every economic activity in the United States; impacted every economic actor in the public and private sector; and covered activities ranging from hiring, work-place actions, set-asides, competitive bidding, and government contracts, to name a few.

Notwithstanding their success or lack thereof, the last 15 years have seen an upsurge of actions on a number of fronts challenging the entire structure of affirmative action policies and programs. While the entire edifice of the civil rights movement and the national effort was directed at correcting past inequalities through expanding the scope of affirmative action programs, more recent efforts have been directed at dismantling the very programs that had become the cornerstone of this nation's affirmative action drive. This dismantling is due, perhaps in part, to a changing political climate. It has also been further reenforced by various court decisions in the judicial arena. Even where the need for such programs is conceded, there is widespread criticism of the existing programs for their relative ineffectiveness. While the minority groups, and their representatives and supporters, overwhelmingly defend the need for such programs, some dissenting voices are being heard from among the minority groups.

In the judicial arena, the Supreme Court, in a 5–4 decision, in the case of *Adarand Constructors* v. *Pena*, held that affirmative action programs must be subject to the most searching constitutional scrutiny. The contract giving rise to the dispute in this case came about as a result of the Surface Transportation and Uniform Relocation Assistance Act of 1987, a D.O.T. appropriations measure. Section 106(c)(1) of STURAA provides that "not less than 10 percent" of the appropriated funds "shall be expended with small-business concerns owned and controlled by socially and economically disadvantaged individuals." The Court held that such quotas, and in particular, the government's use of race-based presumptions in identifying such individuals, violates the equal protection component of the Fifth Amendment's Due Process Clause. The Supreme Court overturned the Appeals Court's decision and remanded the case for further proceedings.

Although the Court's decision was carried out with the narrowest of majorities, it nevertheless signaled a change in the Court's thinking in that it repudiated a number of earlier decisions that had provided the legal foundation for such set-aside programs. The case will most likely span a more vigorous and widespread attack on other government-mandated affirmative action requirements.

Soon after the Supreme Court's decision, the Clinton Administration announced that it would undertake a review of all its affirmative action policies and programs and that the Justice Department would henceforth provide legal guidance on affirmative action to federal agencies. However, the Federal Communication Commission was not waiting for such a review and immediately announced that it planned to scrap its earlier intention to provide preferences to women and minorities in its coming sale of wireless-telephone licenses. Instead, F.C.C. officials said, those advantages will now be given to small business generally. And the process seems to have continued at different levels of state and municipal government. Needless to say, the politicians have been only too quick to join the fray and echo the complaints and resentments of the "angry white male."[1]

THE PROBLEM REMAINS UNRESOLVED

No one would disagree that existing affirmative action programs have not always yielded their desired results. Nor would anyone argue that some of the laws and regulatory procedures have imposed often onerous, time consuming, and expensive reporting and compliance requirements on the business community. By giving preference to minorities, there may have been instances where otherwise equally qualified candidates and businesses may have been left at a competitive disadvantage. The undeniable fact, however, still remains. Despite all the complaints about minority preferences, blacks and other minorities have to yet gain equality in the marketplace. While it is quite legitimate to point out the defects in the existing system, the alternative is not to deny the existence of the problem, but to offer alternative solutions.[2]

The case of *Sears, Roebuck and Co.* v. *Equal Employment Commission* [hereinafter referred to as Sears and EEOC respectively] provides the reader with an illustration of the complexity of issues involved in determining whether and how discrimination on the job has taken place; some of the remedial measures that might be taken with a view to ameliorating the situation and protecting the rights of the disadvantaged; and, how one might go about measuring the results and ensuring compliance.

EEOC AND SEARS ROEBUCK AND COMPANY

On January 31, 1986, the U.S. District court for the Northern District of Illinois Eastern Division dismissed the case against Sears Roebuck and Co. by ruling that EEOC failed to prove that the company had discriminated against women in hiring, promotion, or pay in its employment practices.

The Sears case deals with one of the major attempts by the government to create a broad-scale pattern of enforcement to the law which, in fact, would not base itself so much on proving individual discrimination, but suggest broad patterns of implied discrimination based on the existence of certain employment categories. One of the important assumptions underlying this concept was that any significant difference between the composition of a company's work force and of the relevant qualified population pool from which such a work force is drawn, is evidence of a pattern of discrimination that must be corrected. Most earlier government attempts at equal employment were on a case-by-case basis. It was felt that during the early 1970s this approach was not very efficient or productive because individual cases were time consuming and did not create broad patterns of compliance. The strategy of the EEOC at the time was for the government to initiate a new approach, i.e., to go after major corporations and create settlements that involved large number of employees. The *EEOC* v. *AT&T* case, which was settled without litigation, was the last of this kind. This would thereby set national patterns for hiring and employment practices. A number of cases were filed based on the notion that there are employment categories where the number of employees from different races or sexual categories were disproportionate to the number of employees in the "relevant" group. This led to the assumption of discrimination. Most of the cases did not come to trial; as was the case with GM and At&T, all were settled out of court. Therefore, Sears was the first major case where the concept of "broad pattern of discrimination" was put to judicial test.

BACKGROUND TO THE SEARS CASE

The major struggle that began in 1973 heated up on January 24, 1979 when Sears Roebuck and Company, the nation's largest retailer, filed an unprecedented class action suit against ten federal agencies (Table 1) charging that various federal laws and actions (Table 2) have contributed to the creation of an "unbalanced civilian work force which restricts employment opportunities of American citizens."[3]

Sears and the government had been in disagreement over EEOC policies for some time prior to the initiation of the case. The

company had previously settled two cases with the Labor Department over its alleged violations of the Equal Pay Act, and with the Office of Federal Contract Compliance Programs over its national affirmative action plan. In all these cases, it was found that Sears had not met the requirements of the law. Sears sued to block the release of the 1977 EEOC's finding as well as the disclosure of the company's affirmative action plan and employment data on individual facilities. The EEOC, in responding to the Sears suit, issued a statement stating that the litigation was part of a series of court cases initiated by Sears in an effort to defend its current practices for hiring and firing. The company responded that its affirmative action plan and program were better than anything the

TABLE 1. Federal Agencies Charged in Sears Suit

Attorney General of the United States
Secretary of Labor
Chairman of Equal Opportunity Employment
    Commission (EEOC)
Secretary of Commerce
Secretary of Health, Education, and Welfare (HEW)
Secretary of Housing and Urban Development (HUD)
Director of the Office of Federal Contract and
    Compliances Programs (OFCCP)
Office of Federal Statistical Policy and Standards
Bureau of Census
Federal Agency Council on the 1980 Census

TABLE 2. List of Constitutional Provisions, Statutes, and Executive Orders Cited in Sears Suit

Article I, S1 of the Constitution of the United States
Article I, S2, cl. 3 of the Constitution of the United States
Article II, S1, of the Constitution of the United States
Fifth Amendment of the Constitution of the United States
Section 10 of the Administrative Procedure Act, 5 U.S.C.
    SS701–706
Equal Pay Act of 1963, 29 U.S.C. S206 (d)
Age Discrimination in Employment Act of 1967, 29 U.S.C.
    SS623,633a
Rehabilitation Act of 1973, 29 U.S.C. SS791 (b)–(c),793(a)
Comprehensive Employment and Training Act of 1973, 29
    U.S.C. SS848 (f), 983, 991 (a)
Vietnam Era Veterans' Readjustment and Assistance Act of
    1974, 38 U.S.C. SS2012 (a), 2014, 2021
Title VI, Civil Rights Act of 1966, 42 U.S.C. SS2000d et seq.
Title VII, Civil Rights Act of 1964, 42 U.S.C. SS2000d et seq.
Title VIII, Civil Rights Act of 1968, 42 U.S.C. SS3601 et seq.
Title IX, Education Amendments of 1972, 20 U.S.C. SS1681 et
    seq.
Housing and Community Development Act of 1974, 42 U.S.C.
    SS5309(a)
Age Discrimination Act of 1975, 42 U.S.C. SS 6101, 6102
Budget and Accounting Act, 31 U.S.C. S18b
Executive Order No. 11,246, 30 Fed. Reg. 12,319 (1965),
    reprinted U.S.C. S2000e note, at 1232 (1976) (prohibits
    discrimination by federal contractors on the basis of
    race, color, religion, sex, or national origin)
Reorganization Plan No. 1 of 1978, 43 Fed. Reg. 19,807 (1978)

SOURCE: Departments of State, Justice and Commerce, the
    Judiciary, and Related Agencies Appropriation Act,
    1979, Pub. 95–431, Title V, 92 Stat. 1021 (1978)

EEOC could point to for other companies. The Sears Roebuck case was intended to create a settlement that would set broad patterns to be applied to other cases.

The public policy and political motivation behind such a strategic move was to achieve broad gains in the employment and upward mobility for various minority groups. The government was also counting on broad public support for such a move and the relative reluctance of major corporations to confront the government where there were serious risks of adverse publicity, regardless of the eventual ending of the case.

This strategy had some serious drawbacks because it was based on certain assumptions about the nature of underlying factual data and its casual relationship with the eventual outcome in employment practice. That the reasoning proved to be somewhat faulty is reflected in the eventual dismissal of the government's case against Sears Roebuck. However, of even greater importance, this case reflects the complex nature of the problems involved with defining and correcting discriminatory employment practices on the one hand and creating greater job opportunities for minorities and other disadvantaged groups on the other. The two objectives may not be one and the same thing. Finally, the case should lead us to explore other more proactive ways of ensuring equal employment opportunities for all U.S. citizens.

ISSUES FOR ANALYSIS

The allegations made by Sears against EEOC as well as the company's accusers in defending itself from EEOC's charges have been a bone of contention between American business and federal regulatory agencies for a number of years. Notwithstanding the merits of Sears' charges, the case raises important issues of corporate strategy and public policy that merit serious consideration.

1. It is true that public priorities must change with changing social needs; and public agencies charged with implementing federal laws and policies. However, there is a clear need for setting priorities when the interests of various groups, protected under different laws, come into conflict and cannot be satisfied simultaneously:
   a) Where should the responsibility lie for setting such priorities, and how can they be established?
   b) What are the options available to business firms when caught between conflicting pressures for compliance of various laws and agency regulations representing different constituencies?
2. In case business firms are forced to set priorities on their own, what standards of performance can be accepted as a measure of "good-faith" effort?
3. What is the proper use of statistical data in establishing the existence and magnitude of job discrimination? What factors should federal agencies and courts take into consideration in weighing the credibility of statistical data?
4. What were some of the elements of Sears strategy and tactics during the period the lawsuit was in progress? To what extent can these strategies and tactics be followed in similar and different area of business-government relations or business-social policy issues?

FACTS AND CIRCUMSTANCES OF THE CASE

Headquartered in Chicago, Illinois, Sears maintains more than 2,500 facilities in all 50 states, the District of Columbia, and Puerto Rico. It employs approximately 400,000 people, and is the nation's second largest employer of women. The suit, entitled *Sears v. The Attorney General*, was filed in U.S. District Court in Washington, D.C., on behalf of Sears and all other general merchandise retailers with more than 15 employees. In its suit, Sears pointed out that the laws protecting veterans, the handicapped, and the aged limit the number of jobs and promotions available for women and minorities. Yet, the EEOC and the OFCCP have in the past decade pressed employers for compliance with employment opportunities laws favoring women and minorities. Sears charged that there existed a conflict among many federal employment laws and that "Federal agencies were trying to hold private employers liable for the work force the government itself created." Sears and similarly situated employers, therefore, found it impossible to satisfy the government even if they were committed to equal employment opportunities for all Americans.

In its complaint, Sears strongly defended its hiring and promotion record despite the burdens created by the company's compliance with veterans' laws. According to Sears' then chairman and chief executive officer, Edward Telling:

Of our more than 400,000 employees at the end of 1977, 19.9 percent were minorities compared with 8.7 percent in 1965. Minorities represented 10.5 percent of our officials and managers—up from 1.4 percent in 1956. And 36 percent of the officials and managers were women, compared with 20 percent in 1965.

According to the latest information available from the EEOC, the percentage of women at Sears in the officials and managers category is more than double the average of all other employers reporting to the EEOC. This includes 38,000 companies, employing 34 million workers. And with respect to minorities, we lead other reporting companies by more than a third in the officials and managers category.

We believe this demonstrates our commitment to the spirit and letter of the law. We also believe it is time to end government practices which are working at cross purposes, hampering real progress and discouraging voluntary efforts.[4]

Despite this outstanding record, the company found itself embroiled in conflict with the EEOC for years and could not come to an agreement with that agency. Sears stated that it had filed the lawsuit to "cut through the

impossible conflicting regulations, to force a clarification of irreconcilables, to help to refocus national goals and achievable means towards these goals." The action taken by the firm was not a spur-of-the-moment decision, according to company officials, but "came as a culmination of exasperating circumstances experienced" by Sears.[5]

The Sears Complaint

In 1977, following a lengthy investigation initiated in 1973, the EEOC agreed on the settlements with American Telephone & Telegraph Company, five other employees (Ford, General Motors, General Electric, the International Brotherhood of Electric Workers, and Sears) were charged with nationwide employment discrimination by the then EEOC chairman. Sears sued to block the release of the 1977 EEOC's findings, as well as the disclosure of the company's affirmative action plan and employment data on individual facilities. The company asserted that neither these findings, nor the underlying proprietary information, could be made public by the EEOC. Sears also asserted that the EEOC had made pledges of confidentiality, which the EEOC denied. Critics wondered what Sears had to hide, since on a comparative basis, the company had "the best" equal employment record in the country. Further, decrying the EEOC charges against the firm, Sears observed that it said "something dreadful" about the future of voluntary efforts if a company with the best, or one of the best, records could be dragged into court and assessed with massive back pay.[6]

According to one federal official, "Sears doesn't want to [release the report] because it contains so much damaging information."[7] EEOC investigators had allegedly found that women and minorities were underrepresented in Sears management and in better paying sales jobs and were confined largely to clerical and part-time sales jobs. Critics also contended that Sears' progress in hiring and promoting minorities and women had been too slow. According to one federal official, "When you've got a work force so predominantly white male, you'll never catch up with a representative work force until sometime in the 21st century at the rate Sears is going."[8] Overall, 1,850 discrimination charges had been filed against the company with EEOC since 1965. This amount represents around 200 charges a year, which is a small figure when compared to the large number of employee decisions made by Sears. According to Ray J. Graham, director of equal opportunity at Sears, some of the EEOC charges were dismissed by the commission. In addition, about 50 employment discrimination lawsuits were then pending against the company.

Sears contended that the EEOC charges were unfair because the agency had not taken into account the progress Sears had made or the effects of federal policies on its work force. After informing the company of its findings in 1977, the EEOC was required by law to try to negotiate a settlement out of court. The agency demanded that Sears agree to a large dollar payment, which would be allocated on a proportional basis to all minority and female employees, regardless of whether or not they had been discriminated against. When no agreement could be reached between the parties, the EEOC broke off the negotiations on January 16, 1977. Eight days later, Sears filed its suit.

The thrust of the lawsuit was the firm's claim that employers had been denied "the right to comply" with various federal antidiscrimination statutes and policies because of conflicts between these guidelines, as well as the confusion existing in their interpretation and enforcement. Sears requested an injunction requiring the coordination of all equal opportunity laws and demanded the issuance of uniform guidelines in order "to resolve the existing conflicts between affirmative action requirements based on race and sex and those based on veterans' status, age and physical or mental handicap" (Complaint, Sec. X, Para. 7).[9]

CONFLICTING REQUIREMENTS IN FEDERAL LAW

The complaint lists a long series of actions by federal agencies that imposed conflicting employment policies on private employers.

Until 1964, the federal government actively supported, by statutes and regulations, the family unit with a single breadwinner. Moreover, the federal government, by setting military and civilian policy and by enacting laws pursuant to those policies, has undertaken to create and to shape the national labor force from which private employers must hire.

After World War II, the United States adopted an affirmative action policy that called for a national effort to integrate returning veterans into civilian life by providing them benefits such as job preferences and subsidized educational opportunity under the GI Bill of Rights. Congress also enacted statutes that required private employers to reemploy returning World War II veterans. Similar statutes were enacted during the Korean and Vietnam wars.

Sears complied with government policies by hiring veterans. Trained under the GI Bill, these veterans were able to fill managerial and skilled technical positions. About 97% of these veterans were male, and approximately 92% were white. After the Korean conflict and the Vietnam era, Sears again "complied with and exceeded the requirements" of legislation that provided for reemployment of veterans. Although these veterans were almost exclusively males, a greater proportion than before was now black. Of the Vietnam veterans, for example, less than 4% were women, but 20% were black. Of both Korean and Vietnam veterans, a much smaller percentage took advantage of educational benefits offered by the government than after World War II. The impact this group of veterans had on supervisory and management positions at Sears was consequently less dramatic than that of the World War II veterans. As of the filing of the lawsuit, of 31 senior executives, 27 were veterans. Of these, 23 were veterans of World War II.

In 1964, the federal government altered its stand on employment policy by including women and minority members in the group that should be given special consideration. In that year, Title VII of the Civil Rights Act[10] had been enacted, and in the following year President Johnson issued Executive Order No. 11,246[11] prohibiting discrimination in employment on the basis of race, color, religion, sex, or national origin by federal contractors and requiring them to implement affirmative action plans. Sears, as a federal contractor, voluntarily instituted a formal affirmative action program in 1968. As part of this program, the company inaugurated its Mandatory Achievement Goals (MAG) Plan in 1974. This plan requires, among other things, that each Sears unit "hire one underrepresented group member for every white male hired until the presence of the underrepresented group in a particular job grouping equals or exceeds its presence in the local trade hiring area."[12]

The Age Discrimination in Employment Act (ADEA) of 1967 protects people between the ages of 40 and 65 by prohibiting employers from exercising employment judgments on the basis of the age of the applicant or employee. The 1978 amendment to this act extends the coverage to individuals up to age 70 and raises the mandatory retirement age from 65 to 70. In compliance with the ADEA, Sears in 1978 suspended its mandatory retirement policies under which all hourly personnel had to retire at 65 years of age and most salaried personnel at 63 years of age. Before the suspension took effect, Sears had estimated, that over a six-year period, there would be a loss of 20,000 hourly job opportunities and 3,800 salaried job change opportunities, because in the past each retirement had triggered four hourly and six salaried promotional opportunities. At that time, Sears had estimated that about one-third of its employees would choose to remain beyond their normal retirement age, a figure that was only about half the number of those who actually chose to stay.

Sears claimed that the ADEA amendment considerably slowed its progress in hiring and promoting women and members of minority groups. The company was also disturbed by yet another inconsistency in EEOC's charge about the dominance of women in the part-time worker pool. Sears contended that the government has consistently encouraged part-time employment. The Equal Pay Act of 1963 allows employers to pay part-time employees on a different basis from full-time employees. In 1978, Congress enacted legislation to encourage flexible work schedules and part-time careers in federal employment situations. In 1977, women comprised approximately 75% of part-time federal government workers. Thus, if the government encourages part-time employment and condones the fact that women fill about three-fourths of these jobs at federal agencies, why should the EEOC object to a similar situation in the retail industry where women comprise about 77% of the firm's part-time force, a rate that is approximately equal to the national average of women in nonagricultural and salaried part-time jobs.

With regard to the government's failure to provide a diverse work force, Sears charged that the government's "failure, refusal or inability" to enforce antidiscrimination provisions concerning housing, education, training, and employment had exacerbated the inability of qualified members of minority groups and women to gain employment in management and skilled jobs and the inability of minorities to receive the education and training necessary to secure employment. It has also "deprived employers of an available pool of qualified minority and female applicants" and subjected employers "to liability for employment discrimination in spite of their good faith efforts to comply with the federal government's antidiscrimination mandates" (Complaint, Sec. VII, Para. 56).

Statistics

A core argument underlying Sears' complaint is the government's reliance on statistical sources of information, which Sears claimed are often inadequate and inaccurate (Complaint, Sec. VII). For example, there is no central source of valid and appropriate statistical data collected and disseminated, or recommended, by the federal government. Statistical data are maintained by diverse federal agencies in diverse ways and in diverse locations. OFCCP instructed federal equal employment compliance officers and private employers to use state and local employment and unemployment estimates to measure an employer's compliance with the laws. The National Commission on Employment and Unemployment Statistics and the General Accounting Office (GAO) found that state and local employment and unemployment estimates lack the accuracy of national estimates. EEOC depends on the EEO-1 system of data development, reporting, and collection for use in its educational, litigative, and research work. However, the EEO-1 database was not representative of the private industry civilian force; it was developed without the required participation of public users to ensure maximum usefulness; the published equal employment opportunity reports do not include an appraisal of the accuracy of the statistics; and the EEO-1 reports are not compiled and disseminated promptly. Furthermore, neither the EEOC, the OFCCP, nor other federal agencies that use statistics selected by them were able to determine the relevant labor market for retail sellers of general merchandise because appropriate statistics either were not compiled or, if compiled, were inconsistent, inappropriate, inaccurate, obsolete, or otherwise unavailable.

RELIEF SOUGHT BY SEARS

Because of the government's conflicting employment rules and regulations, their haphazard administration, and the use of inaccu-

rate statistical data to measure an employer's compliance with these guidelines, the Sears suit sought court orders that would:

1. prohibit the use against employers of any statistical disparities from the civilian labor force traceable to compliance with veterans acts and the Age Discrimination in Employment Act;
2. prohibit enforcement of the 1978 amendment of the Age Discrimination in Employment Act;
3. declare the EEOC's contention that employment of women in part-time jobs violates Title VII is an incorrect and invalid interpretation of applicable laws;
4. prohibit the use of a statistical approach to show compliance until the government has taken steps to reshape the national work force and has produced adequate statistics;
5. declare that Sears' voluntary Mandatory Achievement of Goals Plan complies with the law;
6. require the defendants to issue uniform guidelines to instruct employers how to resolve existing conflicts between affirmative action requirements based on race and sex and those based on a veteran's status, age, and physical or mental handicap;
7. bar federal agencies from seeking back pay or other damages from Sears and its class until they have made compliance possible.

THE FEDERAL GOVERNMENT'S RESPONSE

On March 26, 1979, the Justice Department filed a petition for the dismissal of the Sears complaint on grounds of "lack of jurisdiction over subject matter," and Sears' "failure to state a claim upon which relief can be granted."[13] The thrust of the Justice Department's argument was that in the absence of a government's formal charge, Sears has no case against which it sought the protection of the court. Simply put, "the complaint is a political essay, not a lawsuit." (Government's Response, p. 1)

The federal government argued that the issues raised by Sears, i.e., of the allegedly conflicting requirements of various federal antidiscrimination statutes and regulations, are traditionally the province of the legislature and the executive. Moreover, the relief sought by Sears calls on the court to assume continuing regulatory jurisdiction over the national antidiscrimination program. The Constitution (Article III) does not give the court a roving commission to inquire generally into the activities of the two other branches, or to provide government by injunction.

In pursuing its charge of lack of a justiciable claim, i.e., a claim which the courts can decide, on the part of Sears, the government charged that Sears was unable to point to a single instance in which the government had taken enforcement action against it for violations of antidiscrimination statutes, or in which Sears had been denied an opportunity to defend itself on grounds of its compliance with other statutes. Sears could not identify a single instance in which the government had used "statistical disparities" in an enforcement action to prove Sears had not complied with civil rights acts.

DISMISSAL AND APPEAL

On May 15, 1979, the court issued an order concluding that Sears had failed to present a justiciable case or controversy and that the case must be dismissed. In its order, the court essentially relied upon the arguments made by the Justice Department and stated that Sears must recognize that personnel policies reflecting earlier and more limited national attitudes must be modified to widen employment opportunities for all: "To be sure, realization of national policy of genuine equal opportunity for all citizens is a formidable task, but not beyond the notable skill and competence of Sears."[14]

Sears appealed the dismissal of its suit on July 13, 1979. The firm saw its prospects of a court resolution brighten by the Supreme Court's decision in the *Weber* case.[15] This case

resolved the legality of voluntary affirmative action programs after Kaiser Aluminium's plan had been challenged in court. Edward R. Telling, then chairman and chief executive officer at Sears, said: "This supports our own affirmative action program and should allay the concern of a number of black leaders who feared that our suit would delay affirmative action."[16]

EEOC FILES A COMPLAINT AGAINST SEARS

On October 17, 1979, EEOC finally filed a series of complaints against Sears charging the company with intentionally engaging in unlawful employment practices in violation of Title VII of the U.S. Civil Rights Act of 1964.[17]

The legal broadside against Sears consisted of a nationwide sex-discrimination suit brought in a Chicago federal court and four race-discrimination suits brought in federal courts in New York, Atlanta, Memphis, and Montgomery (Alabama). The race-bias complaints charge Sears with discriminating against blacks in its hiring practices at seven specific facilities. The New York suit also alleges discrimination against Hispanic Americans. The lawsuits came more than six years after the date when the EEOC had filed a charge with the commission alleging violation of Title VII by Sears.[18]

The major suit against Sears' home office in Chicago, Illinois, dealt with the issue of sex discrimination and charged that:

1. Since at least July 2, 1965, and continuously to date, Sears had intentionally engaged in unlawful employment practices in the Northern District of Illinois and in each and every state of the Continental United States in violation of Section 703 of Title VII 42 U.S.C. SS2000e–2, including, but not limited to, the following:

    Maintenance of recruitment and selection practices, assignment and transfer practices, training and promotion practices, paying women lower wages than are paid to male employees in the same establishment for equal work, and in general, organizing and conducting its employment practices in a manner that denied female employees employment opportunities, earnings, and on-the-job treatment enjoyed by male applicants and employees.

2. EEOC charged that since at least June 11, 1964, and continuously up until the present time, Sears, an employer having employees subject to the provisions of Section 6 of the FLSA, 29 U.S.C. S206, had willfully violated Sections 6(d) (1) and 15(a) (2) of the FLAA, 29 U.S.C. SS206(d) (1) and 215(a) (2), by discriminating between such employees on the basis of sex in the above mentioned manner.

EEOC requested that the court:

1. Grant a permanent injunction enjoining Sears from engaging in any employment practice which discriminates because of sex in violation of Title VII and FLSA.

2. Order Sears to institute and carry out policies, practices, and affirmative action programs that provide equal employment opportunities for females and that eradicate the effects of its past and present unlawful employment practices.

3. Order Sears to make whole those persons adversely affected by the unlawful employment practices described herein, by providing appropriate back pay, with interest, in the amount to be proved at trial and other affirmative relief necessary to eradicate the effects of its unlawful employment practices.

4. Grant such further relief as the Court deems necessary and appropriate.

5. Award the Commission its costs in this action.

USES AND ABUSES OF NEWS MEDIA BY SEARS AND EEOC AND THE REACTION OF THE BUSINESS COMMUNITY

The nature of the issues raised by Sears and the magnitude of their potential impact was so significant that the case attracted considerable national attention. The legal merits of the case notwithstanding, public opinion was likely to play an important role, for the resolution of some of the underlying issues would take place in the political and legislative arena where the opinion of the public carried considerable weight. It was, therefore, not surprising that both Sears and the EEOC made conscientious use of the news media to cultivate favorable opinion for their respective positions and viewpoints.

To make its case, Sears hired a well-known civil rights attorney, Charles Morgan, Jr., with a record of fighting desegregation cases for over a decade with "a mixture of law, politics and public relations. . . a mixture designed to change the way the government thinks and acts at least as much as it is designed to win a victory in court."[19] The majority view voiced in the news media proclaimed that the filing of the lawsuit by Sears was mainly a preemptive legal and public relations strike to gain the offensive. It was a tactic designed to win sympathy for the firm before the EEOC would file discrimination charges, or "to steal thunder from an anti-Sears suit" by the EEOC.[20] Sears certainly did not drop off the lawsuit quietly at the federal courthouse. Instead, it promoted the action as "loudly as a sale on dishwashers"[21] and billed the suit as a fundamental challenge to big government at news conferences and private press briefings in New York and Washington. Sears publicists distributed over 13,000 press kits to news organizations across the country. The company's president, A. Dean Swift, flew to Washington for briefings, where he announced that his company had filed the suit not only because of its own problems with various federal regulators, but for all corporations and for the country as a whole.

In filing a preemptive suit against the government and doing it with maximum media blitz, Sears was "ignoring a cardinal rule of retailing: '"Don't make enemies for that can hurt sales.'"[22] According to the *Wall Street Journal*, Sears had already alienated women's groups and their sympathizers—

hundreds and thousands of potential customers, but in the eyes of Sears' management, there was no evidence of this being true.

Federal officials viewed the suit as an effort to get in a roundhouse punch before the EEOC filed its own suit charging Sears with hiring discrimination. There was also skepticism in government circles and even among a few knowledgeable attorneys about the fundamental merits of Sears' claim. A federal official familiar with Sears' hiring practices was quoted in the *Wall Street Journal* as saying: "That suit is as spurious as a $7 bill, and any lawyer who would tell you otherwise is a horse's ass."[23]

Another news leakage by the EEOC occurred in August 1979, when the content of an internal memo written by the EEOC acting general counsel, Issie L. Jenkins, found its way to the press.[24] The memo, published by the *Employment Relations Report*, revealed that teams of EEOC lawyers, who in early 1979 had reinvestigated and analyzed the charges against Sears, had found "flaws" and "errors" in the 1977 findings of "reasonable cause." Thus the case against Sears would be weaker and narrower than had first been assumed. According to this memo, Jenkins recommended that the EEOC prepare the suit with no intention of filing it, and then use it as a bargaining chip to negotiate a settlement with Sears. The memo also noted that an EEOC out-of-court settlement with Sears would provide a more reasonable remedy, based on the EEOC's more complete understanding of the merits of the case, than a court would be likely to award. This settlement with Sears "would do more to enhance EEOC enforcement efforts than would immediately filing the suit," the Jenkins memo further said.[25]

SEARS FILES A MOTION TO DISMISS THE EEOC SUIT

Sears' key argument in its motion to dismiss the EEOC lawsuit[26] was based on the commission's alleged misconduct in handling the

Sears investigation before the agency filed its suit. Sears stated:

> The EEOC engaged in a carefully orchestrated pattern of leaks, disclosures, and other unfair and prejudicial acts designed to undermine Sears' business reputation, to coerce and harass Sears into settlement by attempting to "fuel private lawsuits" and to force Sears to forego its right to have its innocence determined by a court of law. It did this by attempting to create "a carefully cultivated public image" of guilt . . . by publicizing the filing of the charge against Sears in violation of Title VII; by intentionally or negligently allowing the Commission Decision to fall into the hands of the National Organization of Women (NOW) and another women's rights group which had charges pending against Sears (despite the existence of a federal Court order forbidding release) and by allowing portions of the decision to be published. (Memorandum in Support of Motion to Dismiss, C.A. 79–C–4373, 3.)

The EEOC actions, according to Sears, were not based upon a valid charge: they denied Sears due process of law, and did not permit conciliation. Sears' most important allegation of misconduct by the EEOC, however, arose from the dual positions of David A. Copus as deputy chief and later acting director of the commission's National Programs Division, while at the same time being an active member of the board of directors of the NOW Legal Defense and Education Fund (NOW-LDEF). Sears stated: "His name appears on a document entitled 'A Litigation strategy for NOW' with the names of others who were in charge of NOW's anti-Sears campaign." (Memorandum in Support of Motion to Dismiss, C.A. 79–C–4373, 12).

In its motion to dismiss the case, Sears thus charged that EEOC members' close affiliation with NOW and the leaks to this and other similar organizations led to harassment of Sears.

In addition to accusing EEOC of misconduct, Sears claimed that the Equal Pay Act allegations made by the commission should be dismissed, since the issue of equal pay had already been decided in an earlier suit by the government against Sears.[27] The court had denied the government's request for an equal pay injunction on a nationwide basis. Sears concluded that the EEOC had no case against it, and charged EEOC with "having sought to brand Sears and having led outside interest groups to expect a large monetary settlement or a lawsuit." (Memorandum in Support of Motion to Dismiss, C.A. 79–C–4373, 21).

Sears Victory in the Court

In Chicago, the location of the major case, Judge Grady denied the motion to dismiss, while expressing himself as sharply critical of the government's conduct. The trial judge in New York granted Sears' motion to dismiss and his judgment in favor of Sears was sustained in the Federal Court of Appeals for the Second Circuit. Judge Freeman in Atlanta also denied the motion in May of 1980, but in the same month Judge Varner in Montgomery granted the motion based upon the failure to timely verify the charges and the EEOC's refusal to engage in a bona fide conciliation issue. The following February, in Tennessee, a magistrate also recommended dismissal, finding that there had been no good faith investigation. All of the cases were eventually dismissed, except for the Chicago case, and all counts of prejudice were cleared. This left the EEOC's case to be resolved in the Chicago courtroom. This was finally resolved on January 31, 1986, following a 10-month protracted trial, when the Federal Court dismissed EEOC's case against Sears.[28]

As this process continued, the EEOC began to dismiss claim after claim, including several so-called "suitable individual charges." At the time of the original complaint, the suit involved 42 distinct claims of nationwide sex discrimination by Sears. By the time of the trial, the EEOC had abandoned all of its Equal Pay Act claims under Title VII. The two allegations the EEOC sought to prove at the trial were that Sears engaged in a nationwide practice of sex discrimination:

1. by saying that female applicants for all selling positions, commission or straight salary, should be deemed to have applied for a commission-selling position and be deemed to be fully qualified for commission selling whether or not they indicated interest in commission selling.
2. by paying female checklist management employees in certain job categories lower compensation than similarly situated male checklist management employees.

SUMMARY OF THE COURT'S DECISION

Legal Standards Applied to the Case

Two separate legal analyses are applied to this case and Title VII cases in general. These are: disparate treatment and disparate impact, each of which has distinct elements of proof. The EEOC claimed that the choice of a theory was unimportant. Under 703(a)(1) of Title VII, 42 U.S.C. 52000e2(a)(1), the disparate treatment theory, employers are prohibited from treating an employee less favorably than the employee's peers because of an employee's sex, color, religion, or national origin.[29] Here, the plaintiff must prove that unlawful discrimination has been the regular policy of the employer, that "discrimination was the company's standard operating procedure and the regular rather than the unusual practice." The focus is on the pattern of discriminatory decision making, not on individual employment decisions.

Under the disparate impact theory, the plaintiff must show that a facially neutral standard for hiring excludes a disproportionate number of members of a protected class. The EEOC admitted to not being able to identify any specific employment practice of Sears that is discriminatory to women, but instead contends that there is something in the subjective process at Sears.

The court concluded that the disparate impact theory could be applied only when a policy had been identified by the plaintiff. Since the EEOC had admitted to not having identified any specific neutral policy of Sears that disproportionately excused women from the job at issue in this case, the court chose to apply only the disparate treatment theory to this case.

Courts Ruling on the Use of Statistical Data by EEOC

An overwhelming majority of the proof given by the EEOC was statistical in nature, and statistical evidence is an acceptable form of evidence for discrimination. The statistics were analyzed in terms of the level of statistical significance of the results. The primary statistical analyses used by the EEOC were multiple regression analysis; the court critically examined the variables in the model and their ability to accurately measure the variables, the weights of the variables, and the importance of variables not included.

In evaluating EEOC's evidentiary data, the court carefully analyzed the quality of data, the type of statistical analyses, used the basic assumptions underlying the use of data and analyses, and the credibility of expert witnesses offered by both EEOC and Sears. The court found the Commission's position deficient and unsustainable on all these grounds.

Evidence and Possible Biases in the EEOC Data on Hiring

One of the most serious flaws in the EEOC's statistical analysis is in the selection of the applicant pool for commission sales jobs at Sears. EEOC's analysis arbitrarily included in its sales-applicant pool all individuals who checked the sales box; it assumed that they were seeking a sales position. The EEOC presented no evidence to support this as Sears presented evidence to prove it was false.

A second major flaw was the failure to include in its analysis the many important factors that significantly affect hiring. The EEOC chose only six factors: (a) job applied for; (b) age; (c) education; (d) job-type experience; (e) product line experience; and (f) commission product expenses. These factors in no way represent the necessary or most important factors. However, other factors were ignored that could be considered quite important in choosing an employee for a particular position, e.g., an applicant's interest in sales and in the product to be sold, or characteristics that could be determined only from an interview.

Faulty Basic Assumptions

EEOC also made certain specific assumptions about the data base which, on closer inspection, turned out to be unsustainable. These assumptions were: (1) all male and female sales applicants were equally likely to accept a job offer for all commission sales positions at Sears, and (2) all male and female sales applicants were equally qualified for commission sales positions at Sears.

The EEOC offered no credible evidence to support these assumptions, whereas Sears proved, with many different kinds of evidence, that men and women tended to have different interests and aspirations regarding work and the differences partially explain the lower percentage of women in commission sales jobs.

With regard to equal qualifications for men and women, the EEOC's own report, the Commission Sales Report, demonstrated this to be false. This, in addition to other deficiencies, e.g., creating artificial territorial and nationwide applicant pools, left the statistical analyses with no real value. Sears did not perform any of its own analyses, but instead offered other evidence to disprove the EEOC's analyses and to prove that a number of women hired and promoted into commission sales at Sears reflected its affirmative action efforts, not discrimination. Sears presented data on hiring and promotion figures that demonstrated the success of the company's efforts in promoting women.

Judge John A. Norberg stated: "viewing all of the evidence together, and considering the credibility of the witnesses and the reasonableness of their testimony, the court finds that EEOC has failed to carry its burden of persuasion on the claim of hiring discrimination. Its statistical evidence is wholly inadequate to support its allegations."

The most flagrant flaw in the EEOC's case was its failure to have "one employee or applicant witness" who claimed to be discriminated against. EEOC also did not account for the interests of applicants in commission sales and products sold on commission at Sears. In addition, the EEOC had also failed to counter Sears' highly convincing evidence of its affirmative action programs and failed to have one witness that could claim discrimination. The judge contended that the EEOC failed to prove its case of discrimination in hiring against women; and found that Sears had proven that it did not have such a pattern as practice.

In regards to promotion, the court stated: "the EEOC has failed to prove its claims of a nationwide pattern or practice of intentional discriminations against women in promotions into commission sales at Sears. To the contrary, the court finds that Sears has proven that it did not have any such pattern as practice. Moreover, Sears has proven legitimate, nondiscriminatory reasons for the alleged disparities and the EEOC has not proven them pretextual."[30]

Both Sears Roebuck and the EEOC Appeal the Lower Court Decision

The EEOC appealed the lower court judgment on the disparate treatment claims and its denial of partial summary judgment regarding a provision that had existed in the Sears Personnel Manual until 1974 allowing a male employee a day off with pay when his wife gave birth.[31] Sears cross-appealed the district court's refusal to dismiss the case on the alleged ground of conflict of interest.

On January 14, 1988, the Appeals Court for the Seventh Circuit decided in favor of Sears Roebuck by affirming the findings and decision of the lower court. In their judgment, the Court stated that "the performance of EEOC [with regards to all aspects of the case] was disappointing and did a disservice not only to Sears, but also to the public and even to NOW and its causes." The Appeals Court also upheld the lower court's decision with regard to the issues raised in Sears' cross- appeal.[32]

NOTES

1. "The Supreme Court," *New York Times* (June 13, 1995) Section D, p. 24; Steven A. Holmes, "Government Acts to Set Its Policy on Race Programs," *New York Times* (June 24, 1995), p. 1; Viveca Novak, "Oregon Easing Minority Hiring for Road Work," *Wall Street Journal* (June 23, 1995), Sec. A, p. 16; Seth Thomas, "A Challenge to the Concept of 'Disadvantaged'," *New York Times* (June 18, 1995), Sec. 1, p. 16.
2. Rochelle Sharpe, "Losing Ground: In Latest Recession, Only Blacks Suffered Net Employment Loss," *Wall Street Journal* (September 14, 1993), p. A12; B. Drummond

Ayers, Jr., "Affirmative Action: The Race to Win over the Angry White Male," *New York Times* (June 4, 1995). Sec. 4, p. 2: Gail Sheehy, "Angry Men, Resilient Women" *New York Times* (June 19, 1995), Sec. A, p. 13; Claudia H. Deutsch, "Affirmative Action: Selling to Big Companies Cautiously in the Mainstream; Minorities Move Ahead as Political Currents Shift," *New York Times* (June 7, 1995), Sec. D, p. 1.
3. Sears, Roebuck and Company, News Release, January 24, 1979.
4. *Ibid.*
5. *Ibid.*

6. Lawrence J. Tell, "EEOC's Secret Struggle with Sears." *Business and Society Review* (Summer 1979), pp. 29–34.

7. *Ibid.*

8. Lawrence Ingrassia, "Sears' Suit Challenging Enforcement of Anti-Bias Laws Raises Some Key Issues." *Wall Street Journal* (March 7, 1979), p. 38.

9. *Sears, Roebuck and Co., etc.* v. *Attorney General of the United States, et al.*, Civil Action No. 79–244, U.S. District Court, District of Columbia, January 1979.

10. Title VII of the Civil Rights Act of 1964, as amended by the Equal Employment Opportunity Act of 1972, forbids discrimination in employment (including firing, upgrading, salaries, fringe benefits, and other conditions of employment) on the basis of race, color, religion, national origin, or sex. Title VII also established the information-gathering and conciliation agency. The EEOC, however, could not enforce any discrimination provisions until 1972, when Congress gave it the power to bring suits to federal district court when it found a pattern of discrimination within a company or other working establishment.

11. Executive Order 11,246, as amended by 11,375, requires government contractors to take "affirmative action" to ensure equality for women and minorities. The Office of Federal Contract Compliance (OFCC) of the Department of Labor was established to enforce this law. Enforcement was almost impossible, however, until the OFCC introduced Order 4. It required every employer with a government contract worth $50,000 or more to file written affirmative action plans with the agency, listing minority categories to be broken down by "utilization rate." Revised Order 4 includes women in these minority categories. It requires companies to set specific goals and timetables for hiring and promoting women on all levels of their work forces. If the company fails to comply, the government can revoke contracts with federal agencies.

12. Sears News Release, January 24, 1979.

13. *Sears, Roebuck and Co., etc.* v. *Attorney General of the United States*, Civil Action No. 79–244, motion to dismiss, filed March 26, 1979.

14. *Sears, Roebuck and Co., etc.* v. *Attorney General of the United States*, Civil Action No. 79–244, filed May 15, 1979.

15. *Steelworkers of America AFL–CIO* v. *Bryan F. Weber et al.* U.S. 621 L. Ed. 2d. 99 S. Ct. 2721 (1979). The United Steelworkers of America, the AFL-CIO, and Kaiser Aluminum and Chemical Corporation entered into a master collective bargaining agreement that contained an affirmative action plan designed to eliminate conspicuous racial imbalances in Kaiser's almost exclusively white craft work force. During the first year of operation, the most junior black trainee selected had less seniority than several white production workers whose bids for admission to the program were rejected. Weber instituted a class action alleging that the affirmative action program discriminated against him and other similarly situated white employees in violation of Sections 703(a) and 703(d) of Title VII of the Civil Rights Act of 1964.

The Supreme Court held that private, voluntary, race-conscious affirmative action plans do not necessarily violate Sections 703(a) and 703(d). Kaiser's affirmative action plan, designed to eliminate traditional patterns of conspicuous racial segregation in the crafts, was permissible under Title VII since it did not require the discharge of white workers and their replacement with new black employees, did not create an absolute bar to the advancement of white employees, and was only a temporary measure designed to eliminate a manifest racial imbalance.

16. "News from Sears," July 13, 1979.

17. *Equal Employment Opportunity Commission* v. *Sears, Roebuck and Co.*, Northern District of Illinois, Civil Action No. 79–C–4373; Middle District of Alabama, C.A. No. 79–507–N; Southern District of Georgia C.A. No. C79–1957; Southern District of New York, C.A. No. 79–CIV–5708; and Western District of Tennessee, C.A. No. 79–2695–B, filed October 17, 1979.

18. The original charge was filed on August 30, 1979.

19. Editorial "Sears' Sweeping Challenge." *Washington Post* (January 29, 1979), p. A22.

20. "A Sears Suit: Calls for Clarification," *Time* (February 5, 1979), pp. 127, 128. Other articles used in preparing this section include the following: Lawrence J. Tell, "EEOC's

Secret Struggle with Sears," *Business and Society Review* (Summer 1979), pp. 29–34; "Sears and the EEOC Dig in for a Long War," *Business Week*, (February 12, 1979), p. 41; "Sears Roebuck Charges U.S. Action Hurt Firm's Efforts to Hire Women, Minorities," *Wall Street Journal* (January 25, 1979), p. 2; Lawrence Ingrassia, "Sears Suit Challenging U.S. Enforcement of Anti-Bias Laws Raises Some Key Issues," *Wall Street Journal* (March 7, 1979), p. 42; Allan Sloan and John J. Donovan, "The Sears Case of Equal Job Opportunity," *New York Law Journal* (February 5, 1979), pp. 86–87; Edward Cowan, "Sears Loses Its Suit Over Job-Bias Rules, *New York Times* (May 16, 1979), p. A1, D18.

21. *Wall Street Journal* (March 7, 1979), p. 42.
22. *Ibid.*
23. *Ibid.*
24. Jerry Knight, "EEOC Hits Sears with Job-Bias Suits." *Washington Post* (October 23, 1979), pp. E1, E6.
25. "The EEOC May Settle Its Case against Sears," *Business Week* (August 20, 1979), p. 24. For further information on this issue, see "EEOC's Lawyers Cushion Plan to Sue Sears over Job Bias," *Wall Street Journal* (August 3, 1979), p. 21; Keith Richburg, "EEOC Staff Recommends Dropping Suit against Sears," *Washington Post* (August 2, 1979), p. A3; "Job-Bias Agency Decides to Proceed in Sears

Suit," *Washington Post* (August 14, 1979), p. A7; "Sears Is Charged in Series in EEOC Suits with Discrimination," *Wall Street Journal* (October 23, 1979), p. 12.
26. *Equal Employment Opportunity Commission* v. *Sears, Roebuck and Co.*, Civil Action No. 79–C–4373, N.D. Illinois, November 1979. Memorandum of Points and Authorities in Support of Defendant's Motion to Dismiss. (This source will hereafter be referred to as Memorandum to Dismiss, C.A. 79–C–4373, followed by the appropriate page number.)
27. *Usery* v. *Sears, Roebuck and Co.*, 421, F. Supp. 411, supplementing *Brennan* v. *Sears, Roebuck and Co.*, 410 F. Supp. 84 (N.D. Iowa, 1976).
28. The U.S. District Court for the Northern District of Illinois Eastern Division *EEOC* v. *Sears, Roebuck and Co.*, No. 79–C–4373, Judge John A. Nordberg, Jan. 31, 1986.
29. *Ibid.*
30. *Ibid.*
31. The motion for partial summary judgement contained four other claims. The EEOC withdrew two of those claims before the court ruled on the motion, and decided not to pursue on appeal the court's denial regarding the two other claims, which involved pregnancy policies.
32. *EEOC* v. *Sears Roebuck and Co.*, Nos. 86–1519 and 86–1621, U.S. Court of Appeals, 7th Circuit.

REFERENCES

Abram, Morris B. "Affirmative Action: Fair Shakers and Social Engineers." *Harvard Law Review,* 99 (April 1986), 1312–26.

"Applying Disparate Impact Theory to Subjective Employer Selection Procedures." *Loyola L.A.L. Review,* 20 (January 1987), 375–419.

Dwyer, P. "Affirmative Action: After the Debate, Opportunity (Supreme Court Decision; Santa Clara County v. D. Joyce Case)," *Business Week* (April 13, 1987), 37.

_____. "Clearing the Confusion over Affirmative Action" (Supreme Court Rulings), *Business Week,* (July 14, 1986), pp. 26, 27.

Fisher, A.B. "Businessmen Like to Hire by the Numbers." *Fortune,* 112 (September 6, 1985), pp. 26–28.

Friedman, J.W. "Redefining the Equality, Discrimination and Affirmative Action under Title VII: The Access Principle." *Texas Law Review,* 65 (November 1986), pp. 41–99.

Leach, D.E. "Affirmative Action Guidelines: An Appropriate Response." *Labor Law Journal,* 27 (September 1978), pp. 555–61.

"Limiting the Role of Statistical Evidence in Affirmative Action Cases." *Boston College Law Review,* 27 (December 1985), 168–73.

O'Meara, J.C. "Whither Affirmative Action? (Supreme Court Justice Scalia's Approach to Affirmative Action Issues). *Personnel Administration ,* 32 (January 1987), pp. 54–55.

Seligman, D. "It Was Foreseeable (No Change in Republican Policy of Affirmative Action Quotas" *Fortune* (July 22, 1985), p. 119.

Sullivan, Kathleen, M. "Sins of Discrimination: Last Term's Affirmative Action Cases" (1985). *Harvard Law Review,* 100 (November 1986), 78–98.

"U.S. Finds for AT&T in Equal Employment Case." *CPA Journal* (April 1979), pp. 72–73.

Vernon–Gerstenfeld, S. and E. Burke,"Affirmative Action in Nine Large Companies: A Field Study," *Personnel,* 62 (April 1985), pp. 54–60.

THE RISE AND FALL OF GM'S X-CAR

*The politicization of the regulatory process:
the role of activist groups and the news media*

On March 8, 1988, a three-judge panel in a federal appeals court ruled that U.S. government had failed to meet its burden of demonstrating a class-wide defect and other violations of the National Highway Traffic and Motor Vehicle Safety Act, arising out of the alleged defective brakes in the 1980 model X-cars of General Motors Corporation.[1] The United States was appealing the decision of a lower court (April 14, 1987) in an earlier trial in favor of GM.[2] In that case, the National Highway Traffic Safety Administration of the Department of Transportation (NHTSA) had charged, among other things, that GM had manufactured an entire generation of cars, its 1980 X-cars,* which were predisposed to a phenomenon known as "premature rear wheel lock-up." The government further argued that GM either determined or should have determined "that the rear braking system, for reasons relating to several distinct components of that system, caused premature rear wheel lock-up with consequent loss of vehicle control. NHTSA also alleged that during postproduction, GM learned that deterioration of front braking components in service were exacerbating the problem. However, in each such instance, the company

failed in its legal duty to notify the Secretary of Transportation and the cars' owners of, and to remedy, the "defect."

As to the two recalls that GM did conduct in 1981 and 1983, with respect to some 1980 X-cars, the government deemed them to be inadequate. Finally, the U.S. government charged that GM failed to submit accurate and complete information in response to NHTSA's queries in the course of its administrative investigation of the 1980 X-cars. Furthermore, GM violated a NHTSA regulation by omitting NHTSA's "hot-line" telephone number in the recall letters the company sent to X-car owners in the 1981 recall campaign. (*District Court's Decision*, pp. 1–2) These latter two charges were made the subject of a separate trial upon GM's request. The U.S. asked for a judgment requiring GM to recall and effectively repair all of its 1.1 million 1980 X-cars. In an unprecedented move, the government also sought $4 million in civil monetary penalties from the company. However, once the court had decided against NHTSA on all other charges, the government agreed to withdraw its complaint on the remaining counts against GM "with prejudice," i.e., the government forfeited its right ever to sue GM again in future on these charges.[3]

This has been a long case, and one of the sorrier sagas in the annals of U.S. regulations.

---

*The term *X-car* has no significance other than as an internal designation assigned by GM to that particular car body.

It demonstrates the excesses to which a regulatory process can be pushed by political and activist group pressures to the extent that concerns for consumer safety are subordinated for high-profile victories in the press. It also shows how the news media is often abused by various parties, including the government agencies, to create favorable public opinion for their relative positions without due regard for accuracy as to facts or fair treatment of other parties' positions.

The investigation had literally started even before the first cars hit the showrooms. After dragging for more than three years, the trial commenced on March 13, 1984, and continued, with intermittent recesses, until May 16, 1985 with the Court's decision being rendered in April 1987. Instead of the six weeks originally allotted, the trial eventually consumed 113 court days. Testimony was received from 33 trial witnesses, including 20 experts. The trial record consisted of 16,000 pages of transcripts and about 3,700 exhibits. This does not include the time taken for appeals that would take another year to resolve. The costs to both GM and the government must be counted in tens of millions of dollars, and it is doubtful whether any more lives were saved as a consequence. It is also unquestionable that both GM and the government could find scores of ways in which these monies could have been spent more productively.

GM had won a victory. However, it came too late. For by then, the X-car had become a casualty of constant controversy, numerous recalls, and bad publicity. GM discontinued building the X-car in 1985. The X-car was GM's high hope of producing an answer to the Japanese competition for a small fuel-efficient car, designed and built from scratch, with state-of-the-art manufacturing and equipment. When the last car came off the assembly line at GM's Willow Run assembly plant, the company had built a total of 3,314,349 cars. The discontinuance of the X-car caused a lay-off of about 5,000 workers. Although the sales decline may have been partially due to the normal life cycle of a model and other market factors, the adverse publicity and government lawsuit no doubt played an important part in the demise of the X-car.

ISSUES FOR ANALYSIS

The case raises a variety of issues as to the nature of regulatory processes that are not only relevant to NHTSA but may have more general applicability to the work of other regulatory agencies. They also throw light on the role of political leaders and activist groups in influencing the direction of regulatory processes and, even more important, in short-circuiting the regulatory procedures that are designed to ensure an orderly investigation and disposition of consumer complaints. Finally, it shows the vulnerability of companies, even as big as General Motors, to adverse news media publicity regardless of the merits of their position. Some of the questions for analysis are:

1. To what extent is NHTSA's mandate adequate in protecting car owners' and drivers' safety against manufacturing defects? How does NHTSA help or hinder the market-related and other legal, e.g., tort, remedies available to car owners?
2. How adequate and effective are NHTSA's procedures in initiating and conducting investigations? Why did it take NHTSA so long to complete its investigation of GM's X-cars?
3. How would one evaluate the use of voluntary, self-initiated consumer complaints as the basis for launching regulatory investigations? How can these processes be made effective in reflecting more realistically the true magnitude of the problem rather than merely the consumer perception?
4. What are some of the other means, e.g., more timely and accurate information on manufacturing defects, that might make markets more effective in protecting consumer interest by affecting the sale of particular cars or other products?

5. How would one evaluate the role of congressional intervention in the regulatory process? Clearly, any political leader has a right, and an obligation, to air his or her concerns and to seek expeditious resolution of problems that concern his or her constituents, and are also in the arena of broad public policy. These concerns, however, can also be manipulated for short-term political gains and thus subvert the regulatory processes that were designed to insulate regulatory agencies from unwarranted political interventions. How can these two competing tendencies be balanced?

6. How would one evaluate the role of activist groups in intervening in the regulatory process? In the U.S. society, do these groups have the right and the obligation to represent public interest as they see it? Is there a need to make these groups more accountable for their actions? If so, what are some of the measures that might be taken in this regard?

7. What was the role of news media, and journalists in particular, in creating public awareness and fanning public concern in the X-car controversy? Was this role merely that of informing the public or did it go beyond that in the direction of influencing public opinion? It is clear that adverse news publicity can have severe consequences on the fortunes of a company. Witness the more recent cases of Audi and Suzuki, which were severely injured by news reports of alleged defects that were later found to be unsubstantiated.[4]

8. How would one evaluate the adequacy of GM's testing procedures for car defects, its responsiveness in warning consumers of potential hazards, and in correcting them promptly and satisfactorily?

GENERAL MOTORS

General Motors Corporation (GM) is the largest manufacturer of automobiles in the world. For the year 1988, GM ranked at the top of the *Fortune* 500 list of largest U.S. industrial corporations. The total sales amounted to $121 billion, with profits of $4.8 billion.[5]

Its passenger car production in the U.S. includes the Chevrolet, Pontiac, Oldsmobile, Buick, and Cadillac lines. The company also produces products and services in the defense and other nonautomotive sectors, which are marketed through distributors and dealers overseas. GM was facing severe market competition at the time of X-car introduction. For example, between 1979 and 1980, annual sales dropped from $66 billion to $57 billion. Subsequently, in 1980, the company suffered a loss of $762 million compared with a profit of $2.2 billion in 1979. Despite all its efforts, the company lost market share during the 1980s. GM's share declined from about 46% of U.S. new car sales in 1980 to about 36% in 1988.[6]

THE BIRTH OF THE X-CAR

The X-car was a long time in the making. The project started in 1973 as GM faced drastically different market conditions for fuel-efficient cars following the first oil shock. GM appointed Robert J. Eaton as the chief of engineering of the X-car project center and responsible for coordinating the resource allocations. In August 1975, Chevrolet Motor Division got the authorization for the engineering design work.[7] In January 1979, James McDonald, executive vice-president of North American Automotive Operations of General Motors was quoted by *Ward's Auto World Magazine*: "There was an absolute dedication that this X-car would have the highest quality of any car we ever brought to market."[8]

The X-car was to be GM's technologically innovative response to the emerging energy crunch. It had an all-new X-body front-wheel drive configuration. Although GM did not have much prior experience with the front-wheel drive technology, especially as coupled with the newer transverse layout, it was, nevertheless, willing to make a frontal attack on the challenge facing it. Thus, X-car got a sophisticated state-of-the-art computer-designed technology to develop its components. About 200 suppliers and hundreds of plant people were trained so that the assembled car would be perfect. The new trans-axle was subjected to prove itself in a nearly 1 million kilometer (about 600,000 miles) test on roads and tracks. X-car also led the onset of their alphabetic-naming of cars.[9]

After four years of research and development and an estimated $3 billion expenditure to build its first small front-wheel drive cars, the X-cars reached the GM dealer showrooms on April 19, 1979. They received a rousing reception and one auto magazine even awarded it the "1980 Car of the Year" honor.[10] Barely two months earlier, in February 1979, the Shah of Iran was ousted, thus precipitating the second energy crisis of the 1970s. Every car customer wanted a fuel-efficient small car, and GM had the hottest, newest, high-mileage car at just the right time. X-car became the crucial new configuration for Chevrolet, Pontiac, Oldsmobile, and Buick divisions. In 1980, GM announced its estimated corporate fuel average as approximately 23 miles per gallon, which was more than 1981 Federal requirements.[11] The car represented a prominent part of GM's product policy. Its different configurations were marketed as Chevrolet Citation, Pontiac Phoenix, Oldsmobile Omega, and Buick Skylark, and were promoted as roomier, fuel-efficient alternatives to hot-selling Japanese small cars.

NATIONAL TRAFFIC AND MOTOR VEHICLE SAFETY ACT OF 1966

The National Traffic and Motor Vehicle Safety Act was enacted by Congress in 1966 for the purpose of reducing traffic accidents and related deaths and injuries.[12] The Act requires automobile manufacturers to notify both NHTSA and the owners of their vehicles when they learn that vehicles possess safety-related defects, and then to remedy those defects without charge to the owners. The term "defect" is defined under Section 1391 in a circular manner, as including any defect

in performance, construction, components, or materials. A *prima facie* proof of a defect in a class of vehicles requires only a showing that a "significant number of them have failed in consequence of the defect, a significant number being merely a "non-*de minimis*" quantity; it need not be "a substantial percentage of the total."[13]

Under Section 1411, the government must also show that the manufacturer not only knows of the supposed defect in its vehicles, but that it made a "good faith" determination that the defect relates to motor vehicle safety as well. A defect is "related to motor vehicle safety" if it presents an "unreasonable risk of accidents." (*District Court's Decision*, pp. 4–6)

Section 1414 of the Act defines the procedures to remedy the defect by any of the alternative routes of repairing the vehicle, replacing it, or refunding the purchase price less depreciation. The Act gives the secretary of transportation authority to administratively order the manufacturer to take remedial action if the secretary (i.e., NHTSA) determines that certain vehicles contain a defect relating to safety. This order is judicially enforceable and violations are subject to federal prosecution. Vehicle manufacturers are required to maintain information, and to produce it upon request, in conjunction with an investigation.

NHTSA'S DEFECT INVESTIGATION PROCEDURES

NHTSA has well-defined procedures for the agency to follow during different phases of a safety investigation.[14] They are designed to ensure a systematic and objective analysis of complaints; determination of present and potential defects and the scope of likely public injury; and implementation of remedial measures. At the same time, they are also intended to provide the car manufacturers with a reasonable opportunity to respond to complaints and offer contrary evidence refuting the allegations in the complaints, and to propose their own corrective measures. The regulatory process is so designed as to insulate it from undue political interference.

NHTSA's defect investigation is carried out by the Office of Defect Investigation (ODI) through its three divisions: Defects Information Systems, Engineering Analysis, and Defects Evaluation.

Defects Information Systems Division. This division gathers and organizes all information NHTSA receives relating to possible safety defects in motor vehicles, vehicle equipment, or tires. The information is received in many forms and is the primary source from which NHTSA first learns of possible safety defects. The division operates a toll-free Auto Safety Hotline (800–424–9393), which gives 24-hour service for consumers to report motor vehicle safety problems or request information on recalls. NHTSA sends a questionnaire to each consumer who calls the hotline about his or her car's potential safety defect so that vital information NHTSA needs in its investigations can be recorded.

The division staff initially reviews and sorts all consumer complaint letters and questionnaire forms for trends and then enters those complaints not related to a formal investigation but determined to be safety-related into the division's computerized data base. Copies of the complaint letters and questionnaire forms are then sent to the respective manufacturers for their records. NHTSA's computerized database contains other information—such as manufacturers' service bulletins that describe specific repair procedures to be followed by dealers, motor vehicle warranty data, and past defect recall reports—which can also be used to support safety defect investigations.

Engineering Analysis Division. This division reviews numerous consumer complaints and other documents to analyze and identify potentially dangerous safety defects. This is accomplished by two types of evaluations—inquiries and engineering analyses. Such an inquiry/analysis may lead the staff to proceed with an engineering analysis, close the inquiry without additional work, or continue the inquiry to obtain more information on the potential problem.

During this phase, a manufacturer may agree to conduct a recall and thereby resolve the issue and close the investigation. However, if a manufacturer decides not to take any action, a NHTSA panel may decide to: open a formal investigation, perform additional engineering analysis work before making a final decision, or close the engineering analysis.

Defects Evaluation Division. This division conducts formal investigations after NHTSA's review panel decides to proceed beyond the engineering analysis phase. ODI also notifies the manufacturer. NHTSA issues a press release to inform the public that it is conducting a formal investigation and to solicit relevant information. This is intended to develop documentary evidence that will bridge the gap between an alleged motor vehicle defect and the official determination that a safety-related defect does or does not exist.

Both the chief counsel and NHTSA's deputy administrator must approve any course of recommended action. Should NHTSA and the manufacturer find no resolution to the problem, and should the manufacturer refuse to conduct a recall, NHTSA can order the manufacturer to do so. If this is not forthcoming, NHTSA will proceed with a court action against the manufacturer.

NHTSA AND AUTOMOTIVE RECALLS

There are three types of product recalls pertaining to automobiles. Type I recall includes problems associated with mislabeled or missing placards, as well as the tire-related troubles. These are classified as minor recalls. Type II, also called intermediate recalls, include defects such as loosened or missing bolts to major assemblies on the automobiles, and the different windshield wiper-related troubles. Type III, or the major recalls, are for severe magnitude major defects affecting the safety of the vehicle, such as the vehicular fire or the loss of steering and braking operations. Other troubles included in Type III are repeated engine stalling, and problems that severely affect vehicle driveability.[15]

It would, however, be incorrect to assume that the number of recalls is an indication of poor product quality. A company may voluntarily recall some of its cars simply because it is conscious of its responsibility to the consumer and, therefore, acts in anticipation of potential problems in order to prevent them from occurring. Note that voluntary recalls have traditionally constituted about 90% of total automotive recalls. On the other hand, a company may indeed have defective cars on the road and is forced to recall them for corrective action by NHTSA. A number of recalls may also be related to genuine disagreements between the manufacturer and NHTSA about the existence of a potential defect and the appropriate corrective action desired.

The effect of recalls and the number of cars affected varies from manufacturer to manufacturer. GM being the largest automobile manufacturer, a major recall for GM involves 40-50,000 cars, but for Ford, the corresponding magnitude would be about 20,000 cars, and for Chrysler, it would be about 10,000 cars. To give an idea of the overall magnitude of auto recalls between the period 1967–1981, there were 116 recalls that were classified as major recalls.[16] (See Table 1.)

AUTOMOTIVE RECALL ANNOUNCEMENT PROCESS

Information regarding automotive recalls is generally given out to people via two public announcements. In the case of voluntary

TABLE 1. Domestic Vehicle Recalls

	1978	1979	1980	1981	1982	1983	1984	1985	1986	1987
American Motors	749,362 / 8	28,641 / 7	11,369 / 2	85,261 / 9	23,741 / 3	40 / 1	71,938 / 7	211,197 / 6	58,056 / 6	219,513 / 4
American General Corporation	21,123 / 2	6,913 / 2	1,143 / 2	399 / 1	3,227 / 1	2,545 / 1	497 / 1	334 / 1	—	24,627 / 3
Chrysler	1,574,244 / 17	227,572 / 14	2,396,533 / 9	290,046 / 5	77,243 / 8	167,403 / 7	445,760 / 10	328,800 / 4	51,506 / 6	59,573 / 7
Ford	3,608,620 / 37	1,405,146 / 34	1,002,852 / 25	399,099 / 18	274,576 / 20	1,621,979 / 21	2,303,924 / 23	1,165,668 / 18	443,967 / 20	3,909,089 / 16
General Motors	1,739,136 / 20	4,813,313 / 36	320,256 / 15	6,476,445 / 15	938,461 / 15	1,214,915 / 20	3,326,057 / 25	3,105,248 / 27	828,303 / 25	2,757,591 / 32
Total	1,141,342 / 72	6,997,667 / 218	3,939,035 / 129	7,379,189 / 129	1,401,192 / 107	3,071,321 / 109	6,283,303 / 127	4,995,186 / 137	1,730,657 / 139	729,717 / 150

NOTE: *x*=total number of cars recalled (upper number)
    y=number of times recalls were made (lower number)

SOURCE: A statement prepared from summary tables in NHTSA's "Annual Reports on Safety-Related Recall Campaigns for Motor Vehicles and Motor Vehicle Equipment, Including tires," 1978–1987. Washington, DC: U.S. Government Printing Office.

recalls, the process gets into motion when a manufacturer discovers a design defect or flaw in the material or workmanship used. The company notifies the NHTSA (National Highway Traffic Safety Administration) with a recall notification memo describing the identity and number of automobiles involved, the specific reasons behind the recall, the ramifications with respect to safety, and the proposed corrective procedure to alleviate the problem. Upon receipt of this memo, NHTSA posts it publicly for general reference. Another public announcement regarding the automotive recalls occurs when the manufacturer has been able to organize itself with its dealer network for the proposed remedial actions for the affected consumers. This may take anywhere up to a few weeks. Thus, the manufacturer issues a corporate press release explaining the relevant information to the consumers. Media, such as the *Wall Street Journal*, publish these materials on the next business day.

DEVELOPMENT AND TESTING OF THE X-CAR

GM introduced the 1980 X-car for public sale in April 1979, under the trade names of Chevrolet Citation, Pontiac Phoenix, Oldsmobile Omega, and Buick Skylark. About 1.1 million X-cars were sold during the 1980 model year ending in September 1980. Like all new cars, X-car also went through an extensive period of engineering studies and field testing. Since certain aspects of these testing procedures and their adequacy in relation to X-car became the subject of controversy and NHTSA complaint, it is important to review briefly the history of X-car engineering studies and field testing.

Formal planning for the 1980 X-car began in 1975. This car was to be GM's first high-volume, front-wheel-drive automobile with a transversely mounted engine to be sold as a "coordinated car line." Because an X-car model was to be offered by each of four of

GM's car divisions, its design and development was coordinated through a "project center," established in early 1976, to which engineers from both car and component divisions were assigned. The project center was administratively a part of GM's corporate engineering staff, but all engineering decisions were ultimately the responsibility of the chief engineers of the several car divisions: Chevrolet, Pontiac, Oldsmobile, and Buick. (*District Court's Decision*, p. 6)

Particular divisions were assigned lead responsibility for the evolution of specific vehicle systems. In the case of brakes, GM brake engineers first selected the generic type of brake components and sized them based on projected vehicle mass. This is standard operating procedure for any GM car program. The procedure started with engineering designs, and proceeded to the development of prototype components, laboratory testing, and field testing on similar-sized peer cars (called "component" cars). As development progressed, the evolving system was installed on various preproduction versions of the proposed X-car itself (called successively, "prototype," "pilot," and "lead unit build" cars). Test results were reviewed, and designs modified to improve performance as the tests indicated. GM at all times contemplated that the 1980 X-car would be equipped with front disc brakes and rear drum brakes, a combination common then and now on both GM and non-GM automobiles. (*District Court's Decision*, pp. 6–7)

Commenting on their field testing procedures, a GM executive stated:

> In the pre-production and pre-announcement period on any car, in the design period, extensive testing is done with cars that are not production cars but are, in various ways, representative, at least for engineering purposes, of what we expect to be manufacturing. Cars were being run on a durability schedule that was itself in the process of being developed.[17]

GM thus developed new ways to test these models. It was decided that rather than develop tests as the needs arose, the company would develop tests that would monitor the car performance under actual driving conditions by representatives of the car-buying public who would eventually buy and use these cars. According to a GM executive:

> We selected a group of potential customers at random, and for a nominal compensation, asked them to drive these cars under different driving conditions. Each car was equipped with a black box monitoring device placed in the trunk to monitor the braking of the customer. The system monitored, among other things, the speed at which the brakes were applied, the rate of deceleration, how long the deceleration occurred, etc. Our objective was to develop a test from the driving pattern of the customer, incorporating the most severe driving conditions.

For the X-cars, the comprehensive durability test was identified as R1523, to be tested over 100,000 miles for 11 months, covering Detroit, over the Rockies to Arizona, and back via a different route. It included roads in Alaska for cold temperature conditioning. GM engineers also developed a modified R1523, with reduced mileage of 57,000, thereby eliminating some areas not requiring extensive use of brakes. It had 11 different cycles—rural cycle, city cycle, etc., in different mixes involving different extents of braking. Having chosen the front disc/rear drum brake design for the X-car, GM brake engineers elected to use semimetallic linings for the disc brakes, believing them to offer superior resistance to fade at the higher brake temperatures they expected to occur at the heavier front end of the vehicle. Organic linings were to be employed on the rear drum brakes because engineers figured they would be less susceptible to environmental degradation. The 1980 X-car was also to be equipped with two "fixed-slope" proportioning valves in its hydraulic system (one valve per rear wheel) to limit the line pressure going to the rear brakes in moderate to heavy breaking. The valves compensate for dynamic force transfer by "proportioning" rear line hydraulic pressure to incremental front-line pressure above a certain "break," or "knee," a point that, in the X-car, was set at 350 psi. (For example, a 41% "fixed-slope" proportioner valve allows, in theory, 41% of the amount of the incremental line pressure applied to the front brakes above the "break" to reach the rear brakes as well.) In harder brake applications, therefore, more line pressure would be directed to the front brakes relative to the rear to compensate for the dynamic transfer of normal force to the front. (*District Court's Decision* pp. 8–9)

GM engineers were generally satisfied with the X-car brake system they had settled upon. Pilot and lead unit built cars passed FMVSS–105 certification tests using either the 3198/3199 or the 4035/4050 rear lining combinations, and the system achieved what GM engineers considered to be acceptable ratings on the Pike's Peak schedule for effectiveness, wear temperature behavior, and overall performance. (*District Court's Decision*, p. 12)

During test driving of X-cars, some of the drivers reported rear wheel lock-up in their "Test Incident Report." Engineers then looked at the cars and found that the linings of the rear wheel were cracked, baked, or burned, and the steel shoes had been glued for excessive heat-generation. This created a sort of divisive crisis within GM. Test engineers said that something was wrong with the cars while the design engineers felt that the test was too severe.

The incidence of wheel lock-up was brought to the attention of a management group gathered in Mesa, Arizona in December 1978, a month before the actual production of the X-car was about to commence. This was a regular annual get-together to review the driving test of the cars that are likely to be produced in the subsequent year. In this meeting, Pete Estes, the GM president, set a task force to evaluate the X-car situation in detail. The loosely defined task force included 15 to 20 members from various departments involved with different aspects of the braking system. On January 23, 1979, the task force unanimously recommended against a delay in the production of the 1980 X-cars as designed, and to proceed with production on schedule. The task force, however, expressed concern that there could be complaints from drivers who drove very excessively and/or braked extremely hard. Consequently, the task force recommended various design changes to take care of these potential problems.

The prop valve setting was recommended to be changed from 41% to 27% so as to change the brake balance and reduce the amount of braking done by the rear wheel in moderate to heavy braking. The task force also recommended a change in the brake lining in automatic transmission cars from 4035/4050 to 4050/4050. The two numbers correspond to the number of linings in a primary and a secondary shoe. The secondary shoe does the principal amount of work, and the 4050 lining had slightly lower friction than the 4035 lining. The brake drum was recommended to be changed from a smooth drum to a finned drum to facilitate quicker dissipation of the heat generated during braking. The recommended changes were introduced in production during the course of the 1980 model year and at different times depending on the extent of change involved or the availability of new components.

ORIGINS OF THE CONTROVERSY

According to a General Motors spokesperson, the controversy started in May 1979 when a 1980 model X-car with "green" brakes was turned over to an automotive magazine reporter for evaluation before the cars were put on the road. A just-manufactured car requires braking for a few times to get the brakes burnished and develop a good mating between the drum (for rear brakes) or the rotor (for front brakes). The 1980 model X-cars rolled off the assembly line in mid-

January 1979, and the magazine reporters started writing critical articles about the brakes between May and July 1979. GM believed that these articles had some influence on the number of public complaints about rear-brake lockup.[18]

Rear Wheel Lock-Up. A few words about the technical terms involved are in order. The alleged defect was the "premature rear wheel lock-up." Here "lock-up" refers to skidding, when a wheel or wheels slide across the road surface instead of rotating. Wheels typically lock-up when the brakes are applied so hard that the braking force at the tire exceeds the frictional adhesion between the tire and the road. Skidding leads to driver's loss of control, because while the tire is locked up, steering is ineffective and it takes longer time for skidding tires to slow down.

The "rear wheel lock-up" refers to the situation when the rear wheel for the automobile locks up before either of the front wheels do. This is also referred to as "fishtailing," "spin-out," or "yawing," and may cause a rotation around the car's vertical axis. "Premature lock-up" refers to the car skidding before the driver would ordinarily expect it to in view of the level of braking force applied. This is the crucial issue in the case, as the District Court explained that skidding results from the interaction of the driver, the brake system, and the tire-road surface. In itself, it is not a failure of a vehicle's performance nor indicative of a brake effect. (*District Court's Decision*, p. 18) An ideal braking system should lock up all four wheels simultaneously, which, the District Court observed, "can never be achieved by any brake design throughout the entire range of operating and evading conditions to which a car is subjected." (*District Court's Decision*, p. 21)

NHTSA's own regulation implicitly encourages rear lock-up bias design over the front-wheel lock-up bias design. The United States government stresses that cars stop quickly, that is, a stopping distance over stability as the paramount objective of effective braking.

In November 1979, NHTSA initiated an engineering analysis of the 1980 X-car following compliance testing conducted by NHTSA that had raised suspicion that these cars might be predisposed to unanticipated lock-ups of the rear wheels while being braked. By the time the engineering analysis was completed in June 1981, NHTSA had received 212 consumer complaints, 58 of them culminating in accidents. A search of NHTSA's computers revealed 54 additional complaints compared to none for any other front-wheel drive cars, including GM's own 1981 X-cars. (*District Court's Decision*, p. 32)

On July 6, 1981, the ODI director wrote to GM stating that NHTSA believed "the rear brake system of the 1980 X-body vehicles (utilizing the 41% valves and aggressive brake linings) contains an engineering defect which has safety-related implications..." and urged GM to commit itself to "corrective action . . . within five (5) working days." GM immediately agreed to a recall of 47,371 manual transmission X-cars fitted with a 41% proportioning valve to be replaced with a 27% proportioning valve, while not conceding the existence of any defect. (*District Court's Decision*, p. 32)

NHTSA continued its investigation and issued an initial determination in January 1983. NHTSA stated that all 1980 X-cars, manuals as well as automatics, with the more aggressive rear-break linings were defective. NHTSA also released a film clip of an X-car spinning out of control to the TV networks, which was featured prominently on nightly news, watched by an estimated 53 million viewers. GM, faced with the adverse publicity, promptly agreed to voluntarily recall all 1980 X-car manuals and some of its automatics.

Between March 1979 and February 1983, GM undertook a total of 10 recalls involving 717,042 cars. Of the 10, the first 8 recalls involving 429,872 cars were voluntary, while the last 2 dated August 5, 1981 and February

18, 1983, were initiated at the direction of NHTSA and involved 287,170 cars. (See Table 2 on page 332.)

On March 4, 1983, NHTSA issued GM a formal administrative subpoena called "Special Order and Documentation Production Request" for production of internal documents relating to premature rear-wheel lock-up problem. GM responded in three installments between March 25 and March 31, 1983. According to NHTSA, the material revealed for the first time that "not only had GM's own test drivers reported 'rear wheel lockup' incidents on preproduction X-body prototypes more than two years before, but also that GM management had felt compelled to create an unprecedented 'task force' to deal with the very problem NHTSA was investigating." (*District Court's Decision*, pp. 34–35)

While the agency's internal procedures were being followed, NHTSA decided to abort the administrative proceedings and instead asked the Department of Justice to take legal action against GM. By the time the legal action was filed against GM, NHTSA claimed that it had received more than 2,000 consumer complaints of "premature wheel lock-up." These complaints included multiple instances of accidents, injuries, and fatalities. Furthermore, where these "incidents were attributable to a vehicle defect, the defect was indisputably safety-related." (*District Court's Decision*, p. 35)

U.S. LAWSUIT AGAINST GENERAL MOTORS

On August 3, 1983, the Justice Department, on behalf of NHTSA, filed a suit against GM, and sought that GM should recall and repair its 1.1 million 1980 model X-cars. The U.S. complaint charged that "GM had filed false and misleading responses to its inquiries in at least 18 instances." The suit claimed that GM itself had doubts about the braking system in 1978, but made no changes to avoid the prob-

TABLE 2. Recall Campaigns For GM's 1980 X-cars

Manufacturer's Notification to NHTSA	Initiator of Recall	Makes and Models	Vehicles Recalled	Likely Problem
1. March 19, 1979	Voluntary by GM	B, C, O	35	Nonconformity to FMVSS 207 "Anchorage of Seats."
2. April 3, 1979	'	B, C, O, P	4,382	Interference between clutch control cable and brake pipes.
3. April 3, 1979	'	B, C, O, P	4,626	Incorrect position of fuel hoses, interfering with front axle.
4. April 3, 1979	'	C, P	10,751	Longitudinal body bars not properly welded.
5. April 12, 1979	'	B, C, O, P	23,725	Over diameter of front suspension coil spring.
6. September 19, 1979	'	B, C, O, P	224,892	Voids in automatic transmission cooler hoses.
7. September 19, 1979	'	B, C, O, P	161,225	Fatigue cracks on steering gear mounting plate.
8. October 19 , 1979	'	B	236	Incorrect turn signal flasher unit installed.
9. August 5, 1981	NHTSA influenced	B,C, O, P	47,371	Rear-brake lock-ups in moderate to hard braking of manual transmission cars.
10. Februry 18, 1983	NHTSA influenced	B, C, O, P	239,799	All manual transmission and automatic transmission cars produced before mid-March 1979 for lock-up in braking.

B = Buick Skylark; C = Chevrolet Citation; O = Oldsmobile Omega; P = Pontiac Phoenix; FMVSS = Federal Motor Vehicle Safety Standard

SOURCE: GAO Report by the Comptroller General of the United States, GAO/RCED-83-195, August 5, 1983. "Department of Transportation's Investigation of Rear Brake Lockup Problems in 1980 X-body cars should have been more timely." Where these "incidents were attributable to a vehicle defect, the defect was indisputably safety-related." (*District Court's Decision*, p. 35)

lem. It alleged that GM had received 1,740 complaints about wheel-locking incidents, numerous accidents, 71 injuries and 15 deaths. The suit further charged that GM had given the government false or misleading information about the X-cars, and had failed to tell the federal officials and the car owners about the defects. The government felt that GM conducted two recalls that it knew would not correct the problem. (*District Court's Decision*, pp. 2, 55, 67) According to J. Paul McGrath, assistant attorney general, "this was the first time that the U.S. Government was asking for civil penalties against an auto maker for providing false data to the safety agency during a defect investigation."[19]

William L. Webber, Jr., GM's assistant general counsel in Detroit, responded to the government's 1983 Washington suit with the following statement:

We are surprised by the unexpected filing of the Justice Department suit. It is especially unwarranted in view of the fact that GM has cooperated extensively with NHTSA to develop the facts which will show clearly that no further recall or corrective action is appropriate. . . .We categorically deny the Government's assertion of misrepresentation. Accordingly, we will vigorously defend the lawsuit.[20]

NEWS MEDIA AND POLITICAL PRESSURES ON NHTSA

On January 5, 1983, Congressman Timothy E. Wirth, chairman of the Subcommittee on Telecommunications, Consumer Protection, and Finance, Committee on Energy and Commerce, asked the General Accounting Office to investigate the National Highway Traffic Safety Administration in connection with possible brake defects in the 1980 General Motors X-body cars: "I am deeply concerned that NHTSA's delay in determining whether there is a defect or ordering a recall of these vehicles may have grave and serious repercussions for the driving public."[21]

Congressman Wirth stated that he had recently received reports that NHTSA was unnecessarily delaying resolution of the various issues pertaining to possible brake defects in the X-car, and, most importantly, might be covering up the existence of very serious defects.

He asked NHTSA to provide answers to the following questions:

- If NHTSA has known about the possibility of a defect since 1979, why has the agency taken so long to order a recall of the X-car or, alternately, to close the defect investigation?
- What further information is needed in order to reach a conclusion regarding the presence of a safety defect, or lack thereof?
- Why did NHTSA allow General Motors to recall only a small number of X-cars—those with manual transmissions produced before July 1979—and not recall other 1980 X-cars with both manual and automatic transmissions?
- In those cars that were recalled, is the remedy chosen adequate or does NHTSA have information which indicates that more should be done to ensure public safety?

In early 1983, NHTSA was also under pressure due to complaints from the Center for Auto Safety, an activist consumer group privately financed and headed by Clarence Ditlow as its director.[22]

Ditlow called the NHTSA action "a preemptive strike" and asked "why it had taken NHTSA two years and 15 deaths to act against GM." Ditlow claimed that NHTSA had tried to cover up the full extent of the brake defect "at the expense of the consumer lives."[23] NHTSA administrator, Raymond A. Peek, Jr. denied the charge and said that "safety was not a partisan question and it was law enforcement."[24]

The GAO Report

The GAO submitted its report on August 5, 1983.[25] Its main findings included the following:

- NHTSA did not follow its established procedures for conducing safety defect investigations.
- Although NHTSA had information that indicated that General Motors' remedy for the braking defect might not be adequate, NHTSA did not formally advise GM of its concern when GM proposed a remedy, aggressively pursue testing affected cars, or initiate an audit of the recall's effectiveness as soon as possible.
- By delaying, or not taking these and related required actions, NHTSA delayed the recall of cars with potential safety defects. Decisions regarding most of these actions were made by a single Safety Administration official, with no apparent review by top agency officials.

The Safety Administration's review of the rear-brake lock-up on X-body cars was conducted in two phases—engineering analysis and formal investigation. GAO found that although the Safety Administration's goal was generally to complete the engineering analysis within 6 months, this phase took 19 months, from November 26, 1979, to July 1, 1981.

Essentially the only action the Safety Administration took during the first 13 months of the engineering analysis was to send a letter to GM requesting basic information for investigating the brake problem. This letter was sent 6 months after the engineering analysis began. Safety Administration guidelines state that such letters should be sent to the manufacturer within 2 weeks of starting an engineering analysis.

The formal investigation phase was from July 1981 to January 1983. From July 1981 through October 1982, numerous actions called for under Safety Administration guidelines were not taken or were delayed. These included the following:

- A press release, which is normal practice, was not issued when the formal investigation was opened.
- The information request letter to the manufacturer was not sent until December 17, 1982, almost 18 months after the formal investigation was opened on July 2, 1981. This letter was usually sent soon after a formal investigation begins.
- A contract to obtain information from consumers directly affected by the defect problem was not awarded until March 22, 1983, nearly 21 months after the formal investigation was opened. This contract is usually awarded to a private contractor early in the investigation.
- An audit of GM's August 1981 recall of 47,371 cars to determine, among other things, the adequacy of the remedy to correct the rear-brake lock-up problem was delayed about 5 months from when it was originally proposed.
- Although the Safety Administration tested 1980 GM X-body cars in July and November 1981 to identify the conditions under which rear-brake lock-up occurred and the causes of such lock-ups, it did not indicate in the public record until January 1983 that these tests were conducted. Normal practice is to disclose that such tests were conducted soon after their completion.

Congressman Wirth said that the GAO report and his preliminary review showed that "NHTSA breached its obligation to the public as required by law." Wirth observed that it was part of a "pattern of non-enforcement and repeal of safety rules which has characterized NHTSA since 1981," and that "it was a sorry state of affairs and an inexcusable track record for an agency whose primary obligation under the law is to remove dangerous vehicles from our roads."[26] Wirth also hoped that the new Secretary of Transportation and a new administrator will return NHTSA to its "congressionally-mandated purpose of protecting the public."[27]

Around that time, Congressman Wirth was getting some information from a staff source in NHTSA. (Later, in January 1984, Wirth was reported to have gone over the head of the then NHTSA's chief, Diane Steed, to ask Transportation Secretary Elizabeth H. Dole to personally look into the X-car brake issue.)[28]

As a result, Robert Helmith, chief of the defects evaluation division at NHTSA, felt there was considerable pressure on NHTSA by Congress. And to alleviate the pressure, NHTSA administrator Raymond A. Peek sent a new request to GM in December 1982 requesting more information and thus escalated the investigation activities.

The January 1983 Initial Determination (ID) was made under the coordination of Peek. The normal procedure in the agency is that recommendation processes up from the individuals doing the analysis at the working level to the associate, and gradually up to the associate administrator of the NHTSA agency, who is then responsible for making the initial determination.

In the case of the X-car, GM felt that there were many clear departures from the set procedure. For instance, as early as June 1982, NHTSA defects engineers had recommended that the X-car case be closed on the grounds that consumer complaints had dropped 75% after GM had voluntarily changed the proportioning valves on 47,000 manual transmission cars.

Furthermore, the NHTSA chief typically stays out of a controversy until the final decision-making stage. He hears the manufacturer to determine the correctness of the Initial Determination made by the associate administrator. But, with respect to the X-car, in December 1982, NHTSA Chief, Raymond A. Peck, Jr., ordered "an initial (defect) determination as soon as possible," just before he faced stiff questioning on the X-car at a congressional hearing. (*Appeals Court Decision*, pp. 5–6)

When GM sought information to investigate the internal process pursued in NHTSA, the government claimed the Deliberative Process Privilege. The law has recognized to some degree the right of a governmental agency to keep the internal processes from being discovered by individuals in lawsuits.

In the case of the X-car, at the time of making Initial Determination, the public relations office of NHTSA on January 13, 1983, released a video film to the television networks showing an X-car dramatically spinning around. In the film, the X-car was proceeding on a wet surface. As the driver applied the brakes, the car went through a 270- to 360-degree spin. According to NHTSA, this was clear evidence supporting the government's determination that the X-car had rear-brake lock-up defect. The film was shown on the nightly newscasts of all three major networks and resulted in an immediate avalanche of added complaints to GM and NHTSA.

However, at the time of releasing this information, NHTSA did not mention to the media that the driver was told not to steer, and the ground surface was wetted to facilitate skidding. The brakes were mechanically applied and adjusted to induce rear-brake lock-up. The brake linings were also taken from a car that had been cited in a consumer complaint. Despite these intentional adverse conditions, in only 19 out of a total of 189 trials (that is, about 10%), the test drivers were able to get the X-car to skid—a fact that was withheld from the television stations and the viewers.

As a result of the broadcast, GM received an immense amount of complaints and criticism from customers, and management started getting calls from dealers about their continued sales. GM realized that fighting with the government to defend itself would take time, thereby forcing dealers to bear enormous losses in market sales.

Since the government had filed the lawsuit against GM, the company decided not to appear and testify at the hearing held by Congressman Timothy E. Wirth's Subcommittee on Telecommunications, Consumer Protection and Finance, Committee on Energy and Commerce.

NHTSA'S LEGAL ARGUMENTS AGAINST GM

The government built its case against GM primarily on the evidence of X-car "consumers" and their personal experiences. This evidence took several forms, including: (1) in-court testimony of 12 live-witness consumers who had lost control of their 1980 X-cars while attempting to slow or stop; (2) depositions of absent consumers in which similar incidents were described; (3) unsolicited written complaints sent to the government or directly to GM; (4) statistical analysis of the complaint data establishing a relationship between reported accidents and early wheel lockups; and (5) comparisons between complaint rates for X-cars and other cars.

According to the government, the 1980 X-car had been the subject of the largest number of reports of "yaw instability" of any car in NHTSA's history. When the trial began, the number of complaints had exceeded 3,500, which went over 4,000 by the end of February 1985, more than two months before the end of the trial. In contrast, the number of similar complaints about other cars was negligible.

The centerpiece of the government's circumstantial proof-of-defect-by-failure-alone evidence was the testimony of 12 "typical" consumers who appeared at the trial. These consumers were considered representative of the variety of the car owners and driving conditions confronted by the totality of complaints that were the basis of the lawsuit. (*Federal Court Decision*, pp. 37–40)

The government also asserted to have corroborated this evidence with the documentation that it secured from GM under subpoena. As evidence of GM's knowledge of, and difficulty with, the X-car brakes, NHTSA introduced an internal GM memorandum by a senior vice-president of engineering which stated, among other things:

- Don't you know that you never lock the rear wheel brakes first?!
- How are such product decisions made?

- What event caused the division responsible for design to change their minds on this matter?
- How could we miss something so obvious?!
- How can GM put out such a system?
- Engineering staff is not doing its job!

As late as May 7th, the same vice-president wrote, "Every time I ask, I am told the "X" car brakes are fixed. These tests do not indicate they are. What do we have that does?" (*District Court's Decision*, p. 43)

According to the government's complaint, GM began receiving complaints soon after the X-cars went on sale in April 1979. In 1980, GM began to catalogue the complaints according to the various brake component configurations then in service. Its records revealed that X-cars with 27% proportioning valves, 4050/4050 rear linings, and finned drums were generating fewer complaints from the field than any of the other configurations. Yet, the company made no effort to do anything about those otherwise equipped until its first recall the following year.

GM'S DEFENSE

GM denied that its cars experienced any of the functional failures alleged by the government. It also asserted that neither skidding nor rear-brake lock-up per se constituted a functional failure, since all cars could be expected to lock wheels under some circumstances, and that the X-car had not been shown to have any peculiar propensity to lock up, rear or front, more frequently than cars generally. (*District Court's Decision*, pp. 56–57)

In addition to the engineering analysis and field test data, GM also presented the court with a "risk analysis" comparing the relative rates of accident involvement of 1980 X-cars with three groups of competitive cars, drawing upon accident data from two of NHTSA's own sources and ten state compilations. Only with "safety-related defects" did the manufacturer have a duty

to notify and repair vehicles under the Act. GM's risk analysis disclosed that, in each database surveyed, 1980 X-cars consistently exhibited a relevant accident rate no worse than, and in most instances better than, the rate not only for peer car groups but also for all 1980 models.

The government did not present its own "risk analysis" and instead argued that this data was not significant to the case because the incidents of rear-brake lock-up were relatively rare and would likely be masked by the vastly greater number of accidents for which "driver error" was responsible. The court, however, concluded that the risk analysis data were consistent with the engineering test data in tending to prove the absence, not the presence, of a "safety-related defect" in the X-car. (*District Court's Decision*, pp. 52–54)

GM also challenged NHTSA's assertion of large numbers of consumer complaints and accidents related to X-cars. The company asserted that the majority of these complaints had poured in after the screening of the video film released by NHTSA's public relations staff, acting on the order of former administrator Raymond Peek on an X-car spinning out of control, and viewed on the network's nightly news.

GM argued that while releasing the film, in conjunction with the 1983 preliminary finding of defects, NHTSA had withheld a number of salient features of the demonstrated car: (1) the test driver of the car was instructed not to steer; (2) the brakes were mechanically applied to induce the desired rear-brake lock-up; (3) the road surface was specially coated for slickness of watered-down ice; and (4) under the above conditions, the X-car skidded out of the prescribed lane only 18 out of 179 instances.

DISTRICT COURT'S DECISION

Based on all the evidence, the court concluded that the government had "failed to meet its burden" that X-cars ever presented an "unreasonable risk of accidents due to a 'defect' in the car." The Court found that the government had stressed "the anecdotal accounts of consumer's personal experiences," whereas the court looked at the NHTSA's voluminous accident and fatality data showing the front-wheel drive compact X-car to be one of the safest cars on the road.

The government's position, according to the District Court, could be summarized as follows:

1. a failure of the vehicle simply to perform as expected was a "defect";
2. consumer experiences alone were sufficient to prove performance failure; and
3. the government was not required to come forward with an "engineering explanation" for that failure of performance.

Moreover, according to the government, the comparative performance of peer cars was irrelevant. That a manufacturer had built to the "state of the art" was not a defense if there were a significant number of failures to perform as expected. The *only* defense, according to the government, was "gross vehicle abuse" by the owner.

Based on its review, the court concluded that the results of engineering analysis and field tests that were conducted both by NHTSA and General Motors conclusively disproved the existence of any common engineering idiosyncrasy in the braking performance of 1980 X-cars not found in their competitors, no matter how configured, and whether or not it could be termed a "defect." (*District Court's Decision*, p. 46) In particular:

1. The percentage of competitive cars found to be rear biased in the "as received" condition, lightly loaded, was not only substantial; it exceeded that of the X-cars.
2. The braking efficiencies of rear-biased competitive cars in customer service were found to be generally lower than the efficiencies of rear biased X-cars, including so-called "complaint cars."
3. The brake balance of all X-cars measured in

terms of their braking efficiencies fell well within the brake balance "envelope" established by the extremes of the competitors from the same and later model years.
4. When the "design intent" brake balance of current configuration X-cars was tested with the brakes "rebuilt and burnished," it was revealed to be front biased, even in the lightly loaded condition.

In short, it appeared that it was the unique character of each application of each vehicle's brakes, and a combination of other factors, never-to-be-replicated, that would ultimately determine whether, and to what extent, a braked vehicle would yaw. There was simply no engineering evidence of any peculiar property of X-cars generally that would render them in any way exceptional insofar as having a predisposition to yaw. (*District Court's Decision*, p. 36)

Since NHTSA could not demonstrate that 1980 test X-cars displayed greater degrees of rear bias than competitive cars, or exhibited any particular propensity to rear-brake lock-up, it postulated the existence of "worst-case" vehicles somewhere in the undiscovered X-car universe by combining the extremes of adverse brake-torque measurements made upon different X-car tests. "Such projections, however, are not only purely hypothetical, and do not even remotely approach by the measurements actually made on more than 100 X-cars, they were all but disavowed by NHTSA engineers who acknowledged that "worst-case" projections are essentially speculation rather than a valid engineering analysis." (*District Court's Decision*, pp. 50–51)

The District Court also concluded that the government did not establish that the X-car braking system represented an unreasonable risk of accidents and injuries of "significance" in either the severity or frequency. The court rejected the government's allegation of GM's prior knowledge of X-car defects and complicity in withholding this information by stating that the internal documents simply demonstrated that despite continuous efforts, the engineers had failed to find an ideal braking system that would be fool proof under any and all driving conditions. In terms of the recalls, the court also rejected the government's charges that GM had failed to notify X-car owners, as required by regulations, of NHTSA's toll-free "Auto Safety Hotline." Instead, the court decided that GM's notification was not required. (*District Court's Decision*, pp. 66–71)

NHTSA LOSES AGAIN ON APPEAL

Dissatisfied with the lower court's decision, the U.S. government filed an appeal before the United States Court of Appeals for the District of Columbia. The Appeals Court also rejected the government's argument about the large number of complaints by indicating that a statistical analysis of complaints showed that these complaints were not large when compared with similar cars, and that a rise in complaints was linked to tremendous adverse publicity generated by NHTSA's film on the X-car test crash. NHTSA had not informed the media of the test protocol or otherwise indicated that the test did not simulate actual driving conditions. (NHTSA has since adopted an internal policy requiring that test protocols be disclosed when test films are released.) The film clip was witnessed by an estimated 53 million viewers on network television. The effects of the flood tide of adverse publicity were all too obvious. GM and NHTSA received more reports of X-car skidding in the two weeks following the television newscast than in the previous 3 1/2 years combined. Under these unusual (indeed unique) circumstances, it was appropriate to find that the government's evidence failed to show that the actual incidence of the phenomenon complained of was greater for the X-car than for comparable vehicle classes. (*Appeals Court's Decision*, p. 31)

The Appeals Court rejected the government's argument against the inapplicability of engineering analysis data developed during the course of litigation. Since the government's case was based on circumstantial evidence of consumer complaints, which were held to be insufficient, it was indeed quite appropriate for the trial court to consider GM's testing data in rebuttal to the charge that vehicle malfunction was responsible for the incidents described by the consumer complaints. (*Appeals Court's Decision*, pp. 32–33)

The Appeals Court also accepted the trial court's decision in concluding that GM's actions as to both 1981 and 1983 recalls were voluntary. According to the Appeals Court, under the regulatory framework established by the Act, GM never incurred an obligation to conduct either recall.

NOTES

1. *United States of America* v. *General Motors Corporation*, U.S. Federal Court, District of Columbia, Civil Action No. 83–2220. (References to this citation in the text would appear as the *District Court's Decision* followed by the appropriate page numbers.)
2. *United States of America* v. *General Motors Corporation*, Federal Court, District of Columbia, Civil Action, 656, F. Supp. 1555 (D.D.C. 1987), Dated March 8, 1988. (References to this citation in the text would appear as *Appeals Court Decision* followed by the appropriate page numbers.)
3. *United States of America* v. *General Motors*

Corporation, Civil Action No. 83–2220, Stipulation and Final Order of Dismissal, U.S. District Court for the Dismissal, U.S. District Court for the District of Columbia, June 14, 1989.
4. See: *Business Week*, "If It Has Wheels and Carries People, Shouldn't It Be Safe?," June 20, 1988, p. 48, and *Business Week* "Revving Without a Cause: When the Car Has a Mind of Its Own," April 4, 1988, pp. 66–67. Also see for Audi: News Release by U.S. Department of Transportation, dated March 7, 1989, "NHTSA Announces Results of 'Sudden Acceleration Study'," and John Tomerlin,

"Solved: The Riddle of Unintended Acceleration," *Road & Track*, February 1988. For Suzuki case, see a letter from George L. Parker, Associate Administrator for Enforcement of NHTSA to Mr. Samuel H. Cole of Center for Auto Safety, dated September 1, 1988, denying a petition to open a defect investigation and order a recall of the Suzuki Samurai and its variants.

5. "The *Fortune* 500, Largest U.S. Industrial Corporations." *Fortune* (April 24, 1989), pp. 354–55.
6. Paul Ingrasia and Jacob M. Schlesinger, "GM's Market Share Declines Last Year, Even as Net Set a Mark." *Wall Street Journal* (February 15, 1989), pp. 1,7.
7. See: *Newsweek* "Slamming the Brakes on GM's X-Car," January 17, 1983.
8. *Ward's Auto World*, January 1979, quoted in an editorial in *Ward's Auto World*, September 1983, p. 6.
9. *Fortune*, "X-Cars Exit: GM Plans to Close the Line," (February 21, 1983), p. 12.
10. John E. Peterson, "Recall Order Denied in GM X-Cars Case; US Claimed Brake Defects." *Business Week* (April 15, 1987).
11. General Motors Corporation, Annual Report, 1980, p. 7.
12. 15 U.S.C. 1381; see generally 1966 U.S. Code Cong. & Admin. News at 2709.
13. *United States* v. *General Motors Corporation*, 518 F 2d. 420, 438 & N. 84 (D.C. Cir. 1975). Cited in District Court's Decision, supra note 1, p. 5.
14. Comptroller General of the United States (GAO), GAO/RCEP–83–195, *Department of Transportation's Investigation of Rear Brake Lockup Problems in 1980 X-Body Cars Should Have Been More Timely*. (Washington, DC: GAO, August 5, 1983).
15. George E. Hoffer, Stephen W. Pruitt, and Robert J. Reilly, "Automotive Recalls and Informational Efficiency." *The Financial Review*, 22, 4, (November 1987), pp. 433–42.
16. George E. Hoffer, Stephen W. Pruitt, and Robert J. Reilly, 116 Recalls Between 1967–1981. "The Impact of Product Recalls on the Wealth of Sellers: A Reexamination." *Journal of Political Economy*, 96, no. 3 (1988), p. 664.
17. Interview with the author. Unless otherwise specifically stated, all direct quotes and paraphrased statements from different people are based on personal interviews or written communications to the author.
18. See also, *Appeals Court's Decision*, p. 30.
19. Helen Kahn, "NHTSA Sues GM to Force 1.1 Million X-Car Recall." *Automotive News* (August 8, 1983), p.1.
20. *Ibid*.
21. Letter from Congressman Timothy E. Wirth, chairman, House of Representatives, Subcommittee on Telecommunications, Consumer Protection, and Finance of the Committee of Energy and Commerce, to Charles A. Borosher, comptroller general, General Accounting Office, dated January 5, 1982, p. 3.
22. "Slamming the Brakes on GM's X-Cars," *Newsweek* (January 17, 1983).
23. Kahn, "NHTSA Sues GM" p.1
24. "Slamming the Brakes on GM's X-Cars," *Newsweek* (January 17, 1983).
25. Kahn, "NHTSA Sues GM" p. 8.
26. Supra note 10, p. 8.
27. "Wirth Wants DOT to Probe GM Brakes," *Automotive News* (January 2, 1984), p. 3.
28. *Ibid*.

CIGARETTE SMOKING AND PUBLIC HEALTH

The role of the tobacco industry in the United States

As America approaches the twenty-first century, the government's tobacco policies remain as contradictory as ever and the country's tobacco wars have entered a new phase.

First, contradictory government tobacco policies. The *agricultural economics of tobacco*—featuring production subsidies, export promotion, and the preservation of the excise tax base—have for some time been on a collision course with the *health economics of tobacco*—measured in terms of the cost of care as well as lost productivity. Since the Surgeon General's report of 1964 launched the crusade against smoking, the government has been unable to reconcile these two sets of policies which it continues to pursue simultaneously. (See Table 1A.)

Not only the government suffers from such a split personality, however. Some of America's largest health maintenance organizations (HMOs), are stockholders in major tobacco companies. In 1995, Prudential owned $12 million in RJR Nabisco stock, $100 million in Philip Morris, $97 million in Loews, and $36 million in American Brands. All together, Prudential's tobacco holdings amounted to over $248 million. Travelers and Metlife (which recently merged to become the second largest health insurer in the country) had investments of over $100 million, while Cigna approached $75 million. These are the same companies that charge clients significantly higher premiums if they have a history of smoking![1]

The tobacco debate is focused upon a wide set of issues, ranging from free enterprise and the rights of legitimate businesses and their customers, to trade, agriculture, and public health economics. The issues raised range from the integrity of scientific evidence and determination of "what is a fact?", to the legitimacy of various methods of communication and truth in advertising, and the exploitation of economic dependencies of certain individuals and groups. While **truth**, **communication** and **economic dependency** may oversimplify the debate, it is nonetheless helpful to keep these variables in mind, for they are the primary focus of proposed legal and regulatory reforms of both the industry and of consumer behavior.

ISSUES FOR ANALYSIS

1. What are the standards of evidence, both scientific and medical, that must be met in cases involving large-scale serious dangers to public health before a strong case can be made for imposing restrictions on the sale, promotion, and even consumption of a product such as cigarettes? To what extent have these standards been met in the case of cigarette smoking?

Table 1. Contradictions in government policy and new weapons in the tobacco wars

---

A. CONTRADICTIONS IN POLICY

The economics of agriculture, trade, and public revenue

The economics of health care

B. NEW WEAPONS IN THE TOBACCO WARS

Secondhand (environmental) smoke: increasing prohibition in public places

Increasing health care liability suits brought by both individuals and state governments

Suppliers: fearing liability, many suppliers seeking to sever or strictly limit relations to the industry

Treating nicotine as an addictive drug, with possible regulation by the FDA

Market focus: severely restricting access to children and young adults

Advertising: making efforts to banish all advertising, including outdoor billboards and direct mail

Image: the growing lack of credibility, especially of top industry executives testifying before Congress

Price: continuing to impose costs on the industry in terms of taxes

---

2. How should the tobacco industry, in general, and individual companies, in particular, conduct themselves? What posture should businesses outside the industry (e.g., health insurance companies, the media, and retailers) adopt?

3. Should there be any self-imposed constraints on promoting certain kinds of cigarettes or promoting them to certain groups, such as teenagers?

4. What role should the government play and what is the rationale for such a role? Mediator? Policymaker/Regulator? Disseminator of information?

5. What are the rights and responsibilities of smokers and nonsmokers in and out of public places or workplaces? Can employers insist that employees not smoke at all—even in private—in the interest of keeping their insurance premiums down?

6. What information should be available? In what form? Presented by whom? To what audience? To what end? Should certain demographic groups (e.g., teenagers) receive special attention?

7. What are the rights and duties of producers and antismoking groups to argue their positions? Is it all right to allow antismoking ads while banning advertisements for cigarettes, a legal product?

The Surgeon General's Report of 1964 brought to a head the long dispute between health authorities and the tobacco industry. The antecedents linking smoking to cancer go back to 1900, when statisticians noted an increase in cancer of the lung associated with smoking. Their data are usually taken as the starting point for studies on the possible relationship of smoking to lung cancer, to diseases of the heart and blood vessels, and to noncancerous diseases of the lower respiratory tract. In contemporary terms, the benchmark study arguing in favor of public regulation of the industry is the Surgeon General's Report of 1964. As a result of its investigation, the president's commission, at that time, reached the conclusion that cigarette smoking is causally related to lung cancer. Further, the magnitude of the effect of cigarette smoking far outweighs all other factors related to such cancer. The commission also found that the risk of developing lung cancer increased with the duration of smoking and the number of cigarettes smoked per day, and diminished with discontinuing smoking. According to the report, the risk of developing cancer of the lung for the combined groups of pipe smokers, cigar smokers, and pipe *and* cigar smokers is greater than for nonsmokers, but much less than for cigarette smokers. In addition, the report stated that cigarette smoking was the greatest cause of chronic bronchitis in the United States and greatly increased the risk of death from that disease and from emphysema. For most Americans, cigarette smoking was a much greater cause of chronic bronchopulmonary disease than atmospheric pollution or occupational exposure. The report also concluded that cigarette smoking was related to cardiovascular diseases.

Subsequent reports have reconfirmed the original findings and added precision to the arguments regarding cancer, cardiovascular and lung diseases. In addition, more attention has been paid in recent years to issues of maternal/fetal health and the question of tobacco as an addictive drug.[2] The U.S. Department of Health and Human Services publishes hundreds of documents each year. The Surgeon General's Reports have a clear policy focus, serving to summarize research and disseminate it to a larger public. They do not so much inform the medical community as provide a basis for public policy initiatives. Such reports appear regularly. During the 1980s they reflected a thematic approach: women (1980), the changing cigarette (1981), cancer (1982), cardiovascular disease (1983), lung disease (1984), passive smoke (1986), and addiction (1988).

ECONOMICS OF THE TOBACCO INDUSTRY: AGRICULTURE, TRADE, AND HEALTH

The tobacco industry accounts for barely 3/10 of 1% of GDP and only slightly more than 1% of trade. Yet on the level of the tobacco farmer and manufacturing industries, it is a profitable sector of the economy. In terms of selected financial indicators, the tobacco industry in 1992 ranked third in sales per employee ($275,000). It was a leader in the growth of profitablity over the previous year (17.5%), with sales averaging $2.06 per $1 of stockholder equity, a 2.6% return on sales, and a 21.9% return on common equity (#872).[3]

Allegations that tobacco use causes disease are almost as old as use of the plant itself. From 1953 to 1984 some 45,000 studies of the health impact of tobacco were conducted.[4] The results of such studies show a high correlation between tobacco use and a number of heart, lung, fetal, and other diseases. At the heart of the debate is whether such correlations establish "cause." The health issues involved are cancer, cardiovascular disease, lung disease, maternal and fetal health, and fire danger and burn injuries. The debates

rage not only over "ordinary 'full flavor' cigarettes," but also over "safer" cigarettes with less tar and nicotine and even over passive or environmental smoke.

It is hard to imagine anyone in the United States who is not familiar with the notion that smoking is injurious to one's health. That this awareness has had some effect on public consciousness is undeniable. Increasing numbers of public and private institutions have imposed restrictions on smoking on the premises, encouraging smokers to quit. Nonsmokers have also become more vociferous in their protests against smokers in the workplace and other public settings. Their stated aim is to create a healthy and smoke-free environment.

The health economics of tobacco paint a different picture. Table 2 summarizes some of the general findings regarding mortality from smoking. A 1994 study by the Centers for Disease Control (CDC) estimated that in 1993 the *medical costs* of smoking approximated $2.06 per pack. Overall, the medical costs of smoking in the economy totaled up to near $50 billion. Of this $26.9 billion was for hospitals, $15.5 billion for doctors, $4.9 billion for nursing homes, $1.8 billion for prescription drugs and $900 million for home health care. The taxpayer foots the bill for $21.9 billion or 43.8% of the medical costs of smoking. The heart of the message is clear: adding up all economic benefits and costs, the tobacco industry inflicts a net cost upon society. [5]

Studies such as the above infuriate the tobacco industry. These and similar studies are based upon multiple assumptions about the progress of various diseases, rates of smoking, costs in the health care industry, and assumptions regarding the economy in general. No doubt such estimates are tendentious. The details ought to be carefully scrutinized. The general message is clear: tobacco is costly to all taxpayers, not just to smokers.

In some ways the health care advocates are winning the day. The number of people smoking has declined steadily from approximately 42% of those 18 and over in 1965 to

Table 2. Mortality Rates from Smoking Expressed as a
Ratio of Deaths Caused by Smoking to Total Deaths

	ALL DEVELOPED COUNTRIES (Thousands)					
	MALES			FEMALES		
	Age 0–34	*Age 35–69*	*Age 70+*	*Age 0–34*	*Age 35–69*	*Age 70+*
Lung Cancer	—/1.2	231/246	141/156	—/0.7	44/64	42/61
All Cancer	—/27	360/736	212/600	—/23	56/500	56/564
Vascular	—/27	318/926	163/1,467	—/13	57/508	92/2,417
Respiratory	—/38	90/140	139/322	—/29	25/66	63/299
All Other	—/413	97/656	40/462	—/179	22/302	25/718
All Causes	—/504	865/2,458	40/462	—/244	160/1,376	236/3,998
	UNITED STATES (Total Number)					
Lung Cancer	—/169	44,725/47,675	32,956/36,010	—/137	19,076/22,720	12,336/15,845
All Cancer	—/5071	62,926/120,869	47,230/120,974	—/4406	24,043/101,432	16,145/108,811
Vascular	—/5040	59,028/179,991	39,260/302,422	—/3137	23,702/88,702	27,983/403,447
Respiratory	—/2341	15,268/25,397	27,743/65,344	—/1723	8834/15,712	14,366/55,672
All Causes	—/98,200	153,739/424,790	122,996/574,768	—/47,889	66,122/260,888	65,473/679,905

SOURCE: Richard Peto, Alan D. Lopez, Jillian Boreham, Michael Thun, and Clark Heath, Jr., *Mortality from Smoking in Developed Countries, 1950–2000*. New York: Oxford University Press, 1994, pp. 2, 534.

25% in 1992 (#212). However, the number of users in the 12–17-year-old group is estimated at 9.6%, with 31.9% of the 18–25 year olds and 33.7% of the 26–33 year olds also smoking. There is apprehension that tobacco use is increasing among the young.

The following statistical material, as well as the data in Table 2, are taken from Richard Peto, Alan D. Lopez, Jillian Boreham, Michael Thun, and Clark Heath, Jr., in their book, *Mortality from Smoking in Developed Countries, 1950–2000.* (New York: Oxford University Press, 1994). This is a very thorough compendium that provides country by country statistics for some 50 different countries. In general, in the United States (pp. 530–535) smoking accounts for some 350,000 to 400,000 deaths per year. This adds up to roughly 36% of all male deaths in the 35–69 age group and 25% of all deaths among the same age of females. For those 70 and over, the figures fall to roughly 21% and 10%, respectively. For men aged 34–69, smoking accounted for 52% (24% for women) of all cancer deaths, as well as 80% (75% for women) of all chronic obstructive pulmonary deaths and roughly 33% (27% for women) of vascular and other respiratory and medical deaths. Putting all ages and sexes together, smoking accounts for 20% of all deaths in the United States, as well as 89% of all lung cancer deaths and 73% of all chronic obstructive pulmonary deaths. For all developed countries, smoking accounts for 16% of all deaths. Furthermore, the mean years lost per death from smoking add up to 22 years for the 35–69 age group and 8 years for those 70 and over (p.4).

THE TOBACCO WARS: OLD AND NEW ISSUES

Notwithstanding all of the above, the tobacco industry continues to argue that scientific evidence linking smoking to cancer and other health hazards is inconclusive. The key issue they dispute is **causality.** They recognize statistical correlations between smoking and various diseases, but steadfastly deny causality. Appearing before Congress in April 1994, the heads of all the major tobacco companies steadfastly denied that tobacco was addictive. While they did concede some possible connections between smoking and lung cancer, on the whole they completely rejected the epidemiological findings of the Surgeon General's Office as marshaled since 1965. They have never really abandoned their mantra: statistical correlation does not prove causality. Indeed, at this point they are caught in a blind alley as far as policy and the law are concerned: an admission of known causality would bury the companies in liability suits.[6]

The tobacco industry has constantly fought a fierce battle against any restrictions on smoking. In this, they have been helped by the immense profits that cigarette sales generate in the United States. The industry maintains that as long as the product is legal, companies have every right to manufacture and sell it. The issue is also presented in terms of freedom of choice. To wit, since adults are aware of the alleged health hazards of smoking, they do so at their own free will and, thereby, absolve the industry of even an indirect responsibility.

The latest controversies (see Table 1B) center around environmental (or passive, second–hand) smoke, the addictive nature of smoking, the attempt to lure young people into smoking, and liability for health care costs. The tobacco industry vigorously disputes all of these issues. It does so on a number of fronts: presenting alternative scientific studies, vigorous advocacy, advertising campaigns for smokers' rights as linked to the American Constitution, and building lobbying coalitions comprised of all those whose economic interests are somehow linked to tobacco.

Secondhand Smoke (Environmental Tobacco Smoke)

The office of the Surgeon General and other investigators have declared passive or secondhand smoke a health hazard. The tobacco industry instantly challenged the scientific basis of the studies.

The following excerpts from the Tobacco Institute's report "Tobacco Smoke and the Nonsmoker: Scientific Integrity at the Crossroads" illustrate the point.[7]

> Three major scientific conferences have concluded within the last five years that there is no persuasive evidence that cigarette smoke in the air, or environmental tobacco smoke (ETS), poses any significant risk to the health of nonsmokers.
>
> When the weekly newspaper of the American Medical Association reported on scientific testimony presented to a committee of the National Academy of Sciences, and referred to the evidence on the health effects of ETS as "inconclusive," the report was denounced as "outrageously wrong" by officials of the heart, lung and cancer associations. As one of the anti-smoking organizations' officials outlined the issue in political—rather than scientific—terms: "It would be truly unfortunate if the AMA's efforts [in opposition to ETS] were undermined by this report." The continued focus on unfounded claims that tobacco smoke compromises the health of nonsmokers will only intensify the current climate of emotionalism and impede the progress of scientific inquiry.
>
> ETS is but one of many potential elements of indoor air. As a matter of scientific fact, exposure to ETS has not been shown to cause lung cancer in nonsmokers. The two most recently published reports on the subject make it clear that the findings are conflicting and inconclusive.

While some regulations on the promotion and smoking of cigarettes have been publicly imposed, they have not unduly hurt the industry. A declining trend among current smokers is more than made up by new young adults who continuously join the ranks of smokers. Nonetheless, over the past five years, many municipalities have been vigorously extending such bans.[8]

The major threat to tobacco companies posed by the environmental smoke debate has been the increasing banning of smoking in public places, whether work or recreational. A number of smaller companies are becoming involved in the anti-smoking campaign by offering incentives to their employees to quit smoking. Neon Electric Corporation of Houston banned smoking by its employees and offered a 50¢-per-hour pay raise to any worker who got rid of the habit. The Alexandria, Virginia, fire department no longer hires smokers as firefighters because 16 of 22 men who retired with disabilities from 1973 to 1978 were smokers. Cybertek Computer Products, Inc., pays $500 to each employee who will quit. In all, about 30% of U.S. businesses have some sort of policy restricting smoking, and about 3 % pay their employees not to smoke. Large companies are more reluctant to ban smoking or to offer bonuses to quitters. One company, AT&T's Bell Laboratories at its Whippany, New Jersey, plant, is experimenting with prohibiting smoking in 70% of its plant. Dow Chemical, Continental Illinois, Kimberly-Clark, and others sponsor educational programs and poster campaigns urging smokers to quit. Larger companies also depend to a certain extent on peer pressure to encourage smokers to quit. In at least one instance, however, smokers have filed suit to reinstitute smoking.

Addictive Nature of Nicotine

A far more ominous charge against cigarette smoking was levelled in the 1988 Report of the U.S. Surgeon General, which labelled tobacco as an addictive entry-level drug.[9] The addiction charge has significantly increased the stakes in the controversy. It has been vigorously pursued by the Food and Drug Administration (FDA), as well as the Surgeon General's Office. By 1994, Dr. David Kessler, head of the FDA, was calling for regulation of tobacco as a drug.[10] In so doing, he rode a crest of public opinion based upon the belief that the tobacco companies: (1) hid their own research that showed nicotine was addictive and, (2) engaged in practices of spiking the nicotine content of tobacco products. The latter point came to light in studies

of tar content in tobacco. For decades, the tobacco companies touted their success in reducing tar. Scientifically, as tar was reduced, nicotine content should also have lessened. However, it did not, which led to the investigation of nicotine spiking.

If addiction is involved, the freedom of smokers to choose to smoke or not would be severely impaired. Furthermore, the addictive nature of smoking makes smokers fairly insensitive to price increases, thus allowing tobacco companies to reach ever greater profit margins from unit sales. From 1986 to 1992, average annual expenditures for tobacco products and smoking supplies rose from $230 to $275 (#704). For another thing, the issue of addiction calls for a reassessment of the tobacco industry as a legitimate business and opens the door to an entirely different type of product liability suit.

Notwithstanding the mountainous accumulation of data and research findings, no end to the controversy is in sight. The tobacco industry continues to dispute the research findings maintaining that: (1) research methodology has been flawed, and even biased; and (2) statistical correlation does not prove causality.[11]

The battle has clearly moved beyond the scientific community and many new fronts have been opened. Most notable among these are legal liability lawsuits, local ordinances restricting smoking, hostility of nonsmokers resulting in smoking being viewed as an anti-social activity, higher insurance rates for smokers, and activities of public interest groups seeking further regulation of marketing and promotion of cigarettes. Adversaries include private voluntary groups and state and local governments, as well as the formidable departments of the Federal Trade Commission, the Federal Communications Commission, and the Surgeon General's Office. These critics are appalled by the industry's steadfast denial of any causal link between cigarette smoking and cancer and other diseases. Says Dr. Alan Blum, editor of the *New York Journal of Medicine* and founder of "Doctors Ought to Care" (an antismoking organization): "We have more evidence to prove that cigarettes cause cancer and heart disease than we have concerning the cause of virtually any other disease entity.[12]

Targeting Young People

Adversaries paint the following scenario: knowing nicotine is an addictive drug, cigarette manufacturers lure the young into smoking. Once hooked, they are a "cash cow" for the industry. However, at the same time, they are set on the path to eventually contract smoking-related diseases. This is a tragedy for those who smoke, but also for the ordinary taxpayer, who ends up footing a good deal of the bill.

In 1995, there was a considerable impetus to prevent the tobacco companies from hooking young smokers, the only segment in American society where smoking is increasing. [13] In addition to the Surgeon General, the FDA has become a major player. The Clinton administration has also promised to move vigorously in the area of smoking by young people and retailers. The target is broad; it includes vending machines, small retailers, and advertising.

The industry has taken notice. RJR has withdrawn its ubiquitous "Joe Camel" ad campaign, which was found to have tremendous appeal to children. Philip Morris has undertaken to curb small retailers and to control vending machines, even announcing that it will stamp "underage sale prohibited" on all packages.[14]

Liability and State Suits to Recover Medicare Costs

A new threat to the tobacco industry has appeared in the form of a wave of product liability lawsuits by victims of lung cancer and other diseases allegedly caused by cigarette smoking.[15] The most celebrated case is that brought against Liggett Tobacco Company by the family of Rose Cipollone,

who claimed that manufacturers deceived her into believing cigarettes were safe. The Cipollone family was successful in the lower courts and for the first time ever, it appeared that a tobacco company had lost a case. Liggett eventually won the suit in 1992; the Supreme Court stated, however, that the federal law requiring warning labels does not protect manufacturers from state damage suits alleging fraud.

The liability issue has been brewing for some time. In 1963, legal considerations emerged when the question of cigarette manufacturers' liability was raised in the case of *Green v. The American Tobacco Company*. A district court in Miami held that, although smoking was a cause of cancer, the company was not liable since it could not have foreseen the consequences. As a result, however, the industry began to give serious consideration to a warning on cigarette packages in order to limit companies' liability. In December 1963, the American Cancer Society issued the results of a survey of more than 1 million Americans. Its conclusion was that "the evidence continues to pile up, and the burden of proof that there is not a causal relationship could soon shift over to the cigarette companies."

Since 1954, some 350 liability suits have been filed against tobacco companies; 207 have been dismissed or withdrawn and, until the Cipollone case, none had even made much progress, let alone been victorious. Prosecutors, however, are pinning their hopes on juries in a society more conscious than ever of the evils of smoking.

Over the past five years the tobacco companies have been hit with several new individual and class action liability lawsuits as well as suits by states to recover Medicare and other related health costs.[16] These cases are based upon assertions that independent research conducted by the tobacco companies themselves over the past fifty years has recognized both the addictive nature of nicotine as well as the various health problems caused by tobacco. Until 1995 the tobacco companies were largely successful in stonewalling such accusations by maintaining a united front as well as by pursuing aggressive legal action.

Then the unimaginable happened. In late 1995 and early 1996, researchers employed by Brown and Williamson as well as by Philip Morris came forward with the damning insider information. In sworn affidavits and court documents they served up the evidence that had long eluded prosecutors: inside company documents, information and corroborating sources that proved the tobacco companies knew of the health problems as well as the addictive nature of nicotine, the levels of which they manipulated. In early March, 1996, the smallest of the U.S. tobacco companies, the Liggett Group, broke ranks with the industry and offered a settlement to both the class action suits it faced as well as to the suits brought by individual states.

Within two year's time, the formal testimony of the CEOs of seven top tobacco companies before Congress in April 1994 was turned on its head. While it appears that tobacco's "united front" is about to crack into pieces, the remaining companies have strongly condemned the Liggett Group's actions and have vowed to fight on. At the same time, the companies have taken a number of steps to improve their image with aggressive public relations campaigns that emphasize the economic and social contributions of tobacco companies. Philip Morris has even announced a program promising strong action to prevent youth access to tobacco.

Despite the mountains of evidence related to all of these issues, the industry shows no sign of giving up the fight. Strongly represented in Congress, the tobacco producers are aggressive lobbyists against restrictive legislation based upon what they term irresponsible and insufficient medical research. In 1958, the cigarette industry formed the Tobacco Institute, which became its primary lobbying arm, and provided a single agency to deal with health-related matters. The Tobacco Institute has taken the lead in efforts to limit the power of the Federal Trade Commission to regulate cigarette advertising and to assure that cigarette warning regulations enacted by Congress are acceptable to the industry. It has also consistently asserted that government action has been based upon political rather than scientific motives.[17]

While all this negative publicity has sent shock waves through the industry, cigarettes are still a big money maker. Emboldened by fat coffers and unwilling to give up enormous profits generated by cigarette sales, the industry is taking on all challengers. From all indications, the battle is likely to be fierce and it is not at all clear what outcomes will emerge.

FEDERAL GOVERNMENT ACTION

Following the Surgeon General's 1964 Report, there was tremendous pressure on Congress for action. Issues of primary concern included: (1) warning labels, (2) advertising, (3) the "equal time" provision, and (4) selective bans on smoking.

Health Warnings

The first official government reaction came from the FTC, when it announced on January 18, 1964, that it was scheduling hearings for March 16.[18] Following these hearings, the FTC announced proposed trade regulation rules to require a warning on cigarette packages and advertisements, the actual wording to be left to the manufacturers. FTC Chairman Paul Rand Dixon notified the House of the Commission's decision and said that the labeling requirement would become effective January 1, 1965. There was so much opposition from the tobacco industry, however, that Chairman Dixon postponed the labeling requirement to July 1, 1965, so that the 89th Congress, which convened on January 4, 1965, would have time to examine the proposal.

The FTC also dropped its regulation on two other ad directives regarding claims of good health and statements that one brand may be less harmful than another.

As the debate ensued three sets of arguments came to dominate discourse: economics, the free market, and health and human habits.[19]

The FTC's position was initially set forth in the Congressional Hearings of 1964. Chairman Paul Dixon contended that the commission had authority to regulate cigarette advertising under Section 5 of the Federal Trade Commission Act, which authorizes the commission "to proceed against any actual or potential deception in sale, or offering for sale, of any product in commerce. . . . Such deception may result either from a direct statement concerning a product or a failure to disclose any material fact relating to such a product." Dixon stated that "the Commission had completed its consideration of the record in this proceeding and has determined that the public interest required the promulgation of a trade regulation rule for the prevention of unfair or deceptive advertising or labeling of cigarettes in relation to the health hazards of smoking." The chairman, however, was more anxious that Congress take the initiative in such a politically sensitive and explosive area.

At the hearings, the industry's position was presented by Bowman Gray, chairman of the board of directors of R.J. Reynolds Tobacco Company, of Winston-Salem, North Carolina. The industry opposed the FTC regulations regarding labeling and advertising for three reasons: (1) The FTC did not have the authority to issue such a trade regulation and the commission, therefore, acted unlawfully; (2) the matter was of such importance that it should be resolved by Congress and not by an agency ("the Commission's rule would not have preemptive effect, and the industry would be exposed to the possibility of diverse State and municipal laws"); and (3) "We oppose it because we believe the Commission's warning requirement is un-wise, unwarranted and is not a fair factual statement of the present state of scientific knowledge."

Should Congress consider that a warning label was absolutely necessary, Gray emphasized the following points:

1. Any such legislation should make it absolutely clear that the congressional statute preempted the field. If there was to be a caution notice, it should be uniform and nationwide in scope.
2. The required caution notice should be fair and factual. It should be phrased in a way that reflected the lack of scientific clinical and laboratory evidence of the relationship between smoking and health.
3. If a warning was to be required on the package, it certainly should not be required in cigarette advertising.

Congress ultimately passed S.559, which required that all cigarette packages bear the label "Caution: Cigarette Smoking May Be Hazardous to Your Health." The bill provided for a uniform and overriding federal labeling requirement that was not expected to affect sales seriously. All action on control of advertising was suspended until July 1969. In its final form, the bill called for a fine of $10,000 for violations and required periodic reports from the FTC and HEW. The bill was strongly opposed by many who saw it as too soft on the industry. The law that was finally passed had little effect on the tobacco industry's sales. A 1965 FTC study reported that 82% of respondents felt the warning label had no effect. For the fiscal year ending June 1965, consumption was at a record level of more than 5.33 billion cigarettes.

The U.S. Public Health Service also noted that, although a million Americans were giving up smoking each year, they were replaced by 1.5 million new smokers, mostly youngsters. In addition, it urged a stronger warning on cigarette packages: "Caution: Cigarette Smoking is Dangerous to Your Health and May Cause Death from Cancer and Other Diseases."

The FTC also recommended to Congress that the Public Health Cigarette Smoking Act be amended to require that the following statement appear clearly and prominently on all cigarette packages: "Warning: Cigarette Smoking Is Dangerous to Health, and May Cause Death from Cancer, Coronary Heart Disease, Chronic Bronchitis, Pulmonary Emphysema and Other Diseases." The Commission also recommended that Congress consider a system of rotational label warnings similar to the present Swedish system. Beginning in 1977, Sweden introduced a labeling system requiring sixteen different warning statements on cigarette packages, to be used interchangeably. In 1979, following an assessment that the system had increased knowledge, sixteen new statements were substituted and the rotational warning requirement was extended to cigarette advertising as well.[20]

Regulation of Advertising

Further hearings were held before both the House and Senate Commerce Committees during the first session of the Eighty-ninth Congress, March 22 to April 1, 1965. The testimony in these hearings emphasized regulation of advertising. The tobacco industry argued, on the basis of the proper role of government and the proper relationship between government and business, that it should not be the government's role to attempt to change the behavior of individual citizens.[21] When an industry demonstrated a willingness to regulate itself, as the cigarette industry had done through its voluntary code, government regulation represented undue interference with business and free enterprise. The government, furthermore, had no right to prohibit the advertising of a product that could be legally manufactured and sold. If action was considered necessary, a warning on the label and not in advertising would be the proper form. The label was the traditional and most effective place for hazard warnings.

Testimony was also given on the nature and purposes of advertising in the cigarette industry. Advertising, it was argued, was a basic means of competition, and prohibiting it would restrict competition in the industry. The intent of cigarette advertising was not to encourage people to smoke, since half the people in the country were already smoking, but to encourage smokers to change brands—that is, to increase a company's market share. The industry was mature and had a mature marketplace. The aim, therefore, was selective and not primary demand.

The FTC, although always in favor of regulating cigarette advertising, had consistently argued that the political and economic implications of such a regulation made Congress the proper initiating body. Congress was also reluctant. In a pressure play in 1965, the FTC announced that it would require a stiffer warning on cigarette packages unless Congress took action. Such a tactic precipitated the 1965 act (which would expire on June 30, 1969). The FTC again used the same tactic it had employed in the labeling debate. In June 1968, in a three-to-two decision, it voted to ban all cigarette advertising from radio and television and strongly suggested to the Senate committee that Congress legislate on the matter. Later in the summer, the Surgeon General's Task Force for Smoking and Health charged that the tobacco industry was encouraging death and disease with its advertising practices and that it was unwilling to face up to the health hazards of smoking.

On February 5, 1969, the FCC, in a six-to-one decision, moved to ban cigarette advertising from radio and television. Chairman Hyde indicated that the Commission would be satisfied only with a complete ban and not with the voluntary restrictions. In defense of its legal power, the commission said: "In the case of such a threat to public health, the authority to act is really a duty to act"; it would appear "wholly at odds with the public interest for broadcasters to present advertising promoting the consumption of a product imposing this unique danger."[22]

The cigarette industry considered the decision arbitrary, and the National Association of Broadcasters charged that the FCC was outside its normal jurisdiction. Despite the heated reaction to the FCC proposal, however, there could be no actual ban without extensive hearings, and there remained the possibility of contrary legislation. Thus, the FTC and FCC made it clear that Congress would have to act.

Although banned from television, the tobacco industry is estimated to spend some $4 billion a year on advertising and promotions. In the past few years, attention has been shifted to banning outdoor advertising, especially in stadiums, where during televised events the billboard messages are broadcast nationally. Opponents also wish to ban the placing of smoking products in film and videos, the use of direct mail, free distribution on street corners, and the sponsoring of sporting and other outdoor recreation events.

The Equal Time Provision

On June 2, 1967, the FCC ordered radio and television stations to allow time for antismoking advertisements. The seven commissioners said that their decision was based on the fairness doctrine, which states that the public should have access to conflicting viewpoints on controversial issues of public importance.[23] This fairness doctrine, a basic principle of the broadcasting field, was made a part of the Communications Act of 1959, although it was not applied to product advertising until 1967.

Thus, stations running cigarette ads had to turn over a significant amount of free time to antismoking commercials—one antismoking for every three smoking commercials. Antismoking groups such as the American Cancer Society filled the air with effective anti-ads. After the ruling, the American Cancer Society distributed 8,900 antismoking commercials in 16 months. The counter-ads were, in effect, the reverse of the cigarette ads. Instead of looking happy and vigorous, smokers were presented as miserable and unhealthy. A number of celebrities were used to advocate quitting smoking, and others refused to perform on programs sponsored by cigarette companies.

The person largely responsible for the FCC's application of the fairness doctrine to cigarette advertising was John F. Banzhaf, III, a 28-year-old New York attorney known as "the Ralph Nader of the cigarette industry."[24] In January 1967, Banzhaf had filed a formal complaint with the FCC against WCBS-TV. The complaint maintained that the fairness doctrine required the station to give equal time to "responsible groups" to present the case against cigarette smoking. Although the FCC rejected the equal time contention, its June 3 ruling responded to Banzhaf's complaint. Banzhaf then formed two organizations. The first, ASH (Action on Smoking and Health), sponsored by noted physicians, raised more than $100,000 to conduct litigation on the fairness doctrine and to enforce its application by monitoring TV stations and filing complaints against those failing to comply. The other organization, LASH (Legislative Action on Smoking and Health), raised funds and enlisted support for the congressional battles.

Despite the voluntary advertising code, the tobacco industry continued to represent smoking as an enjoyable and even healthful activity. Also, much of the advertising was done during prime broadcasting hours and consequently was reaching young people. The industry also fought the fairness doctrine, which mandated "equal time" for opposing views in television advertising. However, since industry regulation was proving ineffectual, the Congress finally acted in March 1970, and cigarette advertising on radio and television was banned effective January 21, 1971.[25] The debate continues over whether all forms of advertising should be banned on the grounds that it is both harmful and deceptive.

Taxes and Selective Bans on Smoking

In January 1983, federal cigarette taxes were raised for the first time in 30 years. The tax was doubled from 8¢ to 16¢ in an effort to discourage consumption. In 1994 it stood at 24¢. Those who want to link smoking to financing health care threaten to raise it to over a dollar.

Studies suggest that to actually decrease cigarette demand, taxes have to be raised to 42¢ for adults and to a whopping $1.42 for teenagers. Some advocates of increased taxes favored using the revenue to defray public health costs due to smoking. The industry objected to the tax and also disputed the public health cost structure rationale. If nicotine is truly addictive, however, price increases by themselves will not be able to control the rate of smoking.

Other government agencies have also gotten into the act. The Civil Aeronautics Board moved in January 1979 to restrict smoking aboard airplanes. The rule required that airlines create as many nonsmoking seats as passengers demanded, that each passenger class must have at least two nonsmoking rows. Further cigar and pipe smoking was completely banned, and nonsmoking passengers between smoking sections were not to be "unreasonably burdened" by smoke. By 1995 most airlines had banned smoking on all domestic U.S. flights.[26] The movement is currently spreading to international flights.

REGULATION BY THE STATES AND LOCAL GOVERNMENTS

A majority of state legislatures have dealt with the regulation of smoking over the past decade. Many local governments have also become active in this area. Legislation centered around certain topics: (1) limitations on smoking in public places, (2) commerce, (3) smoking and schools, (4) advertising of tobacco products, (5) selling to minors, and (6) insurance. By far the two most important topics have been limitations on smoking in public areas and distribution of cigarette tax revenue.

Those who wish to ban smoking in the workplace cite two reasons: (1) the health hazard of environmental smoke, and (2) the increased productivity of workers in a nonsmoking environment. The tobacco industry vigorously disputes the facts behind those proposals and, in addition, has spoken out for "smokers' rights."[27] As pointed out above, such bans have been accelerating over the past five years, going beyond offices and other workplaces to restaurants and any place of public gathering.

The question of labor productivity was raised by the Surgeon General in a 1985 address when he asserted that employees who smoke cost American industry $39 billion a year. Some observers question whether adequate studies have been carried out to justify such an assertion. Micro-level studies, which serve as the basis for broader generalizations, are cited by both sides. At the very least, however, a new battlefield has been demarcated in the seemingly endless smoking controversy. Antismoking activists have succeeded in mobilizing public opinion. In a 1988 poll conducted by the National Center for Health Statistics, 55% of those polled favored a complete ban on smoking in all public places, while 43% were opposed and 2% had no opinion. Among nonsmokers, 69% favored the ban and 30% opposed it, Among smokers, 25% favored it while 72% opposed the ban. The writing on the wall is ominous for the tobacco industry and smokers. Even if they think antismokers are misinformed about the scientific facts, it may not matter. For the U. S. population, when broken down by cigarette-smoking status, breaks down as follows: 45% have never smoked, 24% are former smokers, and 31% are current smokers.[28]

THE CONTINUING DEBATE OVER THE PUBLIC INTEREST

In addition to the activities of the federal government, nonsmokers' rights organizations became increasingly active in the early 1980s. They proved to be successful in achieving restrictions on public smoking in many states and localities. As noted above, the most controversial areas have been nicotine addiction, the targeting of young people by the industry, smoking in public places (as related to the passive or "secondhand smoke" controversy) and product liability suits.

INDUSTRY RESPONSE AND STRATEGY

The industry has objected to the singling out of cigarettes for regulation while the liquor industry escapes such censorship. In denying the health allegations outlined above, the tobacco industry mounted a vigorous strategy of defense against both the onslaught of legislation and the undermining of consumer confidence. The principal measures they adopted aimed to do two things: (1) prevent erosion of the industry itself, and (2) build a vigorous political lobby.

Preventing erosion of the industry involved: making the product safer; vigorously promoting the product; diversifying their lines of business; and expanding overseas. (This last point is treated in a separate accompanying case.)

Building a powerful political lobby has called for the voluntary adoption of a marketing and advertising code to handle critics' demands, continuing to challenge the scientific validity of the antismoking research and also sponsoring independent research, enlisting the active support of economic stakeholders in the industry, and making use of corporate philanthropy.

Product Alterations

Over 25 years ago, the industry began intensive research on the nature of the product itself with respect to the three most toxic byproducts of smoking: tar, nicotine, and carbon monoxide. In February 1964, Dr. Raymond McKeon, American Medical Association president, announced that six tobacco companies had given the AMA $10 million for research, without any restrictions whatsoever. In addition, all the tobacco companies began, or intensified, their own filter research as well as other product innovations.

There was considerable debate over establishing appropriate criteria and procedures for testing. Yet this line of research led to the transformation of the industry. The industry introduced various types of filters, light cigarettes, and the 100mm cigarette—up to half an inch longer than the regular cigarette.

From 1963 to 1985, the nonfilter share of the market fell from 42% to 6%, while filters rose from 58% to 94%. Charcoal filters reached a high of 6% market share from 1968–1972 but fell to 1% by 1985. The most innovative change came with the smokeless cigarette, which was announced in 1987 and test marketed in 1988. This product promised to be safer for the smoker and also not to harm those in the smoking environment.[29]

Marketing

In 1970, total advertising was $314.7 million, with $217.4 going to television and radio. In 1971—after the ban of TV and radio advertising—the total dropped to $251.26 million. By 1975, however, total advertising was $491 million; 10 years later it had increased 5 times to $2.48 billion. In 1994 it was estimated to be around $4 billion.

Marketing did not succeed in increasing the number of cigarettes sold per capita. Per capita consumption dropped from 208 packs in 1966 to 164 packs in 1986 and is projected to decrease by about another 50 packs in the next decade; it peaked with 207 packs in 1973. Overall volume stood at 522.5 billion cigarettes in 1966, peaked in 1981 at 640 billion, and declined to 582 billion in 1986, with another loss of 130 billion estimated by 1995.

With the ever greater taxes assessed by federal, state, and local governments, the pricing of cigarettes came to be recognized as a major problem. For years, the industry had been able to effect significant price increases, especially at manufacturing and wholesale levels. To counter that problem, most major manufacturers introduced discount brands during the 1990s.

In 1994, nearly 20% of Philip Morris sales were discount. Among its premium brands, Marlboro alone accounted for 62.7% of company production and about 25% of the U. S. market. For RJR, discount brands accounted for 40.4% of production and for American Brands 57.3%. Discount brands have been very successful. Philip Morris found, however, that they were eating away at Marlboro; so in a surprise move, it cut Marlboro's prices. [30]

The result is that the cigarette industry has proven to be very profitable. In 1994, Philip Morris's total tobacco sales stood at $28.7 billion, up 10.4% over 1993. Operating income grew by 19.6% to $6.2 billion. Its worldwide cigarette volume grew by 15.4% to 757 billion units; Marlboro grew 14% to 399 billion units. Its premium cigarette business grew 6.3% to 80% of total sales. Internationally, its operating revenues increased 21.9% to $2.9 billion on sales revenues of $17.6 billion, an 11.5% increase over 1993. The cigarette companies find much to dislike about their external operating environment, but they have proven themselves to be very adept at adapting and making profits both at home and abroad.

Industry Diversification and Overseas Expansion

A growing trend in the cigarette industry is a move toward diversification. [31] American Brands produces alcohol, snack foods, fruit products, and office supplies. It owns 27.5% of the outstanding shares of Franklin Life Insurance Company. RJR Nabisco, in addition to tobacco and food, owns a shipping and oil production firm. A comparatively smaller company, Liggett Group Inc., markets wines and liquors, pet foods, cereals, and leisure-time products. Liggett's cigarette market share is the smallest, and there are rumors that Liggett may withdraw from the U.S. cigarette market. Philip Morris has diversified into industrial products, land development, soft drinks, and beer. It also owns General Foods, one of the leading companies in the packaged food industry in the United States, as well as Kraft Co., another major food company with several leading national brands.

Advertising Code

On April 27, 1964, the major tobacco companies announced the formulation of a voluntary advertising code to become effective in January 1965. [32] It outlawed any advertising that would appeal to those under 21, thus barring cigarette commercials before and after television programs designed for minors. It forbade any advertising that portrayed smoking as being essential to social prominence, distinction, success, or sexual attraction. The broadcasting industry also established codes to regulate cigarette advertising. The National Association of Broadcasters' television code board stated that cigarette advertising should not contain false claims and that neither programming nor advertising was to depict smoking as promoting health or as being necessary or desirable to young people. The industry agreed to subject itself to self-regulation, to be enforced by an independent ad-administrator capable of leveling fines of $100,000 for infractions.

Critics questioned the sincerity of the industry and asserted that the above initiative was nothing more than an elegant public relations enterprise. In a sense, these critics have prevailed; regulation of the industry has increased rather than subsided. Proponents of the code suggest that it at least kept things from getting worse.

Challenging the Scientific Evidence

The tobacco industry has never retreated from its stance of challenging the validity of the scientific evidence. This defense has always appeared to lack credibility and the scientific community and larger public have generally ceased to pay any attention to the industry's claims. Nevertheless, the industry has continued to support its argument as a defensive posture for fear that a reversal of this position may expose the tobacco firms to further product liability lawsuits. The industry has pinned its research hopes on the "safer" cigarette (without, however, admitting that ordinary "full flavor" cigarettes are unsafe). They have also bared their fists over environmental smoke and the question of how smoking relates to worker productivity. Perhaps the most critical research issue facing the industry, however, is the controversy over addiction, for it may undermine the legal basis of the industry. That charge may prove to be the most potent weapon in the antismoking arsenal.

Enlisting Economic Stakeholders

The tobacco industry has been hard at working trying to rally all those who make their living off of the industry to become active on its behalf.[33] Tobacco is a major part of the economy. In addition to its advertising budget of $2.5 billion, the tobacco industry employed 46.1 thousand workers in 1986 and met a payroll of $1.31 billion. It paid $6.34 billion to suppliers, including small farmers, local transporters, warehousemen and so forth. It invested $658 million, added value of $12.72 billion and shipped products worth $19.07 billion.

The tobacco industry's health is vital to many states and local communities, not only because of investments and jobs but also because it accounts for millions of dollars in tax revenues. Aside from the 16-cent federal tax per pack, considerable revenue in sales, property, and income taxes is generated.

Philip Morris Corporation also has stressed the "trillion dollar" economic clout of the nation's 55 million smokers. In so doing, it has tried to create an upscale image of smokers as well as to warn establishments such as restaurants not to discriminate against smokers.

The Use of Philanthropy

The tobacco industry has come to realize that a good deal of its prospects for success depend on how it is perceived—its image rather than scientific data. To this end, it has coupled philanthropy with its marketing efforts.[34] In addition to subsidizing the arts, the industry has also been attentive to the needs of minorities. All of this at least helps buy the silence of influential groups in society, if not win their active support.

NOTES

1. J. Wesley Boyd, David U. Himmelstein, and Steffie Woolhandler, "The Tobacco/Health–Insurance Connection." *The Lancet*, 346, July 8, 1995, p. 64.
2. Ed Bean, "Surgeon General's Stature Is Likely to Add Force to Report on Smoking as Addiction." *Wall St. Journal* (May 13, 1988), p. 21.
3. U.S. Department of Commerce, *Statistical Abstract of the United States, 1994*, Washington, DC: U.S. Government Printing Office. In the following section, the numbers in parentheses refer to the number of the table in this source.
4. Joe B. Tye, "A Note on Public Policy Issues in the Cigarette Industry." Stanford Graduate School of Business (photocopy), 1985, p. 11.
5. *San Francisco Chronicle*, "Smoking Costs $2 a Pack in Medical Bills, U. S. Study Says," (July 8, 1994), p. A7, based on the National Medical Expenditures Survey, 1987–1988.
6. Philip J. Hilts, "Tobacco Chiefs Say Cigarettes Aren't Addictive." *New York Times* (April 15, 1994), pp. A1, A20.
7. Tobacco Institute, *Tobacco Smoke and the Non-Smoker: Scientific Integrity at the Crossroads*, Washington, DC, (1987).
8. Jonathan P. Hicks, "Tobacco Industry Battles Council on Smoking Curbs," *New York Times*, September 26, 1994, pp.A1, B2.
9. Martin Tolchin, "Surgeon General Asserts Smoking Is an Addiction." *New York Times* (May 17, 1988), pp. A1, C4.
10. Maggie Mahar, "Tobacco's Smoking Gun: The FDA Puts Nicotine under the Microscope; Where Will It Lead?" *Barrons* (May 16, 1994), pp. 33–37; Eben Shapiro, "The Insider Who Copied Tobacco Firms' Secrets," *Wall Street Journal*, June 20, 1994, pp., B1, B2; Eben Shapiro, "Cigarette Firms Release List of Ingredients," *Wall Street Journal* (April 14, 1994), p. A3; Philip J. Hilts, "Scientists Say Cigarette Company Suppressed Findings on Nicotine," *New York Times* (April 29, 1994), pp. A1, A20; Michael Janofsky, "Majority of Americans Say Cigarettes Spur Addiction," *New York Times*, May 1, 1994, p. 22; Philip J. Hilts, "Major Flaw Cited in Cigarette Data: Testing for Tar and Nicotine Underreports Amounts," *New York Times* (May 2, 1994), pp. A1, A15; Suein

L. Hwang and Yukimo Ono, "Tobacco Dream Team: Experts Who Insist Nicotine Isn't Addictive," *Wall Street Journal* (March 23, 1995), pp. B1, B7; Philip J. Hilts and Glenn Collins, "Documents Disclose Philip Morris Studied Nicotine's Effect on Body," *New York Times* (June 8, 1995), pp. D1, D6; Jerry E. Bishop, "B.A.T. Unit Assails AMA Analysis of Nicotine, Tobacco Documents," *Wall Street Journal* (July 13, 1995), p B7 .
11. The Tobacco Institute, *Cigarette Smoking and Chronic Obstructive Lung Disease: The Major Gaps in the Knowledge*; The Tobacco Institute, *Smoking and Health, 1964–1979: The Continuing Controversy*, 1979.
12. Tye, "A Note on Policy," p. 15.
13. Philip J. Hilts, "Strict Regulations Proposed to Keep Young From Smoking, *New York Times* (September 14, 1994), p. C10; Joseph F. Sullivan, "Bans on Cigarette Machines Are Upheld," *New York Times* (April 1, 1994), p. B5; Laurie McGinley and Rick Wartzman, "Clinton Backs Action to Curb Teen Smoking," *Wall Street Journal* (July 14, 1995), pp. A3, A5; Philip J. Hilts, "Survey Finds Surge in Smoking by Young," *New York Times* (July 20, 1995), p. B9; Suein L. Hwang, Alix M. Freedman, and Michael K. Frisby, "FDA Seeks New Drive to Curb Smoking by Kids, With Industry Limits Possible," *Wall Street Journal* (July 13, 1995), p. A3.
14. Suein L. Hwang,"Philip Morris Co. Unveils Plan Aimed at Curbing Cigarette Smoking by Minors," *Wall Street Journal* (June 28, 1995), p. A3; accompanied by a full double-page ad on pp. A6–A7; the ABC "World News Tonight," and other major broadcasts carried the company's announcement that it would stamp all packages with warnings not to be sold to minors on August 8, 1995.
15. Teri Agins and Alix M. Freedman, "Tobacco Firms Misled Public, U.S. Judge Says," *Wall Street Journal* (April 28, 1988), pp. 2, 26; Laurie P. Cohen and Alix M. Freedman, "Cracks Seen in Tobacco's Liability Dam," *Wall Street Journal* (June 15, 1988), p. 27; Alfonso A. Narvaez, Scientists Fault Tobacco Company," *New York Times* (February 14, 1988), p. 43; Jesus Rangel, "Tobacco Company Testifies It Published Cancer Research," *New York Times* (May 8, 1988), p.

27; Matthew L. Wald, "Using Liability Law to Put Tobacco on Trial" *New York Times* (February 14, 1988), p. F11.

16. Junda Woo, "Cigarette Makers Take on States Seeking Payments for Smokers' Ills," *Wall Street Journal* (July 8, 1994), p. B6; Glenn Collins, "A Tobacco Case's Legal Buccaneers," *New York Times* (March 6, 1995), p. D1, D3; Milo Geyelin, "Smokers' Suit Tries New Approach: The Industry Made Them Do It," *Wall Street Journal* (March 21, 1995), pp. B1, B7; Barnaby Feder, "A United Front by Big Tobacco Starts to Crack," *New York Times,* March 14, 1996, p. A1, D6; Paul Magnusson, "The Smell of Blood," *Business Week,* April 1, 1996, pp. 30–31.

17. The Tobacco Institute, *The Tobacco Observer,* (Monthly). This publication provides an update of issues of interest to the industry.

18. *Congressional Quarterly 1967 Almanac* (1967).

19. U.S. Congress, House Committee on Interstate and Foreign Commerce, *Hearings, Cigarette Labeling and Advertising,* 88th Congress, 2nd session (1964).

20. Federal Trade Commission, *Report to Congress pursuant to the Federal Cigarette Labeling and Advertising Act, 1986,* Washington, DC, (May 1988), pp. 1–6.

21. U.S. Congress, House Committee on Interstate and Foreign Commerce, *Hearings, Cigarette Labeling and Advertising,* 91st Congress, 1st session (1969).

22. *New York Times,* "Showdown in Cigarette Advertising," (May 4, 1969), sec. 6, pp. 36ff.; Federal Trade Commission, *Report to Congress For the Year 1981,* (1984) p. 12.

23. Federal Communication Commission, "Television Station WCBS-TV," *Federal Communication Commission Reports,* 2d. series, vol 8. (May 19–August 4, 1967), pp. 381–387.

24. *Banzhaf* v. *FCC,* U.S. Court of Appeals, Washington, DC Circuit, Case 21285, (November 21, 1968).

25. *Wall Street Journal,* "House, Senate Conferees Agree to Abolish Broadcast Cigarette Ads," (August 10, 1970), p. 9; Irvin Molotsky, "Ban on Cigarette Ads to Be Urged in Congress," *New York Times* (January 19, 1987), pp. A1, A13; Slade Metcalf, "Will Cigarette Advertising Be Banned?" *Folio* (May 1987), p. 135.

26. Laurie McGinley, "Airline Anti-Smoking Drive Gains but Still Faces Strong Opposition." *Wall Street Journal* (August 7, 1987), p. 23.

27. Lawrence Ashe, Jr. and Dennis H. Vaughan, "Smoking in the Workplace: A Management Perspective," *Employee Relations Law Journal,* vol. 11, no. 3, 1988, pp. 383–406; Thomas E. Smith, Jr., "Public Smoking Laws: Who Needs Them? Who Wants Them?" *Legislative Policy,* vol. 3, no. 2 (1982), pp. 51–62; Ann LaForge, "Snuffing Out Smoking in the Office," *New York Times* (February 22, 1987), pp. K1, K2; Ronald Sullivan, "New York Adopts Wide Restrictions on Public Smoking," *New York Times* (January 7, 1987), pp. 1, 30.

28. Alix M. Freedman, "Smokers' Rights Campaign Suffers from Lack of Dedicated Recruits," *New York Times* (April 11, 1988), p. 29.

29. FTC, 1988 Report, p. 15; Alison Leigh Cowan, "Smoke Cut in Reynolds Cigarette," *New York Times* (September 15, 1987), pp. D1, D5.

30. *Tobacco Reporter,* "Year-end Brand Sales and Market Share" (April, 1995), pp. 16–17; *Tobacco Reporter,* "Profile: Philip Morris" (March, 1995), pp. 14–21.

31. Robert Miles, *Coffin Nails and Corporate Strategies.* Englewood Cliffs, NJ: Prentice Hall, 1985.

32. Miles, *Coffin Nails,* pp. 58, 72, 89, 92, 101, 238.

33. Alix M. Freedman, "Philip Morris Ads Tout Demographics of Smokers to Alter 'Low Class' Image." *Wall Street Journal* (June 29, 1988) p. 28.

34. Alix M. Freedman, "Tobacco Firms, Pariahs to Many People, Still Are Angels to the Arts," *Wall Street Journal* (June 8, 1988), pp. 1, 22; Nick Ravo, "Tobacco Companies Gifts to the Arts: A Proper Way to Subsidize Culture?" *New York Times* (March 8, 1987), p. 32.

THE TOBACCO INDUSTRY
IN THE GLOBAL ARENA

*How tobacco companies have set their sights
on global opportunities*

INTRODUCTION

Depending on whom you talk to, smoking is either an insidious habit causing untold harm to one's health and well-being or it is a harmless habit allowing frazzled people to relax. In either case, it takes on ominous proportions in the poverty-stricken countries of the "Third World." These countries, which do not have adequate means to feed their teeming millions and are often unable to provide even the most basic health care for their people, should be doing everything to discourage smoking, whether for health or economic reasons. Unfortunately, this is not so. While the consumption of cigarettes in most of the industrially advanced countries of the world, with the exception of Japan, is either stagnant or declining, the consumption of cigarettes is increasing in most of the Third World.[1]

Whether it is cynicism, gross indifference, or the need for current revenues to meet other, more pressing needs, the fact remains that in most Third World countries, governments are active participants in the production and sale of tobacco products. In a number of countries, tobacco is a state-owned monopoly, while in most others it is a significant source of tax revenues. Therefore, the governments of these countries are less inclined to be active in discouraging cigarette smoking regardless of its long-term costs in human lives, health, and misery. The executive vice–president of Philip Morris International, David E.R. Dangpoor, put it this way:[2] "We have the best partners in the world: the governments. In a lot of countries, it's incredibly important to the whole welfare state that we sell our products to collect taxes."

In many developing countries, Western tobacco companies have been playing a growing role. U.S.-based companies are some of the biggest players, in terms of "modernizing" the production, manufacturing, distribution, and consumption of cigarettes. Often helped by their home governments, these companies have dramatically expanded local markets through sophisticated mass-marketing and promotion techniques. They have, thereby, condemned the people of these countries to a double jeopardy. Not only are they being increasingly "persuaded" to become smokers, but they must also use up their precious foreign exchange resources by consuming cigarettes made by foreign multinationals.

ISSUES FOR ANALYSIS

Some would argue that it is unreasonable to blame foreign multinationals for smoking-related concerns in the Third World, when all they have done is to compete for a share of those markets on a fair and equitable basis.

Furthermore, in most cases they have provided the consumer with a better product and at a relatively lower cost. If smoking is alleged to cause any health-related problems, which tobacco companies consistently deny, it should be up to the governments of these countries to impose restrictions. In addition, it is suggested that it would be the height of cultural arrogance to assume that the governments of these countries did not know what was best for their own people, and that the Western countries were always there to tell the Third World what was good for them.

Such a cynicism has a large measure of truth to it. The problem, however, is not quite that simple and, in any case, it is loaded with serious economic, political, and moral issues.

1. What is the responsibility of the governments of various countries to protect the health and welfare of their people? Does the world have a right to raise such a question in a context that is similar to holding various governments accountable with respect to the human rights of their people? Are governments turning their backs on a hazardous situation in the interest of foreign exchange, jobs, and tax revenues? Or, in places where poverty is endemic, is smoking a rich person's issue?

2. Should the governments of industrially advanced developing countries, e.g., South Korea and Taiwan, be expected to uphold standards of public health that are higher than the governments of poorer and less developed countries? If so, why and by what criteria?

3. To what extent, and under what circumstances, should the governments of industrially advanced countries be expected to regulate the behavior of their multinationals in overseas marketing practices according to the standards operable in their home countries? There are indeed precedents where the U.S. government, and even U.N. agencies, have forbidden companies and countries from even undertaking activities that are condoned by the host countries but considered unacceptable by the home countries. The U.S. government has in the past restricted the sale abroad of textiles and synthetic materials that

were banned for use in the United States. The restriction on overseas bribes by American companies, even in the face of competitors from other countries and their being demanded by host country officials, is another example. Similarly, the use of DDT has been banned under the auspices of WHO because of its serious side-effects on the environment, despite the fact that many underdeveloped countries confronted with the very serious problem of controlling mosquito-related diseases would have preferred to use it.[3]

4. On what basis, if any, should the U.S. government require the U.S.-based tobacco companies to carry health warnings on their cigarettes sold abroad when no such warnings are required by the laws of the host countries, and when the domestic producers, often local government-owned entities, and other foreign producers are unlikely to follow these standards?

5. What is the proper role of the World Health Organization (WHO) in this issue? Should it be more concerned with primary health care needs where people have a low life expectancy due to diseases long controlled in the West?

6. Can we justify an inherently immoral behavior on the part of our companies on economic and competitive grounds or should we hold ourselves to standards that we consider right and proper at home regardless of their economic and social consequences? An example of this type of action is the case of South Africa, where U.S. laws have severely restricted investments by American companies because of South Africa's policies of apartheid, notwithstanding the fact that South Africa's major investment partners, i.e., the United Kingdom and West Germany, have refused to go along with us.

7. U.S. tobacco companies have argued, and with some justification, that their expansion in overseas markets has come at the expense of domestic monopolies and that they are simply better and more efficient marketers. However, equally meritorious arguments can be made that, through the sophisticated and high-pressure mass marketing and advertising techniques, these companies have helped in the glamorization of smoking, especially among the young, and have thereby further aggravated an already serious problem. Clearly, the truth lies somewhere between

these two extremes. In this case, perhaps, inefficient marketing is preferable because it retards the growth of markets. Is this a morally defensible and socially responsible behavior on the part of U.S. companies operating in Third World countries? If not, what new standards of behavior might be instituted and by whom?

8. Is it ethical for First World investors (such as large insurance companies and pension funds) to invest their funds in cigarette companies doing business abroad, especially in poorer Third World countries?

9. The primary, and perhaps the only, significant opposition to the American tobacco companies' marketing practices in Third World countries has been mounted by social activists and public interest groups based in the United States and Western Europe. These groups do not appear to have any constituency in Third World countries or have any mandate, direct or indirect, from Third World governments or their peoples. Why should these groups be so interested in this issue while there are equally as many, if not more, important social issues (e.g., the plight of the homeless, crime, drug addiction), that cry for help and attention within their own countries? The cynics would argue that these concerns reflect the prevailing fads and the need for new and exotic issues that social activists constantly require to legitimize their own existence and social relevance. How relevant are these arguments in assessing the need for doing something to alleviate one obviously bad condition and the right of voluntary groups in a free society to choose any cause that they wish to pursue?

THE INTERNATIONAL TOBACCO ECONOMY AND THE THIRD WORLD

The bulk of world tobacco production is consumed domestically, with only about one-quarter entering world trade (Table 1). Global production of tobacco reached 8.3 million tons in 1992, a 50% increase over the preceding decade. General forecasts are for a steady

TABLE 1. Tobacco: Production, Trade, and Cigarette Production, Selected Countries, 1979–81/1985, 1989, and 1992 (Tobacco: 1,000 metric tons Cigarettes: million units)

	Production			Tobacco Exports		Tobacco Imports	
	Tobacco 1979/81	Tobacco 1992	Cigarettes 1992*	1985	1992	1989	1992
WORLD	5,541	8,255	5,005,247		1,684		1,709
U.S.	813	781	703,134	250	263	194	325
SOUTH AMERICA	565	739	266,609		322	7.6	22
Brazil	397	576	169,000	81	243	0	10
AFRICA	288	483	181,651		279	94	127
Malawi	53	127	1,000		97	0	3
Zimbabwe	104	211	3,025	20	150	0	0.01
EUROPE	722	633	1,064,250		387	728	814
Bulgaria	1,328	66	71,000	156	29	32	11
Italy	131	151	53,799	155	120	61	29
Greece	125	187	29,250	139	115	12	20
ASIA	2,610	5,260	2,612,149		354	231	303
China	1,134	3,515	1,650,000	178	75	20	41
India	458	584	65,270	81	71	0.099	0.09
Indonesia	105	84	145,000	20	28	14	25
Japan	144	789	279,000	98	170	64	117
Turkey	204	321	67,549	103	76	4	21

SOURCES: FAO, *Production Yearbook, 1993*, pp. 176–177; *Trade Yearbook, 1993*, pp. 98–99; and *Commodity Review and Outlook, 1986–1987*, p.98; *Cigarette production: United Nations, *1992 Industrial Commodity Statistics Yearbook*, New York, 1994, pp. 232–34

increase over the short term. Most trade that takes place (between the U.S. and Turkey, for example), is with types of tobacco that manufacturers wish to have to achieve their desired blends.

Nearly 70% of tobacco production comes from developing countries, with nearly 64% from Asian economies (including Turkey), and 42.5% from China alone. On average, developing countries exported 15–20% of their production, while developed countries exported around 30%. In 1992, twelve countries accounted for 7.4 million tons or 90% of production. With 42.5% of world production, China only exports 2% of its crop while the United States, with 9.4% of world production, exports 33% of its crop. In 1992, world tobacco exports were valued at $5.8 billion.

World imports of tobacco stood at some 1,709,000 tons in 1992 (valued at $6.9 billion), showing little change throughout the 1980s. Of this, the U.S. took 19% (325,000 tons) and Europe imported 47.6% (814,000 tons). Both ended up as net importers of unmanufactured tobacco. The major motive for tobacco trade is for producers to achieve desired blends for their final products.

World cigarette production in 1992 stood at slightly over 5 trillion units. The U.S. comprised 14% of the total, Europe 21% and China 32%. As is the case in the United States, so too internationally there is a split between the economics of growers and manufacturers. Africa accounts for barely 3.6% of cigarette manufactures and 5.8% of commercial tobacco production.

Table 2 provides estimates of the percentage of smokers in various countries from 1966 to 1985. Precise data are difficult to obtain, because in many areas the proper surveys have not been carried out. While the numbers may not be precise, the general underlying trends seem to be accurate. During the 1980s, consumption rose throughout the world, ranging from an increase of 54% in developing countries to 12% in Europe. Only in North America did it decline (12%).

TABLE 2. Worldwide Smokers

Country	Male %	Female %	Country	Male %	Female %	Country	Male %	Female %
China	90	3	Tunisia	58	6	Israel	44	30
Morocco	90	—	Yugoslavia	57	10	Soviet Union	44	10
Nepal	87	72	Netherlands	57	42	Czechoslovakia	43	11
Papua New			Malaysia	56	2	Cuba	40	—
Guinea	85	80	Italy	56	32	Norway	40	34
Philippines	78	—	Brazil	54	37	Egypt	40	1
Indonesia	75	10	Nigeria	53	3	East Germany	40	29
Bangladesh	70	20	Kuwait	52	12	U. K.	38	33
Thailand	70	4	Colombia	52	18	Canada	37	29
France	70	50	Rumania	52	9	Australia	37	5
Denmark	68	49	Switzerland	50	37	Hong Kong	37	5
Republic			Turkey	50	50	Guatemala	36	10
of Korea	68	7	Ghana	50	—	United States	35	28*
Spain	66	10	Ireland	49	36	New Zealand	35	29
India	66	26	Guyana	48	4	Peru	34	7
Poland	63	29	Austria	46	13	Uganda	33	—
Zambia	63	56	Hungary	45	23	Sweden	30	30
Japan	63	12	Mexico	45	18	Ivory Coast	24	1
Uruguay	60	32	Chile	45	26			
Argentina	58	18	Venezuela	46	26			

Prevalence of smoking among adults—late 1970s, early 1980s—data not available* current data (1987).

SOURCE: World Health Organization

In general terms, world consumption is divided between the developed Western countries (30%), the former USSR and Eastern Europe (10%), and the developing countries (60%), of which the Asian economies constitute one-half (or 30% of world consumption). In Pakistan, the average per capita consumption of cigarettes has increased 8% each year since 1975. In China, the world's largest producer and consumer of tobacco, there has been an astronomical increase in cigarette consumption. Despite a total ban on advertising, there are an estimated 300 million smokers in that country, and some reports have put the annual rate of increase at close to 10%.[4] Cigarette sales have increased rapidly in Bangladesh, more than doubling over the last 10–15 years. Almost 70% of adult males and 20% of females smoke some form of tobacco product. Consumption in Kenya has been rising at 8% annually. And in Indonesia, per capita cigarette consumption quadrupled between 1973 and 1981.[5]

MARKET STRUCTURES

The world's tobacco business is dominated by five international companies: British American Tobacco/American Brands (U.K./U.S.), Philip Morris (U.S.), R.J. Reynolds (U.S.), Imperial Tobacco (U.K.), and Rupert/Rothmans (West Germany/U.K./U.S.). The biggest U.S. players are Philip Morris, with 43% of the U.S. market (Marlboro consistently holds around a 25% share) and about 7% of the world's market and Reynolds, with 27% of the U.S. market and less than 1% of the world's market. Philip Morris has since acquired Liggett's international operations and also holds a 25% stake in Rothmans International. American Brands is nearly 58% European in its tobacco operations and 40% U.S.A.; and has recently been acquired by B.A.T.[6]

Of non-U. S. companies, B.A.T. industries, which is located in the U.K., has financial interests, subsidiaries, and affiliates in 57 different countries—almost every significant market that is not a state-owned monopoly. It has taken over the U.S. companies Brown and Williamson and American Brands (which had 1993 sales of $7.4 billion). B.A.T. had 1993 sales of $30.7 billion. Of that, 28% came from the U.K and 21% from the rest of Europe. The remaining 51% derived from Latin America (21%), North America (17%), Asia (5%), and other countries (8%).

Rothmans International has subsidiaries and affiliates in 42 countries. It had 1992 sales of $4.2 billion. Exports constituted 81% of its sales. Philip Morris has a stake in its international operations.

Philip Morris and Reynolds are the two major U.S. companies with a predominantly American base while being major players overseas. Philip Morris claimed 7 to 10% of the world market, excluding state monopolies, and sales of 115 billion units (42% of total production) in 1993. Reynolds claimed sales of 192 billion units, of which 51.6 were exported. But while Philip Morris increased exports 16% in 1994, RJR declined 20%. Its fortunes have fluctuated year by year. In the late 1980s, its "Camel" brand reached 3.6% of the European market. "Salem" cigarettes grew by about 18% during the same period. However, in Asia, which accounts for half of the brand's unit volume, sales zoomed 40%. Reynolds' local brands (such as "Mustang" in Brazil) posted a 10% unit volume increase. More revealing, however, were management's comments on R.J. Reynolds Tobacco International's future. "The future markets tagged were Taiwan, South Korea, China, Turkey and Thailand and other major "government-controlled markets."[7]

Philip Morris has subsidiaries and affiliates in 35 countries and licensing agreements in another 20. Tobacco accounted for 42% of the company's 1993 sales of $71.2 billion. At least 37% of its income derived from foreign operations. Tobacco accounted for a full 61% of total company operating profits in 1993. Philip Morris also owns slightly less than

25% of Rothmans International, but is involved in proceedings with the European Community in that regard. The most interesting story in its annual report is the targeting of developing country markets as the areas of high growth potential. To gain access the industry is clearly counting on the U.S. government to bring pressure to bear on those countries to open their markets.

RJR Nabisco has subsidiaries and affiliates in 22 countries and licensing agreements in 23 and sales of $15.7 billion in 1992. In 1993, overseas tobacco operations grew by 9%, while its U.S. tobacco earnings dropped by 43%.

In general terms, these producers account for almost 40% of the world's cigarettes. If countries with state-owned monopolies are excluded, their share rises to 80%[8]

Philip Shepherd has provided an insightful historical perspective to the structural change that took place in the industry in the twentieth century.[9] During the first half of the twentieth century, "Growth in domestic consumption and output was so spectacular that none of the firms showed any real interest in developing foreign operations or exports. The *quid pro quo* U.S. cigarette firms obtained for not entering foreign markets was protection in exploiting the large, rapidly growing

U.S. market. The long period of expansive domestic growth had made overseas markets pale in comparison." Gradually, "The growth rate of the domestic market began to shrink as the market became relatively saturated at high levels of consumption, [so small firms] began to explore the possibilities of foreign operations and increased exports as a way to hedge against uncertainty."

In 1964, the cigarette package labelling controversy broke out in the United States; the leading cigarette companies moved almost immediately to expand overseas where the climate was more favorable. According to Shepherd (p. 81), as sales continued to stagnate, the scramble intensified:

> Historical spheres of influence were abandoned under the immense pressure to diversify out of the U.S. cigarette market. Large-scale demand creation efforts constituted the basic advantage of U.S. cigarette firms. Cigarette companies did not necessarily seek large markets; they went everywhere, large and small.

The market shares of the leading companies in selected markets are provided in Table 3. Clearly, Philip Morris, RJR and B.A.T are the major players in every part of the world where there is not a state monopoly. In such

TABLE 3. Market Share, Selected Countries, 1994

	Philip Morris	*RJR*	*B.A..T.*	*Rothmans*	*Other*	
United States	44.8	26.7	17.7			
Argentina	58.6					
Belgium/Luxembourg	30.8	5.7	12.5			
Brazil	9.8		79.1			
Canada			20.1		Imperial:	65.1
France	29.8	10.2		11.4	Seita:	45.0
Germany	38.7	6.3	18.5		Reemtsma:	23.8
Greece	34.8	17.7/Karelia		31.3/Imports		
Italy	10.4				Monital:	43.5
South Korea					Korea Tobacco:	91.1
Malaysia		18.9		54.9		
Spain	16.4	11.8	4.4	0.4	Tabacalera,S.A.:	62.2
Sweden	13.7	1.5			House of Blend:	83.7

SOURCE: *Tobacco Reporter,* October 1994, March 1995, April 1995, May 1995.

areas, they are not idle, however, as they tend to form licensing agreements for tobacco products as well as market machinery for manufacturing tobacco products.

In general the favored strategy has been to acquire existing companies rather than starting from scratch. In so doing the companies make themselves an attractive sector of the economy by helping local farmers produce tobacco, injecting advertising money into the economy, helping the balance of payments and providing government revenues. Tobacco firms have made judicious use of government policies as well as their industry strengths and opponents' weakness in crafting their strategies.[10]

THE ROLE OF THE U.S. GOVERNMENT IN CREATING A COMPETITIVE ADVANTAGE

U. S. government policies have been a major element in the competitive strategy of tobacco companies. These companies have honed in on both domestic policies of taxes and price supports and foreign policies of "Food for Peace" and economic aid.

Domestic Policies

The tobacco industry has reacted to two government policies that it viewed as contrary to their interest insofar as they impeded their overall ability to compete in the global marketplace, for they affected capital accumulation. The first was taxation. An important side effect of cigarette taxation has been the increasing dependency of all levels of government on cigarette tax revenues. In 1992 (#477), state governments took in $6.1 billion in taxes on tobacco products, compared to $3.7 billion in 1980. The federal excise tax is 24¢ and lawmakers are threatening to quadruple it. The IRS took in $13 billion in excise taxes on alcohol and tobacco, compared to $8 billion in 1980.[11] Not only did the industry want lower domestic taxes, it also wanted (as is noted in more detail below) pressure brought upon foreign governments to lower taxes. For example, between 1981 and 1985, Japan lowered the import tariff on foreign cigarettes from 90% to 20%, but it slapped on a retail tax equivalent to 41% of the price of cigarettes.

The second concern has been price supports. Tobacco price supports historically have been established at levels high enough to assure farmers greater profits than they could realize from any other crop. The USDA tobacco Commodity Credit Corporation program rose from a net cost of $80 million in 1985 to $235 million in 1992 (Table #1094)—there is considerable fluctuation from year to year. Price supports ranged from $1.58 to $1.70 per pound, depending upon the variety. For the tobacco companies, these and other policies maintained domestic prices at higher levels than world prices with the curious result that they subjected American farmers to intense foreign competition. The tobacco industry has not openly opposed price supports, but its members have shifted their suppliers to Third World countries when producing overseas. Philip Morris, however, maintains that American farmers are its primary suppliers. Many developing nations receive substantial assistance from the cigarette companies in establishing their own tobacco agricultural programs. If need be, the five largest companies, which control 40% of the world market, can increasingly internationalize their sources of supply of raw materials. This may be an ominous sign for the U.S. farmers.

U.S. Government Foreign Aid Policies

The initial overseas expansion of U.S. tobacco companies overseas was partially a result of the "Food For Peace" campaign and other United States governmental interventions to help feed the world after World War II. In 1933, the Agricultural Adjustment Act classified tobacco as a basic agricultural commodity. This defined tobacco as a necessity to the farm and the general U.S. economy and paved the way for support payments and for export under the Lend Lease Act during World War II. Through the Commodity Credit Corporation and the price support system, the U.S. Department of Agriculture spent more than $235 million on the U.S. tobacco industry in 1992 alone, compared to less than a third of that spent on antismoking efforts.

When the U.S. government began the "Food For Peace" campaign, its most publicized aim was to feed hungry people. Its other goals, sometimes pursued more vigorously, were to get rid of surplus commodities, to advance U.S. government policy, and to create markets for agricultural products. Since 1955, more than $700 million worth of tobacco was sent to South Vietnam, the Philippines, Cambodia, Egypt, and other Third World Countries. Senator Jesse Helms (R–N.C.) has argued that these sales were important because historically they developed new markets for tobacco. In 1980, tobacco was removed from the Food for Peace program. A program of loan guarantees to commercial lenders who financed tobacco exports was substituted in its place. A second way the U.S. government has helped the industry is through contributions to international development agencies to facilitate further market growth. The U.S. government uses taxpayers' money to finance support of Third World growers both through World Bank funds and support of the UN Development Program.[12]

THE U.S. TOBACCO INDUSTRY'S STRATEGY FOR OVERSEAS EXPANSION

In overseas expansion, the U.S. tobacco companies pursue two principal strategies: investment and trade.

Investment

Beginning in the 1950s, and accelerating after the Surgeon General's Report of 1964, the United States tobacco companies have moved abroad. Actual export of tobacco products has never been the main feature of their strategy. Instead, they opted for marketing arrangements with foreign firms, licensing agreements, and the establishment of their own manufacturing and production facilities.[13] When they moved to establish their own production facilities, the tobacco companies committed themselves to the modernization of a country's entire tobacco industry in order to ensure an adequate supply of quality tobacco. In a survey of the role of tobacco companies in developing countries the *Economist Intelligence Unit* identified six functions:[14] (1) pioneering and developing new areas for tobacco production and subsequent economic growth; (2) providing extension services and materials (usually at cost) to farmers; (3) buying the leaf produced; (4) supporting (overall) family-owned farms; (5) providing financial support and investment on a variety of levels; and (6) conducting research and training. The report is generally benign in interpreting the effects of the companies' activities on the local economy. Critics are not so sanguine.

Trade Policy

A more recent, and quite significant, source of leverage has been the U.S. trade policy to pressure Japan and some of the newly industrializing countries, e.g., South Korea and Taiwan, to remove their discriminatory import and marketing policies against the U.S. tobacco companies and to allow for greater import of U.S. tobacco products. The relevant legislation is section 301 of the revised 1974 Trade Act.[15] The procedure is straightforward and simple. If a company feels that it has been subjected to unfair or discriminatory trade, it files a complaint with the U.S. Trade Representative.[16] Specialists from the departments of Commerce, Trade, and Agriculture are called in to map out a bargaining strategy. The trump card is to threaten tariffs or boycotts of the goods of the nation in question. The industry was driven toward export markets because of stagnant demand and even declining sales in the United States. At home, it has used a combination of defensive and offensive strategies. (See the preceding case, Cigarette Smoking and Public Health.) These have included advertising and lobbying campaigns to slow down the regulatory onslaught, on the one hand, and product innovation and diversification, on the other hand. Furthermore, to offset setbacks in their domestic markets, the U.S. tobacco companies began an aggressive drive to expand their overseas sales by: (1) entering new markets, and (2) by fighting against entry barriers in countries with large markets where their sales were arbitrarily restricted by local regulations and discriminating trade practices.

U. S. exports of cigarettes rose from 6.9 billion cigarettes in 1945 to 205.6 billion in 1992, declining slightly to 195.5 billion in 1993 (Table 4). The main target of the industry is to pry open markets presently controlled by state monopolies.

TABLE 4. U.S. Cigarette Exports, 1993

Country	Billions of Cigarettes
Japan	55.6
Belgium, Luxembourg	51.2
Hong Kong	11.0
Saudi Arabia	9.6
United Arab Emirates	7.8
Singapore	6.5
Turkey	6.1
Former USSR	5.5
Lebanon	5.3
South Korea	4.5

SOURCE: CQ Researcher, "Regulating Tobacco," September 30, 1994, p. 847.

THE EUROPEAN UNION, RUSSIA, AND EASTERN EUROPE

The tobacco companies have long been present in the European Union. On the whole, it has been a far less restrictive market than that of the United States. At present the European Union is still a profit center for many companies. But, it does not possess the potential for growth that the developing countries do. One can, therefore, expect to see a major thrust of U.S. tobacco companies into developing countries.

As pointed out, the major portion (60%) of American Brands' (now part of B.A.T.) sales have been in Europe. In 1993, its domestic sales were $5.4 billion, while international sales (notably U.K.) were $7.8 billion. Surprisingly, however, domestic sales generated operating income of $776 million (56% of the total), nearly 40% more than the $578 million earned by European sales. (It is uncertain what precise role exchange rates played).

The European Union operating environment, however, seems to be changing fast, at least in the UK and Germany.[17] The tobacco companies are banking on their economic clout to forestall further regulation. Overall, in 1990, cigarette manufacturers directly employed 551,601 people in the EU and paid $48 billion in taxes.[18] Italy, Greece, and Spain are major tobacco producing countries and they are likely to forestall community legislation.

The growth markets in Europe are to be found elsewhere, in the former eastern Bloc. The fall of socialism in Russia and eastern Europe has opened up what the tobacco companies consider to be a virtual gold mine. In these countries, the cigarette companies face far less restrictive legislation and a robust consumer market. All the major players have jumped in with significant investment.[19]

In the early 1990s, B.A.T. invested $310 million in 4 joint ventures in Hungary, Ukraine, Russia, and Uzbekistan, developing the capacity to produce 28.5 billion units. In each case, B.A.T. has majority ownership.

RJR invested $300 million in 5 joint ventures; it now has gained 100% ownership in three of them—Czech republic, Hungary, Poland, Russia, Ukraine, and Kazakhstan. In 1995, its annual operating capacity approached 70 billion units.

Philip Morris has developed an eastern European capacity of nearly 86 billion units in 9 joint ventures (to be completely on line by 1998). Precise investment figures are not known, but they exceed $500 million, with $400 million in the Czech Republic alone. Various European concerns (Reetsma, House of Prince/B.A.T., Rothmans and Svenska Tobaks, AB), have come in with some $200 million more and a capacity of a minimum of 56 billion units.

The multinationals have had great success in Eastern Europe. With the break-up of state monopolies, they have grabbed market share. In Hungary, Slovakia, and the Czech Republic, they control 100% of manufacturing capacity. They control 75% in the Ukraine, 71% in the Central Asian Republics, 50% in the Baltics and Belarus, 37% in Russia, and 8% in Poland.[20]

THE ASIA MARKET

To open up the markets in Japan and other Pacific Rim countries, the U.S. Cigarette Export Association enlisted the support of the Reagan administration in 1986. The trade group hired as lobbyists Richard Allen, former national security director, Michael Deaver, former presidential deputy chief of staff, and Michele Laxalt, the daughter of former Senator Paul Laxalt (R–Nevada), a close personal friend of the president. As a result, Section 301 was vigorously applied in the cases of Japan, Taiwan, and South Korea.[21]

The combined effect of these actions has resulted in phenomenal success for the U.S. tobacco industry in Asian markets, both in terms of absolute growth and also in terms of

penetrating specific markets where, hitherto, the tobacco companies had restricted access. In the first 6 months of 1987, Japan quadrupled consumption of U.S. cigarette exports (by volume) compared with the same period in 1986, approaching nearly half the volume of the European Community, which is the largest export market for U.S.-made cigarettes.[22]

More recently, Japan has liberalized pricing and distribution restraints on cigarette imports and, as a result of negotiations with the United States, has suspended its tariffs on cigarettes. These developments have allowed imports to become more price competitive and to increase their share of the Japanese market. Japan is a very large and enticing market from which U.S. and other foreign cigarette makers have been effectively locked out by the Japanese government and its tobacco monopoly. In late 1994 the Japanese government moved to privatize Japan Tobacco.[23] Its 120 million people smoke over 300 billion cigarettes annually. The antismoking movement has to date been very weak. Over 63% of Japanese males and 12% of Japanese females are smokers. Before the Japanese market was pried opened by American negotiators under the pressures of Section 301, the U.S. tobacco companies' market share had hovered around 2% despite spending over $200 million in product promotion. After the application of Section 301, U.S. cigarette sales have had a phenomenal increase, rising from 3% in 1986 to 10% in 1987, with predictions of sales rising to between 15 and 20% by 1992.

Other areas of growth have been the newly industrialized countries (NICs) of East Asia, e.g., South Korea, Taiwan, and Singapore. U.S. government negotiators have pushed open these markets under section 301 of the revised 1974 Trade Act.

In 1987, Taiwanese smokers, according to the U.S. Department of Agriculture, bought 5.1 billion American–made cigarettes worth $119 million, compared with a mere $4.4 million in 1986. Currently, imports account for

18% of cigarette sales in Taiwan, with American cigarettes accounting for over 83% of total imports or a 152 market share.

South Korea is another case in point. In May 1988, the U.S. was able to persuade South Korea to liberalize its cigarette markets and allow U.S. companies to compete with the domestic government monopoly. The agreement lowered taxes on imported cigarettes, allowed the U.S. companies to market their products independent of the government monopoly, and allowed them to be able to advertise and engage in other promotions. As a consequence, it is estimated that the U.S. share of the South Korean market, which was $1.3 million in 1987 (representing a little over 0.5% of the market), was likely to increase to "several hundred million dollars of new sales" in the foreseeable future.[24] Indeed, Asian sales accounted for most of the growth in American cigarettes in 1987. According to the Brown & Williamson Tobacco Corporation, exports of all American–made cigarettes to Asia rose 76% in 1987, resulting in $1 billion in new sales.[25]

There are signs, however, that the industry climate is changing. Health advocates are beginning to gain ground. The municipal assembly in Seoul, South Korea, has moved to ban vending machines. Thailand, Malaysia, and Singapore have banned giving out free samples. For the time being, the antismoking lobby is weak. Over the long term, however, one can expect that it will only strengthen.

CHINA

China, the world's largest producer, also follows a primarily economic strategy.[26] Its present monopoly, China National Tobacco Corporation, was formed in January 1982. About 300 million Chinese smoke regularly (roughly 55% of adults—some say 90% of the men and only 3% of the women). Demand is growing by about 10% a year (from a young demographic base). Some 1.05 trillion cigarettes packaged in 2,500 brands are produced in about 140 plants; some 200 small, uneconomical plants have been closed. China does not allow foreign cigarettes to be marketed to the ordinary population. Of domestic brands, only 13% are filtered and tar delivery is between 20 and 35 mg. By 1985, China was a net exporter of tobacco. It hopes to expand in this direction. For this it is dealing with industry leaders. China's most advanced machines produce about 1,000 cigarettes per minute, as compared to 6,500 and even 8,000 cigarettes per minute in world-class factories. It has contracted with Philip Morris and R.J. Reynolds to build state-of-the art facilities in its special economic zones of Shenzen and Xiamen. The government set aside more than $200 million in foreign exchange for the acquisition of plant and materials. China's counties collected more than $450 in local tobacco levies (40% of the price received by the farmer) in addition to taxes from cigarettes.

Tobacco provides another example of social issues that are ignored in China, because of development priorities. In China, tobacco is a state monopoly. The tobacco economy is flourishing and is one of the areas of the world about which the American tobacco industry is rhapsodic.[27] While paying lip service to health concerns, the Chinese government follows an unabashedly economic policy, because tobacco accounts for over 8% of the government's total revenue.[28] In the past years, China has set aside over $200 million in scarce foreign exchange to update the tobacco industry with state-of-the-art equipment purchased from, among others, the Philip Morris Company and RJR Nabisco.[29] The American cigarette industry itself sees China as an area of tremendous growth potential and lauds the government's open attitude and its provision of special incentives to the industry in terms of high prices, subsidies, and low taxes. The principal problem that American companies express regarding China is that the government seems intent on preserving its market monopoly.

For most Chinese stakeholders, the tobacco issue is not on their list of problems. The World Health Organization's worldwide campaign against smoking has had practically no effect on Chinese policy. Furthermore, the United States government and other Western governments, which actively curtail smoking at home, actively promote it in developing countries.[30] What is notable in this problem, as well as in the previous one, is the regional compartmentalization of stakeholder interests on a given issue. Regarding health and tobacco, cigarette companies in China have not concerned themselves with health warning labels, restricting advertising, and other measures common in the U.S. The Law of the People's Republic of China on Tobacco Monopoly was adopted on June 29, 1991.[31] This law mandates health warnings, restricts advertising, prohibits smoking in some public places, adopts measures to dissuade youth from smoking, and spells out legal liability. So far, however, the manner in which it has been implemented has not dampened the market. Dale Sisel, president and CEO of R.J. Reynolds International, remarks:[32] "RJRTI has put in a request with the government of China to double capacity of its joint-venture Xiamen plant to 5 billion sticks annually. 'We're selling everything we can produce,' Sisel says, 'and there is pent-up demand for our brand Golden Bridge that we haven't been able to supply.'"

It appears that American companies accord top priority to a narrowly conceived economic approach. In this they are joined by the Chinese government (as well as many other developing countries, Eastern Europe, and the former Soviet Union). The impetus for reform clearly emanates from global public health activists who, up to now, have little real clout in China.

The tobacco industry remains enthused about China, representing as it does 1/3 of the world's smokers and an industry growth rate of 10.3% from 1990–1994.[33] There are concerns about smuggling and the underground markets (estimated at 5 billion yuan per year) and high import taxes (264%). There have been some token bans on advertising as the health lobby gains ground. At present, the industry's revenues are still too vital to the government for it to crack down.

SMOKING AND THE WORLD'S POOREST COUNTRIES

There is no question that the smoking habit is increasing among the people of most developing countries. It is also expanding in highly industrialized countries such as Japan, and many of the newly industrialized countries (NICs), e.g., South Korea, Taiwan, Hong Kong, and Singapore. The adverse health effects are, of course, ominous.

It is important to consider why people smoke. In general, smokers find the habit pleasant, at least in the beginning. The pleasure is more than physical. The social meaning of smoking includes such dynamics as: (1) being "American" and "with it" to foreigners, (2) peer pressure and, (3) symbolic of a way of life including "savoir faire," adulthood, and modernity. These psycho-social dynamics of smoking are not lost on the major tobacco companies. The tobacco industry claims that it advertises to increase market share and influence brand choice, not to incite smoking. This is questionable, for advertising is also prevalent in quasi-monopoly markets.[34]

It is quite legitimate to examine the activities of U.S. tobacco companies in promoting cigarette smoking in foreign countries, especially when they use marketing and promotional strategies that have been banned in the United States as endemic to public health and contrary to public policy. However, the issue of public health cannot be viewed in isolation and without any regard to the policies and activities of the governments of those nations. Clearly, the governments of the countries where cigarettes are sold through nationally controlled monopolies must be seen in the same light as private multinational companies, or even domestically controlled private companies. The motives of governments in developing countries are mixed. The characteristics of cigarette addictiveness, and insensitiveness to price elasticities, make them prime, if not major, sources of tax and tariff revenues for the governments to meet other important economic and national security needs.

According to a WHO report, a large part of the world's production of cigarettes is accounted for by state-owned monopolies in centrally planned economies or socialist countries (37%), and state-owned monopolies in nonsocialist countries, such as France, Italy, Austria, and Kenya (17%). With the opening of Russia and Eastern Europe, this has changed. Before that, however, the major international tobacco companies accounted for about 60% of the global production *outside* the centrally planned economies, and almost 80% of the output in the private sector, i.e., *exclusive* of centrally planned economies and state-owned monopolies in other parts of the world.[35]

The principal contrast in analysis is between those who take an economic view (emphasizing income, job, foreign exchange, tax revenue) and those who take a health view. The health problem has not surfaced in a major way among Third World leaders; no one really knows what the people think (if, indeed, they are concerned about the issue). One reason is that health problems related to smoking often do not arise in a stark way due to prevalent malnutrition and low life expectancies. People do not live long enough to develop the problems. This is coupled with a health establishment that is not looking for such data in the first place.

ECONOMIC CONSIDERATIONS: BENEFITS AND COSTS

According to Michael Reich, their are four types of revenues associated with tobacco

and all of them have important political aspects.[36] These revenues are: tax revenues, income to farmers, income to processors, and foreign exchange. There do not seem to be precise aggregate data available for developing countries in all of these areas. We approach them in terms of country examples and some aggregate data generated by the UN's Food and Agriculture Organization.

In many countries, tobacco companies are welcomed because the industry produces jobs, export earnings, and a taxable product. Tobacco is one of the most heavily taxed commodities in the world. To take the example of the United States, The Tobacco Institute claims that in 1983, tobacco accounted for $15.7 billion in U.S. federal, state, local, and export taxes. During the same year, the industry generated directly and indirectly 2.3 million jobs. Such patterns are repeated and often intensified throughout the world. In China, 8% of the government's revenues come from tobacco sales. In financially strapped Brazil, the tobacco industry contributes 1.6% of the country's revenue. "The most important taxpayer in Brazil is the cigarette industry, which contributes 37 to 40 percent of the total amount collected by the Industrialized Products Taxation," reports Dr. Fernando C. Barros of Brazil in the *New York State Journal of Medicine*. Brazilian tobacco consumers pay the highest rate of sales tax in the world, twice that which U.S. consumers pay. In 1983, as much as 75% of the price of a pack of cigarettes in Brazil went to government coffers. Brazil earned $300 million in tobacco exports in 1983 and almost $1 billion in tax revenue. In addition, the tobacco industry provided some 3 million jobs.[37]

The industry's support is crucial to tobacco's attractiveness to farmers who could be making less costly, though not as profitable, use of their land by cultivating food crops. Ten years ago, the Food and Agriculture Organization reported that 10.9 million acres of arable land worldwide had already been converted from food to tobacco production. Approximately 69% of this land was located in the Third World. For example, though surrounded by farmland, Santa Cruz, Brazil must now import the majority of its supply of fresh vegetables and fruits from areas that are more than 100 miles away.

In Egypt, the tobacco monopoly, Eastern Company, produces 180 million cigarettes a day, 30 million over demand. Of the surplus, 7 million are exported (primarily to the Arabic world) and the remainder is used for the production of eight foreign brands by special arrangement with Philip Morris (Marlboro and Merit), R. J. Reynolds (Camel and Winston), B.A.T. and B and W (Kent and DuMaurier), and two brands for Rothmans.[38]

Evidence suggests that outside of areas of state control of tobacco (such as in China, Egypt, and Brazil), trends of international market concentration will continue. Transnational corporations dominate virtually all the major markets outside the state monopoly and socialist nations. Such seller concentration is the result of barriers to entry that prevent potential competitors from entering an industry over relatively long periods of time. In the opinion of Philip Shepherd,[39]

> Bain (1956) identified three basic sets of barriers to entry: (1) absolute cost advantages of existing firms; (2) economies of scale (or other advantages of large-scale production); and, (3) consumer preferences for the products of existing producers. The latter is far and away the most important in the cigarette industry. Process (as opposed to product) technology is not a reason for barriers to entry in the cigarette industry, nor are the supply of raw materials. Process technology does not constitute a barrier to entry because it is not subject to large economies of scale. Small-scale operations are feasible and as efficient as much larger ones. While [a supply of] leaf tobacco is expensive, the basic tendency towards oligopsonistic pressure on growers maintains fairly low prices, so it could be afforded by new entrants in most markets.

The primary barriers to entry may be found, instead, in the factors making for enduring consumer preferences for the products of existing firms: (1) through the location of plants or sales outlets; (2) through the provision of exceptionally good service; (3) by means of physical differences in the product supplied; and, (4) through the creation of a favorable subjective image in the minds of consumers for the product (p. 72). These demand/creation efforts prevent new entry and permit the above-mentioned competitive profits (p. 73).

There are critics of the economic view: they feel that scarce capital resources should be devoted to food production; pricing policy diminishes prospects for meeting basic needs.[40]

Tobacco production also has serious environmental costs. Throughout the Third World, tobacco production leads to accelerated rates of deforestation and erosion as farmers cut trees for the fuel needed to cure tobacco. It can take an acre of woodland to cure a single acre of tobacco in developing countries. Two to three hectares of forest are required to cure one ton of tobacco.

Third World leaders do not seem to be persuaded. Typically less than 1% of arable land is devoted to tobacco, and then only for about six months. While food imports do command foreign exchange, cheap food is available (to pro-U.S. countries) via P.L. 480 subsidy imports. Comparatively, in their view, tobacco contributes more to capital development.

PUBLIC HEALTH: REGULATION OF PROMOTIONAL ACTIVITIES

Where do local public health agencies stand with reference to economic development? Clearly they seem to be in a secondary position. Table 5 provides some notion of antismoking policies in various countries. It is not, however, particularly informative. The poor state of public data is perhaps a sign of neglect. Five of the eight countries listed as totally banning advertising are socialist and

TABLE 5. Cigarette Use and Antismoking Policies in Selected Countries, 1974–84

Country	Annual change in use of cigarettes (%)	Package warning label	Advertising ban		Bans in public places	
			Total	Partial	Strong	Weak
Argentina	+0.1					
Australia	+0.9	x		x		
Brazil	+1.6	x				
Bulgaria	−0.2	x	x		x	
China	+6.2	x				x
Egypt	+8.7	x		x		x
Finland	+0.8	x	x		x	x
France	+0.6	x		x	x	
Hungary	+0.4	x	x		x	
Italy	+1.6		x		x	
Japan	+0.6	x				x
Kenya	+3.9					x
Mexico	+1.0	x		x		
Netherlands	−3.3	x		x		
Norway	−1.6	x	x			
Poland	+0.3	x		x[a]		
Soviet Union	+0.8	x	x		x	
Spain	+1.6			x		
Sweden	−0.3	x		x		
United Kingdom	−3.1	x		x		
United States	0	x		x		x

[a]Includes restrictions on smoking in the workplace.

SOURCE: William U. Chandler, "Tobacco—Strong Words Are Not Enough," in *World Health Forum*, Vol. 7, No. 3(1986), pp. 217–224.

do not feature advertising for much of anything anyway. Furthermore, six of the eight show evidence of increased smoking rates! Ten of sixteen countries with package warning labels show increased rates of cigarette use. It is exceedingly difficult to sort out demographic factors from implementation/enforcement factors. The truth seems to be that, aside from North America and Western Europe, smoking is not an issue that is given high priority. Susan Moreby has gathered some interesting examples.[41]

Brazil, where cigarette consumption grows at a rate of 6% each year, provides an excellent example of the laissez-faire environment available to the tobacco industry. There are no restrictions on tobacco promotion. Billboards litter the countryside. More importantly, the advertising is aggressive and aimed at the young, providing no health

warnings but promising success, happiness, and social status.[42] Throughout the Third World, labels on cigarette packages warning of health hazards are the exception rather than the rule. And the cigarettes sold may "contain twice as much tar as cigarettes sold in Western countries," notes the International Organization of Consumers' Unions. In countries where restrictions on advertising have been initiated, tobacco companies have found ways around them. When the Sudan banned all advertising, Philip Morris altered its billboards: cigarette packs were replaced with cigarette lighters displaying the Marlboro logo.

But despite the sobering prospects, there are encouraging signs. Throughout the world, antismoking groups are springing up, pressuring their respective governments for warning labels and advertising curbs. In the

Middle East, health ministers from several Gulf states joined together to call for mandatory health warnings on all cigarette packages, as well as tar and nicotine contents.

The investments are large and the stakes high. More than 2 million people worldwide now die each year because of tobacco-related ailments. Indeed, if the Third World's consumption of tobacco continues to increase, malnutrition and infectious diseases may soon take a back seat to smoking-related diseases.

In the view of public health experts, the tobacco industry "is expanding unchecked" throughout the Third World, and the results are cause for alarm.

LOCAL GOVERNMENTS, THE TOBACCO INDUSTRY, AND HEALTH PROFESSIONALS

Several major problems encountered in trying to reduce the sale of cigarettes in Third World countries are related to living conditions. Specifically:

1. Life expectancies are not long, so a problem that will affect individuals in their later years will not have a great effect on the choices they make regarding smoking, since they will not live long enough to have the problem.
2. Children become malnourished. The money used for cigarette consumption comes out of the household budget. With barely enough money to get by as it is, the loss of money to cigarette purchases results in fewer funds available for food.
3. A major source of energy is wood. But trees are removed to make space available to grow tobacco, leaving an energy deficit.
4. In addition, using land for tobacco growing means the land cannot be used for farming, which dims the prospects for self-sufficiency.

Some lay the distortion of society's priorities at the door of tobacco multinationals: "The six largest U.S. cigarette manufacturers spend about $2.6 billion a year on advertis-

ing. But, charge antismoking advocates, the money goes much farther than just encouraging smoking and countering the small plain box containing the Surgeon General's warning. They say it also ensures that the carrier of the advertising does not write about smoking and health before it thinks about the ad money that could conceivably be lost."[43] Compound this with the fact that "The big six tobacco companies, all conglomerates, wield much more power when they throw in the advertising budgets of their nontobacco lines." Tobacco companies also alter their advertising images in Third World countries. Realizing the high illiteracy rates, the picture is the primary means of selling; copy is relatively unimportant. Thus, efforts are concentrated on portraying the proper visual image. Also, in different countries, they will adjust the tar levels of their cigarettes; although they won't admit in which countries this practice takes place.

When entering a foreign market, cigarette companies get around local advertising regulations. For example, when Marlboro could not advertise its cigarettes, it began advertising Marlboro lighters. Third world countries don't include adequate warning labels on their cigarette packages. Countries begin to rely on the revenues from the taxes and silent censure on the part of governments fails to work.

An additional social problem of selling to Third World countries is related to the currency. "[Third World countries] are not able to pay in hard currency. This calls for new financing methods and a whole lot of innovation. It's a question of whether the industry will be able to adapt."[44]

Add to this the fact that the First World governments are largely indifferent to the health issue in the Third World, concentrating instead on the balance of payments. In the United Kingdom, Rothman's International was given the 1983 Queen's Award for Export Achievements.[45]

WHAT SHOULD AND CAN BE DONE?

The World Health Organization has claimed that, in the absence of strong and resolute government action, we face the serious probability that the smoking epidemic will ravish the developing world within a decade. A major avoidable public health problem will then be inflicted on countries least able to withstand it for the twin reasons of commercial enterprise and government inactivity.

As Albert Huebner has observed:[46]

If Third World nations follow the example of industrialized countries, antismoking efforts won't begin until lung cancer is epidemic. The scenario had brought untold misery to people in the developed world. For the Third World, it will entail, in addition, an overwhelming economic burden.

NOTES

1. R. Masironi and K. Rothwell, "Smoking in Developing Countries." Geneva: World Health Organization, 1985 (Photocopy: WHO/SMO/85.1); Uma Ram Nath, *Smoking: Third World Alert*. Delhi, India: Oxford University Press, 1986; See also Table 2 in the section that follows.

2. Roger Rosenblatt, "How Do Tobacco Executives Live with Themselves?" *New York Times Magazine* (March 20, 1994), pp. 34–42, 55, 73–75.

3. Thomas R. Dunlap, *DDT: Scientists, Citizens and Public Policy*, Princeton, NJ: Princeton University Press, 1981; Brian Toyne, *The Global Textile Industry*. London: George Allen and Unwin, 1984; United States Congress, *The Foreign Corrupt Practices Act of 1977*, Washington, DC; U.S. Government Printing Office.

4. Masironi and Rothwell, "Smoking," pp. 5–10; M. Khor Kok Peng, "The Urgent Need to Control the Smoking Epidemic In The Third World," , pp. 561–566. in W. F. Forbes, R. C. Frecker, D. Nostbakken, eds., *Proceedings of the Fifth World Conference on Smoking and Health, Winnipeg, Canada*. Ottawa: Canadian Council on Smoking and Health (1983), pp. 281–85.

5. *Tobacco Reporter*, International Cigarette Manufacturers," 27th edition, (April, 1995), pull-out chart; Steve Mufson, "Cigarette Companies Develop Third World As a Growth Market," *Wall Street Journal* (July 5, 1985), p. 1.; David Tucker, *Tobacco: An International Perspective*, London: Euromonitor Publications, Ltd., 1982, pp. 68ff.; Robert Miles, *Coffin Nails and Corporate Strategies*, Englewood Cliffs, NJ: Prentice Hall, 1982.

6. Information on companies is derived from Dun and Bradstreet, *Dun's Business Rankings, 1994, D&B Europa*, as well as Gary Hoover, Alta Campbell, and Patrick J. Spain, eds., *Hoover's Handbook of American Business, 1995*, Austin, TX: Reference Press Inc., 1995; Patrick J. Spain and James R. Talbot, eds., *Hoovers Handbook of World Business, 1995–1996*, Austin TX: Reference Press Inc., 1995, and company reports.

7. *Tobacco Reporter*, "Stronger," March 1995, pp. 12–13.

8. *The Economist* (March 26, 1988), p. 70; Gregory Connolly, "Smoking or Health: The International Marketing of Tobacco," *Tobacco and Health: International Issues in Tobacco Trade and Policy*, Proceedings of a symposium sponsored by The Institute for the Study of Smoking Behavior and Policy, John F. Kennedy School of Government and the Takemi Program in International Health, Harvard School of Public Health (December 8, 1987), pp. 3–4, citing P. Taylor, *The Smoke Ring*, New York: Mentor Press, 1988.

9. Philip L. Shepherd, "Transnational Corporations and the International Cigarette Industry," in Richard S. Newfarmer, ed., *Profits, Progress and Poverty—Case Studies of International Industries in Latin America*, Notre

Dame, IN: University of Notre Dame Press (1985), pp. 63–112, Quoted material appears on pp. 78 and 80.

10. Miles, *Coffin Nails*, ch. 1; U.S. Department of Commerce, *U.S. Industrial Outlook 1988*, "Tobacco Products," (1987), pp. 43–1, 43–3, 43–5; U.S. Department of Commerce, *Statistical Abstract of the United States, 1994*, Washington, DC: U.S. Government Printing Office, 1995; numbers in parentheses in the text refer to table numbers from this publication.

11. U.S. Government, *Statistical Almanac of the United States*, 1994; tables 477, 520.

12. Albert Huebner, "Tobacco's Lucrative Third World Invasion," *Business and Society Review*, 35 (Fall 1980), pp. 51ff; Joe B. Tye, *A Note on Public Policy Issues in the Cigarette Industry*, Palo Alto, CA: Stanford, Graduate School of Businesss (April 15, 1985), (xerox), p. 21–22.

13. Michael Crosby, "Selling Cigarettes to the Third World." *Christianity and Crisis* (May 13, 1983), p. 213.

14. The Economist Intelligence Report, *Tobacco Study II* (April 13, 1984), pp. 6–8, 10, 12–14.

15. Peter Schmiesser, "Pushing Cigarettes Overseas." *New York Times Magazine* (July 10, 1988), p. 18.

16. *The Economist*, "Cigarettes—Trade Liberalization's Dark Shadow," (March 28, 1988), pp. 70–71; Connolly, "Smoking or Health" p. 9ff; and United States District Court for the District of Columbia, "*United States* v. *Michael K. Deaver*, CR– 87–0096. November 3, 1987. Washington, DC: pp. 766–814.

17. Martin DuBois, "Europe's Antismoking Lobby Heats Up." *Wall Street Journal*, (June 26, 1995), p. B8.

18. *Tobacco Reporter*, "European Union: Tobacco a Key Economic Contributor," p. 6.

19. *Tobacco Reporter*, "Multinational Round-up," (August 1994), pp. 36–38.

20. *Tobacco Reporter*, "Rebuilding" (January 1995), pp. 35–40.

21. *The Economist*, "Cigarettes—Trade Liberalization's Dark Shadow," (March 28, 1988), pp. 70–71; Connolly, "Smoking or Health" p. 9ff; and United States District Court for the District of Columbia, *United States* v. *Michael K. Deaver*, CR–87–0096. November 3, 1987. Washington, DC: pp. 766–814.

22. Susan Chira, "U.S. Cigarette Makers Gain in Asia." *New York Times* (May 10, 1988), p. D1.

23. *The Economist*, "Japan Tobacco's Wealth Wizard," September 17, 1994, p. 90; James Sterngold, "When Smoking is a Patriotic Duty," *New York Times* (October 17, 1993,) sec. 3, p. 1.

24. Sally D. Goll, "Tobacco Industry Faces Laws in Asia to Ban Selling, Advertising to Minors," *Wall Street Journal* (August 7, 1995), p. A9F; Pete Engardio, "Asia: The New Front in the War on Smoking," *Business Week* (January 25, 1991), p. 66.

25. M. Ahmad, "Leaf Situation in China," *Pak Tobacco* (January 1984), pp. 23–25; *Tobacco International*, "CNTC, World's Largest Cigarette Maker, Seeks Advice," (September 20, 1985), pp. 7–10; M. Ahmad, "Special Report: The New China," *Tobacco Reporter* (March 1985), pp. 46–48, 50, 52; Tabak Journal International, "China Puts Tobacco Regulations into Effect," (April 1984), pp. 134, 136–137; A. Shelton, "The Quest for Better Quality, *Tobacco Reporter* (March 1986), pp. 26–29.

26. Colleen Zimmerman, "Spotlight on China." *Tobacco Reporter* (February 1993), pp. 24–38.

27. International Tobacco Growers' Association, *Tobacco in the Developing World*. West Sussex, England, 1990.

28. K.K. Chadha and Joe Sokohl, "Spotlight on China; Cautious Optimism in Tobacco Trade." *Tobacco Reporter* (March 1990), pp. 22–23.

29. Editorial Research Report, *Tobacco Industry: On the Defensive, But Still Strong*. Vol. 1, 35 (September 21, 1990), Washington, DC: Congressional Quarterly.

30. Zheng Suping, "Spotlight on China: Monopoly Becomes Law." *Tobacco Reporter* (January 1992), pp. 18–20.

31. David E. Doolittle, "Update: R.J. Reynolds Tobacco International—Major Avenues of Growth." *Tobacco Reporter* (March 1992), pp. 20–24; quote from p. 24.

32. *Tobacco Reporter*, "Spotlight on China," (July 1995), pp. 28–33.

33. Gregory Connolly, "Smoking or Health: The International Marketing of Tobacco," *Tobacco and Health: International Issues in Tobacco Trade and Policy*, proceedings of a symposium sponsored by the Institute for the Study of Smoking Behavior and Policy, John F.

Kennedy School of Government and the Takemi Program in International Health, Harvard School of Public Health (December 8, 1987), pp. 3–4.

34. Susan A. Motely, "Burning the South: U.S. Tobacco Companies in the Third World." *Multinational Monitor* (July/August 1987).

35. Michael Reich, "Tobacco Production and Export Policies in the Third World," in *Ibid.*, pp. 17–28.

36. D. Femi-Pearse, "Aspects of Smoking in Developing Countries in Africa, *New York State Journal of Medicine* (December 1983), pp. 1312–1313; Ruth Roemer, *Recent Developments in Legislation to Combat the World Smoking Epidemic*, Geneva, WHO, 1986.

37. M.R. Naguib, "Increased Cigarette Production and Exports in Egypt." *Tabak Journal International* (April 1986), p. 96.

38. Shepherd, "Transnational Corporation," pp. 65, 72ff.

39. Susan Motely, "Burning the South," p. 9ff.

40. Morton Mintz, "The Smoke Screen: Tobacco and the Press—An Unhealthy Alliance." *Multinational Monitor* (July/August, 1987), pp. 15, 18.

41. Colleen Lowe Morna, "Zimbabwe's Tobacco Addiction." *Multinational Monitor* (July/August 1987), pp. 12–14.

42. *Ibid.*

43. *Lancet*, "Third World Smoking—The New Slave Trade (January 7, 1984), pp. 22–23.

44. *Ibid.*, p. 24.

45. Albert Huebner, "Tobacco's Lucrative Third World Invasion." *Business and Society Review* (Fall 1980), p. 51.

UNION CARBIDE CORPORATION

*Industrial plant accident in Bhopal, India:
responsibility of the multinational corporation**

In the middle of the night of December 3, 1984, J. Mukund, the factory manager of the Union Carbide (India) Ltd. (UCIL), pesticide plant in Bhopal, was awakened up by a telephone call from the night shift supervisor informing him that an accident had occurred at the plant causing a large amount of methyl isocyanate (MIC) gas to leak out from the underground storage tanks. The lethal gas was causing havoc in the plant neighborhoods, injuring and killing an untold number of people as they tried to escape the area. Within a short time, Mr. Mukund had driven to the plant and initiated damage control and emergency procedures. He telephoned the company headquarters in Bombay, who in turn called up Divisional offices in Hong Kong, and the parent company headquarters in Danbury, Connecticut. Within a few hours, news of the disaster had reached all key personnel in the company. The worst corporate crisis in history had just hit Union Carbide Corporation.

The morning of December 4, found death strewn over the stunned Bhopal city. Bodies and animal carcasses lay on sidewalks, streets and railway platforms, and in slum huts, bus stands, and waiting halls. Thousands of injured victims streamed into the city's hospitals. Doctors and other medical personnel struggled to cope with the chaotic rush, knowing neither the cause of the disaster nor how to treat the victims. Groping for anything that might help, they treated immediate symptoms by washing their patients' eyes with water and then soothing their burning with eye drops; and giving the victims aspirins, inhalers, muscle relaxants, and stomach remedies to provide temporary relief. Before the week was over, nearly 3,000 people had died. More than 300,000 others had been affected by exposure to the deadly poison. About 2,000 animals had died, and 7,000 more were severely injured. The worst industrial accident in history was over. But the industrial crisis that made the city of Bhopal international news had just begun.

The impact of the disaster on Union Carbide Corporation was devastating. At the time of the accident, in 1984, Union Carbide had sales revenues of $9.5 billion, net income of $323 million, and total assets of $10.5 billion. Three years later, the sales revenues had fallen to $6 billion, assets had shrunk to about $6.5 billion, and shareholders' equity had fallen from $4.9 billion to under $1 billion. This drastic reduction in size occurred without a single penny being paid in compensation to victims of the disaster.

*This case was prepared by Dr. Paul Shrivastava, Howard I. Scott, Professor of Management, Bucknell University, Lewisburg, PA.

During these turbulent three years, the company's financial survival was threatened more than once. First, in 1985, a few months after the disaster, the Carbide stock price plunged from about $48 a share to about $33 a share. At the depressed price, speculators and arbitrageurs acquired large amounts of the company stock. On August 14, 1985, the GAF Corporation announced that it had acquired a significant stake in Carbide, and would try to take it over. Samuel Heyman, chairman of GAF, said he would sell off Carbide units, which contributed about 40% of its revenues. With the money from those sales (estimated by GAF to be $4.5 billion) he would settle the Bhopal victims' claims. This immediately put the company "in play" in the takeover game. This was followed by frantic bidding and counterbidding wars between GAF and Union Carbide management.

Six months later, GAF gave up its takeover attempt, but only after Carbide management had been maneuvered into a radical financial restructuring. The restructuring involved selling off of 25% of the most profitable assets of the company, closing off several marginally profitable plants, and laying off about 4,000 people.

After more than four years of on-again, off-again legal proceedings, as well as acrimonious and contentious charges and countercharges, a settlement was reached in early February 1989 between the government of India and Union Carbide. The agreement called for the Union Carbide to pay $470 million. The agreement resolves all outstanding issues and claims by any and all parties against Union Carbide. The Supreme Court of India, in settling the claim, did not address the issue of who was to blame for the accident. Also as part of the settlement, the Indian Supreme Court ordered dismissal of all criminal charges and other civil suits in India against Union Carbide.[1]

More than a decade has passed since the accident. In the interim, a great deal has happened and yet a great deal remains unchanged. Union Carbide Corporation of U.S.A. went through the shock of a long, drawn-out hostile takeover battle, which left the company severely battered, highly leveraged, and financially constrained. The accident also attracted worldwide attention to the broad scope of hazards associated with industrial accidents in general, and those in the Third World in particular. Although this accident was the most severe in history, it was by no means unique. Large-scale industrial accidents have created crises for corporations and the public regularly throughout this century. Since the beginning of this century, there have been 28 major industrial accidents in fixed facilities in the free world. These accidents do not include transportation accidents such as airliner crashes or train derailments. These accidents have occurred in both industrialized countries and developing countries. In the U.S., the explosion of a ship with a cargo of ammonium nitrate caused the deaths of over 530 people in Texas City in 1947. In 1948, an explosion of confined dimethyl ether in Ludwigshafen, Germany, killed nearly 250 people. In 1970, an accident at an underground railway construction site in Osaka, Japan, killed 92 people. In 1984, accidents in Mexico City, and Cubatao, Brazil, killed about 500 people each.

Major industrial accidents can occur anywhere—in industrialized as well as developing countries, in small as well as large organizations, in the public as well as the private sectors. Accidents such as Bhopal, Chernobyl, and the NASA Challenger explosion have fundamentally changed the public's awareness of technological hazards facing society. These incidents have highlighted the very limited scope of our knowledge about these hazards and the extreme inadequacy of our ability and resources to cope with such major accidents.

Another sad realization to emerge out of the Bhopal case is the fact that as of this writing (1996) the settlement of the case remains mired in countless legal and bureaucratic tangles. A significant number of victims have died, and those living have yet to receive any meaningful compensation from the Government of India. A great deal of compensation funds have simply disappeared through incompetence and corruption in government bureaucracies and often downright fraud. The survivors of those who died remain desperately poor, with no alternative means of supporting themselves. Those who were partially or totally disabled suffer from a lack of adequate medical care, rehabilitation, loss of employment, and financial hardships. One thing is certain: many more will die before seeing justice done, if ever. Those who live long enough to see the courts resolve the case may not have much time left to make use of the compensation they eventually receive in any settlement.

ISSUES FOR ANALYSIS

The Bhopal case raises a number of important issues around public disclosure of potential hazards, apropriate technology transfers to developing countries, corporate responsibility and liability for overseas plant safety, and the role of host-country governments in direct foreign investments. In addition, it highlights the very important need for developing expeditious and equitable systems for resolving postaccident conflicts and payment of compensation to victims. For example:

1. What are the responsibilities of multinational corporations for their overseas operations, especially in developing countries, to ensure that these plants are operated safely with regard to workers, communities, and the environment? Should a company adopt a single uniform safety standard for all of its plants around the world?
2. To what extent did Union Carbide Corporation (U.S.) and its Indian subsidiary exercise due care in this regard? What more could each of them have done to ensure plant safety and how can MNCs control the safety performance of their overseas operations?
3. How should environmental and safety concerns be incorporated in strategies for technology transfer to developing countries? What corporate and business policies should firms adopt in order to minimize the occurrence of major accidents? How can they trade off between the expense of being safe versus cutting costs to be competitive?
4. What should be the responsibility of government in ensuring plant safety? To what extent should government agencies be held responsible for losses in terms of human lives and property. How would one judge the conduct of the Government of India and its various agencies, state and local authorities in the Bhopal case?
5. What criteria should be used in determining compensation to victims? What kinds of compensation systems should be designed to ensure speedy and fair compensation? How much compensation can Union Carbide pay without going bankrupt?
6. Which country's courts should be responsible for handling cases involving multicountry accidents and liability disputes and why? What role can the International Court of Justice play in this regard?
7. To what extent and under what circumstances are courts an appropriate forum for resolving international liability cases? What alternative forms of dispute resolution mechanisms can be recommended?
8. What ethical issues does the Bhopal case raise? What ethical standards should be applied in making corporate policies regarding the case? Furthermore, in light of Bhopal-type disasters, how should corporate responsibility toward environmental protection and worker and community safety change? What additional actions should corporations undertake voluntarily that were not warranted before Bhopal?

UNION CARBIDE CORPORATION (UCC)

The organizational context of this accident may be understood by examining the position of the Bhopal plant in the overall business of Union Carbide Corporation. In 1984, Union Carbide Corporation (UCC) was the seventh largest chemical company in the

United States, with total assets of $10.51 billion and sales approaching $10 billion. It owned or operated businesses in 40 countries and employed over 33,000 people worldwide. Its main product lines included dry cell batteries, chemicals, industrial gases, specialty alloys, and agricultural products.

The early 1970s were a turbulent period for the chemical industry and the company. The highly cyclical chemical industry became even more volatile because of oil price fluctuations during the early 1970s. The oil embargo created an artificial shortage of petrochemicals and related products and sent their prices skyrocketing. In 1973 and 1974, UCC's sales grew at unprecedented rates of 21% and 35%, respectively. This created an upbeat mood at the company and an aggressive program of growth and expansion was started. Capital expenditure increased annually until 1975. In 1975, the company got the first of a series of jolts. While its sales increased 6% over 1974, the world recession triggered by the 1973 oil embargo reduced demand, resulting in a decline in sales and total employment. Inflation caused reductions in net earnings and led to cost-cutting measures and strategic reorientation. The company outlined three strategies. The first involved strengthening its position in businesses with a good future and in areas where it had a strong market position. Second, it would withdraw from businesses that did not meet Carbide's criteria for financial performance. Third, it would shift the business mix to include a greater proportion of "performance products" (e.g., Sevin and Temik pesticides). Management also decided to diversify into related and unrelated businesses and identified the areas of health, food products, environment, and energy as its future focus. The company estimated that about 60% of its business in 1975 was in growth categories and it planned to allocate about 80% of its capital expenditure during 1975-79 to these growth businesses. Specifically, pesticides and other agricultural products were considered as having high growth potential, whereas old and mature chemical businesses were considered to be less desirable.

In 1976, Congress passed the Toxic Substances Control Act, placing more stringent requirements on the corporation's chemical businesses. Union Carbide set up a new corporate-level Health, Safety and Environmental Affairs Department to ensure compliance with the new act and centralize internal administration.

The year 1977 saw a change in the top management of Union Carbide. W.S. Sneath took over as chairman of the company and Warren Anderson became the new president. Together, they restructured Carbide's business portfolio and started divesting some of its businesses. These decisions resulted in divestiture of over a billion dollars worth of assets over the next four years, including Carbide's petrochemical business in Europe and the entire medical business, in which the company had developed a number of new products.

In 1979, Union Carbide once again benefited from the steep oil-price hike by OPEC. Sales jumped 17% and earnings jumped 41%, and the total number of employees reached an all-time high of 115,763. In the 1980s, Union Carbide continued to refocus its portfolio of businesses away from chemicals, and concentrated on industrial gases and batteries. It had divested almost three dozen business units and product ventures in the late 1970s, to dilute its chemical operations in the U. S. This was done in acknowledgement of increasing competition in the chemicals industry and the lackluster financial performance of the company during the past decade.

In 1982, Warren Anderson took over as chairman, while Alec Flamm became president. The early 1980s were a period of declining performance. Sales dropped, earnings declined, capital expenditures and working capital were reduced, maintenance expenditures were cut back, assets were stripped, and employment level was curtailed. These trends are apparent in the financial figures presented in Table 1.

TABLE 1. Selected Financial Data for Union Carbide Corporation

Dollar Amounts in Millions (Except per Share Figures)	1984ᵃ	1983ᵃ	1982ᵃ	1981	1980
From the Income Statement					
Net sales	$9,508	$9,001	$9,061	$10,168	$9,994
Cost of sales	6,702	6,581	6,687	7,431	7,186
Research and development expense	265	245	240	207	166
Selling, administrative, and other expenses	1,221	1,243	1,249	1,221	1,152
Depreciation	507	477	426	386	326
Interest on long-term and short-term debt	300	252	236	171	153
Other income (expense)—net	77	120	162	164	41
Nonrecurring charge—closing of facilities	—	241	—	—	—
Income before provision for income taxes	590	82	385	916	1,052
Provision for income taxes	277	(10)	58	258	360
Income before extraordinary charge and cumulative					
effect of change in accounting principle	341	79	310	649	673
Extraordinary charge	(18)	—	—	—	—
Cumulative effect of change in accounting					
principle for ITC	—	—	—	—	217
Net income	323	79	310	649	890
Income per share before extraordinary charge					
and cumulative effect of change in accounting					
principleᵇ	4.84	1.13	4.47	9.56	10.08
Extraordinary charge per share	(0.25)	—	—	—	—
Cumulative effect per share of change in					
accounting principle for ITC	—	—	—	—	3.28
Net income per shareᶜ	4.59	1.13	4.47	9.56	13.36
From the balance sheet (at year-end)					
Working capital	$ 1,548	$ 1,483	$ 1,747	$ 2,147	$ 2,124
Total assets	10,518	10,295	10,616	10,423	9,659
Long-term debt	2,362	2,387	2,428	2,101	1,859
Total capitalization	7,962	7,999	8,305	8,018	7,282
UCC stockholders' equity	4,924	4,929	5,159	5,263	4,776
UCC stockholders' equity per share	69.89	69.95	73.54	76.74	70.90
Other data					
Funds from operations—sources	$ 964	$ 708	$ 715	$ 1,172	$ 1,211
Dividends	240	240	235	224	206
Dividends per share	3.40	3.40	3.40	3.30	3.10
Shares outstanding (thousands at year-end)	70,450	70,465	70,153	68,582	67,367
Market price per share—high	$65\frac{1}{4}$	$73\frac{7}{8}$	61	$62\frac{1}{8}$	$52\frac{1}{2}$
Market price per share—low	$32\frac{3}{4}$	51	$40\frac{1}{8}$	$45\frac{1}{4}$	$35\frac{1}{4}$
Capital expenditures	670	761	1,179	1,186	1,129
Number of employees (at year-end)	98,366	99,506	103,229	110,255	116,105

Table 1. *Continued*

Dollar Amounts in Millions (Except per Share Figures)	1984ᵃ	1983ᵃ	1982ᵃ	1981	1980
Selected financial ratios					
Total debt/total capitalization (at year-end)	33.7%	34.0%	33.9%	30.3%	29.9%
Net income/average UCC stockholders' equity	6.6%	1.6%	6.0%	12.9%	15.3%ᵇ
Net income + minority share of income/ average total capitalization	4.5%	1.4%	4.3%	9.1%	10.6%ᵇ
Dividends/net income	74.3%	303.8%	75.8%	34.5%	30.6%ᵇ
Dividends/funds from operations—sources	24.9%	33.9%	32.9%	19.1%	17.0%

ᵃAmounts for 1982 and subsequent years reflect the adoption of Statement of Financial Accounting Standards No. 52.
ᵇNet income in these ratios excludes the nonrecurring credit for the cumulative effect of the change in accounting principle for the investment tax credit (ITC).
ᶜNet income per share is based on weighted average number of shares outstanding during the year. *Funds from operations—source* includes income before extraordinary charge and noncash charges (credits) to income before extraordinary charge. *Total debt* consists of short-term debt, long-term debt, and current installments of long-term debt. *Total capitalization* consists of *total debt* plus *minority stockholders' equity in consolidated subsidiaries*, and UCC *stockholders' equity.*

UNION CARBIDE (INDIA) LTD.

Union Carbide India Limited (UCIL) was incorporated in Calcutta under the name of Eveready Company (India) Ltd. on June 20, 1934. Its name was changed to National Carbon Company (Ltd.) and then to Union Carbide (India) Ltd. in December 1959. The company's most important product was dry cells (batteries). In 1984, more than 50% of the company's revenues came from this product. But over the years, as its product lines in batteries, chemicals, and plastics matured, the company sought out new markets to maintain its growth.

The industries UCIL entered were typically technology-and-capital-intensive. They catered to mass markets and required large-scale production and technically skilled labor. Most often, UCIL would enter industries still in their early stages of development and gain a dominant market position by using the superior technology of its parent company. One such industry was pesticides. In the 1960s, large-scale use of agricultural pesticides was promoted by the Indian government as part of its "green revolution" campaign to modernize agriculture. Pesticides quickly became popular among farmers, and their use tripled between 1956 and 1970.

The Agricultural Products Division was established in 1969. It developed Carbaryl (SEVIN) using Methyl Isocyanate (MIC) as the active agent for a range of pesticides. The Bhopal plant was the key manufacturing facility of the Agricultural Products Division of the company. It began operating in 1969. It was located on the north side of Bhopal, about two miles from the railway station and bus stand—the hub of local commercial and transportation activities. Since the plant was initially used only for "formulation" (the mixing of different stable substances to create pesticides), it did not pose a grave danger to surrounding areas. In 1974 however, it was granted an industrial license to manufacture pesticides and began production of both SEVIN and MIC in 1977 at the Bhopal plant. While these developments occurred inside the company, the pesticide industry underwent major changes. Many small manufacturers entered the industry as formulators. They were less capital intensive and served small market niches.

UCIL was a well-respected company in India. It was considered a good business customer and a responsible and desirable employer. The company worked closely with local, state, and central government agencies to promote the government's family planning and other social programs. It thus developed strong contacts in the government. This excellent relationship with the government facilitated company-government interactions at many levels of operations. The company was easily able to get government permission for dealing with a variety of operating issues. For example, the parent company was allowed to retain 51% of the stock in the Indian company, even after the revised Foreign Exchange Regulations Act (FERA) required foreign companies to hold less than 40% of a domestic (Indian) company's stock.[2] On another occasion, the company was able to have the Bhopal government's objection to its site overruled by the state government.[3]

UCIL had 32.58 million outstanding shares. Of these, 16.58 million shares (50.89%) were held by Carbide Corporation, U.S.A., the holding company. Remaining shares were held by individuals and institutions in India. The company had issued and subscribed-share capital of Rs.325.83 million and accumulated reserves and surplus of Rs.293.89. In 1983, company revenues were Rs.2100 million, ($1 US = Rs.12.8 in 1984), excluding products used internally and valued at Rs.540 million. It reported profit before taxes of Rs.148 million, and profit after taxes and Investment Allowance Reserves of Rs.87 million. It declared a dividend of Rs.1.50 per share. Net worth per share was Rs.19.02 and earnings per share were Rs.2.86. The company employed over 10,000 people, of whom nearly 1,000 earned incomes of over Rs.3,000 per month, making the company one of the best-paying employers in India.[4]

UCIL MANAGEMENT AND ORGANIZATION

UCIL was managed by an eleven-member board of directors, with Keshub Mahindra, a well-known industrialist, as chairman. The vice-chairman was J.B. Law, who also served as the chairman of Union Carbide Eastern, Inc., Hong Kong. V.P. Gokhale served as the managing director (chief executive) of the company. He took up this position on December 26, 1983 and was responsible for overall management of the company. A mechanical engineer by training, he had been with the company since 1959. Each of the five operating divisions were headed by a vice-president reporting to the managing director. Each division was a profit center, organized internally on a functional basis.

Management of the Agricultural Products Division was characterized by frequent changes in top management. During the past fifteen years, it had eight different division heads. Many of them came from nonchemical businesses of the company. Discontinuity in top management created frequent changes in internal systems and procedures, and uncertainty for managers. Many of the more talented managers, particularly those trained in the United States for operating the MIC plant in 1980, had left the company by 1984.[5]

OPERATIONS

The company had 13 manufacturing facilities located in major Indian cities such as Bombay, Calcutta, Madras, Hyderabad, Bhopal, and Srinagar. Production technologies used in these facilities were modern and were supplied by the parent corporation. For example, the Bhopal facility contained plants to manufacture meythyl isocyanate (MIC), and to formulate MIC-based pesticides. The company operated 20 sales offices and sold through a network of 3,000 dealers, who in turn sold to 249,000 retailers all over India. It had dominant market share in its main product (batteries), and was a significant competitor in other product lines, including pesticides, carbons, special metals, chemicals, and plastics. Differences in product lines, marketing philosophies, and operations made each division distinct and independent. For example, the Battery Division operated through a network of distributors and dealers and advertised intensively. The Agricultural Products Division sent distributors to geographical areas where customers (private farmers) were concentrated. Promotion involved programs for farmers aimed at educating them about the usefulness of pesticides.

THE INDUSTRIAL ENVIRONMENT IN BHOPAL AND INDIA

Bhopal is the capital of the state of Madhya Pradesh and the most centrally located city in India. It has a good agricultural and forest base and two large lakes that ensure a steady supply of water to the city. The government controls the most important segments of the local economy. It is the largest employer, the largest producer, and the largest consumer. More than 90% of India's productive industrial resources are controlled directly or indirectly by agencies of the city, state, and central (federal) governments. Virtually all service organizations are nationalized, including banks, insurance companies, postal and telephone systems, radio and television stations, energy production and distribution, railways, airlines, intercity bus service, medical services, and education.

Urbanization and industrialization in Bhopal were not integrated with rural development of the hinterlands. Agricultural production in rural areas was stagnant, while the state's population grew at a rate of more than 2% per year. These conditions forced the rural unemployed to seek work in urban areas, thereby turning Bhopal into a rapidly growing urban area. Bhopal's population grew from 102,000 in 1961 to 385,000 in 1971. It increased to 670,000 in 1981—a growth rate almost three times the average for the state and for the nation as a whole.

Migrants from rural areas were hardly equipped to deal with the difficulties of urban life. In 1971, almost two-thirds of the migrants were unemployed. Of these, half had not completed high school and 20% were totally illiterate. Bhopal's rapidly rising population, coupled with high land and construction costs, caused a severe housing shortage in the city. Government efforts to build housing resulted, for the most part, in the construction of expensive dwellings. Unable to afford housing, many migrants became squatters, illegally occupying land and creating slums and shantytowns. Most of these slums cropped up around industrial plants and other employment centers. Slum dwellers served as a pool of cheap labor for industry, construction, offices, and households seeking domestic help. By 1984, Bhopal had 156 slum colonies, home for nearly 20% of the city's population. Two of them—Jaya Prakash Nagar and Kenchi Chola—were located across the street from Union Carbide's plant, even though the area was not zoned for residential use. In 1974, UCIL was granted an industrial license by the central government to manufacture, rather than simply formulate, pesticides. By 1977, UCIL had begun producing more sophisticated and dangerous pesticides in which carbaryl was the active agent. Component chemicals such as methyl isocyanate (MIC) were imported from the parent company in relatively small quantities. Within a short period of time, however, the pesticides market became very competitive. Fifty different formulations and more than 200 manufacturers came into existence to serve small, regional market niches. Increased competition forced manufacturers to cut costs, improve productivity, take advantage of economies of scale, and resort to "backward integration," (that is, not only to formulate the final products but to manufacture the raw materials and intermediate products as well).

While competitive pressures were mounting, widespread use of pesticides declined. Agricultural production peaked in 1979, declined severely in 1980, and then recovered mildly over the next three years.

Weather conditions, and consequently harvests during 1982 and 1983, were poor, causing farmers temporarily to cut costs by abandoning the use of pesticides. As a result of reduced demand, the pesticides industry became even more competitive in the early 1980s. The expansion and underutilization of production capacity, coupled with a decline in agricultural production, further fueled competition.

During this period of industry decline, UCIL decided to backward integrate into the domestic manufacture of MIC. Until this time, MIC was imported in small drums and did not need to be stored in great quantities. In 1979, the company expanded its Bhopal factory to include facilities that manufactured five pesticide components, including MIC. Using this strategy, UCIL hoped to exploit economies of scale and save transportation costs. Manufacture of MIC required the establishment of a new, hazardous plant and storage facility for MIC. More specifically, this arrangement required MIC to be stored in three large underground tanks with a capacity of about 60 tons each. This made the plant much more hazardous than it had been before.

Municipal authorities in Bhopal objected to the continued use of the UCIL plant at its original location. The city's development plan had earlier designated the plant site for commercial or light industrial use, but not for hazardous industries. With the addition of the MIC facility, this plant had clearly become a hazardous industry. However, at the behest of UCIL, the central and state government authorities overruled the city's objections and granted approval of the backward integration plan.

THE ACCIDENT
AND ITS POSSIBLE CAUSE

At the core of any industrial crisis is a triggering event. In Bhopal, the triggering event was the leakage of a toxic gas, MIC, from storage tanks. Human, organizational, and technological failures in the plant paved the way for the crisis that ensued. The events leading to the accident are murky, which is not unusual when major accidents like the one in Bhopal occur. Moreover, the attributable causes of such accidents become highly contentious because of their impact in establishing culpability and payment of damages to the victims.

MIC is a highly toxic substance used for making carbaryl, the active agent in the pesticide Sevin. It is also very unstable and needs to be kept at low temperatures. UCIL manufactured MIC in batches and stored it in three large underground tanks until it was needed for processing. Two of the tanks that were used for MIC had met specifications, while the third tank that stored MIC had not met specifications and needed reprocessing.

THE PLANT

A schematic layout of the storage tanks and various pipes and valves involved in the accident is shown in Figures 1 and 2. MIC was brought into storage tanks from the MIC refining still through a stainless-steel pipe that branched off into each tank. (See Figure 2 on page 385.) It was transferred out of storage by pressurizing a tank with high-purity nitrogen. Once out of storage, MIC passed through a safety valve to a relief-valve vent header, or pipe, common to all three tanks. This route led to the production reactor unit. Another common line took rejected MIC back to storage for reprocessing and contaminated MIC to the vent-gas scrubber for neutralizing. Excess nitrogen could be forced out of each tank through a process pipe that was regulated by a blow-down valve. Though they served different purposes, the relief-valve pipe and the process pipe were connected by another pipe called the jumper system. This jumper system had been installed about a year before the accident to simplify maintenance.

FIGURE 1. Schematic Layout of Common Headers of MIC Storage Tanks

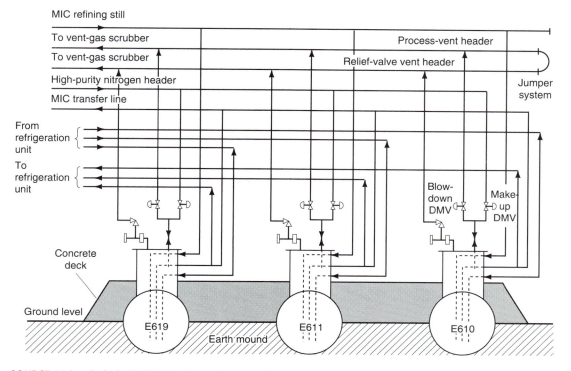

SOURCE: Union Carbide (India) Ltd., Operating Manual Part II: Methyl Isocyanate Unit (Bhopal: Union Carbide (India) Ltd., February 1979).

Normal storage pressure, maintained with the aid of high-purity nitrogen, was 1.0 kilogram per square centimeter (kg/sq cm). Each storage tank was equipped with separate gauges to indicate temperature and pressure, one local and the other inside a remote-control room. Each tank also had a high-temperature alarm, a level indicator, and high- and low-level alarms.

The safety valve through which MIC passed on its way to the Sevin plant operated in conjunction with a mediating graphite rupture disk, which functioned like a pressure cooker. This process held the gas in until it reached a certain pressure, then let it out. The rupture disk could not be monitored from a remote location. Checking it required frequent manual inspection of a pressure indicator located between the disk and the safety valve.

The plant had several safety features. The vent-gas scrubber was a safety device designed to neutralize toxic exhausts from the MIC plant and storage system. Gases leaving the tank were routed to this scrubber, where they were scrubbed with a caustic soda solution and released into the atmosphere at a height of 100 feet or routed to a flare. The gases could also be routed directly to the flare without going through the scrubber. The flare tower was used for burning normally vented gases from the MIC section and other units in the plant. Burning would detoxify the gases before venting them into

FIGURE 2. MIC Storage Tank

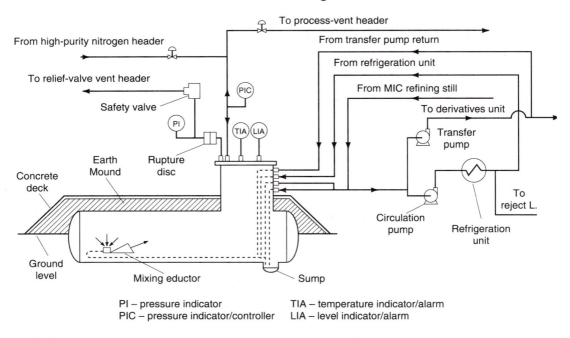

PI – pressure indicator   TIA – temperature indicator/alarm
PIC – pressure indicator/controller   LIA – level indicator/alarm

SOURCE: Bhopal Methyl Isocyanate Incident Investigation Team Report (Danbury, Conn.: Union Carbide
Corporation, March 1985).

the atmosphere. However, the flare was not designed to handle large quantities of MIC vapors. A few weeks before the accident, the scrubber was turned off to a standby position.

Two additional features of the plant were relevant for safety. The first was a refrigeration system, which was used to keep MIC at low temperatures. This was particularly important in the summer when the ambient air could reach temperatures as high as 120°F. However, the refrigeration system was shut down in June of 1984, and its coolant was drained for use in another part of the plant, thus making it impossible to switch on the refrigeration system during an emergency. The second important feature was a set of waterspray pipes that could be used to control escaping gases, over-heated equipment, or fires.

A CHRONOLOGY OF EVENTS

The last batch of MIC manufactured before the accident was produced between October 7 and October 22, 1984. At the end of the manufacturing cycle, one storage tank, called tank E610, contained about 42 tons of MIC, while the second tank, E611, contained about 20 tons. After the MIC production unit was shut down, parts of the plant were dismantled for maintenance. The flare tower was shut down so that a piece of corroded pipe could be replaced. On October 21, nitrogen pressure in tank E610 dropped from 1.25 kg/sq cm, which was about normal, to only 0.25 kg/sq cm. Because the first storage tank lacked sufficient pressure, any MIC needed in the manufacturing process was drawn from the other tank—E611. But on November 30, tank E611 also failed to pressurize because of a defective valve. Plant operators attempted to pressurize tank E610 but failed, so they temporarily abandoned it and, instead, repaired the pressure system in tank E611.

In the normal course of operation, water and MIC react with each other in small quantities in the plant's pipes, creating a plastic substance called trimer. Periodically, the pipes were washed with water to flush out all the trimer that had built up on pipe walls. Because the mixture of water and MIC was so volatile, the pipes were normally blocked off with a physical barrier, known as a slip blind, to prevent the water from going into the storage tank.

On the evening of December 2, the second-shift production superintendent ordered the MIC plant supervisor to flush out several pipes that led from the phosgene system through the MIC storage tanks to the scrubber. Although MIC unit operators were in charge of the flushing operation, insertion of the slip blind was the responsibility of the maintenance supervisor, a position that had been eliminated several days earlier, and no worker had yet been given responsibility for inserting the slip blind. The flushing operation began at 9:30 P.M. Because several bleeder lines, or overflow devices, downstream from the flushing were clogged, water began to accumulate in the pipes. Many of the valves in the plant were leaking, including one that was used to isolate the lines being flushed, so water rose past that valve and into the relief-valve pipe. When the operator noticed that no water was coming out of the bleeder lines, he shut off the flow, but the MIC plant supervisor ordered him to resume the process. The relief-valve pipe was about 20 feet off the ground, thus causing the water to flow downhill toward tank E610. First it flowed through the jumper system to the process pipe. From that pipe, which is normally open, the water flowed to the blow-down valve, which should have been closed. However, the blow-down valve is part of the system used to pressurize the tank with nitrogen—the same tank whose pressurization

system had not been working for weeks. It is possible that this valve had been inadvertently left open or was not sealed properly.

With the blow-down valve open, about 1,100 pounds of water flowed through another isolation valve, normally left open, and entered tank E610, where it began to react with the MIC being stored there. At 10:45 P.M., a change of shift took place. At 11:00 P.M., Suman Dey, the new control-room operator, noticed that the pressure in tank E610 was 10 pounds per square inch (psi), well within the operating range of 2-25 psi. One-half hour later, however, a field operator noticed a leak of MIC near the scrubber. Workers inspected the MIC structure and found MIC and dirty water coming out of a branch of the relief-valve pipe, on the downstream side of the safety valve. They also found that another safety valve, called the process-safety valve, had been removed, and the open end of the relief-valve pipe had not been sealed for flushing. They informed the control room about this. By 12:15 A.M., Dey saw that the pressure in tank E610 had risen to between 25 and 30 psi and was still rising. Within 15 minutes, it showed a reading beyond 55, which was the top of the scale.

Dey ran to the tank. He heard a hissing sound from the safety valve downstream, indicating that it had popped. Local temperature and pressure gauges showed values beyond their maximums of 25°C (77°F) and 55 psi. He heard loud rumbling and screeching noises from the tank and felt heat radiating from it. He went back to the control room and tried to switch on the scrubber, which had been in a standby mode since the last MIC manufacturing run. But his instruments indicated that the caustic soda, the neutralizing agent used in the scrubbers, was not circulating within the scrubber. In the meantime, field operators saw a cloud of gas gushing out of the stack.

Supervisors notified the plant superintendent, who arrived immediately, suspended operation of the MIC plant, and turned on the toxic-gas alarm to warn the community around the plant. A few minutes later, the alarm was turned off, leaving only the inplant siren to warn workers inside the plant. Operators turned on the firewater sprayers to douse the stack, the tank mound, and the relief-valve pipe to the scrubber. Because of low water pressure, the water spray did not reach the gases, which were being emitted at a height of 30 meters. The supervisors tried to turn on the refrigeration system to cool the tanks, but since the coolant from the system was drained, the refrigerator could not work. The safety valve remained open for two hours. A mixture of gases, foam, and liquid escaped at a temperature in excess of 200°C (close to 400°F) and a pressure of 180 psi.

Because the plant was so close to the slums, many thousands of people were affected by exposure to this lethal mixture. Nearly 3,000 people died, although the exact number would never be fully determined. A few months after the accident, the Indian government officially put the death toll at 1,754. But various sources suggest a wide range of higher figures, and the best conclusion one can draw is that the death toll was probably close to 3,000. Thousands more were harmed in some way, many of whom experience illnesses that linger to this day. More than 2,000 animals were killed, and environmental damage was considerable. Bhopal was not equipped to handle an accident of this magnitude. Hospitals and dispensaries could not accommodate the flow of injured victims; likewise, government officials and registered mortuaries could not keep up with the certification and burial of the dead.

There were many reasons for discrepancies in death toll figures. There was no systematic method to certify and accurately count the dead as they were discovered or brought to government hospitals and cremation or burial grounds. For the first three days after the accident, all available medical personnel were engaged in caring for the injured. Few people were left to care for the

dead, register them, perform inquests and autopsies, issue death certificates, or arrange for systematic disposal of bodies.

Dead bodies piled up, one on top of another, in the only city morgue and in temporary tents set up outside of it. Many bodies were released to relatives for disposal without death certificates. Bodies were buried or cremated at unregistered facilities. Graves and funeral pyres registered as single burial units were made to accommodate many corpses because of worker and material shortages. Many people ran from Bhopal and died on roads outside the city and were buried or cremated by the roadside.

THE LONG-TERM HEALTH EFFECTS

The long-term health consequences of exposure to MIC and other toxic gases remain largely unknown and are the subject of considerable controversy in scientific and medical circles. They are likely to be far more serious than originally anticipated.

The most serious permanent damage among the injured was in the respiratory tract. Many victims died of oedema (fluid in the lungs). MIC also damaged mucus membranes, perforated lung tissue, inflamed lungs, and caused secondary lung infections. Many survivors could not be employed because they suffered from bronchitis, pneumonia, asthma, and fibrosis, and were physically unable to work. Long term epidemeological studies have been hampered and not vigorously pursued by the unwillingness of various government agencies in charge of medical studies to share their data with outsiders.

ECONOMIC AND SOCIAL DISRUPTION

The accident did tremendous damage to the local economic and social structures. In addition to the shutdown of the UCIL plant, two mass evacuations—the first at the time of the accident, the second during a fear-ridden "scare" two weeks later—led to the closure of factories, shops, commercial establishments, business and government offices, and schools and colleges. These closures, and labor scarcity resulting from death and injury, disrupted essential services and civil supplies. Establishments that remained open had few employees and few clients.

Estimates of business losses ranged from $8 million to $65 million. The closure of the Union Carbide plant alone eliminated 650 permanent jobs and approximately the same number of temporary jobs—jobs that were particularly important to the local economy because Union Carbide paid high wages. The plant shutdown also dismantled a $25 million investment in the city, which had provided secondary employment to about 1,500 persons. State and local governments lost untold thousands of dollars in taxes. The city, the nation, and the entire developing world suffered a loss of business potential because the accident damaged Union Carbide's business image.

ENVIRONMENTAL CONSEQUENCES

Damage to plant and animal life, while equally devastating, was also not studied systematically because most available resources were deployed for mitigating human losses. Animal deaths probably exceeded 2,000 and included cows, buffaloes, goats, dogs, cats, and birds, although official government records put the figure at only 1,047. About 7,000 animals were given therapeutic care. Postmortems on farm animals suggested the possible presence of an undetected toxin, lending credence to the view that cyanide poisoning was involved. MIC exposure destroyed standing vegetation in surrounding areas. Of 48 plant species examined after the accident, 35 were affected to some degree, and 13 appeared free from damage.

LEGAL PROCEEDINGS

On hearing about the accident, UCC called an emergency meeting of its top executives to develop a crisis management plan. It rushed some medical supplies and teams to Bhopal. Chairman Warren Anderson himself rushed to Bhopal to personally oversee relief and help to victims. Upon his arrival, he was immediately arrested by the local police and confined at the Union Carbide Guest House. After a few hours, and the intervention of the central government, he was released and flown to New Delhi. He returned to the United States without making any headway on the relief mission. On the contrary, his visit and arrest served to create the ferociously adversarial mood that governed the subsequent relations between the company and the government of India.

Government agencies mounted a massive relief and rehabilitation effort to deal with the disaster. However, given their limited resources and the vast magnitude of the accident, they were barely able to give first-aid treatment to victims. The government made interim relief payments of $80 to $800, to help victims tide over their immediate financial needs. Once the immediate crisis subsided however, relief efforts lost their intensity. Since then, government agencies have been criticized in the local press for their indifference and insensitivity to the plight of the victims.

CONSEQUENCES FOR UNION CARBIDE

The accident threatened Union Carbide's very survival. In its aftermath, the company was subject to worldwide humiliation. The day after the accident, the Bhopal plant was shut down and local managers were arrested on criminal charges. The company's reputation came under intense attack by the news media worldwide. The Bhopal accident triggered a series of sanctions and protests against Union Carbide all over the world. Public interest and activist groups initiated a variety of grass-roots campaigns against the company. In Breziers, France, where Union Carbide used MIC made in the United States to make pesticides, the local community objected to reopening the plant after it was shut down following the Bhopal accident. In Rio de Janeiro, Brazil, the state government decreed that MIC could not be produced, stored, or transported within the state. In Scotland, despite a local unemployment rate of 26%, the city of Livingston rejected Union Carbide's proposal to set up a plant to manufacture toxic gases.

During this period of scrutiny and backlash, several accidents occurred at Union Carbide's U.S. plants, which deepened the company's crisis. On March 28, 1985, the chemical mesityl oxide leaked from the company's Institute, West Virginia plant, sickening eight people in a nearby shopping mall. Then, on August 11, 1985, another chemical, aldicarb oxyme, leaked from a storage tank at the same plant, injuring 135 people, 31 of whom were admitted to local hospitals. Two days later, another leak occurred at a sister plant in Charleston, West Virginia. Although no one was injured, the leak was highly publicized and spawned further investigations into company operations. Investigations also revealed that twenty-eight major MIC gas leaks had occurred at the Institute, West Virginia plant during the five years preceding the Bhopal accident. One of them occurred just a month before the Bhopal leak, releasing 14,000 pounds of a MIC/cloroform mixture into the atmosphere.

LEGAL CONSEQUENCES

Soon after the accident, lawyers from the United States arrived in Bhopal, formed partnerships with Indian lawyers, and started arranging to represent victims in multimillion-dollar personal injury lawsuits against Union Carbide. (The chronological development of the legal ramifications of the accident is shown in Table 2) Union Carbide was not the only party taken to court. Many victims also sued the government of India, charging it with negligence in allowing the disaster to occur. Some lawsuits pointed to the delays, incompetence, and corruption involved in relief efforts. Others argued that the Indian government was partly responsible because it had allowed Union Carbide to locate and operate the hazardous facility, and because it had legalized the slums around the plant early in 1984. Critics faulted the government for failing to act on the recommendation of its own Labor Department, which had urged a safety investigation at the plant, and for failing to prepare for the possibility of an emergency at the plant.

In March of 1985, the Indian government passed a law conferring on itself sweeping powers to represent victims in the lawsuit and manage all aspects of registering and processing of legal claims. The following month, it filed a lawsuit in the United States, charging Union Carbide with liability in the deaths of 1,700 persons, the personal injury of 200,000 more persons, and property damages. Union Carbide Corporation developed a multilayered defense strategy. First, it argued that the suits should be dismissed from U.S. courts, because the accident happened in India, victims were mostly Indians, and most material evidence and witnesses were in India. It also suggested that Indian law and compensation standards should be applied in determining victim compensation in this case. The government of India countered by saying that U.S. courts were an appropriate forum for the case because the parent company was a U.S. corporation. This claim was supported by private victim lawyers, who were interested in keeping the case in the U.S., where they could legally represent victims. The battle over the correct forum for trial of cases extended over several months. During this time, Carbide began negotiating an out-of-court settlement of the

TABLE 2. Developments in Lawsuits Against Union Carbide

December 1984 and January 1985	Over 45 suits filed against Carbide in various state and federal courts; 482 personal injury suits filed against UCIL in Bhopal; a $1 billion representative suit filed in Bhopal against UCIL and UCC; a suit in India's Supreme Court against UCIL and the government of India and Madhya Pradesh. Federal suits against UCC consolidated for pretrial proceedings in the Federal Court of the Southern District of New York under Judge J.F. K. Keenan.
March–April 1985	The Bhopal Gas Leak Disaster (Processing of Claims) Ordinance, 1985 passed by Indian Parliament conferring on the government of India powers to secure claims arising out of the disaster. Government of India files **parens patriae** action against UCC.
May 1985	UCC offers $5 million for relief, to be deducted from payment of final settlement. It attaches stringent accounting requirements and demands detailed information on victims' health.
July 1985	UCC moves to dismiss cases against it on **forum non conveniens** grounds.
Through 1985	Out-of-court negotiations
March 1986	Union Carbide and private victim lawyers reach a tentative settlement of $350 million for compensation. Government of India is not party to this settlement and rejects it as absurdly low.
May 1986	Judge Keenan rules on the forum issue sending the case to be tried in Indian courts.
August 1986	Government of India refiles case in Bhopal District Court.
April 1987	Judge Deo of the Bhopal Court revives the attempt to bring about a settlement.
December 1987	Bhopal Court orders UCC to pay to victims $270 million in interim payment. UCC appeals.
April 1988	Madya Pradesh High Court upholds the Bhopal Court ruling, but reduces amount to $190 million.
February 14, 1989	Supreme Court of India orders a settlement of the case whereby Union Carbide agrees to pay $470 million as full and final settlement of all claims arising out of the accident and subsequent litigation. The court also dismisses all criminal and civil charges then pending in India against the company and its executives.

case, with the government of India and the private lawyers.

The government of India had bestowed on itself all rights to represent the victims. It did not accept the role of private lawyers in the case. These lawyers had also lost legitimacy in the eyes of the victims and the world media, because of the insensitive way they had descended upon Bhopal to sign up clients after the accident. They had obtained clients by running newspaper advertisements with affidavit forms attached, which the victims could fill out and mail back to the lawyers' respective offices. Some of them never even met their clients or discussed with them the nature or extent of the damages. Their main interest was in the extremely lucrative attorney fees that were likely to result from the case if it were decided in an American court.

Judge Keenan, the presiding judge in this case, attempted to balance the power of the opposing parties in order to keep them negotiating, but was not very successful. For example, in April of 1985, the court ordered Union Carbide immediately to pay $5 million for interim relief, deductible from the final settlement amount. But the government of India refused to accept the money, saying the corporation had imposed "onerous conditions" on its use. The court was unable to give away the money for 7 months because the litigants could not agree on a plan for using it. This delay was embarrassing for all parties because, all the while, media reports detailed the woefully inadequate relief being provided to the victims.

Initial negotiations led to Union Carbides's offer in August of 1985 of about $200 million to be paid out over 30 years for a total and final settlement of the case. The government rejected the offer without explanation. Two detailed estimates of damage made public in 1985 suggested that the compensation to the victims should range from $1 billion to $2 billion.

In late March of 1986, the *New York Times* reported that a "tentative settlement" of $350 million had been reached between Union Carbide and the private lawyers. The lawyers had a strong economic motive for settling the case early, because if the case was moved to India, they would lose all their fees, which amounted to millions of dollars. But the Indian government's attorneys had not been involved in the negotiations, and they once again rejected the offer as absurdly low. Indeed, even if the agreement was sanctioned by the court, it would be virtually impossible to implement without the cooperation of the Indian government, which was the only party with access to the information and administrative procedures needed to distribute the compensation money fairly.

In May of 1986, Judge Keenan ruled on the forum issue, deciding to send the case to India for trial. In doing so, he imposed three conditions on Union Carbide. First, the corporation had to submit itself to the jurisdiction of Indian courts. Second, Carbide had to agree to satisfy any judgements rendered by Indian courts through due process. And third, the company had to agree to submit to discovery under the U.S. law, which allowed more exploration of company-held information than Indian laws did. This last condition was appealed by Union Carbide, which requested the court to make discovery under U.S. law a reciprocal condition and impose it on the government of India, as well.

Union Carbide's second line of defense was to argue that it was not legally liable for the accident. It said the parent company was not responsible for the accident, because the plant in which it occurred was designed, constructed, owned, and operated by the Indian company Union Carbide (India) Ltd. It argued that the parent company had no control over its Indian subsidiary in matters of day-to-day operations. It suggested that the "corporate veil" between parent and subsidiary prevent it (the parent) from controlling the causes of the accident. Thus, it blamed the accident on the Indian company, which had total assets of only about $80 million. The government of India argued against this position on the basis of Union Carbide's 51% ownership of its subsidiary, and on the legal doctrine of "strict liability." This doctrine says that as long as the source of damage or injury originates within a facility owned by a company, the company is strictly liable for the damages, regardless of whose fault lead to the accident. The acceptability and applicability of this doctrine was contested by Union Carbide.

Finally, the company argued that the accident was caused by sabotage. It said that a disgruntled employee had deliberately poured a large quantity of water into the MIC tank to cause the run-away reaction. However, it did not provide the identity of the saboteur. It argued that since the parent company was not in control of the day-to-day operations of the Indian subsidiary, it should not be held liable for the accident. This issue was being debated in courts in India even four years after the accident.

DRIVE TOWARD A SETTLEMENT: THE UNSETTLED FATE OF VICTIMS

As the case moved slowly through the court system in the U.S., and then in India, the pressure on both parties to reach an out-of-court settlement increased. The government of India wanted a settlement to prevent political backlash from the accident's victims and their families. UCC wanted a settlement to shake off the legal liability and protect its assets. The differences in their motives and objectives, and the backlash from the lawsuits kept them from reaching a settlement even 4 years after the accident.

The board of directors of Union Carbide decided to sell assets of the company and distribute to shareholders the net pretax sale proceeds above the net book value of the businesses. In 1985, the company divested about $2 billion worth of assets. In early 1986, it sold its Battery Division to Ralston Purina for $1.42 billion and announced its intention of selling its home- and automotive-products division for $800 million. Soon thereafter, it sold its corporate headquarters building for $345 million and its agricultural chemicals business for $575 million.

These divestitures alarmed the Indian government. It asked the Bhopal court to bar the company from stripping assets, paying dividends, or buying back debt, until a review ensured that these activities would not disadvantage the victims. The company was able to have the injunction lifted by agreeing to maintain at least $3 billion in assets that could be used to settle the Bhopal claims.

In the Bhopal District Court, the Indian government had demanded $3 billion as compensation for damages. In April 1987, the District Judge M.W. Deo, hearing the case, suggested that the company make an interim relief payment of $4.6 million, and urged the litigants to reach an agreement on the final amount of the settlement. In August 1987, the company agreed to distribute the $4.6 million interim aid, and a few months later offered about $500 million as a final settlement amount. This money was to be paid over a 30-year period. The net present value of this amount was not different from the earlier offer made by the company. The offer was rejected by the government.

Frustrated by the unyielding positions of both sides, and the increasing complexity of the litigation, Judge Deo ordered Union Carbide to pay $270 million as interim aid to victims in December 1987. This money was to be placed with the Commissioner of Claims named by the Indian Government. He suggested that this amount be distributed to victims as follows: $15,500 per death, $8,000 per severe injury, and lesser amounts for remaining victims.

Union Carbide appealed this interim payment on the grounds that it amounted to "a judgement and decree without trial." The issue was moved up to the High Court in Jabalpur. The High Court Judge S.K. Seth in April 1988 upheld the order of the lower court, but reduced the interim relief amount from $270 million to $190 million. He also said that it was not necessary to hold a trial to determine damages to thousands of victims. He suggested that $7,800 should be paid to families of those killed or seriously injured, $3,900 be paid to those injured less seriously, and $1,050 to those with minor injuries.

Finally, in February 1989 a $470 million settlement was ordered by India's Supreme Court ending the intense legal conflict that raged since December 1984. Unfortunately for the victims even the Indian Supreme Court does not change the tragedy of the final outcome. The victims who were poor and unable to work because of their medical condition, continued to die of their ailments and malnourishments.[6]

NOTES

1. Sanjay Hazarika, "Bhopal Payments Set at $470 Million for Union Carbide." *New York Times* (February 15, 1989), p. 1. See also, "Union Carbide Agrees to Settle All Bhopal Litigation for $470 Million in Pact With India's Supreme Court." *Wall Street Journal* (February 15, 1989), p. A-3.

2. *India Today*. "City of Death." Cover story (December 31, 1984), p. 2.

3. Ward Morehouse, and Arun Subramanyam, *The Bhopal Tragedy*. New York: Council on International and Public Affairs (1986), pp. 18, 32.

4. Union Carbide Corporation and Union

Carbide (I) *Limited Annual Reports*, 1983, 1984.

5. Personal interviews with the author.

6. *Chemical Week*, Bhopal: For Victims, Relief, for Carbide. February 22, 1989: p. 8; *Time*, February 27, 1989; *The Economist*, February 18, 1989, p. 65; *Newsweek*, February 27, 1989, p. 54.

U.S. MULTINATIONAL CORPORATIONS IN SOUTH AFRICA

Should there be a conflict between economic interests,
and ethical and political imperatives?

On May 10, 1994, South Africa entered a new era with the successful conclusion of its first ever nonracial elections and with President Nelson Mandela at the helm of the new nation and its government. The transition could not have been more miraculous. The pace of negotiations among the former enemies was indeed tortuous and there were numerous prognostications of various political pundits as to the extreme unlikelyhood of the success of negotiations, and avoidance of violence.

Despite all its problems, the transition to democracy would seem to have been the easier of the two crises confronting the new South Africa. The other problem was the need to jump-start the economy and attract more foreign investment. It would call for an about-face in the strategy of the African National Congress (ANC), which had previously advocated an isolation of the white-controlled South African government from all international forums, thereby making it a pariah in the world family of nations. An important element of this strategy was to urge nations and companies *not* to invest in South Africa, or do business with the South African government and companies.

*This case study was prepared by Dr. Karen Paul, Professor of Business Environment, Florida International University.

Although opinions differ as to the effectiveness of economic sanctions, all sides agree that they played an important role in bringing about the downfall of the white-controlled South African government and moving it toward a negotiated transition to a nonracial, democratic South Africa.

THE ROLE OF U.S. CORPORATIONS IN SOUTH AFRICA

Nowhere else in the world has the "sanctions and divestiture" movement been more pronounced as the one in the United States. A concerted drive by social activists included religious groups, influential political leaders, and other important institutions, notably public pension funds, universities and colleges, and local governments. They combined to bring about a number of major changes in the political posture of the U.S. government and the operations of the U.S. multinational corporations as they pertained to South Africa.

In October 1986, the U.S. Congress—overriding a veto by the then U.S. President Ronald Reagan—passed a law called the Comprehensive Anti-Apartheid Act (CAAA), which set strict operating standards that U.S. companies must comply with in their operations in South Africa. The Act also set conditions that the South African government must meet before such sanctions could be lifted. The CAAA contained a set of proscriptions on sanctions against the South African government and also a set of positive measures toward helping the disenfranchised people of South Africa. In addition, it specified the conditions that must be fulfilled by the South African government before the sanctions can be lifted. A summary of the major provisions of the Act are presented in Appendix A.

A majority of the U.S. companies with significant operations in South Africa agreed to abide by a code of conduct known as the Sullivan Principles. It was created by Rev. Leon Sullivan, a black minister from Philadelphia, who was also a board member of General Motors corporation. During its peak, the Principles were adhered to by over 150 U.S. corporations doing business in South Africa, and represented over 85% of the U.S. direct foreign investments in that country. These companies would spend over $400 million on activities prescribed by the Principles in a 15-year time span.

Notwithstanding the expenditures of millions of dollars, and the companies' insistence that their operations in South Africa were both economically and morally justified, these companies faced enormous pressures and hostility from many sources in South Africa and the United States. These pressures, and the resultant exhaustion from the sheer "hassle" factor—when coupled with growing violence and economic instability in South Africa—propelled a growing number of companies to cease operations in South Africa, with the result that by the time independence came to South Africa—and with it the call for new foreign investments—the number of U.S. companies still operating in South Africa had declined by 2/3 from its peak in the early 1980s.

This case study focuses on two major areas of action pertaining to the operations of the U.S. companies in South Africa. The first one deals with the development and implementation of the Sullivan Principles as

a "voluntary code" on the part of the U.S. companies. (See Appendix B.) The second one discusses some of the approaches used by U.S. companies in the process of divesting their operations in South Africa and withdrawing from that country. This has been done through an examination of the divestiture process used by General Motors Corporation.

ISSUES FOR ANALYSIS

This case raises questions about the moral, legal, and pragmatic considerations a multinational corporation (MNC) must have when operating in host countries whose society differs greatly from the home country. In the case of South Africa, that country's unique system of institutionalized racial discrimination was abhorrent to most Americans. Social activists in churches, trade unions, and universities maintained that U.S. companies should either withdraw in order to demonstrate their support for the oppressed majority of the population; should challenge the South African government to change its practice of apartheid, or at the very least, should serve as a witness for change, demonstrating in their own subsidiaries the extent of their commitment to black empowerment. These demands put multinationals in a new and unique position. Traditionally, MNCs have been asked to stay out of a host country's politics and abstain from attempting to influence government officials. In the case of South Africa, however, they were pressured to become more actively involved so as to become an effective agent of change. This unparalleled situation raises a number of issues for review and analysis:

1. How should a multinational corporation represent the moral, cultural, or political ideals of its home country in a host country? Under what circumstances should it attempt to refrain from imposing home-country standards on a host country? How should a U.S.-based multinational cope with the moral, cul-

tural, and political values of its home country that are universally desirable, but are not respected in a large number of Third World countries?

2. How much responsibility does a multinational have to obey the laws of a host country even if they seem unjust and oppressive? Under what circumstances should a corporation violate such laws, or support employees who violate such laws?

3. The decision to make new investments calls for different criteria than the decision to withdraw from existing commitments or to close an ongoing operation. In the former case, the choice may be among competing investment alternatives and may be easier to make. In the latter case, it is a question of balancing competing interests among different stakeholders and honoring existing commitments. How should a company develop standards to resolve these situations?

4. An associated issue, and the one that is equally important, especially in the case of existing commitments, has to do with the potential loss that a company might incur as a result of such a withdrawal. What if a withdrawal inflicts a significant harm to the company's stockholders? Suppose such a withdrawal has not been forced upon the company because of a legal directive from a government, e.g., the imposition of sanctions forbidding continued investment. Should managers be held responsible for losses to their shareholders accruing from such a withdrawal? What is the responsibility of social activists under these circumstances when they inflict losses on a company's stockholders but do not stand to make any economic sacrifice of their own as a result of their own ethical, political, or social values?

5. When should U.S. corporations exceed local expectations as to working conditions and wages paid to employees? How much responsibility does a business have to pay its work force at a just rate, even when the prevailing local norm is less?

6. What should U.S. companies do to respond to social activists who criticize their presence in South Africa? Can the companies develop any strategies to cope with the pressures of divestment, purchasing restrictions, and the sanctions movement?

7. What contributions have the Sullivan Principles made to the operating practices of U.S. companies, and to the people in South Africa? How can the monitoring system be managed in future years? What changes are necessary, and what changes might be useful?

8. Now that the apartheid has been abolished and the new government is aggressively campaigning for a return of direct foreign investments, what should be the posture of the U.S. multinational companies? In particular, how should the U.S. companies go about defining and implementing social responsibility in the new South Africa?

   a. Should they continue to abide by the provisions of the Sullivan Principles by incurring additional expenditures on social responsibility and community-related activities; or should these expenses now be determined by the laws of the new South African government, good corporate citizenship parctices, and the demands of the market and competition?

   b. When apartheid was dismantled and citizenship extended to all, did multinationals who had campaigned for these changes have an obligation to invest in the country? If noncompliance with ethical standards is cited as a reason to withdraw, does compliance with ethical standards require participation in the economy?

   c. Although the South African government has publicly opposed any and all efforts by the U.S. and South African public interest groups, there are efforts by a number of groups to create new voluntary codes for the U.S. multinationals in particular, and large corporations in general, to be followed in South Africa. How can these efforts be justified, if at all?

9. The success of the "Sullivan Principles," or lack thereof, has prompted many activist groups to seek similar codes of conduct applicable to all multinationals, e.g., the U.N. Code of Conduct for Transnational Corporations, or the more recent code announced by the Clinton Administration. In addition, there are a variety of codes directed at specific activities and regions, e.g., the World Health Organization (WHO) International Code of Marketing of Breast-Milk Substitutes, and the Valdez Principles. Is there a need for such codes? If so, under what conditions, under whose auspices, under what type of

implementation and enforcement mechanisms, and with what objectives and goals?

U.S. INVESTMENTS IN SOUTH AFRICA—A BRIEF HISTORY

U.S. multinationals have invested in South
Africa for many decades, but their investment increased dramatically in the 1950s and
1960s and peaked in 1981. Periodically, however, U.S. business was forced to confront
troubling moral questions about the treatment of black workers in South Africa.
Economic concerns reinforced moral considerations. While U.S. multinationals benefit-
ted in some ways from having available a
large work force of low-paid black workers,
there were disadvantages as well. Large-scale
markets for manufactured goods could not
develop until blacks were paid at a level sufficient to permit them more purchasing
power. As businesses became more dependent on skilled rather than unskilled labor,
the inadequacy of the education system for
blacks, the low level of housing available to
them, and the long commutes they had to the
workplace became serious hindrances to productivity.[1]

South Africa's economy is highly dependent on international linkages. Foreign direct
investment has been of major importance to
the South African economy. In 1984, Great
Britain was represented by 364 companies in
South Africa, with total investments probably approaching 40% of South Africa's direct
foreign investment. The United States and
West Germany each held about 20% of South
Africa's foreign direct investment, with the
U.S. share declining and the West German
share increasing.[2] For 1986, exports (mainly
gold, other minerals, and base metals)
amounted to 30% of the Gross Domestic
Product of South Africa, down about 15%
from the previous year. Imports (mainly
machinery, vehicles and aircraft, chemicals
and base metals) for 1986 were 25% of the
GDP, down about 12% from 1985. Both fig-

ures declined due to the weakness of the
South African economy, the devaluation of
their currency, and the gradual imposition of
sanctions by some trading partners including
the U.S., several Scandinavian countries, and
members of the European Economic
Community.[3] Great Britain was South
Africa's largest trading partner in the 1950s,
1960s, and 1970s, but then was overtaken by
the U.S., which was in turn surpassed by
Japan in 1987. Despite its historical reliance
on international linkages, South Africa has
the potential to be a fairly self-sufficient economy because of its highly developed economic infrastructure, its position as a net
exporter of agricultural goods, and its capacity to supply all raw materials except oil.
Even with regard to its oil needs, it has large
stockpiles as well as a massive gas-to-oil project underway to meet its own energy needs,
albeit at high cost.

THE ORIGINS OF THE SULLIVAN PRINCIPLES

Beginning in the 1960s and intensifying in the
1970s, U.S. companies in South Africa were
under pressure to defend their involvement
in that country. Church groups were particularly biting in their criticism, asserting that by
their very presence there, U.S. companies
were supporting the government of South
Africa and helping to prop up apartheid.

General Motors was under particular
pressure to get out of South Africa as a result
of Project GM, an effort by a group of young
lawyers and campus activists to "democra-
tize the corporation" in 1970. One demand
was that they withdraw from South Africa. A
shareholders' resolution to this effect attracted little support, but the company did nomi-
nate a black clergyman from Philadelphia to
sit on the board of directors. For five years,
this clergyman, Rev. Leon Sullivan, pressed
General Motors to withdraw from South
Africa. Then he developed a unique system

of corporate social monitoring to guide the U.S. companies in South Africa.

The Sullivan Principles [Appendix B] issued in March, 1977, called on U.S. companies to follow these guidelines:

- Nonsegregation of the races in all eating, comfort, and work facilities
- Equal and fair employment practices for all employees
- Equal pay for all employees doing equal or comparable work for the same period of time
- Initiation of and development of training programs that will prepare, in substantial numbers, blacks and other nonwhites for supervisory, administrative, clerical, and technical jobs.
- Increasing the number of blacks and other nonwhites in management and supervisory positions
- Improving the quality of employees' lives outside the work environment in such areas as housing, transportation, schooling, recreation, and health facilities.

The original Signatories of the Principles included GM, Union Carbide, Ford, Otis Elevator, 3M, IBM, International Harvester, American Cyanamide, Citibank, Burroughs, Mobil, and Caltex. Signatories were obliged to provide reports in which they detailed the extent of their efforts to comply with each of these principles. Their reports were compiled and evaluated by Arthur D. Little, Inc., the consulting firm, and a report was issued annually in which a rating was assigned to each company.

Three ratings were possible—Making Good Progress, Making Progress, and Needs to Become More Active. Each company was assigned to one of these categories on the basis of data submitted in response to a questionnaire, which was then analyzed by Arthur D. Little. The "goalposts" changed each year, and companies were evaluated in comparison to the entire set of Signatories. While individual companies knew of the areas in which they achieved high and low marks in the evaluation process, for the outside public, the only information released was each company's final rating.

This set of principles was quite controversial when it was introduced in South Africa. First, it obligated the companies to undertake certain activities that went beyond normal employee practices and in many cases breached existing legal restrictions or social conventions in South Africa. For example, the second principle called for the representation of employees in trade unions, legal for whites but not legal for blacks at the time the principles were introduced. Second, it required businesses to undertake activities *outside* the plant that involved not only their workers but the larger black community as well. Third, it subjected a company's social performance to outside auditors, public reporting, and disclosure.

The Sullivan Principles evolved over the years, with Reverend Sullivan providing several amplifications that emphasized actions he thought U.S. companies should be taking. His first amplification, issued in 1978, called on companies to desegregate the workplace and all its facilities immediately. The second amplification, issued in 1979, stated that companies should support changes in influx control laws to provide for the right of black migrant workers to have a normal family life. (Influx control was the system of restrictions maintained that required blacks to remain outside urban areas unless they could present proof of employment by means of a pass issued by employers.) The third amplification, issued in 1982, required that companies have several items verified by their own accounting firms. However, the fourth amplification, dating from 1985, constituted a significant expansion in the activities expected from Signatories. This amplification required that companies press the South African government to end the laws and regulations that constituted apartheid. This last amplification was institutionalized as a Seventh Principle, "Working to eliminate laws and customs that impede social and political justice," in the Tenth Report, issued in December 1986.

This last amplification put Signatories in the position of outright defiance of the South African government. Normally, multinationals operating abroad are expected to stay out of politics, to refrain from attempting to exert undue influence on the government, and to respect local laws and customs. But U.S. companies in South Africa were being asked to lobby actively to create changes in South African laws, to support those who challenged the government, and to take a public stand on social issues—in short, to become an instrument for social change.

By the mid-1980s, the majority of U.S. companies had joined the Sullivan program as Signatories, with the number subscribing to the principles increasing to 184 in 1986.[4] However, the number of U.S. companies in the Sullivan program decreased to 90 by the end of 1987, mainly due to the fact that 52 of the signatory companies withdrew from South Africa.[5]

DISILLUSIONMENT WITH THE SULLIVAN SYSTEM

Critics charged that despite the efforts of U.S. companies to improve working conditions for blacks, the basic reality was that blacks had the lowest paying jobs, few chances for advancement, and far from equal opportunity in the workplace. Furthermore, the conditions of life for blacks under apartheid remained oppressive. Questions began to be raised about the goals of the Sullivan Principles—did they merely serve to promote incremental change, which would make the conditions of work life more tolerable for the blacks in South Africa? Would they ever lead to fundamental change in the distribution of power or the recognition of basic human rights?[6] Were South African blacks, themselves, represented in the process? Did the companies formulate goals and objectives mainly on the basis of what made sense in U.S. boardrooms, with little attention to the

actual needs defined by the victims of apartheid?[7]

Methodological problems were also raised about the reports. The underlying data that formed the basis for the reports were represented as being "independently verified." However, in reality only a small number of items were verified, leaving unverified such critical areas as the number of job vacancies in various categories, the total number of people in trainee positions, and the total number of blacks in various occupational categories; all of these were critical factors in assessing whether or not blacks were being prepared for, and moved into, jobs requiring higher skills. Even if no intentional distortions were present, this system left considerable room for individual interpretation and, hence, inconsistency. Companies were evaluated on the basis of a check-off system covering a myriad of areas. Hence, efforts tended to become fragmented. The yearly evaluation led many companies to make short-term donations rather than more enduring investments in social responsibility projects.[8]

The emphasis was on inputs to the process—the amount of expenditure in each a wide variety of categories—rather than on outcome. Companies tended to "throw money" at projects rather than to engage in careful planning, implementation, and evaluation, since their rating points came from the donations they made rather than through the effectiveness of their projects. The timing of the monitoring process exacerbated this problem. Companies had to spend their target amounts very quickly in order to be able to report that they had met objectives.

Although the companies were obliged, as part of the monitoring process, to inform employees of their rating categories, and to review the implementation of the Principles with employee groups several times a year, many black employees felt that they were not consulted adequately. There was also some resentment because of the fact that the system was managed by white American management consultants from Arthur D. Little,

Inc. Were no blacks qualified to do the monitoring? Why were black South Africans not represented in the process? Their exclusion made the monitoring system seem a paternalistic gesture on the part of U.S. business.

CHANGES IN SOUTH AFRICA

By the end of the 1970s, the South African government had made some changes to modify and improve economic and social relations among South Africa's racial groups. Whereas Job Reservation had restricted skilled managerial jobs to whites, now blacks were to be allowed to serve as apprentices, to gain skills, and to occupy positions where they would work beside whites, and even supervise whites, a previously forbidden situation. Acknowledgment was made that perhaps some blacks might be entitled to be permanent residents of urban areas, rather than "temporary sojourners" permitted to stay only as long as they held jobs in these areas. The hated "pass books" that blacks were required to carry and produce upon demand, were replaced by identity books which were now issued to all races. Existing "immorality" laws were scrapped, permitting interracial marriages. However, a mixed-race couple would still have no place to live, since residential areas remained limited to one race only. A new Constitution adopted in 1983 provided for a limited form of political representation for "Asians" and "Coloureds." Blacks, however, remained without any political representation.

The United Democratic Front (UDF) was formed to oppose the constitutional changes that continued to deny blacks political representation in the government. UDF, along with black labor unions that have been legalized, became the focal point for new black militancy.

A new sense of urgency was created by the state of emergency declared by the South African government in response to increasing mobilization in the townships. Rising levels of violence in townships were met by brutal repression by police and the military. Thousands of persons were detained without formal charges being filed, and police were not even required to acknowledge who they had in custody. In the black townships, there was increasing hostility towards those who were thought to be collaborating with the government. "Necklacing" became a means of punishment, the necklace being a tire filled with gasoline placed around the neck of the person judged guilty of some offense, and set on fire. Schools ceased to function and a rent boycott spread rapidly. Within a year, the South African government was to declare a state of emergency, impose press censorship, and detain 20,000 individuals, including thousands of children.

THE U.S. CONGRESS TAKES ACTION

During the Carter administration (1976 to 1980), there had been considerable pressure from the U.S. government for isolating the South African economy. However, after President Reagan took office in 1981, the U.S. government's policy toward South Africa became somewhat more conciliatory. The idea that U.S. business could be a liberalizing force in South Africa, and that orderly political change would result from continued economic development, was generally accepted in the executive branch. The notion of "constructive engagement" became the operating principle. It emphasized the need for continued U.S. participation in South Africa to lead that country toward job creation and black socio-economic advancement. The Reagan Administration renewed military contacts and restored nuclear cooperation with South Africa. It also relaxed existing regulations restricting trade with security forces in South Africa.[9]

When constructive engagement failed to produce any positive changes in the actions of the South African government, strong sentiment developed in the U.S. Congress for sanctions. Proposals ranged from the relatively mild demand that trade in krugerrands (South African gold coins) be halted, to the more substantive demand that new investment in South Africa be prohibited or even that all trade be prohibited. Partly in order to forestall congressional action, President Reagan imposed a set of mild sanctions by executive order at the end of 1985. It banned U.S. imports of krugerrands, restricted bank loans to South Africa, and limited computer sales to that country.

In September, 1986, the Comprehensive Anti-Apartheid Bill was passed by the House of Representatives and the U.S. Senate. It was vetoed by President Reagan, and passed by a two-thirds vote over his veto. It banned new investment, prohibited the import of such South African goods as uranium, coal, textiles, steel, and agricultural products; stopped the sale of weapons and computers used by agencies that enforce apartheid; and terminated the landing rights of South African Airways in the United States. The bill went so far as to threaten a cut-off of U.S. aid to countries that continued to supply South Africa with weapons, with Israel as the intended target.

SOCIAL PRESSURE CONTINUES TO BUILD

The movement continued on the part of some religious groups, unions, and social activists to press for increased sanctions against South Africa. Yet, it was far from clear that sanctions were achieving their intended impact on the South African government. Advocates of sanctions asserted that, in time, capital investment, both direct and portfolio investment, from outside South Africa would be reduced; therefore, within South Africa there would have to be an increased use of internal savings for investment, or less investment. This would lead to reduced productive capacity and a decline in the ability to import goods. The results would include: a massive

currency devaluation; diminished per capita GDP; a continuation of the brain drain that already existed; and a lag of technology.[10] There was also a question as to the extent of compliance with international sanctions on the part of all nations. No doubt sanctions-busting would be promoted by both South African government and business interests. South Africa's main export, gold, was extremely susceptible to this type of trade.

Sanctions could have the following confounding effects: Supplies of vital minerals to the Western world could be harmed, since South Africa ranks first among exporters not only of gold, but also chrome ore, ferrochrome, and vanadium; it is the second largest for platinum, manganese, ferromanganese, and titanium.[11] Also, the "front-line states," the nations surrounding South Africa, are dependent on that country's transportation lines for importing goods as well as shipping local products to overseas markets. It was also argued that a decline in the economic situation in South Africa would mean fewer jobs for blacks.

SOUTH AFRICAN RESPONSES TO THE CALL FOR DISINVESTMENT

From South Africa came conflicting responses to the call for disinvestment. The United Democratic Front (UDF), representing more than 600 churches, trade unions, student groups, and community organizations, issued this statement in 1983:

> The UDF welcomes the disinvestment campaign and its gains, especially in so far as it has succeeded in rendering Reagan's "Constructive Engagement" policy hollow and unrepresentative of the majority of American citizens.[12]

The exiled leadership of the African National Congress (ANC) adopted two resolutions in favor of disinvestment in 1985. AZAPO, the Azanian Peoples' Organization, representing the Black Consciousness tradition of Steve Biko, opposed all foreign investment and all foreign involvement in South Africa. However, within South Africa, there was more caution. Among trade union leaders, there was concern that jobs might be lost as a result of disinvestment. And yet the call for disinvestment had a powerful rallying effect in townships. In the end there was cautious support for selective disinvestment, but a general hesitancy to come out unequivocally for total withdrawal of multinationals.

In November 1985, the Congress of South African Trade Unions (COSATU) was formed and soon emerged as the most powerful representative of organized black labor interests in South Africa. Its membership quickly reached 600,000. At its inaugural conference in 1985, COSATU announced its support for disinvestment.[13] Black leaders came out both for and against disinvestment. Archbishop Desmond Tutu, Nobel-prize winning Anglican Archbishop, was a supporter of economic sanctions. On the other hand, Chief M. Buthelezi, head of the Zulu "nation," opposed corporate withdrawals. Helen Suzman, who for many years was the single representative of the opposition party in the South African Parliament, also opposed disinvestment, observing:

> The Pretoria regime will not fall because of sanctions. It will make the changes it intended to make, which will fall far short of what it believes is demanded of it by the undefined expression, "dismantling apartheid and sharing power." Thereafter, if continued pressure is put on it, the Pretoria regime will retreat into the *laager*, bringing with it an even more oppressive system than has been experienced up to now in South Africa.[14]

Various surveys were done purporting to represent black opinion on disinvestment. One commentator observed:

> Anti-sanctions academics tend to ask black people whether they are prepared to support sanctions which will cost them their jobs (they

aren't). Sanctioneers ask them whether they will back sanctions which will end apartheid (they do). Both questions are loaded . . .[15]

POLITICAL DEVELOPMENTS AND BUSINESS PRESSURE

Political unrest continued at high levels throughout South Africa during 1985 and into 1986. As estimated 1 million black students were participating in the school boycott. Rent strikes were attracting wide support, especially since the South African government had decided that local township councils should become self-supporting, leading to an increase in rents and payments for various services. The industrial sector was hard hit by labor unrest. There were 469 strikes during 1984. The beginning of 1985 brought new strikes at about twice that rate. Loosely organized community groups, workers' groups, and student groups in the black townships were confronting security forces on a continuous basis. For many years, outdoor gatherings had been banned in South Africa. This ban was now extended to any meeting, indoors or outdoors, where criticism of the government was aired. The Minister of Law and Order described the ban as applying to "all gatherings held where any government or any principle or any policy principle or any actions of the government, or any statement, or the application or implementation of any act is approved, defended, attacked, criticized or discussed, or which is in protest against or support or in memoriam of anything.[16]

In August 1985 major international banks, led by Chase Manhattan and other U.S. institutions, refused to roll over short-term loans to the private sector in South Africa. Almost two-thirds of South Africa's foreign debt, now amounting to more than $20 billion, was affected. The exchange rate of the rand dropped to an all-time low. The government was left with little choice but to suspend payments. With this set of circumstances, virtually no new foreign capital came into South Africa. Capital investments and modernizing of existing manufacturing plants, mining facilities, and other operations were generally halted. The economy was poised on the brink of a severe contraction.

In August, 1985, South Africa's state president, P.W. Botha, reaffirmed the government's commitment to maintaining apartheid. "I am not prepared to lead white South Africans and other minority groups on a road to abdication and suicide . . . . Destroy white South Africa and our influence and this country will drift into factions, strife, chaos, and poverty."[17]

The message was clear that an end to apartheid was neither anticipated nor desired by those who ruled the country.

Later that fall, 91 South African business leaders issued a statement saying,

> There is a better way. As responsible businessmen committed to South Africa and the welfare of all its people, we are deeply concerned about the current situation. We believe that the reform process should be accelerated by:
>
> • Abolishing statutory race discrimination wherever it exists;
> • Negotiating with acknowledged black leaders about power sharing;
> • Granting full South African citizenship to all our peoples;
> • Restoring and entrenching the rule of law.

We reject violence as a means of achieving change and we support the politics of negotiation. We believe that there is a better way for South Africa and we support equal opportunity, respect for the individual, freedom of enterprise and freedom of movement.

> We believe in the development of the South African economy and the benefit of all of its people and we are, therefore, committed to pursue a role of corporate social responsibility and to play our part in transforming the structures and systems of the country toward fair participation for all.[18]

Signers of the statement were mainly CEOs of South African companies, although some South African subsidiaries of U.S. and European companies were represented. In the U.S., 44 CEOs of multinationals endorsed the statement, running full-page advertisements in the *Wall Street Journal,* as well as in South African newspapers, to publicize their stand. In the U.S., and in most countries with a market economy, this line-up of business leaders would have been regarded as having a formidable influence on government policy. But not so in South Africa. Indeed, the national government seemed almost to become even more determined to handle the demand for reform in its own way and at its own pace.

In the face of this intransigence, a small group of South African business leaders determined to reach out to the banned African National Congress (ANC). So as to establish their own communications with the ANC in September 1985, a delegation of businessmen and journalists flew to Lusaka, Zambia, to meet with ANC leaders, reportedly infuriating State President Botha. The position of the South African government was that the ANC stood for the violent overthrow of the existing government and its replacement by a regime that would embody the worst totalitarian features of Soviet Communism and thereby destroy South Africa's economy.

PRESSURES ON U.S. COMPANIES

American companies were facing considerable pressure from various constituencies in their home country to play a more active role in pressing for social and political change in South Africa. Reverend Sullivan announced in early 1985 that if apartheid were not abolished by May of 1987, he would call upon U.S. companies to withdraw from South Africa.

One issue confronting U.S. corporations was how they could effectively challenge the government of a host country. In most situations, the posture of U.S. companies was to respect and to conform with the laws of the nation where subsidiary operations were located. However, in this case, they had historically skirted the edge of legality, not obeying all apartheid laws, at least in the workplace. They were now being called upon to do more, i.e., to go farther in defying the law.

The divestment movement was picking up steam. Colleges and universities, labor unions, church groups, and a number of pension funds were joining the act. Resolutions to rid portfolios of holdings in companies with holdings in South Africa would not in themselves depress stock prices—after all, if ready buyers came along at the going price, divestment would have no impact on stock price. However, it was one more consideration for managers of U.S. companies. A number of cities and states had adopted resolutions putting restrictions on purchasing from companies with operations in South Africa. This could be a significant economic blow to cities and states that buy a wide range of products—copiers, fleets of vehicles, computers, software, swimming pool chemicals, generators, and food products, to name a few.

The Models of Divestiture: The Case of General Motors Corporation

On October 21, 1986, the front page of the *New York Times* carried this headline: "G.M. Plans to Sell South Africa Unit to a Local Group." Roger B. Smith, chairman of the board, issued this statement:

> There were several factors behind this decision, but our main objective was to create a financially sound organization which will have a greater chance for long-term viability and will continue to be a positive force in the ending of apartheid.
> G.M.S.A. (General Motors South Africa-ed.) has been losing money for several years

in a very difficult South African business climate and, with the current structure, we could not see our operations turning around in the near future.[19]

Although a number of American companies had been withdrawing from South Africa or gradually reducing their investment there, this withdrawal was the largest yet. The reverberations of this announcement would soon fulfill the worst fears of the South African government. U.S. companies, under continuing pressure from activists at home protesting apartheid, were beginning to pull out in droves. Apartheid is the practice of requiring individuals to be registered as White, Black, Coloured, or Asian. Racial classification determines where one may live, go to school, get medical attention, and enjoy recreational facilities and is embodied in the laws and institutions of South Africa. Smith went on to allude to other reasons for withdrawal and expressed his disappointment at the relative lack of progress in dismantling apartheid and solving South Africa's continuing political problems:

> We have been disappointed in the pace of change in ending apartheid. Decisions about our investment in South Africa have depended on an assessment of the economic, social and political environment in that area.
> We had hoped conditions would permit a continued presence there. We have worked hard to maintain a solid business, provide equal economic opportunity and a better quality of life, and also to help move South Africa away from apartheid and toward a society open to all South Africans. In short, we feel our presence there has been a force for constructive change.[20]

He blamed the imposition of sanctions on "the slowness of ending apartheid" and referred to "the ongoing recession in that country," concluding that "the interests of our employees and dealers in South Africa and our own stockholders are better served by local ownership and control."[21]

Smith made no mention of any of the moral arguments that GM and other companies had asserted previously in defense of their determination to stay in South Africa. The basis of the Sullivan Principles, of which GM was a charter signer, was rooted in the conviction that it was morally justifiable to continue operating in South Africa because companies were doing good by staying there. Nor did the press release make any reference to the continuous pressure that social critics in the U.S. had exerted for the past fifteen years to force GM to cease South African operations. Nevertheless, social activists welcomed the announcement that the U.S. company with the second-largest investment in South Africa (Mobil Oil had the largest) had decided to withdraw. "This is a tremendously significant decision," said Timothy Smith, director of the Interfaith Center on Corporate Responsibility. "Business will understand the symbolism of the action, and we expect to see the trickle of companies leaving to turn into a flood."[22]

During 1984 and 1985, 4 and 40 U.S. companies, respectively, had withdrawn from South Africa. The trickle did indeed turn into a flood, with 50 companies leaving in 1986 and 53 in 1987.[23] However, many of the companies retained licensing, franchise, or distribution agreements in South Africa. Although GM, Ford, Xerox, IBM, and Coca Cola had formally withdrawn from South Africa, their products remained available in the South African market. Eastman Kodak was the only U.S. corporation to announce that it was halting sales of its products in South Africa. However, even in this case, middlemen continued to distribute most of the company's film and camera products.

The impact of the withdrawals on the South African economy was not immediately apparent, but would surely be long term and indirect rather than immediate and dramatic. Locally owned companies continued to do business much as they had under U.S. ownership, although in time they might come to be at a disadvantage due to reduced access to technology, international markets, or international lending. Social activists in the U.S., and to some extent in other countries, had been campaigning for multinational corporations to withdraw from South Africa in order to pressure the country to change its practice of apartheid. Yet even after so many corporate withdrawals, the South African government showed little inclination to make the one essential change desired by social activists—to give South African blacks the right of political participation. Indeed, political repression in South Africa grew increasingly severe during the period from 1984 to 1988 when economic sanctions were being applied by the U.S. and multinationals were withdrawing.

THE BEGINNING OF THE END

In June 1987, Reverend Sullivan created further pressure on companies to withdraw. He followed through on the threat he had made two years earlier when he had said that if apartheid had not been dismantled by May of 1987, he would call for U.S. corporations to leave South Africa. Ironically, although Rev. Sullivan dissociated himself from the monitoring process, the Sullivan Principles were now institutionalized in the Comprehensive Anti-Apartheid Bill. This legislation required U.S. companies remaining in South Africa to be monitored either through the Sullivan Principles or by the U.S. Department of State, which developed a similar set of guidelines. A number of the purchasing restrictions adopted by states and municipalities, as well as the portfolio divestment resolutions, specified that companies would be given preferential treatment if they scored acceptably on the Sullivan Principles.

The Signatory Association, now reduced in numbers, had to devise a new way of managing their social responsibility programs and of reporting their ratings to the public. For the next year, the companies agreed to work with what had been called the "Sullivan Principles," but now were known as the "Signatory Principles." Arthur D. Little, Inc., agreed to continue to perform the monitoring function. However, the task forces that the Sullivan Companies had formed in South Africa to work on various aspects of the principles ceased to function. The number of companies working in the Signatory Association was greatly reduced, and many companies were reexamining the extent of their support for the projects previously supported. Some companies even looked at the possibility of opting for State Department monitoring, since this would reduce costs, and the demands being made under this system were considerably less than the demands that had been made in recent years under the Sullivan system.

Epilogue

On the heels of Mandela's ascension to power in South Africa, an initial euphoria boosted the country's economy, bringing with it a renewed interest on the part of foreign investors. President Mandela's, and his cabinet's, efforts to attract and sustain such investment have been difficult, however, due to problems endemic to the South African economy (Appendix C). Economic relief is thwarted by the realities of a long-term secular decline on most measures of economic activity that has plagued South Africa for more than three decades. The latest recession which lasted until 1993, was the steepest in that country's history. The effect of this decline was even more profound and potentially devastating when figures for Gross Domestic Product (GDP) are adjusted for population growth. Between 1981 and 1993, living standards declined by almost 19%. Clearly, a great many reasons for this decline could be attributed to the effects of apartheid and the government's monetary and fiscal policies during that period. Nonetheless, the mere fact of transition to a democratic government is unlikely to change these conditions in the foreseeable future. They relate to factor productivity, government expendi-

tures, savings and investments, and employment, to name a few.

The aforementioned discussion brings us to the important role that foreign investments, and especially the American investments, will need to play in South Africa's economy. A history of operations under the Sullivan Principles has already established a floor of "social expectations," which is breached only at a serious peril to our future credibility. With regard to the Signatory Principles that grew out of the former Sullivan Principles, the Signatory Association met early in 1995 and agreed to dissolve. American corporations will now need to demonstrate a higher level of proactive performance in creating increased opportunities for black-owned businesses, participation in training and skill development of blacks, and, accelerated integration of blacks into the ranks of professional and managerial cadres within their organizations. Furthermore, a continuance of such proactivity will give the American companies a competitive advantage and will also afford them with an opportunity for leadership in good corporate citizenship.

At a superficial level, both the U.S. government and U.S. companies have responded with enthusiasm to President Mandela's call for more foreign investments. Various agencies of the U.S. government have announced grants-in-aid, loans, and technical assistance to South Africa. The number of U.S. companies with employees or investments in South Africa has grown by 20% since Mandela's September 1993 plea for an end to international economic sanctions against his country, following an earlier surge of reinvestment by U.S. firms in South Africa on the heels of former President Bush's lifting of U.S. sanctions in July of 1991. As of October 1994, U.S. companies demonstrated confidence in South Africa to the tune of a 58% increase in their presence in that country since the ban was lifted.

Unfortunately, the rhetoric far exceeds the reality of action. A great many announcements of new investments, however, are just that—announcements—with companies adopting a wait-and-see attitude, and merely establishing a token presence through opening a sales or a representative office. Despite a plethora of press releases, evidence of substantive new investments is scarce. This should not come as a surprise to anyone who understands the nature of risk involved in such decisions. However, it does not make it any easier for the people of South Africa who are anxiously waiting for the Americans to follow through with their strong support for the abolition of apartheid to concrete efforts in building a new South Africa.[24]

An interesting new development has been in the area of social investing in South Africa and, mobilized by the black trade unions, mainly in the mining industry. They had substantial pension funds accumulating and wanted to direct investments into equities of companies traded on the Johannesburg Stock Exchange that exemplified social responsibility, and so formed the Community Growth Fund. This monitoring system used the following weights: job creation (14), industrial relations (14), conditions of employment (13), training (7), equal opportunities for women (7), health and safety (6), product (5), opposition to privatization (5), practicing profit retention rather than reinvesting profits (5), affirmative action (5), location of jobs within South Africa (4), environment (4), worker participation (4), disclosure (4), political profile (2), social spending (1). Racial discrimination was used as a further test of every other dimension. In other words, a company was screened for each of the aforementioned dimensions, then screened again to see if the dimension stood up to the racial discrimination test. For example, in the case of job creation, was it occurring for all racial groups, or was job creation limited to those jobs where only whites are employed? In the first year of active screening, twenty of the first thirty companies are monitored continuously. The main elements of the rating scheme focus on the workplace, specifically whether or not the company is creating jobs, and its industrial relations practices, including the conditions of employment and wages paid.

APPENDIX A: Summary of the Comprehensive Anti-Apartheid Act of 1986* (H.R. 4868)

MAJOR SANCTIONS

Scope

All provisions of the bill apply to South Africa (including the homelands) and Namibia.

Landing Rights

Requires an immediate termination of landing rights for South African aircraft and prohibits U.S. civil aircraft from flying to South Africa.

New Investments

Prohibits any new investment in South Africa, except for investments in black-owned firms. This includes bank loans to the private sector. The term new investment does not include expenses incurred by U.S. companies to comply with the Sullivan-related fair labor standards. The prohibition does not apply to:

1. short-term trade financing (e.g., letters of credit)
2. most rescheduling of existing loans
3. reinvestments of profits
4. transfers of funds necessary to maintain operations in an economically sound manner without expanding operations.

Government Loans

Prohibits all loans to the South African Government (including parastatals), with an exception for certain loans for educational, housing, or humanitarian purposes.

Prohibition of Imports

Prohibits the import of any item produced, grown, manufactured, marketed, or exported by SAG parastatals (i.e., organizations owned, controlled, or subsidized by the SAG).

Krugerrand Imports

Prohibits the import of Krugerrands and other gold coins minted in South Africa as well as Soviet gold coins.

Imports Generally

Prohibits the import of South African (1) uranium ore; (2) uranium oxide; (3) coal; and (4) textiles. These import prohibitions enter into effect 90 days after enactment. The bill also prohibits the import of (5) agricultural commodities and their derivatives and any product suitable for human consumption; (6) iron; and (7) steel.

---

*Adapted from Pauline H. Baker, *The United States and South Africa: The Reagan Years*, (New York: Ford Foundation and the Foreign Policy Association, 1989), pp. 138–145.

In addition to the broad ban on agricultural products, the bill contains a specific prohibition on the import of South African sugar, syrups, and molasses, effective on the date of enactment. The bill also increases the Philippines' quota for such products by an amount corresponding to the South African amount.

Defense Imports

Prohibits the import of defense articles and data produced in South Africa.

Double Taxation

Requires the termination of the bilateral tax treaty and the related protocol in force with South Africa. The relevant provision does not terminate the provisions in the U.S. Code conferring certain double taxation credit/deductions benefits to U.S. firms/nationals regardless of tax treaties.

Government Procurement

Prohibits U.S. government procurement from parastatals except for items necessary for diplomatic or consular purposes.

Bank Accounts

Prohibits the SAG and its parastatals from having bank accounts in the United States, with the exception of those authorized by the U.S. government for diplomatic and consular purposes.

USG Assistance for Trade

Prohibits the use of U.S. government funds for the promotion of tourism in South Africa.

Computer Exports

Prohibits the export of computers and related goods and services to the police, military, and apartheid-enforcing entities.

Nuclear Exports/Trade

Prohibits most nuclear exports/trade involving South Africa (with narrow exceptions for IAEA and for humanitarian/health purposes).

Munitions Exports

Prohibits the export of any item on the U.S. Munitions List (part of the International Traffic in Arms Regulations (ITAR) of the Department of State to South Africa). This provision codifies existing executive branch policy. The current statutory procedures relating to the president's certification of certain ITAR exports and congressional disapproval of individual exports are made applicable to such South Africa exports.

Oil Exports

Prohibits exports of crude oil and petroleum products to South Africa (with an exception for existing contracts).

Agricultural Exports

The bill permits South Africa to participate in Department of Agriculture export credit and promotion programs. This could include credit- and loan-guarantee programs and the export enhancement program recently used with respect to the USSR.

Fair Labor Standards

Requires U.S. nationals employing at least 25 individuals in South Africa to apply certain fair labor standards based on the Sullivan principles. The penalty for failure to implement the principles is a loss of U.S. government export marketing support. The U.S. Embassy and Consulates in South Africa are also required to implement the principles, except that the bill makes it clear that the applicable provision does not confer a right to engage in strikes against the U.S. government.

Unfair Trade Practices

The bill authorizes the president to limit the import into the United States of any products of any foreign country to the extent that the country concerned benefits from, or otherwise takes commercial advantage of, the sanctions contained in the bill.

International Negotiations

The bill requires negotiations with other countries within 180 days on international arrangements to end apartheid. It provides that the secretary of state should convene an international conference to reach agreements and impose multilateral sanctions (as well as certain reporting requirements). Presidential modifications of the bill as a result of such agreements will require congressional approval by joint resolution.

UN Mandatory Sanctions

The bill expresses the sense of the U.S. Congress that the president should seek mandatory Chapter VII Security Council sanctions against South Africa of the kind contained in the bill.

Waivers/Communist Countries

The bill provides that the president may lift any prohibition in the bill if it would increase U.S. dependence upon any member country or observer country of the Council for Mutual Economic Assistance (i.e., the economic entity related to the Warsaw Pact) for the import of (1) coal, or (2) any strategic material, or (3) any critical material. Criteria are established for this purpose.

Military Cooperation

The bill prohibits any agency or entity of the U.S. government from engaging in any form of cooperation with the armed forces of South Africa, except activities reasonably designed to facilitate the collection of necessary intelligence.

Future Sanctions

Requires the president to make a report to Congress 12 months after enactment on progress in South Africa. If he determines that the conditions specified have not been met, the bill requires that the president must recommend which additional measures should be adopted (from a list of potential sanctions).

POSITIVE MEASURES

Scholarships/Assistance

Authorizes assistance for scholarships to the victims of apartheid and assistance generally for disadvantaged South Africans. For example, one provision provides that up to $40 million in economic support funds may be used in FY87 and each year thereafter for assistance in South Africa.

Legal Assistance/Human Rights Fund

Earmarks specific amounts of the Human Rights Fund for South Africa for specified purposes ($500,000 per fiscal year for legal assistance to political prisoners and detainees, and $175,000 for families of the victims of those necklaced).

Export-Import Bank

Requires EXIM to take active steps to encourage the use of its facilities to assist black South African business enterprises and relaxes certain current statutory restrictions on EXIM activities in South Africa.

Housing

Authorizes $10 million for the purchase of housing for black South Africa nationals employed by the U.S. government in South Africa. The housing is to be located in areas open to all population groups.

USG Procurement

Provides that the U.S. Embassy and Consulate in South Africa shall make affirmative efforts to purchase goods and services from the victims of apartheid notwithstanding normal competition in contracting laws.

REPORTING REQUIREMENTS

The Act contains numerous reporting requirements, including reports relating to the following:

Role/activities of the Communist Party in South Africa; Countries violating the Mandatory UN Arms embargo; Health conditions in the homelands; Effect of Sanctions on Front Line States; Bank deposits of South Africans in the U.S.; South African Imports/Strategic minerals; CEMA (Warsaw pact-related) imports; African National Congress compliance with the Foreign Agents Registration Act; and, strategy for assisting disadvantaged South Africans over the next 5 years.

POLICY STATEMENTS

The Senate bill contains numerous policy statements, including praise for U.S. firms that have remained to work in South Africa; the need for negotiations in South Africa and to have all foreign forces removed from the region; and the need for international cooperation and coordination on measures related to South Africa. Other examples including the following.

African National Congress

The bill provides that U.S. policy towards the African National Congress (ANC) shall be designed to bring about a suspension of violence that will lead to the start of negotiations designed to bring about a nonracial and genuine democracy in South Africa. The United States is to encourage the ANC to: (1) suspend terrorist activities; (2) make known its commitment to a free and democratic postapartheid South Africa; (3) agree to enter negotiations; and (4) reexamine its ties to the South African Communist party. It also provides that U.S. policy towards South Africa will be adjusted based on certain actions of both the SAG and the ANC. It provides that it shall be the policy of the U.S. to support negotiations without conditions and abandons unprovoked violence and commits itself to a free and democratic postapartheid South Africa, and if the ANC (1) refuses to participate in negotiations or (2) if the ANC refuses to abandon unprovoked violence during such negotiations and refuses to commit itself to a free and democratic postapartheid South Africa.

Mandela Meeting

The bill expresses the sense of the Congress that the U.S. Ambassador to South Africa should meet with Nelson Mandela.

ENFORCEMENT

Severe criminal and civil penalties are provided for violations of bill and broad regulatory powers are conferred on the president.

TERMINATION

The bill provides that the sanctions contained in the bill shall terminate automatically if the SAG meets five conditions specified in the bill. These conditions related to (1) the release of Nelson Mandela and all political prisoners; (2) the repeal of the state of emergency and all detainees; (3) the unbanning of political parties; (4) the repeal of the Group Area and Population Registration Acts; and (5) agreeing to enter into good-faith negotiations with truly representative members of the black majority without preconditions.

APPENDIX B The Statement of Principles for South Africa
(formerly the Sullivan Principles)

PRINCIPLE I: NONSEGREGATION OF THE RACES IN ALL EATING, COMFORT, AND WORK FACILITIES.

Each signator of the Statement of Principles will proceed immediately to:

- Eliminate all vestiges of racial discrimination.
- Remove all race designation signs.
- Desegregate all eating, comfort, and work facilities.

PRINCIPLE II: EQUAL AND FAIR EMPLOYMENT PRACTICES FOR ALL EMPLOYEES.

Each signator of the Statement of Principles will proceed immediately to:

- Implement equal and fair terms and conditions of employment.
- Provide nondiscriminatory eligibility for benefit plans.
- Establish an appropriate and comprehensive procedure for handling and resolving individual employee complaints.
- Support the elimination of all industrial racial discriminatory laws which impede the implementation of equal and fair terms and conditions of employment, such as abolition of job reservations, job fragmentation, and apprenticeship restrictions for blacks and other nonwhites.
    - Support the elimination of discrimination against the rights of blacks to form or belong to government registered and unregistered unions and acknowledge generally the rights of blacks to form their own unions or be represented by trade unions which already exist.
    - Secure rights of black workers to the freedom of association and assure protection against victimization while pursuing and after attaining these rights.
    - Involve black workers or their representatives in the development of programs that address their educational and other needs and those of their dependents and the local community.

PRINCIPLE III: EQUAL PAY FOR ALL EMPLOYEES DOING EQUAL OR COMPARABLE WORK FOR THE SAME PERIOD OF TIME.

Each signator of the Statement of Principles will proceed immediately to:

- Design and implement a wage and salary administration plan which is applied equally to all employees, regardless of race, who are performing equal or comparable work.
    - Ensure an equitable system of job classifications, including a review of the distinction between hourly and salaried classifications.
    - Determine the extent to which upgrading of personnel and/or jobs in the upper echelons is needed, and accordingly implement programs to accomplish this objective in representative numbers, ensuring the employment of blacks and other nonwhites at all levels of company operations.

- Assign equitable wage and salary ranges, the minimum of these to be well above the appropriate local minimum economic living level.

PRINCIPLE IV: INITIATION AND DEVELOPMENT OF TRAINING PROGRAMS THAT WILL PREPARE, IN SUBSTANTIAL NUMBERS, BLACKS AND OTHER NONWHITES FOR SUPERVISORY, ADMINISTRATIVE, CLERICAL, AND TECHNICAL JOBS.

Each signator of the Statement of Principles will proceed immediately to:

- Determine employee training needs and capabilities, and identify employees with potential for further advancement.
- Take advantage of existing outside training resources and activities, such as exchange programs, technical colleges, and similar institutions or programs.
- Support the development of outside training facilities, individually or collectively—including technical centers, professional training exposure, correspondence and extension courses, as appropriate, for extensive training outreach.
- Initiate and expand inside training programs and facilities.

PRINCIPLE V: INCREASING THE NUMBER OF BLACKS AND OTHER NONWHITES IN MANAGEMENT AND SUPERVISORY POSITIONS.

Each signator of the Statement of Principles will proceed immediately to:

- Identify, actively recruit, train and develop a sufficient and significant number of blacks and other nonwhites to assure that as quickly as possible there will be appropriate representation of blacks and other nonwhites in the management group of each company at all levels of operations.
- Establish management development programs for blacks and nonwhites, as needed, and improve existing programs and facilities for developing management skills of blacks and other nonwhites.
- Identify and channel high management potential blacks and other nonwhite employees into management development programs.

PRINCIPLE VI: IMPROVING THE QUALITY OF EMPLOYEES' LIVES OUTSIDE THE WORK ENVIRONMENT IN SUCH AREAS AS HOUSING, TRANSPORTATION, SCHOOLING, RECREATION, AND HEALTH FACILITIES.

Each signator of the Statement of Principles will proceed immediately to:

- Evaluate existing and/or develop programs, as appropriate, to address the specific needs of black and other nonwhite employees in the areas of housing, health care, transportation, and recreation.
- Evaluate methods for utilizing existing, expanded or newly established in-house medical facilities or other medical programs to improve medical care for all non-whites and their dependents.

- Participate in the development of programs that address the educational needs of employees, their dependents, and the local community. Both individual and collective programs should be considered, in addition to technical education, including such activities as literacy education, business training, direct assistance to local schools, contributions, and scholarships.
- Support changes in influx control laws to provide for the right of black migrant workers to normal family life.
- Increase utilization of and assist in the development of black and other non-white owned and operated business enterprises including distributors, suppliers of goods and services, and manufacturers.

PRINCIPLE VII: WORKING TO ELIMINATE LAWS AND CUSTOMS WHICH IMPEDE SOCIAL, ECONOMIC, AND POLITICAL JUSTICE. (THIS WAS ORIGINALLY KNOWN AS THE "FOURTH AMPLIFICATION.")

Each signator of the Statement of Principles must proceed immediately to:

- Press for a single education system common to all races.
- Use influence and support the unrestricted rights of black businesses to locate in the urban areas of the nation.
- Influence other companies in South Africa to follow the standards of equal rights principles.
- Support the freedom of mobility of black workers, including those from so-called independent homelands, to seek employment opportunities wherever they exist, and make possible provisions for adequate housing for families of employees within the proximity of workers' employment.
- Use financial and legal resources to assist blacks, coloreds and Asians in their efforts to achieve equal access to all health facilities, educational institutions, transportation, housing, beaches, parks and all other accommodations normally reserved for whites.
- Oppose adherence to all apartheid laws and regulations.
- Support the ending of all apartheid laws, practices, and customs.
- Support full and equal participation of blacks, coloreds and Asians in the political process.

With all the foregoing in mind, it is the objective of the companies to involve and assist in the education and training of large and telling numbers of blacks and other nonwhites as quickly as possible. The ultimate impact of this effort is intended to be of massive proportion, reaching and helping millions.

PERIODIC REPORTING

The Signatory Companies of the Statement of Principles will proceed immediately to:

- Report progress on an annual basis to the independent administrative unit Reverend Sullivan established.
- Have all areas specified by Reverend Sullivan audited by a certified public accounting firm.
- Inform all employees of the company's annual periodic report rating and invite their input on ways to improve the rating.

APPENDIX C American Corporations and the Economic Future of South Africa *

South Africa, a vast and resource-rich nation of over 40 million people, offers a vastly complex, and potentially rich landscape for growth and development with excellent long-term opportunities for direct foreign investment. The country has achieved a miraculously peaceful transition to a nonracial majority rule. The political leadership is stable, intent on consensus building, and has staked its political future on economic growth through private enterprise and competitive markets.

On the surface, South Africa seems to have all the ingredients of the beginning of a successful economic transformation. It has excellent infrastructure, functioning civil service and governmental administrative structures, ample raw materials and other physical resources, a vibrant private sector, and a large and growing domestic market. It is also strategically situated to become a nerve center for the economies of surrounding countries in southern Africa. The country has adopted a conservative fiscal and monetary agenda with a promise to curtail government spending, public debt, and government bureaucracy and regulation. Even in the area of providing a minimal social safety net to the vast majority of poor people, the government has emphasized building the infrastructure—through its Reconstruction and Development Program (RDP)—which would simultaneously create jobs and uplift the economy, rather than put primary emphasis on welfare, subsidies, and income transfers. There are, however, a number of fundamental structural weaknesses that are embedded in South Africa's economic fabric, raising serious concerns about its near- and long-term prospects.

South Africa's economy has witnessed a secular decline in overall employment, worker productivity, and wage levels. The employment decline in the private sector has been even more precipitous than the rate of decline in overall employment and employment in the public sector. Labor output declined by 20% between 1980–91, while the growth in employee earnings remained essentially stagnant. This problem is further compounded by the low productivity of investment. The highly protected and regulated economy of South Africa, encumbered with high tariff barriers and exchange controls, invested heavily in domestic sectors and yet received little, if any, benefits from those investments. During the past 20 years, South Africa's manufacturing sector has suffered from low and often negative productivity marked with massive capital investment and accompanied by sluggish employment and output growth. The situation in mining, one of South Africa's premier industries, is equally discouraging. Despite stagnation since the early 1970s, the growth of capital stock increased rapidly between 1970–1980 averaging 6.6% a year while output declined by 1% per year. Similar trends continued during the 1980s. In agriculture, white-owned commercial farms are highly capital intensive—the capital/output ratio in agriculture has been as high as three times that of manufacturing. While agricultural productivity is quite high when compared with the rest of Africa, it compares quite unfavorably with the rest of the world both in absolute terms and in terms of capital/output ratios.

The good news is that the economy is growing again. GDP rose by 2.3% in 1994, leaving the average South African better off for the first time since 1988. Inflation saw its lowest dip in 22 years, at 9%. These good tidings need to be considered, however, in the context of South Africa's debt picture, which shows foreign debt at a modest 15% of total GDP,

---

*Adapted from S. Prakash Sethi, "American Corporations and the Economic Future of South Africa." *Business and Society Review* (Winter, 1995), pp. 10–18.

but public-sector debt accounting for 55% of GDP, accompanied by a growing budget deficit.

THE HORNS OF THE REAL DILEMMA

No process of economic growth, however, is likely to succeed, or even be acceptable to the vast majority of South Africa's people, unless it takes cognizance of: (a) current disparities in the income and wealth among whites and blacks; and, (b) the gap between the two groups in terms of their control of income-producing assets characterized by the ability of the two groups to influence the direction of South Africa's economy in terms of its orientation, sectoral emphasis, and thereby distribution of income, creations of savings, and future wealth creation, i.e., Black Economic Empowerment.

In an open economy, and under ordinary conditions, this process is benign and evolves out of the working of markets where incomes flow to various stakeholders in proportion to their contribution to economic output. However, South Africa's economy is neither open nor competitive as far as blacks are concerned. For example, six industrial groups control over 85% of the value of shares listed on the Johannesburg Stock Exchange—with Anglo-American alone accounting for over 52% of the share capital. It is not a competitive economy when 5% of all firms control over 63% of a nation's sales turnover. For all intents and purposes, the system is closed to outsiders. When we look at what the system does, rather than what it says, it should be obvious to everyone that blacks are still the outsiders as far as the system is concerned.

At one level, South Africa's blacks can look at the future with a great deal of optimism. At the aggregate level, some indicators of blacks' economic health look promising. For example, in the area of personal income, in 1985, whites accounted for 55.5% of personal disposable income while blacks accounted for 31.8%. According to UNISA estimates, by the year 2000, whites' share of disposable income is expected to decline to 42.5% while that of blacks is expected to increase to 40.7%. Blacks currently account for over 40% of all retail purchases, a figure that is likely to increase to 50% or higher by the year 2000. These numbers are interesting but they do not even begin to address the serious deficiencies that persist. An overwhelming majority of blacks earn wages and live under conditions that are barely above the poverty level. This leaves them with little discretionary income for saving or investment in human capital, i.e., education and skills development. Unemployment rates among blacks average over 25-30% while those among black youths could be as high as 50%. These are the highest rates among all groups and affect those who can least afford it.

Regardless of all the progress made by the blacks in small business, this effort alone will not be enough to pull them out of poverty or enable them to compete with white-owned businesses. The informal sector and small business are highly desirable, but they are not a panacea. Estimates show that black business accounts for less than 2% of the nation's GDP, and it still would not amount to much even if it were to increase to 3 or 4%.

Nor are blacks doing well in the area of professional- and managerial-level employment in the formal economic sector. They are grossly underrepresented in the managerial and professional ranks even given the very low percentage rate of blacks graduating from professional and technical institutions. Current estimates suggest that there are fewer than 250,000 blacks employed in the professional, administrative, and technical capacities where they occupy mostly the lower ranks of occupational ladders. In the largest 100 South African companies, 97.5% of managers are white, and 92.5% are men. Furthermore, according to a recent study by the International Monetary Fund, a large part of the increase in the income share of the black work force in South Africa has come about through a narrowing of the wage differential between whites and Non-whites in similar job categories and *not* by increasing the number of Blacks in higher-paying, more skilled categories.

The new South Africa will have to compete with other parts of the world for its share of direct foreign investments. South Africa needs these investments not only to expand its domestic economy, but even more importantly, to create a large export sector for labor-intensive industries. However, the competition for these investments is quite intense and the progress is likely to be painstaking and slow. The paramount question for the new South Africa government is whether it can create a stable political fiscal and monetary environment while maintaining a competitive economy on the one hand; and, on the other hand, contain the explosion of rising expectations while providing the beginning of a social safety net to alleviate the misery of abject poverty to which a large majority of people have been subjected during the apartheid era.

NOTES

1. Merle Lipton, *Capitalism and Apartheid.* Claremont, Cape Province, South Africa: David Philip, 1986.
2. Merle Lipton, *Sanctions and South Africa.* London: The Economist Intelligence Unit, 1988, p. 40.
3. *S.A. Barometer,* vol. 1 no. 2. March 27, 1987, p. 19.
4. According to the U.S. Department of State, there were 29 U.S. companies in South Africa remaining outside the Sullivan program at the end of 1986.
5. Of the remaining companies, 8 withdrew from the program, 2 were dropped for non-payment of dues, and in a merger Burroughs and Sperry became a single company, Unisys.
6. Elizabeth Schmidt, *One Step in the Wrong Direction: An Analysis of the Sullivan Principles as a Strategy for Opposing Apartheid.* New York: Episcopal Church People for a Free South Africa, 1985.
7. David Beaty and Oren Harari, "Divestment and Disinvestment from South Africa: A Reappraisal." *California Management Review,* 29 (Summer, 1987), pp. 31-50.
8. Karen Paul, "The Inadequacy of Sullivan Reporting." *Business and Society Review,* 57 (Spring, 1986), pp. 61-65.
9. Elizabeth Schmidt, "Marching to Pretoria: Reagan's South Africa Policy on the Move." *TransAfrica Forum,* 2, no. 2, 1983, pp. 1-12.
10. J.P. Hayes, *Economic Effects of Sanctions on Southern Africa.* London: Trade Policy Research Centre, 1987.
11. Merle Lipton, *Sanctions and South Africa.* London: The Economist Intelligence Unit, 1988, p. 42.
12. Jack Brian Bloom, *Black South Africa and the Disinvestment Dilemma.* Johannesburg: Jonathan Ball Publishers, 1986, p. 86.
13. "A New Political Force." *Financial Mail,* December 6, 1985.
14. Helen Suzman, "The Folly of Economic Sanctions." *Business and Society Review,* no. 57 (Spring, 1986), p. 87.
15. Steven Friedman, "What the Figures Say Is Not What They Mean." *The South African Foundation News,* Dec., 1987.
16. Martin Murray, *South Africa: Time of Agony, Time of Destiny.* London: Verson, 1987, p. 250.
17. "South African National Union of Mine Workers Threatens Boycott." *New York Times,* Aug. 15, 1985.
18. Advertisement, "There Is a Better Way," *Wall Street Journal,* October 18, 1986.
19. "G.M. Statement on Sale." *New York Times,* Oct. 21, 1986.
20. *Ibid.*
21. *Ibid.*

22. "G.M. Plans to Sell South Africa Unit to a Local Group." *New York Times*, October 21, 1986.
23. Data from Investor Responsibility Research Center, Washington, DC.

24. S. Prakash Sethi, "American Corporations and the Economic Future of South Africa." *Business and Society Review* (Winter 1995), pp. 10-18.

REFERENCES

Adam, Heribert. "Options for Transforming South Africa." *Journal of International Affairs* 40 2, (1987), pp 287-302.

Adam, Heribert and Kogila Moodley. *The Opening of the Apartheid Mind: Options for the New South Africa.* Berkeley: University of California Press, 1993.

Baker, Pauline, *The United States and South Africa: The Reagan Years.* New York: Ford Foundation and the Foreign Policy Association (1989).

Baker, Pauline, et al., eds. *South Africa and the World Economy in the 1990s.* Washington, DC: Brookings Institution, 1993.

Berger, Peter L., and Bobby Godsell, eds. *A Future South Africa: Visions, Strategies and Realities.* Boulder, Co: Westview Press, 1988.

Borstelmann, Thomas. *Apartheid's Reluctant Uncle: the United States and Southern Africa in the Early Cold War.* New York: Oxford University Press, 1993.

Christopher, A.J. *The Atlas of Apartheid.* New York: Routledge, 1994.

Cole, Ken, ed. *Sustainable Development for a Democratic South Africa,* New York: St. Martin's Press, 1994.

Cooper, Alison, and Micheline Tusenius. *International Investment in South Africa.* Washington, DC: Investor Responsibility Research Center, 1987.

Economist. "A Giant for Africa." May 20, 1995, pp. 9-14.

Hauck, David. *Can Pretoria Be Moved?* Washington, DC: Investor Responsibility Research Center, 1986.

Investor Responsibility Research Center, Inc. *South African Review Service* (various issues). Washington, DC: 1319 F Street, N.W., Suite 900, Washington, D.C. 20004.

Lapping, Brian. *Apartheid: A History.* New York: George Braziller, Inc., 1987.

Leape, Jonathan, Bo Baskin, and Stefan Underhill. *Business in the Shadow of Apartheid: U.S. Firms in South Africa.* Lexington, MA: Lexington Books, 1985.

Lipton, Merle. *Sanctions and South Africa: The Dynamics of Economic Isolation.* London: The Economist Intelligence Unit Special Report #1119, 1988.

Maasdorp, Gavind, and Whiteside, Alan, eds. *Towards a Post-Apartheid Future: Political and Economic Relations in Southern Africa.* New York: St. Martin's Press, 1992.

Oden, Bertil, ed. *Southern Africa after Apartheid: Regional Integration and External Resources.* Uppsala, Sweden: The Scandinavian Institute of African Studies, 1993.

Paul, Karen, and Dominic A. Aquila. "Political Consequences of Ethical Investing: The Case of South Africa." *Journal of Business Ethics* 7 1988.

Paul, Karen, and Sharyn Duffy. "Corporate Responses to the Call for South African Withdrawal." *Research in Social Performance and Policy* 10, ed. by Lee Preston. Greenwich, CT: JAI Press, 1988. pp. 211-40.

Report on the Signatory Companies to the Statement of Principles for South Africa (formerly the Sullivan Signatory Companies). Reports annually from 1977. New York: Industry Support Unit, Room 21WO11 150 East 42nd Street, New York, NY 10017.

Sampson, Anthony. *Black and Gold: Tycoons, Revolutionaries, and Apartheid.* New York: Pantheon Books, 1987.

Sethi, S. Parakash. "American Corporations and the Economic Future of South Africa." *Business and Society Review* 92 (Winter 1995), pp.10-18.

Sethi, S. Prakash, ed. *The South African Quagmire: In Search of a Peaceful Path to Democratic Pluralism.* Cambridge, MA: Ballinger Publishers, 1987.

South Africa: Time Running Out: The Report on the Study Commission on U.S. Policy Toward

Southern Africa. Berkeley, CA: University of California Press, 1986.

Spence, J.E., ed. *Change in South Africa.* London: Printer Publishers, 1994, p. 114.

Stedman, Stephen John, ed. *South Africa: the Political Economy of Transformation.* Boulder, CO: Lynn Rienner, 1994, p. 213.

Thede, Nancy, and Pierre Beaudet, eds., *A Post-Apartheid Southern Africa?* Basingstroke: Macmillan, 1993, p. 117.

Unger, Sanford, and Peter Vale. "South Africa: Why Constructive Engagement Failed." *Foreign Affairs* 64 2, 1985-86, pp. 234–258.

U.S. Government. *South Africa: Summary Report on Trade, Lending, Investment, and Strategic Minerals.* Washington, DC: GAO/NSIAD-88-228, September, 1988.

Viljoen, John. "Corporate Social Responsibility in Third World Countries: The South African Case." *International Journal of Management* 2, 1987, pp. 138-45.

Worden, Nigel. *The Making of Modern South Africa: Conquest, Segregation, and Apartheid.* Cambridge, MA: Oxford, 1994, p. 166.

THE BENEVOLENT CORPORATION?

Merck and Co., Inc. gives away the cure for river blindness

In the mounting domestic and international debates over health care, the giant pharmaceutical companies have often been the objects of strident criticism. They are principally accused of price gouging and a hardhearted indifference to the plight of those who cannot afford health care and the products they have for sale. The world was astonished, therefore, when, in October 1987, Merck and Co., Inc., announced its intentions to give away a drug that could cure river blindness (Merck and Co., Inc., 1987; Lindley, 1987; *New York Times*, 1987). Merck was the discoverer of ivermectin, a drug with proven commercial value in the treatment of animals (under the brand name Ivomec). A different formulation of the drug was also found to be an effective treatment for river blindness (onchocerciasis) in humans (under the brand name mectizan). This gift was made without cost and, apparently, with few strings attached.

By various estimates, some 18 million people in tropical Africa and Latin America are afflicted by the disease of river blindness, while more than 85 million people are at risk of contracting it (FDC, 1987; Waldholz, 1987; *New York Tmes*, 1987; WHO, 1987). Merck's decision to donate Mectizan, rather than sell it, derived partially from the fact that the countries most in need of the drug were hardly in a position to buy it. Mectizan was an "orphan drug." In the terminology of the pharmaceutical industry, an orphan drug is one whose potential users are so poor that they do not constitute an effective market. There is, therefore, no economic incentive to develop and distribute it—the drug is an orphan in the marketplace (Merck and Co., Inc., 1987).

Merck chose to make its gift through the World Health Organization, which has long led vigorous efforts to eradicate river blindness, accompanied by some $4 million in funding from the United States Agency for International Development (FDC, 1987). Mectizan [ivermectin] does not restore the sight of those people who have already been blinded by the disease. However, it does kill the larvae of the worms that carry the disease and prevents the adult worms from reproducing. Its principal effect is to prevent people from becoming blinded, not to cure those who have already become blind. Although the drug has minor side effects (fever, some tenderness of lymph nodes, mild hypertension, possible adverse effects for pregnant women), it is considered safe (Aziz, 1986; *American Family Physician*, 1988; Abiose et al, 1993; Ankomah, 1989).

Merck's gift has sparked considerable controversy. Those suspicious of the company's motives have pondered what they are "really up to" and have suggested that Merck is giving away something of little market value in order to extract market concessions for other products that would be worth millions at a later date. Others suggest that what Merck has done voluntarily should in some way be mandated for the rest of the industry, that the basic needs of the world's poor and sick should take priority over the profit motive. Such critics call for strict regulation of drug prices, as well as stringent limits on the monopoly powers granted pharmaceutical companies through patent rights. As a case in point, in the early 1990s Ciba–Geigy developed a drug (amocarzine) that promises in some ways to be even more effective against river blindness than ivermectin is (Poltera et al, 1991; *New York Times*, June 1991). Many other scientific advances against the disease are also in the offing. The question is whether the pharmaceutical companies involved should be made to follow Merck's example.

ISSUES FOR ANALYSIS

1. Who are the stakeholders in this case and what are their respective responsibilities? How would you diagram a stakeholder map?
2. If poor people are in need of a drug that would cure an illness, who in society is responsible for seeing that they get the drug? In the end, who is responsible for bringing about the needed socioeconomic development and the delivery of health care programs?
3. Current patent laws allow a company to have monopoly rights over a drug for 17 years, whether they exploit the patent commercially or not. Should patent rights in the area of medicine be modified to provide for compulsory licensing or other measures to ensure that a patent is "worked" and that the related drugs are made available to the public?
4. Should monopoly pricing of important drugs be allowed or, on the contrary, should generic drugs be allowed to come to the market earlier? What role do patents play in providing adequately for the longer-term and broader-based health care of the world's poor?

5. To what extent did the management of Merck take care of the interests of its important stakeholders when it gave away the drug?
6. How can very poor people be drawn into health care markets? Is it sensible to think that large, market-based pharmaceutical companies can effectively respond to the public health needs of developing countries?
7. What is the role of governments, local and foreign, as well as international governmental agencies, such as the World Health Organization, in solving the underlying development and public health problems?
8. What is the appropriate role for private voluntary organizations of all types? What is the responsibility of poor people themselves?
9. What are the "critical success factors" in delivering adequate health care to poor people in developing countries?

THE NATURE OF RIVER BLINDNESS AND ASSESSMENT OF ITS EFFECTS

River blindness (onchocerciasis) has been the object of intense scientific attention since the late nineteenth century (Manson–Bahr, 1982). According to the World Health Organization (1985, p. 7):

> Onchocerciasis is a filiarlial disease caused by the development in the human dermis of the filarial worm *Onchocerca volvulus*. This parasitic worm is 'viviparous' and for the greater part of its life, around 10 years, emits embryos or microfilaria into the dermal tissues, where they provoke itching and skin lesions; these microfilaria may invade the eye, causing severe eye disorders culminating in blindness. It is the microfilaria which are the pathogenic stages of the parasite.
>
> Some of these microfilaria are ingested by a fly of the genus *Simulium*, inside of which they undergo morphological changes and are transformed into infected larvae, which find their way into the mouths of the insect, and are inoculated into man during a subsequent bite. This passage through the vector is an essential stage in the spread of onchocerciasis.
>
> The distribution of the disease is, therefore, dependent on that of the vector which

has an aquatic stage, developing in the rapids of rivers. Thus the disease is essentially concentrated in foci alongside watercourses, whence its name "river blindness."

The life cycle of the parasite *onchocerca volvulus* is depicted in Figure 1. In general terms there are 5 basic stages (Eckholm, 1989).

1. A black fly that carries the onchocerca larvae bites a human, infecting that person with the parasite.
2. The larvae quickly grow into adult worms that have a threadlike structure. Male larvae may be 1 to 2 inches long, while female larvae may reach 2 feet. They live under the person's skin for up to 12 years.
3. The abundant offspring of the worm (called microfilaria) cause the disease's symptoms.
4. The microfilaria migrate through the skin, causing severe itching and, eventually, blindness.
5. When another fly bites the infected person and carries the parasite to another human, the cycle is completed.

There are various symptoms of the disease. In what follows we present the description provided by WHO (1985, p. 8). Among the general symptoms of the disease are visible nodules that surround adult female parasites of the human victim. They are located primarily around the hips and on the rib cage, but very often also on the head and legs. The nodules are generally 1cm to 2cm in size but may exceed 5cm. When they are touched they almost roll beneath the fingers. The frequency and severity of the symptoms are associated with the number of microfilaria. Clinical onchocerciasis manifests only after several years, during which infections are continuously accumulated.

In addition to nodules, skin and eye lesions are observed. The most common skin symptom is a rash accompanied by violent and persistent itching. In severe cases the skin becomes atrophied and depigmented. The WHO summarizes the final stages in this way (1985, p. 8):

In the case of intense and prolonged invasion of the eye by microfilaria, permanent lesions appear: keratitis which opacifies the cornea, iridocyclitis causing glaucoma, and inflammation of the retina and optic nerve.

Up until recently, blindness has received most of the attention in the public health literature. As of early 1995, more and more attention is being paid to the skin diseases caused by the parasite, with studies suggesting that they should be attacked as a separate health problem (Leary, 1995).

MERCK'S MECTIZAN (IVERMECTIN) POLICY: STRATEGIC AND ETHICAL ANALYSIS

While people, in general, view Merck's gift of its drug mectizan [ivermectin] as a definite advantage for the millions of people afflicted by a horrible disease, most analysts also think it added up to a beneficial strategic move. In what follows, we review how the drug was discovered, the strategic implications of the giveaway, the rationale for choosing a definite structure to administer the giveaway, and an overall assessment of benefits and costs.

Discovery of the Drug Mectizan [Ivermectin]

Merck makes drugs to treat a wide variety of diseases. To maintain its competitive edge in the industry, it invests heavily in research. During the mid-1970s, its scientists came across the drug ivermectin and discovered that it was extraordinarily effective against parasitic worms. According to then company president and CEO, Roy Vagelos, "This ivermectin was unusual in that it killed a number of different worms and we spent years trying to figure out where it would be most effective."(National Public Radio, 1987). Very early on, Merck discovered that the drug was

FIGURE 1. The Life Cycle of *Onchocerca Volvulus*

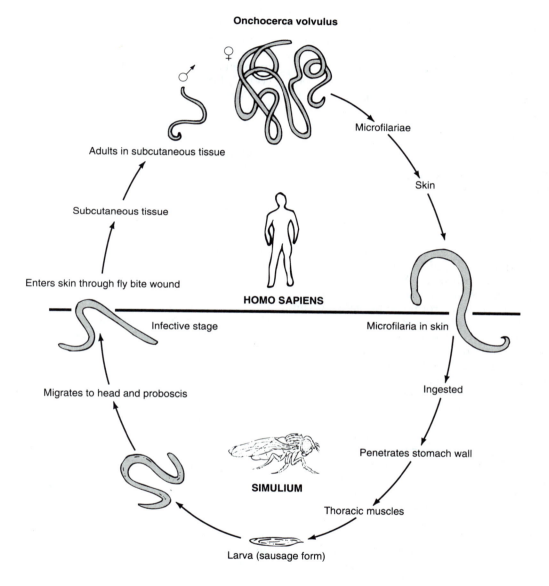

Onchocerca volvulus

Microfilariae

Skin

Adults in subcutaneous tissue

Microfilaria in skin

Subcutaneous tissue

HOMO SAPIENS

Enters skin through fly bite wound

Infective stage

Ingested

Migrates to head and proboscis

Penetrates stomach wall

SIMULIUM

Thoracic muscles

Larva (sausage form)

very effective in combatting a number of animal parasites and that there was a very lucrative market for the drug. At the time, it was widely used on cattle, horses, sheep, hogs, and some canine diseases, with estimated sales of $250–300 million (FDC, 1987). From 1980 on, the company engaged in clinical trials of ivermectin in humans (Kaufman, 1990). Over a seven-year research program, the drug was found to be very effective against river blindness, even with a low dosage of one tablet per year.

The Strategic Rationale for Merck's Decision

For all its effectiveness against river blindness, ivermectin was essentially an orphan drug in market terms. Those who needed it could not afford it. "Need" did not translate into "demand" and, therefore, no effective market materialized. According to World Bank sources, the initial costs of ivermectin would have been around $3 per tablet (Wigg, 1993). That was too expensive, given the economic circumstances of the regions where the disease was most prevalent. The head of the Onchocerciasis Control Program (OCP) in West Africa, Dr. Ebrahim M. Samba, credits the generosity of Merck's chairman, Dr. P. Roy Vagelos, with the gift of the drug. In making this decision, Dr. Vagelos and his wife were apparently swayed by a film showing the devastation of river blindness in West Africa. In deciding to donate the drug, he had to overcome the opposition of other drug companies, as well as his own board of directors, who feared that such a move would set a dangerous precedent and spoil future markets. Many within Merck also feared that the drug might be surreptitiously funneled to the black market and would, thereby, undermine the lucrative veterinary trade.

The Social Structure of the Giveaway

In deciding to give away ivermectin, Merck could easily have announced that it would no longer protect its patent rights and been done with it. Instead, it chose a highly visible and structured set of institutional arrangements to administer the giveaway. This was announced by simultaneous press conferences in New York and Paris, under the umbrella of the World Health Organization (WHO, 1987).

Merck decided to channel the giveaway through an international committee of experts. The first five years were not without significant problems (Tanouye, 1992). Overall, however, the general scheme has worked out.

The Mectizan Expert Committee was set up and funded by Merck and was based in the Carter Presidential Center in Atlanta. The Center's executive director, Dr. William Foege, was appointed chairman. Other members of the committee were drawn from public health and tropical disease experts: Dr. Bruce Greene, University of Alabama Birmingham; Dr. Michel LaRiviere, University of Paris; Dr. Adertokunbo, Carnegie Corporation of New York and former UNDP, World Bank, and WHO official; Dr. Eric Ottesen, of the National Institute of Allergy and Infectious Diseases; and Dr. Guillermo E. Zera–Flores, of the Ministry of Public Health of Guatemala and a member of WHO's Expert Committee on Onchocerciasis (Merck and Co., Inc., 1990).

The review committee was charged with providing the infrastructure for the proper distribution and use of the drug and, most important, preventing the diversion of free ivermectin to agricultural markets. In addition, costs of distribution would be partially assumed by the World Health Organization and U. S. Government Programs (some $4 million was funneled through the U.S. Agency for International Development [US AID]) (FDC Report, 1987).

Assessment of Merck's Benefits and Costs

The benefits to Merck include very positive worldwide publicity, some tax advantages, and a well of goodwill among developing countries and public health officials that could possibly benefit other Merck product development and marketing strategies.

Merck structured the giveaway through government and private voluntary organizations (PVOs), so that it would not bear the costs of distribution and oversight. Nonetheless, the company faced two significant potential costs. First, many in the pharmaceutical industry feared that the decision might establish some sort of precedent for product pricing and distribution policies of pharmaceuticals operating in developing countries. Second, the company itself feared that the drug given freely for human use might be diverted for use in animals and, thus, undermine the lucrative agricultural market for ivermectin. As of this date, neither of those potential costs has materialized in a significant way.

THE ONCHOCERCIASIS CONTROL PROGRAM: 1974–1994

Significant public awareness of river blindness as a public health problem and an obstacle to social and economic development emerged through extensive research conducted in West Africa from 1950 through 1965 (Webbe, 1992). The disease is rampant in West and Central Africa and also afflicts parts of Latin America, as shown in the accompanying maps.

By the late 1960s, several West African nations, together with multilateral sponsoring agencies from the UN, began a control program based upon aerial campaigns to kill larvae. The boundaries of the control program were set with reference to the blinding savanna forms of the disease and excluded the nonblinding forest forms. By 1986 the program area covered 1,235,000 sq. km,

FIGURE 2. Geographical Distribution of Onchocerciasis in Africa and Arabic Peninsula

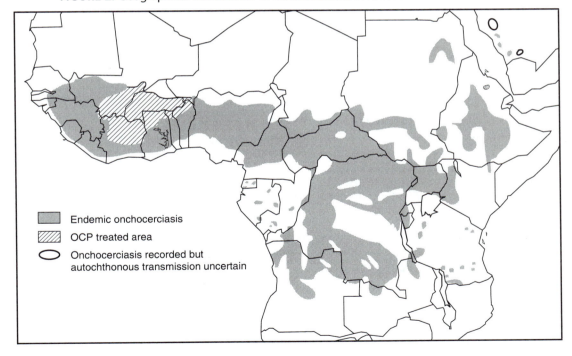

Endemic onchocerciasis

OCP treated area

Onchocerciasis recorded but autochthonous transmission uncertain

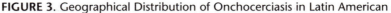

FIGURE 3. Geographical Distribution of Onchocerciasis in Latin American

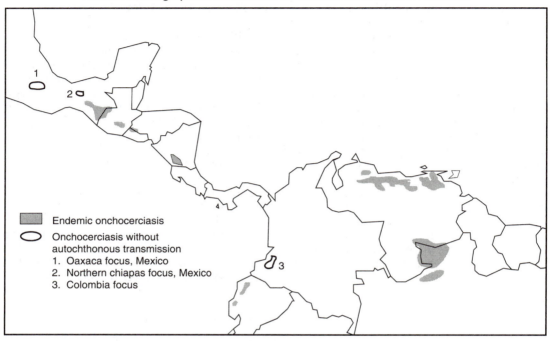

including 50,000 km of rivers, and covered a population of 30 million (the cross-hatched area in Figure 2). The program developed a two-pronged attack: to eliminate larvae in new areas and to prevent the reemergence of the fly in areas already protected.

The lifespan of the female worm was thought to average eleven years. Accordingly, eleven years of larviciding were deemed necessary to eliminate the human reservoir of *onchocerca volvulus*. Some studies suggest that a fourteen-year time period is more realistic. At this rate, the Onchocerciasis Control Program is scheduled to continue larviciding through 1997.

The program has averaged about $1 U.S. per person in protected areas and has proven to be effective. In the original program area, after sixteen years of larviciding, river blindness ceased to be a public health problem and larviciding has actually been discontin-

ued in 90% of the original area attacked in 1974. Various indicators, such as skin infections, infected newborn children, freeing infected people from the parasite, and prevention of total blindness, have shown steady—and in some cases, remarkable—improvement (Mabey, 1993; Pacque et al. 1990a; 1990b).

At the outset of the program, six different larvicides were used. As time went on, resistance to some larvicides was noted and adjustments made so that overall accuracy and cost-effectiveness improved. Computer programming was used in this endeavor, as well as in determining when spraying could safely be discontinued. The computer program (PERLES) helped minimize larvicide and application costs by simultaneously interrelating larvicidal and hydrological factors with aircraft delivery programs. According to Webbe (1992, p. 113):

Epidemiological mapping and entomological surveillance procedures are complemented by another computer model (ONCHOISM), which predicts long-term epidemiological trends given control methods based on specific combinations of vector control and chemotherapy.

In this program, ivermectin formed part of clinical trials by the Onchocerciasis Chemotherapy Project (OCT) and was found to be an effective *microfilaricidal* agent. However, the chemotherapy project continues to seek what it terms a *macrofilaricidal* agent. Initial studies indicated that annual treatment with ivermectin alone was unable to effectively control transmission of the disease. The effectiveness of ivermectin, however, varies according to different treatment combinations and schedules (Ottosen et al., 1990).

The OCP's distribution of ivermectin was at first hampered by both reliance on too highly sophisticated technology, as well as highly vertical management. It was not sufficiently integrated into the delivery of general health systems, accompanied by training, epidemiological surveillance, or technical assistance.

Overall, the OCP has been considered a successful program (World Bank, 1990). The success is due primarily to the fact that it had: (1) clearly defined objectives, (2) a realistic and feasible time-frame, (3) choice of the right technology, (4) the susceptibility of onchocerciasis transmission to the applied control strategy, (5) contracting out of highly specialized operations, and (6) a strong emphasis on operational research. In addition, a number of administrative features fostered success. Namely, a high degree of program autonomy within WHO allowed operational flexibility. Planning was medium term, based on 6 years, with sustained donor financial commitments. There was unrestricted information flow, which enabled a system of clear accountability and internal checks and balances to develop. And there was strong management and high-quality staff.

SOCIOECONOMIC REDEVELOPMENT

As a region is liberated from the scourge of river blindness, countries must devote resources to the land settlement and socio-economic development of the afflicted regions. Webbe (1992, p. 114) cites the World Bank (1990) review of the OCP as stating that 15 million acres of riverain and tillable land have been recovered for resettlement and cultivation and that, by the end of the century, 25 million hectares will have been recovered.

The Committee of Sponsoring Agencies (UNDP, FAO, WHO, and the World Bank) that oversees the OCP has urged the examination of the development potential of the area freed from river blindness (McMillan et al., 1993). This initiative has resulted in an approach termed "land settlement review" (LSR). The motivation for such a review was based on the opinion that (McMillan et al., 1993, p. v) "unassisted and unguided, spontaneous or anarchic settlement, may result in local systems of agricultural production that have negative long term consequences for people and natural resources." Such consequences range from environmental deterioration and declining productivity to declining real income levels—all leading to the abandonment of once productive lands.

The resettlement programs aim to facilitate development, based upon a five-stage model of settlement-related development planning (McMillan, et al., 1993, p. 23).

Other aspects of the redevelopment program focus upon technical issues, such as knowledge of the natural resource base and

TABLE 1. A Five-Stage Model of Settlement-Related Development Planning

Stage 1	Planning
Stage 2	Initial infrastructure development, recruitment of personnel, and installation of program facilities
Stage 3	Adaptation, transition, settling in
Stage 4	Economic and social development
Stage 5	Handing over and incorporation

farming systems, to socio-institutional factors, including land tenure; the traditional relationships between pastoralists, settlers, and the original population; the household and community-level participation; the establishment of both markets and service/administration centers; and the integration of the local area into the national economy and institutions.

PUBLIC HEALTH IN DEVELOPING COUNTRIES: THE STRUCTURE OF SOCIAL RESPONSIBILITY

In the literature on economic development and public health, one encounters many diverse and even conflicting theories. The most significant bone of contention is "whether the market reaches the poor." That is, do poor people have sufficient market access and participation, such that market-based health programs will effectively meet their needs? We briefly examine the role of governments, markets, and private voluntary organizations.

Governments

In the countries where river blindness holds sway, the governments have been almost completely ineffectual in combating it. The "state" or "government" does not represent a universal reality throughout the world. The nature, function, and limits of the state are differentiated from place to place on the basis of social structure, the formal objective tasks of the government, and the constraints and social crises it faces. It is very clear that the development of efficient and stable political institutions is, itself, a necessary condition of economic development and effective public health programs. It is evident that the local governments in the areas affected by river blindness are severely handicapped in almost every way.

The various international and governmental organizations involved in the public health and resettlement aspects of river blindness areas all focused on the importance of building strong local political institutions. In so doing, they fostered development in a variety of functional ways.

Multinational Pharmaceutical Enterprises

Multinational enterprises (MNEs) are very often richer and more powerful than the governments of many small, developing countries. They are also active political lobbyists on both the national and international scene as they seek to forge what they call a positive environment in which to do business. Pharmaceutical multinationals potentially can make a contribution to the development of public health. Experience suggests, however, that they frequently fail to do so. What needs to happen for their presence to become a positive factor?

To answer that question, one must begin by examining why pharmaceutical companies do what they do. For a MNE to undertake an investment, there must first be a market with a promise of a profitable return on investment that compares favorably with other investment opportunities. For the corporation, the health sector must offer an attractive market.

Secondly, the company looks for a "hospitable social and political climate." Above all, this means that the government takes a "positive approach" to the private sector and sets up policies that make private enterprise viable. This entails ensuring the stability of the government, minimizing corruption, reducing the burden of regulations, and so forth.

Third, a "hospitable economic climate" is expected. This basically means that a government accepts the concept of profitability (and, in the case of multinationals, the repatriation of profits). More hard-nosed business people suggest that the government either must pay to provide health care for the poorest of the poor, or it must generate a process that brings the poorest of the poor from the noncash into the cash economy, enabling them to pay for themselves.

The fourth element a company desires is that it not be viewed as a development agency, but as an agent in the development process. The general business view is that overall development and attainment of public welfare are the responsibility of the local host government, as well as outside governments. The corporation's business is business.

In the case of river blindness, Merck departed from the norm by donating its product in a rather unique partnership with governmental agencies and private voluntary organizations.

Private Voluntary Organizations

In addition to government and business organizations, there are many organizations and interest groups that have a direct impact on development policy because they occupy positions of power and influence in society. Such groups are families and kinship units, religions, universities and research groups, the arts and mass media, and various interest groups (organized around issues such as environment and ecology, population control, or community-based development).

Many of the rural poor are the landless, women, and children. They have few productive assets. The corporate strategic scenario is not likely to include members of such households or even consider them stakeholders. Some suggest that the only effective redistributive agent is the government. Yet, the governments in question are frequently either inept, repressive, or responsive only to special interests with clout.

The poor often enough end up voiceless and marginated. It is frequently only private voluntary organizations that can exercise influence upon governments and corporations on their behalf, as well as effectively deliver services to the poor. For example, in the first two years of the Clinton Admin-

istration, the amount of U.S. aid channelled through private voluntary organizations rose from 17% to 30% (Crossette, 1995).

What private voluntary organizations have to contribute varies according to their nature and purposes. Frequently enough, they are indigenous to the local scene and possess an aura of both social and political acceptability. Secondly, they generally possess some grass-roots structures and can elicit popular participation. Finally, their administrative structures are often quite efficient due to the small scale of organization, the high motivation of members, low costs of delivery associated with volunteers, and relatively unencumbered procedures.

The main social structure in most Third World countries is the extended family. In many countries, the sense of being a nation is weak. People's primary identity is that of family and clan or tribe. Their loyalties are to these groups and their "policies" rather than to government and its policies. This reality is perhaps more important in Africa than anywhere else. If development planners neglect these dynamics, their prospects for success are bleak, indeed. For family, elders, and traditions have tremendous persuasive power over attitudes regarding outside agents of change and innovations.

Next to family and kinship systems, religious groupings are social institutions of major importance. They deserve special comment, for so often they are seen as tradition-bound and major obstacles to development. Religious groups can be development agents. Whether for good or ill, they do, in fact, have tremendous social power. There are a number of specific areas of development cooperation that suggest themselves in light of the above remarks. Because of the actual structures and activities of many churches, there are four that are more important: health, education, community organization, and media.

In addition to kinship and religious institutions, a third major set of voluntary organizations are found in educational institutions and research centers. Educational associations and personnel are not only technical agents of change. They are also very important in effecting changes in kinship and religious traditions and values and, in this way, forging new cultural forms and institutions.

In the same way, the arts and mass media are likewise of pivotal importance. More than any other medium, the fine arts are capable of creating a new sociocultural vision. For their part, the communication arts are powerful tools to transcend narrow kinship, religious, and other traditional biases. Some of the greatest problems in development are in galvanizing political will. The arts and mass media have tremendous persuasive power in transforming values and building social unity. They also have tremendous educational potential in areas of extension and the diffusion of technology.

In the area of health, it is well known that private voluntary organizations have developed significant communication networks as well as actual institutions such as hospitals, infirmaries, and out-patient programs. While in developed countries many such functions have been overtaken by the state, private enterprise, or other agencies, in the developing countries the contributions of private voluntary organizations are frequently vital. Churches, for example, generally have some form of health care system in place. Furthermore, many voluntary organizations, such as Doctors without Borders, have a strong international base that draws in global support.

DEVELOPING SUCCESSFUL PROGRAMS

By all accounts, the OCP (Onchocerciasis Control Program) has been successful in combating river blindness. Its structure and implementation have featured a unique partnership between a powerful pharmaceutical multinational, Merck; many local and international governmental agencies; as well as many local and international private volun-

tary organizations. Many people wonder whether this model should be adopted in combating other diseases in the developing world.

It is clear that a particular disease, such as river blindness, must be seen as but a piece in a far larger mosaic of overall social and economic development and the crafting of viable public health programs. The *World Health Report 1995: Bridging the Gaps* (WHO, 1995) provides a chilling reminder of just how many millions of people are suffering and dying from preventable diseases. The OCP success against river blindness provides a ray of hope. It is a complex world of donors, recipients, and providers that aims simultaneously to provide for the basic economic development of a country while successfully targeting a specific disease.

The multinational—governmental—voluntary organization model that emerges in the river blindess case suggests that, in order to be fruitful, any program has to consider a number of targets. Each participant attacks the target at different levels, and with different resources.

First, a number of steps can be taken to improve rural health services. Structures already in place could be transformed with relatively little effort by channeling efforts towards nutrition and preventive medicine, by employing oral rehydration therapy (ORT), by improving birth control information, maternal training, child care, sanitation practices, and so forth.

Secondly, education must be a major area of focus for both development and public health. There is considerable scope for cooperation in areas of teacher training and curriculum development and the reshaping of educational endeavors so that they directly serve development needs. What is needed, therefore, are both financial aid and technical cooperation to expand and improve the basic educational system already in place.

A number of other themes might at the same time be usefully explored. Namely, schooling for girls and disadvantaged minority groups, the use of nonformal education to improve adult literacy and to impart technical skills, refugee education, and preschool education and child care. In all of these areas, the churches and other PVOs already have some structures in place. With the proper technical and financial assistance, they could be improved and targeted upon certain priority objectives and groups in the development scene.

A third area of program activity is community development projects. Admittedly, the term is nebulous and is used to cover anything from housing and water projects, to sewage, rural electrification, roads, warehouses, and so forth. Clearly, PVO leaders, as such, are not particularly trained in the technical aspects that such projects call for. Nor do they possess the raw materials, or the financial and technical resources that are needed. What they do have to offer, however, is a respected forum for public discussions, a somewhat efficient social organization that can help in getting things done, and a social system beyond family or clan that is trusted. These qualities are of fundamental importance for community development projects and the scope for their utilization in development is quite positive. Private voluntary organizations can provide a venue for popular participation in development, enabling the people to identify their needs, help design a project, implement it, and then evaluate it.

A fourth area of specific cooperation involves the mass media. In most parts of the world, the PVOs have developed considerable capacity in the print and radio media. In some places there are television facilities. These media are of considerable interest in the public health and development context. In fact, they could rather easily be harmonized with efforts in the health, education, and community development spheres.

Finally, there are numerous potential roles for private voluntary associations—interest groups—in shaping development. The free association, which both transcends family and clan ties and is free of government or business domination, is a central feature of Western social thought. On the development scene today, many such groups have proliferated; a significant number are international. The focus of interest ranges from population and ecological resource management to technology transfer, scientific exchanges, international *fora* on development and so forth. These groups tend to be small and low-cost, with a dedicated core focused on achieving very specific results. Hence, they can be quite efficient on a small scale. The conclusion to be drawn from this brief survey of river blindness is that public health and socioeconomic development are too important to be left merely to government and business circles or to blind faith in either government programs or market fundamentalism.

REFERENCES

Abiose, A., B.R. Jones, S.N., Cousins, I. Murdoch, A. Casseis–Brown, O.E. Babalola, N.D.E. Alexander, I. Nuhu, J. Evans, U.F. Ibrahim and A.O. Mahmood. 1993. "Reduction in Incidence of Optic Nerve Disease with Annual Ivermectin to Control Onchocerciasis," *The Lancet*, 341, n.8838, January 16, pp. 130–34.

American Family Physician, 1988. "Onchocerciasis (Treated With Ivermectin)," p. 376.

Ankomah, Baffour, 1989. "Drug Company Gives Away River Blindness Cure for Free: A Multinational Pharmaceutical Company Has Developed What the WHO Believes Is a Cure," *African Business*, April, pp. 14–16.

Aziz, Mohammed A., 1986. "Chemotherapeutic Approach to Control of Onchocerciasis," *Reviews of Infectious Diseases*, 8, 1, May–June, pp. 500–04

Crossette, Barbara, 1995. "Gore Says U.S. Will Shift More Foreign Aid to Private Groups," *New York Times*, March 13, p. A7.

434   *Multinational Corporations and Developing Countries*

Eckholm, Eric, 1989. "River Blindness: Conquering an Ancient Scourge," *New York Times Magazine*, January 8, p. 20.

FDC Report, 1987. "Merck's Mectizan (Ivermectin) Third World Giveaway," October 26, Washington, DC, U.S. Food and Drug Commission, [photocopy].

Gray, Bradford H., 1992. "World Blindness and the Medical Profession: Conflicting Medical Cultures and the Ethical Dilemmas of Helping," *Milford Quarterly*, 3, 70, pp. 535–56.

Greene, Bruce M., Hugh R. Taylor, and Eddie W. Cupp, 1985. "Comparison of Ivermectin and Diethylcarbamazine in the Treatment of Onchocerciasis," *The New England Journal of Medicine*, July 18, pp. 133–38.

Kaufman, Art, Merck Sharp & Dohme International, 1990. "Onchocerciasis: Its Treatment With 'Mectizan'—A Backgrounder for the Press," Rahway, NJ, March 28.

Leary, Warren E., 1995. "River Blindness Disease Has 2d Devastating Side," *New York Times*, March 28, p. C7.

Lindley, David, 1987. "Merck's New Drug Free to WHO for River Blindness Programme," *Nature*, October 29, p. 752.

Mabey, David, 1993. "Onchocerciasis: Ivermectin and Onchocercal Optic Nerve Lesions," *Lancet* (North American Edition), January 16, pp. 153–54; followed by a discussion piece, March 6, 1993, pp. 634–35.

Manson–Bahr, P.E.C., 1982. "Onchocerciasis," in *Manson's Tropical Diseases*, London, Baslliere Tindall, 18th. edition, pp. 164–74 and Appendix II.

McMillan, Della E., Jean–Baptiste Nana, Kimseyinga Savadogo, 1993. *Settlement and Development in the River Blindness Control Zone: Case Study Burkina Faso*, World Bank Technical Paper No. 200, Series on River Blindness Control in West Africa, Washington, DC.

Merck and Co., Inc., 1987. "Merck to Donate Worldwide Supply of Drug to Treat River Blindness," *The Daily*, October 21, p. 1.

Merck and Co., Inc., 1990. "Officials Visit Nigeria on Mission to Make New Drug Available Free of Charge for Treatment of River Blindness," News Release, March 26.

National Public Radio, 1987. "All Things Considered," 8:00pm Broadcast; [photocopy transcript].

New York Times, 1991. "Advances on Two Fronts Are Reported in Fight on River Blindness," June 11, pp. B6, C3.

New York Times, 1987. "Merck Offers Free Distribution of New River Blindness Drug," October 22.

Okie, Susan, 1990. "500 Million Infected with Tropical Ills, Control Efforts Lagging," *Washington Post*, March 28, p. A4.

Ottosen, Eric A., V. Vijayasekaran, V. Kumaraswami, S.V. Perumal Pillai, A. Sandanandam, Sheila Frederick, R. Prabhakar and Sriram P. Tripathy, 1990. "A Controlled Trial of Ivermectin and Diethylcarbamazine in Lymphatic Filariasis," *The New England Journal of Medicine*, 322, 16, April 19, pp. 1113–37.

Pacque, Michael, Beatriz Munoz, Gretchen Poetschke, Jeanne Foose, Bruce M. Greene and Hugh R. Taylor. 1990a. "Pregnancy Outcome after Ivermectin Treatment During Community-based Distribution," *The Lancet*, 336, 8729, December 15, pp. 1486–90.

_____. 1990b. "Safety of and Compliance with Community-based Ivermectin Therapy," *The Lancet*, 335, 8702, December 1, pp. 1377–80.

Poltera, Anton A., Guillermo Zea–Flores, Ronald Guderian, Fernando Beltranana, Roberto Proana, Michael Moran, Frantisek Zak and Heini P. Streibel, 1991. "Onchocercicidal Effects of Amocarzine," *The Lancet*, 337, 8741, March 9, p. 583–84.

Quarcoopome, C.D., 1983. "Onchocerciasis: A Major Social Problem in West Africa," *Social Science and Medicine*, 17, 22, pp. 1703–07.

Rothova, Aniki, Jan S. Stilma, Allegonda van der Lelij, William R. Wilson, and Robert F. Barbe, 1989. "Side-effects of Ivermectin in Treatment of Onchocerciasis," *The Lancet*, 334, 8652, June 24, pp. 1439–41.

Science, 1993. "Project Sought Treatment for River Blindness," January 29, p. 593.

Tanouye, Elysee, 1992. "Merck and Co. Encounters Problems Distributing the Drug Ivermectin Which Can Cure Onchocerciasis," *Wall Street Journal*, September 23, p. B1.

Taylor, Hugh R., Carlos Gonzales, and Brown Duke, 1993. "Simplified Dose Schedule of Ivermectin," *Lancet* (North American Edition), January 2, pp. 50–51.

Taylor, Hugh R., Michel Pacque, and Beatriz Munoz, 1990. "Impact of Mass Treatment of

Onchocerciasis With Ivermectin on the Transmission of Infection," *Science*, October 5, pp. 116–18.

The Lancet, 1990. "Global Scale of Avoidable Blindness," (editorial) 3365, 8722, p. 1038.

United States Government, Department of State, 1978. "Regional Onchocerciasis Area Satellite (LANDSAT) Related Study: Agreement between the United States of America and the African Development Bank Signed at Abijan, June 30, 1976," Washington, DC: U.S. Government Printing Office.

Waldholz, Michael, 1987. "Merck, in Unusual Gesture, Will Donate Drug to Fight Leading Cause of Blindness," *Wall St. Journal*, October 22.

Walsh, John, 1987. "Merck Donates Drug for River Blindness (Mectizan)," *Science*, October 30, p. 610.

Webbe, G., 1992. "The Onchocerciasis Control Programme," *Transactions of the Royal Society of Tropical Medicine and Hygiene*, 86, pp. 113–14.

Wigg, David, 1993. *And Then Forgot to Tell Us Why . . . A Look at the Campaign Against River Blindness in West Africa*, Washington, DC: World Bank Development Essays.

World Bank, 1990. *External Review of the Onchocerciasis Program*, Washington, DC.

World Health Organization, 1987. "Notes for Remarks by Dr. Halfdan Mahler, Director General, World Health Organization, at a Press Conference Held by Merck and Co., Inc.," Washington, DC and Paris, October 21.

World Health Organization, 1985. "Review of the Work of the Onchocerciasis Control Programme in the Volta River Basin, " extracted from "Ten Years of Onchocerciasis Control in West Africa," COP/GVA/85.1B; R386–786, [photocopy], p. 7.

World Health Organization, 1995, *World Health Report 1995: Bridging the Gaps*, Geneva.